EDWARD GIBBON

Born 27th April 1737 at Putney. Educated at
Westminster School, Oxford, and privately
at Lausanne. Toured Italy, 1764–5, and conceived the plan of his 'History'. Settled in
London in 1772 and sat in Parliament from
1774 to 1783. Lived in Lausanne, 1784–93,
and died in London 16th January 1794.

EDWARD GIBBON

Decline and Fall
of the Roman Empire

IN SIX VOLUMES · VOLUME ONE

INTRODUCTION BY
CHRISTOPHER DAWSON

DENT: LONDON AND TORONTO
EVERYMAN'S LIBRARY
DUTTON: NEW YORK

All rights reserved
Printed in Great Britain by
Biddles Ltd, Guildford, Surrey
and bound at the
Aldine Press · Letchworth · Herts
for
J. M. DENT & SONS LTD
Aldine House · Albemarle Street · London
This edition was first published in
Everyman's Library in 1910
Last reprinted 1977

Published in the U.S.A. by arrangement
with J. M. Dent & Sons Ltd

No. 434 Hardback ISBN 0 460 00434 4

INTRODUCTION

THE best introduction to Gibbon's *Decline and Fall of the Roman Empire* is his own autobiography, which is hardly less a classic than the History itself and which gives us an extraordinarily faithful image of the mind of the writer and his intellectual preparation for the work which was his life. Few men have had a clearer sense of their literary vocation. He lived a dedicated life and even in that literary age there is no writer who devoted himself more whole-heartedly to the cultivation of his peculiar talent. The origins of this vocation go back to his childhood when his providential ill health spared him the hardships of a regular education and left him free to indulge his omnivorous appetite for books—"that early and invincible love of reading which I would not exchange for the treasures of India." And so when he was sent to Oxford in 1752, just before he was fifteen, he "arrived with a stock of erudition that might have puzzled a doctor and a degree of ignorance of which a schoolboy would have been ashamed." Eighteenth-century Oxford was not well equipped for dealing with infant prodigies, and Gibbon has described his time there as "the most idle and unprofitable of my whole life." However it was very brief, for after fourteen months his academic career was cut short by his sudden conversion to Catholicism. This is perhaps the most surprising event in Gibbon's life, for there was nothing in his character or environment to explain such a defiance of the established order.[1] But, as he himself points out, nothing he ever did had a more decisive influence on his intellectual destiny. "If," he writes, "my childish revolt against the religion of my country had not stripped me in time of my academic gown, the five important years, so liberally improved in the studies and conversation of Lausanne, would have been steeped in port and prejudice among the monks of Oxford. . . . I should have grown to manhood ignorant of the life and language of Europe, and my knowledge of the world would have been confined to an English cloister. But my religious error fixed me at Lausanne, in a state of banishment and disgrace. The rigid course of discipline and abstinence to which I was condemned

---

[1] Nevertheless by a curious coincidence the same step was taken about the same time by his Acton cousins, including the grandfather and great-grandfather of the nineteenth-century historian.

invigorated the constitution of my mind and body; poverty and pride estranged me from my fellow countrymen." [1] At Lausanne Gibbon soon ceased to be a Catholic, but at the same time, as he confesses, he "ceased to be an Englishman," his "opinions, thoughts, and sentiments were cast in a foreign mould," so that he became the most cosmopolitan and un-English of all the great English writers.

French Switzerland at this period was becoming the centre of the European Enlightenment. At the very moment when Gibbon was making up his mind to return to Protestantism, an even more famous convert, Jean Jacques Rousseau, was taking the same step at Geneva,[2] and a few months later Voltaire arrived as a voluntary exile to establish his permanent headquarters by the Lake of Geneva.[2] Gibbon was never altogether the disciple of Voltaire and still less of Rousseau. Although he was the youngest of the three, he belonged mentally to an older generation—that of the Protestant rationalists like Bayle and Le Clerc and Barbeyrac. But while he criticized the superficiality and partisanship of the French philosophers, he shared their fundamental ideals and prejudices, and it is impossible to find any European writer, not even Voltaire himself, whose work reflects more perfectly the spirit of what is called "The Enlightenment" in all its strength and all its limitations.

During the fifteen years between his return to England in 1758 and the commencement of his History in 1773 Gibbon continued to pursue his intellectual vocation in the unfavourable circumstances of his life as a country gentleman and an officer in the militia. Nothing indeed is more impressive than the contrast between his easy-going adaptability to an uncongenial environment and the indomitable persistence with which he continued to pursue his distant goal. In this respect, at least, his life and method of work were totally unlike those of the French philosophers, as Byron points out so well in his famous parallel between Voltaire and Gibbon:

> "The other deep and slow, exhausting thought,
>   And hiving wisdom with each passing year,
>   In meditation dwelt, with learning wrought,
>   And shaped his weapon with an edge severe,
>   Sapping a solemn creed with solemn sneer; . . ."

[1] *Autobiography*, p. 81.
[2] Rousseau made his abjuration at Geneva in July 1754 and Gibbon at Lausanne on 25th December of the same year.   Voltaire settled at Prangins near Nyon in December 1754 and bought a house close to Lausanne at Monrion in 1755.

After his father's death, Gibbon came to London in 1772 and began to take an active part in public life, entering Parliament in 1774 and obtaining office in Lord North's Government in 1779. It was during these active years that he wrote and published the first three volumes of the *Decline and Fall*. Finally in 1784 after the fall of Lord North's Government he decided to carry out his long meditated plan of retiring to his beloved Lausanne. There in ideal surroundings he completed the history and prepared to enjoy that autumnal felicity in which "our passions are supposed to be calmed, our duties fulfilled, our ambitions satisfied, our fame and fortune established on a solid basis." But the sands were running out. The History was hardly completed before the world of the Enlightenment collapsed in the storm and ruin of revolution and Gibbon himself died at the age of fifty-six during his last visit to England, on 16th January 1794.

He was perhaps fortunate in the moment of his death. His age was finished and his work was done, and nothing he might have added to it could have increased his fame. From the moment that the first volume of his History was published in 1776 it had been accepted as a classic, and thenceforward for a century and more his work has continued to be published and sold and read in spite of all the changes of literary taste and the progress of historical knowledge.

What is the explanation of this extraordinary success? Above all, no doubt, it is due to his extraordinary literary gifts, which surpass those of every other English historian with the exception of Macaulay. It was the classical age of the literary historian and Gibbon was the greatest and the most learned of them all. But this is not the only explanation. In addition to his literary gifts, he had found a theme which was precisely adapted to those gifts and to the spirit of the age. The field of classical antiquity had been cultivated until the soil had become exhausted, and the late eighteenth century was awakening to the existence of the new world of medieval culture which had still to be explored. It was Gibbon's achievement to provide the link between these two worlds. As Carlyle wrote in one of his happiest moments: "Gibbon is a kind of bridge that connects the ancient with the modern ages. And how gorgeously does it swing across the gloomy and tumultuous chasm of these barbarous centuries." To a generation that had been reared on Livy and Tacitus and which was anxious to explore the world of Froissart and Ville-hardouin Gibbon provided the necessary introduction, and his work was read as eagerly as the latest novel. To the present generation his style is too ornate, his pace too slow, and his philosophy too antiquated to make an immediate appeal.   But his own contemporaries and the two generations that followed were enchanted by the music of his style and enthralled by the imaginative power with which he marshalled the pageantry of thirteen centuries of history.

Where Gibbon stands without a peer, alike among the literary historians of the eighteenth century and the scientific historians of later times, is in the supreme architectonic power with which he disposes of his vast material and creates out of the shapeless mass an ordered and intelligible whole.

It is true that he does not follow a uniform scheme of treatment and the two main parts of his work differ in plan as well as in scale as he explains in the important introduction to the second part which is to be found on pp. 72–6 of the fifth volume of this edition.   The first four volumes contain a consecutive history of the Empire from the Antonines to Heraclius—a period of some five centuries.   But in the last two volumes he abandons this method and deals with the last 800 years from Mohammed to the fall of Constantinople in a series of brilliant but discontinuous surveys.   This method put Gibbon's remarkable powers of synthesis to a very severe test, and even in his own time it evoked the criticism of Horace Walpole, who complained that he was "a little confounded by his leaping backwards and forwards and could not recollect all those *fainéant* emperors of Constantinople who came again and again, like the same ships in a moving picture." [1]

Nevertheless with the exception of the two chapters which form the introduction to the second part,[2] Gibbon is justified in his claim that "the seeming neglect of chronological order is surely compensated by the superior merits of interest and perspicuity," produced by "the method of grouping my picture by nations."   The real fault of these later volumes lies not in their discontinuity, but in his complete lack of sympathy with his main subject—the Byzantine empire itself.   No modern historian can agree with Gibbon's supercilious dismissal of the Byzantine history as "a tedious and uniform tale of weakness and misery," presenting "a dead uniformity of abject vices which are neither softened by the weakness of humanity nor animated by the vigour of memorable crimes." [3]

[1] Letter of 10th February 1789.
[2] Chapters xlviii and xlix: Vol. v, pp. 72–206 of this edition.
[3] Vol. v, p. 3.

The fact is that Gibbon's clarity of vision and unity of design have been achieved at the cost of the depth of his understanding and the width of his sympathies. His thought had been so moulded by the culture of the Renaissance and the philosophy of the Enlightenment that he could recognize no other values. Everything that was of value in the world came from antiquity or from the modern classical culture that was rooted in antiquity. The world between was a world of darkness and disorder, of superstition and barbarism. Hence he could not see the Byzantine world as a new form of culture with its own specific character and achievements and values. It was to him merely the ghost of a vanished majesty—a spectre reigning over a world of shadows.

This failure of understanding is even more disastrous when he has to deal with the problem of the rise of Christianity. For Christianity was essentially something new—the spiritual source of new life which came into a declining civilization "like the day-spring from on high: to give light to those who live in darkness and in the shadow of death and to guide our feet into the way of peace."

All this was invisible and unintelligible to Gibbon. He had no understanding of specifically religious values. They were for him an unknown dimension. That is his real difficulty in dealing with Christianity: not the scientific incredibility of miracles, or the metaphysical absurdity of dogmas, but the fundamental concepts of religious faith and divine revelation—in short the idea of what Christianity was about.

Consequently Gibbon's famous chapters on The Rise of Christianity [1] entirely fail to touch the root of the matter. Assuming that Christianity in the religious sense of the word does not exist, the historian still has to account for the vast development of creeds and sects and ecclesiastical establishments which play such a large part in Byzantine and medieval history. This Gibbon proceeds to do by describing the five secondary causes which favoured the spread of the new religion. But, as Leslie Stephen, who was himself no believer, points out, these secondary causes are much more satisfactory to one who accepts the reality of the Christian revelation than to the religious sceptic. For Gibbon's causes, on his own showing, are essentially second-ary and "the true causes of the greatest of all spiritual move-ments lay in a region altogether inscrutable by his methods of inquiry." "Gibbon, indeed, is as incapable of understanding

[1] Chapters xv and xvi, vol. I, pp. 430–500; vol. II, pp. 1–69.

the spiritual significance of the phenomenon as of assigning a cause for it." [1]

It has often been said that Gibbon's attitude to Christianity is marked by a note of personal animosity and the cause of this has sometimes been sought in the circumstances of his early conversion to Catholicism and his later reaction against it. But it seems to me that the real explanation is to be found in the intellectual discomfort caused by the constant intervention in his history of a factor which he had eliminated from his philosophy and which is essentially inexplicable. And since Christianity has no place in his philosophy, he is compelled to reduce its place in history by treating it with irony and seeking to discredit it with sneers and innuendoes. The most notorious example of this method is to be seen in his treatment of the martyrs and the great persecutions, but it runs through the whole work and reaches its climax in his chapter on medieval heresy and the Reformation in the last volume, where he contrives to inflict the maximum of damage on both parties, concluding with a surprisingly bitter attack on the Unitarians, like Dr. Priestley, as "those men who preserve the name without the substance of religion, who indulge the license without the temper of philosophy." [2]

This complete lack of sympathy and understanding for the religious forces which have exerted such an immense influence on western culture is Gibbon's great defect as a historian: and it is a very serious one, since it invalidates his judgment on the very issues which are most vital to his subject. His most learned modern editor, the late J. B. Bury, cannot be suspected of any partiality in this matter, but on the two chief issues his judgment agrees with that of Gibbon's Christian critics. On the theological issue he writes "neither the historian nor the man of letters will any longer subscribe, without a thousand reserves, to the theological chapters of the *Decline and Fall*, and no discreet inquirer would go there for his ecclesiastical history." [3] And on the historical issue, he says: "Gibbon's account of the internal history of the Empire after Heraclius is not only superficial; it gives an entirely false impression of the facts."

[1] Leslie Stephen's *History of English Thought in the 18th Century*, vol. 1, p. 449 (3rd ed.).
[2] Vol. v, pp. 501-5. Here Gibbon even goes so far as to suggest that Priestley's opinions were so subversive as to require the attention of the Government, a deplorable lapse from his own standards of toleration and enlightenment.
[3] *The Decline and Fall of the Roman Empire*, edited by J. B. Bury; 4th ed., vol. 1, xxxix.

"The designation of the story of the later Empire as a uniform tale of weakness and misery is one of the most untrue, and most effective, judgments ever uttered by a thoughtful historian." [1]

If this is true, how can Gibbon retain his position as the classical historian of the Decline of the Roman Empire? It is not simply due to his superb literary gifts, nor yet to his remarkably high standard of historical accuracy which distinguishes him from other literary historians. I believe the reason is that he has identified himself with his subject as no other historian has done. A contemporary critic said of him that he came at last to believe he was the Roman Empire, and though this was said in jest by an unfriendly critic it contains a real element of truth. For this somewhat absurd little man—"Monsieur Pomme de Terre"—with his pug face and his pot belly, was possessed and obsessed by the majestic spirit of Rome. His conversion to the Church may have been transitory and superficial, but his conversion to the City and the Empire was profound and governed his whole life and work. He felt as a Roman; he thought as a Roman; he wrote as a Roman. Even when he is most representative of the spirit of his own age, as in the famous pages which conclude the first part of the History where he makes his profession of faith in the permanence and progress of European civilization, he sees that civilization as a kind of revived and extended Pax Romana: "one great republic whose various inhabitants have attained almost the same level of politeness and cultivation."

Anyone who lives in his subject, as Gibbon has done, is bound to be a partisan, and Gibbon was a partisan of Rome, of antiquity and of the classical tradition. No doubt this makes him unjust to Christianity, the Catholic Church, and the Byzantine empire, for all of them were guilty in his eyes of *lèse majesté* against the indivisible authority of Rome and Reason and Civilization. Nevertheless, the cause with which he identified himself was neither trifling nor imaginary. It represents a permanent element in history, though it is not the whole of history. If Gibbon was a bad Christian, he was a good European, and we may apply to him the great verse of the Christian poet concerning his hero, the Emperor Julian:

"Perfidus ille Deo, quamvis non perfidus Urbi."

CHRISTOPHER DAWSON

[1] Ibid i, lii–liii.

SELECT BIBLIOGRAPHY
OF IMPERIAL HISTORY

I. HISTORY. i. General: *The Cambridge Ancient History*, vols. xi, xii; *The Cambridge Medieval History*, vols. i–iv; H. Stuart Jones: *The Roman Empire*, 1916; G. H. Stevenson: *The Roman Empire*, 1920; M. P. Nilsson: *Imperial Rome* (trans. G. C. Richards), 1926; C. W. C. Oman: *The Byzantine Empire*, 1892; N. H. Baynes: *The Byzantine Empire*, 1925; A. A. Vasiliev: *History of the Byzantine Empire*, 1928–9; H. R. Hall: *Ancient History: the Near East*, 11th ed., 1950; M. Cary: *Geographical Background of Greek and Roman History*, 1949; L. Gregorovius: *Rome in the Middle Ages* (trans.), 8 vols., 1894–1902.

ii. Special Periods: J. B. Bury: *History of the Roman Empire from its Foundation to the Death of Marcus Aurelius*, 1937; M. Cary: *A History of Rome to the Reign of Constantine*, 1935; J. N. Miller: *The Roman Empire During the First Three Centuries*. 1935; H. M. D. Parker: *A History of the Roman World*, A.D. *138–337*, 1935; A. E. Boak: *A History of Rome to* A.D. *565*, 1925; B. W. Henderson: *Five Roman Emperors*, 1927; *Life and Principate of the Emperor Hadrian*, 1923; E. E. Bryant: *The Reign of Antoninus Pius*, 1895; H. D. Sedgwick: *Marcus Aurelius : a Biography*. 1921; M. Platnauer: *The Life and Reign of the Emperor L. Septimus Severus*, 1918; H. J. Basset: *Macrinus and Diadumenianus*, 1920; R. V. N. Hopkins: *The Life of Alexander Severus*, 1907; J. H. E. Crees: *The Reign of the Emperor Probus*, 1907; G. H. Rendall: *The Emperor Julian*, 1879; T. Hodgkin: *The Dynasty of Theodosius*, 1889; F. H. Dudden: *The Life and Times of St Ambrose*, 1935; J. B. Bury: *A History of the Later Roman Empire from Arcadius to Irene*, 1889; extended to Justinian, 1923; *A History of the Eastern Empire from the Fall of Irene to the Accession of Basil I*, 1912; W. G. Holmes: *The Age of Justinian and Theodora*, 2 vols., 1905–7; G. Finlay: *History of the Byzantine Empire* (Everyman's Library), 1906; H. St L. B. Moss and N. H. Baynes: *Byzantium* (with valuable bibliographies), 1948; C. Diehl: *History of the Byzantine Empire* (trans. G. B. Ives), 1925; W. Stevenson: *The Crusades in the East*, 1907; J. LaMonte: *Feudal Monarchy in the Latin Kingdom of Jerusalem*, 1932; D. C. Munro: *The Kingdom of the Crusades*, 1935; S. Runciman: *A History of the Crusades*, 3 vols., 1950–4; E. Pears: *The Fall of Constantinople*, 1885; *The Destruction of the Greek Empire*, 1903; G. W. Bussell: *The Roman Empire : Essays on the Constitutional History 81* B.C.–A.D. *1081*, 1910; J. B. Bury: *The Constitution of the Later Empire*, 1910; C. Diehl: *Byzantine Portraits* (trans. H. Bell), 1927.

iii. Administration, Social and Economic: W. T. Arnold: *The Roman System of Provincial Administration to the Accession of Constantine the Great*, 1879; G. H. Stevenson: *Roman Provincial Administration*, 1909; Th. Mommsen: *The Provinces of the Roman*

Select Bibliography xiii

Empire (trans. W. P. Dickson), 1909; H. Mattingly; *The Imperial Civil Service of Rome*, 1900; F. F. Abbot and A. C. Johnson: *Municipal Administration in the Roman Empire*, 1926; A. W. Greenidge: *Roman Public Life*, 1901; S. Dill: *Roman Society from Nero to Marcus Aurelius*, 1904; R. H. Barrow: *Slavery in the Roman Empire*, 1928; M. Rostovtzeff: *Social and Economic History of Rome*, 1926; T. Frank (ed.): *An Economic Survey of Ancient Rome*, 1933–40; W. S. Davis: *The Influence of Wealth in Imperial Rome*, 1910; W. S. Heitland: *Agricola*, 1921; H. Mattingly and E. A. Sydenham: *The Roman Imperial Coinage*, vols. ii. iii. 1951; H. Mattingly: *Roman Coins*, 1928; G. Runciman: *Byzantine Civilization*, 1933; W. Wroth: *Catalogue of the Imperial Byzantine Coins in the British Museum*, 1908.

iv. The Invaders: T. Hodgkin: *Italy and her Invaders*, 8 vols., 1880–99; J. B. Bury: *Invasion of Europe by the Barbarians*, 1928; L. Halphen: *Les Barbares*, 4th ed., 1940; F. Lot: *Les Invasions Germaniques*, 2nd ed., 1945; H. Bradley: *History of the Goths*, 1888; E. A. Thompson: *History of Attila and the Huns*, 1948; Sir P. Sykes: *History of Persia*, 1930; N. C. Debevoise, *A Political History of Parthia*, 1938; R. K. Douglas: art. 'Mongols' in *Encyclopaedia Britannica* (indispensable); H. H. Howorth: *History of the Mongols*, 1876–88; E. H. Parker: *A Thousand Years of the Tartars*, 1924; D. S. Margoliouth: *Mahomet and the Rise of Islam*, 1905; *The Early Development of Mohammedanism*, 1914; T. W. Arnold: *The Preaching of Islam*, 1896; S. Lane-Poole: *Turkey*, 1888; P. Wittek: *The Rise of the Ottoman Empire*, 1938.

v. Military and Naval: H. M. D. Parker: *The Roman Legions*, 1928; G. L. Cheesman: *The Auxilia of the Roman Army*, 1914; C. G. Starr: *The Roman Imperial Navy*, 1941.

II. LAW. H. F. Jolowicz: *Historical Introduction to the Study of Roman Law*, 1932; H. J. Roby: *Introduction to Justinian's Digest*, 1884; J. Muirhead: *Historical Introduction to the Private Law of Rome*, 2nd ed., 1899; J. L. Strachan-Davidson: *Problems of the Roman Criminal Law*, 1912; P. Vinogradoff: *Roman Law in Medieval Europe*, 1909.

III. CHRISTIANITY AND PAGANISM. F. Altheim: *A History of Roman Religion*, 1938; F. Cumont: *Oriental Religions in Roman Paganism*, 4th ed., 1929; L. Duchesne: *History of the Christian Church* (trans.), 1909–24; H. F. Tozer: *The Church and the Eastern Empire*, 1888; A. Harnack: *The Expansion of Christianity in the First Three Centuries* (trans. J. Moffat), 1904; E. G. Hardy: *Christianity and the Roman Government*, 1906; T. R. Glover: *Conflict of Religions in the Early Roman Empire*, 10th ed., 1923; S. Angus: *The Mystery Religions and Christianity*, 1925; N. H. Baynes: 'Constantine the Great and the Christian Church' (*Proceedings of the British Academy*), 1929; C. N. Cochrane; *Christianity and Classical Culture*, 1940; P. de Labriolle: *History of Latin Christian Literature*, (trans. H. Wilson), 1924.

SELECT BIBLIOGRAPHY OF GIBBON

1. *Decline and Fall of the Roman Empire*; 1st ed., 1776–88. Later editions by H. H. Milman: 12 vols. 1838–9; 6 vols. 1846; 8 vols. 1854–5; H. G. Bohn: 7 vols. 1853–5; J. B. Bury: 7 vols. 1896–1900; 7 vols. 1909–14; 7 vols. 1926–9.

2. MINOR WORKS. *Essai sur l'Étude de la Littérature*, 1761 (Eng. trans. 1764); *Mémoires Littéraires de la Grande Bretagne pour l'an 1767*, 1768; *Critical Observations on the Sixth Book of the Aeneid*, 1770; *A Vindication of Some Passages in . . . the 'Decline and Fall,'* 1779; *Mémoire Justicatif pour servir de Réponse a l'Exposé etc. de la Cour de France*, 1779.

3. MISCELLANEOUS WORKS. Ed. John Lord Sheffield: *Miscellaneous Works of Edward Gibbon*, 2 vols. 1796; 4th English ed., 1837.

4. AUTOBIOGRAPHIES. J. Murray (ed.): *The Autobiographies of Edward Gibbon*, 1896; G. Birkbeck Hill (ed.): *The Memoirs of the Life of Edward Gibbon*, 1900; O. Smeaton (ed.): *The Autobiography of Edward Gibbon*, 1911.

5. LETTERS AND JOURNALS. R. E. Prothero (ed.): *Private Letters of Edward Gibbon, 1753–94*, 2 vols. 1896; D. M. Low (ed.): *Gibbon's Journal to January 28th 1763*, 1929.

6. BIOGRAPHY. J. C. Morrison: *Gibbon* (English Men of Letters series), 1878; E. Clodd: *Gibbon and Christianity*, 1916; J. M. Robertson: *Gibbon*, 1925; J. B. Black: *The Art of History*, 1926; G. M. Young: *Gibbon*, 1932; S. T. McCloy: *Gibbon's Antagonism to Christianity*, 1933; C. Dawson: *Edward Gibbon* (British Academy Lecture), 1934; E. Blunden: *Edward Gibbon and his Age*, 1935; R. B. Mowat: *Gibbon*, 1936; D. M. Low: *Gibbon*, 1937; H. L. Bond: *The Literary Art of Edward Gibbon*, 1960. See also studies by Sir L. Stephen: *History of English Thought in the Eighteenth Century* (vol. i), 1876; *Hours in a Library*, 4 vols. 1907; *Cambridge History of English Literature*, vol. x, chapter xiii (by Sir A. W. Warde), 1921; W. Bagehot: *Literary Studies*, vol. ii, 1879; ed. E. Bagehot, 1906; also articles in the *Encyclopaedia Britannica* and *Dictionary of National Biography*.

AUTHORITIES

The ancient authorities to which Gibbon had recourse in preparing his great work were as follows:

I. DION CASSIUS, whose *History of Rome* from the earliest time to his own day is a work of immense value. He completed it in eighty books, but of this work there are only extant Books xxxvi.–lx., covering the period 68 B.C. to A.D. 60. Zonaras, however, whose *Epitome* is extant, was largely indebted to the earlier books, and we have a number of fragments of the other books in the *Excerpta de Virtutibus et Vitiis* and the *Excerpta de Legationibus*, compilations authorized to be made in the tenth century by Constantine VII. Xiphilin also made, in the eleventh century, an abridgment of the last twenty books, save in Book lxx. which is amissing in his abridgment.

II. HERODIAN, whose work *Histories of the Empire after Marcus* embraced in the eight books the reigns from Commodus to Gordianus III.

III. THE HISTORIA AUGUSTA is aptly styled by Bury "a composite work in which six different authors, who lived and wrote in the reigns of Diocletian and Constantine, had a hand," viz., (1) AELIUS SPARTIANUS who, at the order of Diocletian, wrote a series of Imperial biographies, including the Caesars and the Augusti, as far as Caracalla. (2) VULCACIUS GALLICANUS wrote a work on the lives of the emperors who bore the title of Augustus. (3) TREBELLIUS POLLIO wrote the lives of all the emperors from the two Philips, reaching as far as Claudius and his brother Quintillus. (4) FLAVIUS VOPISCUS continued the work of Pollio, carrying it down as far as the death of Carinus and accession of Diocletian. (5) JULIUS CAPITOLINUS also wrote a series of Imperial biographies, but many of them are lost. The earliest extant one is that of Antoninus Pius, the latest Maximus and Balbinus. (6) AELIUS LAMPRIDIUS wrote Imperial biographies, which he dedicated to Constantine. He began with Commodus and reached Alexander Severus.

IV. SEXTUS AURELIUS VICTOR was the governor of the second Pannonia, being appointed by the Emperor Julian in A.D. 361. He was thought to have written a long History of the Roman Emperors now lost, of which the *Caesares* (still extant) is an abridgment.

V. EUTROPIUS was the *Magister Memoriae* at the court of Valens, to whom he dedicated his *Short Roman History*.

VI. RUFUS FESTUS, also a *Magister Memoriae* to Valens. His volume was written about A.D. 369, because he refers to the great victory over the Goths gained by Valens in that year.

VII. L. CAELIUS LACTANTIUS FIRMIANUS lived in the reigns of Diocletian and Constantine at Nicomedia, where he taught rhetoric.

Later in life he acted as tutor to Constantine's son Crispus. His works were chiefly theological. The most important is the *De Mortibus Persecutorum*, written about A.D. 314 and relating the deaths of those who persecuted the Christians. Doubts have been thrown on the authorship, but no satisfactory reason has been assigned which would lead one to withdraw the volume from the works of Lactantius.

VIII. EUSEBIUS OF CAESAREA.—He succeeded to the chronographic work of Sextus Julius Africanus, who (as Bury says) flourished in the early part of the third century, and wrote his chronographic work between A.D. 212 and 221. *The Ecclesiastical History* of Eusebius corrects the numerous errors which occur in the *Chronographies* of Africanus. The latter began his chronicle with Adam, but Eusebius with Abraham.

LIBANIUS, who lived from A.D. 314 to *c.* 395, was another authority to which Gibbon was under great obligations; also the *Orations* of Themistius who was a friend of Libanius.

AMMIANUS MARCELLINUS was a native of Antioch where he was born about 330, and went through all Julian's campaigns. His *Res Gestae* in thirty-one books are of value as throwing the light of contemporary ideas on the events of the time. He was known to have been alive in A.D. 391.

EUNAPIUS OF SARDIS (A.D. 347–414) wrote a continuation of the *Chronicle of Dexippus* from A.D. 270 to 404; also the *Lives of the Philosophers and Sophists*.

ZOSIMUS who, as L. Mendelssohn has shown, was a *Count* and an *ex-advocatus fisci*, wrote his history between the dates A.D. 450 and 501.

IDATIUS or HYDATIUS, a Spaniard, wrote the *Consular Fasti*, which consists of three parts, the first extending from the first Consuls to the founding of Constantinople, A.D. 330; the second from A.D. 330 to 395; the third from 395 to 468. As Mommsen points out, the first two parts are an abridgment of the *Chronicon Paschale*.

Then we have the four Greek ecclesiastical historians, who flourished in the first half of the fifth century:

PHILOSTORGIUS, born *c.* 365, died 412. His *Ecclesiastical History* is unfortunately only known by Photius's epitome of it in the ninth century.

SOCRATES, who was a native of Constantinople, brought down his History to A.D. 439. He was an orthodox writer as also was

SOZOMEN, his contemporary, who intended to trace the History of the Church from 324 to 439, where Socrates ended, but the work as it has come down to us ends in 425, the last books having been lost.

. THEODORET, who, like Socrates and Sozomen, was also orthodox, wrote his History, which comes down to A.D. 429, between A.D. 441 and 449.

SYNESIUS OF CYRENE (360–*c.* 415), the friend of Aurelian, was converted to Christianity under Theophilus of Alexandria and became

Bishop of Ptolemais. Was a satirist, a poet, and a letter-writer, in which occur valuable descriptions of the period.

PALLADIUS, Bishop of Helenopolis, wrote a biographical work on John Chrysostom, also short biographies of men and women contemporary with him who had followed the ascetic rule. This was called *Historia Lausiaca*.

OLYMPIODORUS, the Pagan of Thebes (in Egypt), wrote a valuable History in twenty-two books. Unluckily it is no longer extant, but extracts have been preserved in Photius's *Bibliotheca*. Other valuable works of this period are the fragments of the History of PRISCUS OF PANIUM in Thrace, whose History began about A.D. 435 and continued down to 474, and whom Bury considers as the best historian of the fifth century; also Q. AURELIUS SYMMACHUS, born about 340 and died about 405, whose works consist of nine books of letters descriptive of the age; also DECIUS MAGNUS AUSONIUS, born about A.D. 310 at Burdigala and died *c.* 395, whose poems reflect the customs of the time with rare fidelity; PONTIUS PAULINUS OF NOLA (354–431), who wrote a description of the Churches of the time, and in his poems limned the chief characters of the age; PAULINUS OF PELLA, his father, was Praetorian Praefect of Illyricum, and wrote a valuable poem, *Eucharisticon Deo Sub ephemerdis meae textu*, which gives an interesting description of Aquitania at the time of Ataulf's invasion; also CLAUDIUS CLAUDIANUS, the celebrated poet, born probably at Alexandria where he lived and wrote, being the laureate of Honorius from about 396 to 404; and AURELIUS PRUDENTIUS CLEMENS, who was at once the earliest and the greatest of the Christian poets. His *Contra Symmachum* is a most important work from an historical sense, dealing with the victory over Alaric at Pollentia. Another great Christian poet was FLAVIUS MEROBAUDES, whose *Carmina* are of great value. Other chronicles for the period are that of PROSPER TIRO of Aquitaine, who compiled an *Epitome Chronicon*, also the *Chronica Gallica* and the *Chronica Italica* (made up of the Fasti Vindobonenses and the Continuation of Prosper, etc.), while Gibbon unquestionably drew much of his material for the fourth and fifth centuries from the work of PAULUS OROSIUS of Tarraco, *Historiae adversum Paganos*, the *De Gubernatione Dei* of SALVIAN, and the *Ecclesiastical History* of TYRANNIUS RUFINUS.

In the fifth, sixth, and seventh centuries Malchus of Philadelphia, Eustathius of Epiphania, Hesychius of Miletus, Theodoros Anagnostes, Procopius of Caesarea (whose *Secret History* and *Military History* are of priceless value), Agathias of Myrina, Joannes Rhetor, or Malalas, John of Antioch, Joshua Stylites, Zacharias Rhetor, C. Apollinaris Sidonius, Cassiodorus, Corippus, Victor Tonnennensis, Isidorus Junior, Gregory of Tours, have all been laid under levy by Gibbon; while the principal authorities consulted by Gibbon in the period dating from the eighth to the twelfth century are John of Ephesus, Evagrius, Theophylactus Simocattes, the poems of George Pisides (the *Heracliad*, etc.), Sebaeos, John of Damascus, Nicephorus of Constantinople, Theodore of Studion, George the Monk, Leo the Armenian, Joseph Gennesius, the Sicilian Chronicle,

Leo Diacorus, Constantine Psellus, Michael Attaleiates, Nicephorus Bryennius, Anna Comnena, John Cinnamus, Nicetas Acominatos, John Scylitzes, John Zonaras, among Greek sources; and the *Liber Pontificalis*, Letters of Pope Gregory the Great, Paul the Deacon, Fredegarius; while for the Mohammedan period, the extant authorities which Gibbon consulted in addition to the Koran, were *The Life of Mohammed* by Al-Tabari, also by Wakidi, by Ibn Kutaiba, by Ibn Abd-al-Hakam, by Masudi, by Eutychius, John of Nikiu, Michael of Mitylene, Bar Hebraeus, or Abulpharagius. On the ninth to fourteenth centuries Photius, Constantine Porphyrogennetos, George Codinus, Eustathius, George Acropolites, George Pachymeres, Nicephorus Blemmydes, the *Gesta Francorum*, the *Chronicle of Morea*, Hugo Falcandus, Albert of Aachen, William of Tyre, Marshal Villehardouin, Nicetas, Abu-L-Fide, were all placed under contribution; while for the siege and fall of Constantinople the chief authorities relied on were Laonicus Chalcondyles, Ducas, George Phrantzes, Critobulus of Imbros, Minhaj-i-Siraj Juzjani, Mirza Haidar, the Yuan Shi, John Cananus, Cardinal Isidore, Leonardus of Chios.

[Footnotes printed in square brackets were written by Oliphant Smeaton for the 1910 edition.]

CONTENTS

xx   Gibbon's Decline and Fall of Rome

THE
HISTORY OF THE DECLINE AND FALL
OF THE
ROMAN EMPIRE

CHAPTER I

The Extent and Military Force of the Empire in the Age of the Antonines

In the second century of the Christian era, the Empire of Rome comprehended the fairest part of the earth, and the most civilised portion of mankind. The frontiers of that extensive monarchy were guarded by ancient renown and disciplined valour. The gentle but powerful influence of laws and manners had gradually cemented the union of the provinces. Their peaceful inhabitants enjoyed and abused the advantages of wealth and luxury. The image of a free constitution was preserved with decent reverence: the Roman senate appeared to possess the sovereign authority, and devolved on the emperors all the executive powers of government. During a happy period (A.D. 98–180) of more than fourscore years, the public administration was conducted by the virtue and abilities of Nerva, Trajan, Hadrian, and the two Antonines. It is the design of this, and of the two succeeding chapters, to describe the prosperous condition of their empire; and afterwards, from the death of Marcus Antoninus, to deduce the most important circumstances of its decline and fall; a revolution which will ever be remembered, and is still felt by the nations of the earth.

The principal conquests of the Romans were achieved under the republic; and the emperors, for the most part, were satisfied with preserving those dominions which had been acquired by the policy of the senate, the active emulation of the consuls, and the martial enthusiasm of the people. The seven first centuries were filled with a rapid succession of triumphs; but it was reserved for Augustus to relinquish the ambitious design of subduing the whole earth, and to introduce a spirit of moderation into the public councils. Inclined to peace by his temper and situation, it was easy for him to discover that Rome, in her present exalted situation, had much less to hope than to fear from the chance of arms; and that, in the prosecution of remote wars, the undertaking became every day more difficult, the event more doubtful, and the possession more precarious, and less beneficial. The experience of Augustus added weight to these salutary reflections, and effectually convinced him that, by the prudent vigour of his counsels, it would be easy to secure every concession which the safety or the dignity of Rome might require from the most formidable Barbarians. Instead of exposing his person and his legions to the arrows of the Parthians, he obtained, by an honourable treaty, the restitution of the standards and prisoners which had been taken in the defeat of Crassus.[1]

His generals, in the early part of his reign, attempted the reduction of Æthiopia and Arabia Felix. They marched near a thousand miles to the south of the tropic; but the heat of the climate soon repelled the invaders, and protected the unwarlike natives of those sequestered regions.[2] The northern countries of Europe scarcely deserved the expense and labour of conquest. The forests and morasses of Germany were filled with a hardy race of barbarians, who despised life when it was separated from freedom; and though, on the first attack, they seemed to yield to the weight of the Roman power, they soon, by a signal act of despair, regained their independence, and reminded Augustus

---

[1] Dion Cassius (l. liv. p. 736), with the annotations of Reimar, who has collected all that Roman vanity has left upon the subject. The marble of Ancyra, on which Augustus recorded his own exploits, asserts that *he compelled* the Parthians to restore the ensigns of Crassus.

[2] Strabo (l. xvi. p. 780), Pliny the elder (Hist. Natur. l. vi. c. 28, 29), and Dion Cassius (l. liii. p. 723 and l. liv. p. 734), have left us very curious details concerning these wars. The Romans made themselves masters of Mariaba, a city of Arabia Felix, well known to the Orientals (see Abulfeda and the Nubian geography, p. 52). They were arrived within three days' journey of the Spice country, the rich object of their invasion.

[Gibbon has fallen into error here. Strabo says that the Romans under Aelius Gallus advanced as far as Marsyaba or Marsyabæ, within two days' journey of the Spice country, not three as stated. To this place they laid siege, but were unable to take it owing to the want of water. They therefore commenced their retreat. Gibbon (as Dr. W. Smith says) not only assumes that this place is the same as Mariaba, which Pliny mentions among the conquests of Aelius Gallus, but also, blindly adopting the theory of D'Anville, identifies Mariaba with Mâreb, the celebrated capital of the Sabaeans of Yemen upon the borders of the Southern province. Strabo, however, mentions Mariaba, the capital of the Sabaeans as distinct from Marsyaba (cf. Strabo).—O. S.]

of the vicissitude of fortune.[1] On the death of that emperor, his testament was publicly read in the senate. He bequeathed, as a valuable legacy to his successors, the advice of confining the empire within those limits, which Nature seemed to have placed as its permanent bulwarks and boundaries; on the west the Atlantic ocean; the Rhine and Danube on the north; the Euphrates on the east; and towards the south, the sandy deserts of Arabia and Africa.[2]

Happily for the repose of mankind, the moderate system recommended by the wisdom of Augustus, was adopted by the fears and vices of his immediate successors. Engaged in the pursuit of pleasure, or in the exercise of tyranny, the first Cæsars seldom showed themselves to the armies, or to the provinces; nor were they disposed to suffer, that those triumphs which *their* indolence neglected should be usurped by the conduct and valour of their lieutenants. The military fame of a subject was considered as an insolent invasion of the Imperial prerogative; and it became the duty, as well as interest, of every Roman general, to guard the frontiers intrusted to his care, without aspiring to conquests which might have proved no less fatal to himself than to the vanquished barbarians.[3]

The only accession which the Roman empire received, during the first century of the Christian era, was the province of Britain. In this single instance the successors of Cæsar and Augustus were persuaded to follow the example of the former, rather than the precept of the latter. The proximity of its situation to the coast of Gaul seemed to invite their arms; the pleasing, though doubtful intelligence, of a pearl fishery, attracted their avarice;[4] and as Britain was viewed in the light of a distinct and insulated world, the conquest scarcely formed any exception to the general system of continental measures. After a war of about forty

---

[1] By the slaughter of Varus and his three legions. First book of the Annals of Tacitus. Sueton. in August, c. 23 and Velleius Paterculus, l. ii. c. 117, etc. Augustus did not receive the melancholy news with all the temper and firmness that might have been expected from his character.

[2] Tacit. Annal. l. ii., Dion Cassius, l. lvi. p. 833, and the speech of Augustus himself, in Julian's Cæsars. It receives great light from the learned notes of his French translator M. Spanheim.

[3] Germanicus, Suetonius Paulinus, and Agricola, were checked and recalled in the course of their victories. Corbulo was put to death. Military merit, as it is admirably expressed by Tacitus, was, in the strictest sense of the word, *imperatoria virtus*.

[4] Cæsar himself conceals that ignoble motive; but it is mentioned by Suetonius, c. 47. The British pearls proved, however, of little value, on account of their dark and livid colour. Tacitus observes, with reason (in Agricola, c. 12), that it was an inherent defect. " Ego facilius crediderim, naturam margaritis deesse quam nobis avaritiam."

years, undertaken by the most stupid, maintained by the most dissolute, and terminated by the most timid of all the emperors, the far greater part of the island submitted to the Roman yoke.[1] The various tribes of Britons possessed valour without conduct, and the love of freedom without the spirit of union. They took up arms with savage fierceness; they laid them down, or turned them against each other with wild inconstancy; and while they fought singly, they were successively subdued. Neither the fortitude of Caractacus, nor the despair of Boadicea, nor the fanaticism of the Druids, could avert the slavery of their country, or resist the steady progress of the Imperial generals, who maintained the national glory, when the throne was disgraced by the weakest, or the most vicious of mankind. At the very time when Domitian, confined to his palace, felt the terrors which he inspired; his legions, under the command of the virtuous Agricola, defeated the collected force of the Caledonians at the foot of the Grampian hills;[2] and his fleets, venturing to explore an unknown and dangerous navigation, displayed the Roman arms round every part of the island. The conquest of Britain was considered as already achieved;[3] and it was the design of Agricola to complete and ensure his success by the easy reduction of Ireland, for which in his opinion, one legion and a few auxiliaries were sufficient.[4] The western isle might be improved into a valuable possession, and the Britons would wear their chains with the less reluctance, if the prospect and example of freedom were on every side removed from before their eyes.

But the superior merit of Agricola soon occasioned his removal from the government of Britain; and for ever disappointed this rational, though extensive scheme of conquest. Before his departure, the prudent general had provided for security as well as for dominion. He had observed that the island is almost divided into two unequal parts by the opposite gulfs, or, as they are now called, the Friths of Scotland. Across the narrow interval of about forty miles, he had drawn a line of military stations, which was afterwards fortified in the reign of Antoninus

---

[1] Claudius, Nero, and Domitian. A hope is expressed by Pomponius Mela, l. iii. c. 6 (he wrote under Claudius) that, by the success of the Roman arms, the island and its savage inhabitants would soon be better known.

[2] [*Grampian Hills*—Later investigation has thrown grave doubt upon the assertion that the *Mons Graupius* of Tacitus referred to any peak in the Grampian range. The spot cannot now be identified.—O. S.]

[3] The admirable abridgment given by Tacitus, in the Life of Agricola, and copiously, though perhaps not completely, illustrated by our own antiquarians, Camden and Horsley.

[4] The Irish writers, jealous of their national honour, are extremely provoked on this occasion, both with Tacitus and with Agricola.

Pius, by a turf rampart erected on foundations of stone.[1] This wall of Antoninus, at a small distance beyond the modern cities of Edinburgh [2] and Glasgow,[3] was fixed as the limit of the Roman province. The native Caledonians preserved in the northern extremity of the island their wild independence, for which they were not less indebted to their poverty than to their valour. Their incursions were frequently repelled and chastised; but their country was never subdued.[4] The masters of the fairest and most wealthy climates of the globe turned with contempt from gloomy hills assailed by the winter tempest, from lakes concealed in a blue mist, and from cold and lonely heaths, over which the deer of the forest were chased by a troop of naked barbarians.[5]

Such was the state of the Roman frontiers, and such the maxims of Imperial policy, from the death of Augustus to the accession of Trajan. That virtuous and active prince had received the education of a soldier, and possessed the talents of a general.[6] The peaceful system of his predecessors was inter-

[1] Horsley's Britannia Romana, l. i. c. 10.

[2] [Carriden on the Firth of Forth, about 14 miles from Edinburgh, mentioned by Gildas (500 A.D.) as being a very ancient town. Its name, " Cair-Edon " means in Gaelic " The town in the front."—O. S.]

[3] [Chapel Hill on the Clyde, 11 miles W.N.W. of Glasgow.—O. S.]

[4] The poet Buchanan celebrates, with elegance and spirit (see his Sylvæ v.), the unviolated independence of his native country. But, if the single testimony of Richard of Cirencester was sufficient to create a Roman province of Vespasiana to the north of the wall, that independence would be reduced within very narrow limits.

[Buchanan refers to Scotland and the independence of his countrymen in Sylvæ No. iv., i.e. in the " Epithalamium on the marriage of Francis, the Dauphin of France, and Mary Stuart of Scotland," not, as Gibbon says, in Sylvæ No. v., which is entitled " The Lamentation of France on the Death of Francis II., its King." With regard to the matter of the independence of the people being preserved by the walls, the fact should be noted that there really were two Roman walls, the remains of which are extant to-day, one extending from the Forth to the Clyde, and the other from the Solway to the mouth of the Tyne. The stone wall from the Solway to the Tyne has been ascribed to Severus, and the parallel earthen mound to Hadrian. But there is every reason to believe that the two are complimentary to each other and coeval in date, and the results of the most recent investigation has inclined to ascribe both to Hadrian. In confirmation of this view it may be stated that neither Dion Cassius nor Herodian attributes the erection of any wall to Severus.—O. S.]

[5] Appian (in Procem.) and the uniform imagery of Ossian's Poems, which, according to every hypothesis, were composed by a native Caledonian.

[Ossian, " a native Caledonian." This statement was made by Gibbon under the belief that the compositions of James Macpherson were genuine translations from the Gaelic. Now Macpherson's *Ossian* has never been satisfactorily explained. Macpherson was not a Gaelic scholar, and there are only original texts for about one half of the poems published by Macpherson as translations of extant works. For the remainder of the poems no originals, either ancient or modern, have ever been found.—O. S.]

[6] Pliny's Panegyric, which seems founded on facts.

rupted by scenes of war and conquest; and the legions, after
a long interval, beheld a military emperor at their head. The
first exploits of Trajan were against the Dacians, the most warlike of men, who dwelt beyond the Danube, and who, during
the reign of Domitian, had insulted with impunity the Majesty
of Rome.[1] To the strength and fierceness of barbarians, they
added a contempt for life, which was derived from a warm persuasion of the immortality and transmigration of the soul.[2]
Decebalus, the Dacian king, approved himself a rival not unworthy of Trajan; nor did he despair of his own and the public
fortune, till, by the confession of his enemies, he had exhausted
every resource both of valour and policy.[3] This memorable war,
with a very short suspension of hostilities, lasted five years; and
as the emperor could exert, without control, the whole force of
the state, it was terminated by an absolute submission of the
barbarians.[4] The new province of Dacia, which formed a second
exception to the precept of Augustus, was about 1300 miles
in circumference. Its natural boundaries were the Dniester,
the Teyss [Theiss modern form], or Tibiscus, the Lower Danube,
and the Euxine Sea. The vestiges of a military road may still
be traced from the banks of the Danube to the neighbourhood
of Bender, a place famous in modern history, and the actual
frontier of the Turkish and Russian empires.[5]

Trajan was ambitious of fame; and as long as mankind shall
continue to bestow more liberal applause on their destroyers
than on their benefactors, the thirst of military glory will ever
be the vice of the most exalted characters. The praises of Alexander, transmitted by a succession of poets and historians, had
kindled a dangerous emulation in the mind of Trajan. Like
him the Roman emperor undertook an expedition against the
nations of the east, but he lamented with a sigh, that his
advanced age scarcely left him any hopes of equalling the re-

[1] Dion Cassius, l. lxvii.
[2] Herodotus, l. iv. c. 94. Julian in the Cæsars, with Spanheim's observations.
[3] Plin. Epist. viii. 9.
[4] Dion Cassius, l. lxviii. p. 1123, 1131. Julian in Cæsaribus, Eutropius,
viii. 2, 6. Aurelius Victor in Epitome.
[The two Dacian Wars of Trajan lasted from A.D. 101-107, the first of
these continuing throughout 101-102, Trajan being accorded a triumph in
102, with the agnomen *Dacicus*.—O. S.]
[5] Memoir of M. d'Anville, on the Province of Dacia, in the Académie des
Inscriptions, tom. xxviii. p. 444-468.
[*Bender* is now in the Russian province of Bessarabia, on the line to
Odessa, being distant therefrom about 82 miles.—O. S.]

nown of the son of Philip.[1] Yet the success of Trajan, however
transient, was rapid and specious. The degenerate Parthians,
broken by intestine discord, fled before his arms. He descended
the river Tigris in triumph, from the mountains of Armenia to
the Persian gulf. He enjoyed the honour of being the first, as
he was the last, of the Roman generals, who ever navigated that
remote sea. His fleets ravaged the coasts of Arabia; and Trajan
vainly flattered himself that he was approaching towards the
confines of India.[2] Every day the astonished senate received
the intelligence of new names and new nations, that acknowledged his sway. They were informed that the kings of
Bosphorus, Colchos, Iberia, Albania, Osrhoene, and even the
Parthian monarch himself, had accepted their diadems from the
hands of the emperor; that the independent tribes of the Median
and Carduchian hills had implored his protection; and that
the rich countries of Armenia, Mesopotamia, and Assyria, were
reduced into the state of provinces.[3] But the death of Trajan
soon clouded the splendid prospect; and it was justly to be
dreaded, that so many distant nations would throw off the unaccustomed yoke, when they were no longer restrained by the
powerful hand which had imposed it.

It was an ancient tradition, that when the Capitol was founded
by one of the Roman kings, the god Terminus (who presided
over boundaries, and was represented according to the fashion
of that age by a large stone) alone, among all the inferior deities,
refused to yield his place to Jupiter himself. A favourable inference was drawn from his obstinacy, which was interpreted by
the augurs as a sure presage that the boundaries of the Roman
power would never recede.[4] During many ages, the prediction,
as it is usual, contributed to its own accomplishment. But
though Terminus had resisted the majesty of Jupiter, he submitted to the authority of the emperor Hadrian.[5] The resignation of all the eastern conquests of Trajan was the first measure
of his reign. He restored to the Parthians the election of an

---

[1] Trajan's sentiments are represented in a very just and lively manner in
the Cæsars of Julian.
[2] Eutropius and Sextus Rufus have endeavoured to perpetuate the illusion. See a very sensible dissertation of M. Freret in the Académie des Inscriptions, tom. xxi. p. 55.
[3] Dion Cassius, l. lxviii.
[4] Ovid, Fast. l. ii. ver. 667. Livy, under the reign of Tarquin.
[5] St. Augustin is highly delighted with the proof of the weakness of Terminus, and the vanity of the Augurs. De Civitate Dei, iv. 29.
[But an instance of the shrinkage of the Roman frontiers had already
occurred in the loss of Trans-Rhenane Germany.—O. S.]

independent sovereign, withdrew the Roman garrisons from the
provinces of Armenia, Mesopotamia, and Assyria, and, in compliance with the precept of Augustus, once more established the
Euphrates as the frontier of the empire.[1] Censure, which
arraigns the public actions and the private motives of princes,
has ascribed to envy, a conduct, which might be attributed to
the prudence and moderation of Hadrian. The various character of that emperor, capable, by turns, of the meanest and the
most generous sentiments, may afford some colour to the suspicion. It was, however, scarcely in his power to place the
superiority of his predecessor in a more conspicuous light, than
by thus confessing himself unequal to the task of defending the
conquests of Trajan.

The martial and ambitious spirit of Trajan formed a very
singular contrast with the moderation of his successor. The
restless activity of Hadrian was not less remarkable, when compared with the gentle repose of Antoninus Pius. The life of the
former was almost a perpetual journey; and as he possessed the
various talents of the soldier, the statesman, and the scholar, he
gratified his curiosity in the discharge of his duty. Careless of
the difference of seasons and of climates, he marched on foot,
and bare-headed, over the snows of Caledonia, and the sultry
plains of the Upper Egypt; nor was there a province of the
empire which, in the course of his reign, was not honoured with
the presence of the monarch.[2] But the tranquil life of Antoninus Pius was spent in the bosom of Italy; and, during the
twenty-three years that he directed the public administration,
the longest journeys of that amiable prince extended no farther
than from his palace in Rome to the retirement of his Lanuvian
Villa.[3]

Notwithstanding this difference in their personal conduct, the
general system of Augustus was equally adopted and uniformly
pursued by Hadrian and by the two Antonines. They persisted

---

[1] Augustan History, p. 5. Jerome's Chronicle, and all the Epitomisers.
It is somewhat surprising that this memorable event should be omitted by
Dion, or rather by Xiphilin.

[Hadrian preferred security of frontiers to the prestige of extensive new
dominions that were insufficiently conquered. Therefore he not only made
the Euphrates the boundary in the east, but he strengthened the frontier of
Dacia in the north: he built the fortified wall between the Rhine and the
Danube, and in Britain he erected the Roman wall between the Tyne and
the Solway.—O. S.]

[2] Dion, l. lxix. p. 1158. Hist. August. p. 5, 8. If all our historians were
lost, medals, inscriptions, and other monuments, would be sufficient to
record the travels of Hadrian.

[3] Augustan History.

in the design of maintaining the dignity of the empire, without attempting to enlarge its limits. By every honourable expedient they invited the friendship of the barbarians; and endeavoured to convince mankind that the Roman power, raised above the temptation of conquest, was actuated only by the love of order and justice. During a long period of forty-three years their virtuous labours were crowned with success; and if we except a few slight hostilities that served to exercise the legions of the frontier, the reigns of Hadrian and Antoninus Pius offer the fair prospect of universal peace.[1] The Roman name was revered among the most remote nations of the earth. The fiercest barbarians frequently submitted their differences to the arbitration of the emperor; and we are informed by a contemporary historian, that he had seen ambassadors who were refused the honour which they came to solicit, of being admitted into the rank of subjects.[2]

The terror of the Roman arms added weight and dignity to the moderation of the emperors. They preserved peace by a constant preparation for war; and while justice regulated their conduct, they announced to the nations on their confines that they were as little disposed to endure as to offer an injury. The military strength, which it had been sufficient for Hadrian and the elder Antoninus to display, was exerted against the Parthians and the Germans by the emperor Marcus. The hostilities of the barbarians provoked the resentment of that philosophic monarch, and, in the prosecution of a just defence, Marcus and his generals obtained many signal victories, both on the Euphrates and on the Danube.[3] The military establishment of the Roman empire, which thus assured either its tranquillity or success, will now become the proper and important object of our attention.

In the purer ages of the commonwealth, the use of arms was reserved for those ranks of citizens who had a country to love, a property to defend, and some share in enacting those laws,

---

[1] We must, however, remember, that, in the time of Hadrian, a rebellion of the Jews raged with religious fury, though only in a single province: Pausanias (l. viii. c. 43) mentions two necessary and successful wars, conducted by the generals of Pius. 1st. Against the wandering Moors, who were driven into the solitudes of Atlas. 2nd, Against the Brigantes of Britain, who had invaded the Roman province. Both these wars (with several other hostilities) are mentioned in the Augustan History, p. 19.

[2] Appian of Alexándria, in the preface to his History of the Roman Wars.

[3] Dion, l. lxxi. Hist. August. in Marco, b. iv. 9-22. The Parthian victories gave birth to a crowd of contemptible historians, whose memory has been rescued from oblivion, and exposed to ridicule, in a very lively piece of criticism of Lucian.

which it was their interest, as well as duty, to maintain. But in proportion as the public freedom was lost in extent of conquest, war was gradually improved into an art, and degraded into a trade.[1] The legions themselves, even at the time when they were recruited in the most distant provinces, were supposed to consist of Roman citizens. That distinction was generally considered either as a legal qualification or as a proper recompense for the soldier; but a more serious regard was paid to the essential merit of age, strength, and military stature.[2] In all levies, a just preference was given to the climates of the North over those of the South: the race of men born to the exercise of arms was sought for in the country rather than in cities; and it was very reasonably presumed, that the hardy occupations of smiths, carpenters, and huntsmen, would supply more vigour and resolution than the sedentary trades which are employed in the service of luxury.[3] After every qualification of property had been laid aside, the armies of the Roman emperors were still commanded, for the most part, by officers of a liberal birth and education; but the common soldiers, like the mercenary troops of modern Europe, were drawn from the meanest, and very frequently from the most profligate, of mankind.

That public virtue which among the ancients was denominated patriotism, is derived from a strong sense of our own interest in the preservation and prosperity of the free government of which we are members. Such a sentiment, which had rendered the legions of the republic almost invincible, could make but a very feeble impression on the mercenary servants of a despotic prince; and it became necessary to supply that defect by other motives, of a different, but not less forcible nature; honour and religion. The peasant, or mechanic, imbibed the useful prejudice that he was advanced to the more dignified profession of arms, in which his rank and reputation would depend on his own valour; and that, although the prowess of a private soldier must often escape the notice of fame, his own behaviour might sometimes confer glory or disgrace on the company, the legion, or even the army, to whose honours he was associated. On his first entrance into

---

[1] The poorest rank of soldiers possessed above forty pounds sterling (Dionys. Halicarn. iv. 17), a very high qualification, at a time when money was so scarce, that an ounce of silver was equivalent to seventy pound weight of brass. The populace, excluded by the ancient constitution, were indiscriminately admitted by Marius. Sallust. de Bell. Jugurth. c. 91.

[2] Cæsar formed his legion Alauda, of Gauls and strangers: but it was during the licence of civil war; and after the victory, he gave them the freedom of the city for their reward.

[3] Vegetius de Re Militari, l i c 2-7.

the service, an oath was administered to him, with every circumstance of solemnity. He promised never to desert his standard.
to submit his own will to the commands of his leaders, and to
sacrifice his life for the safety of the emperor and the empire.[1]
The attachment of the Roman troops to their standards was
inspired by the united influence of religion and of honour. The
golden eagle, which glittered in the front of the legion, was the
object of their fondest devotion; nor was it esteemed less impious
than it was ignominious, to abandon that sacred ensign in the
hour of danger.[2] These motives, which derived their strength
from the imagination, were enforced by fears and hopes of a
more substantial kind. Regular pay, occasional donatives, and
a stated recompense, after the appointed time of service, alleviated the hardships of the military life,[3] whilst, on the other
hand, it was impossible for cowardice or disobedience to escape
the severest punishment. The centurions were authorised to
chastise with blows, the generals had a right to punish with
death; and it was an inflexible maxim of Roman discipline, that
a good soldier should dread his officers far more than the enemy.
From such laudable arts did the valour of the Imperial troops
receive a degree of firmness and docility, unattainable by the
impetuous and irregular passions of barbarians.

And yet so sensible were the Romans of the imperfection of
valour without skill and practice, that, in their language, the
name of an army was borrowed from the word which signified
exercise.[4] Military exercises were the important and unremitted
object of their discipline. The recruits and young soldiers were
constantly trained both in the morning and in the evening, nor
was age or knowledge allowed to excuse the veterans from the
daily repetition of what they had completely learnt. Large

[1] The oath of service and fidelity to the emperor, was annually renewed
by the troops, on the first of January.

[2] Tacitus calls the Roman eagles, Bellorum Deos. They were placed in
a chapel in the camp, and with the other deities received the religious worship of the troops.

[3] Gronovius de Pecunia vetere, l. iii. p. 120, etc. The emperor Domitian
raised the annual stipend of the legionaries to twelve pieces of gold, which,
in his time, was equivalent to about ten of our guineas. This pay, somewhat higher than our own, had been, and was afterwards, gradually increased, according to the progress of wealth and military government.
After twenty years' service, the veteran received three thousand denarii
(about one hundred pounds sterling), or a proportionable allowance of land.
The pay and advantages of the guards were, in general, about double those
of the legions.

[4] Exercitus ab exercitando, Varro de Linguâ Latinâ, l. iv. Cicero in
Tusculan. l. ii. 37. There is room for a very interesting work, which should
lay open the connection between the languages and manners of nations.

sheds were erected in the winter-quarters of the troops, that their useful labours might not receive any interruption from the most tempestuous weather; and it was carefully observed, that the arms destined to this imitation of war, should be of double the weight which was required in real action.[1] It is not the purpose of this work to enter into any minute description of the Roman exercises. We shall only remark, that they comprehended whatever could add strength to the body, activity to the limbs, or grace to the motions. The soldiers were diligently instructed to march, to run, to leap, to swim, to carry heavy burdens, to handle every species of arms that was used either for offence or for defence, either in distant engagement or in a closer onset; to form a variety of evolutions; and to move to the sound of flutes, in the Pyrrhic or martial dance.[2] In the midst of peace, the Roman troops familiarised themselves with the practice of war; and it is prettily remarked by an ancient historian who had fought against them, that the effusion of blood was the only circumstance which distinguished a field of battle from a field of exercise.[3] It was the policy of the ablest generals, and even of the emperors themselves, to encourage these military studies by their presence and example; and we are informed that Hadrian, as well as Trajan, frequently condescended to instruct the unexperienced soldiers, to reward the diligent, and sometimes to dispute with them the prize of superior strength or dexterity.[4] Under the reigns of those princes, the science of tactics was cultivated with success; and as long as the empire retained any vigour, their military instructions were respected as the most perfect model of Roman discipline.

Nine centuries of war had gradually introduced into the service many alterations and improvements. The legions, as they are described by Polybius,[5] in the time of the Punic wars, differed very materially from those which achieved the victories of Cæsar, or defended the monarchy of Hadrian and the Antonines. The constitution of the Imperial legion may be described in a few words.[6] The heavy-armed infantry, which composed its prin-

[1] Vegetius, l. ii. and the rest of his first book.
[2] The Pyrrhic dance is extremely well illustrated by M. le Beau, in the Académie des Inscriptions, tom. xxxv. p. 262, etc. That learned academician, in a series of memoirs, has collected all the passages of the ancients that relate to the Roman legion.
[3] Joseph. de Bell. Judaico, l. iii. c. 5. We are indebted to this Jew for some very curious details of Roman discipline.
[4] Plin. Panegyr. c. 13. Life of Hadrian, in the Augustan History, 1-14.
[5] See an admirable digression on the Roman discipline, in the sixth book of his history.
[6] Vegetius de Re Militari, l. ii. c. 4, etc. Considerable part of his very

cipal strength,[1] was divided into ten cohorts, and fifty-five companies, under the orders of a correspondent number of tribunes and centurions. The first cohort, which always claimed the post of honour and the custody of the eagle, was formed of eleven hundred and five soldiers, the most approved for valour and fidelity. The remaining nine cohorts consisted each of five hundred and fifty-five; and the whole body of legionary infantry amounted to six thousand one hundred men. Their arms were uniform, and admirably adapted to the nature of their service:[2] an open helmet, with a lofty crest; a breast-plate, or coat of mail; greaves on their legs, and an ample buckler on their left arm. The buckler was of an oblong and concave figure, four feet in length, and two and an half in breadth, framed of a light wood, covered with a bull's hide, and strongly guarded with plates of brass. Besides a lighter spear, the legionary soldier grasped in his right hand the formidable *pilum*, a ponderous javelin, whose utmost length was about six feet, and which was terminated by a massy triangular point of steel of eighteen inches.[3] This instrument was indeed much inferior to our

perplexed abridgment was taken from the regulations of Trajan and Hadrian; and the legion, as he describes it, cannot suit any other age of the Roman empire.

[1] Vegetius de Re Militari, l. ii. c. 1. In the purer age of Cæsar and Cicero, the word *miles* was almost confined to the infantry. Under the lower empire, and in the times of chivalry, it was appropriated almost as exclusively to the men at arms, who fought on horseback.

[Gibbon's account of the military system of the Romans contains several errors that must be corrected. The legion was not a fixed quantity. It varied in the several epochs of development of the Roman military system. Usually it is stated to have consisted of 6000 footmen, and from 120 to 132 horse, otherwise ten cohorts containing six centuries.—O. S.]

[2] [The Roman arms were, as Gibbon says, admirably fitted for service in the field. The Roman helmet (*cassis galea*) differed from the Greek in lacking a visor. The breastplate (*lorica pectoralis*) consisted of from five to seven stripes of beaten iron or bronze, each equal in width to about three fingers, and all attached to leather straps. They were then fastened round the body with hooks from the waist up to the armpit, thus forming the breast-armour (*pectorale*), while similar stripes were laid across the shoulders (*humeralia*), and fastened by means of hooks to the upper stripes of the *pectorale*. Several stripes hanging down in front protected the lower part of the body. The bronze or metal greaves were in use in republican times, but the imperial legionaries had wholly abandoned them, in favour of stockings made of wool or leather.—O. S.]

[3] In the time of Polybius and Dionysius of Halicarnassus (l. v. c. 45), the steel point of the *pilum* seems to have been much longer. In the time of Vegetius, it was reduced to a foot, or even nine inches. I have chosen a medium.

[The pilum in late Imperial times gave place to the *spiculum*, about 5½ feet long, the size of the three-edged spearhead being 9 inches to 1 foot, also to the *vericulum* (called in Vegetius's time the *verutum*) which was about 3½ feet long with an iron point 5 inches long.—O. S.]

modern fire-arms; since it was exhausted by a single discharge, at the distance of only ten or twelve paces. Yet when it was launched by a firm and skilful hand, there was not any cavalry that durst venture within its reach, nor any shield or corslet that could sustain the impetuosity of its weight. As soon as the Roman had darted his *pilum*, he drew his sword, and rushed forwards to close with the enemy. His sword was a short well-tempered Spanish blade, that carried a double edge, and was alike suited to the purpose of striking or of pushing; but the soldier was always instructed to prefer the latter use of his weapon, as his own body remained less exposed, whilst he inflicted a more dangerous wound on his adversary.[1] The legion was usually drawn up eight deep; and the regular distance of three feet was left between the files as well as ranks.[2] A body of troops, habituated to preserve this open order, in a long front and a rapid charge, found themselves prepared to execute every disposition which the circumstances of war, or the skill of their leader, might suggest. The soldier possessed a free space for his arms and motions, and sufficient intervals were allowed, through which seasonable reinforcements might be introduced to the relief of the exhausted combatants.[3] The tactics of the Greeks and Macedonians were formed on very different principles. The strength of the phalanx depended on sixteen ranks of long pikes, wedged together in the closest array.[4] But it was soon discovered by reflection, as well by the event, that the strength of the phalanx was unable to contend with the activity of the legion.[5]

The cavalry, without which the force of the legion would have remained imperfect, was divided into ten troops or squadrons; the first, as the companion of the first cohort, consisted of an hundred and thirty-two men; whilst each of the other nine amounted only to sixty-six. The entire establishment formed a regiment, if we may use the modern expression, of seven hundred and twenty-six horse, naturally connected with its respective legion, but occasionally separated to act in the line, and to compose a part of the wings of the army.[6] The cavalry

---

[1] For the legionary arms, see Lipsius de Militiâ Romanâ, l. iii. c. 2-7.

[2] See the beautiful comparison of Virgil, Georgic. ii. v. 279.

[3] M. Guichard, Mémoires Militaires, tom. i. c. 4. and Nouveaux Mémoires, tom. i. p. 293-311 has treated the subject like a scholar and an officer.

[4] Arrian's Tactics. With the true partiality of a Greek, Arrian rather chose to describe the phalanx, of which he had read, than the legions which he had commanded.

[5] Polyb. l. xvii.

[6] Veget, de Re Militari, l. ii. c. 6. His positive testimony, which might

of the emperors was no longer composed, like that of the ancient
republic, of the noblest youths of Rome and Italy, who, by per-
forming their military service on horseback, prepared themselves
for the offices of senator and consul; and solicited, by deeds of
valour, the future suffrages of their countrymen.[1] Since the
alteration of manners and government, the most wealthy of the
equestrian order were engaged in the administration of justice,
and of the revenue;[2] and whenever they embraced the profession of arms, they were immediately intrusted with a troop of
horse, or a cohort of foot.[3] Trajan and Hadrian formed their
cavalry from the same provinces, and the same class of their
subjects, which recruited the ranks of the legion. The horses
were bred, for the most part, in Spain or Cappadocia. The
Roman troopers despised the complete armour with which the
cavalry of the East was encumbered. *Their* more useful arms
consisted in a helmet, an oblong shield, light boots, and a coat
of mail. A javelin, and a long broad-sword, were their principal
weapons of offence. The use of lances and of iron maces they
seem to have borrowed from the barbarians.[4]

The safety and honour of the empire were principally intrusted
to the legions, but the policy of Rome condescended to adopt
every useful instrument of war. Considerable levies were regularly made among the provincials, who had not yet deserved
the honourable distinction of Romans. Many dependant princes
and communities, dispersed round the frontiers, were permitted,
for a while, to hold their freedom and security by the tenure
of military service.[5] Even select troops of hostile barbarians
were frequently compelled or persuaded to consume their
dangerous valour in remote climates, and for the benefit of the
state.[6] All these were included under the general name of
auxiliaries; and howsoever they might vary according to the
difference of times and circumstances, their numbers were seldom

be supported by circumstantial evidence, ought surely to silence those
critics who refuse the Imperial legion its proper body of cavalry.

[1] Livy almost throughout, particularly xlii. 61.

[2] Plin. Hist. Natur. xxxiii. 2. The true sense of that very curious passage
was first discovered and illustrated by M. de Beaufort, République
Romaine, l. ii. c. 2.

[3] As in the instance of Horace and Agricola. This appears to have been
a defect in the Roman discipline; which Hadrian endeavoured to remedy,
by ascertaining the legal age of a tribune.

[4] Arrian's Tactics, 4.

[5] Such, in particular, was the state of the Batavians. Tacit. Germania,
c. 29.

[6] Marcus Antoninus obliged the vanquished Quadi and Marcomanni to
supply him with a large body of troops, which he immediately sent into
Britain. Dion Cassius, l. lxxi.

much inferior to those of the legions themselves.[1] Among the auxiliaries, the bravest and most faithful bands were placed under the command of præfects and centurions, and severely trained in the arts of Roman discipline; but the far greater part retained those arms, to which the nature of their country, or their early habits of life, more peculiarly adapted them. By this institution each legion, to whom a certain proportion of auxiliaries was allotted, contained within itself every species of lighter troops, and of missile weapons; and was capable of encountering every nation, with the advantages of its respective arms and discipline.[2] Nor was the legion destitute of what, in modern language, would be styled a train of artillery. It consisted in ten military engines of the largest, and fifty-five of a smaller size; but all of which, either in an oblique or horizontal manner, discharged stones and darts with irresistible violence.[3]

The camp of a Roman legion presented the appearance of a fortified city.[4] As soon as the space was marked out, the pioneers carefully levelled the ground, and removed every impediment that might interrupt its perfect regularity. Its form was an exact quadrangle; and we may calculate that a square of about seven hundred yards was sufficient for the encampment of twenty thousand Romans; though a similar number of our own troops would expose to the enemy a front of more than treble that extent. In the midst of the camp, the prætorium, or general's quarters, rose above the others; the cavalry, the infantry, and the auxiliaries occupied their respective stations; the streets

---

[1] Tacit. Annal. iv. 5. Those who fix a regular proportion of as many foot, and twice as many horse, confound the auxiliaries of the emperors, with the Italian allies of the republic.

[2] Vegetius, ii. 2. Arrian, in his order of march and battle against the Alani.

[3] The subject of the ancient machines is treated with great knowledge and ingenuity by the Chevalier Folard (Polybe, tom. ii. p. 233-290). He prefers them in many respects to our modern cannon and mortars. We may observe, that the use of them in the field gradually became more prevalent, in proportion as personal valour and military skill declined with the Roman empire. When men were no longer found, their place was supplied by machines. See Vegetius, ii. 25. Arrian.

[The Roman military machines (*tormenta*), or engines of warfare, which supplied the place of our modern artillery were the battering-ram (*aries*), the *catapulta*, for discharging arrows and javelins, and the *ballista* for hurling large rocks and heavy stone bullets. For representation of these see Cæsar's *Gallic War*, B. 1, in *Temple Series of Classical Texts ;* also Rüstow and Köchly, " *Geschichte des griechischen Kriegswesens,*" p. 196 *et seq.*—O. S.]

[4] Vegetius finishes his second book, and the description of the legion, with the following emphatic words: " Universa quæ in quoque belli genere necessaria esse creduntur, secum legio debet ubique portare, ut in quovis loco fixerit castra, armatam faciat civitatem."

were broad and perfectly straight, and a vacant space of two hundred feet was left on all sides, between the tents and the rampart. The rampart itself was usually twelve feet high, armed with a line of strong and intricate palisades, and defended by a ditch of twelve feet in depth as well as in breadth. This important labour was performed by the hands of the legionaries themselves, to whom the use of the spade and the pick-axe was no less familiar than that of the sword or *pilum*. Active valour may often be the present of nature; but such patient diligence can be the fruit only of habit and discipline.[1]

Whenever the trumpet gave the signal of departure, the camp was almost instantly broke up, and the troops fell into their ranks without delay or confusion. Besides their arms, which the legionaries scarcely considered as an encumbrance, they were laden with their kitchen furniture, the instruments of fortification, and the provision of many days.[2] Under this weight, which would oppress the delicacy of a modern soldier, they were trained by a regular step to advance, in about six hours, near twenty miles.[3] On the appearance of an enemy, they threw aside their baggage, and by easy and rapid evolutions converted the column of march into an order of battle.[4] The slingers and archers skirmished in the front; the auxiliaries formed the first line, and were seconded or sustained by the strength of the legions: the cavalry covered the flanks, and the military engines were placed in the rear.

Such were the arts of war by which the Roman emperors defended their extensive conquests, and preserved a military spirit, at a time when every other virtue was oppressed by luxury and despotism. If, in the consideration of their armies, we pass from their discipline to their numbers, we shall not find it easy to define them with any tolerable accuracy. We may compute, however, that the legion, which was itself a body of six thousand eight hundred and thirty-one Romans, might, with its attendant auxiliaries, amount to about twelve thousand five hundred men. The peace establishment of Hadrian and his successors was composed of no less than thirty of these formid-

---

[1] For the Roman Castrametation, Polybius, l. vi. with Lipsius de Militiâ Romanâ, Joseph. de Bell. Jud. l. iii. c. 5. Vegetius, i. 21-25, iii. 9 and Mémoires de Guichard, tom. i. c. 1.

[2] Cicero in Tusculan. ii. 37. Joseph. de Bell. Jud. l. iii. 5. Frontinus, iv. 1.

[3] Vegetius, i. 9. Mémoires de l'Académie des Inscriptions, tom. xxv. p. 187.

[4] Those evolutions are admirably well explained by M. Guichard, Nouveaux Mémoires, tom. i. p. 141-234.

able brigades; and most probably formed a standing force of three hundred and seventy-five thousand men. Instead of being confined within the walls of fortified cities, which the Romans considered as the refuge of weakness or pusillanimity, the legions were encamped on the banks of the great rivers, and along the frontiers of the barbarians. As their stations, for the most part, remained fixed and permanent, we may venture to describe the distribution of the troops. Three legions were sufficient for Britain. The principal strength lay upon the Rhine and Danube, and consisted of sixteen legions, in the following proportions: two in the Lower and three in the Upper Germany; one in Rhætia, one in Noricum, four in Pannonia, three in Mæsia, and two in Dacia. The defence of the Euphrates was entrusted to eight legions, six of whom were planted in Syria, and the other two in Cappadocia. With regard to Egypt, Africa, and Spain, as they were far removed from any important scene of war, a single legion maintained the domestic tranquillity of each of those great provinces. Even Italy was not left destitute of a military force. Above twenty thousand chosen soldiers, distinguished by the titles of City Cohorts and Prætorian Guards, watched over the safety of the monarch and the capital. As the authors of almost every revolution that distracted the empire, the Prætorians will, very soon, and very loudly, demand our attention; but in their arms and institutions, we cannot find any circumstance which discriminated them from the legions, unless it were a more splendid appearance, and a less rigid discipline.[1]

The navy maintained by the emperors might seem inadequate to their greatness; but it was fully sufficient for every useful purpose of government. The ambition of the Romans was confined to the land; nor was that warlike people ever actuated by the enterprising spirit which had prompted the navigators of Tyre, of Carthage, and even of Marseilles, to enlarge the bounds of the world, and to explore the most remote coasts of the ocean. To the Romans the ocean remained an object of terror rather than of curiosity;[2] the whole extent of the Mediterranean, after the destruction of Carthage, and the extirpation of the pirates, was included within their provinces. The policy of the emperors

---

[1] Tacitus (Annal. iv. 5) has given us a state of the legions under Tiberius: and Dion Cassius (l. lv. p. 794) under Alexander Severus. I have endeavoured to fix on the proper medium between these two periods. See likewise Lipsius de Magnitudine Romanâ, l. i. c. 4, 5.

[2] The Romans tried to disguise, by the pretence of religious awe, their ignorance and terror. Tacit. Germania. c. 34.

was directed only to preserve the peaceful dominion of that sea, and to protect the commerce of their subjects. With these moderate views, Augustus stationed two permanent fleets in the most convenient ports of Italy, the one at Ravenna, on the Adriatic, the other at Misenum, in the bay of Naples. Experience seems at length to have convinced the ancients, that as soon as their galleys exceeded two, or at the most three ranks of oars, they were suited rather for vain pomp than for real service. Augustus himself, in the victory of Actium, had seen the superiority of his own light frigates (they were called Liburnians) over the lofty but unwieldy castles of his rival.[1] Of these Liburnians he composed the two fleets of Ravenna and Misenum, destined to command, the one the eastern, the other the western division of the Mediterranean; and to each of the squadrons he attached a body of several thousand marines. Besides these two ports, which may be considered as the principal seats of the Roman navy, a very considerable force was stationed at Frejus, on the coast of Provence, and the Euxine was guarded by forty ships, and three thousand soldiers. To all these we add the fleet which preserved the communication between Gaul and Britain, and a great number of vessels constantly maintained on the Rhine and Danube, to harass the country, or to intercept the passage of the barbarians.[2] If we review this general state of the Imperial forces; of the cavalry as well as infantry; of the legions, the auxiliaries, the guards, and the navy; the most liberal computation will not allow us to fix the entire establishment by sea and by land at more than four hundred and fifty thousand men; a military power, which, however formidable it may seem, was equalled by a monarch of the last century, whose kingdom was confined within a single province of the Roman empire.[3]

We have attempted to explain the spirit which moderated, and

[1] Plutarch, in Marc. Anton. And yet, if we may credit Orosius, these monstrous castles were no more than ten feet above the water, vi. 19.

[2] Lipsius, de Magnitud. Rom. l. i. c. 5. The sixteen last chapters of Vegetius relate to naval affairs.

[3] Voltaire, Siècle de Louis XIV. c. 29. It must, however, be remembered, that France still feels that extraordinary effort.

[The complete list of Roman naval stations was:—Forum Julium, Aquileia, Alexandria, Seleucia, Carpathos, Britain, the Euxine, the Rhine, the Danube, and the Euphrates. Concerning the construction of the Roman ships and the destructive differences between trading vessels or ships of burden (naves onerariæ) and war-vessels (naves longæ), which after the naval battle of Actium in which the light two-banked vessels of the Liburnian pirates defeated the heavy Greek-Egyptian fleet of Antony. See Graser De Veterum re Navali.—O. S.]

the strength which supported, the power of Hadrian and the
Antonines. We shall now endeavour, with clearness and precision, to describe the provinces once united under their sway,
but, at present, divided into so many independent and hostile
states.

Spain, the western extremity of the empire, of Europe, and of
the ancient world, has, in every age, invariably preserved the
same natural limits; the Pyrenæan mountains, the Mediterranean, and the Atlantic Ocean. That great peninsula, at
present so unequally divided between two sovereigns, was distributed by Augustus into three provinces, Lusitania, Bætica,
and Tarraconensis. The kingdom of Portugal now fills the place
of the warlike country of the Lusitanians; and the loss sustained
by the former, on the side of the East, is compensated by an
accession of territory towards the North. The confines of
Grenada and Andalusia correspond with those of ancient Bætica.
The remainder of Spain, Gallicia and the Asturias, Biscay and
Navarre, Leon and the two Castilles, Murcia, Valencia, Catalonia,
and Arragon, all contributed to form the third and most considerable of the Roman governments, which, from the name of
its capital, was styled the province of Tarragona.[1] Of the native
barbarians, the Celtiberians were the most powerful, as the
Cantabrians and Asturians proved the most obstinate. Confident in the strength of their mountains, they were the last who
submitted to the arms of Rome, and the first who threw off the
yoke of the Arabs.

Ancient Gaul, as it contained the whole country between the
Pyrenees, the Alps, the Rhine, and the Ocean, was of greater
extent than modern France. To the dominions of that powerful monarchy, with its recent acquisitions of Alsace and Lorraine,
we must add the duchy of Savoy, the cantons of Switzerland,
the four electorates of the Rhine, and the territories of Liege,
Luxemburg, Hainault, Flanders, and Brabant. When Augustus
gave laws to the conquests of his father, he introduced a division
of Gaul equally adapted to the progress of the legions, to the
course of the rivers, and to the principal national distinctions,
which had comprehended above an hundred independent states.[2]

[1] Strabo, l. ii. It is natural enough to suppose, that Arragon is derived
from Tarraconensis, and several moderns who have written in Latin, use
those words as synonymous. It is however certain, that the Arragon, a
little stream which falls from the Pyrenees into the Ebro, first gave its
name to a country, and gradually to a kingdom. D'Anville, Géographie
du Moyen Age, p. 181.
[2] One hundred and fifteen *cities* appear in the Notitia of Gaul; and it is
well known that this appellation was applied not only to the capital town,

The sea-coast of the Mediterranean, Languedoc, Provence, and Dauphiné, received their provincial appellation from the colony of Narbonne. The government of Aquitaine was extended from the Pyrenees to the Loire. The country between the Loire and the Seine was styled the Celtic Gaul, and soon borrowed a new denomination from the celebrated colony of Lugdunum, or Lyons. The Belgic lay beyond the Seine, and in more ancient times had been bounded only by the Rhine; but a little before the age of Cæsar the Germans, abusing their superiority of valour, had occupied a considerable portion of the Belgic territory. The Roman conquerors very eagerly embraced so flattering a circumstance, and the Gallic frontier of the Rhine, from Basil to Leyden, received the pompous names of the Upper and the Lower Germany.[1] Such, under the reign of the Antonines, were the six provinces of Gaul; the Narbonnese, Aquitaine, the Celtic, or Lyonnese, the Belgic, and the two Germanies.

We have already had occasion to mention the conquest of Britain, and to fix the boundary of the Roman province in this island. It comprehended all England, Wales, and the Lowlands of Scotland, as far as Dumbarton and Edinburgh. Before Britain lost her freedom, the country was irregularly divided between thirty tribes of barbarians, of whom the most considerable were the Belgæ in the West, the Brigantes in the North, the Silures in South Wales, and the Iceni in Norfolk and Suffolk.[2] As far as we can either trace or credit the resemblance of manners and language, Spain, Gaul, and Britain were peopled by the same hardy race of savages. Before they yielded to the Roman arms, they often disputed the field, and often renewed the contest. After their submission they constituted the western division of the European provinces, which extended from the columns of Hercules to the wall of Antoninus[3] and

but to the whole territory of each state. But Plutarch and Appian increase the number of tribes to three or four hundred.

[1] D'Anville. Notice de l'Ancienne Gaule.

[2] Whitaker's History of Manchester, vol. i. c. 3.

[3] [*Wall of Antoninus*.—Extending from Carriden on the Forth to Chapel-hill, near Old Kilpatrick on the Clyde. It was erected in 140 A.D. by the imperial legate, Lollius Urbicus, and named by him after the Emperor Marcus Antoninus Pius. The work consisted of a ditch about 20 feet deep and 40 feet wide; also a rampart about 20 feet high and 24 feet thick at the base, and on the inner or south side of the rampart, a paved military road, with a chain of 21 forts. It is commonly called *Graham's or Grime's Dyke*, some say after the Pictish king, Grime, who was Buchanan's eighty-second king in line from Fergus I., and lived about 990 A.D. But the wall was immensely anterior to his reign.—O. S. (See, however, Sir George Macdonald, *The Roman Wall in Scotland*, 2nd edition, 1934.)]

from the mouth of the Tagus to the sources of the Rhine and Danube.

Before the Roman conquest, the country which is now called Lombardy was not considered as a part of Italy. It had been occupied by a powerful colony of Gauls, who settling themselves along the banks of the Po, from Piedmont to Romagna, carried their arms and diffused their name from the Alps to the Apennine. The Ligurians dwelt on the rocky coast, which now forms the republic of Genoa. Venice was yet unborn; but the territories of that state, which lie to the east of the Adige, were inhabited by the Venetians.[1] The middle part of the peninsula that now composes the duchy of Tuscany and the ecclesiastical state, was the ancient seat of the Etruscans and Umbrians; to the former of whom Italy was indebted for the first rudiments of civilised life.[2] The Tiber rolled at the foot of the seven hills of Rome, and the country of the Sabines, the Latins, and the Volsci, from that river to the frontiers of Naples, was the theatre of her infant victories. On that celebrated ground the first consuls deserved triumphs; their successors adorned villas, and *their* posterity have erected convents.[3] Capua and Campania possessed the immediate territory of Naples; the rest of the kingdom was inhabited by many warlike nations, the Marsi, the Samnites, the Apulians, and the Lucanians; and the sea-coasts had been covered by the flourishing colonies of the Greeks. We may remark, that when Augustus divided Italy into eleven regions, the little province of Istria was annexed to that seat of Roman sovereignty.[4]

The European provinces of Rome were protected by the course of the Rhine and the Danube. The latter of those mighty streams, which rises at the distance of only thirty miles from the former, flows above thirteen hundred miles, for the most part, to the south-east, collects the tribute of sixty navigable rivers, and is, at length, through six mouths, received into the Euxine, which appears scarcely equal to such an accession of waters.[5] The provinces of the Danube soon acquired the general appellation of Illyricum, or the Illyrian frontier,[6] and were esteemed

---

[1] The Italian Veneti, though often confounded with the Gauls, were more probably of Illyrian origin. M. Freret, Memoires de l'Academie des Inscriptions, tom. xviii.　　　[2] Maffei, Verona illustrata, l. i.

[3] The first contrast was observed by the ancients. Florus, i. 11. The second must strike every modern traveller.

[4] Pliny (Hist. Natur. l. iii.) [6] follows the division of Italy by Augustus.

[5] Tournefort, Voyages en Grèce et Asie Mineure, lettre xviii.

[6] The name of Illyricum originally belonged to the sea-coast of the Adriatic, and was gradually extended by the Romans from the Alps to the Euxine Sea. Severini Pannonia, i. l. c. 3.

the most warlike of the empire; but they deserve to be more particularly considered under the names of Rhætia, Noricum, Pannonia, Dalmatia, Dacia, Mæsia, Thrace, Macedonia, and Greece.

The province of Rhætia, which soon extinguished the name of the Vindelicians, extended from the summit of the Alps to the banks of the Danube; from its source, as far as its conflux with the Inn. The greatest part of the flat country is subject to the elector of Bavaria; the city of Augsburg is protected by the constitution of the German empire; the Grisons are safe in their mountains, and the country of Tyrol is ranked among the numerous provinces of the house of Austria.

The wide extent of territory, which is included between the Inn, the Danube, and the Save; Austria, Styria, Carinthia, Carniola, the Lower Hungary, and Sclavonia, was known to the ancients under the names of Noricum and Pannonia. In their original state of independence, their fierce inhabitants were intimately connected. Under the Roman government they were frequently united, and they still remain the patrimony of a single family. They now contain the residence of a German prince, who styles himself Emperor of the Romans, and form the centre, as well as strength, of the Austrian power. It may not be improper to observe, that if we except Bohemia, Moravia, the northern skirts of Austria, and a part of Hungary, between the Theiss and the Danube, all the other dominions of the House of Austria were comprised within the limits of the Roman empire.

Dalmatia, to which the name of Illyricum more properly belonged, was a long but narrow tract between the Save and the Adriatic. The best part of the sea-coast, which still retains its ancient appellation, is a province of the Venetian state, and the seat of the little republic of Ragusa.[1] The inland parts have assumed the Sclavonian names of Croatia and Bosnia; the former obeys an Austrian governor, the latter a Turkish pasha; but the whole country is still infested by tribes of barbarians, whose savage independence irregularly marks the doubtful limit of the Christian and Mahometan power.[2]

[1] [Ragusa, after being Greek first, then Roman, then an independent republic, was later a dependent republic under the protection successively of Byzantium, Venice, Hungary, and the Porte. From 1808 to 1814 it was part of Illyria. In 1814 it was included in the Austrian empire, and is now in Jugoslavia.

[2] A Venetian traveller, the Abbate Fortis, has lately given us some account of those very obscure countries. But the geography and antiquities of the western Illyricum can be expected only from the munificence of the emperor, its sovereign.

After the Danube had received the waters of the Theiss and the Save, it acquired, at least among the Greeks, the name of Ister.[1] It formerly divided Mæsia and Dacia, the latter of which, as we have already seen, was a conquest of Trajan, and the only province beyond the river. If we inquire into the present state of those countries, we shall find that, on the left hand of the Danube, Temeswar and Transylvania have been annexed, after many revolutions, to the crown of Hungary; whilst the principalities of Moldavia and Wallachia acknowledge the supremacy of the Ottoman Porte. On the right hand of the Danube, Mæsia, which, during the middle ages, was broken into the barbarian kingdoms of Servia and Bulgaria, is again united in Turkish slavery.

The appellation of Roumelia,[2] which is still bestowed by the Turks on the extensive countries of Thrace, Macedonia, and Greece, preserves the memory of their ancient state under the Roman empire. In the time of the Antonines, the martial regions of Thrace, from the mountains of Hæmus and Rhodope, to the Bosphorus and the Hellespont, had assumed the form of a province. Notwithstanding the change of masters and of religion, the new city of Rome, founded by Constantine on the banks of the Bosphorus, has ever since remained the capital of a great monarchy. The kingdom of Macedonia, which, under the reign of Alexander, gave laws to Asia, derived more solid advantages from the policy of the two Philips; and with its dependencies of Epirus and Thessaly, extended from the Ægean to the Ionian Sea. When we reflect on the fame of Thebes and Argos, of Sparta and Athens, we can scarcely persuade ourselves that so many immortal republics of ancient Greece were lost in a single province of the Roman empire, which, from the superior influence of the Achæan league, was usually denominated the province of Achaia.

Such was the state of Europe under the Roman emperors. The provinces of Asia, without excepting the transient conquests of Trajan, are all comprehended within the limits of the Turkish

[1] The Save rises near the confines of *Istria*, and was considered by the more early Greeks as the principal stream of the Danube.

[2] [Roumelia has during the last thirty or forty years undergone many changes alike in territory and title. Western Roumelia embraced Greece and Macedonia, while Eastern Roumelia comprehended Thrace. Since Gibbon wrote the situation has wholly changed. Greece and Servia are independent wholly of Turkey, while Bulgaria is practically so, and Montenegro was always so. Roumania has been constituted a kingdom out of Moldavia and Wallachia, while Austria has acquired Dalmatia, Bosnia, and Herzegovina.—O. S.]

power. But, instead of following the arbitrary divisions of despotism and ignorance, it will be safer for us, as well as more agreeable, to observe the indelible characters of nature. The name of Asia Minor is attributed with some propriety to the peninsula, which, confined betwixt the Euxine and the Mediterranean, advances from the Euphrates towards Europe. The most extensive and flourishing district, westward of Mount Taurus and the river Halys, was dignified by the Romans with the exclusive title of Asia. The jurisdiction of that province extended over the ancient monarchies of Troy, Lydia, and Phrygia, the maritime countries of the Pamphylians, Lycians, and Carians, and the Grecian colonies of Ionia, which equalled in arts, though not in arms, the glory of their parent. The kingdoms of Bithynia and Pontus possessed the northern side of the peninsula from Constantinople to Trebizond. On the opposite side, the province of Cilicia was terminated by the mountains of Syria: the inland country, separated from the Roman Asia by the river Halys, and from Armenia by the Euphrates, had once formed the independent kingdom of Cappadocia. In this place we may observe that the northern shores of the Euxine, beyond Trebizond in Asia, and beyond the Danube in Europe, acknowledged the sovereignty of the emperors, and received at their hands either tributary princes or Roman garrisons. Budzak, Crim Tartary, Circassia, and Mingrelia, are the modern appellations of those savage countries.[1]

Under the successors of Alexander, Syria was the seat of the Seleucidæ, who reigned over Upper Asia, till the successful revolt of the Parthians confined their dominions between the Euphrates and the Mediterranean. When Syria became subject to the Romans, it formed the eastern frontier of their empire; nor did that province, in its utmost latitude, know any other bounds than the mountains of Cappadocia to the north, and towards the south the confines of Egypt, and the Red Sea. Phœnicia and Palestine were sometimes annexed to, and sometimes separated from, the jurisdiction of Syria. The former of these was a narrow and rocky coast; the latter was a territory scarcely superior to Wales, either in fertility or extent. Yet Phœnicia and Palestine will for ever live in the memory of mankind; since America, as well as Europe, has received letters from the one, and religion from the other.[2] A sandy desert alike destitute of wood and

---

[1] Periplus of Arrian. He examined the coasts of the Euxine, when he was governor of Cappadocia.

[2] The progress of religion is well known. The use of letters was introduced among the savages of Europe about fifteen hundred years before

water skirts along the doubtful confine of Syria, from the
Euphrates to the Red Sea. The wandering life of the Arabs was
inseparably connected with their independence; and wherever,
on some spots less barren than the rest, they ventured to form
any settled habitation, they soon became subjects to the Roman
empire.[1]

The geographers of antiquity have frequently hesitated to
what portion of the globe they should ascribe Egypt.[2] By its
situation that celebrated kingdom is included within the immense
peninsula of Africa; but it is accessible only on the side of Asia,
whose revolutions, in almost every period of history, Egypt has
humbly obeyed. A Roman præfect was seated on the splendid
throne of the Ptolemies; and the iron sceptre of the Mamalukes
is now in the hands of a Turkish pasha. The Nile flows down
the country, above five hundred miles from the tropic of Cancer
to the Mediterranean, and marks, on either side, the extent of
fertility by the measure of its inundations. Cyrene, situate
towards the west, and along the sea-coast, was first a Greek
colony, afterwards a province of Egypt, and is now lost in the
desert of Barca.

From Cyrene to the ocean, the coast of Africa extends above
fifteen hundred miles; yet so closely is it pressed between the
Mediterranean and the Sahara, or sandy desert, that its breadth
seldom exceeds fourscore or an hundred miles. The eastern
division was considered by the Romans as the more peculiar and
proper province of Africa. Till the arrival of the Phœnician
colonies, that fertile country was inhabited by the Libyans, the
most savage of mankind. Under the immediate jurisdiction of
Carthage, it became the centre of commerce and empire; but
the republic of Carthage is now degenerated into the feeble and
disorderly states of Tripoli and Tunis. The military government
of Algiers oppresses the wide extent of Numidia, as it was once
united under Massinissa and Jugurtha: but in the time of
Augustus, the limits of Numidia were contracted; and, at least,
two-thirds of the country acquiesced in the name of Mauritania,

Christ; and the Europeans carried them to America, about fifteen centuries
after the Christian era. But in a period of three thousand years, the
Phœnician alphabet received considerable alterations, as it passed through
the hands of the Greeks and Romans.

[1] Dion Cassius, lib. lxviii. p. 1131 [c. 14].

[2] Ptolemy and Strabo, with the modern geographers, fix the Isthmus of
Suez as the boundary of Asia and Africa. Dionysius, Mela, Pliny, Sallust,
Hirtius, and Solinus, have preferred for that purpose the western branch of
the Nile, or even the great Catabathmus, or descent, which last would
assign to Asia, not only Egypt, but part of Libya.

with the epithet of Cæsariensis. The genuine Mauritania, or
country of the Moors, which, from the ancient city of Tingi, or
Tangier, was distinguished by the appellation of Tingitana, is
represented by the modern kingdom of Fez. Sallé, on the Ocean,
long infamous for its piratical depredations, was noticed by the
Romans, as the extreme object of their power, and almost of their
geography. A city of their foundation may still be discovered
near Mequinez, the residence of the barbarian whom we condescend to style the Emperor of Morocco; but it does not appear
that his more southern dominions, Morocco itself, and Segel-
messa, were ever comprehended within the Roman province.
The western parts of Africa are intersected by the branches of
Mount Atlas, a name so idly celebrated by the fancy of poets; [1]
but which is now diffused over the immense ocean that rolls
between the ancient and the new continent. [2]

Having now finished the circuit of the Roman empire, we may
observe, that Africa is divided from Spain by a narrow strait of
about twelve miles, through which the Atlantic flows into the
Mediterranean. The columns of Hercules, so famous among the
ancients, were two mountains which seemed to have been torn
asunder by some convulsion of the elements; and at the foot of
the European mountain the fortress of Gibraltar is now seated.
The whole extent of the Mediterranean Sea, its coasts, and its
islands, were comprised within the Roman dominion. Of the
larger islands, the two Baleares, which derive their name of
Majorca and Minorca from their respective size, are subject at
present, the former to Spain, the latter to Great Britain. It is
easier to deplore the fate, than to describe the actual condition,
of Corsica. Two Italian sovereigns assume a regal title from
Sardinia and Sicily. Crete, or Candia, with Cyprus, and most
of the smaller islands of Greece and Asia, have been subdued by
the Turkish arms; whilst the little rock of Malta defies their
power, and has emerged, under the government of its military
Order, into fame and opulence.

This long enumeration of provinces, whose broken fragments
have formed so many powerful kingdoms, might almost induce
us to forgive the vanity or ignorance of the ancients. Dazzled

---

[1] The long range, moderate height, and gentle declivity of mount Atlas
are very unlike a solitary mountain which rears its head into the clouds,
and seems to support the heavens. The peak of Teneriffe, on the contrary,
rises a league and a half above the surface of the sea, and as it was frequently
visited by the Phœnicians, might engage the notice of the Greek poets.
Buffon, Histoire Naturelle, tom. i. p. 312. Histoire des Voyages, tom. ii.

[2] M. de Voltaire, tom. xiv. p. 297, unsupported by either fact or probability, has generously bestowed the Canary Islands on the Roman empire.

with the extensive sway, the irresistible strength, and the real or affected moderation of the emperors, they permitted themselves to despise, and sometimes to forget, the outlying countries which had been left in the enjoyment of a barbarous independence; and they gradually usurped the licence of confounding the Roman monarchy with the globe of the earth.[1] But the temper, as well as knowledge, of a modern historian require a more sober and accurate language. He may impress a juster image of the greatness of Rome, by observing that the empire was above two thousand miles in breadth, from the wall of Antoninus and the northern limits of Dacia, to mount Atlas and the tropic of Cancer; that it extended, in length, more than three thousand miles from the Western Ocean to the Euphrates; that it was situated in the finest part of the Temperate Zone, between the twenty-fourth and fifty-sixth degrees of northern latitude; and that it was supposed to contain above sixteen hundred thousand square miles, for the most part of fertile and well-cultivated land.[2]

CHAPTER II

Of the Union and internal Prosperity of the Roman Empire, in the Age of the Antonines

IT is not alone by the rapidity, or extent of conquest, that we should estimate the greatness of Rome. The sovereign of the Russian deserts commands a larger portion of the globe. In the seventh summer after his passage of the Hellespont, Alexander erected the Macedonian trophies on the banks of the Hyphasis.[3] Within less than a century, the irresistible Zingis, and the Mogul princes of his race, spread their cruel devastations and transient empire from the sea of China to the confines of Egypt and Germany.[4] But the firm edifice of Roman power was raised and preserved by the wisdom of ages. The obedient provinces of Trajan and the Antonines were united by laws and adorned by arts. They might occasionally suffer from the partial abuse of delegated authority; but the general principle of government

---

[1] Bergier, Hist. des Grands Chemins, l. iii. c. 1, 2, 3, 4, a very useful collection.

[2] Templeman's Survey of the Globe: but I distrust both the doctor's learning and his maps.

[3] They were erected about midway between Lahor and Delhi. The conquests of Alexander in Hindostan were confined to the Punjab, a country watered by the five great streams of the Indus.

[4] M. de Guignes, Histoire des Huns, l. xv. xvi. and xvii.

was wise, simple, and beneficent. They enjoyed the religion of their ancestors, whilst in civil honours and advantages they were exalted, by just degrees, to an equality with their conquerors.

I. The policy of the emperors and the senate, as far as it concerned religion, was happily seconded by the reflections of the enlightened, and by the habits of the superstitious, part of their subjects. The various modes of worship, which prevailed in the Roman world, were all considered by the people, as equally true; by the philosopher, as equally false; and by the magistrate, as equally useful. And thus toleration produced not only mutual indulgence, but even religious concord.

The superstition of the people was not embittered by any mixture of theological rancour; nor was it confined by the chains of any speculative system. The devout polytheist, though fondly attached to his national rites, admitted with implicit faith the different religions of the earth.[1] Fear, gratitude, and curiosity, a dream or an omen, a singular disorder, or a distant journey, perpetually disposed him to multiply the articles of his belief, and to enlarge the list of his protectors. The thin texture of the Pagan mythology was interwoven with various but not discordant materials. As soon as it was allowed that sages and heroes, who had lived, or who had died for the benefit of their country, were exalted to a state of power and immortality, it was universally confessed that they deserved, if not the adoration, at least the reverence of all mankind. The deities of a thousand groves and a thousand streams possessed, in peace, their local and respective influence; nor could the Roman who deprecated the wrath of the Tiber, deride the Egyptian who presented his offering to the beneficent genius of the Nile. The visible powers of Nature, the planets, and the elements, were the same throughout the universe. The invisible governors of the moral world were inevitably cast in a similar mould of fiction and allegory. Every virtue, and even vice, acquired its divine representative; every art and profession its patron, whose attributes, in the most distant ages and countries, were uniformly derived from the character of their peculiar votaries. A republic of gods of such opposite tempers and interest required, in every system, the

[1] There is not any writer who describes in so lively a manner as Herodotus, the true genius of Polytheism. The best commentary may be found in Mr. Hume's Natural History of Religion; and the best contrast in Bossuet's Universal History. Some obscure traces of an intolerant spirit appear in the conduct of the Egyptians (Juvenal, Sat. xv.); and the Christians as well as Jews, who lived under the Roman empire, formed a very important exception: so important, indeed, that the discussion will require a distinct chapter of this work.

moderating hand of a supreme magistrate, who, by the progress
of knowledge and flattery, was gradually invested with the
sublime perfections of an Eternal Parent, and an Omnipotent
Monarch.[1] Such was the mild spirit of antiquity, that the
nations were less attentive to the difference than to the resemblance of their religious worship. The Greek, the Roman, and
the Barbarian, as they met before their respective altars, easily
persuaded themselves, that under various names, and with
various ceremonies, they adored the same deities. The elegant
mythology of Homer gave a beautiful, and almost a regular form,
to the polytheism of the ancient world.[2]

The philosophers of Greece deduced their morals from the
nature of man, rather than from that of God. They meditated,
however, on the Divine Nature, as a very curious and important
speculation; and in the profound inquiry, they displayed the
strength and weakness of the human understanding.[3] Of the
four most celebrated schools, the Stoics and the Platonists endeavoured to reconcile the jarring interests of reason and piety.
They have left us the most sublime proofs of the existence and
perfections of the first cause; but, as it was impossible for them
to conceive the creation of matter, the workman in the Stoic
philosophy was not sufficiently distinguished from the work;
whilst, on the contrary, the spiritual God of Plato and his disciples resembled an idea rather than a substance. The opinions
of the Academics and Epicureans were of a less religious cast;
but whilst the modest science of the former induced them to
doubt, the positive ignorance of the latter urged them to deny,
the providence of a Supreme Ruler. The spirit of inquiry,
prompted by emulation, and supported by freedom, had divided
the public teachers of philosophy into a variety of contending
sects; but the ingenuous youth who, from every part, resorted
to Athens, and the other seats of learning in the Roman empire,
were alike instructed in every school to reject and to despise the
religion of the multitude. How, indeed, was it possible, that a
philosopher should accept, as divine truths, the idle tales of the
poets, and the incoherent traditions of antiquity; or, that he

[1] The rights, powers, and pretensions of the sovereign of Olympus, are
very clearly described in the xvth book of the Iliad: in the Greek original,
I mean; for Mr. Pope, without perceiving it, has improved the theology of
Homer.

[2] Cæsar de Bell. Gall. vi. 17. Within a century or two the Gauls themselves applied to their gods the names of Mercury, Mars, Apollo, etc.

[3] The admirable work of Cicero, de Naturâ Deorum, is the best clue we
have to guide us through the dark and profound abyss. He represents
with candour, and confutes with subtlety, the opinions of the philosophers.

should adore, as gods, those imperfect beings whom he must
have despised, as men! Against such unworthy adversaries,
Cicero condescended to employ the arms of reason and eloquence;
but the satire of Lucian was a much more adequate, as well as
more efficacious weapon. We may be well assured, that a writer
conversant with the world would never have ventured to expose
the gods of his country to public ridicule, had they not already
been the objects of secret contempt among the polished and
enlightened orders of society.[1]

Notwithstanding the fashionable irreligion which prevailed in
the age of the Antonines, both the interests of the priests and
the credulity of the people were sufficiently respected. In their
writings and conversation, the philosophers of antiquity asserted
the independent dignity of reason; but they resigned their
actions to the commands of law and of custom. Viewing, with
a smile of pity and indulgence, the various errors of the vulgar,
they diligently practised the ceremonies of their fathers, devoutly
frequented the temples of the gods; and sometimes condescend-
ing to act a part on the theatre of superstition, they concealed the
sentiments of an Atheist under the sacerdotal robes. Reasoners
of such a temper were scarcely inclined to wrangle about their
respective modes of faith, or of worship. It was indifferent to
them what shape the folly of the multitude might choose to
assume; and they approached, with the same inward contempt,
and the same external reverence, the altars of the Libyan, the
Olympian, or the Capitoline Jupiter.[2]

It is not easy to conceive from what motives a spirit of persecution could introduce itself into the Roman councils. The
magistrates could not be actuated by a blind, though honest
bigotry, since the magistrates were themselves philosophers;
and the schools of Athens had given laws to the senate. They
could not be impelled by ambition or avarice, as the temporal
and ecclesiastical powers were united in the same hands. The
pontiffs were chosen among the most illustrious of the senators;
and the office of Supreme Pontiff was constantly exercised by
the emperors themselves. They knew and valued the advantages of religion, as it is connected with civil government. They
encouraged the public festivals which humanise the manners of

---

[1] I do not pretend to assert, that, in this irreligious age, the natural
terrors of superstition, dreams, omens, apparitions, etc., had lost their
efficacy.

[2] Socrates, Epicurus, Cicero, and Plutarch, always inculcated decent
reverence for the religion of their own country, and of mankind. The devotion of Epicurus was assiduous and exemplary. Diogen. Laert. x. 10.

the people. They managed the arts of divination, as a convenient instrument of policy; and they respected as the firmest
bond of society, the useful persuasion that, either in this or in
a future life, the crime of perjury is most assuredly punished
by the avenging gods.[1] But whilst they acknowledged the
general advantages of religion, they were convinced that the
various modes of worship contributed alike to the same salutary
purposes; and that, in every country, the form of superstition,
which had received the sanction of time and experience, was the
best adapted to the climate and to its inhabitants. Avarice
and taste very frequently despoiled the vanquished nations of
the elegant statues of their gods, and the rich ornaments of their
temples;[2] but, in the exercise of the religion which they derived
from their ancestors, they uniformly experienced the indulgence,
and even protection, of the Roman conquerors. The province of
Gaul seems, and indeed only seems, an exception to this universal
toleration. Under the specious pretext of abolishing human
sacrifices, the emperors Tiberius and Claudius suppressed the
dangerous power of the Druids,[3] but the priests themselves, their
gods and their altars, subsisted in peaceful obscurity till the final
destruction of Paganism.[4]

Rome, the capital of a great monarchy, was incessantly filled
with subjects and strangers from every part of the world,[5] who
all introduced and enjoyed the favourite superstitions of their
native country.[6] Every city in the empire was justified in maintaining the purity of its ancient ceremonies; and the Roman
senate, using the common privilege, sometimes interposed, to
check this inundation of foreign rites. The Egyptian superstition, of all the most contemptible and abject, was frequently
prohibited; the temples of Serapis and Isis demolished and their
worshippers banished from Rome and Italy.[7] But the zeal of

[1] Polybius, l. vi. c. 53, 54 [cap. 56]. Juvenal, Sat. xiii. laments, that in
his time this apprehension had lost much of its effect.
[2] See the fate of Syracuse, Tarentum, Ambracia, Corinth, etc., the
conduct of Verres, in Cicero (Actio ii. Orat. 4), and the usual practice of
governors, in the viiith Satire of Juvenal.
[3] Sueton. in Claud.—Plin. Hist. Nat. xxx. i.
[4] Pelloutier Histoire des Celtes, tom. vi. p. 230-252.
[5] Seneca, Consolat. ad Helviam, p. 74. Edit. Lips.
[6] Dionysius Halicarn. Antiquitat. Roman. l. ii.
[7] In the year of Rome 701, the temple of Isis and Serapis was demolished
by the order of the Senate (Dion Cassius, l. xl. p. 252), and even by the
hands of the consul (Valerius Maximus, 1, 3). After the death of Cæsar, it
was restored at the public expense (Dion, l. xlvii. p. 501). When Augustus
was in Egypt, he revered the majesty of Serapis (Dion, l. ii. p. 647); but in
the Pomærium of Rome, and a mile round it, he prohibited the worship of
the Egyptian gods (Dion. l. liii. p. 679, l. liv. p. 735). They remained

fanaticism prevailed over the cold and feeble efforts of policy.
The exiles returned, the proselytes multiplied, the temples were
restored with increasing splendour, and Isis and Serapis at length
assumed their place among the Roman deities.[1] Nor was this
indulgence a departure from the old maxims of government. In
the purest ages of the commonwealth, Cybele and Æsculapius
had been invited by solemn embassies;[2] and it was customary
to tempt the protectors of besieged cities, by the promise of
more distinguished honours than they possessed in their native
country.[3] Rome gradually became the common temple of her
subjects; and the freedom of the city was bestowed on all the
gods of mankind.[4]

II. The narrow policy of preserving, without any foreign
mixture, the pure blood of the ancient citizens, had checked the
fortune, and hastened the ruin, of Athens and Sparta. The aspiring genius of Rome sacrificed vanity to ambition, and deemed
it more prudent, as well as honourable, to adopt virtue and merit
for her own wheresoever they were found, among slaves or
strangers, enemies or barbarians.[5] During the most flourishing
era of the Athenian commonwealth, the number of citizens gradually decreased from about thirty [6] to twenty-one thousand.[7] If,
on the contrary, we study the growth of the Roman republic, we
may discover, that, nowithstanding the incessant demands of
wars and colonies, the citizens, who, in the first census of Servius
Tullius, amounted to no more than eighty-three thousand, were
multiplied, before the commencement of the social war, to the
number of four hundred and sixty-three thousand men, able to
bear arms in the service of their country.[8] When the allies of

however, very fashionable under his reign (Ovid. de Art. Amand. l. i.) and
that of his successor, till the justice of Tiberius was provoked to some acts
of severity. (Tacit. Annal. ii. 85. Joseph. Antiquit. l. xviii. c. 3).

[1] Tertullian in Apologetic, c. 6, p. 74. Edit. Havercamp. I am inclined
to attribute their establishment to the devotion of the Flavian family.

[2] See Livy, l. xi. and xxix.

[3] Macrob. Saturnalia, l. iii. c. 9. He gives us a form of evocation.

[4] Minutius Felix in Octavio, p. 54. Arnobius, l. vi. p. 115.

[5] Tacit. Annal. xi. 24. The Orbis Romanus of the learned Spanheim is a
complete history of the progressive admission of Latium, Italy, and the
provinces, to the freedom of Rome.

[6] Herodotus, v. 97. It should seem, however, that he followed a large
and popular estimation.

[7] Athenæus Deipnosophist, l. vi. p. 272. Edit. Casaubon. Meursius de
Fortunâ Atticâ, c. 4. [Regarding the number of the inhabitants of Athens
cf. Boeckh, *Public Economy of Athens*, and Clinton's Essay on *Fasti Hel-
lenici*, in which he estimates the population of Athens between 30,000 and
40,000 at the epoch named.—O. S.]

[8] See a very accurate collection of the numbers of each Lustrum in M. de
Beaufort, Republique Romaine, l. iv. c. 4.

[These questions (says Milman) are placed in an entirely new light by

Rome claimed an equal share of honours and privileges, the
senate indeed preferred the chance of arms to an ignominious
concession. The Samnites and the Lucanians paid the severe
penalty of their rashness; but the rest of the Italian states, as
they successively returned to their duty, were admitted into the
bosom of the republic,[1] and soon contributed to the ruin of public
freedom. Under a democratical government, the citizens exercise
the powers of sovereignty; and those powers will be first abused,
and afterwards lost, if they are committed to an unwieldy multitude. But when the popular assemblies had been suppressed
by the administration of the emperors, the conquerors were distinguished from the vanquished nations, only as the first and
most honourable order of subjects; and their increase, however
rapid, was no longer exposed to the same dangers. Yet the
wisest princes, who adopted the maxims of Augustus, guarded
with the strictest care the dignity of the Roman name, and
diffused the freedom of the city with a prudent liberality.[2]

Till the privileges of Romans had been progressively extended
to all the inhabitants of the empire, an important distinction was
preserved between Italy and the provinces. The former was
esteemed the centre of public unity, and the firm basis of the
constitution. Italy claimed the birth, or at least the residence,
of the emperors and the senate.[3] The estates of the Italians
were exempt from taxes, their persons from the arbitrary jurisdiction of governors. Their municipal corporations, formed
after the perfect model of the capital, were intrusted, under the
immediate eye of the supreme power,[4] with the execution of the
laws. From the foot of the Alps to the extremity of Calabria,
all the natives of Italy were born citizens of Rome. Their partial
distinctions were obliterated, and they insensibly coalesced into

Niebuhr in his *Romische Geschichte*, vol. i. p. 464. He rejects the census of
Servius Tullius as historic and establishes the principle that the census
comprehends all the confederate cities which had the right of isopolity, or
equal political rights.—O. S.]

[1] Appian. de Bell. civil. l. i. Velleius Paterculus, l. ii. c. 15, 16, 17.

[2] Mæcenas had advised him to declare by one edict, all his subjects,
citizens. But we may justly suspect that the historian Dion was the
author of a counsel, so much adapted to the practice of his own age, and so
little to that of Augustus.

[3] The senators were obliged to have one-third of their own landed property
in Italy. Plin. l. vi. ep. 19. The qualification was reduced by Marcus to
one-fourth. Since the reign of Trajan, Italy had sunk nearer to the level
of the provinces.

[4] [It may be doubted (adds Dean Milman) whether the municipal government was not the old Italian constitution, rather than a transcript from
that of Rome. The free government of the cities (says Savigny) was the
leading characteristic of Italy, *Geschichte der Romischen Rechts.*—O. S.]

one great nation, united by language, manners, and civil institutions, and equal to the weight of a powerful empire. The republic gloried in her generous policy, and was frequently rewarded by the merit and services of her adopted sons. Had she always confined the distinction of Romans to the ancient families within the walls of the city, that immortal name would have been deprived of some of its noblest ornaments. Virgil was a native of Mantua; Horace was inclined to doubt whether he should call himself an Apulian or a Lucanian: it was in Padua that an historian was found worthy to record the majestic series of Roman victories. The patriot family of the Catos emerged from Tusculum; and the little town of Arpinum claimed the double honour of producing Marius and Cicero, the former of whom deserved, after Romulus and Camillus, to be styled the Third Founder of Rome; and the latter, after saving his country from the designs of Catiline, enabled her to contend with Athens for the palm of eloquence.[1]

The provinces of the empire (as they have been described in the preceding chapter) were destitute of any public force, or constitutional freedom. In Etruria, in Greece,[2] and in Gaul,[3] it was the first care of the senate to dissolve those dangerous confederacies, which taught mankind, that as the Roman arts prevailed by division, they might be resisted by union. Those princes, whom the ostentation of gratitude or generosity permitted for a while to hold a precarious sceptre, were dismissed from their thrones as soon as they had performed their appointed task of fashioning to the yoke the vanquished nations. The free states and cities which had embraced the cause of Rome, were rewarded with a nominal alliance, and insensibly sunk into real servitude. The public authority was everywhere exercised by the ministers of the senate and of the emperors, and that authority was absolute, and without control. But the same salutary maxims of government, which had secured the peace and obedience of Italy, were extended to the most distant conquests. A nation of Romans was gradually formed in the provinces, by the double expedient of introducing colonies, and of admitting the most faithful and deserving of the provincials to the freedom of Rome.

[1] The first part of the Verona Illustrata of the Marquis Maffei, gives the clearest and most comprehensive view of the state of Italy under the Cæsars.

[2] Pausanias, l. vii. [c]. The Romans condescended to restore the names of those assemblies, when they could no longer be dangerous.

[3] They are frequently mentioned by Cæsar. The Abbé Dubos attempts, with very little success, to prove that the assemblies of Gaul were continued under the emperors. Histoire de l'Etablissement de la Monarchie Françoise, l. i. c. 4.

"Wheresoever the Roman conquers, he inhabits," [1] is a very just observation of Seneca, confirmed by history and experience. The natives of Italy, allured by pleasure or by interest, hastened to enjoy the advantages of victory; and we may remark, that about forty years after the reduction of Asia, eighty thousand Romans were massacred in one day, by the cruel orders of Mithridates.[2] These voluntary exiles were engaged, for the most part, in the occupations of commerce, agriculture, and the farm of the revenue. But after the legions were rendered permanent by the emperors, the provinces were peopled by a race of soldiers; and the veterans, whether they received the reward of their service in land or in money, usually settled with their families in the country where they had honourably spent their youth. Throughout the empire, but more particularly in the western parts, the most fertile districts, and the most convenient situations, were reserved for the establishment of colonies; some of which were of a civil, and others of a military nature. In their manners and internal policy, the colonies formed a perfect representation of their great parent; and they were soon endeared to the natives by the ties of friendship and alliance, they effectually diffused a reverence for the Roman name, and a desire, which was seldom disappointed, of sharing, in due time, its honours and advantages.[3] The municipal cities insensibly equalled the rank and splendour of the colonies; and in the reign of Hadrian, it was disputed which was the preferable condition, of those societies which had issued from, or those which had been received into the bosom of Rome.[4] The right of Latium, as it was called, conferred on the cities to which it had been granted a more partial favour. The magistrates only, at the expiration of their office, assumed the quality of Roman citizens; but as those offices were annual, in a few years they circulated round the principal families.[5] Those of the provincials who were per-

---

[1] Seneca in Consolat. ad Helviam, c. 6.

[2] Memnon apud Photium, c. 33 [p. 231 edit. Bekker]. Valer. Maxim. ix. 2. Plutarch [Sulla cap. 24] and Dion Cassius swell the massacre to 150,000 citizens; but I should esteem the smaller number to be more than sufficient.

[3] Twenty-five colonies were settled in Spain (Plin. Hist. Natur. iii. 3, 4 iv. 35): and nine in Britain, of which London, Colchester, Lincoln, Chester, Gloucester, and Bath, still remain considerable cities (Richard of Cirencester, p. 36, and Whitaker's History of Manchester, l. i. c. 3).

[4] Aul. Gell. Noctes Atticæ, xvi. 13. The emperor Hadrian expressed his surprise, that the cities of Utica, Gades, and Italica, which already enjoyed the rights of *Municipia*, should solicit the title of *colonies*. Their example, however, became fashionable, and the empire was filled with honorary colonies. Spanheim, de Usu Numismatum, Dissertat. xiii.

[5] Spanheim, Orbis Roman, c. 8, p. 62.

mitted to bear arms in the legions;[1] those who exercised any
civil employment; all, in a word, who performed any public
service, or displayed any personal talents, were rewarded with a
present, whose value was continually diminished by the increasing liberality of the emperors. Yet even, in the age of the
Antonines, when the freedom of the city had been bestowed on
the greater number of their subjects, it was still accompanied
with very solid advantages. The bulk of the people acquired,
with that title, the benefit of the Roman laws, particularly in
the interesting articles of marriage, testaments, and inheritances;
and the road of fortune was open to those whose pretensions were
seconded by favour or merit. The grandsons of the Gauls, who
had besieged Julius Cæsar in Alesia, commanded legions, governed
provinces, and were admitted into the senate of Rome.[2] Their
ambition, instead of disturbing the tranquillity of the state, was
intimately connected with its safety and greatness.

So sensible were the Romans of the influence of language over
national manners, that it was their most serious care to extend,
with the progress of their arms, the use of the Latin tongue.[3]
The ancient dialects of Italy, the Sabine, the Etruscan, and the
Venetian, sunk into oblivion; but in the provinces, the east was
less docile than the west, to the voice of its victorious preceptors.
This obvious difference marked the two portions of the empire
with a distinction of colours, which, though it was in some degree
concealed during the meridian splendour of prosperity, became
gradually more visible as the shades of night descended upon the
Roman world. The western countries were civilised by the same
hands which subdued them. As soon as the barbarians were
reconciled to obedience, their minds were opened to any new
impressions of knowledge and politeness. The language of Virgil
and Cicero, though with some inevitable mixture of corruption,
was so universally adopted in Africa, Spain, Gaul, Britain, and
Pannonia,[4] that the faint traces of the Punic or Celtic idioms were

---

[1] Aristid. in Romæ Encomio, tom. i. p. 218. Edit. Jebb.
[2] Tacit. Annal. xi. 23, 24. Hist. iv. 74.
[3] Plin. Hist. Natur. iii. 5. Augustin. de Civitate Dei, xix. 7. Lipsius de
pronunciatione Linguæ Latinæ, c. 3.
[4] Apuleius and Augustin will answer for Africa; Strabo for Spain and
Gaul; Tacitus, in the Life of Agricola, for Britain; and Velleius Paterculus,
for Pannonia. To them we may add the language of the Inscriptions.
[Mr. Hallam declines to admit the truth of this assertion as regards
Britain. He says, " Nor did the Roman ever establish their language, I
know not whether they wished to do so, in this island, as we perceive by
that stubborn British tongue which has survived two conquests " (*Middle
Ages*, iii. 314). Dean Milman also refers to the matter and points that the
passage from Tacitus referred to by Gibbon merely asserts the progress of

preserved only in the mountains, or among the peasants.[1] Education and study insensibly inspired the natives of those countries with the sentiments of Romans; and Italy gave fashions as well as laws to her Latin provincials. They solicited with more ardour, and obtained with more facility, the freedom and honours of the state; supported the national dignity in letters[2] and in arms; and, at length, in the person of Trajan, produced an emperor whom the Scipios would not have disowned for their countryman. The situation of the Greeks was very different from that of the Barbarians. The former had been long since civilised and corrupted. They had too much taste to relinquish their language, and too much vanity to adopt any foreign institutions. Still preserving the prejudices after they had lost the virtues of their ancestors, they affected to despise the unpolished manners of the Roman conquerors, whilst they were compelled to respect their superior wisdom and power.[3] Nor was the influence of the Grecian language and sentiments confined to the narrow limits of that once celebrated country. Their empire, by the progress of colonies and conquest, had been diffused from the Hadriatic to the Euphrates and the Nile. Asia was covered with Greek cities, and the long reign of the Macedonian kings had introduced a silent revolution into Syria and Egypt. In their pompous courts those princes united the elegance of Athens with the luxury of the East, and the example of the court was imitated, at an humble distance, by the higher ranks of their subjects. Such was the general division of the Roman empire into the Latin and Greek languages. To these we may add a third distinction for the body of the natives in Syria, and especially in Egypt. The use of their ancient dialects, by secluding them from the commerce of mankind, checked the improvements of those barbarians.[4] The

Latin studies among the higher orders. He thinks that it was a kind of court language and that of public affairs, and that it prevailed in the Roman colonies.—O. S.]

[1] The Celtic was preserved in the mountains of Wales, Cornwall, and Armorica. We may observe that Apuleius reproaches an African youth, who lived among the populace, with the use of the Punic; whilst he had almost forgot Greek, and neither could nor would speak Latin (Apolog. p. 596). The greater part of St. Austin's congregations were strangers to the Punic.

[2] Spain alone produced Columella, the Senecas, Lucan, Martial, and Quintilian.

[3] There is not, I believe, from Dionysius to Libanius, a single Greek critic who mentions Virgil or Horace. They seem ignorant that the Romans had any good writers.

[4] The curious reader may see in Dupin (Bibliothèque Ecclésiastique, tom. xix. p. 1, c. 8), how much the use of the Syriac and Egyptian languages was still preserved.

slothful effeminacy of the former, exposed them to the contempt; the sullen ferociousness of the latter, excited the aversion of the conquerors.[1] Those nations had submitted to the Roman power, but they seldom desired or deserved the freedom of the city; and it was remarked that more than two hundred and thirty years elapsed after the ruin of the Ptolemies before an Egyptian was admitted into the senate of Rome.[2]

It is a just though trite observation, that victorious Rome was herself subdued by the arts of Greece. Those immortal writers who still command the admiration of modern Europe, soon became the favourite object of study and imitation in Italy and the western provinces. But the elegant amusements of the Romans were not suffered to interfere with their sound maxims of policy. Whilst they acknowledged the charms of the Greek, they asserted the dignity of the Latin tongue, and the exclusive use of the latter was inflexibly maintained in the administration of civil as well as military government.[3] The two languages exercised at the same time their separate jurisdiction throughout the empire: the former as the natural idiom of science; the latter as the legal dialect of public transactions. Those who united letters with business were equally conversant with both; and it was almost impossible, in any province, to find a Roman subject of a liberal education, who was at once a stranger to the Greek and to the Latin language.

It was by such institutions that the nations of the empire insensibly melted away into the Roman name and people. But there still remained, in the centre of every province and of every family, an unhappy condition of men who endured the weight, without sharing the benefits, of society. In the free states of antiquity the domestic slaves were exposed to the wanton rigour of despotism. The perfect settlement of the Roman empire was preceded by ages of violence and rapine. The slaves consisted, for the most part, of barbarian captives, taken in thousands by the chance of war, purchased at a vile price,[4] accustomed to a life of independence, and impatient to break and to revenge their fetters. Against such internal enemies, whose desperate insurrections had more than once reduced the republic to the brink of

[1] Juvenal, Sat. iii. and xv. Ammian. Marcellin. xxii. 16.
[2] Dion Cassius, l. lxxvii. [5] p. 1275. The first instance happened under the reign of Septimius Severus.
[3] Valerius Maximus, l. ii. c. 2, n. 2. The emperor Claudius disfranchised an eminent Grecian for not understanding Latin. He was probably in some public office. Suetonius in Claud. c. 16.
[4] In the camp of Lucullus, an ox sold for a drachma, and a slave for four drachmæ, or about three shillings. Plutarch. in Lucull. p. 580.

destruction,[1] the most severe regulations,[2] and the most cruel
treatment, seemed almost justified by the great law of self-
preservation. But when the principal nations of Europe, Asia,
and Africa, were united under the laws of one sovereign, the
source of foreign supplies flowed with much less abundance,
and the Romans were reduced to the milder but more tedious
method of propagation.[3] In their numerous families, and particularly in their country estates, they encouraged the marriage
of their slaves. The sentiments of nature, the habits of education, and the possession of a dependent species of property, contributed to alleviate the hardships of servitude.[4] The existence
of a slave became an object of greater value, and though his
happiness still depended on the temper and circumstances of the
master, the humanity of the latter, instead of being restrained
by fear, was encouraged by the sense of his own interest. The
progress of manners was accelerated by the virtue or policy of
the emperors; and by the edicts of Hadrian and the Antonines,
the protection of the laws was extended to the most abject part
of mankind. The jurisdiction of life and death over the slaves,
a power long exercised and often abused, was taken out of private
hands, and reserved to the magistrates alone. The subterraneous prisons were abolished; and, upon a just complaint of
intolerable treatment, the injured slave obtained either his
deliverance, or a less cruel master.[5]

Hope, the best comfort of our imperfect condition, was not
denied to the Roman slave; and if he had any opportunity of
rendering himself either useful or agreeable, he might very
naturally expect that the diligence and fidelity of a few years
would be rewarded with the inestimable gift of freedom. The
benevolence of the master was so frequently prompted by the
meaner suggestions of vanity and avarice, that the laws found it
more necessary to restrain than to encourage a profuse and undistinguishing liberality, which might degenerate into a very
dangerous abuse.[6] It was a maxim of ancient jurisprudence,
that a slave had not any country of his own, he acquired with

---

[1] Diodorus Siculus in Eclog. Hist. l. xxxiv. and xxxvi.   Florus, iii. 19, 20.
[2] See a remarkable instance of severity in Cicero in Verrem, v. 3.
[3] [Milman says an active slave-trade was carried on in Britain.—O. S.]
[4] See in Gruter, and the other collectors, a great number of inscriptions
addressed by slaves to their wives, children, fellow-servants, masters, etc.
They are all most probably of the Imperial age.
[5] Augustan History [Spartian Hadr. 18] and Dissertation of M. de
Burigny, in the xxxvth volume of the Academy of Inscriptions, upon the
Roman slaves.
[6] Dissertation of M. de Burigny in the xxxviith volume, on the Roman
freedmen.

his liberty an admission into the political society of which his patron was a member. The consequences of this maxim would have prostituted the privileges of the Roman city to a mean and promiscuous multitude. Some seasonable exceptions were therefore provided; and the honourable distinction was confined to such slaves only, as for just causes, and with the approbation of the magistrate, should receive a solemn and legal manumission. Even these chosen freed-men obtained no more than the private rights of citizens, and were rigorously excluded from civil or military honours. Whatever might be the merit or fortune of their sons, *they* likewise were esteemed unworthy of a seat in the senate; nor were the traces of a servile origin allowed to be completely obliterated till the third or fourth generation.[1] Without destroying the distinction of ranks, a distant prospect of freedom and honours was presented, even to those whom pride and prejudice almost disdained to number among the human species.

It was once proposed to discriminate the slaves by a peculiar habit; but it was justly apprehended that there might be some danger in acquainting them with their own numbers.[2] Without interpreting, in their utmost strictness, the liberal appellations of legions and myriads;[3] we may venture to pronounce, that the proportion of slaves, who were valued as property, was more considerable than that of servants, who can be computed only as an expense.[4] The youths of a promising genius were instructed in the arts and sciences, and their price was ascertained by the degree of their skill and talents.[5] Almost every profession, either liberal[6] or mechanical, might be found in the household of an opulent senator. The ministers of pomp and sensuality were multiplied beyond the conception of modern luxury.[7] It was more for the interest of the merchant or manu-

[1] Spanheim, Orbis Roman, l. i. c. 16, p. 124, etc.

[2] Seneca de Clementiâ, l. i. c. 24. The original is much stronger, " Quantum periculum immineret si servi nostri numerare nos cœpissent."

[3] Pliny (Hist. Natur. l. xxxiii.) and Athenæus (Deipnosophist. l. vi. p. 272). The latter boldly asserts, that he knew very many (παμπόλλοι) Romans who possessed, not for use, but ostentation, ten and even twenty thousand slaves.

[4] In Paris there are not more than 43,700 domestics of every sort, and not a twelfth part of the inhabitants. Messange, Recherches sur la Population, p. 186.

[5] A learned slave sold for many hundred pounds sterling : Atticus always bred and taught them himself. Cornel. Nepos in Vit. c. 13.

[6] Many of the Roman physicians were slaves. Middleton's Dissertation and Defence.

[7] Their ranks and offices are very copiously enumerated by Pignorius de Servis.

facturer to purchase than to hire his workmen; and in the country, slaves were employed as the cheapest and most laborious instruments of agriculture. To confirm the general observation, and to display the multitude of slaves, we might allege a variety of particular instances. It was discovered, on a very melancholy occasion, that four hundred slaves were maintained in a single palace of Rome.[1] The same number of four hundred belonged to an estate which an African widow, of a very private condition, resigned to her son, whilst she reserved for herself a much larger share of her property.[2] A freed-man, under the reign of Augustus, though his fortune had suffered great losses in the civil wars, left behind him three thousand six hundred yoke of oxen, two hundred and fifty thousand head of smaller cattle, and, what was almost included in the description of cattle, four thousand one hundred and sixteen slaves.[3]

The number of subjects who acknowledged the laws of Rome, of citizens, of provincials, and of slaves, cannot now be fixed with such a degree of accuracy, as the importance of the object would deserve. We are informed that when the emperor Claudius exercised the office of censor, he took an account of six millions nine hundred and forty-five thousand Roman citizens, who, with the proportion of women and children, must have amounted to about twenty millions of souls. The multitude of subjects of an inferior rank was uncertain and fluctuating. But, after weighing with attention every circumstance which could influence the balance, it seems probable that there existed, in the time of Claudius, about twice as many provincials as there were citizens, of either sex, and of every age; and that the slaves were at least equal in number to the free inhabitants of the Roman world.[4] The total amount of this imperfect calculation would rise to about one hundred and twenty millions of persons; a degree of population which possibly exceeds that of modern

---

[1] Tacit. Annal. xiv. 43. They were all executed for not preventing their master's murder.

[2] Apuleius in Apolog. p. 548, edit. Delphin.

[3] Plin. Hist. Natur. l. xxxiii. 47.

[4] [Zumpt in his Dissertation on the Population of the Roman state, regards it as a gross error on the part of Gibbon to estimate the number of the slaves as being at least equal to that of the free population. The luxury and magnificence of the great at the commencement of the empire must not (he reckons) be taken as the groundwork of calculations for the whole Roman world. The agricultural labourer and the artisan, in Spain, Gaul, Britain, Syria, Egypt, maintained himself as in the present day by his own labour and that of his household without possessing a single slave. —O. S.]

Europe,[1] and forms the most numerous society that has ever been united under the same system of government.

Domestic peace and union were the natural consequences of the moderate and comprehensive policy embraced by the Romans. If we turn our eyes towards the monarchies of Asia, we shall behold despotism in the centre, and weakness in the extremities; the collection of the revenue, or the administration of justice, enforced by the presence of an army; hostile barbarians established in the heart of the country, hereditary satraps usurping the dominion of the provinces, and subjects inclined to rebellion, though incapable of freedom. But the obedience of the Roman world was uniform, voluntary, and permanent. The vanquished nations, blended into one great people, resigned the hope, nay even the wish, of resuming their independence, and scarcely considered their own existence as distinct from the existence of Rome. The established authority of the emperors pervaded without an effort the wide extent of their dominions, and was exercised with the same facility on the banks of the Thames, or of the Nile, as on those of the Tiber. The legions were destined to serve against the public enemy, and the civil magistrate seldom required the aid of a military force.[2] In this state of general security, the leisure as well as opulence both of the prince and people were devoted to improve and to adorn the Roman empire.

Among the innumerable monuments of architecture constructed by the Romans, how many have escaped the notice of history, how few have resisted the ravages of time and barbarism! And yet even the majestic ruins that are still scattered over Italy and the provinces, would be sufficient to prove that those countries were once the seat of a polite and powerful empire. Their greatness alone, or their beauty, might deserve our attention; but they are rendered more interesting by two important circumstances, which connect the agreeable history of the arts with the more useful history of human manners. Many of those works were erected at private expense, and almost all were intended for public benefit.

[1] Compute twenty millions in France, twenty-two in Germany, four in Hungary, ten in Italy with its islands, eight in Great Britain and Ireland, eight in Spain and Portugal, ten or twelve in the European Russia, six in Poland, six in Greece and Turkey, four in Sweden, three in Denmark and Norway, four in the Low Countries. The whole would amount to one hundred and five or one hundred and seven millions. Voltaire, Histoire Generale.

[2] Joseph. de Bell. Judaico. l. ii. c. 16. The oration of Agrippa, or rather of the historian is a fine picture of the Roman empire.

It is natural to suppose that the greatest number, as well as the most considerable of the Roman edifices, were raised by the emperors, who possessed so unbounded a command both of men and money. Augustus was accustomed to boast that he had found his capital of brick, and that he had left it of marble.[1] The strict economy of Vespasian was the source of his magnificence. The works of Trajan bear the stamp of his genius. The public monuments with which Hadrian adorned every province of the empire, were executed not only by his orders, but under his immediate inspection. He was himself an artist; and he loved the arts, as they conduced to the glory of the monarch. They were encouraged by the Antonines, as they contributed to the happiness of the people. But if the emperors were the first, they were not the only architects of their dominions. Their example was universally imitated by their principal subjects, who were not afraid of declaring to the world that they had spirit to conceive, and wealth to accomplish, the noblest undertakings. Scarcely had the proud structure of the Coliseum been dedicated at Rome, before the edifices of a smaller scale indeed, but of the same design and materials, were erected for the use, and at the expense, of the cities of Capua and Verona.[2] The inscription of the stupendous bridge of Alcantara attests that it was thrown over the Tagus by the contribution of a few Lusitanian communities. When Pliny was intrusted with the government of Bithynia and Pontus, provinces by no means the richest or most considerable of the empire, he founded the cities within his jurisdiction striving with each other in every useful and ornamental work, that might deserve the curiosity of strangers, or the gratitude of their citizens. It was the duty of the Proconsul to supply their deficiencies, to direct their taste, and sometimes to moderate their emulation.[3] The opulent senators of Rome and the provinces esteemed it an honour, and

[1] Sueton. in August. c. 28. Augustus built in Rome the temple and forum of Mars the Avenger; the temple of Jupiter Tonans in the Capitol; that of Apollo Palatine, with public libraries; the portico and basilica of Caius and Lucius, the porticos of Livia and Octavia, and the theatre of Marcellus. The example of the sovereign was imitated by his ministers and generals; and his friend Agrippa left behind him the immortal monument of the Pantheon.

[2] Maffei, Verona illustrata, l. iv. p. 68.

[3] Xth book of Pliny's Epistles. He mentions the following works, carried on at the expense of the cities. At Nicomedia, a new forum, an aqueduct, and a canal, left unfinished by a king; at Nice, a gymnasium, and a theatre which had already cost near ninety thousand pounds; baths at Prusa and Claudiopolis; and an aqueduct of sixteen miles in length for the use of Sinope.

almost an obligation, to adorn the splendour of their age and country; and the influence of fashion very frequently supplied the want of taste or generosity. Among a crowd of these private benefactors, we may select Herodes Atticus, an Athenian citizen, who lived in the age of the Antonines. Whatever might be the motive of his conduct, his magnificence would have been worthy of the greatest kings.

The family of Herod, at least after it had been favoured by fortune, was lineally descended from Cimon and Miltiades, Theseus and Cecrops, Æacus and Jupiter. But the posterity of so many gods and heroes was fallen into the most abject state. His grandfather had suffered by the hands of justice, and Julius Atticus, his father, must have ended his life in poverty and contempt, had he not discovered an immense treasure buried under an old house, the last remains of his patrimony. According to the rigour of law, the emperor might have asserted his claim, and the prudent Atticus prevented, by a frank confession, the officiousness of informers. But the equitable Nerva, who then filled the throne, refused to accept any part of it, and commanded him to use, without scruple, the present of fortune. The cautious Athenian still insisted that the treasure was too considerable for a subject, and that he knew not how to *use it*. *Abuse it, then*, replied the monarch, with a good-natured peevishness; for it is your own.[1] Many will be of opinion that Atticus literally obeyed the emperor's last instructions; since he expended the greatest part of his fortune, which was much increased by an advantageous marriage, in the service of the Public. He had obtained for his son Herod the prefecture of the free cities of Asia; and the young magistrate, observing that the town of Troas was indifferently supplied with water, obtained from the munificence of Hadrian three hundred myriads of drachms (about a hundred thousand pounds) for the construction of a new aqueduct. But in the execution of the work the charge amounted to more than double the estimate, and the officers of the revenue began to murmur, till the generous Atticus silenced their complaints, by requesting that he might be permitted to take upon himself the whole additional expense.[2]

The ablest preceptors of Greece and Asia had been invited by liberal rewards to direct the education of young Herod. Their pupil soon became a celebrated orator according to the useless

[1] Hadrian afterwards made a very equitable regulation, which divided all treasure-trove between the right of property and that of discovery. Hist. August. p. 9 [Spartian Hadr. c. 18].

[2] Philostrat. in Vit. Sophist. l. ii. p. 548.

rhetoric of that age, which, confining itself to the schools, disdained to visit either the Forum or the Senate. He was honoured with the consulship at Rome; but the greatest part of his life was spent in a philosophic retirement at Athens, and his adjacent villas; perpetually surrounded by sophists, who acknowledged, without reluctance, the superiority of a rich and generous rival.[1] The monuments of his genius have perished; some considerable ruins still preserve the fame of his taste and munificence: modern travellers have measured the remains of the stadium which he constructed at Athens. It was six hundred feet in length, built entirely of white marble, capable of admitting the whole body of the people, and finished in four years, whilst Herod was president of the Athenian games. To the memory of his wife Regilla he dedicated a theatre, scarcely to be paralleled in the empire; no wood except cedar, very curiously carved, was employed in any part of the building. The Odeum,[2] designed by Pericles for musical performances, and the rehearsal of new tragedies, had been a trophy of the victory of the arts over Barbaric greatness; as the timbers employed in the construction consisted chiefly of the masts of the Persian vessels. Notwithstanding the repairs bestowed on that ancient edifice by a king of Cappadocia, it was again fallen to decay. Herod restored its ancient beauty and magnificence. Nor was the liberality of that illustrious citizen confined to the walls of Athens. The most splendid ornaments bestowed on the temple of Neptune in the Isthmus, a theatre at Corinth, a stadium at Delphi, a bath at Thermopylæ, and an aqueduct at Canusium in Italy, were insufficient to exhaust his treasures. The people of Epirus, Thessaly, Eubœa, Bœotia, and Peloponnesus, experienced his favours; and many inscriptions of the cities of Greece and Asia gratefully style Herodes Atticus their patron and benefactor.[3]

[1] Aulus Gellius, in Noct. Attic. i. 2. ix. 2, xviii. 10, xix. 12, Philostrat. p. 564.
[2] [The Odeum of Pericles and the Odeum of Herodes were altogether different structures. Gibbon confounds them here. The former was under the south-eastern extremity of the Acropolis, the latter under the south-western extremity. The Odeum served for the rehearsal of new comedies as well as tragedies. They were read or repeated before representation without music or decorations. No piece could be represented in the theatre if it had not been previously approved by judges for this purpose. The King of Cappadocia, who restored the Odeum which had been burned by Sylla, was Ariobarzanes. Cf. Martini, Dissertat. on Odeons of Ancients, Leipsic, 1767.—O. S.]
[3] Philostrat. l. ii. p. 548, 560. Pausanias, l. i. and vii. 10. The Life of Herodes, in the xxxth volume of the Memoirs of the Academy of Inscriptions.

In the commonwealths of Athens and Rome, the modest
simplicity of private houses announced the equal condition of
freedom; whilst the sovereignty of the people was represented
in the majestic edifices destined to the public use; [1] nor was this
republican spirit totally extinguished by the introduction of
wealth and monarchy. It was in works of national honour and
benefit, that the most virtuous of the emperors affected to display their magnificence. The golden palace of Nero excited a
just indignation, but the vast extent of ground which had been
usurped by his selfish luxury, was more nobly filled under the
succeeding reigns by the Coliseum, the baths of Titus, the
Claudian portico, and the temples dedicated to the goddess of
Peace, and to the genius of Rome.[2] These monuments of architecture, the property of the Roman people, were adorned with
the most beautiful productions of Grecian painting and sculpture; and in the temple of Peace a very curious library was open
to the curiosity of the learned. At a small distance from thence
was situated the Forum of Trajan. It was surrounded with a
lofty portico, in the form of a quadrangle, into which four
triumphal arches opened a noble and spacious entrance: in the
centre arose a column of marble, whose height, of one hundred
and ten feet, denoted the elevation of the hill that had been cut
away. This column, which still subsists in its ancient beauty,
exhibited an exact representation of the Dacian victories of its
founder. The veteran soldier contemplated the story of his own
campaigns, and by an easy illusion of national vanity, the peaceful citizen associated himself to the honours of the triumph.
All the other quarters of the capital, and all the provinces of the
empire, were embellished by the same liberal spirit of public
magnificence, and were filled with amphitheatres, theatres,
temples, porticos, triumphal arches, baths, and aqueducts, all
variously conducive to the health, the devotion, and the pleasures

[1] It is particularly remarked of Athens by Dicæarchus, de Statu Græciæ,
p. 8, inter Geographos Minores, edit. Hudson.
[2] Donatus de Roma Vetere, l. iii. c. 4, 5, 6. Nardini, Roma Antica, l. iii.
11, 12, 13, and a MS. description of ancient Rome, by Bernardus Oricel-
larius, or Rucellai, of which I obtained a copy from the library of the Canon
Ricardi at Florence. Two celebrated pictures of Timanthes and of Proto-
genes are mentioned by Pliny, as in the Temple of Peace: and the Laocoon
was found in the baths of Titus.
[It was the Emperor Vespasian who caused the Temple of Peace to be
built, and who ordered to be transported to it the greatest part of the
pictures, statues, and other works of art which had escaped the civil
tumults. It was there that every day the artists and the literati of Rome
assembled, and on its site many antiques have been dug up. Cf. Notes of
Reimarus on Dion Cassius, lxvi. c. 15.—O. S.]

of the meanest citizen. The last mentioned of those edifices deserve our peculiar attention. The boldness of the enterprise, the solidity of the execution, and the uses to which they were subservient, rank the aqueducts among the noblest monuments of Roman genius and power. The aqueducts of the capital claim a just pre-eminence; but the curious traveller, who, without the light of history, should examine those of Spoleto, of Metz, or of Segovia, would very naturally conclude that those provincial towns had formerly been the residence of some potent monarch. The solitudes of Asia and Africa were once covered with flourishing cities, whose populousness, and even whose existence, was derived from such artificial supplies of a perennial stream of fresh water.[1]

We have computed the inhabitants and contemplated the public works of the Roman empire. The observation of the number and greatness of its cities will serve to confirm the former, and to multiply the latter. It may not be unpleasing to collect a few scattered instances relative to that subject, without forgetting, however, that from the vanity of nations and the poverty of language, the vague appellation of city has been indifferently bestowed on Rome and upon Laurentum. *Ancient* Italy is said to have contained eleven hundred and ninety-seven cities; and for whatsoever era of antiquity the expression might be intended,[2] there is not any reason to believe the country less populous in the age of the Antonines than in that of Romulus. The petty states of Latium were contained within the metropolis of the empire, by whose superior influence they had been attracted. Those parts of Italy which have so long languished under the lazy tyranny of priests and viceroys, had been afflicted only by the more tolerable calamities of war; and the first symptoms of decay which *they* experienced were amply compensated by the rapid improvements of the Cisalpine Gaul. The splendour of Verona may be traced in its remains: yet Verona was less celebrated than Aquileia or Padua, Milan or Ravenna. II. The spirit of improvement had passed the Alps, and been felt even in the woods of Britain, which were gradually cleared away to open a free space for convenient and elegant habitations. York was the seat of government; London was already enriched by commerce; and Bath was celebrated for the salutary effects of its medicinal waters. Gaul could boast

---

[1] Montfaucon, l'Antiquité Expliquée, tom. iv. p. 2, l. i. c. 9. Fabretti has composed a very learned treatise on the aqueducts of Rome.

[2] Ælian. Hist. Var. l. ix. c. 16. He lived in the time of Alexander Severus. See Fabricius, Biblioth. Græca, l. iv. c. 21.

of her twelve hundred cities;[1] and though, in the northern
parts, many of them, without excepting Paris itself, were little
more than the rude and imperfect townships of a rising people;
the southern provinces imitated the wealth and elegance of
Italy.[2] Many were the cities of Gaul, Marseilles, Arles, Nismes,
Narbonne, Thoulouse, Bourdeaux, Autun, Vienna, Lyons,
Langres, and Treves, whose ancient condition might sustain an
equal, and perhaps advantageous comparison with their present
state. With regard to Spain, that country flourished as a province, and has declined as a kingdom. Exhausted by the abuse
of her strength, by America, and by superstition, her pride might
possibly be confounded, if we required such a list of three hundred
and sixty cities, as Pliny has exhibited under the reign of Vespasian.[3] III. Three hundred African cities had once acknowledged the authority of Carthage,[4] nor is it likely that their
numbers diminished under the administration of the emperors:
Carthage itself rose with new splendour from its ashes; and that
capital, as well as Capua and Corinth, soon recovered all the
advantages which can be separated from independent sovereignty.
IV. The provinces of the east present the contrast of Roman
magnificence with Turkish barbarism. The ruins of antiquity
scattered over uncultivated fields, and ascribed, by ignorance,
to the power of magic, scarcely afford a shelter to the oppressed
peasant or wandering Arab. Under the reign of the Cæsars, the
proper Asia alone contained five hundred populous cities,[5] enriched with all the gifts of nature, and adorned with all the
refinements of art. Eleven cities of Asia had once disputed the
honour of dedicating a temple to Tiberius, and their respective
merits were examined by the senate.[6] Four of them were

---

[1] Joseph. de Bell. Jud. ii. 16. The number, however, is mentioned, and
should be received with a degree of latitude.

[2] Plin. Hist. Natur. iii. 5.

[3] Plin. Hist. Natur. iii. 3, 4, iv. 35. The list seems authentic and accurate: the division of the provinces, and the different condition of the cities,
are minutely distinguished.

[4] Strabon. Geograph. l. xvii. p. 1189.

[5] Joseph. de Bell. Jud. ii. 16. Philostrat. in Vit. Sophist. l. ii. p. 548,
edit. Olear.

[6] Tacit. Annal. iv. 55. I have taken some pains in consulting and comparing modern travellers, with regard to the fate of those eleven cities of
Asia: seven or eight are totally destroyed, Hypæpe, Tralles, Laodicea,
Ilium, Halicarnassus, Miletus, Ephesus, and we may add Sardis. Of the
remaining three, Pergamus is a straggling village of two or three thousand
inhabitants; Magnesia, under the name of Guzel-hissar, a town of some
consequence, and Smyrna, a great city, peopled by an hundred thousand
souls. But even at Smyrna, while the Franks have maintained commerce,
the Turks have ruined the arts.

immediately rejected as unequal to the burden; and among these was Laodicea, whose splendour is still displayed in its ruins.[1] Laodicea collected a very considerable revenue from its flocks of sheep, celebrated for the fineness of their wool, and had received, a little before the contest, a legacy of above four hundred thousand pounds by the testament of a generous citizen.[2] If such was the poverty of Laodicea, what must have been the wealth of those cities, whose claim appeared preferable, and particularly of Pergamus, of Smyrna, and of Ephesus, who so long disputed with each other the titular primacy of Asia.[3] The capitals of Syria and Egypt held a still superior rank in the empire: Antioch and Alexandria looked down with disdain on a crowd of dependent cities,[4] and yielded, with reluctance, to the majesty of Rome itself.

All these cities were connected with each other, and with the capital, by the public highways, which issuing from the Forum of Rome, traversed Italy, pervaded the provinces, and were terminated only by the frontiers of the empire. If we carefully trace the distance from the wall of Antoninus to Rome, and from thence to Jerusalem, it will be found that the great chain of communication, from the north-west to the south-east point of the empire, was drawn out to the length of four thousand and eighty Roman miles.[5] The public roads were accurately divided by mile-stones, and ran in a direct line from one city to another, with very little respect for the obstacles either of nature or private property. Mountains were perforated, and bold arches thrown over the broadest and most rapid streams.[6] The middle

[1] See a very exact and pleasing description of the ruins of Laodicea, in Chandler's Travels through Asia Minor, p. 225, etc.

[2] Strabo, l. xii. p. 866. He had studied at Tralles.

[3] Dissertation of M. de Boze, Mém. de l'Académie, tom. xviii. Aristides pronounced an oration which is still extant, to recommend concord to the rival cities.

[4] The inhabitants of Egypt, exclusive of Alexandria, amounted to seven millions and a half (Joseph. de Bell. Jud. ii. 16). Under the military government of the Mamalukes, Syria was supposed to contain sixty thousand villages (Histoire de Timur Bec, l. v. c. 20).

[5] The following Itinerary may serve to convey some idea of the direction of the road, and of the distance between the principal towns. I. From the wall of Antoninus to York, 222 Roman miles. II. London 227. III. Rhutupiæ or Sandwich 67. IV. The navigation to Boulogne 45. V. Rheims 174. VI. Lyons 330. VII. Milan 324. VIII. Rome 426. IX. Brundusium 360. X. The navigation to Dyrrachium 40. XI. Byzantium 711. XII. Ancyra 283. XIII. Tarsus 301. XIV. Antioch 141. XV. Tyre 252. XVI. Jerusalem 168. In all 4080 Roman, or 3740 English miles. See the Itineraries published by Wesseling, his annotations; Gale and Stukeley for Britain, and M. d'Anville for Gaul and Italy.

[6] Montfaucon, l'Antiquité Expliquée (tom. iv. p. 2, l. i. c. 5), has described the bridges of Narni, Alcantara, Nismes, etc.

part of the road was raised into a terrace which commanded the adjacent country, consisted of several strata of sand, gravel, and cement, and was paved with large stones, or in some places, near the capital, with granite.[1] Such was the solid construction of the Roman highways, whose firmness has not entirely yielded to the effort of fifteen centuries. They united the subjects of the most distant provinces by an easy and familiar intercourse; but their primary object had been to facilitate the marches of the legions; nor was any country considered as completely subdued, till it had been rendered, in all its parts, pervious to the arms and authority of the conqueror. The advantage of receiving the earliest intelligence, and of conveying their orders with celerity, induced the emperors to establish throughout their extensive dominions, the regular institution of posts.[2] Houses were everywhere erected at the distance only of five or six miles; each of them was constantly provided with forty horses, and by the help of these relays it was easy to travel an hundred miles in a day along the Roman roads.[3] The use of the posts was allowed to those who claimed it by an Imperial mandate; but though originally intended for the public service, it was sometimes indulged to the business or conveniency of private citizens.[4] Nor was the communication of the Roman empire less free and open by sea than it was by land. The provinces surrounded and inclosed the Mediterranean; and Italy, in the shape of an immense promontory, advanced into the midst of that great lake. The coasts of Italy are, in general, destitute of safe harbours; but human industry had corrected the deficiencies of nature; and the artificial port of Ostia, in particular, situate at the mouth of the Tyber, and formed by the emperor Claudius, was a useful monument of Roman greatness.[5] From this port, which was only sixteen miles from the capital, a favourable

---

[1] Bergier, Histoire des grands Chemins de l'Empire Romain, l. ii. c. 1-28.

[2] Procopius in Hist. Arcanâ, c. 30. Bergier Hist. des grands Chemins, l. iv. Codex Theodosian. l. viii. tit. v. vol. ii. p. 506-563, with Godefroy's learned commentary.

[3] In the time of Theodosius, Cæsarius, a magistrate of high rank, went post from Antioch to Constantinople. He began his journey at night, was in Cappadocia (165 miles from Antioch) the ensuing evening, and arrived at Constantinople the sixth day about noon. The whole distance was 725 Roman, or 665 English miles. See Libanius Orat. xxii. and the Itineraria, p. 572-581.

[4] Pliny, though a favourite and a minister, made an apology for granting post-horses to his wife on the most urgent business. Epist. x. 121, 122.

[5] Bergier, Hist. des grands Chemins, l. iv. c. 49.

breeze frequently carried vessels in seven days to the columns of Hercules, and in nine or ten, to Alexandria in Egypt.[1]

Whatever evils either reason or declamation have imputed to extensive empire, the power of Rome was attended with some beneficial consequences to mankind; and the same freedom of intercourse which extended the vices, diffused likewise the improvements of social life. In the more remote ages of antiquity, the world was unequally divided. The east was in the immemorial possession of arts and luxury; whilst the west was inhabited by rude and warlike barbarians, who either disdained agriculture, or to whom it was totally unknown. Under the protection of an established government, the productions of happier climates, and the industry of more civilised nations, were gradually introduced into the western countries of Europe; and the natives were encouraged, by an open and profitable commerce, to multiply the former, as well as to improve the latter. It would be almost impossible to enumerate all the articles, either of the animal or the vegetable reign, which were successively imported into Europe, from Asia and Egypt; [2] but it will not be unworthy of the dignity, and much less of the utility, of an historical work, slightly to touch on a few of the principal heads. 1. Almost all the flowers, the herbs, and the fruits, that grow in our European gardens, are of foreign extraction, which, in many cases, is betrayed even by their names: the apple was a native of Italy, and when the Romans had tasted the richer flavour of the apricot, the peach, the pomegranate, the citron, and the orange, they contented themselves with applying to all these new fruits the common denomination of apple, discriminating them from each other by the additional epithet of their country. 2. In the time of Homer, the vine grew wild in the island of Sicily, and most probably in the adjacent continent; but it was not improved by the skill, nor did it afford a liquor grateful to the taste, of the savage inhabitants.[3] A thousand years afterwards, Italy could boast, that of the fourscore most generous and celebrated wines, more than two-thirds were produced from her soil.[4] The blessing was soon communicated to the Narbonnese province of Gaul; but so intense was the cold to

---

[1] Plin. Hist. Natur. xix. 1.

[From Puteoli (says Pliny), which seems to have been the usual landing place from the East. Cf. Voyages of St. Paul, Acts xxviii. 13, and Josephus, *Vita*, cap. 3.—O. S.]

[2] It is not improbable that the Greeks and Phœnicians introduced some new arts and productions into the neighbourhood of Marseilles and Gades.

[3] Homer, Odyss. l. ix. v. 358.

[4] Plin. Hist. Natur. l. xiv.

the north of the Cevennes, that, in the time of Strabo, it was thought impossible to ripen the grapes in those parts of Gaul.[1] This difficulty, however, was gradually vanquished; and there is some reason to believe, that the vineyards of Burgundy are as old as the age of the Antonines.[2] The olive, in the western world, followed the progress of peace, of which it was considered as the symbol. Two centuries after the foundation of Rome, both Italy and Africa were strangers to that useful plant; it was naturalised in those countries; and at length carried into the heart of Spain and Gaul. The timid errors of the ancients, that it required a certain degree of heat, and could only flourish in the neighbourhood of the sea, were insensibly exploded by industry and experience.[3] The cultivation of flax was transported from Egypt to Gaul, and enriched the whole country, however it might impoverish the particular lands on which it was sown.[4] 5. The use of artificial grasses became familiar to the farmers both of Italy and the provinces, particularly the Lucerne, which derived its name and origin from Media.[5] The assured supply of wholesome and plentiful food for the cattle during winter, multiplied the number of the flocks and herds, which in their turn contributed to the fertility of the soil. To all these improvements may be added an assiduous attention to mines and fisheries, which, by employing a multitude of laborious hands, serve to increase the pleasures of the rich, and the subsistence of the poor. The elegant treatise of Columella describes the advanced state of the Spanish husbandry, under the reign of Tiberius; and it may be observed, that those famines which so

[1] Strab. Geograph. l. iv. p. 223. The intense cold of a Gallic winter was almost proverbial among the ancients.
[It appears from the treatise of Cicero, De Republica (iii. 9), that there was a law of the Republic prohibiting the culture of the vine and the olive beyond the Alps, in order to keep up the value of those in Italy. This restriction was veiled under the pretext of encouraging the growth of grain—O. S.]

[2] In the beginning of the fourth century, the orator Eumenius (Panegyric. Veter. viii. 6, edit. Delphin.) speaks of the vines in the territory of Autun, which were decayed through age, and the first plantation of which was totally unknown. The Pagus Arebrignus is supposed by M. d'Anville to be the district of Beaune, celebrated, even at present, for one of the first growths of Burgundy.
[This (says Wenck) is proved by a passage of Pliny the Elder where he speaks of a certain kind of grape (vitis picata : vinum picatum) which grows naturally in the district of Vienne, and had recently been transplanted into the country of the Arverni (Auvergne) and neighbouring states. Pliny wrote in A.D. 77. Cf. Hist. Nat. xiv. 1.—O. S.]

[3] Plin. Hist. Natur. l. xv.

[4] Plin. Hist. Natur. l. xix.

[5] Harte's Essays on Agriculture, in which he has collected all that the ancients and moderns have said of lucerne.

frequently afflicted the infant republic, were seldom or never experienced by the extensive empire of Rome. The accidental scarcity, in any single province, was immediately relieved by the plenty of its more fortunate neighbours.

Agriculture is the foundation of manufactures; since the productions of nature are the materials of art. Under the Roman empire, the labour of an industrious and ingenious people was variously, but incessantly employed, in the service of the rich. In their dress, their table, their houses, and their furniture, the favourites of fortune united every refinement of conveniency, of elegance, and of splendour, whatever could soothe their pride or gratify their sensuality. Such refinements, under the odious name of luxury, have been severely arraigned by the moralists of every age; and it might perhaps be more conducive to the virtue, as well as happiness, of mankind, if all possessed the necessaries, and none the superfluities, of life. But in the present imperfect condition of society, luxury, though it may proceed from vice or folly, seems to be the only means that can correct the unequal distribution of property. The diligent mechanic, and the skilful artist, who have obtained no share in the division of the earth, receive a voluntary tax from the possessors of land; and the latter are prompted, by a sense of interest, to improve those estates, with whose produce they may purchase additional pleasures. This operation, the particular effects of which are felt in every society, acted with much more diffusive energy in the Roman world. The provinces would soon have been exhausted of their wealth, if the manufactures and commerce of luxury had not insensibly restored to the industrious subjects the sums which were exacted from them by the arms and authority of Rome. As long as the circulation was confined within the bounds of the empire, it impressed the political machine with a new degree of activity, and its consequences, sometimes beneficial, could never become pernicious.

But it is no easy task to confine luxury within the limits of an empire. The most remote countries of the ancient world were ransacked to supply the pomp and delicacy of Rome. The forests of Scythia afforded some valuable furs. Amber was brought over land from the shores of the Baltic to the Danube; and the barbarians were astonished at the price which they received in exchange for so useless a commodity.[1] There was a

---

[1] Tacit. Germania, c. 45. Plin. Hist. Nat. xxxviii. 11. The latter observed, with some humour, that even fashion had not yet found out the use of amber. Nero sent a Roman knight to purchase great quantities on the spot where it was produced, the coast of modern Prussia.

considerable demand for Babylonian carpets and other manufactures of the East; but the most important and unpopular
branch of foreign trade was carried on with Arabia and India.
Every year, about the time of the summer solstice, a fleet of an
hundred and twenty vessels sailed from Myos-hormos, a port of
Egypt, on the Red Sea. By the periodical assistance of the
Monsoons, they traversed the ocean in about forty days. The
coast of Malabar, or the island of Ceylon,[1] was the usual term of
their navigation, and it was in those markets that the merchants
from the more remote countries of Asia expected their arrival. The
return of the fleet of Egypt was fixed to the months of December
or January; and as soon as their rich cargo had been transported
on the backs of camels, from the Red Sea to the Nile, and had
descended that river as far as Alexandria, it was poured, without
delay, into the capital of the empire.[2] The objects of oriental
traffic were splendid and trifling: silk, a pound of which was
esteemed not inferior in value to a pound of gold;[3] precious
stones, among which the pearl claimed the first rank after the
diamond;[4] and a variety of aromatics, that were consumed in
religious worship and the pomp of funerals. The labour and
risk of the voyage was rewarded with almost incredible profit;
but the profit was made upon Roman subjects, and a few individuals were enriched at the expense of the Public. As the
natives of Arabia and India were contented with the productions
and manufactures of their own country, silver, on the side of
the Romans, was the principal, if not the only instrument of
commerce. It was a complaint worthy of the gravity of the
senate, that in the purchase of female ornaments, the wealth
of the state was irrecoverably given away to foreign and hostile
nations.[5] The annual loss is computed, by a writer of an inquisitive but censorious temper, at upwards of eight hundred
thousand pounds sterling.[6] Such was the style of discontent,
brooding over the dark prospect of approaching poverty. And

---

[1] Called Taprobana by the Romans, and Serendib by the Arabs. It was
discovered under the reign of Claudius, and gradually became the principal
mart of the East.

[2] Plin. Hist. Natur. l. vi. Strabo, l. xvii.

[3] Hist. August. p. 224. A silk garment was considered as an ornament
to a woman, but as a disgrace to a man.

[4] The two great pearl fisheries were the same as at present, Ormuz and
Cape Comorin. As well as we can compare ancient with modern geography,
Rome was supplied with diamonds from the mine of Jumelpur, in Bengal,
which is described in the Voyages de Tavernier, tom. ii. p. 281.

[5] Tacit. Annal. iii. 52 (in a speech of Tiberius).

[6] Plin. Hist. Natur. xii. 18. In another place he computes half that
sum; Quingenties H. S. for India exclusive of Arabia.

yet, if we compare the proportion between gold and silver, as it stood in the time of Pliny, and as it was fixed in the reign of Constantine, we shall discover within that period a very considerable increase.[1] There is not the least reason to suppose that gold was become more scarce; it is therefore evident that silver was grown more common; that whatever might be the amount of the Indian and Arabian exports, they were far from exhausting the wealth of the Roman world; and that the produce of the mines abundantly supplied the demands of commerce.

Notwithstanding the propensity of mankind to exalt the past, and to depreciate the present, the tranquil and prosperous state of the empire was warmly felt, and honestly confessed, by the provincials as well as Romans. " They acknowledged that the true principles of social life, laws, agriculture, and science, which had been first invented by the wisdom of Athens, were now firmly established by the power of Rome, under whose auspicious influence the fiercest barbarians were united by an equal government and common language. They affirm, that with the improvement of arts, the human species was visibly multiplied. They celebrate the increasing splendour of the cities, the beautiful face of the country, cultivated and adorned like an immense garden; and the long festival of peace, which was enjoyed by so many nations, forgetful of their ancient animosities, and delivered from the apprehension of future danger." [2] Whatever suspicions may be suggested by the air of rhetoric and declamation, which seems to prevail in these passages, the substance of them is perfectly agreeable to historic truth.

It was scarcely possible that the eyes of contemporaries should discover in the public felicity the latent causes of decay and corruption. This long peace, and the uniform government of the Romans, introduced a slow and secret poison into the vitals of the empire. The minds of men were gradually reduced to the same level, the fire of genius was extinguished, and even the military spirit evaporated. The natives of Europe were brave and robust, Spain, Gaul, Britain, and Illyricum supplied the legions with excellent soldiers, and constituted the real strength of the monarchy. Their personal valour remained, but they no longer possessed that public courage which is nourished by the love of independence, the sense of national honour, the presence of danger, and the habit of command. They received laws and

[1] The proportion which was 1 to 10, and 12½, rose to 14 2-5ths, the legal regulation of Constantine. See Arbuthnot's Tables of ancient Coins, c. v.
[2] Among many other passages, see Pliny (Hist. Natur. iii. 5), Aristides (de Urbe Romá), and Tertullian (de Animâ, c. 30).

governors from the will of their sovereign, and trusted for their defence to a mercenary army. The posterity of their boldest leaders was contented with the rank of citizens and subjects. The most aspiring spirits resorted to the court or standard of the emperors; and the deserted provinces, deprived of political strength or union, insensibly sunk into the languid indifference of private life.

The love of letters, almost inseparable from peace and refinement, was fashionable among the subjects of Hadrian and the Antonines, who were themselves men of learning and curiosity. It was diffused over the whole extent of their empire; the most northern tribes of Britons had acquired a taste for rhetoric; Homer as well as Virgil were transcribed and studied on the banks of the Rhine and Danube; and the most liberal rewards sought out the faintest glimmerings of literary merit.[1] The sciences of physic and astronomy were successfully cultivated by the Greeks; the observations of Ptolemy and the writings of Galen are studied by those who have improved their discoveries and corrected their errors; but if we except the inimitable Lucian, this age of indolence passed away without having produced a single writer of original genius, or who excelled in the arts of elegant composition. The authority of Plato and Aristotle, of Zeno and Epicurus, still reigned in the schools; and their systems, transmitted with blind deference from one generation of disciples to another, precluded every generous attempt to exercise the powers, or enlarge the limits, of the human mind. The beauties of the poets and orators, instead of kindling a fire like their own, inspired only cold and servile imitations: or if any ventured to deviate from those models, they deviated at the same time from good sense and propriety. On the revival of

[1] Herodes Atticus gave the sophist Polemo above eight thousand pounds for three declamations. Philostrat. l. i. p. 558 [vita Herodes, cap. 7]. The Antonines founded a school at Athens, in which professors of grammar, rhetoric, politics, and the four great sects of philosophy, were maintained at the public expense for the instruction of youth. The salary of a philosopher was ten thousand drachmæ, between three and four hundred pounds a year. Similar establishments were formed in the other great cities of the empire. Lucian in Eunuch. tom. ii. p. 353 edit. Reitz. Philostrat. l. ii. p. 566. Hist. August. p. 21. Dion Cassius, l. lxxi. p. 1195. Juvenal himself, in a morose satire, which in every line betrays his own disappointment and envy, is obliged, however, to say—

——O Juvenes, circumspicit et agitat vos.
Materiamque sibi Ducis indulgentia quærit.—Satir. vii. 20.

[Vespasian (says Guizot) was the first to assign salaries to professors. He gave to each professor of rhetoric, Greek, and Roman centena sestertia. Hadrian and the Antonines (adds Wenck), though liberal, were less profuse. —O. S.]

letters, the youthful vigour of the imagination, after a long repose, national emulation, a new religion, new languages, and a new world, called forth the genius of Europe. But the provincials of Rome, trained by a uniform artificial foreign education, were engaged in a very unequal competition with those bold ancients, who, by expressing their genuine feelings in their native tongue, had already occupied every place of honour. The name of Poet was almost forgotten; that of Orator was usurped by the sophists. A cloud of critics, of compilers, of commentators, darkened the face of learning, and the decline of genius was soon followed by the corruption of taste.

The sublime Longinus, who in somewhat a later period, and in the court of a Syrian queen, preserved the spirit of ancient Athens, observes and laments this degeneracy of his contemporaries, which debased their sentiments, enervated their courage, and depressed their talents. " In the same manner," says he, " as some children always remain pigmies, whose infant limbs have been too closely confined; thus our tender minds, fettered by the prejudices and habits of a just servitude, are unable to expand themselves, or to attain that well-proportioned greatness which we admire in the ancients; who living under a popular government, wrote with the same freedom as they acted." [1] This diminutive stature of mankind, if we pursue the metaphor, was daily sinking below the old standard, and the Roman world was indeed peopled by a race of pygmies; when the fierce giants of the north broke in, and mended the puny breed. They restored a manly spirit of freedom; and after the revolution of ten centuries, freedom became the happy parent of taste and science.

CHAPTER III

Of the Constitution of the Roman Empire, in the Age of the Antonines

THE obvious definition of a monarchy seems to be that of a state, in which a single person, by whatsoever name he may be distinguished, is entrusted with the execution of the laws, the management of the revenue, and the command of the army. But, unless

---

[1] Longin. de Sublim. c. 43, p. 229, edit. Toll. Here too we may say of Longinus, "his own example strengthens all his laws." Instead of proposing his sentiments with a manly boldness, he insinuates them with the most guarded caution, puts them into the mouth of a friend; and, as far as we can collect from a corrupted text, makes a show of refuting them himself. [The author of the treatise *On the Sublime* is now recognised to have been an otherwise unknown rhetor of the 1st century A.D.]

public liberty is protected by intrepid and vigilant guardians, the authority of so formidable a magistrate will soon degenerate into despotism. The influence of the clergy, in an age of super-stition, might be usefully employed to assert the rights of man-kind; but so intimate is the connection between the throne and the altar, that the banner of the church has very seldom been seen on the side of the people.[1] A martial nobility and stubborn commons, possessed of arms, tenacious of property, and collected into constitutional assemblies, form the only balance capable of preserving a free constitution against enterprises of an aspiring prince.

Every barrier of the Roman constitution had been levelled by the vast ambition of the dictator; every fence had been extir-pated by the cruel hand of the Triumvir. After the victory of Actium, the fate of the Roman world depended on the will of Octavianus, surnamed Cæsar, by his uncle's adoption, and after-wards Augustus, by the flattery of the senate.[2] The conqueror was at the head of forty-four veteran legions,[3] conscious of their own strength, and of the weakness of the constitution, habituated, during twenty years civil war, to every act of blood and violence, and passionately devoted to the house of Cæsar, from whence alone they had received, and expected, the most lavish rewards. The provinces, long oppressed by the ministers of the republic, sighed for the government of a single person, who would be the master, not the accomplice, of those petty tyrants. The people of Rome, viewing, with a secret pleasure, the humiliation of the aristocracy, demanded only bread and public shows; and were supplied with both by the liberal hand of Augustus. The rich and polite Italians, who had almost universally embraced the philosophy of Epicurus, enjoyed the present blessings of ease and tranquillity, and suffered not the pleasing dream to be inter-rupted by the memory of their old tumultuous freedom. With its power, the senate had lost its dignity; many of the most noble families were extinct. The republicans of spirit and ability had perished in the field of battle, or in the proscription. The door of the assembly had been designedly left open, for a mixed multitude of more than a thousand persons, who reflected dis-grace upon their rank, instead of deriving honour from it.[4]

---

[1] [Gibbon's remark here is wholly incorrect.—O. S.]

[2] [His patronymic was Caius Octavius.—O. S.]

[3] Orosius, vi. 18. [Regarding this point Dion says 25 legions. The United Triumvirs' had been 43.—O. S.]

[4] Julius Cæsar introduced soldiers, strangers, and half-barbarians, into the senate (Sueton. in Cæsar, c. 77, 80). The abuse became still more scandalous after his death.

The reformation of the senate was one of the first steps in which Augustus laid aside the tyrant, and professed himself the father of his country. He was elected censor; and, in concert with his faithful Agrippa, he examined the list of the senators, expelled a few members, whose vices or whose obstinacy required a public example, persuaded near two hundred to prevent the shame of an expulsion by a voluntary retreat, raised the qualification of a senator to about ten thousand pounds, created a sufficient number of Patrician families, and accepted for himself the honourable title of Prince of the Senate, which had always been bestowed, by the censors, on the citizen the most eminent for his honours and services.[1] But whilst he thus restored the dignity, he destroyed the independence of the senate. The principles of a free constitution are irrecoverably lost, when the legislative power is nominated by the executive.

Before an assembly thus modelled and prepared, Augustus pronounced a studied oration, which displayed his patriotism, and disguised his ambition. " He lamented, yet excused, his past conduct. Filial piety had required at his hands the revenge of his father's murder; the humanity of his own nature had sometimes given way to the stern laws of necessity, and to a forced connection with two unworthy colleagues: as long as Antony lived, the republic forbade him to abandon her to a degenerate Roman, and a barbarian queen. He was now at liberty to satisfy his duty and his inclination. He solemnly restored the senate and people to all their ancient rights; and wished only to mingle with the crowd of his fellow-citizens, and to share the blessings which he had obtained for his country." [2]

It would require the pen of Tacitus (if Tacitus had assisted at this assembly) to describe the various emotions of the senate;

---

[1] Dion Cassius, l. iii. [c. 42]. p. 693. Suetonius in August. c. 55.
[The title of " Princeps Senatus " (says Dr. W. Smith) was an honorary distinction which neither was connected with any office nor conferred any privileges. Under the Republic the censor usually bestowed this title on the oldest of those who had filled the office of censor (Livy, xxvii. 11); but the censor in office seems sometimes to have received this title from his colleague. As Augustus was appointed Princeps Senatus when he discharged the duties of the censorship in his sixth consulship (B.C. 28: Dion Cassius, l. iii. 1), there is no doubt that he received the title from his colleague Agrippa in accordance with ancient precedent. The name of the Princeps Senatus was the name which stood first in the album senatorum, a list of the senate, which was made public. The title which only declared Augustus the chief of the senators was the one he chose beyond all others. Cf. Tacitus, Annals. b. i. cc. 1-9; Ovid, Fasti, b. ii. 412.—O. S.]
[2] Dion (l. iii. p. 698) gives us a prolix and bombast speech on this great occasion. I have borrowed from Suetonius and Tacitus the general language of Augustus.

those that were suppressed, and those that were affected. It was dangerous to trust the sincerity of Augustus; to seem to distrust it was still more dangerous. The respective advantages of monarchy and a republic have often divided speculative inquirers; the present greatness of the Roman state, the corruption of manners, and the licence of the soldiers, supplied new arguments to the advocates of monarchy, and these general views of government were again warped by the hopes and fears of each individual. Amidst this confusion of sentiments, the answer of the senate was unanimous and decisive. They refused to accept the resignation of Augustus; they conjured him not to desert the republic, which he had saved. After a decent resistance, the crafty tyrant submitted to the orders of the senate; and consented to receive the government of the provinces, and the general command of the Roman armies, under the well-known names of PROCONSUL and IMPERATOR.[1] But he would receive them only for ten years. Even before the expiration of that period, he hoped that the wounds of civil discord would be completely healed, and that the republic, restored to its pristine health and vigour, would no longer require the dangerous interposition of so extraordinary a magistrate. The memory of this comedy, repeated several times during the life of Augustus, was preserved to the last ages of the empire, by the peculiar pomp with which the perpetual monarchs of Rome always solemnised the tenth years of their reign.[2]

Without any violation of the principles of the constitution, the general of the Roman armies might receive and exercise an authority almost despotic over the soldiers, the enemies, and the subjects of the republic. With regard to the soldiers, the jealousy of freedom had, even from the earliest ages of Rome, given way to the hopes of conquest, and a just sense of military discipline. The dictator, or consul, had a right to command the service of the Roman youth; and to punish an obstinate or cowardly disobedience by the most severe and ignominious penalties, by

---

[1] *Imperator* (from which we have derived Emperor) signified under the republic no more than *general*, and was emphatically bestowed by the soldiers, when on the field of battle they proclaimed their victorious leader worthy of that title. When the Roman *emperors* assumed it in that sense, they placed it after their name, and marked how often they had taken it. [Gibbon does not state with sufficient clearness the double use of the word " Imperator " made by the Roman emperors. There was first the ancient use of the title (referred to by Gibbon in the note upon the word). Then there was, second, the new use of the title, which was conferred on the emperor by the senate, and was prefixed to the imperial name (*prænomen imperatoris*. Cf. Suetonius, lib. c. 26).—O. S.]

[2] Dion, l. liii. p. 703, etc.

striking the offender out of the list of citizens, by confiscating his property, and by selling his person into slavery.[1] The most sacred rights of freedom, confirmed by the Porcian and Sempronian laws, were suspended by the military engagement. In his camp the general exercised an absolute power of life and death; his jurisdiction was not confined by any forms of trial or rules of proceeding, and the execution of the sentence was immediate and without appeal.[2] The choice of the enemies of Rome was regularly decided by the legislative authority. The most important resolutions of peace and war were seriously debated in the senate, and solemnly ratified by the people. But when the arms of the legions were carried to a great distance from Italy, the generals assumed the liberty of directing them against whatever people, and in whatever manner, they judged most advantageous for the public service. It was from the success, not from the justice, of their enterprises, that they expected the honours of a triumph. In the use of victory, especially after they were no longer controlled by the commissioners of the senate, they exercised the most unbounded despotism. When Pompey commanded in the east, he rewarded his soldiers and allies, dethroned princes, divided kingdoms, founded colonies, and distributed the treasures of Mithridates. On his return to Rome, he obtained, by a single act of the senate and people, the universal ratification of all his proceedings.[3] Such was the power over the soldiers, and over the enemies of Rome, which was either granted to, or assumed by, the generals of the republic. They were, at the same time, the governors, or rather monarchs, of the conquered provinces, united the civil with the military character, administered justice as well as the finances, and exercised both the executive and legislative power of the state.

From what has been already observed in the first chapter of this work, some notion may be formed of the armies and provinces thus intrusted to the ruling hand of Augustus. But as it was impossible that he could personally command the legions of so

[1] Livy, Epitom. l. xiv. Valer. Maxim. vi. 3.

[2] See in the viiith book of Livy, the conduct of Manlius Torquatus and Papirius Cursor. They violated the laws of nature and humanity, but they asserted those of military discipline; and the people, who abhorred the action, was obliged to respect the principle.

[3] By the lavish but unconstrained suffrages of the people, Pompey had obtained a military command scarcely inferior to that of Augustus. Among the extraordinary acts of power executed by the former, we may remark the foundation of twenty-nine cities, and the distribution of three or four millions sterling to his troops. The ratification of his acts met with some opposition and delays in the senate. See Plutarch, Appian, Dion Cassius, and the first book of the epistles to Atticus.

many distant frontiers, he was indulged by the senate, as Pompey
had already been, in the permission of devolving the execution of
his great office on a sufficient number of lieutenants.   In rank
and authority these officers seemed not inferior to the ancient
proconsuls; but their station was dependent and precarious.
They received and held their commissions at the will of a superior,
to whose *auspicious* influence the merit of their action was legally
attributed.[1] They were the representatives of the emperor.
The emperor alone was the general of the republic, and his jurisdiction, civil as well as military, extended over all the conquests
of Rome.   It was some satisfaction, however, to the senate, that
he always delegated his power to the members of their body.
The Imperial lieutenants were of consular or prætorian dignity;
the legions were commanded by senators, and the præfecture of
Egypt was the only important trust committed to a Roman
knight.

Within six days after Augustus had been compelled to accept
so very liberal a grant, he resolved to gratify the pride of the
senate by an easy sacrifice.   He represented to them, that they
had enlarged his powers, even beyond that degree which might
be required by the melancholy condition of the times.   They had
not permitted him to refuse the laborious command of the armies
and the frontiers; but he must insist on being allowed to restore
the more peaceful and secure provinces, to the mild administration of the civil magistrate.   In the division of the provinces,
Augustus provided for his own power, and for the dignity of the
republic.   The proconsuls of the senate, particularly those of
Asia, Greece, and Africa, enjoyed a more honourable character
than the lieutenants of the emperor, who commanded in Gaul
or Syria.   The former were attended by lictors, the latter by
soldiers.[2]   A law was passed that wherever the emperor was

---

[1] Under the commonwealth, a triumph could only be claimed by the
general, who was authorised to take the Auspices in the name of the people.
By an exact consequence drawn from this principle of policy and religion,
the triumph was reserved to the emperor; and his most successful lieutenants were satisfied with some marks of distinction, which, under the
name of triumphal honours, were invented in their favour.

[2] [With regard to the difference between the various kinds of province, it
may be well to note the following:—1. *Provinces of the Senate.*—These were
divided into two classes, consular and prætorian: Asia and Africa being
the consular provinces, all the rest being prætorian.   The governors of
these provinces were appointed in the ancient fashion by lot, and for a
single year (Sueton. Aug. 47; Dion Cass. l. iii. 13; Tacit. Ann. iii. 58), the
two oldest consulars drawing lots for the consular provinces, and the two
oldest prætorians for the prætorian provinces.   All the governors of senatorial provinces, whether consulars or prætorians, had the title of proconsul.
2. *The Provinces of the Cæsar.*—These were governed by the emperor him-

present, his extraordinary commission should supersede the
ordinary jurisdiction of the governor; a custom was introduced,
that the new conquest belonged to the Imperial portion; and
it was soon discovered that the authority of the *Prince*, the
favourite epithet of Augustus, was the same in every part of the
empire.

In return for this imaginary concession, Augustus obtained an
important privilege, which rendered him master of Rome and
Italy. By a dangerous exception to the ancient maxims, he was
authorised to preserve his military command, supported by a
numerous body of guards, even in time of peace, and in the heart
of the capital. His command, indeed, was confined to those
citizens who were engaged in the service by the military oath;
but such was the propensity of the Romans to servitude, that
the oath was voluntarily taken by the magistrates, the senators,
and the equestrian order, till the homage of flattery was insensibly converted into an annual and solemn protestation of fidelity.

Although Augustus considered a military force as the firmest
foundation, he wisely rejected it, as a very odious instrument
of government. It was more agreeable to his temper, as well
as to his policy, to reign under the venerable names of ancient
magistracy, and artfully to collect, in his own person, all the
scattered rays of civil jurisdiction. With this view, he permitted
the senate to confer upon him, for his life, the powers of the consular [1] and tribunitian offices,[2] which were, in the same manner,
continued to all his successors. The consuls had succeeded to the
kings of Rome, and represented the dignity of the state. They
superintended the ceremonies of religion, levied and commanded
the legions, gave audience to foreign ambassadors, and presided
in the assemblies both of the senate and people. The general

self by means of his Legati, the larger ones being administered by officers
who bore the title *Legati Augusti pro prætore*. Like the proconsuls of the
senatorial provinces these *legati* were divided into two classes according to
their rank as *consulars* or *prætorians*. The most important provinces in
which were several legions were administered by *legati consulares*, while
those in which there was only one legion had *legati prætorii*, but the official
title for both was as above—*Legati Augusti pro prætore*. The legati were
nominated by the emperor and continued in the government of the province
as long as he pleased.—O. S.]

[1] Cicero (de Legibus, iii. 3) gives the consular office the name of *Regia
potestas ;* and Polybius (l. vi. c. 3) observes three powers in the Roman
constitution. The monarchical was represented and exercised by the
consuls.

[2] As the tribunitian power (distinct from the annual office) was first invented for the Dictator Cæsar (Dion, l. xliv. p. 384), we may easily conceive
that it was given as a reward for having so nobly asserted, by arms, the
sacred rights of the tribunes and people. Commentaries, De Bell. Civil. l. i.

control of the finances was intrusted to their care; and though they seldom had leisure to administer justice in person, they were considered as the supreme guardians of law, equity, and the public peace. Such was their ordinary jurisdiction; but whenever the senate empowered the first magistrate to consult the safety of the commonwealth, he was raised by that degree above the laws, and exercised, in the defence of liberty, a temporary despotism.[1] The character of the tribunes was, in every respect, different from that of the consuls. The appearance of the former was modest and humble; but their persons were sacred and inviolable. Their force was suited rather for opposition than for action. They were instituted to defend the oppressed, to pardon offences, to arraign the enemies of the people, and, when they judged it necessary, to stop, by a single word, the whole machine of government. As long as the republic subsisted, the dangerous influence, which either the consul or the tribune might derive from their respective jurisdiction, was diminished by several important restrictions. Their authority expired with the year in which they were elected; the former office was divided between two, the latter among ten persons; and, as both in their private and public interest they were averse to each other, their mutual conflicts contributed, for the most part, to strengthen rather than to destroy the balance of the constitution. But when the consular and tribunitian powers were united, when they were vested for life in a single person, when the general of the army was, at the same time, the minister of the senate, and the representative of the Roman people, it was impossible to resist the exercise, nor was it easy to define the limits, of his Imperial prerogative.[2]

To these accumulated honours, the policy of Augustus soon added the splendid as well as important dignities of supreme pontiff, and of censor.[3] By the former he acquired the management of the religion, and by the latter a legal inspection over the

[1] Augustus exercised nine annual consulships without interruption. He then most artfully refused that magistracy, as well as the dictatorship, absented himself from Rome, and waited till the fatal effects of tumult and faction forced the senate to invest him with a perpetual consulship. Augustus, as well as his successors, affected, however, to conceal so invidious a title.

[2] [The imperial authority in the city rested mainly on the *tribunitia potestas*, which corresponded to the *jus tribunitium* of the republic. The former secured to the emperor the inviolability of his person, the right of intercession against the resolution of the senate and the people, and the right of summoning the senate and the people.—O. S.]

[3] [Though Augustus refused to accept the title of "Censor," he really possessed all the authority and powers of the office, the duties thereof being discharged by him under the title *prefectus morum*.—O. S.]

manners and fortunes, of the Roman people. If so many distinct and independent powers did not exactly unite with each other, the complaisance of the senate was prepared to supply every deficiency by the most ample and extraordinary concessions. The emperors, as the first ministers of the republic, were exempted from the obligation and penalty of many inconvenient laws: they were authorised to convoke the senate, to make several motions in the same day, to recommend candidates for the honours of the state, to enlarge the bounds of the city, to employ the revenue at their discretion, to declare peace and war, to ratify treaties; and by a most comprehensive clause, they were empowered to execute whatsoever they should judge advantageous to the empire, and agreeable to the majesty of things private or public, human or divine.[1]

When all the various powers of executive government were committed to the *Imperial magistrate*, the ordinary magistrates of the commonwealth languished in obscurity, without vigour, and almost without business. The names and forms of the ancient administration were preserved by Augustus with the most anxious care. The usual number of consuls, prætors, and tribunes,[2] were annually invested with their respective ensigns of office, and continued to discharge some of their least important functions. Those honours still attracted the vain ambition of the Romans; and the emperors themselves, though invested for life with the powers of the consulship, frequently aspired to the title of that annual dignity, which they condescended to share with the most illustrious of their fellow-citizens.[3] In the election of these magistrates, the people, during the reign of Augustus, were permitted to expose all the inconveniences of a wild democracy.

[1] See a fragment of a Decree of the Senate, conferring on the emperor Vespasian all the powers granted to his predecessors, Augustus, Tiberius, and Claudius. This curious and important monument is published in Gruter's Inscriptions, No. ccxlii.

[2] Two consuls were created on the Calends of January; but in the course of the year others were substituted in their places, till the annual number seems to have amounted to no less than twelve. The prætors were usually sixteen or eighteen (Lipsius in Excurs. D. ad Tacit. Annal. l. i.). I have not mentioned the Ædiles or Quæstors. Officers of the police or revenue easily adapt themselves to any form of government. In the time of Nero, the tribunes legally possessed the right of *intercession*, though it might be dangerous to exercise it (Tacit. Annal. xvi. 26). In the time of Trajan, it was doubtful whether the tribuneship was an office or a name (Plin. Epist. i. 23).

[3] The tyrants themselves were ambitious of the consulship. The virtuous princes were moderate in the pursuit, and exact in the discharge of it. Trajan revived the ancient oath, and swore before the consul's tribunal that he would observe the laws (Plin. Panegyric. c. 64).

That artful prince, instead of discovering the least symptom of impatience, humbly solicited their suffrages for himself or his friends, and scrupulously practised all the duties of an ordinary candidate.[1] But we may venture to ascribe to his councils, the first measure of the succeeding reign, by which the elections were transferred to the senate.[2] The assemblies of the people were for ever abolished, and the emperors were delivered from a dangerous multitude, who, without restoring liberty, might have disturbed, and perhaps endangered, the established government.

By declaring themselves the protectors of the people, Marius and Cæsar had subverted the constitution of their country. But as soon as the senate had been humbled and disarmed, such an assembly, consisting of five or six hundred persons, was found a much more tractable and useful instrument of dominion. It was on the dignity of the senate, that Augustus and his successors founded their new empire; and they affected, on every occasion, to adopt the language and principles of Patricians. In the administration of their own powers they frequently consulted the great national council, and *seemed* to refer to its decision the most important concerns of peace and war. Rome, Italy, and the internal provinces, were subject to the immediate jurisdiction of the senate. With regard to civil objects, it was the supreme court of appeal; with regard to criminal matters, a tribunal constituted for the trial of all offences that were committed by men in any public station, or that affected the peace and majesty of the Roman people. The exercise of the judicial power became the most frequent and serious occupation of the senate; and the important causes that were pleaded before them afforded a last refuge to the spirit of ancient eloquence. As a council of state, and as a court of justice, the senate possessed very considerable prerogatives; but in its legislative capacity, in which it was supposed virtually to represent the people, the rights of sovereignty were acknowledged to reside in that assembly. Every power was derived from their authority, every law was ratified by their sanction. Their regular meetings were held on three stated days in every month, the Calends, the Nones, and the Ides. The debates were conducted with decent freedom; and the

---

[1] Quoties Magistratuum Comitiis interesset. Tribus cum candidatis suis circuibat: supplicabatque more solemni. Ferebat et ipse suffragium in tribubus, ut unus e populo. Suetonius in August. c. 56.

[2] Tum primum Comitia e campo ad patres translata sunt. Tacit. Annal. i. 15. The word *primum* seems to allude to some faint and unsuccessful efforts, which were made towards restoring them to the people.

emperors themselves, who glorified in the name of senators, sat, voted, and divided with their equals.[1]

To resume, in a few words, the system of the Imperial government, as it was instituted by Augustus, and maintained by those princes who understood their own interest and that of the people, it may be defined an absolute monarchy disguised by the forms of a commonwealth. The masters of the Roman world surrounded their throne with darkness, concealed their irresistible strength, and humbly professed themselves the accountable ministers of the senate, whose supreme decrees they dictated and obeyed.[2]

The face of the court corresponded with the forms of the administration. The emperors, if we except those tyrants whose capricious folly violated every law of nature and decency, disdained that pomp and ceremony which might offend their countrymen, but could add nothing to their real power. In all the offices of life they affected to confound themselves with their subjects, and maintained with them an equal intercourse of visits and entertainments. Their habit, their palace, their table, were suited only to the rank of an opulent senator. Their family, however numerous or splendid, was composed entirely of their domestic slaves and freedmen.[3] Augustus or Trajan would have blushed at employing the meanest of the Romans in those menial offices, which, in the household and bed-chamber of a limited monarch, are so eagerly solicited by the proudest nobles of Britain.

The deification of the emperors [4] is the only instance in which

---

[1] [Dr. W. Smith points out that Gibbon had omitted to notice an important institution of Augustus, which eventually superseded the senate in many of its functions. This was the *Consilium* or kind of Privy Council, which consisted of twenty members selected by the emperor from the senate, and in which all important matters were discussed before they were submitted to the senate. In course of time the power of the Consilium was augmented.—O. S.]

[2] Dion Cassius (l. liii. p. 703-714) has given a very loose and partial sketch of the Imperial system. To illustrate and often to correct him, I have meditated Tacitus, examined Suetonius, and consulted the following moderns: the Abbé de la Bleterie, in the Memoires de l'Academie des Inscriptions, tom. xix. xxi. xxiv. xxv. xxvii. Beaufort, Republique Romaine, tom. i. p. 255-275. The Dissertations of Noodt and Gronovius, *de lege Regia*, printed at Leyden, in the year 1731. Gravina de Imperio Romano, p. 479-544 of his Opuscula. Maffei, Verona Illustrata, t. i. p. 245, etc.

[3] A weak prince will always be governed by his domestics. The power of slaves aggravated the shame of the Romans; and the senate paid court to a Pallas or a Narcissus. There is a chance that a modern favourite may be a gentleman.

[4] Treatise of Vandale *de Consecratione Principum*. It would be easier for me to copy than it has been to verify the quotations of that learned Dutchman.

they departed from their accustomed prudence and modesty. The Asiastic Greeks were the first inventors, the successors of Alexander the first objects, of this servile and impious mode of adulation. It was easily transferred from the kings to the governors of Asia; and the Roman magistrates very frequently were adored as provincial deities, with the pomp of altars and temples, of festivals and sacrifices.[1] It was natural that the emperors should not refuse what the proconsuls had accepted; and the divine honours which both the one and the other received from the provinces, attested rather the despotism than the servitude of Rome. But the conquerors soon imitated the vanquished nations in the arts of flattery; and the imperious spirit of the first Cæsar too easily consented to assume, during his lifetime, a place among the tutelar deities of Rome. The milder temper of his successor declined so dangerous an ambition, which was never afterwards revived, except by the madness of Caligula and Domitian. Augustus permitted indeed some of the provincial cities to erect temples to his honour, on condition that they should associate the worship of Rome with that of the sovereign; he tolerated private superstition, of which he might be the object;[2] but he contented himself with being revered by the senate and people in his human character, and wisely left to his successor the care of his public deification. A regular custom was introduced, that on the decease of every emperor who had neither lived nor died like a tyrant, the senate by a solemn decree should place him in the number of the gods: and the ceremonies of his Apotheosis were blended with those of his funeral.[3] This legal, and, as it should seem, injudicious profanation, so abhorrent to our stricter principles, was received with a faint murmur,[4] by the easy nature of polytheism; but it was received as an institution, not of religion, but of policy. We should disgrace the virtues of the Antonines, by comparing them with the vices of Hercules or Jupiter. Even the character of Cæsar or Augustus were far superior to those of the popular deities. But it was the misfortune of the former to live in an enlightened age, and their actions were too faithfully recorded

---

[1] Dissertation of the Abbé Mongault in the first volume of the Academy of Inscriptions.

[2] Jurandasque tuum per nomen ponimus aras, says Horace to the emperor himself, and Horace was well acquainted with the court of Augustus.

[3] See Seneca's Satire 'Αποκολοκύντωσις.—[O.S.]

[4] See Cicero in Philippic. i. 6. Julian in Cæsaribus. Inque Deûm templis jurabit Roma per umbras, is the indignant expression of Lucan, but it is a patriotic, rather than a devout indignation.

to admit of such a mixture of fable and mystery, as the devotion of the vulgar requires. As soon as their divinity was established by law, it sunk into oblivion, without contributing either to their own fame, or to the dignity of succeeding princes.

In the consideration of the Imperial government, we have frequently mentioned the artful founder, under his well-known title of Augustus, which was not however conferred upon him till the edifice was almost completed. The obscure name of Octavianus he derived from a mean family in the little town of Aricia. It was stained with the blood of the proscription; and he was desirous, had it been possible, to erase all memory of his former life. The illustrious surname of Cæsar he had assumed as the adopted son of the dictator; but he had too much good sense, either to hope to be confounded, or to wish to be compared, with that extraordinary man. It was proposed in the senate, to dignify their minister with a new appellation: and after a very serious discussion, that of Augustus was chosen, among several others, as being the most expressive of the character of peace and sanctity, which he uniformly affected.[1] *Augustus* was therefore a personal, *Cæsar* a family distinction. The former should naturally have expired with the prince on whom it was bestowed; and however the latter was diffused by adoption and female alliance, Nero was the last prince who could allege any hereditary claim to the honours of the Julian line. But, at the time of his death, the practice of a century had inseparably connected those appellations with the Imperial dignity, and they have been preserved by a long succession of emperors, Romans, Greeks, Franks, and Germans, from the fall of the republic to the present time. A distinction was, however, soon introduced. The sacred title of Augustus was always reserved for the monarch, whilst the name of Cæsar was more freely communicated to his relations; and, from the reign of Hadrian, at least, was appropriated to the second person in the state, who was considered as the presumptive heir of the empire.[2]

The tender respect of Augustus for a free constitution which he had destroyed, can only be explained by an attentive consideration of the character of that subtle tyrant. A cool head,

---

[1] Dion Cassius, l. liii. p. 710, with the curious Annotations of Reimar.

[2] [Wenck says that the princes who by their birth or their adoption belonged to the family of the Cæsars, took the name of Cæsar. After the death of Nero, this name was applied to the imperial dignity itself, and afterwards the appointed successor. The time at which it was employed in the latter sense cannot be fixed with certainty. It is probable that Ælius Verus was the first who was called Cæsar, when adopted by Hadrian. —O. S.]

an unfeeling heart, and a cowardly disposition, prompted him, at the age of nineteen, to assume the mask of hypocrisy, which he never afterwards laid aside. With the same hand, and probably with the same temper, he signed the proscription of Cicero, and the pardon of Cinna. His virtues, and even his vices, were artificial; and according to the various dictates of his interest, he was at first the enemy, and at last the father, of the Roman world.[1] When he framed the artful system of the Imperial authority, his moderation was inspired by his fears. He wished to deceive the people by an image of civil liberty, and the armies by an image of civil government.

I. The death of Cæsar was ever before his eyes. He had lavished wealth and honours on his adherents; but the most favoured friends of his uncle were in the number of the conspirators. The fidelity of the legions might defend his authority against open rebellion; but their vigilance could not secure his person from the dagger of a determined republican; and the Romans, who revered the memory of Brutus,[2] would applaud the imitation of his virtue. Cæsar had provoked his fate, as much by the ostentation of his power as by his power itself. The consul or the tribune might have reigned in peace. The title of king had armed the Romans against his life. Augustus was sensible that mankind is governed by names; nor was he deceived in his expectation, that the senate and people would submit to slavery, provided they were respectfully assured that they still enjoyed their ancient freedom. A feeble senate and enervated people cheerfully acquiesced in the pleasing illusion, as long as it was supported by the virtue, or even by the prudence, of the successors of Augustus. It was a motive of self-preservation, not a principle of liberty, that animated the conspirators against Caligula, Nero, and Domitian. They attacked the person of the tyrant, without aiming their blow at the authority of the emperor.

There appears, indeed, *one* memorable occasion, in which the senate, after seventy years of patience, made an ineffectual

---

[1] As Octavianus advanced to the banquet of the Cæsars, his colour changed like that of the Camelion; pale at first, then red, afterwards black, he at last assumed the mild livery of Venus and the graces (Cæsars, p. 309). This image employed by Julian, in his ingenious fiction, is just and elegant; but when he considers this change of character as real, and ascribes it to the power of philosophy, he does too much honour to philosophy, and to Octavianus.

[2] Two centuries after the establishment of monarchy, the emperor Marcus Antoninus recommends the character of Brutus as a perfect model of Roman virtue.

attempt to reassume its long-forgotten rights. When the throne was vacant by the murder of Caligula, the consuls convoked that assembly in the Capitol, condemned the memory of the Cæsars, gave the watchword *liberty* to the few cohorts who faintly adhered to their standard, and during eight and forty hours acted as the independent chiefs of a free commonwealth. But while they deliberated, the Prætorian Guards had resolved. The stupid Claudius, brother of Germanicus, was already in their camp, invested with the Imperial purple, and prepared to support his election by arms. The dream of liberty was at an end; and the senate awoke to all the horrors of inevitable servitude. Deserted by the people, and threatened by a military force, that feeble assembly was compelled to ratify the choice of the Prætorians, and to embrace the benefit of an amnesty, which Claudius had the prudence to offer, and the generosity to observe.[1]

II. The insolence of the armies inspired Augustus with fears of a still more alarming nature. The despair of the citizens could only attempt what the power of the soldiers was, at any time, able to execute. How precarious was his own authority over men whom he had taught to violate every social duty! He had heard their seditious clamours; he dreaded their calmer moments of reflection. One revolution had been purchased by immense rewards; but a second revolution might double those rewards. The troops professed the fondest attachment to the house of Cæsar; but the attachments of the multitude are capricious and inconstant. Augustus summoned to his aid whatever remained in those fierce minds of Roman prejudices; enforced the rigour of discipline by the sanction of law; and interposing the majesty of the senate between the emperor and the army, boldly claimed their allegiance, as the first magistrate of the republic.[2]

During a long period of two hundred and twenty years, from the establishment of this artful system to the death of Commodus, the dangers inherent to a military government were, in a great measure, suspended. The soldiers were seldom roused to that fatal sense of their own strength, and of the weakness of the civil authority, which was, before and afterwards, productive of such dreadful calamities. Caligula and Domitian were assas-

---

[1] It is much to be regretted that we have lost the part of Tacitus which treated of that transaction. We are forced to content ourselves with the popular rumours of Josephus, and the imperfect hints of Dion and Suetonius.

[2] Augustus restored the ancient severity of discipline. After the civil wars, he dropped the endearing name of Fellow-Soldiers, and called them only Soldiers (Sueton. in August. c. 25). See the use Tiberius made of the senate in the mutiny of the Pannonian legions (Tacit. Annals, i. [25]).

sinated in their palace by their own domestics;[1] the convulsions which agitated Rome on the death of the former, were confined to the walls of the city. But Nero involved the whole empire in his ruin. In the space of eighteen months, four princes perished by the sword; and the Roman world was shaken by the fury of the contending armies. Excepting only this short, though violent, eruption of military licence, the two centuries from Augustus to Commodus passed away unstained with civil blood, and undisturbed by revolutions. The emperor was elected by *the authority of the senate*, and *the consent of the soldiers*.[2] The legions respected their oath of fidelity; and it requires a minute inspection of the Roman annals to discover three inconsiderable rebellions, which were all suppressed in a few months, and without even the hazard of a battle.[3]

In elective monarchies, the vacancy of the throne is a moment big with danger and mischief. The Roman emperors, desirous to spare the legions that interval of suspense, and the temptation of an irregular choice, invested their designed successor with so large a share of present power, as should enable him, after their decease, to assume the remainder, without suffering the empire to perceive the change of masters. Thus Augustus, after all his fairer prospects had been snatched from him by untimely deaths rested his last hopes on Tiberius, obtained for his adopted son the censorial and tribunitian powers, and dictated a law by which the future prince was invested with an authority equal to his own, over the provinces and the armies.[4] Thus Vespasian subdued the generous mind of his eldest son. Titus was adored by the eastern legions, which, under his command, had recently achieved the conquest of Judæa. His power was dreaded, and, as his virtues were clouded by the intemperance of youth, his designs were suspected. Instead of listening to such unworthy suspicions, the prudent monarch associated Titus to the full powers of the Imperial dignity; and the grateful son ever

---

[1] [Caligula perished by a conspiracy formed by officers of the Prætorian Guard.—O. S.]

[2] These words seem to have been the constitutional language. See Tacit. Annal. xiii. 4.

[3] The first was Camillus Scribonianus, who took up arms in Dalmatia against Claudius, and was deserted by his own troops in five days. The second, L. Antonius, in Germany, who rebelled against Domitian; and the third, Avidius Cassius, in the reign of M. Antoninus. The two last reigned but a few months, and were cut off by their own adherents. We may observe, that both Camillus and Cassius coloured their ambition with the design of restoring the republic, a task, said Cassius, peculiarly reserved for his name and family.

[4] Velleius Paterculus, l. ii. c. 121. Sueton. in Tiber. c. 20.

approved himself the humble and faithful minister of so indulgent a father.[1]

The good sense of Vespasian engaged him indeed to embrace
every measure that might confirm his recent and precarious
elevation. The military oath, and the fidelity of the troops, had
been consecrated by the habits of an hundred years, to the name
and family of the Cæsars; and although that family had been
continued only by the fictitious rite of adoption, the Romans still
revered, in the person of Nero, the grandson of Germanicus, and
the lineal successor of Augustus. It was not without reluctance
and remorse that the Prætorian Guards had been persuaded to
abandon the cause of the tyrant.[2] The rapid downfall of Galba,
Otho, and Vitellius, taught the armies to consider the emperors
as the creatures of *their* will, and the instruments of *their* licence.
The birth of Vespasian was mean; his grandfather had been a
private soldier, his father a petty officer of the revenue;[3] his
own merit had raised him, in an advanced age, to the empire;
but his merit was rather useful, than shining, and his virtues
were disgraced by a strict and even sordid parsimony. Such a
prince consulted his true interest by the association of a son,
whose more splendid and amiable character might turn the
public attention from the obscure origin to the future glories of
the Flavian house. Under the mild administration of Titus,
the Roman world enjoyed a transient felicity, and his beloved
memory served to protect, above fifteen years, the vices of his
brother Domitian.

Nerva had scarcely accepted the purple from the assassins of
Domitian before he discovered that his feeble age was unable to
stem the torrent of public disorders, which had multiplied under
the long tyranny of his predecessor. His mild disposition was
respected by the good; but the degenerate Romans required a
more vigorous character, whose justice should strike terror into
the guilty. Though he had several relations, he fixed his choice
on a stranger. He adopted Trajan, then about forty years of
age, and who commanded a powerful army in the Lower
Germany; and immediately, by a decree of the senate, declared
him his colleague and successor in the empire.[4] It is sincerely to

---

[1] Sueton. in Tit. c. 6. Plin. in Præfat. Hist. Natur.

[2] This idea is frequently and strongly inculcated by Tacitus. Hist. i. 5,
16; ii. 76.

[3] The emperor Vespasian, with his usual good sense, laughed at the
genealogists, who deduced his family from Flavius, the founder of Reate
(his native country), and one of the companions of Hercules. Suet. in
Vespasian. c. 12.

[4] Dion. l. lxviii. p. 1121. Plin. Secund. in Panegyric.

be lamented, that whilst we are fatigued with the disgustful relation of Nero's crimes and follies, we are reduced to collect the actions of Trajan from the glimmerings of an abridgment, or the doubtful light of a panegyric. There remains, however, one panegyric far removed beyond the suspicion of flattery. Above two hundred and fifty years after the death of Trajan, the senate, in pouring out the customary acclamations on the accession of a new emperor, wished that he might surpass the felicity of Augustus, and the virtue of Trajan.[1]

We may readily believe, that the father of his country hesitated whether he ought to intrust the various and doubtful character of his kinsman Hadrian with sovereign power. In his last moments, the arts of the empress Plotina either fixed the irresolution of Trajan, or boldly supposed a fictitious adoption;[2] the truth of which could not be safely disputed, and Hadrian was peaceably acknowledged as his lawful successor. Under his reign, as has been already mentioned, the empire flourished in peace and prosperity. He encouraged the arts, reformed the laws, asserted military discipline, and visited all his provinces in person. His vast and active genius was equally suited to the most enlarged views, and the minute details of civil policy. But the ruling passions of his soul were curiosity and vanity. As they prevailed, and as they were attracted by different objects, Hadrian was, by turns, an excellent prince, a ridiculous sophist, and a jealous tyrant. The general tenor of his conduct deserved praise for its equity and moderation. Yet in the first days of his reign, he put to death four consular senators, his personal enemies, and men who had been judged worthy of empire; and the tediousness of a painful illness rendered him, at last, peevish and cruel. The senate doubted whether they should pronounce him a god or a tyrant; and the honours decreed to his memory were granted to the prayers of the pious Antoninus.[3]

The caprice of Hadrian influenced his choice of a successor. After revolving in his mind several men of distinguished merit, whom he esteemed and hated, he adopted Ælius Verus, a gay and voluptuous nobleman, recommended by uncommon beauty

---

[1] Felicior Augusto, MELIOR TRAJANO. Eutrop. viii. 5.

[2] Dion (l. lxix. p. 1249) affirms the whole to have been a fiction, on the authority of his father, who being governor of the province where Trajan died, had very good opportunities of sifting this mysterious transaction. Yet Dodwell (Prælect. Camden. xvii.) has maintained that Hadrian was called to the certain hope of the empire during the lifetime of Trajan.

[3] Dion (lxx. p. 1171). Aurel. Victor.

to the lover of Antinous.[1] But while Hadrian was delighting
himself with his own applause, and the acclamations of the
soldiers, whose consent had been secured by an immense donative, the new Cæsar [2] was ravished from his embraces by an
untimely death. He left only one son. Hadrian commended
the boy to the gratitude of the Antonines. He was adopted by
Pius; and, on the accession of Marcus, was invested with an
equal share of sovereign power. Among the many vices of this
younger Verus he possessed one virtue; a dutiful reverence for
his wiser colleague, to whom he willingly abandoned the ruder
cares of empire. The philosophic emperor dissembled his follies,
lamented his early death, and cast a decent veil over his
memory.

As soon as Hadrian's passion was either gratified or disappointed, he resolved to deserve the thanks of posterity, by
placing the most exalted merit on the Roman throne. His
discerning eye easily discovered a senator about fifty years of age,
blameless in all the offices of life, and a youth of about seventeen,
whose riper years opened the fair prospect of every virtue: the
elder of these was declared the son and successor of Hadrian, on
condition, however, that he himself should immediately adopt
the younger. The two Antonines (for it is of them that we are
now speaking) governed the Roman world forty-two years, with
the same invariable spirit of wisdom and virtue. Although Pius
had two sons,[3] he preferred the welfare of Rome to the interest of
his family, gave his daughter Faustina in marriage to young
Marcus, obtained from the senate the tribunitian and proconsular powers, and with a noble disdain, or rather ignorance of
jealousy, associated him to all the labours of government.
Marcus, on the other hand, revered the character of his benefactor, loved him as a parent, obeyed him as his sovereign,[4] and,
after he was no more, regulated his own administration by the
example and maxims of his predecessor. Their united reigns
are possibly the only period of history in which the happiness of
a great people was the sole object of government.

[1] The deification of Antinous, his medals, statues, temples, city, oracles,
and constellation, are well known, and still dishonour the memory of
Hadrian. Yet we may remark, that of the first fifteen emperors, Claudius
was the only one whose taste in love was entirely correct. For the honours
of Antinous, see Spanheim, Commentaire sur les Césars de Julien, p. 80.

[2] Hist. August. p. 13. Aurelius Victor in Epitom.

[3] Without the help of medals and inscriptions we should be ignorant of
this fact, so honourable to the memory of Pius.

[4] During the twenty-three years of Pius's reign, Marcus was only two
nights absent from the palace, and even those were at different times.
Hist. August. p. 25.

Titus Antoninus Pius has been justly denominated a second Numa. The same love of religion, justice, and peace, was the distinguishing characteristic of both princes. But the situation of the former opened a much larger field for the exercise of those virtues. Numa could only prevent a few neighbouring villages from plundering each other's harvests. Antoninus diffused order and tranquillity over the greatest part of the earth. His reign is marked by the rare advantage of furnishing very few materials for history; which is, indeed, little more than the register of the crimes, follies, and misfortunes of mankind. In private life, he was an amiable as well as a good man. The native simplicity of his virtue was a stranger to vanity or affectation. He enjoyed with moderation the conveniencies of his fortune, and the innocent pleasures of society:[1] and the benevolence of his soul displayed itself in a cheerful serenity of temper.

The virtue of Marcus Aurelius Antoninus was of a severer and more laborious kind.[2] It was the well-earned harvest of many a learned conference, of many a patient lecture, and many a midnight lucubration. At the age of twelve years he embraced the rigid system of the Stoics, which taught him to submit his body to his mind, his passions to his reason; to consider virtue as the only good, vice as the only evil, all things external as things indifferent.[3] His meditations, composed in the tumult of a camp, are still extant; and he even condescended to give lessons of philosophy in a more public manner than was perhaps consistent with the modesty of a sage, or the dignity of an emperor.[4] But his life was the noblest commentary on the precepts of Zeno. He was severe to himself, indulgent to the imperfections of others, just and beneficent to all mankind. He regretted that Avidius Cassius, who excited a rebellion in Syria,

[1] He was fond of the theatre, and not insensible to the charms of the fair sex. Marcus Antoninus, i. 16. Hist. August. p. 20, 21. Julian in Cæsar.

[2] The enemies of Marcus charged him with hypocrisy, and with a want of that simplicity which distinguished Pius and even Verus (Hist. August. 6, 34). This suspicion, unjust as it was, may serve to account for the superior applause bestowed upon personal qualifications, in preference to the social virtues. Even Marcus Antoninus has been called a hypocrite; but the wildest scepticism never insinuated that Cæsar might possibly be a coward, or Tully a fool. Wit and valour are qualifications more easily ascertained, than humanity or the love of justice.

[3] Tacitus has characterised, in a few words, the principles of the portico: Doctores sapientiæ secutus est, qui sola bona quæ honesta, mala tantum quæ turpia; potentiam, nobilitatem, cæteraque extra animum, neque bonis neque malis adnumerant. Tacit. Hist. iv. 5.

[4] Before he went on the second expedition against the Germans, he read lectures of philosophy to the Roman people, during three days. He had already done the same in the cities of Greece and Asia. Hist. August. in Cassio, c. 3.

had disappointed him, by a voluntary death, of the pleasure of converting an enemy into a friend; and he justified the sincerity of that sentiment, by moderating the zeal of the senate against the adherents of the traitor.[1] War he detested, as the disgrace and calamity of human nature; but when the necessity of a just defence called upon him to take up arms, he readily exposed his person to eight winter campaigns on the frozen banks of the Danube, the severity of which was at last fatal to the weakness of his constitution. His memory was revered by a grateful posterity, and above a century after his death, many persons preserved the image of Marcus Antoninus, among those of their household gods.[2]

If a man were called to fix the period in the history of the world, during which the condition of the human race was most happy and prosperous, he would, without hesitation, name that which elapsed from the death of Domitian to the accession of Commodus. The vast extent of the Roman empire was governed by absolute power, under the guidance of virtue and wisdom. The armies were restrained by the firm but gentle hand of four successive emperors, whose characters and authority commanded involuntary respect. The forms of the civil administration were carefully preserved by Nerva, Trajan, Hadrian, and the Antonines, who delighted in the image of liberty, and were pleased with considering themselves as the accountable ministers of the laws. Such princes deserved the honour of restoring the republic had the Romans of their days been capable of enjoying a rational freedom.

The labours of these monarchs were overpaid by the immense reward that inseparably waited on their success; by the honest pride of virtue, and by the exquisite delight of beholding the general happiness of which they were the authors. A just, but melancholy reflection embittered, however, the noblest of human enjoyments. They must often have recollected the instability of a happiness which depended on the character of a single man. The fatal moment was perhaps approaching, when some licentious youth, or some jealous tyrant, would abuse, to the destruction, that absolute power which they had exerted for the benefit of their people. The ideal restraints of the senate and the laws might serve to display the virtues, but could never correct the vices, of the emperor. The military force was a blind and irresistible instrument of oppression; and the corruption of Roman

---

[1] Dion, l. lxxi. [c. 23] p. 1190. Hist. August. in Avid. Cassio [c. 8].
[2] Hist. August. in Marc. Antonin. c. 18.

manners would always supply flatterers eager to applaud, and
ministers prepared to serve the fear or the avarice, the lust or the
cruelty, of their masters.

These gloomy apprehensions had been already justified by the
experience of the Romans. The annals of the emperors exhibit
a strong and various picture of human nature, which we should
vainly seek among the mixed and doubtful characters of modern
history. In the conduct of those monarchs we may trace the
utmost lines of vice and virtue; the most exalted perfection, and
the meanest degeneracy of our own species. The golden age of
.Trajan and the Antonines had been preceded by an age of iron.
It is almost superfluous to enumerate the unworthy successors
of Augustus. Their unparalleled vices, and the splendid theatre
on which they were acted, have saved them from oblivion.
The dark unrelenting Tiberius, the furious Caligula, the feeble
Claudius, the profligate and cruel Nero, the beastly Vitellius,[1]
and the timid inhuman Domitian, are condemned to everlasting
infamy. During fourscore years (excepting only the short and
doubtful respite of Vespasian's reign [2]) Rome groaned beneath
an unremitting tyranny, which exterminated the ancient families
of the republic, and was fatal to almost every virtue, and every
talent, that arose in that unhappy period.

Under the reign of these monsters the slavery of the Romans
was accompanied with two peculiar circumstances, the one
occasioned by their former liberty, the other by their extensive
conquests, which rendered their condition more completely
wretched than that of the victims of tyranny in any other age
or country. From these causes were derived, 1. The exquisite
sensibility of the sufferers; and, 2, the impossibility of escaping
from the hand of the oppressor.

I. When Persia was governed by the descendants of Sefi, a
race of princes whose wanton cruelty often stained their divan,
their table, and their bed, with the blood of their favourites,
there is a saying recorded of a young nobleman, that he never
departed from the sultan's presence without satisfying himself

---

[1] Vitellius consumed in mere eating, at least six millions of our money in
about seven months. It is not easy to express his vices with dignity, or
even decency. Tacitus fairly calls him a hog; but it is by substituting to a
coarse word a very fine image. " At Vitellius, umbraculis hortorum abditus,
ut *ignava animalia*, quibus si cibum suggeras jacent torpentque, præterita,
instantia, futura, pari oblivione dimiserat. Atque illum nemore Arcino
desidem et marcentem, etc." Tacit. Hist. iii. 36, ii. 95. Sueton. in Vitell.
c. 13. Dion Cassius, l. lxv. p. 1062.
[2] The execution of Helvidius Priscus, and of the virtuous Eponina, disgraced the reign of Vespasian.

whether his head was still on his shoulders. The experience
of every day might almost justify the scepticism of Rustan.[1]
Yet the fatal sword, suspended above him by a single thread,
seems not to have disturbed the slumbers, or interrupted the
tranquillity, of the Persian. The monarch's frown, he well knew,
could level him with the dust; but the stroke of lightning or
apoplexy might be equally fatal; and it was the part of a wise
man to forget the inevitable calamities of human life in the enjoyment of the fleeting hour. He was dignified with the appellation
of the king's slave; had, perhaps, been purchased from obscure
parents in a country which he had never known; and was
trained up from his infancy in the severe discipline of the seraglio.[2]
His name, his wealth, his honours, were the gift of a master,
who might, without injustice, resume what he had bestowed.
Rustan's knowledge, if he possessed any, could only serve to
confirm his habits by prejudices. His language afforded not
words for any form of government, except absolute monarchy.
The history of the East informed him, that such had ever been
the condition of mankind.[3] The Koran, and the interpreters of
that divine book, inculcated to him, that the sultan was the
descendant of the prophet, and the vice-regent of heaven; that
patience was the first virtue of a Mussulman, and unlimited
obedience the great duty of a subject.

The minds of the Romans were very differently prepared for
slavery. Oppressed beneath the weight of their own corruption
and of military violence, they for a long while preserved the
sentiments, or at least the ideas, of their free-born ancestors.
The education of Helvidius and Thrasea, of Tacitus and Pliny,
was the same as that of Cato and Cicero. From Grecian philosophy they had imbibed the justest and most liberal notions of
the dignity of human nature, and the origin of civil society. The
history of their own country had taught them to revere a free,
a virtuous, and a victorious commonwealth; to abhor the successful crimes of Cæsar and Augustus; and inwardly to despise
those tyrants whom they adored with the most abject flattery.
As magistrates and senators, they were admitted into the great
council which had once dictated laws to the earth, whose name

[1] Voyage de Chardin en Perse, vol. iii. p. 293.

[2] The practice of raising slaves to the great offices of state is still more
common among the Turks than among the Persians. The miserable
countries of Georgia and Circassia supply rulers to the greatest part of the
East.

[3] Chardin says, that European travellers have diffused among the Persians some ideas of the freedom and mildness of our governments. They
have done them a very ill office.

still gave a sanction to the acts of the monarch, and whose authority was so often prostituted to the vilest purposes of tyranny. Tiberius, and those emperors who adopted this maxim attempted to disguise their murders by the formalities of justice, and perhaps enjoyed a secret pleasure in rendering the senate their accomplice as well as their victim. By this assembly the last of the Romans were condemned for imaginary crimes and real virtues. Their infamous accusers assumed the language of independent patriots, who arraigned a dangerous citizen before the tribunal of his country; and the public service was rewarded by riches and honours.[1] The servile judges professed to assert the majesty of the commonwealth, violated in the person of its first magistrate;[2] whose clemency they most applauded when they trembled the most at his inexorable and impending cruelty.[3] The tyrant beheld their baseness with just contempt, and encountered their secret sentiments of detestation with sincere and avowed hatred for the whole body of the senate.

II. The division of Europe into a number of independent states, connected, however, with each other, by the general resemblance of religion, language, and manners, is productive of the most beneficial consequences to the liberty of mankind. A modern tyrant, who should find no resistance either in his own breast, or in his people, would soon experience a gentle restraint from the example of his equals, the dread of present censure, the advice of his allies, and the apprehension of his enemies. The object of his displeasure, escaping from the narrow limits of his dominions, would easily obtain, in a happier climate, a secure refuge, a new fortune adequate to his merit, the freedom of complaint, and perhaps the means of revenge. But the empire of the Romans filled the world, and when that empire fell into the hands of a single person, the world became a safe and dreary prison for his enemies. The slave of Imperial despotism, whether he was con-

---

[1] They alleged the example of Scipio and Cato (Tacit. Annal. iii. 66). Marcellus Epirus and Crispus Vibius had acquired two millions and a half under Nero. Their wealth, which aggravated their crimes, protected them under Vespasian. Tacit. Hist. iv. 43. Dialog. de Orator. c. 8. For one accusation, Regulus, the just object of Pliny's satire, received from the senate the consular ornaments, and a present of sixty thousand pounds.

[2] The crime of *majesty* was formerly a treasonable offence against the Roman people. As tribunes of the people, Augustus and Tiberius applied it to their own persons, and extended it to an infinite latitude.

[3] After the virtuous and unfortunate widow of Germanicus had been put to death, Tiberius received the thanks of the senate for his clemency. She had not been publicly strangled; nor was the body drawn with a hook to the Gemoniæ, where those of common malefactors were exposed. Tacit. Annal. vi. 25. Sueton. in Tiberio, c. 53.

demned to drag his gilded chain in Rome and the senate, or to
wear out a life of exile on the barren rock of Seriphus, or the
frozen banks of the Danube, expected his fate in silent despair.[1]
To resist was fatal, and it was impossible to fly. On every side
he was encompassed with a vast extent of sea and land, which
he could never hope to traverse without being discovered, seized,
and restored to his irritated master. Beyond the frontiers, his
anxious view could discover nothing, except the ocean, inhospitable deserts, hostile tribes of barbarians, of fierce manners and
unknown language, or dependent kings, who would gladly purchase the emperor's protection by the sacrifice of an obnoxious
fugitive.[2] "Wherever you are," said Cicero to the exiled Marcellus, "remember that you are equally within the power of the
conqueror."[3]

CHAPTER IV

The Cruelty, Follies, and Murder of Commodus—Election of Pertinax
—His Attempts to reform the State—His Assassination by the Prætorian Guards

THE mildness of Marcus, which the rigid discipline of the Stoics
was unable to eradicate, formed, at the same time, the most
amiable, and the only defective, part of his character. His excellent understanding was often deceived by the unsuspecting
goodness of his heart. Artful men, who study the passions of
princes, and conceal their own, approached his person in the
disguise of philosophic sanctity, and acquired riches and honours
by affecting to despise them.[4] His excessive indulgence to his
brother,[5] his wife, and his son, exceeded the bounds of private
virtue, and became a public injury, by the example and consequences of their vices.

[1] Seriphus was a small rocky island in the Ægean Sea, the inhabitants
of which were despised for their ignorance and obscurity. The place of
Ovid's exile is well known, by his just, but unmanly lamentations. It
should seem, that he only received an order to leave Rome in so many days,
and to transport himself to Tomi. Guards and gaolers were unnecessary.
[2] Under Tiberius, a Roman knight attempted to fly to the Parthians
He was stopt in the Straits of Sicily; but so little danger did there appear
in the example, that the most jealous of tyrants disdained to punish it.
Tacit. Annal. vi. 14.
[3] Cicero ad Familiares, iv. 7.
[4] See the complaints of Avidius Cassius, Hist. August. p. 45. These are,
it is true, the complaints of faction; but even faction exaggerates, rather
than invents.
[5] [His brother—his brother by adoption, L. Verus.—O. S.]

Faustina, the daughter of Pius and the wife of Marcus, has been
as much celebrated for her gallantries as for her beauty. The
grave simplicity of the philosopher was ill calculated to engage
her wanton levity, or to fix that unbounded passion for variety,
which often discovered personal merit in the meanest of mankind. The Cupid of the ancients was, in general, a very sensual
deity; and the amours of an empress, as they exact on her
side the plainest advances, are seldom susceptible of much sentimental delicacy. Marcus was the only man in the empire who
seemed ignorant or insensible of the irregularities of Faustina;
which, according to the prejudices of every age, reflected some
disgrace on the injured husband. He promoted several of her
lovers to posts of honour and profit,[1] and during a connection of
thirty years, invariably gave her proofs of the most tender confidence, and of a respect which ended not with her life. In his
Meditations, he thanks the gods, who had bestowed on him a
wife, so faithful, so gentle, and of such a wonderful simplicity
of manners. The obsequious senate, at his earnest request,
declared her a goddess. She was represented in her temples,
with the attributes of Juno, Venus, and Ceres; and it was
decreed, that on the day of their nuptials, the youth of either
sex should pay their vows before the altar of their chaste
patroness.[2]

The monstrous vices of the son have cast a shade on the purity
of the father's virtues. It has been objected to Marcus, that he
sacrificed the happiness of millions to a fond partiality for a
worthless boy; and that he chose a successor in his own family,
rather than in the republic. Nothing, however, was neglected
by the anxious father, and by the men of virtue and learning
whom he summoned to his assistance, to expand the narrow
mind of young Commodus, to correct his growing vices, and to
render him worthy of the throne, for which he was designed.
But the power of instruction is seldom of much efficacy, except in
those happy dispositions where it is almost superfluous. The dis-
tasteful lesson of a grave philosopher was in a moment obliterated
by the whisper of a profligate favourite; and Marcus himself
blasted the fruits of this laboured education, by admitting his
son, at the age of fourteen or fifteen, to a full participation of the
Imperial power. He lived but four years afterwards; but he

---

[1] Hist. August. p. 34.
[2] Dion Cassius, l. lxxi. p. 1195. Hist. August. p. 33. Commentaire de
Spanheim sur les Césars de Julien, p. 289. The deification of Faustina is
the only defect which Julian's criticism is able to discover in the all-accom-
plished character of Marcus.

lived long enough to repent a rash measure, which raised the
impetuous youth above the restraint of reason and authority.

Most of the crimes which disturb the internal peace of society
are produced by the restraints which the necessary, but unequal,
laws of property have imposed on the appetites of mankind, by
confining to a few the possession of those objects that are coveted
by many. Of all our passions and appetites, the love of power
is of the most imperious and unsociable nature, since the pride
of one man requires the submission of the multitude. In the
tumult of civil discord, the laws of society lose their force, and
their place is seldom supplied by those of humanity. The ardour
of contention, the pride of victory, the despair of success, the
memory of past injuries, and the fear of future dangers, all contribute to inflame the mind, and to silence the voice of pity.
From such motives almost every page of history has been
stained with civil blood; but these motives will not account for
the unprovoked cruelties of Commodus, who had nothing to wish
and everything to enjoy. The beloved son of Marcus succeeded
(A.D. 180) to his father, amidst the acclamations of the senate
and armies,[1] and when he ascended the throne the happy youth
saw round him neither competitor to remove nor enemies to
punish. In this calm elevated station it was surely natural that
he should prefer the love of mankind to their detestation, the
mild glories of his five predecessors, to the ignominious fate of
Nero and Domitian.

Yet Commodus was not, as he has been represented, a tiger
born with an insatiate thirst of human blood, and capable,
from his infancy, of the most inhuman actions.[2] Nature had
formed him of a weak, rather than a wicked, disposition. His
simplicity and timidity rendered him the slave of his attendants,
who gradually corrupted his mind. His cruelty, which at first
obeyed the dictates of others, degenerated into habit, and at
length became the ruling passion of his soul.[3]

Upon the death of his father, Commodus found himself embarrassed with the command of a great army, and the conduct of a
difficult war against the Quadi and Marcomanni.[4] The servile

[1] Commodus was the first *Porphyrogenetus* (born since his father's accession to the throne). By a new strain of flattery, the Egyptian medals date
by the years of his life; as if they were synonymous to those of his reign.
Tillemont, Hist. des Empereurs, tom. ii. p. 752.

[2] Hist. August. p. 46.

[3] Dion Cassius, l. lxxii. p. 1203.

[4] According to Tertullian (Apolog. c. 25), he died at Sirmium. But the
situation of Vindobona, or Vienna, where both the Victors place his death,
is better adapted to the operations of the war against the Marcomanni and
Quadi.

and profligate youths whom Marcus had banished, soon regained their station and influence about the new emperor. They exaggerated the hardships and dangers of a campaign in the wild countries beyond the Danube; and they assured the indolent prince, that the terror of his name and the arms of his lieutenants would be sufficient to complete the conquest of the dismayed barbarians; or to impose such conditions as were more advantageous than any conquest. By a dexterous application to his sensual appetites, they compared the tranquillity, the splendour, the refined pleasures of Rome, with the tumult of a Pannonian camp, which afforded neither leisure nor materials for luxury.[1] Commodus listened to the pleasing advice; but whilst he hesitated between his own inclination and the awe which he still retained for his father's counsellors, the summer insensibly elapsed, and his triumphal entry into the capital was deferred till the autumn. His graceful person,[2] popular address, and imagined virtues, attracted the public favour; the honourable peace which he had recently granted to the barbarians diffused an universal joy;[3] his impatience to revisit Rome was fondly ascribed to the love of his country; and his dissolute course of amusements was faintly condemned in a prince of nineteen years of age.

During the three first years of his reign, the forms, and even the spirit, of the old administration were maintained by those faithful counsellors, to whom Marcus had recommended his son, and for whose wisdom and integrity Commodus still entertained a reluctant esteem. The young prince and his profligate favourites revelled in all the licence of sovereign power; but his hands were yet unstained with blood; and he had even displayed a generosity of sentiment, which might perhaps have ripened into solid virtue.[4] A fatal incident decided his fluctuating character.

One evening (A.D. 183), as the emperor was returning to the palace through a dark and narrow portico in the amphitheatre,[5] an assassin, who waited his passage, rushed upon him with a drawn sword, loudly exclaiming, " *The senate sends you this.*" The menace prevented the deed; the assassin was seized by the

---

[1] Herodian, l. i. p. 12.
[2] Herodian, l. i. p. 16.
[3] This universal joy is well described (from the medals as well as historians) by Mr. Wotton, Hist. of Rome, p. 192, 193.
[4] Manilius, the confidential secretary of Avidius Cassius, was discovered after he had lain concealed several years. The emperor nobly relieved the public anxiety by refusing to see him and burning his papers without opening them. Dion Cassius, l. lxxii. p. 1200.
[5] Maffei degli Amphitheatri, p. 126.

guards, and immediately revealed the authors of the conspiracy. It had been formed, not in the state, but within the walls of the palace. Lucilla, the emperor's sister, and widow of Lucius Verus, impatient of the second rank, and jealous of the reigning empress, had armed the murderer against her brother's life. She had not ventured to communicate the black design to her second husband Claudius Pompeianus, a senator of distinguished merit and unshaken loyalty; but among the crowd of her lovers (for she imitated the manners of Faustina), she found men of desperate fortunes and wild ambition, who were prepared to serve her more violent as well as her tender passions. The conspirators experienced the rigour of justice, and the abandoned princess was punished, first with exile, and afterwards with death.[1]

But the words of the assassin sunk deep into the mind of Commodus, and left an indelible impression of fear and hatred against the whole body of the senate. Those whom he had dreaded as importunate ministers, he now suspected as secret enemies. The Delators, a race of men discouraged, and almost extinguished, under the former reigns, again became formidable, as soon as they discovered that the emperor was desirous of finding disaffection and treason in the senate. That assembly, whom Marcus had ever considered as the great council of the nation, was composed of the most distinguished of the Romans; and distinction of every kind soon became criminal. The possession of wealth stimulated the diligence of the informers; rigid virtue implied a tacit censure of the irregularities of Commodus; important services implied a dangerous superiority of merit; and the friendship of the father always insured the aversion of the son. Suspicion was equivalent to proof; trial to condemnation. The execution of a considerable senator was attended with the death of all who might lament or revenge his fate; and when Commodus had once tasted human blood, he became incapable of pity or remorse.

Of these innocent victims of tyranny, none died more lamented than the two brothers of the Quintilian family, Maximus and Condianus; whose fraternal love has saved their names from oblivion, and endeared their memory to posterity. Their studies and their occupations, their pursuits and their pleasures, were still the same. In the enjoyment of a great estate, they never admitted the idea of a separate interest; some fragments are now extant of a treatise which they composed in common;

[1] Dion, l. lxxii. p. 1205.   Herodian, l. i. p. 16.   Hist. August. p. 46.

and in every action of life it was observed that their two bodies
were animated by one soul. The Antonines, who valued their
virtues, and delighted in their union, raised them, in the same
year, to the consulship: and Marcus afterwards intrusted to
their joint care the civil administration of Greece, and a great
military command, in which they obtained a signal victory over
the Germans. The kind cruelty of Commodus united them in
death.[1]

The tyrant's rage, after having shed the noblest blood of the
senate, at length recoiled on the principal instrument of his
cruelty. Whilst Commodus was immersed in blood and luxury,
he devolved the detail of the public business on Perennis; a
servile and ambitious minister, who had obtained his post by
the murder of his predecessor, but who possessed a considerable
share of vigour and ability. By acts of extortion, and the forfeited estates of the nobles sacrificed to his avarice, he had
accumulated an immense treasure. The Prætorian guards were
under his immediate command; and his son, who already discovered a military genius, was at the head of the Illyrian legions.
Perennis aspired to the empire; or what, in the eyes of Commodus, amounted to the same crime, he was capable of aspiring
to it, had he not been prevented, surprised, and (A.D. 186) put
to death. The fall of a minister is a very trifling incident in the
general history of the empire; but it was hastened by an extraordinary circumstance, which proved how much the nerves of
discipline were already relaxed. The legions of Britain, discontented with the administration of Perennis, formed a deputation of fifteen hundred select men, with instructions to march
to Rome, and lay their complaints before the emperor. These
military petitioners, by their own determined behaviour, by
inflaming the divisions of the guards, by exaggerating the
strength of the British army, and by alarming the fears of
Commodus, exacted and obtained the minister's death, as the
only redress of their grievances.[2] This presumption of a distant
army, and their discovery of the weakness of government, was
a sure presage of the most dreadful convulsions.

The negligence of the public administration was betrayed soon
afterwards by a new disorder which arose from the smallest
beginnings. A spirit of desertion began to prevail among the

[1] In a note upon the Augustan History, p. 96, Casaubon has collected a
number of particulars concerning these celebrated brothers.
[2] Dion, l. lxxii. p. 1210. Herodian, l. i. p. 22. Hist. August. p. 48.
Dion gives a much less odious character of Perennis than the other historians. His moderation is almost a pledge of his veracity.

troops; and the deserters, instead of seeking their flight in safety
or concealment, infested the highways. Maternus, a private
soldier, of a daring boldness above his station, collected these
bands of robbers into a little army, set open the prisons, invited
the slaves to assert their freedom, and plundered with impunity
the rich and defenceless cities of Gaul and Spain. The governors
of the provinces, who had long been the spectators, and perhaps
the partners, of his depredations, were, at length, roused from
their supine indolence by the threatening commands of the
emperor. Maternus found that he was encompassed, and foresaw that he must be overpowered. A great effort of despair was
his last resource. He ordered his followers to disperse, to pass
the Alps in small parties and various disguises, and to assemble
at Rome, during the licentious tumult of the festival of Cybele.[1]
To murder Commodus, and to ascend the vacant throne, was the
ambition of no vulgar robber. His measures were so ably concerted, that his concealed troops already filled the streets of
Rome. The envy of an accomplice discovered and ruined this
singular enterprise, in the moment when it was ripe for execution.[2]

Suspicious princes often promote the last of mankind from a
vain persuasion, that those who have no dependence, except on
their favour, will have no attachment, except to the person of
their benefactor. Cleander, the successor of Perennis, was a
Phrygian by birth; of a nation, over whose stubborn, but
servile temper, blows only could prevail.[3] He had been sent
from his native country to Rome, in the capacity of a slave.
As a slave he entered the Imperial palace, rendered himself
useful to his master's passions, and rapidly ascended to the most
exalted station which a subject could enjoy. His influence over
the mind of Commodus was much greater than that of his predecessor; for Cleander was devoid of any ability or virtue which
could inspire the emperor with envy or distrust. Avarice was
the reigning passion of his soul, and the great principle of his
administration. The rank of Consul, of Patrician, of Senator,
was exposed to public sale; and it would have been considered
as disaffection if any one had refused to purchase these empty

---

[1] During the second Punic war, the Romans imported from Asia the worship of the mother of the gods. Her festival, the *Megalesia*, began on the
fourth of April, and lasted six days. The streets were crowded with mad
processions, the theatres with spectators, and the public tables with un-
bidden guests. Order and police were suspended, and pleasure was the
only serious business of the city. See Ovid. de Fastis, l. iv. 189, etc.
[2] Herodian, l. i. p. 23, 28.
[3] Cicero pro Flacco, c. 27.

and disgraceful honours with the greatest part of his fortune.[1] In the lucrative provincial employments, the minister shared with the governor the spoils of the people. The execution of the laws was venal and arbitrary. A wealthy criminal might obtain, not only the reversal of the sentence by which he was justly condemned; but might likewise inflict whatever punishment he pleased on the accuser, the witnesses, and the judge.

By these means, Cleander, in the space of three years, had accumulated more wealth than had ever yet been possessed by any freedman.[2] Commodus was perfectly satisfied with the magnificent presents which the artful courtier laid at his feet in the most seasonable moments. To divert the public envy, Cleander, under the emperor's name, erected baths, porticos, and places of exercise, for the use of the people.[3] He flattered himself that the Romans, dazzled and amused by this apparent liberality, would be less affected by the bloody scenes which were daily exhibited; that they would forget the death of Byrrhus, a senator to whose superior merit the late emperor had granted one of his daughters; and that they would forgive the execution of Arrius Antoninus, the last representative of the name and virtues of the Antonines. The former, with more integrity than prudence, had attempted to disclose, to his brother-in-law, the true character of Cleander. An equitable sentence pronounced by the latter, when Proconsul of Asia, against a worthless creature of the favourite, proved fatal to him.[4] After the fall of Perennis, the terrors of Commodus had, for a short time, assumed the appearance of a return to virtue. He repealed the most odious of his acts, loaded his memory with the public execration, and ascribed to the pernicious counsels of that wicked minister, all the errors of his inexperienced youth. But his repentance lasted only thirty days; and, under Cleander's tyranny, the administration of Perennis was often regretted.

Pestilence and famine contributed to fill up the measure of the calamities of Rome.[5] The first could be only imputed to the

---

[1] One of these dear-bought promotions occasioned a current bon mot, that Julius Solon was *banished* into the senate.

[2] Dion (l. lxxii. p. 12, 13) observes, that no freedman had possessed riches equal to those of Cleander. The fortune of Pallas amounted, however, to upwards of five and twenty hundred thousand pounds; *Ter millies.*

[3] Dion, l. lxxii. p. 12, 13. Herodian, l. i. p. 29. Hist. August. p. 52. These baths were situated near the *Porta Capena.* Nardini, Roma Antica, p. 79.

[4] Hist. August. p. 48.

[5] Herodian, l. i. p. 28.   Dion, l. lxxii. p. 1215.   The latter says, that two thousand persons died every day at Rome, during a considerable length of time.

just indignation of the gods; but (A.D. 189) a monopoly of corn, supported by the riches and power of the minister, was considered as the immediate cause of the second. The popular discontent, after it had long circulated in whispers, broke out in the assembled circus. The people quitted their favourite amusements for the more delicious pleasure of revenge, rushed in crowds towards a palace in the suburbs, one of the emperor's retirements, and demanded, with angry clamours, the head of the public enemy. Cleander, who commanded the Prætorian guards,[1] ordered a body of cavalry to sally forth, and disperse the seditious multitude. The multitude fled with precipitation towards the city; several were slain, and many more were trampled to death: but when the cavalry entered the streets, their pursuit was checked by a shower of stones and darts from the roofs and windows of the houses. The foot guards,[2] who had been long jealous of the prerogatives and insolence of the Prætorian cavalry, embraced the party of the people. The tumult became a regular engagement, and threatened a general massacre. The Prætorians, at length, gave way, oppressed with numbers; and the tide of popular fury returned with redoubled violence against the gates of the palace, where Commodus lay, dissolved in luxury, and alone unconscious of the civil war. It was death to approach his person with the unwelcome news. He would have perished in this supine security, had not two women, his elder sister Fadilla, and Marcia, the most favoured of his concubines, ventured to break into his presence. Bathed in tears, and with dishevelled hair, they threw themselves at his feet; and with all the pressing eloquence of fear, discovered to the affrighted emperor, the crimes of the minister, the rage of the people, and the impending ruin, which, in a few minutes, would burst over his palace and person. Commodus started from his dream of pleasure, and commanded that the head of Cleander should be thrown out to the people. The desired spectacle instantly appeased the tumult; and the son of Marcus might even yet have regained the affection and confidence of his outraged subjects.[3]

[1] Tuncque primum tres præfecti prætorio fuere: inter quos libertinus. From some remains of modesty, Cleander declined the title, whilst he assumed the powers, of Prætorian præfect. As the other freedmen were styled, from their several departments, a rationibus, ab epistolis ; Cleander called himself a pugione, as intrusted with the defence of his master's person. Salmasius and Casaubon seem to have talked very idly upon this passage.

[2] Οἱ τῆς πόλεως πέζοι στρατιῶται. Herodian, l. i. p. 31. It is doubtful whether he means the Prætorian infantry, or the cohortes urbanæ, a body of six thousand men, but whose rank and discipline were not equal to their numbers. Neither Tillemont nor Wotton choose to decide this question.

[3] Dion Cassius, l. lxxii. p. 1215. Herodian, l. i. p. 32. Hist. August. p. 48.

But every sentiment of virtue and humanity was extinct in the mind of Commodus. Whilst he thus abandoned the reins of empire to these unworthy favourites, he valued nothing in sovereign power, except the unbounded licence of indulging his sensual appetites. His hours were spent in a seraglio of three hundred beautiful women, and as many boys, of every rank, and of every province; and, wherever the arts of seduction proved ineffectual, the brutal lover had recourse to violence. The ancient historians have expatiated on these abandoned scenes of prostitution, which scorned every restraint of nature or modesty; but it would not be easy to translate their too faithful descriptions into the decency of modern language. The intervals of lust were filled up with the basest amusements. The influence of a polite age, and the labour of an attentive education, had never been able to infuse into his rude and brutish mind the least tincture of learning; and he was the first of the Roman emperors totally devoid of taste for the pleasures of the understanding. Nero himself excelled, or affected to excel, in the elegant arts of music and poetry; nor should we despise his pursuits had he not converted the pleasing relaxation of a leisure hour into the serious business and ambition of his life. But Commodus, from his earliest infancy, discovered an aversion to whatever was rational or liberal, and a fond attachment to the amusements of the populace; the sports of the circus and amphitheatre, the combats of gladiators, and the hunting of wild beasts. The masters in every branch of learning, whom Marcus provided for his son, were heard with inattention and disgust; whilst the Moors and Parthians, who taught him to dart the javelin and to shoot with the bow, found a disciple who delighted in his application, and soon equalled the most skilful of his instructors, in the steadiness of the eye, and the dexterity of the hand.

The servile crowd, whose fortune depended on their master's vices, applauded these ignoble pursuits. The perfidious voice of flattery reminded him that by exploits of the same nature, by the defeat of the Nemæan lion, and the slaughter of the wild boar of Erymanthus, the Grecian Hercules had acquired a place among the gods, and an immortal memory among men. They only forgot to observe, that, in the first ages of society, when the fiercer animals often dispute with man the possession of an unsettled country, a successful war against those savages is one of the most innocent and beneficial labours of heroism. In the civilised state of the Roman empire, the wild beasts had long since retired from the face of man, and the neighbourhood of populous cities. To surprise them in their solitary haunts, and to transport them to Rome, that they might be slain in pomp by the hand of an emperor, was an enterprise equally ridiculous for the prince, and oppressive for the people.[1] Ignorant of these distinctions, Commodus eagerly embraced the glorious resemblance, and styled himself (as we still read on his medals[2]) the *Roman Hercules*. The club and the lion's hide were placed by the side of the throne, amongst the ensigns of sovereignty; and statues were erected, in which Commodus was represented in the character, and with the attributes, of the god, whose valour and dexterity he endeavoured to emulate in the daily course of his ferocious amusements.[3]

Elated with these praises, which gradually extinguished the innate sense of shame, Commodus resolved to exhibit, before the eyes of the Roman people, those exercises, which till then he had decently confined within the walls of his palace, and to the presence of a few favourites. On the appointed day, the various motives of flattery, fear, and curiosity, attracted to the amphitheatre an innumerable multitude of spectators: and some degree of applause was deservedly bestowed on the uncommon skill of the Imperial performer. Whether he aimed at the head or heart of the animal, the wound was alike certain and mortal. With arrows, whose point was shaped into the form of a crescent, Commodus often intercepted the rapid career, and cut asunder the long bony neck of the ostrich.[4] A panther was let loose; and the archer waited till he had leaped upon a trembling malefactor. In the same instant the shaft flew, the beast dropped dead, and the man remained unhurt. The dens of the amphitheatre disgorged at once a hundred lions; a hundred darts from the unerring hand of Commodus laid them dead as they ran raging round the *Arena*. Neither the huge bulk of the elephant, nor the scaly hide of the rhinoceros, could defend them from his stroke. Ethiopia and India yielded their most extraordinary productions; and several animals were slain in

[1] The African lions, when pressed by hunger, infested the open villages and cultivated country, and they infested them with impunity. The royal beast was reserved for the pleasures of the emperor and the capital; and the unfortunate peasant, who killed one of them, though in his own defence, incurred a very heavy penalty. This extraordinary *game-law* was mitigated by Honorius, and finally repealed by Justinian. Codex Theodos. tom. v. p. 92, et Comment Gothofred.

[2] Spanheim de Numismat. Dissertat. xii. tom. ii. p. 493.

[3] Dion, l. lxxii. p. 1216. Hist. August. p. 49.

[4] The ostrich's neck is three feet long, and composed of seventeen vertebræ. Buffon, Hist. Naturelle.

the amphitheatre, which had been seen only in the representations of art, or perhaps of fancy.[1] In all these exhibitions, the
securest precautions were used to protect the person of the
Roman Hercules from the desperate spring of any savage; who
might possibly disregard the dignity of the emperor, and the
sanctity of the god.[2]

But the meanest of the populace were affected with shame
and indignation when they beheld their sovereign enter the lists
as a gladiator, and glory in a profession which the laws and
manners of the Romans had branded with the justest note of
infamy.[3] He chose the habit and arms of the *Secutor*, whose
combat with the *Retiarius* formed one of the most lively scenes
in the bloody sports of the amphitheatre. The *Secutor* was
armed with an helmet, sword, and buckler; his naked antagonist
had only a large net and a trident; with the one he endeavoured
to entangle, with the other to dispatch, his enemy. If he missed
the first throw, he was obliged to fly from the pursuit of the
Secutor, till he had prepared his net for a second cast.[4] The
emperor fought in this character seven hundred and thirty-five
several times. These glorious achievements were carefully recorded in the public acts of the empire; and that he might omit
no circumstance of infamy, he received from the common fund
of gladiators, a stipend so exorbitant, that it became a new and
most ignominious tax upon the Roman people.[5] It may be
easily supposed that in these engagements the master of the
world was always successful: in the amphitheatre his victories
were not often sanguinary; but when he exercised his skill in
the school of gladiators, or his own palace, his wretched antagonists were frequently honoured with a mortal wound from the
hand of Commodus, and obliged to seal their flattery with their

---

[1] Commodus killed a camelopardalis or giraffe (Dion, l. lxxii. p. 1211),
the tallest, the most gentle, and the most useless of the large quadrupeds.
This singular animal, a native only of the interior parts of Africa, has not
been seen in Europe since the revival of letters, and though M. de Buffon
(Hist. Naturelle, tom. xiii.) has endeavoured to describe, he has not ventured to delineate, the giraffe.

[2] Herodian, l. i. p. 37. Hist. August. p. 50.

[3] The virtuous and even the wise princes forbade the senators and knights
to embrace this scandalous profession, under pain of infamy, or, what was
more dreaded by those profligate wretches, of exile. The tyrants allured
them to dishonour by threats and rewards. Nero once produced, in the
arena, forty senators and sixty knights. Lipsius, Saturnalia, l. ii. c. 2.
He has happily corrected a passage of Suetonius, in Nerone, c. 12.

[4] Lipsius, l. ii. c. 7, 8. Juvenal, in the eighth satire, gives a picturesque
description of this combat.

[5] Hist. August. p. 50. Dion, l. lxxii. p. 1220. He received for each time,
decies about £8000 sterling.

blood.[1] He now disdained the appellation of Hercules. The name of Paulus, a celebrated Secutor, was the only one which delighted his ear. It was inscribed on his colossal statues, and repeated in the redoubled acclamations [2] of the mournful and applauding senate.[3] Claudius Pompeianus, the virtuous husband of Lucilla, was the only senator who asserted the honour of his rank. As a father, he permitted his sons to consult their safety by attending the amphitheatre. As a Roman, he declared, that his own life was in the emperor's hands, but that he would never behold the son of Marcus prostituting his person and dignity. Notwithstanding his manly resolution, Pompeianus escaped the resentment of the tyrant, and with his honour had the good fortune to preserve his life.[4]

Commodus had now attained the summit of vice and infamy. Amidst the acclamations of a flattering court, he was unable to disguise, from himself, that he had deserved the contempt and hatred of every man of sense and virtue in his empire. His ferocious spirit was irritated by the consciousness of that hatred, by the envy of every kind of merit, by the just apprehension of danger, and by the habit of slaughter, which he contracted in his daily amusements. History has preserved a long list of consular senators sacrificed to his wanton suspicion, which sought out, with peculiar anxiety, those unfortunate persons connected, however remotely, with the family of the Antonines, without sparing even the ministers of his crimes or pleasures.[5] His cruelty proved at last fatal to himself. He had shed with impunity the noblest blood of Rome: he perished as soon as he was dreaded by his own domestics. Marcia his favourite concubine, Eclectus his chamberlain, and Lætus his Prætorian præfect, alarmed by the fate of their companions and predecessors, resolved to prevent the destruction which every hour hung over their heads, either from the mad caprice of the tyrant,[6] or the sudden indignation

---

[1] Victor tells us, that Commodus only allowed his antagonists a leaden weapon, dreading most probably the consequences of their despair.

[2] They were obliged to repeat six hundred and twenty-six times, *Paulus first of the Secutors*, etc.

[3] Dion, l. lxxii. p. 1221. He speaks of his own baseness and danger.

[4] He mixed, however, some prudence with his courage, and passed the greatest part of his time in a country retirement; alleging his advanced age, and the weakness of his eyes. " I never saw him in the senate," says Dion, " except during the short reign of Pertinax." All his infirmities had suddenly left him, and they returned as suddenly upon the murder of that excellent prince. Dion, l. lxxiii. p. 1227.

[5] The præfects were changed almost hourly or daily; and the caprice of Commodus was often fatal to his most favourite chamberlains. Hist. August. p. 46, 51.

[6] [Wenck says that Commodus had already given orders for their death. — O S.]

of the people. Marcia seized the occasion of presenting a draught
of wine to her lover, after he had fatigued himself with hunting
some wild beasts. Commodus retired to sleep; but whilst he
was labouring with the effects of poison and drunkenness, a
robust youth, by profession a wrestler, entered his chamber, and
strangled him without resistance. The body was secretly conveyed out of the palace, before the least suspicion was entertained
in the city, or even in the court, of the emperor's death. Such
was the fate of the son of Marcus, and so easy was it to destroy
a hated tyrant, who, by the artificial powers of government, had
oppressed, during thirteen years, so many millions of subjects,
each of whom was equal to their master in personal strength
and personal abilities.[1]

The measures of the conspirators were conducted with the
deliberate coolness and celerity which the greatness of the occasion required. They resolved instantly to fill the vacant throne
with an emperor whose character would justify and maintain
the action that had been committed. They fixed on Pertinax,
præfect of the city, an ancient senator of consular rank, whose
conspicuous merit had broke through the obscurity of his birth,
and raised him to the first honours of the state. He had successively governed most of the provinces of the empire; and in
all his great employments, military as well as civil, he had
uniformly distinguished himself by the firmness, the prudence,
and the integrity of his conduct.[2] He now remained almost
alone of the friends and ministers of Marcus; and when, at a
late hour of the night, he was awakened with the news, that the
chamberlain and the præfect were at his door, he received them
with intrepid resignation, and desired they would execute their

[1] Dion, l. lxxii. p. 1222. Herodian, l. i. p. 43. Hist. August. p. 52.
[2] Pertinax was a native of Alba Pompeia, in Piedmont, and son of a
timber-merchant. The order of his employments (it is marked by Capitolinus) well deserves to be set down, as expressive of the form of government
and manners of the age. 1. He was a centurion. 2. Præfect of a cohort
in Syria, in the Parthian war, and in Britain. 3. He obtained an *Ala*, or
squadron of horse, in Mæsia. 4. He was commissary of provisions on the
Æmilian way. 5. He commanded the fleet upon the Rhine. 6. He was
procurator of Dacia, with a salary of about £1600 a year. 7. He commanded the Veterans of a legion. 8. He obtained the rank of senator. 9.
Of prætor. 10. With the command of the first legion in Rhætia and
Noricum. 11. He was consul about the year 175. 12. He attended
Marcus into the east. 13. He commanded an army on the Danube. 14.
He was consular legate of Mæsia. 15. Of Dacia. 16. Of Syria. 17. Of
Britain. 18. He had the care of the public provisions at Rome. 19. He
was proconsul of Africa. 20. Præfect of the city. Herodian (l. i. p. 48)
does justice to his disinterested spirit; but Capitolinus, who collected
every popular rumour, charges him with a great fortune acquired by
bribery and corruption.

master's orders. Instead of death, they offered him the throne
of the Roman world. During some moments he distrusted their
intentions and assurances. Convinced at length of the death
of Commodus, he accepted the purple with a sincere reluctance,
the natural effect of his knowledge both of the duties and of the
dangers of the supreme rank.[1]

Lætus conducted without delay his new emperor to the camp
of the Prætorians, diffusing at the same time through the city a
seasonable report that Commodus died suddenly of an apoplexy;
and that the virtuous Pertinax had *already* succeeded to the
throne. The guards were rather surprised than pleased with
the suspicious death of a prince whose indulgence and liberality
they alone had experienced; but the emergency of the occasion,
the authority of their præfect, the reputation of Pertinax, and
the clamours of the people, obliged them to stifle their secret
discontents, to accept the donative promised of the new emperor,
to swear allegiance to him, and with joyful acclamations and
laurels in their hands to conduct him to the senate-house, that
the military consent might be ratified by the civil authority.

This important night was now far spent; with the dawn of day,
and (A.D. 193, 1st January) the commencement of the new year,
the senators expected a summons to attend an ignominious
ceremony.[2] In spite of all remonstrances, even of those of his
creatures, who yet preserved any regard for prudence or decency,
Commodus had resolved to pass the night in the gladiators'
school, and from thence to take possession of the consulship,
in the habit and with the attendance of that infamous crew.
On a sudden, before the break of day, the senate was called
together in the temple of Concord, to meet the guards, and to
ratify the election of a new emperor. For a few minutes they
sat in silent suspense, doubtful of their unexpected deliverance,
and suspicious of the cruel artifices of Commodus; but when at
length they were assured that the tyrant was no more, they
resigned themselves to all the transports of joy and indignation.
Pertinax, who modestly represented the meanness of his extraction, and pointed out several noble senators more deserving than
himself of the empire, was constrained by their dutiful violence
to ascend the throne, and received all the titles of Imperial power,
confirmed by the most sincere vows of fidelity. The memory of
Commodus was branded with eternal infamy. The names of

[1] Julian in the Cæsars taxes him with being accessory to the death of
Commodus.
[2] [The senate always assembled on the eve of the 1st January to dedicate themselves to the service of the state.—O. S.]

tyrant, of gladiator, of public enemy, resounded in every corner of the house. They decreed in tumultuous votes,[1] that his honours should be reversed, his titles erased from the public monuments, his statues thrown down, his body dragged with a hook into the stripping-room of the gladiators, to satiate the public fury; and they expressed some indignation against those officious servants who had already presumed to screen his remains from the justice of the senate. But Pertinax could not refuse those last rites to the memory of Marcus, and the tears of his first protector Claudius Pompeianus, who lamented the cruel fate of his brother-in-law, and lamented still more that he had deserved it.[2]

These effusions of impotent rage against a dead emperor, whom the senate had flattered when alive with the most abject servility, betrayed a just but ungenerous spirit of revenge. The legality of these decrees was however supported by the principles of the Imperial constitution. To censure, to depose, or to punish with death, the first magistrate of the republic, who had abused his delegated trust, was the ancient and undoubted prerogative of the Roman senate;[3] but that feeble assembly was obliged to content itself with inflicting on a fallen tyrant that public justice, from which, during his life and reign, he had been shielded by the strong arm of military despotism.[4]

Pertinax found a nobler way of condemning his predecessor's memory; by the contrast of his own virtues with the vices of Commodus. On the day of his accession, he resigned over to his wife and son his whole private fortune; that they might have no pretence to solicit favours at the expense of the state. He refused to flatter the vanity of the former with the title of Augusta; or to corrupt the inexperienced youth of the latter by the rank of Cæsar. Accurately distinguishing between the duties of a parent and those of a sovereign, he educated his son with a severe simplicity, which, while it gave him no assured prospect of the

---

[1] [What Gibbon calls " tumultuous votes " were only the applause and acclamations which recurred so often in the senate.—O. S.]

[2] Capitolinus gives us the particulars of these tumultuary votes, which were moved by one senator, and repeated, or rather chanted, by the whole body. Hist. August. p. 52.

[3] The senate condemned Nero to be put to death *more majorum*. Sueton. c. 49.

[4] [No particular law assigned this right to the senate: it was deduced from the ancient principles of the republic. Gibbon appears to infer (says Wenck), from the passage of Suetonius, that the senate, according to its ancient right, punished Nero with death. The words, however, were *more majorum*, and they refer not to the decrees of the senate, but to the kind of death he was to die, which was taken from an old law of Romulus.—O. S.]

throne, might in time have rendered him worthy of it. In public, the behaviour of Pertinax was grave and affable. He lived with the virtuous part of the senate (and in a private station, he had been acquainted with the true character of each individual), without either pride or jealousy; considered them as friends and companions, with whom he had shared the dangers of the tyranny, and with whom he wished to enjoy the security of the present time. He very frequently invited them to familiar entertainments, the frugality of which was ridiculed by those who remembered and regretted the luxurious prodigality of Commodus.[1]

To heal, as far as it was possible, the wounds inflicted by the hand of tyranny, was the pleasing, but melancholy, task of Pertinax. The innocent victims, who yet survived, were recalled from exile, released from prison, and restored to the full possession of their honours and fortunes. The unburied bodies of murdered senators (for the cruelty of Commodus endeavoured to extend itself beyond death) were deposited in the sepulchres of their ancestors; their memory was justified; and every consolation was bestowed on their ruined and afflicted families. Among these consolations, one of the most grateful was the punishment of the Delators; the common enemies of their master, of virtue, and of their country. Yet even in the inquisition of these legal assassins, Pertinax proceeded with a steady temper, which gave everything to justice, and nothing to popular prejudice and resentment.

The finances of the state demanded the most vigilant care of the emperor. Though every measure of injustice and extortion had been adopted, which could collect the property of the subject into the coffers of the prince; the rapaciousness of Commodus had been so very inadequate to his extravagance, that, upon his death, no more than eight thousand pounds were found in the exhausted treasury,[2] to defray the current expenses of government, and to discharge the pressing demand of a liberal donative, which the new emperor had been obliged to promise to the Prætorian guards. Yet under these distressed circumstances, Pertinax had the generous firmness to remit all the oppressive taxes invented by Commodus, and to cancel all the unjust claims of the treasury; declaring, in a decree of the senate, " that he

---

[1] Dion (l. lxxiii. p. 1223) speaks of these entertainments, as a senator who had supped with the emperor; Capitolinus (Hist. August. p. 58), like a slave, who had received his intelligence from one of the scullions.
[2] *Decies.* The blameless economy of Pius left his successors a treasure of *vicies septies millies,* above two and twenty millions sterling. Dion, l. lxxiii. p. 1231.

was better satisfied to administer a poor republic with innocence, than to acquire riches by the ways of tyranny and dishonour." Economy and industry he considered as the pure and genuine sources of wealth; and from them he soon derived a copious supply for the public necessities. The expense of the household was immediately reduced to one half. All the instruments of luxury, Pertinax exposed to public auction,[1] gold and silver plate, chariots of a singular construction, a superfluous wardrobe of silk and embroidery, and a great number of beautiful slaves of both sexes; excepting only, with attentive humanity, those who were born in a state of freedom, and had been ravished from the arms of their weeping parents. At the same time that he obliged the worthless favourites of the tyrant to resign a part of their ill-gotten wealth, he satisfied the just creditors of the state, and unexpectedly discharged the long arrears of honest services. He removed the oppressive restrictions which had been laid upon commerce, and granted all the uncultivated lands in Italy and the provinces to those who would improve them; with an exemption from tribute, during the term of ten years.[2]

Such an uniform conduct had already secured to Pertinax the noblest reward of a sovereign, the love and esteem of his people. Those who remembered the virtues of Marcus were happy to contemplate in their new emperor the features of that bright original; and flattered themselves that they should long enjoy the benign influence of his administration. A hasty zeal to reform the corrupted state, accompanied with less prudence than might have been expected from the years and experience of Pertinax, proved fatal to himself and to his country. His honest indiscretion united against him the servile crowd, who found their private benefit in the public disorders, and who preferred the favour of a tyrant to the inexorable equality of the laws.[3]

Amidst the general joy, the sullen and angry countenance of the Prætorian guards betrayed their inward dissatisfaction. They had reluctantly submitted to Pertinax; they dreaded the strictness of the ancient discipline, which he was preparing to restore; and they regretted the licence of the former reign. Their discontents were secretly fomented by Lætus their præfect, who

---

[1] Besides the design of converting these useless ornaments into money, Dion (l. lxxiii. p. 1229) assigns two secret motives of Pertinax. He wished to expose the vices of Commodus and to discover by the purchasers those who most resembled him.

[2] Though Capitolinus has picked up many idle tales of the private life of Pertinax, he joins with Dion and Herodian in admiring his public conduct.

[3] Leges, rem surdam, inexorabilem esse. T. Liv. ii. 3.

found, when it was too late, that his new emperor would reward
a servant, but would not be ruled by a favourite. On the third
day of his reign the soldiers seized on a noble senator, with a
design to carry him to the camp, and to invest him with the
Imperial purple. Instead of being dazzled by the dangerous
honour, the affrighted victim escaped from their violence, and
took refuge at the feet of Pertinax. A short time afterwards
Sosius Falco, one of the consuls of the year, a rash youth,[1] but
of an ancient and opulent family, listened to the voice of ambition; and a conspiracy was formed during a short absence of
Pertinax, which was crushed by his sudden return to Rome, and
his resolute behaviour. Falco was on the point of being justly
condemned to death as a public enemy, had he not been saved
by the earnest and sincere entreaties of the injured emperor;
who conjured the senate, that the purity of his reign might not
be stained by the blood even of a guilty senator.

These disappointments served only to irritate the rage of the
Prætorian guards. On the twenty-eighth of March, eighty-six
days only after the death of Commodus, a general sedition broke
out in the camp, which the officers wanted either power or
inclination to suppress. Two or three hundred of the most
desperate soldiers marched at noon-day, with arms in their hands
and fury in their looks, towards the Imperial palace. The gates
were thrown open by their companions upon guard; and by the
domestics of the old court, who had already formed a secret
conspiracy against the life of the too virtuous emperor. On the
news of their approach, Pertinax, disdaining either flight or
concealment, advanced to meet his assassins; and recalled to
their minds his own innocence, and the sanctity of their recent
oath. For a few moments they stood in silent suspense, ashamed
of their atrocious design, and awed by the venerable aspect and
majestic firmness of their sovereign, till at length the despair
of pardon reviving their fury, a barbarian of the country of
Tongres [2] levelled the first blow against Pertinax, who was
instantly dispatched with a multitude of wounds. His head

---

[1] If we credit Capitolinus (which is rather difficult), Falco behaved with
the most petulant indecency to Pertinax, on the day of his accession. The
wise emperor only admonished him of his youth and inexperience. Hist.
August. p. 55.
[2] The modern bishopric of Liege. This soldier probably belonged to the
Batavian horseguards, who were mostly raised in the dutchy of Gueldres
and the neighbourhood, and were distinguished by their valour, and by the
boldness with which they swam their horses across the broadest and most
rapid rivers. Tacit. Hist. iv. 12. Dion, l. lv. p. 797. Lipsius de magnitudine Romanâ, l. i. c. 4.

separated from his body, and placed on a lance, was carried in triumph to the Prætorian camp, in the sight of a mournful and indignant people, who lamented the unworthy fate of that excellent prince, and the transient blessings of a reign, the memory of which could serve only to aggravate their approaching misfortunes.[1]

CHAPTER V

Public Sale of the Empire to Didius Julianus by the Prætorian Guards—Clodius Albinus in Britain, Pescennius Niger in Syria, and Septimius Severus in Pannonia, declare against the Murderers of Pertinax—Civil Wars and Victory of Severus over his three Rivals—Relaxation of Discipline—New Maxims of Government

THE power of the sword is more sensibly felt in an extensive monarchy than in a small community. It has been calculated by the ablest politicians, that no state, without being soon exhausted, can maintain above the hundredth part of its members in arms and idleness. But although this relative proportion may be uniform, the influence of the army over the rest of the society will vary according to the degree of its positive strength. The advantages of military science and discipline cannot be exerted, unless a proper number of soldiers are united into one body, and actuated by one soul. With a handful of men, such an union would be ineffectual; with an unwieldy host, it would be impracticable; and the powers of the machine would be alike destroyed by the extreme minuteness, or the excessive weight, of its springs. To illustrate this observation we need only reflect, that there is no superiority of natural strength, artificial weapons, or acquired skill, which could enable one man to keep in constant subjection one hundred of his fellow-creatures: the tyrant of a single town, or a small district, would soon discover that an hundred armed followers were a weak defence against ten thousand peasants or citizens; but an hundred thousand well-disciplined soldiers will command, with despotic sway, ten millions of subjects; and a body of ten or fifteen thousand guards will strike terror into the most numerous populace that ever crowded the streets of an immense capital.

The Prætorian bands, whose licentious fury was the first symptom and cause of the decline of the Roman empire, scarcely

[1] Dion, l. lxxiii. p. 1232. Herodian, l. ii. p. 60. Hist. August. p. 58. Victor in Epitom. and in Cæsarib. Eutropius, viii. 16.

amounted to the last-mentioned number.[1] They derived their
institution from Augustus. That crafty tyrant, sensible that laws
might colour, but that arms alone could maintain, his usurped
dominion, had gradually formed this powerful body of guards in
constant readiness to protect his person, to awe the senate, and
either to prevent or to crush the first motions of rebellion. He
distinguished these favoured troops by a double pay, and superior
privileges; but, as their formidable aspect would at once have
alarmed and irritated the Roman people, three cohorts only were
stationed in the capital; whilst the remainder was dispersed in
the adjacent towns of Italy.[2] But after fifty years of peace and
servitude, Tiberius ventured on a decisive measure, which for
ever riveted the fetters of his country. Under the fair pretences
of relieving Italy from the heavy burthen of military quarters,
and of introducing a stricter discipline among the guards,
he assembled them at Rome, in a permanent camp,[3] which
was fortified with skilful care,[4] and placed on a commanding
situation.[5]

Such formidable servants are always necessary, but often fatal
to the throne of despotism. By thus introducing the Prætorian
guards, as it were into the palace and the senate, the emperors
taught them to perceive their own strength, and the weakness
of the civil government; to view the vices of their masters with
familiar contempt, and to lay aside that reverential awe, which
distance only, and mystery, can preserve towards an imaginary
power. In the luxurious idleness of an opulent city, their pride
was nourished by the sense of their irresistible weight; nor was
it possible to conceal from them, that the person of the sovereign,
the authority of the senate, the public treasure, and the seat of
empire, were all in their hands. To divert the Prætorian bands
from these dangerous reflections, the firmest and best established
princes were obliged to mix blandishments with commands,

---

[1] They were originally nine or ten thousand men (for Tacitus and Dion
are not agreed upon the subject), divided into as many cohorts. Vitellius
increased them to sixteen thousand, and as far as we can learn from inscriptions, they never afterwards sunk much below that number. Lipsius de
magnitudine Româ, i. 4.

[2] Sueton. in August. c. 49.

[3] Tacit. Annal. iv. 2. Sueton. in Tiber. c. 37. Dion Cassius, l. lvii.
p. 867.

[4] In the civil war between Vitellius and Vespasian, the Prætorian camp
was attacked and defended with all the machines used in the siege of the
best fortified cities. Tacit. Hist. iii. 84.

[5] Close to the walls of the city, on the broad summit of the Quirinal and
Viminal hills. Nardini, Roma Antica, p. 174. Donatus de Roma Antiqua,
p. 46.

rewards with punishments, to flatter their pride, indulge their pleasures, connive at their irregularities, and to purchase their precarious faith by a liberal donative; which, since the elevation of Claudius, was exacted as a legal claim, on the accession of every new emperor.[1]

The advocates of the guards endeavoured to justify by arguments, the power which they asserted by arms; and to maintain that, according to the purest principles of the constitution, *their* consent was essentially necessary in the appointment of an emperor. The election of consuls, of generals, and of magistrates, however it had been recently usurped by the senate, was the ancient and undoubted right of the Roman people.[2] But where was the Roman people to be found? Not surely amongst the mixed multitude of slaves and strangers that filled the streets of Rome; a servile populace, as devoid of spirit as destitute of property. The defenders of the state, selected from the flower of the Italian youth,[3] and trained in the exercise of arms and virtue, were the genuine representatives of the people, and the best entitled to elect the military chief of the republic. These assertions, however defective in reason, became unanswerable, when the fierce Prætorians increased their weight, by throwing, like the barbarian conqueror of Rome, their swords into the scale.[4]

The Prætorians had violated the sanctity of the throne, by the atrocious murder of Pertinax; they dishonoured the majesty of it, by their subsequent conduct. The camp was without a leader, for even the Præfect Lætus, who had excited the tempest, prudently declined the public indignation. Amidst the wild disorder Sulpicianus, the emperor's father-in-law, and governor of the city, who had been sent to the camp on the first alarm of mutiny, was endeavouring to calm the fury of the multitude,

---

[1] Claudius, raised by the soldiers to the empire, was the first who gave a donative. He gave *quina dena*, £120 (Sueton. in Claud. c. 10): when Marcus, with his colleague Lucius Verus, took quiet possession of the throne, he gave *vicena*, £160 to each of the guards. Hist. August. p. 25. (Dion, l. lxxiii. p. 1231.) We may form some idea of the amount of these sums, by Hadrian's complaint, that the promotion of a Cæsar had cost him *ter millies*, two millions and a half sterling.

[2] Cicero de Legibus, iii. 3. The first book of Livy, and the second of Dionysius of Halicarnassus, show the authority of the people, even in the election of the kings.

[3] They were originally recruited in Latium, Etruria, and the old colonies (Tacit. Annal. iv. 5). The emperor Otho compliments their vanity, with the flattering titles of Italiæ Alumni Romana vere juventus. Tacit. Hist. i. 84.

[4] In the siege of Rome by the Gauls. See Livy, v. 48. Plutarch, in Camill. p. 143.

when he was silenced by the clamorous return of the murderers, bearing on a lance the head of Pertinax. Though history has accustomed us to observe every principle and every passion yielding to the imperious dictates of ambition, it is scarcely credible that, in these moments of horror, Sulpicianus should have aspired to ascend a throne polluted with the recent blood of so near a relation, and so excellent a prince. He had already begun to use the only effectual argument, and to treat for the Imperial dignity; but the more prudent of the Prætorians, apprehensive that, in this private contract, they should not obtain a just price for so valuable a commodity, ran out upon the ramparts; and, with a loud voice, proclaimed that the Roman world was to be disposed of to the best bidder by public auction.[1]

This infamous offer, the most insolent excess of military licence, diffused an universal grief, shame, and indignation throughout the city. It reached at length the ears of Didius Julianus, a wealthy senator, who, regardless of the public calamities, was indulging himself in the luxury of the table.[2] His wife and his daughter, his freedmen and his parasites, easily convinced him that he deserved the throne, and earnestly conjured him to embrace so fortunate an opportunity. The vain old man (A.D. 193, March 28th) hastened to the Prætorian camp, where Sulpicianus was still in treaty with the guards; and began to bid against him from the foot of the rampart. The unworthy negotiation was transacted by faithful emissaries, who passed alternately from one candidate to the other, and acquainted each of them with the offers of his rival. Sulpicianus had already promised a donative of five thousand drachms (above one hundred and sixty pounds) to each soldier; when Julian, eager for the prize, rose at once to the sum of six thousand two hundred and fifty drachms, or upwards of two hundred pounds sterling. The gates of the camp were instantly thrown open to the purchaser; he was declared emperor, and received an oath of allegiance from the soldiers, who retained humanity enough to stipulate that he should pardon and forget the competition of Sulpicianus.

It was now incumbent on the Prætorians to fulfil the conditions of the sale. They placed their new sovereign, whom they served and despised, in the centre of their ranks, surrounded

---

[1] Dion, l. lxxiii. p. 1234. Herodian, l. ii. p. 63. Hist. August. p. 60. Though the three historians agree that it was in fact an auction, Herodian alone affirms that it was proclaimed as such by the soldiers.

[2] Spartianus softens the most odious parts of the character and elevation of Julian.

him on every side with their shields, and conducted him in close
order of battle through the deserted streets of the city.   The
senate was commanded to assemble; and those who had been
the distinguished friends of Pertinax, or the personal enemies
of Julian, found it necessary to affect a more than common
share of satisfaction at this happy revolution.[1]   After Julian
had filled the senate-house with armed soldiers, he expatiated
on the freedom of his election, his own eminent virtues, and his
full assurance of the affections of the senate.   The obsequious
assembly congratulated their own and the public felicity;
engaged their allegiance, and conferred on him all the several
branches of the Imperial power.[2]   From the senate Julian was
conducted, by the same military procession, to take possession
of the palace.   The first objects that struck his eyes were the
abandoned trunk of Pertinax and the frugal entertainment
prepared for his supper.   The one he viewed with indifference;
the other with contempt.   A magnificent feast was prepared by
his order, and he amused himself till a very late hour with dice,
and the performances of Pylades, a celebrated dancer.   Yet it
was observed, that after the crowd of flatterers dispersed, and
left him to darkness, solitude, and terrible reflection, he passed
a sleepless night; revolving most probably in his mind his own
rash folly, the fate of his virtuous predecessor, and the doubtful
and dangerous tenure of an empire, which had not been acquired
by merit, but purchased by money.[3]

   He had reason to tremble.   On the throne of the world he
found himself without a friend, and even without an adherent.
The guards themselves were ashamed of the prince whom their
avarice had persuaded them to accept; nor was there a citizen
who did not consider his elevation with horror, as the last insult
on the Roman name.   The nobility, whose conspicuous station
and ample possessions exacted the strictest caution, dissembled
their sentiments, and met the affected civility of the emperor
with smiles of complacency and professions of duty.   But the
people, secure in their numbers and obscurity, gave a free
vent to their passions.   The streets and public places of Rome
resounded with clamours and imprecations.   The enraged multi-

   [1] Dion Cassius, at that time prætor, had been a personal enemy to Julian,
l. lxxiii. p. 1235.
   [2] Hist. August. p. 61.   We learn from thence one curious circumstance,
that the new emperor, whatever had been his birth, was immediately aggre-
gated to the number of Patrician families.
   [3] Dion, l. lxxiii. p. 1235.   Hist. August. p. 61.   I have endeavoured to
blend into one consistent story the seeming contradictions of the two
writers.

tude affronted the person of Julian, rejected his liberality, and conscious of the impotence of their own resentment, they called aloud on the legions of the frontiers to assert the violated majesty of the Roman empire.

The public discontent was soon diffused from the centre to the frontiers of the empire. The armies of Britain, of Syria, and of Illyricum, lamented the death of Pertinax, in whose company, or under whose command, they had so often fought and conquered. They received with surprise, with indignation, and perhaps with envy, the extraordinary intelligence that the Prætorians had disposed of the empire by public auction; and they sternly refused to ratify the ignominious bargain. Their immediate and unanimous revolt was fatal to Julian, but it was fatal at the same time to the public peace; as the generals of the respective armies, Clodius Albinus, Pescennius Niger, and Septimius Severus, were still more anxious to succeed than to revenge the murdered Pertinax. Their forces were exactly balanced. Each of them was at the head of three legions,[1] with a numerous train of auxiliaries; and however different in their characters, they were all soldiers of experience and capacity.

Clodius Albinus, governor of Britain, surpassed both his competitors in the nobility of his extraction, which he derived from some of the most illustrious names of the old republic.[2] But the branch from whence he claimed his descent was sunk into mean circumstances, and transplanted into a remote province. It is difficult to form a just idea of his true character. Under the philosophic cloak of austerity, he stands accused of concealing most of the vices which degrade human nature.[3] But his accusers are those venal writers who adored the fortune of Severus, and trampled on the ashes of an unsuccessful rival. Virtue, or the appearances of virtue, recommended Albinus to the confidence and good opinion of Marcus; and his preserving with the son the same interest which he had acquired with the father, is a proof at least that he was possessed of a very flexible disposition. The favour of a tyrant does not always suppose a want of merit in the object of it; he may, without intending it, reward a man of worth and ability, or he may find such a man useful to his own

---

[1] Dion, l. lxxiii. p. 1235.

[2] The Postumian and the Cejonian; the former of whom was raised to the consulship in the fifth year after its institution.

[3] Spartianus, in his undigested collections, mixes up all the virtues and all the vices that enter into the human composition, and bestows them on the same object. Such, indeed, are many of the characters in the Augustan History.

service. It does not appear that Albinus served the son of Marcus, either as the minister of his cruelties, or even as the associate of his pleasures. He was employed in a distant honourable command, when he received a confidential letter from the emperor, acquainting him of the treasonable designs of some discontented generals, and authorising him to declare himself the guardian and successor of the throne, by assuming the title and ensigns of Cæsar.[1] The governor of Britain wisely declined the dangerous honour, which would have marked him for the jealousy, or involved him in the approaching ruin, of Commodus. He courted power by nobler, or, at least, by more specious arts. On a premature report of the death of the emperor, he assembled his troops; and, in an eloquent discourse, deplored the inevitable mischiefs of despotism, described the happiness and glory which their ancestors had enjoyed under the consular government, and declared his firm resolution to reinstate the senate and people in their legal authority. This popular harangue was answered by the loud acclamations of the British legions, and received at Rome with a secret murmur of applause. Safe in the possession of this little world, and in the command of an army less distinguished indeed for discipline than for numbers and valour,[2] Albinus braved the menaces of Commodus, maintained towards Pertinax a stately ambiguous reserve, and instantly declared against the usurpation of Julian. The convulsions of the capital added new weight to his sentiments, or rather to his professions of patriotism. A regard to decency induced him to decline the lofty titles of Augustus and Emperor; and he imitated perhaps the example of Galba, who, on a similar occasion, had styled himself the Lieutenant of the senate and people.[3]

Personal merit alone had raised Pescennius Niger from an obscure birth and station to the government of Syria; a lucrative and important command, which in times of civil confusion gave him a near prospect of the throne. Yet his parts seem to have been better suited to the second than to the first rank; he was an unequal rival, though he might have approved himself an excellent lieutenant, to Severus, who afterwards displayed the greatness of his mind by adopting several useful institutions from a vanquished enemy.[4] In his government, Niger acquired the esteem of the soldiers, and the love of the provincials. His

---

[1] Hist. August. p. 80, 84.

[2] Pertinax, who governed Britain a few years before, had been left for dead, in a mutiny of the soldiers. Hist August. p. 54. Yet they loved and regretted him; admirantibus eam virtutem cui irasœbantur.

[3] Suetonius in. Galba, c. 10.   [4] Hist. August. p. 76.

rigid discipline fortified the valour and confirmed the obedience
of the former, whilst the voluptuous Syrians were less delighted
with the mild firmness of his administration, than with the
affability of his manners, and the apparent pleasure with which
he attended their frequent and pompous festivals.[1] As soon as
the intelligence of the atrocious murder of Pertinax had reached
Antioch, the wishes of Asia invited Niger to assume the Imperial
purple and revenge his death. The legions of the eastern frontier
embraced his cause; the opulent but unarmed provinces from
the frontiers of Æthiopia [2] to the Hadriatic cheerfully submitted
to his power; and the kings beyond the Tigris and the Euphrates
congratulated his election, and offered him their homage and
services. The mind of Niger was not capable of receiving this
sudden tide of fortune; he flattered himself that his accession
would be undisturbed by competition, and unstained by civil
blood; and whilst he enjoyed the vain pomp of triumph, he
neglected to secure the means of victory. Instead of entering
into an effectual negotiation with the powerful armies of the west,
whose resolution might decide, or at least must balance, the
mighty contest; instead of advancing without delay towards
Rome and Italy, where his presence was impatiently expected,[3]
Niger trifled away in the luxury of Antioch those irretrievable
moments which were diligently improved by the decisive activity
of Severus.[4]

The country of Pannonia and Dalmatia, which occupied the
space between the Danube and the Hadriatic, was one of the
last and most difficult conquests of the Romans. In the defence
of national freedom, two hundred thousand of these barbarians
had once appeared in the field, alarmed the declining age of
Augustus, and exercised the vigilant prudence of Tiberius at
the head of the collected force of the empire.[5] The Pannonians
yielded at length to the arms and institutions of Rome. Their
recent subjection, however, the neighbourhood, and even the

[1] Herod. l. ii. p. 68. The chronicle of John Malala, of Antioch, shows the
zealous attachment of his countrymen to these festivals, which at once
gratified their superstition and their love of pleasure.

[2] A king of Thebes, in Egypt, is mentioned in the Augustan History, as
an ally, and, indeed, as a personal friend of Niger. If Spartianus is not, as
I strongly suspect, mistaken, he has brought to light a dynasty of tributary
princes totally unknown to history.

[3] Dion, l. lxxiii. p. 1238. Herod. l. ii. p. 67. A verse in every one's
mouth at that time seems to express the general opinion of the three rivals;
Optimus est *Niger*, bonus *Afer*, pessimus *Albus*. Hist. August. p. 75.

[4] Herodian, l. ii. p. 71.

[5] See an account of that memorable war in Velleius Paterculus, ii. 110,
etc., who served in the army of Tiberius.

mixture, of the unconquered tribes, and perhaps the climate, adapted, as it has been observed, to the production of great bodies and slow minds,[1] all contributed to preserve some remains of their original ferocity, and under the tame and uniform countenance of Roman provincials, the hardy features of the natives were still to be discerned. Their warlike youth afforded an inexhaustible supply of recruits to the legions stationed on the banks of the Danube, and which, from a perpetual warfare against the Germans and Sarmatians, were deservedly esteemed the best troops in the service.

The Pannonian army was at this time commanded by Septimius Severus, a native of Africa, who, in the gradual ascent of private honours, had concealed his daring ambition, which was never diverted from its steady course by the allurements of pleasure, the apprehension of danger, or the feelings of humanity.[2] On the first news of the murder of Pertinax, he assembled his troops, painted in the most lively colours the crime, the insolence, and the weakness of the Prætorian guards, and animated the legions to arms and to revenge. He concluded (and the peroration was thought extremely eloquent) with promising every soldier about four hundred pounds; an honourable donative, double in value to the infamous bribe with which Julian had purchased the empire.[3] The acclamations of the army immediately saluted Severus with the names of Augustus, Pertinax, and Emperor; and he (A.D. 193, April 13th) thus attained the lofty station to which he was invited, by conscious merit and a long train of dreams and omens, the fruitful offspring either of his superstition or policy.[4]

The new candidate for empire saw and improved the peculiar advantage of his situation. His province extended to the Julian Alps, which gave an easy access into Italy; and he remembered the saying of Augustus, That a Pannonian army might in ten

[1] Such is the reflection of Herodian, l. ii. p. 74. Will the modern Austrians allow the influence?

[2] In the letter to Albinus, already mentioned, Commodus accuses Severus, as one of the ambitious generals who censured his conduct, and wished to occupy his place. Hist. August. p. 80.

[3] Pannonia was too poor to supply such a sum. It was probably promised in the camp, and paid at Rome, after the victory. In fixing the sum, I have adopted the conjecture of Casaubon. Hist. August. p. 66. Comment. p. 115.

[4] Herodian, l. ii. p. 78. Severus was declared emperor on the banks of the Danube, either at Carnuntum, according to Spartianus (Hist. August. p. 65), or else at Sabaria, according to Victor. Mr. Hume, in supposing that the birth and dignity of Severus were too much inferior to the Imperial crown, and that he marched in Italy as general only, has not considered this transaction with his usual accuracy (Essay on the original contract).

days appear in sight of Rome.[1] By a celerity proportioned to the
greatness of the occasion, he might reasonably hope to revenge
Pertinax, punish Julian, and receive the homage of the senate
and people, as their lawful emperor, before his competitors,
separated from Italy by an immense tract of sea and land, were
apprised of his success, or even of his election.   During the whole
expedition he scarcely allowed himself any moments for sleep or
food; marching on foot, and in complete armour, at the head
of his columns, he insinuated himself into the confidence and
affection of his troops, pressed their diligence, revived their
spirits, animated their hopes, and was well satisfied to share the
hardships of the meanest soldier, whilst he kept in view the
infinite superiority of this reward.

The wretched Julian had expected, and thought himself prepared, to dispute the empire with the governor of Syria; but in
the invincible and rapid approach of the Pannonian legions, he
saw his inevitable ruin.   The hasty arrival of every messenger
increased his just apprehensions.   He was successively informed
that Severus had passed the Alps; that the Italian cities, unwilling or unable to oppose his progress, had received him with
the warmest professions of joy and duty; that the important
place of Ravenna had surrendered without resistance, and that
the Hadriatic fleet was in the hands of the conqueror.   The
enemy was now within two hundred and fifty miles of Rome;
and every moment diminished the narrow span of life and empire
allotted to Julian.

He attempted, however, to prevent, or at least to protract, his
ruin.   He implored the venal faith of the Prætorians, filled the
city with unavailing preparations for war, drew lines round the
suburbs, and even strengthened the fortifications of the palace;
as if those last intrenchments could be defended without hope
of relief against a victorious invader.   Fear and shame prevented
the guards from deserting his standard; but they trembled at the
name of the Pannonian legions, commanded by an experienced
general, and accustomed to vanquish the barbarians on the
frozen Danube.[2]   They quitted, with a sigh, the pleasures of the
baths and theatres, to put on arms, whose use they had almost
forgotten, and beneath the weight of which they were oppressed.
The unpractised elephants, whose uncouth appearance, it was

[1] Velleius Paterculus, l. ii. c. 3.   We must reckon the march from the
nearest verge of Pannonia, and extend the sight of the city as far as two
hundred miles.
[2] This is not a puerile figure of rhetoric, but an allusion to a real fact
recorded by Dion, l. lxxi. p. 1181.   It probably happened more than once.

hoped, would strike terror into the army of the north, threw their
unskilful riders; and the awkward evolutions of the marines,
drawn from the fleet of Misenum, were an object of ridicule to the
populace; whilst the senate enjoyed, with secret pleasure, the
distress and weakness of the usurper.[1]

Every motion of Julian betrayed his trembling perplexity. He
insisted that Severus should be declared a public enemy by the
senate. He intreated that the Pannonian general might be
associated to the empire. He sent public ambassadors of consular rank to negotiate with his rival; he dispatched private
assassins to take away his life. He designed that the Vestal
virgins, and all the colleges of priests, in their sacerdotal habits,
and bearing before them the sacred pledges of the Roman religion,
should advance, in solemn procession, to meet the Pannonian
legions; and, at the same time, he vainly tried to interrogate,
or to appease, the fates, by magic ceremonies, and unlawful
sacrifices.[2]

Severus, who dreaded neither his arms nor his enchantments,
guarded himself from the only danger of secret conspiracy, by
the faithful attendance of six hundred chosen men, who never
quitted his person or their cuirasses, either by night or by day,
during the whole march. Advancing with a steady and rapid
course, he passed, without difficulty, the defiles of the Apennine,
received into his party the troops and ambassadors sent to retard
his progress, and made a short halt at Interamnia, about seventy
miles from Rome. His victory was already secure; but the
despair of the Prætorians might have rendered it bloody; and
Severus had the laudable ambition of ascending the throne without drawing the sword.[3] His emissaries, dispersed in the capital,
assured the guards, that provided they would abandon their
worthless prince, and the perpetrators of the murder of Pertinax,
to the justice of the conqueror, he would no longer consider that
melancholy event as the act of the whole body. The faithless
Prætorians, whose resistance was supported only by sullen
obstinacy, gladly complied with the easy conditions, seized the
greatest part of the assassins, and signified to the senate that
they no longer defended the cause of Julian. That assembly,
convoked by the consul, unanimously acknowledged Severus

---

[1] Dion, l. lxxiii. p. 1233. Herodian, l. ii. p. 81. There is no surer proof
of the military skill of the Romans, than their first surmounting the idle
terror, and afterwards disdaining the dangerous use, of elephants in war.
[2] Hist. August. p. 62, 63.
[3] Victor and Eutropius, viii. 17, mention a combat near the Milvian
bridge, the Ponte Molle, unknown to the better and more ancient writers.

as lawful emperor, decreed divine honours to Pertinax, and
pronounced a sentence of deposition and death against his unfortunate successor. Julian was conducted into a private apartment of the baths of the palace, and (A.D. 193, June 2) beheaded
as a common criminal, after having purchased, with an immense
treasure, an anxious and precarious reign of only sixty-six days.[1]
The almost incredible expedition of Severus, who, in so short a
space of time, conducted a numerous army from the banks of the
Danube to those of the Tiber, proves at once the plenty of
provisions produced by agriculture and commerce, the goodness
of the roads, the discipline of the legions, and the indolent subdued temper of the provinces.[2]

The first cares of Severus were bestowed on two measures, the
one dictated by policy, the other by decency; the revenge, and
the honours, due to the memory of Pertinax. Before the new
emperor entered Rome, he issued his commands to the Prætorian
guards, directing them to wait his arrival on a large plain near
the city, without arms, but in the habits of ceremony, in which
they were accustomed to attend their sovereign. He was obeyed
by those haughty troops, whose contrition was the effect of their
just terrors. A chosen part of the Illyrian army encompassed
them with levelled spears. Incapable of flight or resistance, they
expected their fate in silent consternation. Severus mounted
the tribunal, sternly reproached them with perfidy and cowardice,
dismissed them with ignominy from the trust which they had
betrayed, despoiled them of their splendid ornaments, and
banished them, on pain of death, to the distance of an hundred
miles from the capital. During the transaction, another detachment had been sent to seize their arms, occupy their camp, and
prevent the hasty consequences of their despair.[3]

The funeral and consecration of Pertinax was next solemnised
with every circumstance of sad magnificence.[4] The senate, with
a melancholy pleasure, performed the last rites to that excellent
prince, whom they had loved, and still regretted. The concern

---

[1] Dion, l. lxxiii. p. 1240. Herodian, l. ii. p. 83. Hist. August. p. 63.

[2] From these sixty-six days, we must first deduct sixteen, as Pertinax
was murdered on the 28th of March, and Severus most probably elected
on the 13th of April (see Hist. August. p. 65, and Tillemont, Hist. des
Empereurs, tom. iii. p. 393, Note 7). We cannot allow less than ten days
after his election, to put a numerous army in motion. Forty days remain
for this rapid march, and as we may compute about eight hundred miles
from Rome to the neighbourhood of Vienna, the army of Severus marched
twenty miles every day, without halt or intermission.

[3] Dion, l. lxxiv. p. 1241. Herodian, l. ii. p. 84.

[4] Dion (l. lxxiv. p. 1244), who assisted at the ceremony as a senator,
gives a most pompous description of it.

of his successor was probably less sincere. He esteemed the virtues of Pertinax, but those virtues would for ever have confined his ambition to a private station. Severus pronounced his funeral oration with studied eloquence, inward satisfaction, and well-acted sorrow; and by this pious regard to his memory, convinced the credulous multitude that *he alone* was worthy to supply his place. Sensible, however, that arms, not ceremonies, must assert his claim to the empire, he left Rome at the end of thirty days, and, without suffering himself to be elated by this easy victory, prepared to encounter his more formidable rivals.

The uncommon abilities and fortune of Severus have induced an elegant historian to compare him with the first and greatest of the Cæsars.[1] The parallel is, at least, imperfect. Where shall we find, in the character of Severus, the commanding superiority of soul, the generous clemency, and the various genius, which could reconcile and unite the love of pleasure, the thirst of knowledge, and the fire of ambition? [2] In one instance only they may be compared with some degree of propriety, in the celerity of their motions and their civil victories. In less than four years [3] (A.D. 193–197), Severus subdued the riches of the east, and the valour of the west. He vanquished two competitors of reputation and ability, and defeated numerous armies, provided with weapons and discipline equal to his own. In that age, the art of fortification, and the principles of tactics, were well understood by all the Roman generals; and the constant superiority of Severus was that of an artist who uses the same instruments with more skill and industry than his rivals. I shall not, however, enter into a minute narrative of these military operations; but as the two civil wars against Niger and against Albinus were almost the same in their conduct, event, and consequences, I shall collect into one point of view the most striking circumstances, tending to develop the character of the conqueror, and the state of the empire.

Falsehood and insincerity, unsuitable as they seem to the dignity of public transactions, offend us with a less degrading idea of meanness than when they are found in the intercourse of private life. In the latter, they discover a want of courage;

[1] Herodian, l. iii. [c. 7] p. 112.

[2] Though it is not, most assuredly, the intention of Lucan, to exalt the character of Cæsar, yet the idea he gives of that hero, in the tenth book of the Pharsalia, where he describes him, at the same time, making love to Cleopatra, sustaining a siege against the power of Egypt, and conversing with the sages of the country, is, in reality, the noblest panegyric.

[3] Reckoning from his election, April 13, 193, to the death of Albinus, February 19, 197. Tillemont's Chronology.

in the other, only a defect of power: and, as it is impossible
for the most able statesman to subdue millions of followers and
enemies by their own personal strength, the world, under the
name of policy, seems to have granted them a very liberal indulgence of craft and dissimulation. Yet the arts of Severus cannot
be justified by the most ample privileges of state reason. He
promised only to betray, he flattered only to ruin; and however
he might occasionally bind himself by oaths and treaties, his
conscience, obsequious to his interest, always released him from
the inconvenient obligation.[1]

If his two competitors, reconciled by their common danger, had
advanced upon him without delay, perhaps Severus would have
sunk under their united effort. Had they even attacked him,
at the same time, with separate views and separate armies, the
contest might have been long and doubtful. But they fell, singly
and successively, an easy prey to the arts as well as arms of their
subtle enemy, lulled into security by the moderation of his professions, and overwhelmed by the rapidity of his action. He
first marched against Niger, whose reputation and power he the
most dreaded: but he declined any hostile declarations, suppressed the name of his antagonist, and only signified to the
senate and people, his intention of regulating the eastern provinces. In private he spoke of Niger, his old friend and intended
successor,[2] with the most affectionate regard, and highly applauded his generous design of revenging the murder of Pertinax.
To punish the vile usurper of the throne, was the duty of every
Roman general. To persevere in arms, and to resist a lawful
emperor, acknowledged by the senate, would alone render him
criminal.[3] The sons of Niger had fallen into his hands among
the children of the provincial governors, detained at Rome as
pledges for the loyalty of their parents.[4] As long as the power
of Niger inspired terror, or even respect, they were educated with
the most tender care, with the children of Severus himself; but
they were soon involved in their father's ruin, and removed, first

---

[1] Herodian, l. ii. [c. 13] p. 85.
[2] Whilst Severus was very dangerously ill, it was industriously given out
that he intended to appoint Niger and Albinus his successors. As he could
not be sincere with respect to both, he might not be so with regard to either.
Yet Severus carried his hypocrisy so far as to profess that intention in the
memoirs of his own life.
[3] Hist. August. p. 65.
[4] This practice, invented by Commodus, proved very useful to Severus.
He found, at Rome, the children of many of the principal adherents of his
rivals; and he employed them more than once to intimidate, or seduce, the
parents.

by exile, and afterwards by death, from the eye of public compassion.[1]

Whilst Severus was engaged in his eastern war, he had reason to apprehend that the governor of Britain might pass the sea and the Alps, occupy the vacant seat of empire, and oppose his return with the authority of the senate and the forces of the west. The ambiguous conduct of Albinus, in not assuming the Imperial title, left room for negotiation. Forgetting, at once, his professions of patriotism, and the jealousy of sovereign power, he accepted the precarious rank of Cæsar, as a reward for his fatal neutrality. Till the first contest was decided, Severus treated the man, whom he had doomed to destruction, with every mark of esteem and regard. Even in the letter, in which he announced his victory over Niger, he styles Albinus the brother of his soul and empire, sends him the affectionate salutations of his wife Julia, and his young family, and intreats him to preserve the armies and the republic faithful to their common interest. The messengers charged with this letter were instructed to accost the Cæsar with respect, to desire a private audience, and to plunge their daggers into his heart.[2] The conspiracy was discovered, and the too credulous Albinus, at length, passed over to the continent, and prepared for an unequal contest with his rival, who rushed upon him at the head of a veteran and victorious army.

The military labours of Severus seem inadequate to the importance of his conquests. Two engagements, the one near the Hellespont, the other in the narrow defiles of Cilicia, decided the fate of his Syrian competitor; and the troops of Europe asserted their usual ascendant over the effeminate natives of Asia.[3] The battle of Lyons, where one hundred and fifty thousand [4] Romans were engaged, was equally fatal to Albinus. The valour of the British army maintained, indeed, a sharp and doubtful contest with the hardy discipline of the Illyrian legions. The fame and person of Severus appeared, during a few moments, irrecoverably lost, till that warlike prince rallied his fainting troops, and led

[1] Herodian, l. iii. p. 96. Hist. August. p. 67, 68.

[2] Hist. August. p. 84. Spartianus has inserted this curious letter at full length.

[3] Consult the third book of Herodian, and the seventy-fourth book of Dion Cassius.

[There were really three battles, one near Cyzicus on the Hellespont, one near Nicæa in Bithynia, the third near the Issus in Cilicia, where Alexander conquered Darius. Dion, l. lxxiv. c, 6 and 7. Herodian, l. iii. 2-4. —O. S.]

[4] Dion, l. lxxv. p. 1260.

them on to a decisive victory.[1] The war was finished by that memorable day.

The civil wars of modern Europe have been distinguished, not only by the fierce animosity, but likewise by the obstinate perseverance, of the contending factions. They have generally been justified by some principle, or, at least, coloured by some pretext, of religion, freedom, or loyalty. The leaders were nobles of independent property and hereditary influence. The troops fought like men interested in a decision of the quarrel; and as military spirit and party zeal were strongly diffused throughout the whole community, a vanquished chief was immediately supplied with new adherents, eager to shed their blood in the same cause. But the Romans, after the fall of the republic, combated only for the choice of masters. Under the standard of a popular candidate for empire, a few enlisted from affection, some from fear, many from interest, none from principle. The legions, uninflamed by party zeal, were allured into civil war by liberal donatives, and still more liberal promises. A defeat, by disabling the chief from the performance of his engagements, dissolved the mercenary allegiance of his followers; and left them to consult their own safety, by a timely desertion of an unsuccessful cause. It was of little moment to the provinces, under whose name they were oppressed or governed; they were driven by the impulsion of the present power, and as soon as that power yielded to a superior force, they hastened to implore the clemency of the conqueror, who, as he had an immense debt to discharge, was obliged to sacrifice the most guilty countries to the avarice of his soldiers. In the vast extent of the Roman empire, there were few fortified cities capable of protecting a routed army; nor was there any person, or family, or order of men, whose natural interest, unsupported by the powers of government, was capable of restoring the cause of a sinking party.[2]

Yet, in the contest between Niger and Severus, a single city deserves an honourable exception. As Byzantium was one of the greatest passages from Europe into Asia, it had been provided with a strong garrison, and a fleet of five hundred vessels was anchored in the harbour.[3] The impetuosity of Severus disap-

---

[1] Dion, l. lxxv. [c. 6] p. 1261. Herodian, l. iii. p. 110. Hist. August. p. 68. The battle was fought in the plain of Trevoux, three or four leagues from Lyons. Tillemont, tom. iii. p. 406, Note 18.

[2] Montesquieu, Considérations sur la Grandeur et la Décadence des Romains, c. xii.

[3] Most of these, as may be supposed, were small open vessels; some, however, were galleys of two, and a few of three ranks of oars.

pointed this prudent scheme of defence; he left to his generals the siege of Byzantium, forced the less guarded passage of the Hellespont, and, impatient of a meaner enemy, pressed forward to encounter his rival. Byzantium, attacked by a numerous and increasing army, and afterwards by the whole naval power of the empire, sustained a siege of three years, and remained faithful to the name and memory of Niger. The citizens and soldiers (we know not from what cause) were animated with equal fury, several of the principal officers of Niger, who despaired of, or who disdained, a pardon, had thrown themselves into this last refuge: the fortifications were esteemed impregnable, and, in the defence of the place, a celebrated engineer displayed all the mechanical powers known to the ancients.[1] Byzantium, at length, surrendered to famine. The magistrates and soldiers were put to the sword, the walls demolished, the privileges suppressed, and the destined capital of the east subsisted only as an open village, subject to the insulting jurisdiction of Perinthus. The historian Dion, who had admired the flourishing, and lamented the desolate, state of Byzantium, accused the revenge of Severus, for depriving the Roman people of the strongest bulwark against the barbarians of Pontus and Asia.[2] The truth of this observation was but too well justified in the succeeding age, when the Gothic fleets covered the Euxine, and passed through the undefended Bosphorus into the centre of the Mediterranean.

Both Niger and Albinus were discovered and put to death in their flight from the field of battle. Their fate excited neither surprise nor compassion. They had staked their lives against the chance of empire, and suffered what they would have inflicted; nor did Severus claim the arrogant superiority of suffering his rivals to live in a private station. But his unforgiving

[1] The engineer's name was Priscus. His skill saved his life, and he was taken into the service of the conqueror. For the particular facts of the siege consult Dion Cassius (l. lxxv. [c. 10] p. 1251), and Herodian (l. iii. [c. 6] p. 95): for the theory of it, the fanciful chevalier de Folard may be looked into. Polybe, tom. i. p. 76.

[2] Notwithstanding the authority of Spartianus and some modern Greeks, we may be assured from Dion and Herodian, that Byzantium, many years after the death of Severus, lay in ruins.

[Milman considers that there is no contradiction between the account of Dion and that of Spartianus and the modern Greeks. Dion does not say that Severus destroyed Byzantium, but that he stripped it of its franchises and privileges, deprived the inhabitants of their property, razed the fortifications, and subjected the city to the jurisdiction of Perinthus. But Severus came to regret his harshness and restored to Byzantium its rights and franchises, and ordered temples to be built. Zosimus mentions a portico which was built by Severus in Byzantium and called by his name. —O. S.]

temper, stimulated by avarice, indulged a spirit of revenge where there was no room for apprehension. The most considerable of the provincials, who, without any dislike to the fortunate candidate, had obeyed the governor under whose authority they were accidentally placed, were punished by death, exile, and especially by the confiscation of their estates. Many cities of the east were stript of their ancient honours, and obliged to pay, into the treasury of Severus, four times the amount of the sums contributed by them for the service of Niger.[1]

Till the final decision of the war, the cruelty of Severus was, in some measure, restrained by the uncertainty of the event, and his pretended reverence for the senate. The head of Albinus, accompanied with a menacing letter, announced to the Romans, that he was resolved to spare none of the adherents of his unfortunate competitors. He was irritated by the just suspicion, that he had never possessed the affections of the senate, and he concealed his old malevolence under the recent discovery of some treasonable correspondences. Thirty-five senators, however, accused of having favoured the party of Albinus, he freely pardoned; and, by his subsequent behaviour, endeavoured to convince them that he had forgotten, as well as forgiven, their supposed offences. But, at the same time, he condemned forty-one[2] other senators, whose names history has recorded; their wives, children, and clients, attended them in death, and the noblest provincials of Spain and Gaul were involved in the same ruin. Such rigid justice, for so he termed it, was, in the opinion of Severus, the only conduct capable of ensuring peace to the people, or stability to the prince; and he condescended slightly to lament, that, to be mild, it was necessary that he should first be cruel.[3]

The true interest of an absolute monarch generally coincides with that of his people. Their numbers, their wealth, their order, and their security, are the best and only foundations of his real greatness; and were he totally devoid of virtue, prudence might supply its place, and would dictate the same rule of conduct. Severus considered the Roman empire as his property, and had no sooner secured the possession, than he bestowed his care on the cultivation and improvement of so valuable an

---

[1] Dion, l. lxxiv. p. 1250.

[2] Dion (l. lxxv. p. 1264); only 29 senators are mentioned by him, but 41 are named in the Augustan History, p. 69, among whom were six of the name of Pescennius. Herodian (l. iii. p. 115) speaks in general of the cruelties of Severus.

[3] Aurelius Victor.

acquisition. Salutary laws, executed with inflexible firmness, soon corrected most of the abuses with which, since the death of Marcus, every part of the government had been infected. In the administration of justice, the judgments of the emperor were characterised by attention, discernment, and impartiality; and whenever he deviated from the strict line of equity, it was generally in favour of the poor and oppressed; not so much indeed from any sense of humanity, as from the natural propensity of a despot, to humble the pride of greatness, and to sink all his subjects to the same common level of absolute dependence. His expensive taste for building, magnificent shows, and above all a constant and liberal distribution of corn and provisions, were the surest means of captivating the affection of the Roman people.[1] The misfortunes of civil discord were obliterated. The calm of peace and prosperity was once more experienced in the provinces; and many cities, restored by the munificence of Severus, assumed the title of his colonies, and attested by public monuments their gratitude and felicity.[2] The fame of the Roman arms was revived by that warlike and successful emperor,[3] and he boasted with a just pride, that, having received the empire oppressed with foreign and domestic wars, he left it established in profound, universal, and honourable peace.[4]

Although the wounds of civil war appeared completely healed, its mortal poison still lurked in the vitals of the constitution. Severus possessed a considerable share of vigour and ability; but the daring soul of the first Cæsar, or the deep policy of Augustus, were scarcely equal to the task of curbing the insolence of the victorious legions. By gratitude, by misguided policy, by seeming necessity, Severus was induced to relax the nerves of discipline.[5] The vanity of his soldiers was flattered with the honour

---

[1] Dion, l. lxxvi. p. 1272. Hist. August. p. 67 [Spartian. Severus, c. 8]. Severus celebrated the secular games with extraordinary magnificence, and he left in the public granaries a provision of corn for seven years, at the rate of 75,000 modii, or about 2500 quarters per day. I am persuaded, that the granaries of Severus were supplied for a long term; but I am not less persuaded, that policy on one hand, and admiration on the other, magnified the hoard far beyond its true contents. [Hist. Aug. p. 73. Spar. Sev. c. 23.]

[2] See Spanheim's treatise of ancient medals, the inscriptions, and our learned travellers, Spon and Wheeler, Shaw, Pocock, etc., who, in Africa, Greece, and Asia, have found more monuments of Severus than of any other Roman emperor whatsoever.

[3] He carried his victorious arms to Seleucia and Ctesiphon, the capitals of the Parthian monarchy. I shall have occasion to mention this war in its proper place.

[4] *Etiam in Britannis* was his own just and emphatic expression. Hist. August. 72 [Spart. Sev. c. 23].

[5] Herodian, l. iii. p. 115. Hist. August. p. 68.

of wearing gold rings; their ease was indulged in the permission of living with their wives in the idleness of quarters. He increased their pay beyond the example of former times, and taught them to expect, and soon to claim, extraordinary donatives on every public occasion of danger or festivity. Elated by success, enervated by luxury, and raised above the level of subjects by their dangerous privileges,[1] they soon became incapable of military fatigue, oppressive to the country, and impatient of a just subordination. Their officers asserted the superiority of rank by a more profuse and elegant luxury. There is still extant a letter of Severus, lamenting the licentious state of the army, and exhorting one of his generals to begin the necessary reformation from the tribunes themselves; since, as he justly observes, the officer who has forfeited the esteem, will never command the obedience, of his soldiers.[2] Had the emperor pursued the train of reflection, he would have discovered that the primary cause of this general corruption might be ascribed, not indeed to the example, but to the pernicious indulgence, however, of the commander in chief.

The Prætorians, who murdered their emperor and sold the empire, had received the just punishment of their treason; but the necessary, though dangerous, institution of guards, was soon restored on a new model by Severus, and increased to four times the ancient number.[3] Formerly these troops had been recruited in Italy; and as the adjacent provinces gradually imbibed the softer manners of Rome, the levies were extended to Macedonia, Noricum, and Spain. In the room of these elegant troops, better adapted to the pomp of courts than to the uses of war, it was established by Severus, that from all the legions of the frontiers, the soldiers most distinguished for strength, valour, and fidelity, should be occasionally draughted; and promoted, as an honour and reward, into the more eligible service of the guards.[4] By this new institution, the Italian youth were diverted from the exercise of arms, and the capital was terrified by the strange aspect and manners of a multitude of barbarians. But Severus flattered himself that the legions would consider these chosen Prætorians as the representatives of the whole military order; and that the present aid of fifty thousand men, superior in arms

---

[1] Upon the insolence and privileges of the soldiers, the 16th Satire, falsely ascribed to Juvenal, may be consulted; the style and circumstances of it would induce me to believe that it was composed under the reign of Severus, or that of his son.

[2] Hist. August. p. 75.   [3] Herodian, l. iii. p. 131.

[4] Dion, l. lxxiv. p. 1243.

and appointments to any force that could be brought into the field against them, would for ever crush the hopes of rebellion, and secure the empire to himself and his posterity.

The command of these favoured and formidable troops soon became the first office of the empire. As the government degenerated into military despotism, the Prætorian Præfect, who in his origin had been a simple captain of the guards, was placed, not only at the head of the army, but of the finances, and even of the law. In every department of administration he represented the person and exercised the authority of the emperor.[1] The first Præfect who enjoyed and abused this immense power was Plautianus, the favourite minister of Severus. His reign lasted above ten years, till the marriage of his daughter with the eldest son of the emperor, which seemed to assure his fortune, proved the occasion of his ruin.[2] The animosities of the palace, by irritating the ambition and alarming the fears of Plautianus, threatened to produce a revolution, and obliged the emperor, who still loved him, to consent with reluctance to his death.[3] After the fall of Plautianus an eminent lawyer, the celebrated Papinian, was appointed to execute the motley office of Prætorian Præfect.

Till the reign of Severus, the virtue and even the good sense of the emperors had been distinguished by their zeal or affected reverence for the senate, and by a tender regard to the nice frame of civil policy instituted by Augustus. But the youth of Severus had been trained in the implicit obedience of camps, and his riper years spent in the despotism of military command.

[1] [The Prætorian Præfect was at first only the Commander of the Guard and far inferior to the Præfectus Urbi, yet from his very position he had from the first great power and influence. To guard against the misuse of that power, Augustus took two precautions, first by dividing the command between two præfects, and secondly by choosing them exclusively from the equestrian order. The wisdom of the first precaution was shown by the peril to which Tiberius was exposed by entrusting to Sejanus the sole command, and the second continued until the reign of Severus. The power of the præfects was immense. As they were regarded as the representatives of the emperors, they came to exercise all the functions of emperors. Thus they held not only the supreme military and judicial authority, but even legislative power and the control of the finances and the provinces.—O. S.]

[2] One of his most daring and wanton acts of power, was the castration of an hundred free Romans, some of them married men, and even fathers of families; merely that his daughter, on her marriage with the young emperor, might be attended by a train of eunuchs worthy of an eastern queen. Dion, l. lxxvi. p. 1271.

[3] Dion, l. lxxvi. p. 1274. Herodian, l. iii. p. 122, 129. The grammarian of Alexandria seems, as it is not unusual, much better acquainted with this mysterious transaction, and more assured of the guilt of Plautianus, than the Roman senator ventures to be.

His haughty and inflexible spirit could not discover, or would not acknowledge, the advantage of preserving an intermediate power, however imaginary, between the emperor and the army. He disdained to profess himself the servant of an assembly that detested his person and trembled at his frown; he issued his commands, where his request would have proved as effectual; assumed the conduct and style of a sovereign and a conqueror, and exercised, without disguise, the whole legislative as well as the executive power.

The victory over the senate was easy and inglorious. Every eye and every passion was directed to the supreme magistrate, who possessed the arms and treasure of the state; whilst the senate, neither elected by the people, nor guarded by military force, nor animated by public spirit, rested its declining authority on the frail and crumbling basis of ancient opinion. The fine theory of a republic insensibly vanished, and made way for the more natural and substantial feelings of monarchy. As the freedom and honours of Rome were successively communicated to the provinces, in which the old government had been either unknown, or was remembered with abhorrence, the tradition of republican maxims was gradually obliterated. The Greek historians of the age of the Antonines [1] observe with a malicious pleasure, that although the sovereign of Rome, in compliance with an obsolete prejudice, abstained from the name of king, he possessed the full measure of regal power. In the reign of Severus, the senate was filled with polished and eloquent slaves from the eastern provinces, who justified personal flattery by speculative principles of servitude. These new advocates of prerogative were heard with pleasure by the court, and with patience by the people, when they inculcated the duty of passive obedience, and descanted on the inevitable mischiefs of freedom. The lawyers and the historians concurred in teaching, that the Imperial authority was held, not by the delegated commission, but by the irrevocable resignation of the senate; that the emperor was freed from the restraint of civil laws, could command by his arbitrary will the lives and fortunes of his subjects, and might dispose of the empire as of his private patrimony.[2] The most eminent of the civil lawyers, and particularly Papinian, Paulus, and Ulpian, flourished under the house of Severus; and the Roman jurisprudence having closely united itself with the system

---

[1] Appian in Proem [cap. 6].

[2] Dion Cassius seems to have written with no other view, than to form these opinions into an historical system. The Pandects will show how assiduously the lawyers, on their side, laboured in the cause of prerogative.

of monarchy, was supposed to have attained its full maturity and perfection.

The contemporaries of Severus, in the enjoyment of the peace and glory of his reign, forgave the cruelties by which it had been introduced. Posterity, who experienced the fatal effects of his maxims and example, justly considered him as the principal author of the decline of the Roman empire.

CHAPTER VI

The Death of Severus—Tyranny of Caracalla—Usurpation of Macrinus— Follies of Elagabalus—Virtues of Alexander Severus—Licentiousness of the Army—General State of the Roman Finances

THE ascent to greatness, however steep and dangerous, may entertain an active spirit with the consciousness and exercise of its own powers; but the possession of a throne could never yet afford a lasting satisfaction to an ambitious mind. This melancholy truth was felt and acknowledged by Severus. Fortune and merit had, from an humble station, elevated him to the first place among mankind. "He had been all things," as he said himself, "and all was of little value." [1] Distracted with the care, not of acquiring, but of preserving an empire, oppressed with age and infirmities, careless of fame,[2] and satiated with power, all his prospects of life were closed. The desire of perpetuating the greatness of his family was the only remaining wish of his ambition and paternal tenderness.

Like most of the Africans, Severus was passionately addicted to the vain studies of magic and divination, deeply versed in the interpretation of dreams and omens, and perfectly acquainted with the science of judicial astrology; which, in almost every age, except the present, has maintained its dominion over the mind of man. He had lost his first wife whilst he was governor of the Lyonnese Gaul.[3] In the choice of a second, he sought only to connect himself with some favourite of fortune; and as soon as he had discovered that a young lady of Emesa in Syria had

[1] Hist. August. p. 71 [Spart. Sever. c. 18]. "Omnia fui et nihil expedit."

[2] Dion Cassius, l. lxxvi. [c. 16] p. 1284.

[3] About the year 186 M. de Tillemont is miserably embarrassed with a passage of Dion, in which the empress Faustina, who died in the year 175, is introduced as having contributed to the marriage of Severus and Julia (l. lxxiv. p. 1243). The learned compiler forgot, that Dion is relating, not a real fact, but a dream of Severus; and dreams are circumscribed to no limits of time or space. Hist. des Empereurs, tom. iii. p. 389, Note 6.

a royal nativity, he solicited, and obtained her hand.[1] Julia
Domna (for that was her name) deserved all that the stars could
promise her. She possessed, even in an advanced age, the
attractions of beauty,[2] and united to a lively imagination, a
firmness of mind, and strength of judgment, seldom bestowed on
her sex. Her amiable qualities never made any deep impression
on the dark and jealous temper of her husband; but in her son's
reign she administered the principal affairs of the empire, with
a prudence that supported his authority; and with a moderation that sometimes corrected his wild extravagancies.[3] Julia
applied herself to letters and philosophy, with some success, and
with the most splendid reputation. She was the patroness of
every art, and the friend of every man of genius.[4] The grateful
flattery of the learned has celebrated her virtue; but, if we may
credit the scandal of ancient history, chastity was very far from
being the most conspicuous virtue of the empress Julia.[5]

Two sons, Caracalla [6] and Geta, were the fruit of this marriage,
and the destined heirs of the empire. The fond hopes of the
father, and of the Roman world, were soon disappointed by these
vain youths, who displayed the indolent security of hereditary
princes; and a presumption that fortune would supply the place
of merit and application. Without any emulation of virtue or
talents, they discovered, almost from their infancy, a fixed and
implacable antipathy for each other. Their aversion, confirmed
by years, and fomented by the arts of their interested favourites,
broke out in childish, and gradually in more serious, competitions;
and, at length, divided the theatre, the circus, and the court, into
two factions; actuated by the hopes and fears of their respective
leaders. The prudent emperor endeavoured, by every expedient
of advice and authority, to allay this growing animosity. The
unhappy discord of his sons clouded all his prospects, and
threatened to overturn a throne raised with so much labour,
cemented with so much blood, and guarded with every defence
of arms and treasure. With an impartial hand he maintained

---

[1] Hist. August. p. 65 [Spart. Sev. c. 3].
[2] Hist. August. [Spart. Carac. c. 10] p. 85.
[3] Dion Cassius, l. lxxvii. [c. 18] p. 1304, 1314.
[4] See a Dissertation of Menage, at the end of his edition of Diogenes Laer-
tius, de Fœminis Philosophis.
[5] Dion, l. lxxvi. [c. 16] p. 1285. Aurelius Victor [De Cæs. xx. 23].
[6] Bassianus was his first name, as it had been that of his maternal grandfather. During his reign he assumed the appellation of Antoninus, which
is employed by lawyers and ancient historians. After his death, the public
indignation loaded him with the nick-names of Tarantus and Caracalla.
The first was borrowed from a celebrated gladiator, the second from a long
Gallic gown which he distributed to the people of Rome.

between them an exact balance of favour, conferred on both the
rank of Augustus, with the revered name of Antoninus; and for
the first time the Roman world beheld three emperors.[1] Yet
even this equal conduct served only to inflame the contest, whilst
the fierce Caracalla asserted the right of primogeniture, and the
milder Geta courted the affections of the people and the soldiers.
In the anguish of a disappointed father, Severus foretold that the
weaker of his sons would fall a sacrifice to the stronger; who, in
his turn, would be ruined by his own vices.[2]

In these circumstances the intelligence of a war in Britain and
of an invasion (A.D. 208) of the province by the barbarians of the
North, was received with pleasure by Severus. Though the
vigilance of his lieutenants might have been sufficient to repel the
distant enemy, he resolved to embrace the honourable pretext
of withdrawing his sons from the luxury of Rome, which enervated their minds and irritated their passions; and of inuring
their youth to the toils of war and government. Notwithstanding his advanced age (for he was above three-score), and his gout,
which obliged him to be carried in a litter, he transported himself
in person into that remote island, attended by his two sons, his
whole court, and a formidable army. He immediately passed
the walls of Hadrian and Antoninus, and entered the enemy's
country, with a design of completing the long-attempted conquest of Britain. He penetrated to the northern extremity of
the island without meeting an enemy. But the concealed
ambuscades of the Caledonians, who hung unseen on the rear
and flanks of his army, the coldness of the climate, and the
severity of a winter march across the hills and morasses of Scotland, are reported to have cost the Romans above fifty thousand
men. The Caledonians at length yielded to the powerful and
obstinate attack, sued for peace, and surrendered a part of their
arms, and a large tract of territory. But their apparent submission lasted no longer than the present terror. As soon as the
Roman legions had retired, they resumed their hostile independence. Their restless spirit provoked Severus to send a new army
into Caledonia, with the most bloody orders, not to subdue but
to extirpate the natives. They were saved by the death of their
haughty enemy.[3]

This Caledonian war, neither marked by decisive events, nor

---

[1] The elevation of Caracalla is fixed by the accurate M. de Tillemont to
the year 198: the association of Geta to the year 208.

[2] Herodian, l. iii. p. 130. The Lives of Caracalla and Geta in the
Augustan History.

[3] Dion, l. lxxvi. p. 1280, etc. Herodian, l. iii. p. 132, etc.

attended with any important consequences, would ill deserve our
attention; but it is supposed, not without a considerable degree
of probability, that the invasion of Severus is connected with
the most shining period of the British history or fable. Fingal,
whose fame, with that of his heroes and bards, has been revived
in our language by a recent publication, is said to have commanded the Caledonians in that memorable juncture, to have
eluded the power of Severus, and to have obtained a signal
victory on the banks of the Carun, in which the son of *the King
of the World,* Caracalla fled from his arms along the fields 'of
his pride.[1] Something of a doubtful mist still hangs over these
Highland traditions; nor can it be entirely dispelled by the most
ingenious researches of modern criticism: [2] but if we could, with
safety, indulge the pleasing supposition, that Fingal lived, and
that Ossian sung, the striking contrast of the situation and
manners of the contending nations might amuse a philosophic
mind. The parallel would be little to the advantage of the
more civilised people, if we compared the unrelenting revenge of
Severus with the generous clemency of Fingal; the timid and
brutal cruelty of Caracalla, with the bravery, the tenderness,
the elegant genius of Ossian; the mercenary chiefs who, from
motives of fear or interest, served under the Imperial standard,
with the freeborn warriors who started to arms at the voice of
the king of Morven; if, in a word, we contemplated the untutored
Caledonians, glowing with the warm virtues of nature, and the
degenerate Romans, polluted with the mean vices of wealth and
slavery.

The declining health and last illness of Severus inflamed the
wild ambition and black passions of Caracalla's soul. Impatient
of any delay or division of empire, he attempted, more than once,
to shorten the small remainder of his father's days, and endeavoured, but without success, to excite a mutiny among the
troops.[3] The old emperor had often censured the misguided lenity
of Marcus, who, by a single act of justice, might have saved the

---

[1] Ossian's Poems, vol. i. p. 175.
[2] That the Caricul of Ossian is the Caracalla of the Roman History is,
perhaps, the only point of British antiquity in which Mr. Macpherson and
Mr. Whitaker are of the same opinion, and yet the opinion is not without
difficulty. In the Caledonian war, the son of Severus was known only by
the appellation of Antoninus; and it may seem strange that the Highland
bard should describe him by a nick-name, invented four years afterwards,
scarcely used by the Romans till after the death of that emperor, and
seldom employed by the most ancient historians. Dion, l. lxxvii. p. 1317.
Hist. August. p. 89. Aurel. Victor. Euseb. in Chron. ad ann. 214.
[3] Dion, l. lxxvi. p. 1282. Hist. August. p. 71. Aurel. Victor.

Romans from the tyranny of his worthless son. Placed in the
same situation, he experienced how easily the rigour of a judge
dissolves away in the tenderness of a parent. He deliberated, he
threatened, but he could not punish; and this last and only
instance of mercy was more fatal to the empire than a long
series of cruelty.[1] The disorder of his mind irritated the pains
of his body; he wished impatiently for death, and hastened the
instant of it by his impatience. He expired (A.D. 211, February
4th) at York in the sixty-fifth year of his life, and in the eighteenth
of a glorious and successful reign. In his last moments he recommended concord to his sons, and his sons to the army. The
salutary advice never reached the heart, or even the understanding, of the impetuous youths; but the more obedient troops,
mindful of their oath of allegiance, and of the authority of their
deceased master, resisted the solicitations of Caracalla, and proclaimed both brothers emperors of Rome. The new princes soon
left the Caledonians in peace, returned to the capital, celebrated
their father's funeral with divine honours, and were cheerfully
acknowledged as lawful sovereigns, by the senate, the people,
and the provinces. Some pre-eminence of rank seems to have
been allowed to the elder brother; but they both administered
the empire with equal and independent power.[2]

Such a divided form of government would have proved a source
of discord between the most affectionate brothers. It was impossible that it could long subsist between two implacable
enemies, who neither desired nor could trust a reconciliation. It
was visible that one only could reign, and that the other must
fall; and each of them judging of his rival's designs by his own,
guarded his life with the most jealous vigilance from the repeated
attacks of poison or the sword. Their rapid journey through
Gaul and Italy, during which they never eat at the same table,
or slept in the same house, displayed to the provinces the odious
spectacle of fraternal discord. On their arrival at Rome, they
immediately divided the vast extent of the Imperial palace.[3] No

[1] Dion, l. lxxvi. p. 1283. Hist. August. p. 89.
[2] Dion, l. lxxvi. p. 1284. Herodian, l. iii. p. 135.
[3] Mr. Hume is justly surprised at a passage in Herodian (l. iv. p. 139),
who, on this occasion, represents the Imperial palace as equal in extent to
the rest of Rome. The whole region of the Palatine Mount on which it was
built, occupied, at most, a circumference of eleven or twelve thousand feet
(Notitia and Victor, in Nardini's Roma Antica). But we should recollect
that the opulent senators had almost surrounded the city with their extensive gardens and suburban palaces, the greatest part of which had been
gradually confiscated by the emperors. If Geta resided in the gardens that
bore his name in the Janiculum; and if Caracalla inhabited the gardens of
Mæcenas on the Esquiline, the rival brothers were separated from each

communication was allowed between their apartments: the doors
and passages were diligently fortified, and guards posted and
relieved with the same strictness as in a besieged place. The
emperors met only in public, in the presence of their afflicted
mother; and each surrounded by a numerous train of armed
followers. Even on these occasions of ceremony, the dissimulation of courts could ill disguise the rancour of their hearts.[1]

This latent civil war already distracted the whole government,
when a scheme was suggested that seemed of mutual benefit to
the hostile brothers. It was proposed, that since it was impossible to reconcile their minds, they should separate their interest,
and divide the empire between them. The conditions of the
treaty were already drawn with some accuracy. It was agreed
that Caracalla, as the elder brother, should remain in possession
of Europe and the western Africa; and that he should relinquish
the sovereignty of Asia and Egypt to Geta, who might fix his
residence at Alexandria or Antioch, cities little inferior to Rome
itself in wealth and greatness; that numerous armies should be
constantly encamped on either side of the Thracian Bosphorus,
to guard the frontiers of the rival monarchies; and that the
senators of European extraction should acknowledge the sover-
reign of Rome, whilst the natives of Asia followed the emperor
of the East. The tears of the empress Julia interrupted the
negotiation, the first idea of which had filled every Roman breast
with surprise and indignation. The mighty mass of conquest
was so intimately united by the hand of time and policy, that
it required the most forcible violence to rend it asunder. The
Romans had reason to dread that the disjointed members would
soon be reduced by a civil war under the dominion of one master;
but if the separation was permanent, the division of the provinces
must terminate in the dissolution of an empire whose unity had
hitherto remained inviolate.[2]

Had the treaty been carried into execution, the sovereign of
Europe might soon have been the conqueror of Asia; but Caracalla obtained an easier though a more guilty victory. He
artfully listened to his mother's entreaties, and consented (A.D.
212, 27th February) to meet his brother in her apartment, on

other by the distance of several miles; and yet the intermediate space was
filled by the imperial gardens of Sallust, of Lucullus, of Agrippa, of Domitian, of Caius, etc., all skirting round the city, and all connected with each
other, and with the palace, by bridges thrown over the Tiber and the
streets. But this explanation of Herodian would require, though it ill
deserves, a particular dissertation, illustrated by a map of ancient Rome.
[1] Herodian, l. iv. p. 139.   [2] Herodian, l. iv. p. 144.

terms of peace and reconciliation. In the midst of their conversation, some centurions, who had contrived to conceal themselves, rushed with drawn swords upon the unfortunate Geta. His distracted mother strove to protect him in her arms; but, in the unavailing struggle, she was wounded in the hand, and covered with the blood of her younger son, while she saw the elder animating and assisting [1] the fury of the assassins. As soon as the deed was perpetrated, Caracalla, with hasty steps, and horror in his countenance, ran towards the Prætorian camp as his only refuge, and threw himself on the ground before the statues of the tutelar deities.[2] The soldiers attempted to raise and comfort him. In broken and disordered words he informed them of his imminent danger and fortunate escape; insinuating that he had prevented the designs of his enemy, and declared his resolution to live and die with his faithful troops. Geta had been the favourite of the soldiers; but complaint was useless, revenge was dangerous, and they still reverenced the son of Severus. Their discontent died away in idle murmurs, and Caracalla soon convinced them of the justice of his cause, by distributing in one lavish donative the accumulated treasures of his father's reign.[3] The real *sentiments* of the soldiers alone were of importance to his power or safety. Their declaration in his favour, commanded the dutiful *professions* of the senate. The obsequious assembly was always prepared to ratify the decision of fortune; but as Caracalla wished to assuage the first emotions of public indignation, the name of Geta was mentioned with decency, and he received the funeral honours of a Roman emperor.[4] Posterity, in pity to his misfortune, has cast a veil over his vices. We consider that young prince as the innocent victim of his brother's ambition, without recollecting that he himself wanted power, rather than inclination, to consummate the same attempts of revenge and murder.

The crime went not unpunished. Neither business, nor pleasure, nor flattery, could defend Caracalla from the stings of

---

[1] Caracalla consecrated, in the temple of Serapis, the sword, with which as he boasted, he had slain his brother Geta. Dion, l. lxxvii. p. 1307.

[2] Herodian, l. iv. p. 147. In every Roman camp there was a small chapel near the head quarters, in which the statues of the tutelar deities were preserved and adored; and we may remark, that the eagles, and other military ensigns, were in the first rank of these deities: an excellent institution, which confirmed discipline by the sanction of religion. Lipsius de Militia Romana, iv. 5, v. 2.

[3] Herodian, l. iv. p. 148. Dion, l. lxxvii. p. 1289.

[4] Geta was placed among the gods. Sit *divus*, dum non sit *vivus*, said his brother. Hist. August. p. 91. Some marks of Geta's consecration are still found upon medals.

a guilty conscience; and he confessed, in the anguish of a
tortured mind, that his disordered fancy often beheld the angry
forms of his father and his brother rising into life, to threaten
and upbraid him.[1]   The consciousness of his crime should have
induced him to convince mankind, by the virtues of his reign,
that the bloody deed had been the involuntary effect of fatal
necessity.   But the repentance of Caracalla only prompted him
to remove from the world whatever could remind him of his
guilt, or recall the memory of his murdered brother.   On his
return from the senate to the palace, he found his mother in the
company of several noble matrons, weeping over the untimely
fate of her younger son.   The jealous emperor threatened them
with instant death; the sentence was executed against Fadilla,
the last remaining daughter of the emperor Marcus; and even
the afflicted Julia was obliged to silence her lamentations, to
suppress her sighs, and to receive the assassin with smiles of joy
and approbation.   It was computed that, under the vague
appellation of the friends of Geta, above twenty thousand persons
of both sexes suffered death.   His guards and freedmen, the
ministers of his serious business, and the companions of his looser
hours, those who by his interest had been promoted to any
commands in the army or provinces, with the long-connected
chain of their dependents, were included in the proscription;
which endeavoured to reach every one who had maintained the
smallest correspondence with Geta, who lamented his death, or
who even mentioned his name.[2]   Helvius Pertinax, son to the
prince of that name, lost his life by an unseasonable witticism.[3]
It was a sufficient crime of Thrasea Priscus, to be descended from
a family in which the love of liberty seemed an hereditary quality.[4]
The particular causes of calumny and suspicion were at length

---

[1] Dion, l. lxxvii. p. 1301.

[2] Dion, l. lxxvii. p. 1290.   Herodian, l. iv. p. 150.   Dion (p. 1298) says,
that the comic poets no longer durst employ the name of Geta in their
plays, and that the estates of those who mentioned it in their testaments,
were confiscated.

[3] Caracalla had assumed the names of several conquered nations; Pertinax observed that the name of *Geticus* (he had obtained some advantage
of the Goths or Getæ) would be a proper addition to Parthicus, Alemannicus,
etc.   Hist. August. p. 89.

[4] Dion, l. lxxvii. p. 1291.   He was probably descended from Helvidius
Priscus and Thrasea Pætus, those patriots whose firm, but useless and
unseasonable, virtue has been immortalised by Tacitus.

[Caracalla reproached those who demanded no favours of him: " It is
clear that if you make me no requests, you do not trust me; if you do not
trust me, you suspect me; if you suspect me, you fear me; and if you fear
me, you hate me," and forthwith condemned them as conspirators.   A good
specimen of the sorites in a tyrant's logic, says Milman.—O. S.]

exhausted; and when a senator was accused of being a secret enemy to the government, the emperor was satisfied with the general proof that he was a man of property and virtue. From this well-grounded principle he frequently drew the most bloody inferences.

The execution of so many innocent citizens was bewailed by the secret tears of their friends and families. The death of Papinian, the Prætorian præfect, was lamented as a public calamity. During the last seven years of Severus, he had exercised the most important offices of the state, and, by his salutary influence, guided the emperor's steps in the paths of justice and moderation. In full assurance of his virtues and abilities, Severus, on his death-bed, had conjured him to watch over the prosperity and union of the Imperial family.[1] The honest labours of Papinian served only to inflame the hatred which Caracalla had already conceived against his father's minister. After the murder of Geta, the Præfect was commanded to exert the powers of his skill and eloquence in a studied apology for that atrocious deed. The philosophic Seneca had condescended to compose a similar epistle to the senate, in the name of the son and assassin of Agrippina.[2] That it was easier to commit than to justify a " parricide," was the glorious reply of Papinian,[3] who did not hesitate between the loss of life and that of honour. Such intrepid virtue, which had escaped pure and unsullied from the intrigues of courts, the habits of business, and the arts of his profession, reflects more lustre on the memory of Papinian, than all his great employments, his numerous writings, and the superior reputation as a lawyer, which he has preserved through every age of the Roman jurisprudence.[4]

It had hitherto been the peculiar felicity of the Romans, and in the worst of times their consolation, that the virtue of the emperors was active, and their vice indolent. Augustus, Trajan, Hadrian, and Marcus, visited their extensive dominions in person, and their progress was marked by acts of wisdom and beneficence. The tyranny of Tiberius, Nero, and Domitian, who resided almost constantly at Rome, or in the adjacent villas, was confined to the

---

[1] It is said that Papinian was himself a relation of the empress Julia.

[Papinian was said to be no longer Prætorian Prefect. Caracalla had deprived him of that office after the death of Severus. So says Dion, and the testimony of Spartianus is of little weight against this other testimony. —O. S.]

[2] Tacit. Annal. xiv. ii.

[3] Hist. August. p. 88.

[4] With regard to Papinian, see Heineccius's Historia Juris Romani, I 330, etc.

senatorial and equestrian orders.[1]　But Caracalla was the common enemy of mankind.　He left (A.D. 213) the capital (and he never returned to it) about a year after the murder of Geta.　The rest of his reign was spent in the several provinces of the empire, particularly those of the East, and every province was by turns the scene of his rapine and cruelty.　The senators, compelled by fear to attend his capricious motions, were obliged to provide daily entertainments at an immense expense, which he abandoned with contempt to his guards; and to erect, in every city, magnificent palaces and theatres, which he either disdained to visit, or ordered to be immediately thrown down.　The most wealthy families were ruined by partial fines and confiscations, and the great body of his subjects oppressed by ingenious and aggravated taxes.[2]　In the midst of peace, and upon the slightest provocation, he issued his commands, at Alexandria in Egypt, for a general massacre.　From a secure post in the temple of Serapis, he viewed and directed the slaughter of many thousand citizens, as well as strangers, without distinguishing either the number or the crime of the sufferers; since, as he coolly informed the senate, *all* the Alexandrians, those who had perished and those who had escaped, were alike guilty.[3]

The wise instructions of Severus never made any lasting impression on the mind of his son, who, although not destitute of imagination and eloquence, was equally devoid of judgment and humanity.[4]　One dangerous maxim, worthy of a tyrant, was remembered and abused by Caracalla, " To secure the affections of the army, and to esteem the rest of his subjects as of little moment." [5]　But the liberality of the father had been restrained

[1] Tiberius and Domitian never moved from the neighbourhood of Rome. Nero made a short journey into Greece. " Et laudatorum Principum usus ex æquo quamvis procul agentibus.　Sævi proximis ingruunt." Tacit. Hist. iv. 75.

[2] Dion, l. lxxvii. p. 1294.

[3] Dion, l. lxxvii. p. 1307.　Herodian, l. iv. p. 158.　The former represents it as a cruel massacre, the latter as a perfidious one too.　It seems probable, that the Alexandrians had irritated the tyrant by their railleries, and perhaps by their tumults.

[After these massacres Caracalla also deprived the Alexandrians of their spectacles and public feasts.　He divided the city into two parts by a wall, with towers at intervals, to prevent the peaceful communication of the citizens.　Thus was treated the unhappy Alexandria (says Dion) by " the savage beast of Ausonia."　This was the title the oracle had applied to Caracalla, and it was said he was so pleased with it that he ordered it to be always used.—O. S.]

[4] Dion, l. lxxvii. p. 1296.

[5] Dion, l. lxxvi. p. 1284.　Mr. Wotton (Hist. of Rome, p. 330) suspects that this maxim was invented by Caracalla himself, and attributed to his father.

by prudence, and his indulgence to the troops was tempered by
firmness and authority. The careless profusion of the son was
the policy of one reign, and the inevitable ruin both of the army
and of the empire. The vigour of the soldiers, instead of being
confirmed by the severe discipline of camps, melted away in the
luxury of cities. The excessive increase of their pay and donatives [1] exhausted the state to enrich the military order, whose
modesty in peace, and service in war, is best secured by an
honourable poverty. The demeanour of Caracalla was haughty
and full of pride; but with the troops he forgot even the proper
dignity of his rank, encouraged their insolent familiarity, and,
neglecting the essential duties of a general, affected to imitate
the dress and manners of a common soldier.

It was impossible that such a character, and such a conduct as
that of Caracalla, could inspire either love or esteem; but as long
as his vices were beneficial to the armies, he was secure from the
danger of rebellion. A secret conspiracy, provoked by his own
jealousy, was fatal to the tyrant. The Prætorian præfecture
was divided between two ministers. The military department
was intrusted to Adventus, an experienced rather than an able
soldier; and the civil affairs were transacted by Opilius Macrinus,
who, by his dexterity in business, had raised himself, with a fair
character, to that high office. But his favour varied with the
caprice of the emperor, and his life might depend on the slightest
suspicion, or the most casual circumstance. Malice or fanaticism
had suggested to an African, deeply skilled in the knowledge of
futurity, a very dangerous prediction, that Macrinus and his son
were destined to reign over the empire. The report was soon
diffused through the province; and when the man was sent in
chains to Rome, he still asserted, in the presence of the Præfect
of the city, the faith of his prophecy. That magistrate, who had
received the most pressing instructions to inform himself of the
successors of Caracalla, immediately communicated the examina-

---

[1] Dion (l. lxxviii. p. 1343) informs us, that the extraordinary gifts of Caracalla to the army amounted annually to seventy millions of drachmæ (about
two millions three hundred and fifty thousand pounds). There is another
passage in Dion, concerning the military pay, infinitely curious; were it not
obscure, imperfect, and probably corrupt. The best sense seems to be,
that the Prætorian guards received twelve hundred and fifty drachmæ
(forty pounds) a year (Dion, l. lxxvii. p. 1307). Under the reign of
Augustus, they were paid at the rate of two drachmæ, or denarii, per day,
720 a year (Tacit. Annal. i. 17). Domitian, who increased the soldiers' pay
one fourth, must have raised the Prætorians to 960 drachmæ (Gronovius de
Pecuniâ Veteri, l. iii. c. 2). These successive augmentations ruined the
empire, for, with the soldiers' pay, their numbers too were increased. We
have seen the Prætorians alone increased from 10,000 to 50,000 men.

tion of the African to the Imperial court, which at that time
resided in Syria. But, notwithstanding the diligence of the
public messengers, a friend of Macrinus found means to apprise
him of the approaching danger. The emperor received the letters
from Rome; and as he was then engaged in the conduct of a
chariot-race, he delivered them unopened to the Prætorian
Præfect, directing him to dispatch the ordinary affairs, and to
report the more important business that might be contained in
them. Macrinus read his fate, and resolved to prevent it. He
inflamed the discontents of some inferior officers, and employed
the hand of Martialis, a desperate soldier, who had been refused
the rank of centurion. The devotion of Caracalla prompted him
to make a pilgrimage from Edessa to the celebrated temple of
the Moon at Carrhæ.[1] He (A.D. 217, 8th March) was attended
by a body of cavalry; but having stopped on the road for some
necessary occasion, his guards preserved a respectful distance,
and Martialis approaching his person under a pretence of duty,
stabbed him with a dagger. The bold assassin was instantly
killed by a Scythian archer of the Imperial guard. Such was
the end of a monster whose life disgraced human nature, and
whose reign accused the patience of the Romans. The grateful
soldiers forgot his vices, remembered only his partial liberality,
and obliged the senate to prostitute their own dignity and that of
religion by granting him a place among the gods. Whilst he
was upon earth, Alexander the Great was the only hero whom
this god deemed worthy his admiration. He assumed the name
and ensigns of Alexander, formed a Macedonian phalanx of
guards, persecuted the disciples of Aristotle, and displayed with
a puerile enthusiasm the only sentiment by which he discovered
any regard for virtue or glory. We can easily conceive, that
after the battle of Narva, and the conquest of Poland, Charles
the Twelfth (though he still wanted the more elegant accomplishments of the son of Philip) might boast of having rivalled his
valour and magnanimity; but in no one action of his life did
Caracalla express the faintest resemblance of the Macedonian
hero, except in the murder of a great number of his own and of
his father's friends.[2]

[1] Dion, l. lxxviii. p. 1312. Herodian, l. iv. p. 168.
[Carrhæ, now Harran, between Edessa and Nisibis, famous for the
defeat of Crassus, the Haran from which Abraham set out for the land of
Canaan. This city, says M. Guizot, has always been remarkable for its
attachment to Sabaism.—O. S.]

[2] The fondness of Caracalla for the name and ensigns of Alexander, is
still preserved on the medals of that emperor. Spanheim de Usu Numismatum, Dissertat. xii. Herodian (l. iv. p. 154) had seen very ridiculous

After the distinction of the house of Severus, the Roman world remained three days without a master. The choice of the army (for the authority of a distant and feeble senate was little regarded) hung in an anxious suspense; as no candidate presented himself whose distinguished birth and merit could engage their attachment and unite their suffrages. The decisive weight of the Prætorian guards elevated the hopes of their præfects, and these powerful ministers began to assert their *legal* claim to fill the vacancy of the Imperial throne. Adventus, however, the senior præfect, conscious of his age and infirmities, of his small reputation, and his smaller abilities, resigned the dangerous honour to the crafty ambition of his colleague Macrinus, whose well-dissembled grief removed all suspicion of his being accessory to his master's death.[1] The troops neither loved nor esteemed his character. They cast their eyes around in search of a competitor, and at last yielded with reluctance to his promises of unbounded liberality and indulgence. A short time after his accession (A.D. 217, March 11) he conferred on his son Diadumenianus, at the age of only ten years, the Imperial title and the popular name of Antoninus. The beautiful figure of the youth, assisted by an additional donative, for which the ceremony furnished a pretext, might attract, it was hoped, the favour of the army, and secure the doubtful throne of Macrinus.

The authority of the new sovereign had been ratified by the cheerful submission of the senate and provinces. They exulted in their unexpected deliverance from a hated tyrant, and it seemed of little consequence to examine into the virtues of the successor of Caracalla. But as soon as the first transports of joy and surprise had subsided, they began to scrutinise the merits of Macrinus with a critical severity, and to arraign the hasty choice of the army. It had hitherto been considered as a fundamental maxim of the constitution, that the emperor must be always chosen in the senate, and the sovereign power, no longer exercised by the whole body, was always delegated to one of its members. But Macrinus was not a senator.[2] The sudden

pictures, in which a figure was drawn, with one side of the face like Alexander, and the other like Caracalla.

[1] Herodian, l. iv. p. 169. Hist. August. p. 94.

[2] Dion, l. lxxxviii. p. 1350. Elagabalus reproached his predecessor, with daring to seat himself on the throne, though, as Prætorian præfect, he could not have been admitted into the senate after the voice of the crier had cleared the house. The personal favour of Plautianus and Sejanus had broken through the established rule. They rose indeed from the equestrian order; but they preserved the præfecture with the rank of senator, and even with the consulship.

elevation of the Prætorian præfects betrayed the meanness of
their origin; and the equestrian order was still in possession of
that great office, which commanded with arbitrary sway the lives
and fortunes of the senate. A murmur of indignation was heard,
that a man whose obscure [1] extraction had never been illustrated
by any signal service, should dare to invest himself with the
purple, instead of bestowing it on some distinguished senator,
equal in birth and dignity to the splendour of the Imperial
station.

As soon as the character of Macrinus was surveyed by the
sharp eye of discontent, some vices, and many defects, were
easily discovered. The choice of his ministers was in many
instances justly censured, and the dissatisfied people, with their
usual candour, accused at once his indolent tameness and his
excessive severity.[2]

His rash ambition had climbed a height where it was difficult
to stand with firmness, and impossible to fall without instant
destruction. Trained in the arts of courts, and the forms of
civil business, he trembled in the presence of the fierce and undisciplined multitude, over whom he had assumed the command;
his military talents were despised, and his personal courage
suspected; a whisper that circulated in the camp, disclosed the
fatal secret of the conspiracy against the late emperor, aggravated
the guilt of murder by the baseness of hypocrisy, and heightened
contempt by detestation. To alienate the soldiers, and to provoke inevitable ruin, the character of a reformer was only want-
ing: and such was the peculiar hardship of his fate, that Macrinus
was compelled to exercise that invidious office. The prodigality of Caracalla had left behind it a long train of ruin and
disorder; and if that worthless tyrant had been capable of reflecting on the sure consequences of his own conduct, he would
perhaps have enjoyed the dark prospect of the distress and
calamities which he bequeathed to his successors.

In the management of this necessary reformation, Macrinus

---

[1] He was a native of Cæsarea, in Numidia, and began his fortune by
serving in the household of Plautian, from whose ruin he narrowly escaped.
His enemies asserted that he was born a slave, and had exercised, among
other infamous professions, that of gladiator. The fashion of aspersing
the birth and condition of an adversary, seems to have lasted from the
time of the Greek orators to the learned grammarians of the last age.

[2] Both Dion and Herodian speak of the virtues and vices of Macrinus,
with candour and impartiality; but the author of his Life, in the Augustan
History, seems to have implicitly copied some of the venal writers, employed by Elagabalus, to blacken the memory of his predecessor.

proceeded with a cautious prudence, which would have restored
health and vigour to the Roman army, in an easy and almost
imperceptible manner. To the soldiers already engaged in the
service, he was constrained to leave the dangerous privileges and
extravagant pay given by Caracalla; but the new recruits were
received on the more moderate though liberal establishment of
Severus, and gradually formed to modesty and obedience.[1] One
fatal error destroyed the salutary effects of this judicious plan.
The numerous army, assembled in the East by the late emperor,
instead of being immediately dispersed by Macrinus through the
several provinces, was suffered to remain united in Syria, during
the winter that followed his elevation. In the luxurious idleness of their quarters, the troops viewed their strength and
numbers, communicated their complaints, and revolved in their
minds the advantages of another revolution. The veterans,
instead of being flattered by the advantageous distinction, were
alarmed by the first steps of the emperor, which they considered
as the presage of his future intentions. The recruits, with sullen
reluctance, entered on a service, whose labours were increased
while its rewards were diminished by a covetous and unwarlike
sovereign. The murmurs of the army swelled with impunity
into seditious clamours; and the partial mutinies betrayed a
spirit of discontent and disaffection, that waited only for the
slightest occasion to break out on every side into a general
rebellion. To minds thus disposed, the occasion soon presented
itself.

The empress Julia had experienced all the vicissitudes of
fortune. From an humble station she had been raised to greatness, only to taste the superior bitterness of an exalted rank.
She was doomed to weep over the death of one of her sons, and
over the life of the other. The cruel fate of Caracalla, though
her good sense must have long taught her to expect it, awakened
the feelings of a mother and of an empress. Notwithstanding
the respectful civility expressed by the usurper towards the
widow of Severus, she descended with a painful struggle into
the condition of a subject, and soon withdrew herself by a
voluntary death from the anxious and humiliating dependence. Julia Mæsa, her sister, was ordered to leave the court and

---

[1] Dion, l. lxxxiii. p. 1336. The sense of the author is as clear as the intention of the emperor; but M. Wotton has mistaken both, by understanding the distinction, not of veterans and recruits, but of old and new
legions. History of Rome, p. 347.

Antioch.[1] She retired to Emesa with an immense fortune, the fruit of twenty years' favour, accompanied by her two daughters, Soæmias and Mamæa, each of whom was a widow, and each had an only son. Bassianus,[2] for that was the name of the son of Soæmias, was consecrated to the honourable ministry of high priest of the Sun; and this holy vocation, embraced either from prudence or superstition, contributed to raise the Syrian youth to the empire of Rome. A numerous body of troops was stationed at Emesa; and, as the severe discipline of Macrinus had constrained them to pass the winter encamped, they were eager to revenge the cruelty of such unaccustomed hardships. The soldiers, who resorted in crowds to the temple of the Sun, beheld with veneration and delight the elegant dress and figure of a young Pontiff: they recognised, or they thought that they recognised, the features of Caracalla, whose memory they now adored. The artful Mæsa saw and cherished their rising partiality, and readily sacrificing her daughter's reputation to the fortune of her grandson, she insinuated that Bassianus was the natural son of their murdered sovereign. The sums distributed by her emissaries with a lavish hand silenced every objection, and the profusion sufficiently proved the affinity, or at least the resemblance, of Bassianus with the great original. The young Antoninus (for he had assumed and polluted that respectable name) was (A.D. 218, May 16) declared emperor by the troops of Emesa, asserted his hereditary right, and called aloud on the armies to follow the standard of a young and liberal prince, who

[1] Dion, l. lxxviii. p. 1330. The abridgment of Xiphilin, though less particular, is in this place clearer than the original.

[2] [The following is the genealogical table of the young emperor:—

BASSIANUS
|
Severus Imperator=Julia Domna . Julia Mæsa=Avitus
|
Caracalla Imperator Geta Imperator

Varius Marcellus=Soæmias   Mamæa=Gessius Marcianus
|
Elagabalus Imper.   Alexander Severus Imper.

Bassianus was originally called Varius Avitus Bassianus, a series of names derived from his father, maternal grandfather (Avitus), and maternal great-grandfather (Bassianus).—O. S.]

had taken up arms to revenge his father's death and the oppression of the military order.[1]

Whilst a conspiracy of women and eunuchs was concerted with
prudence, and conducted with rapid vigour, Macrinus, who, by
a decisive motion, might have crushed his infant enemy, floated
between the opposite extremes of terror and security, which
alike fixed him inactive at Antioch. A spirit of rebellion diffused
itself through all the camps and garrisons of Syria, successive
detachments murdered their officers,[2] and joined the party of
the rebels; and the tardy restitution of military pay and privileges was imputed to the acknowledged weakness of Macrinus.
At length he marched out of Antioch, to meet the increasing and
zealous army of the young pretender. His own troops seemed
to take the field with faintness and reluctance; but (A.D. 218,
June 7), in the heat of the battle,[3] the Prætorian guards,
almost by an involuntary impulse, asserted the superiority of
their valour and discipline. The rebel ranks were broken;
when the mother and grandmother of the Syrian prince, who,
according to their eastern custom, had attended the army, threw
themselves from their covered chariots, and, by exciting the compassion of the soldiers, endeavoured to animate their drooping
courage. Antoninus himself, who, in the rest of his life, never acted
like a man, in this important crisis of his fate approved himself
a hero, mounted his horse, and, at the head of his rallied troops,
charged sword in hand among the thickest of the enemy; whilst
the eunuch Gannys, whose occupations had been confined to
female cares and the soft luxury of Asia, displayed the talents of
an able and experienced general. The battle still raged with
doubtful violence, and Macrinus might have obtained the
victory, had he not betrayed his own cause by a shameful and
precipitate flight. His cowardice served only to protract his
life a few days, and to stamp deserved ignominy on his misfor-

[1] According to Lampridius (Hist. August. p. 135), Alexander Severus
lived twenty-nine years, three months, and seven days. As he was killed
March 19, 235, he was born December 12, 205, and was consequently about
this time thirteen years old, as his elder cousin might be about seventeen.
This computation suits much better the history of the young princes, than
that of Herodian (l. v. p. 181), who represents them as three years younger;
whilst, by an opposite error of chronology, he lengthens the reign of Elagabalus two years beyond its real duration. For the particulars of the conspiracy, see Dion, l. lxxviii. p. 1339. Herodian, l. v. p. 184.
[2] By a most dangerous proclamation of the pretended Antoninus, every
soldier who brought in his officer's head, became entitled to his private
estate, as well as to his military commission.
[3] Dion, l. lxxviii. p. 1345. Herodian, l. v. p. 186. The battle was fought
near the village of Immæ, about two and twenty miles from Antioch.

tunes. It is scarcely necessary to add, that his son Diadumenianus was involved in the same fate.   As soon as the stubborn
Prætorians could be convinced that they fought for a prince who
had basely deserted them, they surrendered to the conqueror;
the contending parties of the Roman army, mingling tears of joy
and tenderness, united under the banners of the imagined son of
Caracalla, and the East acknowledged with pleasure the first
emperor of Asiatic extraction.

The letters of Macrinus had condescended to inform the senate
of the slight disturbance occasioned by an impostor in Syria, and
a decree immediately passed, declaring the rebel and his family
public enemies; with a promise of pardon, however, to such of
his deluded adherents as should merit it by an immediate return
to their duty.   During the twenty days that elapsed from the
declaration to the victory of Antoninus (for in so short an
interval was the fate of the Roman world decided), the capital
and the provinces, more especially those of the East, were distracted with hopes and fears, agitated with tumult, and stained
with a useless effusion of civil blood, since whosoever of the
rivals prevailed in Syria, must reign over the empire.   The
specious letters in which the young conqueror announced his
victory to the obedient senate, were filled with professions of
virtue and moderation; the shining examples of Marcus and
Augustus he should ever consider as the great rule of his administration; and he affected to dwell with pride on the striking
resemblance of his own age and fortunes with those of Augustus,
who in the earliest youth had revenged by a successful war the
murder of his father.   By adopting the style of Marcus Aurelius
Antoninus, son of Antoninus and grandson of Severus, he tacitly
asserted his hereditary claim to the empire; but, by assuming
the tribunitian and proconsular powers before they had been conferred on him by a decree of the senate, he offended the delicacy of
Roman prejudice.   This new and injudicious violation of the
constitution was probably dictated either by the ignorance of his
Syrian courtiers, or the fierce disdain of his military followers.[1]

As the attention of the new emperor was diverted by the most
trifling amusements, he (A.D. 219) wasted many months in his
luxurious progress from Syria to Italy, passed at Nicomedia his
first winter after his victory, and deferred till the ensuing summer
his triumphal entry into the capital.   A faithful picture,
however, which preceded his arrival, and was placed by his
immediate order over the altar of Victory in the senate-house,

[1] Dion, l. lxxix. [c. 4] p. 1353.

conveyed to the Romans the just but unworthy resemblance of
his person and manners. He was drawn in his sacerdotal robes
of silk and gold, after the loose flowing fashion of the Medes and
Phœnicians; his head was covered with a lofty tiara, his
numerous collars and bracelets were adorned with gems of an
inestimable value. His eyebrows were tinged with black, and
his cheeks painted with an artificial red and white.[1] The grave
senators confessed with a sigh, that, after having long experienced the stern tyranny of their own countrymen, Rome was
at length humbled beneath the effeminate luxury of Oriental
despotism.

The Sun was worshipped at Emesa, under the name of Elagabalus,[2] and under the form of a black conical stone, which, as it
was universally believed, had fallen from heaven on that sacred
place. To this protecting deity, Antoninus, not without some
reason, ascribed his elevation to the throne. The display of
superstitious gratitude was the only serious business of his reign.
The triumph of the God of Emesa over all the religions of the
earth, was the great object of his zeal and vanity: and the
appellation of Elagabalus (for he presumed as pontiff and
favourite to adopt that sacred name) was dearer to him than all
the titles of Imperial greatness. In a solemn procession through
the streets of Rome, the way was strewed with gold dust; the
black stone, set in precious gems, was placed on a chariot drawn
by six milk-white horses richly caparisoned. The pious emperor
held the reins, and, supported by his ministers, moved slowly
backwards, that he might perpetually enjoy the felicity of the
divine presence. In a magnificent temple raised on the Palatine
Mount, the sacrifices of the god of Elagabalus were celebrated
with every circumstance of cost and solemnity. The richest
wines, the most extraordinary victims, and the rarest aromatics,
were profusely consumed on his altar. Around the altar a chorus
of Syrian damsels performed their lascivious dances to the sound
of barbarian music, whilst the gravest personages of the state
and army, clothed in long Phœnician tunics, officiated in the

---

[1] Dion, l. lxxix. [c. 14] p. 1363. Herodian, l. v. [c. 5] p. 189.
[2] This name is derived by the learned from two Syriac words, *Ela* a God
and *Gabal*, to form, the forming or plastic God, a proper, and even happy
epithet for the Sun. Wotton's History of Rome, p. 378.
[The name Elagabalus was corrupted by Lampridius and the later
writers into Heliogabalus, because the God was identified with Helios or the
Sun. Herodian writes the name Ἐλαιαγάβαλος, and Dion Ἐλεγάβαλος,
but Elagabalus is the correct form (says Smith), as is testified to by the
witness of the medals of the epoch.—O. S.]

meanest functions, with affected zeal and secret indignation.[1]

To this temple, as to the common centre of religious worship,
the Imperial fanatic attempted to remove the Ancilia, the
Palladium,[2] and all the sacred pledges of the faith of Numa. A
crowd of inferior deities attended in various stations the majesty
of the god of Emesa; but his court was still imperfect, till a
female of distinguished rank was admitted to his bed. Pallas
had been first chosen for his comfort; but as it was dreaded lest
her warlike terrors might affright the soft delicacy of a Syrian
deity, the Moon, adored by the Africans under the name of
Astarte, was deemed a more suitable companion for the Sun.
Her image, with the rich offerings of her temple as a marriage
portion, was transported with solemn pomp from Carthage to
Rome, and the day of these mystic nuptials was a general festival
in the capital and throughout the empire.[3]

A rational voluptuary adheres with invariable respect to the
temperate dictates of nature, and improves the gratifications of
sense by social intercourse, endearing connections, and the soft
colouring of taste and the imagination. But Elagabalus (I
speak of the emperor of that name), corrupted by his youth, his
country, and his fortune, abandoned himself to the grossest
pleasures with ungoverned fury, and soon found disgust and
satiety in the midst of his enjoyments. The inflammatory
powers of art were summoned to his aid: the confused multitude
of women, of wines, and of dishes, and the studied variety of
attitudes and sauces, served to revive his languid appetites.
New terms and new inventions in these sciences, the only ones
cultivated and patronised by the monarch,[4] signalised his reign,
and transmitted his infamy to succeeding times. A capricious
prodigality supplied the want of taste and elegance; and whilst
Elagabalus lavished away the treasures of his people in the
wildest extravagance, his own voice and that of his flatterers

---

[1] Herodian, l. v. [c. 5] p. 190.

[2] He broke into the sanctuary of Vesta, and carried away a statue, which
he supposed to be the Palladium; but the vestals boasted, that, by a pious
fraud, they had imposed a counterfeit image on the profane intruder.
Hist. August. p. 103.

[3] Dion, l. lxxix. [c. 12] p. 1360. Herodian, l. v. [c. 6] p. 193. The subjects
of the empire were obliged to make liberal presents to the new-married
couple; and whatever they had promised during the life of Elagabalus, was
carefully exacted under the administration of Mamæa.

[4] The invention of a new sauce was liberally rewarded; but if it was not
relished, the inventor was confined to eat of nothing else, till he had discovered another more agreeable to the Imperial palate. Hist. August.
[Lamprid. Heliog. ᴄ. 29], p. 111.

applauded a spirit and magnificence unknown to the tameness of his predecessors. To confound the order of seasons and climates,[1] to sport with the passions and prejudices of his subjects, and to subvert every law of nature and decency, were in the number of his most delicious amusements. A long train of concubines, and a rapid succession of wives, among whom was a vestal virgin, ravished by force from her sacred asylum,[2] were insufficient to satisfy the impotence of his passions. The master of the Roman world affected to copy the dress and manners of the female sex, preferred the distaff to the sceptre, and dishonoured the principal dignities of the empire by distributing them among his numerous lovers; one of whom was publicly invested with the title and authority of the emperor's, or, as he more properly styled himself, of the empress's husband.[3]

It may seem probable, the vices and follies of Elagabalus have been adorned by fancy, and blackened by prejudice.[4] Yet confining ourselves to the public scenes displayed before the Roman people, and attested by grave and contemporary historians, their inexpressible infamy surpasses that of any other age or country. The licence of an eastern monarch is secluded from the eye of curiosity by the inaccessible walls of his seraglio. The sentiments of honour and gallantry have introduced a refinement of pleasure, a regard for decency, and a respect for the public opinion, into the modern courts of Europe; but the corrupt and opulent nobles of Rome gratified every vice that could be collected from the mighty conflux of nations and manners. Secure of impunity, careless of censure, they lived without restraint in the patient and humble society of their slaves and parasites. The emperor, in his turn, viewing every rank of his subjects with the same contemptuous indifference, asserted without control his sovereign privilege of lust and luxury.

The most worthless of mankind are not afraid to condemn in others the same disorders which they allow in themselves; and can readily discover some nice difference of age, character, or

---

[1] He never would eat sea-fish except at a great distance from the sea; he then would distribute vast quantities of the rarest sorts, brought at an immense expense, to the peasants of the inland country. Hist. Aug. [Lamprid. Heliog. c. 23], p. 109.

[2] Dion, l. lxxix. p. 1358. Herodian, l. v. p. 192.

[3] Hierocles enjoyed that honour. Dion, l. lxxix. p. 1363, 1364. A dancer was made præfect of the city, a charioteer præfect of the watch, a barber præfect of the provisions. Hist. August. p. 105.

[4] Even the credulous compiler of his Life, in the Augustan History (p. 111), is inclined to suspect that his vices may have been exaggerated.

station, to justify the partial distinction.   The licentious soldiers,
who had raised to the throne the dissolute son of Caracalla,
blushed at their ignominious choice, and turned with disgust
from that monster, to contemplate with pleasure the opening
virtues of his cousin Alexander the son of Mamæa.   The crafty
Mæsa, sensible that her grandson Elagabalus must inevitably
destroy himself by his own vices, had provided another and surer
support of her family.   Embracing a favourable moment of
fondness and devotion, she had persuaded the young emperor to
adopt Alexander, and to invest him (A.D. 221) with the title of
Cæsar, that his own divine occupations might be no longer interrupted by the care of the earth.   In the second rank that amiable
prince soon acquired the affections of the public, and excited the
tyrant's jealousy, who resolved to terminate the dangerous competition, either by corrupting the manners, or by taking away
the life, of his rival.   His arts proved unsuccessful; his vain
designs were constantly discovered by his own loquacious folly,
and disappointed by those virtuous and faithful servants whom
the prudence of Mamæa had placed about the person of her son.
In a hasty sally of passion, Elagabalus resolved to execute by
force what he had been unable to compass by fraud, and by a
despotic sentence degraded his cousin from the rank and honours
of Cæsar.   The message was received in the senate with silence,
and in the camp with fury.   The Prætorian guards swore to
protect Alexander, and to revenge the dishonoured majesty of
the throne.   The tears and promises of the trembling Elagabalus,
who only begged them to spare his life, and to leave him in the
possession of his beloved Hierocles, diverted their just indignation; and they contented themselves with empowering their
præfects to watch over the safety of Alexander, and the conduct
of the emperor.[1]

It was impossible that such a reconciliation should last, or
that even the mean soul of Elagabalus could hold an empire on
such humiliating terms of dependence.   He soon attempted, by
a dangerous experiment, to try the temper of the soldiers.   The
report of the death of Alexander, and the natural suspicion that
he had been murdered, inflamed their passions into fury, and the
tempest of the camp could only be appeased by the presence and
authority of the popular youth.   Provoked at this new instance
of their affection for his cousin, and their contempt for his person,

---

[1] Dion, l. lxxix. p. 1365.   Herodian, l. v. p. 195-201.   Hist. August.
p. 105.   The last of the three historians seems to have followed the best
authors in his account of the revolution.

the emperor ventured to punish some of the leaders of the mutiny.
His unseasonable severity proved instantly fatal to his minions,
his mother, and himself. Elagabalus was (A.D. 222, 10th
March) massacred by the indignant Prætorians, his mutilated
corpse dragged through the streets of the city, and thrown into
the Tiber. His memory was branded with eternal infamy by
the senate; the justice of whose decree has been ratified by
posterity.[1]

In the room of Elagabalus, his cousin Alexander was raised to
the throne by the Prætorian guards. His relation to the family
of Severus, whose name he assumed, was the same as that of his
predecessor; his virtue and his danger had already endeared him
to the Romans, and the eager liberality of the senate conferred
upon him, in one day, the various titles and powers of the Imperial
dignity.[2] But as Alexander was a modest and dutiful youth,
of only seventeen years of age, the reins of government were in
the hands of two women, of his mother Mamæa, and of Mæsa, his
grandmother. After the death of the latter, who survived but
a short time the elevation of Alexander, Mamæa remained the
sole regent of her son and of the empire.

In every age and country, the wiser, or at least the stronger,
of the two sexes, has usurped the powers of the state, and confined the other to the cares and pleasures of domestic life. In
hereditary monarchies, however, and especially in those of
modern Europe, the gallant spirit of chivalry, and the law of
succession, have accustomed us to allow a singular exception;
and a woman is often acknowledged the absolute sovereign of a
great kingdom, in which she would be deemed incapable of exercising the smallest employment, civil or military. But as the
Roman emperors were still considered as the generals and
magistrates of the republic, their wives and mothers, although
distinguished by the name of Augusta, were never associated to

---

[1] The era of the death of Elagabalus, and of the accession of Alexander,
has employed the learning and ingenuity of Pagi, Tillemont, Valsecchi,
Vignoli, and Torre bishop of Adria. The question is most assuredly intricate; but I still adhere to the authority of Dion; the truth of whose
calculations is undeniable, and the purity of whose text is justified by the
agreement of Xiphilin, Zonaras, and Cedrenus. Elagabalus reigned three
years, nine months, and four days, from his victory over Macrinus, and was
killed March 10, 222. But what shall we reply to the medals, undoubtedly
genuine, which reckon the fifth year of his tribunitian power? We shall
reply, with the learned Valsecchi, that the usurpation of Macrinus was annihilated, and that the son of Caracalla dated his reign from his father's
death. After resolving this great difficulty, the smaller knots of this question may be easily untied, or cut asunder.

[2] Hist. August. p. 114. By this unusual precipitation, the senate meant
to confound the hopes of pretenders, and prevent the factions of the armies.

their personal honours; and a female reign would have appeared
an inexpiable prodigy in the eyes of those primitive Romans,
who married without love, or loved without delicacy and respect.[1]
The haughty Agrippina aspired, indeed, to share the honours of
the empire, which she had conferred on her son; but her mad
ambition, detested by every citizen who felt for the dignity of
Rome, was disappointed by the artful firmness of Seneca and
Burrhus.[2] The good sense, or the indifference, of succeeding
princes, restrained them from offending the prejudices of their
subjects; and it was reserved for the profligate Elagabalus, to
discharge the acts of the senate, with the name of his mother
Soæmias, who was placed by the side of the consuls, and subscribed, as a regular member, the decrees of the legislative
assembly. Her more prudent sister, Mamæa, declined the useless and odious prerogative, and a solemn law was enacted, excluding women for ever from the senate, and devoting to the
infernal gods, the head of the wretch by whom this sanction
should be violated.[3] The substance, not the pageantry, of power
was the object of Mamæa's manly ambition. She maintained
an absolute and lasting empire over the mind of her son, and in
his affection the mother could not brook a rival. Alexander,
with her consent, married the daughter of a Patrician; but his
respect for his father-in-law, and love for the empress, were
inconsistent with the tenderness or interest of Mamæa. The
Patrician was executed on the ready accusation of treason, and
the wife of Alexander driven with ignominy from the palace, and
banished into Africa.[4]

Notwithstanding this act of jealous cruelty, as well as some
instances of avarice, with which Mamæa is charged; the general
tenor of her administration was equally for the benefit of her
son and of the empire. With the approbation of the senate,
she chose sixteen of the wisest and most virtuous senators, as a

---

[1] Metellus Numidicus, the censor, acknowledged to the Roman people in
a public oration that had kind Nature allowed us to exist without the help
of women, we should be delivered from a very troublesome companion;
and he could recommend matrimony, only as the sacrifice of private
pleasure to public duty. Aulus Gellius, i. 6.

[2] Tacit. Annal. xiii. 5.

[3] Hist. August. p. 102, 107 [Lamprid. Heliog. c. 4 and 18].

[4] Dion, l. lxxx. [c. 2] p. 1369. Herodian, l. vi. [c. 1] p. 206. Hist. August.
[Lamprid. Alexander Sev. c. 49] p. 131. Herodian represents the Patrician
as innocent. The Augustan History, on the authority of Dexippus, condemns him, as guilty of a conspiracy against the life of Alexander. It is
impossible to pronounce between them: but Dion is an irreproachable
witness of the jealousy and cruelty of Mamæa toward the young empress,
whose hard fate Alexander lamented, but durst not oppose.

perpetual council of state, before whom every public business of
moment was debated and determined. The celebrated Ulpian,
equally distinguished by his knowledge of, and his respect for,
the laws of Rome, was at their head; and the prudent firmness
of this aristocracy restored order and authority to the government. As soon as they had purged the city from foreign superstition and luxury, the remains of the capricious tyranny of
Elagabalus, they applied themselves to remove his worthless
creatures from every department of public administration, and
to supply their places with men of virtue and ability. Learning,
and the love of justice, became the only recommendations for
civil offices. Valour, and the love of discipline, the only qualifications for military employments.[1]

But the most important care of Mamæa and her wise counsellors, was to form the character of the young emperor, on whose
personal qualities the happiness or misery of the Roman world
must ultimately depend. The fortunate soil assisted, and even
prevented, the hand of cultivation. An excellent understanding soon convinced Alexander of the advantages of virtue, the
pleasure of knowledge, and the necessity of labour. A natural
mildness and moderation of temper preserved him from the
assaults of passion, and the allurements of vice. His unalterable
regard for his mother, and his esteem for the wise Ulpian,
guarded his inexperienced youth from the poison of flattery.

The simple journal of his ordinary occupations exhibits a
pleasing picture of an accomplished emperor,[2] and with some
allowance for the difference of manners, might well deserve the
imitation of modern princes. Alexander rose early; the first
moments of the day were consecrated to private devotion, and
his domestic chapel was filled with the images of those heroes,
who, by improving or reforming human life, had deserved the
grateful reverence of posterity. But, as he deemed the service
of mankind the most acceptable worship of the gods, the greatest
part of his morning hours was employed in his council, where he
discussed public affairs, and determined private causes, with a
patience and discretion above his years. The dryness of business
was relieved by the charms of literature: and a portion of time

[1] Herodian, l. vi. p. 203. Hist. August. p. 119. The latter insinuates,
that when any law was to be passed, the council was assisted by a number
of able lawyers and experienced senators, whose opinions were separately
given and taken down in writing.
[2] See his Life in the Augustan History. The undistinguishing compiler
has buried these interesting anecdotes under a load of trivial and unmeaning circumstances.

was always set apart for his favourite studies of poetry, history, and philosophy. The works of Virgil and Horace, the Republics of Plato and Cicero, formed his taste, enlarged his understanding, and gave him the noblest ideas of man and government. The exercises of the body succeeded to those of the mind; and Alexander, who was tall, active, and robust, surpassed most of his equals in the gymnastic arts. Refreshed by the use of the bath and a slight dinner, he resumed, with new vigour, the business of the day; and, till the hour of supper, the principal meal of the Romans, he was attended by his secretaries, with whom he read and answered the multitude of letters, memorials, and petitions, that must have been addressed to the master of the greatest part of the world. His table was served with the most frugal simplicity; and whenever he was at liberty to consult his own inclination, the company consisted of a few select friends, men of learning and virtue, amongst whom Ulpian was constantly invited. Their conversation was familiar and instructive; and the pauses were occasionally enlivened by the recital of some pleasing composition, which supplied the place of the dancers, comedians, and even gladiators, so frequently summoned to the tables of the rich and luxurious Romans.[1] The dress of Alexander was plain and modest, his demeanour courteous and affable: at the proper hours his palace was open to all his subjects, but the voice of a crier was heard, as in the Eleusinian mysteries, pronouncing the same salutary admonition; " Let none enter those holy walls, unless he is conscious of a pure and innocent mind." [2]

Such an uniform tenor of life, which left not a moment for vice or folly, is a better proof of the wisdom and justice of Alexander's government, than all the trifling details preserved in the compilation of Lampridius. Since the accession of Commodus, the Roman world had experienced, during a term of forty years, the successive and various vices of four tyrants. From the death of Elagabalus it enjoyed (A.D. 222–235) an auspicious calm of thirteen years. The provinces, relieved from the oppressive taxes invented by Caracalla and his pretended son, flourished in peace and prosperity, under the administration of magistrates, who were convinced by experience, that to deserve the love of the subjects was their best and only method of obtaining the favour of their sovereign. While some gentle restraints were imposed on the innocent luxury of the Roman

---

[1] See the 13th Satire of Juvenal.
[2] Hist. August. p. 119.

people, the price of provisions, and the interest of money, were reduced, by the paternal care of Alexander, whose prudent liberality, without distressing the industrious, supplied the wants and amusements of the populace. The dignity, the freedom, the authority of the senate were restored; and every virtuous senator might approach the person of the emperor, without fear, and without a blush.

The name of Antoninus, ennobled by the virtues of Pius and Marcus, had been communicated by adoption to the dissolute Verus, and by descent to the cruel Commodus. It became the honourable appellation of the sons of Severus, was bestowed on young Diadumenianus, and at length prostituted to the infamy of the high priest of Emesa. Alexander, though pressed by the studied, and perhaps sincere, importunity of the senate, nobly refused the borrowed lustre of a name; whilst in his whole conduct he laboured to restore the glories and felicity of the age of the genuine Antonines.[1]

In the civil administration of Alexander, wisdom was enforced by power, and the people, sensible of the public felicity, repaid their benefactor with their love and gratitude. There still remained a greater, a more necessary, but a more difficult enterprise; the reformation of the military order, whose interest and temper, confirmed by long impunity, rendered them impatient of the restraints of discipline, and careless of the blessings of public tranquillity. In the execution of his design the emperor affected to display his love, and to conceal his fear, of the army. The most rigid economy in every other branch of the administration, supplied a fund of gold and silver for the ordinary pay and the extraordinary rewards of the troops. In their marches he relaxed the severe obligation of carrying seventeen days' provision on their shoulders. Ample magazines were formed along the public roads, and as soon as they entered the enemy's country, a numerous train of mules and camels waited on their haughty laziness. As Alexander despaired of correcting the luxury of his soldiers, he attempted, at least, to direct it to objects of martial pomp and ornament, fine horses, splendid armour, and shield enriched with silver and gold. He shared whatever

---

[1] See in the Hist. August. p. 116, 117, the whole contest between Alex-ander and the senate, extracted from the journals of that assembly. It happened on the sixth of March, probably of the year 223, when the Romans had enjoyed, almost a twelvemonth, the blessings of his reign. Before the appellation of Antoninus was offered him as a title of honour, the senate waited to see whether Alexander would not assume it, as a family name.

fatigues he was obliged to impose, visited, in person, the sick
and wounded, preserved an exact register of their services and
his own gratitude, and expressed, on every occasion, the warmest
regard for a body of men, whose welfare, as he affected to declare,
was so closely connected with that of the state.[1] By the most
gentle arts he laboured to inspire the fierce multitude with a
sense of duty, and to restore at least a faint image of that discipline to which the Romans owed their empire over so many
other nations, as warlike and more powerful than themselves.
But his prudence was vain, his courage fatal, and the attempt
towards a reformation served only to inflame the ills it was
meant to cure.

The Prætorian guards were attached to the youth of Alexander.
They loved him as a tender pupil, whom they had saved from a
tyrant's fury, and placed on the Imperial throne. That amiable
prince was sensible of the obligation; but as his gratitude was
restrained within the limits of reason and justice, they soon were
more dissatisfied with the virtues of Alexander, than they had
ever been with the vices of Elagabalus. Their præfect, the wise
Ulpian, was the friend of the laws and of the people; he was considered as the enemy of the soldiers, and to his pernicious counsels
every scheme of reformation was imputed. Some trifling accident
blew up their discontent into a furious mutiny; and a civil war
raged, during three days, in Rome, whilst the life of that excellent
minister was defended by the grateful people. Terrified, at
length, by the sight of some houses in flames, and by the threats
of a general conflagration, the people yielded with a sigh, and
left the virtuous, but unfortunate, Ulpian to his fate. He was
pursued into the Imperial palace, and massacred at the feet of
his master, who vainly strove to cover him with the purple, and
to obtain his pardon from the inexorable soldiers. Such was
the deplorable weakness of government, that the emperor was
unable to revenge his murdered friend and his insulted dignity,
without stooping to the arts of patience and dissimulation.
Epagathus, the principal leader of the mutiny, was removed
from Rome, by the honourable employment of præfect of Egypt;
from that high rank he was gently degraded to the government of
Crete; and when, at length, his popularity among the guards was
effaced by time and absence, Alexander ventured to inflict the
tardy, but deserved punishment of his crimes.[2] Under the reign

---

[1] It was a favourite saying of the emperor's, Se milites magis servare
quam seipsum; quod salus publica in his esset. Hist. August. p. 130.

[2] Though the author of the Life of Alexander (Hist. August. p. 132) mentions the sedition raised against Ulpian by the soldiers, he conceals the

of a just and virtuous prince, the tyranny of the army threatened
with instant death his most faithful ministers, who were suspected of an intention to correct their intolerable disorders. The
historian Dion Cassius had commanded the Pannonian legions
with the spirit of ancient discipline. Their brethren of Rome,
embracing the common cause of military licence, demanded the
head of the reformer. Alexander, however, instead of yielding
to their seditious clamours, showed a just sense of his merit and
services, by appointing him his colleague in the consulship, and
defraying from his own treasury the expense of that vain dignity:
but as it was justly apprehended, that if the soldiers beheld him
with the ensigns of his office, they would revenge the insult in
his blood, the nominal first magistrate of the state retired, by the
emperor's advice, from the city, and spent the greatest part of
his consulship at his villas in Campania.[1]

The lenity of the emperor confirmed the insolence of the
troops; the legions imitated the example of the guards, and
defended their prerogative of licentiousness with the same furious
obstinacy. The administration of Alexander was an unavailing
struggle against the corruption of his age. In Illyricum, in
Mauritania, in Armenia, in Mesopotamia, in Germany, fresh
mutinies perpetually broke out; his officers were murdered, his
authority was insulted, and his life at last sacrificed to the fierce
discontents of the army.[2] One particular fact well deserves to
be recorded, as it illustrates the manners of the troops, and exhibits a singular instance of their return to a sense of duty and
obedience. Whilst the emperor lay at Antioch, in his Persian

catastrophe, as it might discover a weakness in the administration of his
hero. From this designed omission, we may judge of the weight and candour of that author.

[In this account of the slaughter of Ulpian (says Wenck), Gibbon has confounded two events altogether different, the quarrel of the people with the
Prætorians, which lasted three days, and the assassination of Ulpian by
the latter. Dion relates first the death of Ulpian; afterwards turning
back, according to a manner which is usual with him, he says that during
the life of Ulpian there had been a war of three days between the Prætorians
and the people. But Ulpian was not the cause. Ulpian's death was due
to his condemnation of his predecessors in the Prætorian præfectship,
Chrestus and Florian, and the determination of the soldiers to revenge
them. Zosimus attributes the condemnation of these men to Mamæa,
but Ulpian reaped the advantage.—O. S.]

[1] For an account of Ulpian's fate and his own danger, see the mutilated
conclusion of Dion's History, l. lxxx. p. 1371.

[The statement that Dion retired to his estates in Campania is erroneous.
He was not rich, and possessed no villas or estates in Campania. He
resided during his consulship at Rhegium, and on its expiry returned to
Rome, where he had an interview with the emperor, from whom he obtained
permission to retire to his native city Nicæa, in Bithynia.—O. S.]

[2] Annot. Reimar. ad Dion Cassius, l. lxxx. p. 1369.

expedition, the particulars of which we shall hereafter relate, the punishment of some soldiers, who had been discovered in the baths of women, excited a sedition in the legion to which they belonged. Alexander ascended his tribunal, and with a modest firmness represented to the armed multitude, the absolute necessity as well as his inflexible resolution of correcting the vices introduced by his impure predecessor, and of maintaining the discipline, which could not be relaxed without the ruin of the Roman name and empire. Their clamours interrupted his mild expostulation. " Reserve your shouts," said the undaunted emperor, " till you take the field against the Persians, the Germans, and the Sarmatians. Be silent in the presence of your sovereign and benefactor, who bestows upon you the corn, the clothing, and the money of the provinces; Be silent, or I shall no longer style you soldiers, but *citizens*,[1] if those indeed who disclaim the laws of Rome deserve to be ranked among the meanest of the people." His menaces inflamed the fury of the legion, and their brandished arms already threatened his person. " Your courage," resumed the intrepid Alexander, " would be more nobly displayed in the field of battle; *me* you may destroy, you cannot intimidate; and the severe justice of the republic would punish your crime, and revenge my death." The legion still persisted in clamorous sedition, when the emperor pronounced, with a loud voice, the decisive sentence, " *Citizens !* lay down your arms, and depart in peace to your respective habitations." The tempest was instantly appeased; the soldiers, filled with grief and shame, silently confessed the justice of their punishment and the power of discipline, yielded up their arms and military ensigns, and retired in confusion, not to their camp, but to the several inns of the city. Alexander enjoyed, during thirty days, the edifying spectacle of their repentance; nor did he restore them to their former rank in the army, till he had punished with death those tribunes whose connivance had occasioned the mutiny. The grateful legion served the emperor, whilst living, and revenged him when dead.[2]

The resolutions of the multitude generally depend on a moment; and the caprice of passion might equally determine the seditious legion to lay down their arms at the emperor's feet, or to plunge them into his breast. Perhaps, if the singular

---

[1] Julius Cæsar had appeased a sedition with the same word *Quirites ;* which thus opposed to *Soldiers*, was used in a sense of contempt, and reduced the offenders to the less honourable condition of mere citizens. Tacit. Annal. i. 42.

[2] Hist. August. p. 132.

transaction had been investigated by the penetration of a philosopher, we should discover the secret causes which on that occasion authorised the boldness of the prince, and commanded the
obedience of the troops; and perhaps, if it had been related by
a judicious historian, we should find this action, worthy of Cæsar
himself, reduced nearer to the level of probability and the common
standard of the character of Alexander Severus. The abilities
of that amiable prince seem to have been inadequate to the
difficulties of his situation, the firmness of his conduct inferior to
the purity of his intentions. His virtues, as well as the vices of
Elagabalus, contracted a tincture of weakness and effeminacy
from the soft climate of Syria, of which he was a native; though
he blushed at his foreign origin, and listened with a vain complacency to the flattering genealogists, who derived his race from
the ancient stock of Roman nobility.[1] The pride and avarice
of his mother cast a shade on the glories of his reign; and by
exacting from his riper years the same dutiful obedience which
she had justly claimed from his inexperienced youth, Mamæa
exposed to public ridicule, both her son's character and her
own.[2] The fatigues of the Persian war irritated the military
discontent; the unsuccessful event degraded the reputation of
the emperor as a general, and even as a soldier. Every cause
prepared, and every circumstance hastened, a revolution, which
distracted the Roman empire with a long series of intestine
calamities.

The dissolute tyranny of Commodus, the civil wars occasioned
by his death, and the new maxims of policy introduced by the
house of Severus, had all contributed to increase the dangerous
power of the army, and to obliterate the faint image of laws and
liberty that was still impressed on the minds of the Romans.
This internal change, which undermined the foundations of the
empire, we have endeavoured to explain with some degree of

---

[1] From the Metelli. Hist. August. [Lamprid. Alexander Sev. c. 44] p. 119.
The choice was judicious. In one short period of twelve years, the Metelli
could reckon seven consulships and five triumphs. Velleius Paterculus,
ii. 11, and the Fasti.

[2] The Life of Alexander, in the Augustan History, is the mere idea of a
perfect prince, an awkward imitation of the Cyropædia. The account of
his reign, as given by Herodian, is rational and moderate, consistent with
the general history of the age; and, in some of the most invidious particulars, confirmed by the decisive fragments of Dion. Yet from a very
paltry prejudice, the greater number of our modern writers abuse Herodian,
and copy the Augustan History. Mess. de Tillemont and Wotton. From
the opposite prejudice, the emperor Julian (in Cæsarib. p. 315) dwells with
a visible satisfaction on the effeminate weakness of the *Syrian*, and the
ridiculous avarice of his mother.

order and perspicuity. The personal characters of the emperors, their victories, laws, follies, and fortunes, can interest us no farther than as they are connected with the general history of the Decline and Fall of the monarchy. Our constant attention to that great object will not suffer us to overlook a most important edict of Antoninus Caracalla, which communicated to all the free inhabitants of the empire the name and privileges of Roman citizens. His unbounded liberality flowed not, however, from the sentiments of a generous mind; it was the sordid result of avarice, and will naturally be illustrated by some observations on the finances of that state, from the victorious ages of the commonwealth to the reign of Alexander Severus.

The siege of Veii in Tuscany, the first considerable enterprise of the Romans, was protracted to the tenth year, much less by the strength of the place than by the unskilfulness of the besiegers. The unaccustomed hardships of so many winter campaigns, at the distance of near twenty miles from home,[1] required more than common encouragements; and the senate wisely prevented the clamours of the people, by the institution of a regular pay for the soldiers, which was levied by a general tribute, assessed according to an equitable proportion on the property of the citizens.[2] During more than two hundred years after the conquest of Veii, the victories of the republic added less to the wealth than to the power of Rome. The states of Italy paid their tribute in military service only, and the vast force both by sea and land, which was exerted in the Punic wars, was maintained at the expense of the Romans themselves. That high-spirited people (such is often the generous enthusiasm of freedom) cheerfully submitted to the most excessive but voluntary burdens, in the just confidence that they should speedily enjoy the rich harvest of their labours. Their expectations were not

---

[1] According to the more accurate Dionysius, the city itself was only an hundred stadia, or twelve miles and a half, from Rome; though some outposts might be advanced farther on the side of Etruria. Nardini, in a professed treatise, has combated the popular opinion and the authority of two popes, and has removed Veii from Civita Castellana, to a little spot called Isola, in the midway between Rome and the lake Bracciano.

[2] Cf. Livy, b. iv. c. 59 and b. v. c. 7. In the Roman Census, property, power, and taxation, were commensurate with each other.

[The most important part of the revenue of the Roman state under the Republic was derived from the *tributum* or property-tax, imposed by the constitution of Servius Tullius, upon the assessed value of every kind of property belonging to Roman citizens; but as the chief part of the property of Roman citizens was land, the tributum was chiefly a land-tax. The tax was abolished in B.C. 147 on the conquest of Macedonia, and was never imposed again. From that date Italy was free from direct taxation.— O. S.]

disappointed. In the course of a few years, the riches of
Syracuse, of Carthage, of Macedonia, and of Asia, were brought
in triumph to Rome. The treasures of Perseus alone amounted
to near two millions sterling, and the Roman people, the
sovereign of so many nations, was for ever delivered from the
weight of taxes.[1] The increasing revenue of the provinces was
found sufficient to defray the ordinary establishment of war and
government, and the superfluous mass of gold and silver was
deposited in the temple of Saturn, and reserved for any unfore-
seen emergency of the state.[2]

History has never perhaps suffered a greater or more irreparable
injury, than in the loss of the curious register bequeathed by
Augustus to the senate, in which that experienced prince so
accurately balanced the revenues and expenses of the Roman
empire.[3] Deprived of this clear and comprehensive estimate,
we are reduced to collect a few imperfect hints from such of the
ancients as have accidentally turned aside from the splendid to
the more useful parts of history. We are informed that, by the
conquests of Pompey, the tributes of Asia were raised from fifty
to one hundred and thirty-five millions of drachms; or about
four millions and a half sterling.[4] Under the last and most
indolent of the Ptolemies, the revenue of Egypt is said to have
amounted to twelve thousand five hundred talents; a sum
equivalent to more than two millions and a half of our money,
but which was afterwards considerably improved by the more
exact economy of the Romans, and the increase of the trade of
Æthiopia and India.[5] Gaul was enriched by rapine, as Egypt
was by commerce, and the tributes of those two great provinces
have been compared as nearly equal to each other in value.[6]
The ten thousand Euboic or Phœnician talents, about four
millions sterling,[7] which vanquished Carthage was condemned

[1] Plin. Hist. Natur. l. xxxiii. c. 3. Cicero de Offic. ii. 22. Plutarch in
P. Æmil. p. 275.
[2] See a fine description of this accumulated wealth of ages, in Lucan's
Phars. l. iii. v. 155.
[3] Tacit. in Annal. i. 11. It seems to have existed in the time of Appian.
[4] Plutarch. in Pompeio. p. 642.   [5] Strabo, l. xvii. p. 798.
[6] Velleius Paterculus, l. ii. c. 39. He seems to give the preference to the
revenue of Gaul.
[When Cæsar conquered Gaul he imposed on it a tribute of 40 millions of
sesterces, or £429,000. This was increased, however, and in the time of
Constantine the tribute of the Gallic provinces amounted to £4,200,000.—
O. S.]
[7] The Euboic, the Phœnician, and the Alexandrian talents were double
in weight to the Attic. Hooper on ancient weights and measures, p. iv.
c. 5. It is very probable, that the same talent was carried from Tyre to
Carthage.
[It is not correct to say that the Euboic, Phœnician, and Alexandrian

to pay within the term of fifty years, were a slight acknowledgment of the superiority of Rome,[1] and cannot bear the least proportion with the taxes afterwards raised both on the lands and
on the persons of the inhabitants, when the fertile coast of Africa
was reduced into a province.[2]

Spain, by a very singular fatality, was the Peru and Mexico
of the old world. The discovery of the rich western continent by
the Phœnicians, and the oppression of the simple natives, who
were compelled to labour in their own mines for the benefit of
strangers, form an exact type of the more recent history of
Spanish America.[3] The Phœnicians were acquainted only with
the sea-coast of Spain; avarice, as well as ambition, carried the
arms of Rome and Carthage into the heart of the country, and
almost every part of the soil was found pregnant with copper,
silver, and gold. Mention is made of a mine near Carthagena
which yielded every day twenty-five thousand drachms of silver,
or about three hundred thousand pounds a year.[4] Twenty
thousand pound weight of gold was annually received from the
provinces of Asturia, Gallicia, and Lusitania.[5]

We want both leisure and materials to pursue this curious
inquiry through the many potent states that were annihilated
in the Roman empire. Some notion, however, may be formed
of the revenue of the provinces where considerable wealth had
been deposited by nature, or collected by man, if we observe the
severe attention that was directed to the abodes of solitude and
sterility. Augustus once received a petition from the inhabitants of Gyarus, humbly praying that they might be relieved
from one-third of their excessive impositions. Their whole tax
amounted indeed to no more than one hundred and fifty drachms,
or about five pounds; but Gyarus was a little island, or rather a
rock, of the Ægean Sea, destitute of fresh water and every
necessary of life, and inhabited only by a few wretched fishermen.[6]

talents were double the weight of the Attic. The Euboic was the same as
the old Attic talent, *i.e.* that in use in Solon's time, and was not double in
weight to the later Attic. It has been shown by Boeckh that the true
ratio between the Euboic and the later Attic talents was 100 to 72, or nearly
4 to 3.—O. S.]

[1] Polyb. l. xv. c. 2.   [2] Appian in Punicis, p. 84.

[3] Diodorus Siculus, l. v.   Cadiz was built by the Phœnicians a little
more than a thousand years before Christ. Vell. Paterc. i. 2.

[4] Strabo, l. iii. p. 148.

[5] Plin. Hist. Natur. l. xxxiii. c. 3.   He mentions likewise a silver mine in
Dalmatia, that yielded every day fifty pounds to the state.

[6] Strabo, l. x. p. 485.   Tacit. Annal. iii. 69 and iv. 30.   Tournefort
(Voyages au Levant, Lettre viii.) gives a very lively picture of the actual
misery of Gyarus.

From the faint glimmerings of such doubtful and scattered lights we should be inclined to believe, 1st, That (with every fair allowance for the difference of times and circumstances) the general income of the Roman provinces could seldom amount to less than fifteen or twenty millions of our money;[1] and, 2ndly, That so ample a revenue must have been fully adequate to all the expenses of the moderate government instituted by Augustus, whose court was the modest family of a private senator, and whose military establishment was calculated for the defence of the frontiers, without any aspiring views of conquest, or any serious apprehension of a foreign invasion.

Notwithstanding the seeming probability of both these conclusions, the latter of them at least is positively disowned by the language and conduct of Augustus. It is not easy to determine whether, on this occasion, he acted as the common father of the Roman world, or as the oppressor of liberty; whether he wished to relieve the provinces, or to impoverish the senate and the equestrian order. But no sooner had he assumed the reins of government than he frequently intimated the insufficiency of the tributes, and the necessity of throwing an equitable proportion of the public burden upon Rome and Italy. In the prosecution of this unpopular design, he advanced, however, by cautious and well-weighed steps. The introduction of customs was followed by the establishment of an excise, and the scheme of taxation was completed by an artful assessment on the real and personal property of the Roman citizens, who had been exempted from any kind of contribution above a century and a half.

I. In a great empire like that of Rome, a natural balance of money must have gradually established itself. It has been already observed, that as the wealth of the provinces was attracted to the capital by the strong hand of conquest and power, so a considerable part of it was restored to the industrious provinces by the gentle influence of commerce and arts. In the reign of Augustus and his successors, duties were imposed on every kind of merchandise, which through a thousand channels flowed to the great centre of opulence and luxury; and in whatsoever manner the law was expressed, it was the Roman purchaser, and not the provincial merchant, who paid the tax.[2] The rate of the customs varied from the eighth to the fortieth part of the value of the commodity; and we have a right to suppose

[1] Lipsius de magnitudine Romanâ (l. ii. c. 3) computes the revenue at one hundred and fifty millions of gold crowns; but his whole book, though learned and ingenious, betrays a very heated imagination.
[2] Tacit. Annal. xiii. 31.

that the variation was directed by the unalterable maxims of policy: that a higher duty was fixed on the articles of luxury than on those of necessity, and that the productions raised or manufactured by the labour of the subjects of the empire, were treated with more indulgence than was shown to the pernicious, or at least the unpopular, commerce of Arabia and India.[1] There is still extant a long but imperfect catalogue of eastern commodities, which about the time of Alexander Severus were subject to the payment of duties; cinnamon, myrrh, pepper, ginger, and the whole tribe of aromatics, a great variety of precious stones, among which the diamond was the most remarkable for its price, and the emerald for its beauty.[2] Parthian and Babylonian leather, cottons, silks, both raw and manufactured, ebony, ivory, and eunuchs.[3] We may observe that the use and value of those effeminate slaves gradually rose with the decline of the empire.

II. The excise, introduced by Augustus after the civil wars, was extremely moderate, but it was general. It seldom exceeded one per cent.; but it comprehended whatever was sold in the markets or by public auction, from the most considerable purchases of lands and houses to those minute objects which can only derive a value from their infinite multitude and daily consumption. Such a tax, as it affects the body of the people, has ever been the occasion of clamour and discontent. An emperor well acquainted with the wants and resources of the state, was obliged to declare by a public edict that the support of the army depended in a great measure on the produce of the excise.[4]

III. When Augustus resolved to establish a permanent military force for the defence of his government against foreign and domestic enemies, he instituted a peculiar treasury for the pay of the soldiers, the rewards of the veterans, and the extraordinary expenses of war. The ample revenue of the excise, though peculiarly appropriated to those uses, was found inadequate. To supply the deficiency, the emperor suggested a new tax of five per cent. on all legacies and inheritances. But the nobles of

---

[1] Pliny (Hist. Natur. l. vi. c. 28 [s. 32]; l. xii. c. 18). His observation, that the Indian commodities were sold at Rome at a hundred times their original price, may give us some notion of the produce of the customs, since that original price amounted to more than eight hundred thousand pounds.

[2] The ancients were unacquainted with the art of cutting diamonds.

[3] M. Bouchaud, in his treatise de l'Impot chez les Romains, has transcribed this catalogue from the Digest, and attempts to illustrate it by a very prolix commentary. [In the Pandects, 39 (tit. 6, l. 16, § 7), de Publican. See also Cicero in Verrem.—O. S.]

[4] Tacit. Annal. i. 78. Two years afterwards, the reduction of the poor kingdom of Cappadocia gave Tiberius a pretence for diminishing the excise to one half; but the relief was of very short duration.

Rome were more tenacious of property than of freedom. Their indignant murmurs were received by Augustus with his usual temper. He candidly referred the whole business to the senate, and exhorted them to provide for the public service by some other expedient of a less odious nature. They were divided and perplexed. He insinuated to them that their obstinacy would oblige him to *propose* a general land-tax and capitation. They acquiesced in silence.[1] The new imposition on legacies and inheritances was however mitigated by some restrictions. It did not take place unless the object was of a certain value, most probably of fifty or an hundred pieces of gold,[2] nor could it be exacted from the nearest of kin on the father's side.[3] When the rights of nature and poverty were thus secured, it seemed reasonable that a stranger, or a distant relation, who acquired an unexpected accession of fortune, should cheerfully resign a twentieth part of it for the benefit of the state.[4]

Such a tax, plentiful as it must prove in every wealthy community, was most happily suited to the situation of the Romans, who could frame their arbitrary wills, according to the dictates of reason or caprice, without any restraint from the modern fetters of entails and settlements. From various causes the partiality of paternal affection often lost its influence over the stern patriots of the commonwealth and the dissolute nobles of the empire; and if the father bequeathed to his son the fourth part of his estate, he removed all ground of legal complaint.[5] But a rich childless old man was a domestic tyrant, and his power increased with his years and infirmities. A servile crowd, in which he frequently reckoned prætors and consuls, courted his smiles, pampered his avarice, applauded his follies, served his passions, and waited with impatience for his death. The arts of attendance and flattery were formed into a most lucrative science; those who professed it acquired a peculiar appellation;

---

[1] Dion Cassius, l. lv. p. 794, l. lvi. p. 825.

[The tax of five per cent. on all legacies and inheritances (vicesima hereditatium et legatorum) was only levied on property bequeathed by Roman citizens, and was therefore paid chiefly by the inhabitants of Italy. It was an ingenious mode of imposing a property-tax upon the inhabitants of Italy, and was a sort of equivalent of the land-tax paid by the provinces. All inheritances below 100,000 sesterces and the nearest relations by blood were exempt.—O. S.]

[2] The sum is only fixed by conjecture.

[3] As the Roman law subsisted for many ages, the *Cognati*, or relations on the mother's side, were not called to the succession. This harsh institution was gradually undermined by humanity, and finally abolished by Justinian.

[4] Plin. Panegyric. c. 37.

[5] Heineccius in the Antiquit. Juris Romani, l. ii.

and the whole city, according to the lively descriptions of satire,
was divided between two parties, the hunters and their game.[1]
Yet, while so many unjust and extravagant wills were every day
dictated by cunning, and subscribed by folly, a few were the
result of rational esteem and virtuous gratitude. Cicero, who
had so often defended the lives and fortunes of his fellow-citizens,
was rewarded with legacies to the amount of an hundred and
seventy thousand pounds;[2] nor do the friends of the younger
Pliny seem to have been less generous to that amiable orator.[3]
Whatever was the motive of the testator, the treasury claimed,
without distinction, the twentieth part of his estate; and in the
course of two or three generations, the whole property of the subject must have gradually passed through the coffers of the state.

In the first and golden years of the reign of Nero, that prince,
from a desire of popularity, and perhaps from a blind impulse of
benevolence, conceived a wish of abolishing the oppression of the
customs and excise. The wisest senators applauded his magnanimity; but they diverted him from the execution of a design,
which would have dissolved the strength and resources of the
republic.[4] Had it indeed been possible to realise this dream of
fancy, such princes as Trajan and the Antonines would surely
have embraced with ardour the glorious opportunity of conferring so signal an obligation on mankind. Satisfied, however,
with alleviating the public burden, they attempted not to
remove it. The mildness and precision of their laws ascertained
the rule and measure of taxation, and protected the subject of
every rank against arbitrary interpretations, antiquated claims,
and the insolent vexation of the farmers of the revenue.[5] For
it is somewhat singular that, in every age, the best and wisest
of the Roman governors persevered in this pernicious method of
collecting the principal branches at least of the excise and
customs.[6]

The sentiments, and, indeed, the situation of Caracalla, were
very different from those of the Antonines. Inattentive, or
rather averse, to the welfare of his people, he found himself

[1] Horat. l. ii. Sat. v.   Petron. c. 116, etc.   Plin. l. ii. Epist. 20.
[2] Cicero in Philipp. ii. c. 16.
[3] See his Epistles. Every such will gave him an occasion of displaying
his reverence to the dead, and his justice to the living. He reconciled both
in his behaviour to a son who had been disinherited by his mother (v. 1).
[4] Tacit. Annal. xiii. 50.   Esprit des Loix, l. xii. c. 19.
[5] Pliny's Panegyric, the Augustan History, and Burman de Vectigal,
passim.
[6] The tributes (properly so called) were not farmed; since the good
princes often remitted many millions of arrears.

under the necessity of gratifying the insatiate avarice, which he had excited in the army. Of the several impositions introduced by Augustus, the twentieth on inheritances and legacies was the most fruitful, as well as the most comprehensive. As its influence was not confined to Rome or Italy, the produce continually increased with the gradual extension of the ROMAN CITY. The new citizens, though charged, on equal terms,[1] with the payment of new taxes, which had not affected them as subjects, derived an ample compensation from the rank they obtained, the privileges they acquired, and the fair prospect of honours and fortune that was thrown open to their ambition. But the favour which implied a distinction, was lost in the prodigality of Caracalla, and the reluctant provincials were compelled to assume the vain title, and the real obligations, of Roman citizens. Nor was the rapacious son of Severus contented with such a measure of taxation, as had appeared sufficient to his moderate predecessors. Instead of a twentieth, he exacted a tenth of all legacies and inheritances; and during his reign (for the ancient proportion was restored after his death) he crushed alike every part of the empire under the weight of his iron sceptre.[2]

When all the provincials became liable to the peculiar impositions of Roman citizens, they seemed to acquire a legal exemption from the tributes which they had paid in their former condition of subjects. Such were not the maxims of government adopted by Caracalla and his pretended son. The old as well as the new taxes were, at the same time, levied in the provinces. It was reserved for the virtue of Alexander to relieve them in a great measure from this intolerable grievance, by reducing the tributes to a thirtieth part of the sum exacted at the time of his accession.[3]

[1] The situation of the new citizens is minutely described by Pliny (Pane gyric, c. 37, 38, 39). Trajan published a law very much in their favour.

[2] Dion, l. lxxvii. p. 1295. [This tax was abrogated in the sixth century. —O. S.]

[3] He who paid ten *aurei*, the usual tribute, was charged with no more than the third part of an aureus, and proportional pieces of gold were coined by Alexander's order. Hist. August. p. 127, with the commentary of Salmasius.

[Gibbon has omitted to mention the important change introduced during the first two centuries of the empire in the system of taxation in the provinces. The following information may therefore be useful, taken from Sartigny's Essay: In the time of the Republic the system of taxation differed in the various provinces. All the provinces save Sicily paid either a fixed land-tax (*vectigal stipendiarium*) or variable duties such as tithes or other portion of the produce. Without respect to their differences all land in the provinces bore the general name " agri vectigales," which consequently was the name for all land which paid taxes, since Italy was exempt. At the outset of Imperial rule, an attempt was made to introduce uniformity of taxation in provinces by abolishing variable duties and sub-

It is impossible to conjecture the motive that engaged him to spare so trifling a remnant of the public evil; but the noxious weed, which had not been totally eradicated, again sprang up with the most luxuriant growth, and in the succeeding age darkened the Roman world with its deadly shade. In the course of this history, we shall be too often summoned to explain the land-tax, the capitation, and the heavy contributions of corn, wine, oil, and meat, which were exacted from the provinces for the use of the court, the army, and the capital.

As long as Rome and Italy were respected as the centre of government, a national spirit was preserved by the ancient, and insensibly imbibed by the adopted, citizens. The principal commands of the army were filled by men who had received a liberal education, were well instructed in the advantages of laws and letters, and who had risen, by equal steps, through the regular succession of civil and military honours.[1] To their influence and example we may partly ascribe the modest obedience of the legions during the two first centuries of the Imperial history.

But when the last enclosure of the Roman constitution was trampled down by Caracalla, the separation of professions gradually succeeded to the distinction of ranks. The more polished citizens of the internal provinces were alone qualified to act as lawyers and magistrates. The rougher trade of arms was abandoned to the peasants and barbarians of the frontiers, who knew no country but their camp, no science but that of war, no civil laws, and scarcely those of military discipline. With bloody hands, savage manners, and desperate resolutions, they sometimes guarded, but much oftener subverted, the throne of the emperors.

stituting a land-tax. With this view a census of property was taken by order of Augustus, and the land-tax was introduced by him into some, but it did not become general until the age of M. Aurelius, when the new system of taxation was completed.—O. S.]

[1] See the Lives of Agricola, Vespasian, Trajan, Severus, and his three competitors; and indeed of all the eminent men of those times.

CHAPTER VII

The Elevation and Tyranny of Maximin—Rebellion in Africa and Italy,
under the Authority of the Senate—Civil Wars and Seditions—Violent
Deaths of Maximin and his Son, of Maximus and Balbinus, and of the
three Gordians—Usurpation and secular Games of Philip

OF the various forms of government which have prevailed in the
world, an hereditary monarchy seems to present the fairest scope
for ridicule.   Is it possible to relate, without an indignant smile,
that, on the father's decease, the property of a nation, like that
of a drove of oxen, descends to his infant son, as yet unknown
to mankind and to himself; and that the bravest warriors and
the wisest statesmen, relinquishing their natural right to empire,
approach the royal cradle with bended knees and protestations
of inviolable fidelity?   Satire and declamation may paint these
obvious topics in the most dazzling colours, but our more serious
thoughts will respect a useful prejudice, that establishes a rule of
succession, independent of the passions of mankind; and we shall
cheerfully acquiesce in any expedient which deprives the multitude of the dangerous, and indeed the ideal, power of giving
themselves a master.

In the cool shade of retirement, we may easily devise imaginary
forms of government, in which the sceptre shall be constantly
bestowed on the most worthy, by the free and incorrupt suffrage of the whole community.   Experience overturns these airy
fabrics, and teaches us that, in a large society, the election
of a monarch can never devolve to the wisest, or to the most
numerous, part of the people.   The army is the only order of
men sufficiently united to concur in the same sentiments, and
powerful enough to impose them on the rest of their fellow-
citizens: but the temper of soldiers, habituated at once to
violence and to slavery, renders them very unfit guardians of a
legal, or even a civil, constitution.   Justice, humanity, or
political wisdom, are qualities they are too little acquainted
with in themselves, to appreciate them in others.   Valour will
acquire their esteem, and liberality will purchase their suffrage;
but the first of these merits is often lodged in the most savage
breasts; the latter can only exert itself at the expense of the
public; and both may be turned against the possessor of the
throne, by the ambition of a daring rival.

The superior prerogative of birth, when it has obtained the
sanction of time and popular opinion, is the plainest and least

invidious of all distinctions among mankind. The acknowledged right extinguishes the hopes of faction, and the conscious security disarms the cruelty of the monarch. To the firm establishment of this idea, we owe the peaceful succession, and mild administration, of European monarchies. To the defect of it, we must attribute the frequent civil wars, through which an Asiatic despot is obliged to cut his way to the throne of his fathers. Yet, even in the East, the sphere of contention is usually limited to the princes of the reigning house, and as soon as the more fortunate competitor has removed his brethren, by the sword and the bow-string, he no longer entertains any jealousy of his meaner subjects. But the Roman empire, after the authority of the senate had sunk into contempt, was a vast scene of confusion. The royal, and even noble, families of the provinces, had long since been led in triumph before the car of the haughty republicans. The ancient families of Rome had successively fallen beneath the tyranny of the Cæsars; and whilst those princes were shackled by the forms of a commonwealth, and disappointed by the repeated failure of their posterity,[1] it was impossible that any idea of hereditary succession should have taken root in the minds of their subjects. The right to the throne, which none could claim from birth, every one assumed from merit. The daring hopes of ambition were set loose from the salutary restraints of law and prejudice; and the meanest of mankind might, without folly, entertain a hope of being raised by valour and fortune to a rank in the army, in which a single crime would enable him to wrest the sceptre of the world from his feeble and unpopular master. After the murder of Alexander Severus, and the elevation of Maximin, no emperor could think himself safe upon the throne, and every barbarian peasant of the frontier might aspire to that august, but dangerous station.

About thirty-two years before that event, the emperor Severus, returning from an eastern expedition, halted in Thrace, to celebrate, with military games, the birthday of his younger son, Geta. The country flocked in crowds to behold their sovereign, and a young barbarian of gigantic stature earnestly solicited, in his rude dialect, that he might be allowed to contend for the prize of wrestling. As the pride of discipline would have been disgraced in the overthrow of a Roman soldier by a Thracian peasant, he was matched with the stoutest followers of the camp,

---

[1] There had been no example of three successive generations on the throne; only three instances of sons who succeeded their fathers. The marriages of the Cæsars (notwithstanding the permission, and the frequent practice, of divorces) were generally unfruitful.

sixteen of whom he successively laid on the ground. His victory was rewarded by some trifling gifts, and a permission to inlist in the troops. The next day, the happy barbarian was distinguished above a crowd of recruits, dancing and exulting after the fashion of his country. As soon as he perceived that he had attracted the emperor's notice, he instantly ran up to his horse, and followed him on foot, without the least appearance of fatigue, in a long and rapid career. "Thracian," said Severus, with astonishment, "art thou disposed to wrestle after thy race?" Most willingly, Sir, replied the unwearied youth, and, almost in a breath, overthrew seven of the strongest soldiers in the army. A gold collar was the prize of his matchless vigour and activity, and he was immediately appointed to serve in the horse-guards who always attended on the person of the sovereign.[1]

Maximin, for that was his name, though born on the territories of the empire, descended from a mixed race of barbarians. His father was a Goth, and his mother of the nation of the Alani.[2] He displayed, on every occasion, a valour equal to his strength; and his native fierceness was soon tempered or disguised by the knowledge of the world. Under the reign of Severus and his son, he obtained the rank of centurion, with the favour and esteem of both those princes, the former of whom was an excellent judge of merit. Gratitude forbade Maximin to serve under the assassin of Caracalla. Honour taught him to decline the effeminate insults of Elagabalus. On the accession of Alexander he returned to court, and was placed by that prince in a station useful to the service and honourable to himself. The fourth legion, to which he was appointed tribune, soon became, under his care, the best disciplined of the whole army. With the general applause of the soldiers, who bestowed on their favourite hero the names of Ajax and Hercules, he was successively promoted to the first military command;[3] and had not he still retained too much of his savage origin, the emperor might perhaps have given his own sister in marriage to the son of Maximin.[4]

Instead of securing his fidelity, these favours served only to inflame the ambition of the Thracian peasant, who deemed his

---

[1] Hist. August. p. 138 [Capitol. Max. c. 1 seqq.].

[2] [The name of the father was Micca, and of the mother Ababa.—O. S.]

[3] Hist. August. p. 140. Herodian, l. vi. p. 223. Aurelius Victor. By comparing these authors, it should seem, that Maximin had the particular command of the Triballian horse, with the general commission of disciplining the recruits of the whole army. His Biographer ought to have marked, with more care, his exploits, and the successive steps of his military promotions.

[4] Original letter of Alexander Severus, Hist. August. p. 149.

fortune inadequate to his merit, as long as he was constrained to acknowledge a superior. Though a stranger to real wisdom, he was not devoid of a selfish cunning, which showed him that the emperor had lost the affection of the army, and taught him to improve their discontent to his own advantage. It is easy for faction and calumny to shed their poison on the administration of the best of princes, and to accuse even their virtues, by artfully confounding them with those vices to which they bear the nearest affinity. The troops listened with pleasure to the emissaries of Maximin. They blushed at their own ignominious patience, which, during thirteen years, had supported the vexatious discipline imposed by an effeminate Syrian, the timid slave of his mother and of the senate. It was time, they cried, to cast away that useless phantom of the civil power, and to elect for their prince and general a real soldier, educated in camps, exercised in war, who would assert the glory, and distribute among his companions the treasures, of the empire. A great army was at that time assembled on the banks of the Rhine, under the command of the emperor himself, who, almost immediately after his return from the Persian war, had been obliged to march against the barbarians of Germany. The important care of training and reviewing the new levies was intrusted to Maximin. One day (A.D. 235, March 19), as he entered the field of exercise, the troops, either from a sudden impulse or a formed conspiracy, saluted him emperor, silenced by their loud acclamations his obstinate refusal, and hastened to consummate their rebellion by the murder of Alexander Severus.

The circumstances of his death are variously related. The writers, who suppose that he died in ignorance of the ingratitude and ambition of Maximin, affirm that, after taking a frugal repast in the sight of the army, he retired to sleep, and that, about the seventh hour of the day, a part of his own guards broke into the imperial tent, and with many wounds assassinated their virtuous and unsuspecting prince.[1] If we credit another,

---

[1] Hist. August. p. 135. I have softened some of the most improbable circumstances of this wretched biographer. From this ill-worded narration, it should seem, that the prince's buffoon having accidentally entered the tent, and awakened the slumbering monarch, the fear of punishment urged him to persuade the disaffected soldiers to commit the murder.

[Maximin was rapidly promoted both by Septimius Severus and Alexander Severus. The latter promoted him to the command of a legion, the discipline of which was soon restored by Maximin. This shows that after all he cannot have been merely an ordinary man. He must have had a true soldier's nature; a person who was able to make himself popular with a demoralised army, notwithstanding his strictness and cruelty, must have

and indeed a more probable account, Maximin was invested with
the purple by a numerous detachment, at the distance of several
miles from the head-quarters; and he trusted for success rather
to the secret wishes than to the public declarations of the great
army. Alexander had sufficient time to awaken a faint sense
of loyalty among his troops; but their reluctant professions of
fidelity quickly vanished on the appearance of Maximin, who
declared himself the friend and advocate of the military order,
and was unanimously acknowledged emperor of the Romans
by the applauding legions. The son of Mamæa, betrayed and
deserted, withdrew into his tent, desirous at least to conceal his
approaching fate from the insults of the multitude. He was
soon followed by a tribune and some centurions, the ministers
of death; but, instead of receiving with manly resolution the
inevitable stroke, his unavailing cries and entreaties disgraced
the last moments of his life, and converted into contempt some
portion of the just pity which his innocence and misfortunes
must inspire. His mother Mamæa, whose pride and avarice he
loudly accused as the cause of his ruin, perished with her son.
The most faithful of his friends were sacrificed to the first fury
of the soldiers. Others were reserved for the more deliberate
cruelty of the usurper; and those who experienced the mildest
treatment, were stripped of their employments, and ignominiously driven from the court and army.[1]

The former tyrants, Caligula and Nero, Commodus and
Caracalla, were all dissolute and inexperienced youths,[2] educated
in the purple, and corrupted by the pride of empire, the luxury
of Rome, and the perfidious voice of flattery. The cruelty of
Maximin was derived from a different source, the fear of contempt. Though he depended on the attachment of the soldiers,
who loved him for virtues like their own, he was conscious that
his mean and barbarian origin, his savage appearance, and his
total ignorance of the arts and institutions of civil life,[3] formed
a very unfavourable contrast with the amiable manners of the
unhappy Alexander. He remembered that, in his humbler for-

been an extraordinary man. He was the first Roman emperor who was
altogether without literary education. Niebuhr's Lectures on the History
of Rome, Lecture cxxxvii. See also the *Maximin* by J. Capitolin.—O. S.]
[1] Herodian, l. vi. p. 223-227.
[2] Caligula, the eldest of the four, was only twenty-five years of age when
he ascended the throne; Caracalla was twenty-three, Commodus nineteen,
and Nero no more than seventeen.
[3] It appears that he was totally ignorant of the Greek language: which,
from its universal use in conversation and letters, was an essential part of
every liberal education.

tune, he had often waited before the door of the haughty nobles
of Rome, and had been denied admittance by the insolence of
their slaves. He recollected too the friendship of a few who had
relieved his poverty, and assisted his rising hopes. But those
who had spurned, and those who had protected the Thracian,
were guilty of the same crime, the knowledge of his original
obscurity. For this crime many were put to death; and by the
execution of several of his benefactors, Maximin published, in
characters of blood, the indelible history of his baseness and
ingratitude.[1]

The dark and sanguinary soul of the tyrant was open to every
suspicion against those among his subjects who were the most
distinguished by their birth or merit. Whenever he was alarmed
with the sound of treason, his cruelty was unbounded and unrelenting. A conspiracy against his life was either discovered or
imagined, and Magnus, a consular senator, was named as the
principal author of it. Without a witness, without a trial, and
without an opportunity of defence, Magnus, with four thousand
of his supposed accomplices, were put to death. Italy and the
whole empire were infested with innumerable spies and informers.
On the slightest accusation, the first of the Roman nobles, who
had governed provinces, commanded armies, and been adorned
with the consular and triumphal ornaments, were chained on the
public carriages, and hurried away to the emperor's presence.
Confiscation, exile, or simple death, were esteemed uncommon
instances of his lenity. Some of the unfortunate sufferers he
ordered to be sewed up in the hides of slaughtered animals, others
to be exposed to wild beasts, others again to be beaten to death
with clubs. During the three years of his reign, he disdained to
visit either Rome or Italy. His camp, occasionally removed
from the banks of the Rhine to those of the Danube, was the seat
of his stern despotism, which trampled on every principle of law
and justice, and was supported by the avowed power of the
sword.[2] No man of noble birth, elegant accomplishments, or
knowledge of civil business, was suffered near his person; and
the court of a Roman emperor revived the idea of those ancient

---

[1] Hist. August. p. 141. Herodian, l. vii. p. 237. The latter of these
historians has been most unjustly censured for sparing the vices of Maximin.

[2] The wife of Maximin, by insinuating wise counsels with female gentle-
ness, sometimes brought back the tyrant to the way of truth and
humanity. See Ammianus Marcellinus, l. xiv. c. 1, where he alludes to the
fact which he had more fully related under the reign of the Gordians. We
may collect from the medals, that Paullina was the name of this benevolent
empress; and from the title of *Diva*, that she died before Maximin.
(Valesius ad loc. cit. Ammian.) Spanheim de U. et P. N. tom. ii. p. 300.

chiefs of slaves and gladiators, whose savage power had left a deep impression of terror and detestation.[1]

As long as the cruelty of Maximin was confined to the illustrious senators, or even to the bold adventurers, who in the court or army expose themselves to the caprice of fortune, the body of the people viewed their sufferings with indifference, or perhaps with pleasure. But the tyrant's avarice, stimulated by the insatiate desires of the soldiers, at length attacked the public property. Every city of the empire was possessed of an independent revenue, destined to purchase corn for the multitude, and to supply the expenses of the games and entertainments. By a single act of authority, the whole mass of wealth was at once confiscated for the use of the Imperial treasury. The temples were stripped of their most valuable offerings of gold and silver, and the statues of gods, heroes, and emperors, were melted down and coined into money. These impious orders could not be executed without tumults and massacres, as in many places the people chose rather to die in the defence of their altars, than to behold in the midst of peace their cities exposed to the rapine and cruelty of war. The soldiers themselves, among whom this sacrilegious plunder was distributed, received it with a blush; and, hardened as they were in acts of violence, they dreaded the just reproaches of their friends and relations. Throughout the Roman world a general cry of indignation was heard, imploring vengeance on the common enemy of human kind; and at length, by an act of private oppression, a peaceful and unarmed province was driven into rebellion against him.[2]

The procurator of Africa was a servant worthy of such a master, who considered the fines and confiscations of the rich as one of the most fruitful branches of the Imperial revenue. An iniquitous sentence had been (A.D. 237, April) pronounced against some opulent youths of that country, the execution of which would have stripped them of far the greater part of their patrimony. In this extremity, a resolution that must either complete or prevent their ruin, was dictated by despair. A respite of three days, obtained with difficulty from the rapacious treasurer, was employed in collecting from their estates a great number of slaves and peasants, blindly devoted to the commands of their lords, and armed with the rustic weapons of clubs and axes. The leaders of the conspiracy, as they were admitted to the audience of the procurator, stabbed him with the daggers

---

[1] He was compared to Spartacus and Athenio. Hist. August. p. 141.
[2] Herodian, l. vii. [c. 3 and 4] p. 238. Zosim. l. i. [c. 13 and 18] p. 15.

concealed under their garments, and, by the assistance of their tumultuary train, seized on the little town of Thysdrus,[1] and erected the standard of rebellion against the sovereign of the Roman empire. They rested their hopes on the hatred of mankind against Maximin, and they judiciously resolved to oppose to that detested tyrant, an emperor whose mild virtues had already acquired the love and esteem of the Romans, and whose authority over the province would give weight and stability to the enterprise. Gordianus, their proconsul, and the object of their choice, refused, with unfeigned reluctance, the dangerous honour, and begged with tears that they would suffer him to terminate in peace a long and innocent life, without staining his feeble age with civil blood. Their menaces compelled him to accept the Imperial purple, his only refuge indeed against the jealous cruelty of Maximin; since, according to the reasoning of tyrants, those who have been esteemed worthy of the throne deserve death, and those who deliberate have already rebelled.[2]

The family of Gordianus was one of the most illustrious of the Roman senate. On the father's side, he was descended from the Gracchi; on his mother's, from the emperor Trajan. A great estate enabled him to support the dignity of this birth, and, in the enjoyment of it, he displayed an elegant taste and beneficent disposition. The palace in Rome, formerly inhabited by the great Pompey, had been, during several generations, in the possession of Gordian's family.[3] It was distinguished by ancient trophies of naval victories, and decorated with the works of modern painting. His villa on the road to Præneste was celebrated for baths of singular beauty and extent, for three stately rooms of an hundred feet in length, and for a magnificent portico, supported by two hundred columns of the four most curious and costly sorts of marble.[4] The public shows exhibited at his ex-

---

[1] In the fertile territory of Byzacium, one hundred and fifty miles to the south of Carthage. This city was decorated, probably by the Gordians, with the title of colony, and with a fine amphitheatre, which is still in a very perfect state. See Itinerar. Wesseling, p. 59, and Shaw's Travels, p. 117.

[2] Herodian, l. vii. [c. 4 and 5] p. 239. Hist. August. p. 153 [Capitol. Gordiani, c. 7 seq.].

[3] Hist. Aug. p. 152. The celebrated house of Pompey *in carinis*, was usurped by Marc Antony, and consequently became, after the Triumvir's death, a part of the Imperial domain. The emperor Trajan allowed and even encouraged the rich senators to purchase those magnificent and useless places (Plin. Panegyric. c. 50): and it may seem probable that, on this occasion, Pompey's house came into the possession of Gordian's great-grandfather.

[4] The Claudian, the Numidian, the Carystian, and the Synnadian. The colours of Roman marbles have been faintly described and imperfectly

pense, and in which the people were entertained with many hundreds of wild beasts and gladiators,[1] seem to surpass the fortune of a subject; and whilst the liberality of other magistrates was confined to a few solemn festivals in Rome, the magnificence of Gordian was repeated, when he was ædile, every month in the year, and extended, during his consulship, to the principal cities of Italy. He was twice elevated to the last-mentioned dignity, by Caracalla and by Alexander; for he possessed the uncommon talent of acquiring the esteem of virtuous princes, without alarming the jealousy of tyrants. His long life was innocently spent in the study of letters and the peaceful honours of Rome; and, till he was named proconsul of Africa by the voice of the senate and the approbation of Alexander,[2] he appears prudently to have declined the command of armies and the government of provinces. As long as that emperor lived, Africa was happy under the administration of his worthy representative; after the barbarous Maximin had usurped the throne, Gordianus alleviated the miseries which he was unable to prevent. When he reluctantly accepted the purple, he was above fourscore years old; a last and valuable remains of the happy age of the Antonines, whose virtues he revived in his own conduct and celebrated in an elegant poem of thirty books. With the venerable proconsul, his son, who had accompanied him into Africa as his lieutenant, was likewise declared emperor. His manners were less pure, but his character was equally amiable with that of his father. Twenty-two acknowledged concubines, and a library of sixty-two thousand volumes, attested the variety of his inclinations, and from the productions which he left behind him, it appears that the former as well as the latter were designed for use rather than ostentation.[3] The Roman people acknowledged in the features of the younger Gordian the resemblance of Scipio Africanus, recollected with pleasure that his mother was the

distinguished. It appears, however, that the Carystian was a sea-green, and that the marble of Synnada was white mixed with oval spots of purple. Salmasius ad Hist. August. p. 164.

[1] Hist. August. p. 151, 152. He sometimes gave five hundred pair of gladiators, never less than one hundred and fifty. He once gave for the use of the circus one hundred Sicilian, and as many Cappadocian horses. The animals designed for hunting were chiefly bears, boars, bulls, stags, elks, wild asses, etc. Elephants and lions seem to have been appropriated to Imperial magnificence.

[2] See the original letter, in the Augustan History, p. 152, which at once shows Alexander's respect for the authority of the senate, and his esteem for the proconsul appointed by that assembly.

[3] By each of his concubines, the younger Gordian left three or four children. His literary productions were by no means contemptible.

grand-daughter of Antoninus Pius, and rested the public hope on those latent virtues which had hitherto, as they fondly imagined, lain concealed in the luxurious indolence of a private life.

As soon as the Gordians had appeased the first tumult of a popular election, they removed their court to Carthage. They were received with the acclamations of the Africans, who honoured their virtues, and who, since the visit of Hadrian, had never beheld the majesty of a Roman emperor. But these vain acclamations neither strengthened nor confirmed the title of the Gordians. They were induced by principle, as well as interest, to solicit the approbation of the senate; and a deputation of the noblest provincials was sent, without delay, to Rome, to relate and justify the conduct of their countrymen, who, having long suffered with patience, were at length resolved to act with vigour. The letters of the new princes were modest and respectful, excusing the necessity which had obliged them to accept the Imperial title; but submitting their election and their fate to the supreme judgment of the senate.[1]

The inclinations of the senate were neither doubtful nor divided. The birth and noble alliances of the Gordians had intimately connected them with the most illustrious houses of Rome. Their fortune had created many dependents in that assembly, their merit had acquired many friends. Their mild administration opened the flattering prospect of the restoration not only of the civil but even of the republican government. The terror of military violence, which had first obliged the senate to forget the murder of Alexander, and to ratify the election of a barbarian peasant,[2] now produced a contrary effect, and provoked them to assert the injured rights of freedom and humanity. The hatred of Maximin towards the senate was declared and implacable; the tamest submission had not appeased his fury, the most cautious innocence would not remove his suspicions; and even the care of their own safety urged them to share the fortune of an enterprise, of which (if unsuccessful) they were sure to be the first victims. These considerations, and perhaps others of a more private nature, were debated in a previous conference of the consuls and the magistrates. As soon as their resolution was decided, they convoked in the temple of Castor the whole body of the senate, according to an ancient form of secrecy,[3]

---

[1] Herodian, l. vii. p. 243.   Hist. August. p. 144.

[2] Quod tamen patres dum periculosum existimant inermes armato resistere, approbaverunt. *Aurelius Victor.*

[3] Even the servants of the house, the scribes, etc., were excluded, and

calculated to awaken their attention, and to conceal their decrees.
" Conscript fathers," said the consul Syllanus, " the two
Gordians, both of consular dignity, the one your proconsul, the
other your lieutenant, have been declared emperors by the
general consent of Africa. Let us return thanks," he boldly
continued, " to the youth of Thysdrus; let us return thanks to
the faithful people of Carthage, our generous deliverers from an
horrid monster—Why do you hear me thus coolly, thus timidly?
Why do you cast those anxious looks on each other? why hesitate? Maximin is a public enemy! may his enmity soon expire
with him, and may we long enjoy the prudence and felicity of
Gordian the father, the valour and constancy of Gordian the
son!" [1] The noble ardour of the consul revived the languid
spirit of the senate. By an unanimous decree the election of the
Gordians was ratified, Maximin, his son, and his adherents, were
pronounced enemies of their country, and liberal rewards were
offered to whomsoever had the courage and good fortune to
destroy them.

During the emperor's absence, a detachment of the Prætorian
guards remained at Rome, to protect, or rather to command, the
capital. The Præfect Vitalianus had signalised his fidelity to
Maximin, by the alacrity with which he had obeyed, and even
prevented, the cruel mandates of the tyrant. His death alone
could rescue the authority of the senate, and the lives of the
senators, from a state of danger and suspense. Before their
resolves had transpired, a quæstor and some tribunes were com-
missioned to take his devoted life. They executed the order with
equal boldness and success; and, with their bloody daggers in
their hands, ran through the streets proclaiming to the people
and the soldiers the news of the happy revolution. The enthusiasm of liberty was seconded by the promise of a large donative,
in lands and money; the statues of Maximin were thrown down;
the capital of the empire acknowledged, with transport, the
authority of the two Gordians and the senate,[2] and the example
of Rome was followed by the rest of Italy.

A new spirit had arisen in that assembly, whose long patience
had been insulted by wanton despotism and military licence.
The senate assumed the reins of government, and, with a calm

their office was filled by the senators themselves. We are obliged to the
Augustan History, p. 159, for preserving this curious example of the old
discipline of the commonwealth.

[1] This spirited speech, translated from the Augustan historian, p. 156,
seems transcribed by him from the original registers of the senate.

[2] Herodian, l. vii. p. 244.

intrepidity, prepared to vindicate by arms the cause of freedom.
Among the consular senators recommended by their merit and
services to the favour of the emperor Alexander, it was easy to
select twenty, not unequal to the command of an army, and the
conduct of a war. To these was the defence of Italy intrusted.
Each was appointed to act in his respective department,
authorised to enrol and discipline the Italian youth; and
instructed to fortify the ports and highways against the impending invasion of Maximin. A number of deputies, chosen
from the most illustrious of the senatorian and equestrian orders,
were dispatched at the same time to the governors of the several
provinces, earnestly conjuring them to fly to the assistance of
their country, and to remind the nations of their ancient ties of
friendship with the Roman senate and people. The general
respect with which these deputies were received, and the zeal of
Italy and the provinces in favour of the senate, sufficiently prove
that the subjects of Maximin were reduced to that uncommon
distress, in which the body of the people has more to fear from
oppression than from resistance. The consciousness of that
melancholy truth inspires a degree of persevering fury seldom
to be found in those civil wars which are artificially supported for
the benefit of a few factious and designing leaders.[1]

For while the cause of the Gordians was embraced with such
diffusive ardour, the Gordians themselves (A.D. 237, 3rd July)
were no more. The feeble court of Carthage was alarmed with
the rapid approach of Capelianus, governor of Mauritania, who,
with a small band of veterans, and a fierce host of barbarians,
attacked a faithful but unwarlike province. The younger
Gordian sallied out to meet the enemy at the head of a few
guards, and a numerous undisciplined multitude, educated in
the peaceful luxury of Carthage. His useless valour served only
to procure him an honourable death, in the field of battle. His
aged father, whose reign had not exceeded thirty-six days, put
an end to his life on the first news of the defeat. Carthage,
destitute of defence, opened her gates to the conqueror, and
Africa was exposed to the rapacious cruelty of a slave, obliged
to satisfy his unrelenting master with a large account of blood
and treasure.[2]

[1] Herodian, l. vii. p. 247, l. viii. p. 277.   Hist. August. p. 156-158.
[2] Herodian, l. vii. p. 254.   Hist. August. p. 150-160.   We may observe,
that one month and six days, for the reign of Gordian, is a just correction
of Casaubon and Panvinius, instead of the absurd reading of one year and
six months.   Commentar. p. 193.   Zosimus relates, l. i. p. 17, that the two
Gordians perished by a tempest in the midst of their navigation.   A strange
ignorance of history, or a strange abuse of metaphors!

The fate of the Gordians filled Rome with just, but unexpected terror. The senate convoked in the temple of Concord, affected to transact the common business of the day; and seemed to decline, with trembling anxiety, the consideration of their own and the public danger. A silent consternation prevailed on the assembly, till a senator, of the name and family of Trajan, awakened his brethren from their fatal lethargy. He represented to them, that the choice of cautious dilatory measures had been long since out of their power; that Maximin, implacable by nature, and exasperated by injuries, was advancing towards Italy, at the head of the military force of the empire; and that their only remaining alternative was either to meet him bravely in the field, or tamely to expect the tortures and ignominious death reserved for unsuccessful rebellion. " We have lost," continued he, " two excellent princes; but unless we desert ourselves, the hopes of the republic have not perished with the Gordians. Many are the senators, whose virtues have deserved, and whose abilities would sustain, the Imperial dignity. Let us elect two emperors, one of whom may conduct the war against the public enemy, whilst his colleague remains at Rome to direct the civil administration. I cheerfully expose myself to the danger and envy of the nomination, and give my vote in favour of Maximus and Balbinus. Ratify my choice, conscript fathers, or appoint, in their place, others more worthy of the empire." The general apprehension silenced the whispers of jealousy; the merit of the candidates was universally acknowledged; and the house resounded with the sincere acclamations, of " long life and victory to the emperors Maximus and Balbinus. You are happy in the judgment of the senate; may the republic be happy under your administration! " [1]

The virtues and the reputation of the new emperors justified the most sanguine hopes of the Romans. The various nature of their talents seemed to appropriate to each his peculiar department of peace and war, without leaving room for jealous emulation. Balbinus was an admired orator, a poet of distinguished fame, and a wise magistrate, who had exercised with innocence and applause the civil jurisdiction in almost all the interior provinces of the empire. His birth was noble,[2] his fortune affluent,

---

[1] Augustan History, p. 166, from the registers of the senate; the date is confessedly faulty, but the coincidence of the Apollinarian games enables us to correct it.

[2] He was descended from Cornelius Balbus, a noble Spaniard, and the adopted son of Theophanes the Greek historian. Balbus obtained the freedom of Rome by the favour of Pompey, and preserved it by the elo-

his mar.ners liberal and affable. In him the love of pleasure was
corrected by a sense of dignity, nor had the habits of ease deprived him of a capacity for business. The mind of Maximus
was formed in a rougher mould. By his valour and abilities he
had raised himself from the meanest origin to the first employments of the state and army. His victories over the Sarmatians
and the Germans, the austerity of his life, and the rigid impartiality of his justice, whilst he was Præfect of the city, commanded the esteem of a people, whose affections were engaged
in favour of the more amiable Balbinus. The two colleagues
had both been consuls (Balbinus had twice enjoyed that honourable office), both had been named among the twenty lieutenants
of the senate; and since the one was sixty and the other seventy-
four years old,[1] they had both attained the full maturity of age
and experience.

After the senate had conferred on Maximus and Balbinus an
equal portion of the consular and tribunitian powers, the title
of Fathers of their country, and the joint office of Supreme
Pontiff, they ascended to the Capitol, to return thanks to the
gods, protectors of Rome.[2] The solemn rites of sacrifice were
disturbed by a sedition of the people. The licentious multitude
neither loved the rigid Maximus, nor did they sufficiently fear
the mild and humane Balbinus. Their increasing numbers surrounded the temple of Jupiter; with obstinate clamours they
asserted their inherent right of consenting to the election of their
sovereign; and demanded, with an apparent moderation, that,
besides the two emperors chosen by the senate, a third should be
added of the family of the Gordians, as a just return of gratitude
to those princes who had sacrificed their lives for the republic.
At the head of the city-guards, and the youth of the equestrian
order, Maximus and Balbinus attempted to cut their way through
the seditious multitude. The multitude, armed with sticks and

quence of Cicero (see Orat. pro Cornel. Balbo). The friendship of Cæsar
(to whom he rendered the most important secret services in the civil war)
raised him to the consulship and the pontificate, honours never yet possessed by a stranger. The nephew of this Balbus triumphed over the
Garamantes. See Dictionnaire de Bayle, au mot *Balbus*, where he distinguishes the several persons of that name, and rectifies, with his usual
accuracy, the mistakes of former writers concerning them.

[1] Zonaras, l. xii. p. 622. But little dependence is to be had on the
authority of a moderate Greek, so grossly ignorant of the history of the
third century, that he creates several imaginary emperors, and confounds
those who really existed.

[2] Herodian, l. vii. p. 250, supposes that the senate was at first convoked
in the Capitol, and is very eloquent on the occasion. The Augustan History, p. 116, seems much more authentic.

stones, drove them back into the Capitol. It is prudent to yield when the contest, whatever may be the issue of it, must be fatal to both parties. A boy, only thirteen years of age, the grandson of the elder, and nephew of the younger, Gordian, was produced to the people, invested with the ornaments and title of Cæsar. The tumult was appeased by this easy condescension; and the two emperors, as soon as they had been peaceably acknowledged in Rome, prepared to defend Italy against the common enemy.

Whilst in Rome and Africa revolutions succeeded each other with such amazing rapidity, the mind of Maximin was agitated by the most furious passions. He is said to have received the news of the rebellion of the Gordians, and of the decree of the senate against him, not with the temper of a man, but the rage of a wild beast; which, as it could not discharge itself on the distant senate, threatened the life of his son, of his friends, and of all who ventured to approach his person. The grateful intelligence of the death of the Gordians was quickly followed by the assurance that the senate, laying aside all hopes of pardon or accommodation, had substituted in their room two emperors, with whose merit he could not be unacquainted. Revenge was the only consolation left to Maximin, and revenge could only be obtained by arms. The strength of the legions had been assembled by Alexander from all parts of the empire. Three successful campaigns against the Germans and the Sarmatians had raised their fame, confirmed their discipline, and even increased their numbers, by filling the ranks with the flower of the barbarian youth. The life of Maximin had been spent in war, and the candid severity of history cannot refuse him the valour of a soldier, or even the abilities of an experienced general.[1] It might naturally be expected, that a prince of such a character, instead of suffering the rebellion to gain stability by delay, should immediately have marched from the banks of the Danube to those of the Tiber, and that his victorious army, instigated by contempt for the senate, and eager to gather the spoils of Italy, should have burned with impatience to finish the easy and lucrative conquest. Yet as far as we can trust to the obscure chronology of that period,[2] it appears that the operations of

[1] In Herodian, l. vii. p. 249, and in the Augustan History, we have three several orations of Maximin to his army, on the rebellion of Africa and Rome: M. de Tillemont has very justly observed, that they neither agree with each other, nor with truth. Histoire des Empereurs, tom. iii. p. 799.

[2] The carelessness of the writers of that age leaves us in a singular perplexity. 1. We know that Maximus and Balbinus were killed during the Capitoline games. Herodian, l. viii p. 285. The authority of Censorinus (de Die Natali, c. 18) enables us to fix those games with certainty to the

some foreign war deferred the Italian expedition till the ensuing spring. From the prudent conduct of Maximin, we may learn that the savage features of his character have been exaggerated by the pencil of party, that his passions, however impetuous, submitted to the force of reason, and that the barbarian possessed something of the generous spirit of Sylla, who subdued the enemies of Rome before he suffered himself to revenge his private injuries.[1]

When the troops of Maximin, advancing in excellent order, arrived at the foot of the Julian Alps, they were terrified by the silence and desolation that reigned on the frontiers of Italy. The villages and open towns had been abandoned on their approach by the inhabitants, the cattle was driven away, the provisions removed, or destroyed, the bridges broke down, nor was anything left which could afford either shelter or give subsistence to an invader. Such had been the wise orders of the generals of the senate, whose design was to protract the war, to ruin the army of Maximin by the slow operation of famine, and to consume his strength in the sieges of the principal cities of Italy, which they had plentifully stored with men and provisions from the deserted country. Aquileia received and withstood the first shock of the invasion. The streams that issue from the head of the Hadriatic gulf, swelled by the melting of the winter snows,[2] opposed an unexpected obstacle to the arms of Maximin. At length, on a singular bridge, constructed with art and difficulty of large hogsheads, he transported his army to the opposite

year 238, but leaves us in ignorance of the month or day. 2. The election of Gordian by the senate is fixed, with equal certainty, to the 27th of May; but we are at a loss to discover whether it was in the same or the preceding year. Tillemont and Muratori, who maintain the two opposite opinions, bring into the field a desultory troop of authorities, conjectures, and probabilities. The one seems to draw out, the other to contract, the series of events between those periods, more than can be well reconciled to reason and history. Yet it is necessary to choose between them.

[1] Velleius Paterculus, l. ii. c. 24. The president de Montesquieu (in his dialogue between Sylla and Eucrates) expresses the sentiments of the dictator, in a spirited and even a sublime manner.

[2] Muratori (Annali d'Italia, tom. ii. p. 294) thinks the melting of the snows suits better with the months of June or July, than with that of February. The opinion of a man who passed his life between the Alps and the Apennines, is undoubtedly of great weight; yet I observe, 1. That the long winter, of which Muratori takes advantage, is to be found only in the Latin version, and not in the Greek text of Herodian. 2. That the vicissitude of suns and rains, to which the soldiers of Maximin were exposed (Herodian, l. viii. p. 277) denotes the spring rather than the summer. We may observe likewise, that these several streams, as they melted into one, composed the Timavus, so poetically (in every sense of the word) described by Virgil. They are about twelve miles to the east of Aquileia. See Cluver. Italia Antiqua, tom. i. p. 189, etc.

bank, rooted up the beautiful vineyards in the neighbourhood of Aquileia, demolished the suburbs, and employed the timber of the buildings in the engines and towers, with which on every side he attacked the city. The walls, fallen to decay during the security of a long peace, had been hastily repaired on this sudden emergency; but the firmest defence of Aquileia consisted in the constancy of the citizens; all ranks of whom, instead of being dismayed, were animated by the extreme danger, and their knowledge of the tyrant's unrelenting temper. Their courage was supported and directed by Crispinus and Menophilus, two of the twenty lieutenants of the senate, who, with a small body of regular troops, had thrown themselves into the besieged place. The army of Maximin was repulsed on repeated attacks, his machines destroyed by showers of artificial fire; and the generous enthusiasm of the Aquileians was exalted into a confidence of success, by the opinion, that Belenus, their tutelar deity, combated in person in the defence of his distressed worshippers.[1]

The emperor Maximus, who had advanced as far as Ravenna, to secure that important place, and to hasten the military preparations, beheld the event of the war in the more faithful mirror of reason and policy. He was too sensible, that a single town could not resist the persevering efforts of a great army; and he dreaded lest the enemy, tired with the obstinate resistance of Aquileia, should on a sudden relinquish the fruitless siege, and march directly towards Rome. The fate of the empire and the cause of freedom must then be committed to the chance of a battle; and what arms could he oppose to the veteran legions of the Rhine and the Danube? Some troops newly levied among the generous but enervated youth of Italy; and a body of German auxiliaries, on whose firmness, in the hour of trial, it was dangerous to depend. In the midst of these just alarms, the stroke of domestic conspiracy punished the crimes of Maximin, and delivered Rome and the senate from the calamities that would surely have attended the victory of an enraged barbarian.

The people of Aquileia had scarcely experienced any of the common miseries of a siege, their magazines were plentifully supplied, and several fountains within the walls assured them of an inexhaustible resource of fresh water. The soldiers of Maximin were, on the contrary, exposed to the inclemency of the season, the contagion of disease, and the horrors of famine. The open

[1] Herodian, l. viii. p. 272. The Celtic deity was supposed to be Apollo, and received under that name the thanks of the senate. A temple was likewise built to Venus the bald, in honour of the women of Aquileia, who had given up their hair to make ropes for the military engines.

country was ruined, the rivers filled with the slain, and polluted
with blood. A spirit of despair and disaffection began to diffuse
itself among the troops; and as they were cut off from all intelligence, they easily believed that the whole empire had embraced
the cause of the senate, and that they were left as devoted
victims to perish under the impregnable walls of Aquileia. The
fierce temper of the tyrant was exasperated by disappointments,
which he imputed to the cowardice of his army; and his wanton
and ill-timed cruelty, instead of striking terror, inspired hatred
and a just desire of revenge. A party of Prætorian guards, who
trembled for their wives and children in the camp of Alba, near
Rome, executed the sentence of the senate. Maximin, abandoned
by his guards, was (A.D. 238, April) slain in his tent, with his
son (whom he had associated to the honours of the purple),
Anulinus the præfect, and the principal ministers of his tyranny.[1]
The sight of their heads, borne on the point of spears, convinced
the citizens of Aquileia, that the siege was at an end; the gates
of the city were thrown open, a liberal market was provided for
the hungry troops of Maximin, and the whole army joined in
solemn protestations of fidelity to the senate and the people of
Rome, and to their lawful emperors Maximus and Balbinus.
Such was the deserved fate of a brutal savage, destitute, as he
has generally been represented, of every sentiment that distinguishes a civilised, or even a human being. The body was suited
to the soul. The stature of Maximin exceeded the measure of
eight feet, and circumstances almost incredible are related of his
matchless strength and appetite.[2] Had he lived in a less enlightened age, tradition and poetry might well have described
him as one of those monstrous giants, whose supernatural power
was constantly exerted for the destruction of mankind.

It is easier to conceive than to describe the universal joy of the
Roman world on the fall of the tyrant, the news of which is said
to have been carried in four days from Aquileia to Rome. The
return of Maximus was a triumphal procession, his colleague and

[1] Herodian, l. viii. p. 279. Hist. August. p. 146. The duration of
Maximin's reign has not been defined with much accuracy, except by
Eutropius, who allows him three years and a few days (l. ix. 1); we may
depend on the integrity of the text, as the Latin original is checked by the
Greek version of Pæanius.

[2] Eight Roman feet and one third, which are equal to above eight
English feet, as the two measures are to each other in the proportion of 967
to 1000. See Greaves's discourse on the Roman foot. We are told that
Maximin could drink in a day an amphora (or about seven gallons of wine),
and eat thirty or forty pounds of meat. He could move a loaded waggon,
break a horse's leg with his fist, crumble stones in his hand, and tear up
small trees by the roots. See his Life in the Augustan History.

young Gordian went out to meet him, and the three princes made
their entry into the capital, attended by the ambassadors of
almost all the cities of Italy, saluted with the splendid offerings
of gratitude and superstition, and received with the unfeigned
acclamations of the senate and people, who persuaded themselves that a golden age would succeed to an age of iron.[1] The
conduct of the two emperors correspond with these expectations.
They administered justice in person; and the rigour of the one
was tempered by the other's clemency. The oppressive taxes
with which Maximin had loaded the rights of inheritance and
succession were repealed, or at least moderated. Discipline was
revived, and with the advice of the senate many wise laws were
enacted by their imperial ministers, who endeavoured to restore
a civil constitution on the ruins of military tyranny. " What
reward may we expect for delivering Rome from a monster? "
was the question asked by Maximus, in a moment of freedom
and confidence. Balbinus answered it without hesitation. " The
love of the senate, of the people, and of all mankind." " Alas ! "
replied his more penetrating colleague, " Alas ! I dread the hatred
of the soldiers, and the fatal effects of their resentment." [2] His
apprehensions were but too well justified by the event.

Whilst Maximus was preparing to defend Italy against the
common foe, Balbinus, who remained at Rome, had been engaged
in scenes of blood and intestine discord. Distrust and jealousy
reigned in the senate; and even in the temples where they
assembled, every senator carried either open or concealed arms.
In the midst of their deliberations, two veterans of the guards,
actuated either by curiosity or a sinister motive, audaciously
thrust themselves into the house, and advanced by degrees
beyond the altar of Victory. Gallicanus, a consular, and
Mæcenas, a Prætorian senator, viewed with indignation their
insolent intrusion: drawing their daggers, they laid the spies,
for such they deemed them, dead at the foot of the altar, and
then advancing to the door of the senate, imprudently exhorted
the multitude to massacre the Prætorians, as the secret adherents
of the tyrant. Those who escaped the first fury of the tumult
took refuge in the camp, which they defended with superior
advantage against the reiterated attacks of the people, assisted
by the numerous bands of gladiators, the property of opulent
nobles. The civil war lasted many days, with infinite loss and

---

[1] See the congratulatory letter of Claudius Julianus the consul, to the
two emperors, in the Augustan History.
[2] Hist. August. p. 171 [Capitol. c. 15].

confusion on both sides. When the pipes were broken that supplied the camp with water, the Prætorians were reduced to intolerable distress; but in their turn they made desperate sallies into the city, set fire to a great number of houses, and filled the street with the blood of the inhabitants. The emperor Balbinus attempted, by ineffectual edicts and precarious truces, to reconcile the factions at Rome. But their animosity, though smothered for a while, burnt with redoubled violence. The soldiers, detesting the senate and the people, despised the weakness of a prince who wanted either the spirit or the power to command the obedience of his subjects.[1]

After the tyrant's death, his formidable army had acknowledged, from necessity rather than from choice, the authority of Maximus, who transported himself without delay to the camp before Aquileia. As soon as he had received their oath of fidelity, he addressed them in terms full of mildness and moderation; lamented, rather than arraigned, the wild disorders of the times, and assured the soldiers, that of all their past conduct, the senate would remember only their generous desertion of the tyrant, and their voluntary return to their duty. Maximus enforced his exhortations by a liberal donative, purified the camp by a solemn sacrifice of expiation, and then dismissed the legions to their several provinces, impressed, as he hoped, with a lively sense of gratitude and obedience.[2] But nothing could reconcile the haughty spirit of the Prætorians. They attended the emperors on the memorable day of their public entry into Rome; but amidst the general acclamations, the sullen dejected countenance of the guards sufficiently declared that they considered themselves as the object, rather than the partners, of the triumph. When the whole body was united in their camp, those who had served under Maximin, and those who had remained at Rome, insensibly communicated to each other their complaints and apprehensions. The emperors chosen by the army had perished with ignominy; those elected by the senate were seated on the throne.[3] The long discord between the civil and military powers was decided by a war, in which the former had obtained a complete victory. The soldiers must now learn a new doctrine of submission to the senate; and whatever clemency was affected by that politic assembly, they dreaded a slow revenge, coloured

---

[1] Herodian, l. viii. [c. 12] p. 258.
[2] Herodian, l. viii. [c. 7] p. 213.
[3] The observation had been made imprudently enough in the acclamations of the senate, and with regard to the soldiers it carried the appearance of a wanton insult. Hist. August. p. 170.

by the name of discipline, and justified by fair pretences of the public good. But their fate was still in their own hands; and if they had courage to despise the vain terrors of an impotent republic, it was easy to convince the world that those who were masters of the arms were masters of the authority, of the state.

When the senate elected two princes, it is probable that, besides the declared reason of providing for the various emergencies of peace and war, they were actuated by the secret desire of weakening by division the despotism of the supreme magistrate. Their policy was effectual, but it proved fatal both to their emperors and to themselves. The jealousy of power was soon exasperated by the difference of character. Maximus despised Balbinus as a luxurious noble, and was in his turn disdained by his colleague as an obscure soldier. Their silent discord was understood rather than seen;[1] but the mutual consciousness prevented them from uniting in any vigorous measures of defence against their common enemies of the Prætorian camp. The whole city was (A.D. 238, July 15) employed in the Capitoline games, and the emperors were left almost alone in the palace. On a sudden they were alarmed by the approach of a troop of desperate assassins. Ignorant of each other's situation or designs, for they already occupied very distant apartments, afraid to give or to receive assistance, they wasted the important moments in idle debates and fruitless recriminations. The arrival of the guards put an end to the vain strife. They seized on these emperors of the senate, for such they called them with malicious contempt, stripped them of their garments, and dragged them in insolent triumph through the streets of Rome, with a design of inflicting a slow and cruel death on those unfortunate princes. The fear of a rescue from the faithful Germans of the Imperial guards, shortened their tortures; and their bodies, mangled with a thousand wounds, were left exposed to the insults or to the pity of the populace.[2]

In the space of a few months, six princes had been cut off by the sword. Gordian, who had already received the title of Cæsar, was the only person that occurred to the soldiers as proper to fill the vacant throne.[3] They carried him to the camp, and unanimously saluted him Augustus and Emperor. His name was

---

[1] Discordiæ tacitæ, et quæ intelligerentur potius quam viderentur. Hist. August. p. 170. This well-chosen expression is probably stolen from some better writer.

[2] Herodian, l. viii. p. 287, 288.

[3] Quia non alius erat in præsenti, is the expression of the Augustan History.

dear to the senate and people; his tender age promised a long impunity of military licence; and the submission of Rome and the provinces to the choice of the Prætorian guards, saved the republic, at the expense indeed of its freedom and dignity, from the horrors of a new civil war in the heart of the capital.[1]

As the third Gordian was only nineteen years of age at the time of his death, the history of his life, were it known to us with greater accuracy than it really is, would contain little more than the account of his education, and the conduct of the ministers, who by turns abused or guided the simplicity of his inexperienced youth. Immediately after his accession, he fell into the hands of his mother's eunuchs, that pernicious vermin of the East, who, since the days of Elagabalus, had infested the Roman palace. By the artful conspiracy of these wretches, an impenetrable veil was drawn between an innocent prince and his oppressed subjects, the virtuous disposition of Gordian was deceived, and the honours of the empire sold without his knowledge, though in a very public manner, to the most worthless of mankind. We are ignorant by what fortunate accident the emperor escaped from this ignominious slavery, and devolved his confidence on a minister whose wise counsels had no object except the glory of his sovereign and the happiness of the people. It should seem that (A.D. 240) love and learning introduced Misitheus to the favour of Gordian. The young prince married the daughter of his master of rhetoric, and promoted his father-in-law to the first offices of the empire. Two admirable letters that passed between them are still extant. The minister, with the conscious dignity of virtue, congratulates Gordian that he is delivered from the tyranny of the eunuchs,[2] and still more that he is sensible of his deliverance. The emperor acknowledges, with an amiable confusion, the errors of his past conduct; and laments, with singular propriety, the misfortune

---

[1] Quintus Curtius (l. x. c. 9) pays an elegant compliment to the emperor of the day, for having, by his happy accession, extinguished so many firebrands, sheathed so many swords, and put an end to the evils of a divided government. After weighing with attention every word of the passage, I am of opinion that it suits better with the elevation of Gordian, than with any other period of the Roman History. In that case, it may serve to decide the age of Quintus Curtius. Those who place him under the first Cæsars, argue from the purity of his style, but are embarrassed by the silence of Quintilian, in his accurate list of Roman historians.

[2] Hist. August. p. 161. From some hints in the two letters, I should expect that the eunuchs were not expelled the palace without some degree of gentle violence, and that young Gordian rather approved of, than consented to, their disgrace.

of a monarch, from whom a venal tribe of courtiers perpetually labour to conceal the truth.[1]

The life of Misitheus had been spent in the profession of letters, not of arms; yet such was the versatile genius of that great man, that, when (A.D. 242) he was appointed Prætorian Præfect, he discharged the military duties of his place with vigour and ability. The Persians had invaded Mesopotamia, and threatened Antioch. By the persuasion of his father-in-law, the young emperor quitted the luxury of Rome, opened, for the last time recorded in history, the temple of Janus, and marched in person into the East. On his approach with a great army, the Persians withdrew their garrisons from the cities which they had already taken, and retired from the Euphrates to the Tigris. Gordian enjoyed the pleasure of announcing to the senate the first success of his arms, which he ascribed with a becoming modesty and gratitude to the wisdom of his father and Præfect. During the whole expedition, Misitheus watched over the safety and discipline of the army; whilst he prevented their dangerous murmurs by maintaining a regular plenty in the camp, and by establishing ample magazines of vinegar, bacon, straw, barley, and wheat, in all the cities of the frontier.[2] But the prosperity of Gordian expired with Misitheus, who died of a flux, not without very strong suspicions of poison. Philip, his successor (A.D. 243) in the præfecture, was an Arab by birth, and consequently, in the earlier part of his life, a robber by profession. His rise from so obscure a station to the first dignities of the empire, seems to prove that he was a bold and able leader. But his boldness prompted him to aspire to the throne, and his abilities were employed to supplant, not to serve, his indulgent master. The minds of the soldiers were irritated by an artificial scarcity, created by his contrivance in the camp; and the distress of the

---

[1] Duxit uxorem filiam Misithei, quem causâ eloquentiæ dignum parentela suâ putavit; et præfectum statim fecit; post quod, non puerile jam et contemptibile videbatur imperium.

[The name " Misitheus " which is found in Capitolinus has been justly suspected by scholars. It seems improbable that such a name as " God-hater "—for that is its signification—could be borne by an individual of eminence. Gruter thinks that the inscription in which the name is found is a forgery, because Zosimus calls the father-in-law of Gordian Timesicles. Eckhel also thinks that the form Temesitheus is more likely to be correct than Misitheus. Bury gives the name in full as C. Furius Sabinius Aquila Timesitheus, and the name of the daughter, the wife of the young emperor, as Tranquillina.—O. S.]

[2] Hist. August. p. 162. Aurelius Victor. Porphyrius in Vit. Plotin. ap. Fabricium Biblioth. Græc. l. iv. c. 36. The philosopher Plotinus accompanied the army, prompted by the love of knowledge, and by the hope of penetrating as far as India.

army was attributed to the youth and incapacity of the prince.
It is not in our power to trace the successive steps of the secret
conspiracy and open sedition, which were at length fatal to
Gordian. A sepulchral monument was erected to his memory
on the spot [1] where (A.D. 244, March) he was killed, near the
conflux of the Euphrates with the little river Aboras.[2] The
fortunate Philip, raised to the empire by the votes of the soldiers,
found a ready obedience from the senate and the provinces.[3]

We cannot forbear transcribing the ingenious, though somewhat fanciful description, which a celebrated writer of our own
times has traced of the military government of the Roman empire.
" What in that age was called the Roman empire, was only an
irregular republic, not unlike the Aristocracy [4] of Algiers,[5] where
the militia, possessed of the sovereignty, creates and deposes a
magistrate, who is styled a Dey. Perhaps, indeed, it may be
laid down as a general rule, that a military government is, in
some respects, more republican than monarchical. Nor can it be
said that the soldiers only partook of the government by their
disobedience and rebellions. The speeches made to them by the
emperors, were they not at length of the same nature as those
formerly pronounced to the people by the consuls and the
tribunes? And although the armies had no regular place or
forms of assembly; though their debates were short, their action
sudden, and their resolves seldom the result of cool reflection,
did they not dispose, with absolute sway, of the public fortune?
What was the emperor, except the minister of a violent government elected for the private benefit of the soldiers?

" When the army had elected Philip, who was Prætorian
præfect to the third Gordian; the latter demanded that he
might remain sole emperor; he was unable to obtain it. He
requested that the power might be equally divided between
them; the army would not listen to his speech. He consented

---

[1] About twenty miles from the little town of Circesium, on the frontier
of the two empires.

[2] The inscription (which contained a very singular pun) was erased by the
order of Licinius, who claimed some degree of relationship to Philip (Hist.
August. p. 165); but the *tumulus* or mound of earth which formed the
sepulchre, still subsisted in the time of Julian. Ammian. Marcellin. xxiii. 5.

[3] Aurelius Victor. Eutrop. ix. 2. Orosius, vii. 20. Ammianus Marcellinus, xxiii. 5. Zosimus, l. i. p. 19. Philip, who was a native of Bostra,
was about forty years of age.

[4] Can the epithet of *Aristocracy* be applied, with any propriety, to the
government of Algiers? Every military government floats between the
extremes of absolute monarchy and wild democracy.

[5] The military republic of the Mamalukes in Egypt, would have afforded
M. de Montesquieu (Considérations sur la Grandeur et la Décadence des
Romains, c. 16) a juster and more noble parallel.

to be degraded to the rank of Cæsar; the favour was refused
him. He desired, at least, he might be appointed Prætorian
præfect; his prayer was rejected. Finally, he pleaded for his
life. The army, in these several judgments, exercised the
supreme magistracy." According to the historian, whose doubtful narrative the president De Montesquieu has adopted, Philip,
who, during the whole transaction, had preserved a sullen silence,
was inclined to spare the innocent life of his benefactor; till,
recollecting that his innocence might excite a dangerous compassion in the Roman world; he commanded, without regard to
his suppliant cries, that he should be seized, stript, and led away
to instant death. After a moment's pause the inhuman sentence
was executed.[1]

On his return from the East to Rome, Philip, desirous of
obliterating the memory of his crimes, and of captivating the
affections of the people, solemnised (A.D. 248, April 21) the
secular games with infinite pomp and magnificence. Since their
institution or revival by Augustus,[2] they had been celebrated
by Claudius, by Domitian, and by Severus, and were now renewed the fifth time, on the accomplishment of the full period
of a thousand years from the foundation of Rome. Every circumstance of the secular games was skilfully adapted to inspire
the superstitious mind with deep and solemn reverence. The
long interval between them [3] exceeded the term of human life;
and as none of the spectators had already seen them, none could
flatter themselves with the expectation of beholding them a
second time. The mystic sacrifices were performed, during
three nights, on the banks of the Tiber; and the Campus
Martius resounded with music and dances, and was illuminated
with innumerable lamps and torches. Slaves and strangers were

[1] The Augustan History (p. 163, 164) cannot, in this instance, be reconciled with itself or with probability. How could Philip condemn his predecessor, and yet consecrate his memory? How could he order his public
execution, and yet, in his letters to the senate, exculpate himself from the
guilt of his death? Philip, though an ambitious usurper, was by no means
a mad tyrant. Some chronological difficulties have likewise been discovered by the nice eyes of Tillemont and Muratori, in this supposed
association of Philip to the empire.

[2] The account of the last supposed celebration, though in an enlightened
period of history, was so very doubtful and obscure, that the alternative
seems not doubtful. When the popish jubilees, the copy of the secular
games, were invented by Boniface VIII., the crafty pope pretended that
he only revived an ancient institution. M. de Chais Lettres sur les Jubilès.

[3] Either of a hundred, or a hundred and ten years. Varro and Livy
adopted the former opinion, but the infallible authority of the Sibyl consecrated the latter (Censorinus de Die Natal. c. 17). The emperors
Claudius and Philip, however, did not treat the oracle with implicit respect.

excluded from any participation in these national ceremonies. A chorus of twenty-seven youths, and as many virgins, of noble families, and whose parents were both alive, implored the propitious gods in favour of the present, and for the hope of the rising generation; requesting, in religious hymns, that, according to the faith of their ancient oracles, they would still maintain the virtue, the felicity, and the empire of the Roman people.[1] The magnificence of Philip's shows and entertainments dazzled the eyes of the multitude. The devout were employed in the rites of superstition, whilst the reflecting few revolved in their anxious minds the past history and the future fate of the empire.

Since Romulus, with a small band of shepherds and outlaws, fortified himself on the hills near the Tiber, ten centuries had already elapsed.[2] During the first four ages, the Romans, in the laborious school of poverty, had acquired the virtues of war and government; by the vigorous exertion of those virtues, and by the assistance of fortune, they had obtained, in the course of the three succeeding centuries, an absolute empire over many countries of Europe, Asia, and Africa. The last three hundred years had been consumed in apparent prosperity and internal decline. The nation of soldiers, magistrates, and legislators, who composed the thirty-five tribes of the Roman people, was dissolved into the common mass of mankind and confounded with the millions of servile provincials, who had received the name without adopting the spirit of Romans. A mercenary army, levied among the subjects and barbarians of the frontier, was the only order of men who preserved and abused their independence. By their tumultuary election, a Syrian, a Goth, or an Arab, was exalted to the throne of Rome, and invested with despotic power over the conquests and over the country of the Scipios.

The limits of the Roman empire still extended from the Western Ocean to the Tigris, and from Mount Atlas to the Rhine and the Danube. To the undiscerning eye of the vulgar, Philip appeared a monarch no less powerful than Hadrian or Augustus had formerly been. The form was still the same, but the animating health and vigour were fled. The industry of the people was discouraged and exhausted by a long series of oppres-

---

[1] The idea of the secular games is best understood from the poem of Horace, and the description of Zosimus, l. ii. p. 167, etc.

[2] The received calculation of Varro assigns to the foundation of Rome an era that corresponds with the 754th year before Christ. But so little is the chronology of Rome to be depended on, in the more early ages, that Sir Isaac Newton has brought the same event as low as the year 627.

sion. The discipline of the legions, which alone, after the extinction of every other virtue, had propped the greatness of the state,
was corrupted by the ambition, or relaxed by the weakness, of
the emperors. The strength of the frontiers, which had always
consisted in arms rather than in fortifications, was insensibly
undermined; and the fairest provinces were left exposed to the
rapaciousness or ambition of the barbarians, who soon discovered the decline of the Roman empire.

CHAPTER VIII

Of the State of Persia after the Restoration of the Monarchy by Artaxerxes

WHENEVER Tacitus indulges himself in those beautiful episodes,
in which he relates some domestic transaction of the Germans or
of the Parthians, his principal object is to relieve the attention of
the reader from a uniform scene of vice and misery. From the
reign of Augustus to the time of Alexander Severus, the enemies
of Rome were in her bosom; the tyrants, and the soldiers;
and her prosperity had a very distant and feeble interest in
the revolutions that might happen beyond the Rhine and the
Euphrates. But when the military order had levelled, in wild
anarchy, the power of the prince, the laws of the senate, and even
the discipline of the camp, the barbarians of the north and of the
east, who had long hovered on the frontier, boldly attacked the
provinces of a declining monarchy. Their vexatious inroads
were changed into formidable irruptions, and, after a long vicissitude of mutual calamities, many tribes of the victorious invaders
established themselves in the provinces of the Roman empire.
To obtain a clearer knowledge of these great events, we shall
endeavour to form a previous idea of the character, forces, and
designs of those nations who avenged the cause of Hannibal and
Mithridates.

In the more early ages of the world, whilst the forest that
covered Europe afforded a retreat to a few wandering savages,
the inhabitants of Asia were already collected into populous
cities, and reduced under extensive empires, the seat of the arts,
of luxury, and of despotism. The Assyrians reigned over the

East,[1] till the sceptre of Ninus and Semiramis dropt from the hands of their enervated successors. The Medes and the Babylonians divided their power, and were themselves swallowed up in the monarchy of the Persians, whose arms could not be confined within the narrow limits of Asia. Followed, as it is said, by two millions of *men*, Xerxes, the descendant of Cyrus, invaded Greece. Thirty thousand *soldiers*, under the command of Alexander, the son of Philip, who was intrusted by the Greeks with their glory and revenge, were sufficient to subdue Persia. The princes of the house of Seleucus usurped and lost the Macedonian command over the East. About the same time that, by an ignominious treaty, they resigned to the Romans the country on this side Mount Taurus, they were driven by the Parthians, an obscure horde of Scythian origin, from all the provinces of Upper Asia. The formidable power of the Parthians, which spread from India to the frontiers of Syria, was in its turn subverted by Ardshir, or Artaxerxes; the founder of a new dynasty, which, under the name of Sassanides, governed Persia till the invasion of the Arabs. This great revolution, whose fatal influence was soon experienced by the Romans, happened in the fourth year of Alexander Severus, two hundred and twenty-six years after the Christian era.[2]

Artaxerxes had served with great reputation in the armies of Artaban, the last king of the Parthians, and it appears that he was driven into exile and rebellion by royal ingratitude, the customary reward for superior merit. His birth was obscure, and the obscurity equally gave room to the aspersions of his enemies, and the flattery of his adherents. If we credit the scandal of the former, Artaxerxes sprang from the illegitimate commerce of a tanner's wife with a common soldier.[3] The latter

[1] An ancient chronologist quoted by Velleius Paterculus (l. i. c. 6) observes, that the Assyrians, the Medes, the Persians, and the Macedonians, reigned over Asia one thousand nine hundred and ninety-five years, from the accession of Ninus to the defeat of Antiochus by the Romans. As the latter of these great events happened 289 years before Christ, the former may be placed 2184 years before the same era. The Astronomical Observations, found at Babylon by Alexander, went fifty years higher.

[2] In the five hundred and thirty-eighth year of the era of Seleucus. Agathias, l. ii. p. 63. This great event (such is the carelessness of the Orientals) is placed by Eutychius as high as the tenth year of Commodus, and by Moses of Chorene as low as the reign of Philip. Ammianus Marcellinus has so servilely copied (xxiii. 6) his ancient materials, which are indeed very good, that he describes the amily of the Arsacides as still seated on the Persian throne in the middle of the fourth century.

[3] The tanner's name was Babec; the soldier's, Sassan: from the former Artaxerxes obtained the surname of Babegan: from the latter all his descendants have been styled *Sassanides*.

represent him as descended from a branch of the ancient kings of Persia, though time and misfortune had gradually reduced his ancestors to the humble station of private citizens.[1] As the lineal heir of the monarchy, he asserted his right to the throne, and challenged the noble task of delivering the Persians from the oppression under which they groaned above five centuries since the death of Darius. The Parthians were defeated in three great battles. In the last of these their king Artaban was slain, and the spirit of the nation was for ever broken.[2] The authority of Artaxerxes was solemnly acknowledged in a great assembly held at Balch in Khorasan. Two younger branches of the royal house of Arsaces were confounded among the prostrate satraps. A third, more mindful of ancient grandeur than of present necessity, attempted to retire, with a numerous train of vassals, towards their kinsman, the king of Armenia; but this little army of deserters was intercepted, and cut off, by the vigilance of the conqueror,[3] who boldly assumed the double diadem, and the title of King of Kings, which had been enjoyed by his predecessor. But these pompous titles, instead of gratifying the vanity of the Persian, served only to admonish him of his duty, and to inflame in his soul the ambition of restoring, in their full splendour, the religion and empire of Cyrus.

I. During the long servitude of Persia under the Macedonian and the Parthian yoke, the nations of Europe and Asia had mutually adopted and corrupted each other's superstitions. The Arsacides, indeed, practised the worship of the Magi; but they disgraced and polluted it with a various mixture of foreign idolatry. The memory of Zoroaster, the ancient prophet and philosopher of the Persians,[4] was still revered in the East; but

[1] D'Herbelot. Bibliotheque Orientale. Ardshir.
[2] Dion Cassius, l. lxxx. Herodian, l. vi. p. 207. Abulpharagius Dynast. p. 80.

[On the field of Hoormuz (or Ormuz) the son of Babec was saluted on the field with the lofty title " Shahan Shah, Ruler of Rulers," and this name has ever since been adopted by the sovereigns of Persia. Cf. Malcolm, *History of Persia*, i. 71. The name Ardshir should be written Ardeshir.—O. S.]

[3] Moses Chorenensis, l. ii. c. 65-71.

[4] Hyde and Prideaux, working up the Persian legends and their own conjectures into a very agreeable story, represent Zoroaster as a contemporary of Darius Hystaspes. But it is sufficient to observe, that the Greek writers, who lived almost in the age of Darius, agree in placing the era of Zoroaster many hundred, or even thousand, years before their own time. The judicious criticism of Mr. Moyle perceived, and maintained against his uncle Dr. Prideaux, the antiquity of the Persian prophet. See his work, vol. ii.

[Zoroaster, who is styled Zarathustra in the Zendavesta, and Zerdusht by the Persians, is universally represented as the founder of the Magian

the obsolete and mysterious language in which the Zendavesta was composed,[1] opened a field of dispute to seventy sects, who variously explained the fundamental doctrines of their religion, and were all indifferently derided by a crowd of infidels, who rejected the divine mission and miracles of the Prophet. To suppress the idolaters, reunite the schismatics, and confute the unbelievers, by the infallible decision of a general council, the pious Artaxerxes summoned the Magi from all parts of his dominions. These priests, who had so long sighed in contempt and obscurity, obeyed the welcome summons; and on the appointed day appeared, to the number of about eighty thousand. But as the debates of so tumultuous an assembly could not have been directed by the authority of reason, or influenced by the art of policy, the Persian synod was reduced, by successive operations, to forty thousand, to four thousand, to four hundred, to forty, and at last to seven Magi, the most respected for their learning and piety. One of these, Erdaviraph, a young but holy prelate, received from the hands of his brethren three cups of soporiferous wine. He drank them off, and instantly fell into a long and profound sleep. As soon as he waked, he related to the king and to the believing multitude his journey to Heaven, and his intimate conferences with the Diety. Every doubt was silenced by this supernatural evidence; and the articles of the faith of Zoroaster were fixed with equal authority and precision.[2] A short delineation of that celebrated system will be found useful, not only to display the character of the Persian nation, but to illustrate many of their most important transactions, both in peace and war, with the Roman empire.[3]

---

religion. There has been the most complete divergence of opinion as to the time at which he lived. In the Zendavesta, Zarathustra is said to have lived in the reign of Vitacpa, called Gushtasp by the Persians, who belonged to the dynasty of the Kavja or Kayanians. This Gushtasp has been identified by some with Darius Hystaspes. But a more critical examination of the Zendavesta has shown that the religion of Zarathustra was known in the eastern parts of Iran, Bactria, and Sogdiana, not later than one thousand years before Christ. Cf. Duncker, Geschichte des Alterthums, vol. ii. p. 307. —O. S.]

[1] That ancient idiom was called the *Zend*. The language of the commentary, the Pehlvi, though much more modern, has ceased many ages ago to be a living tongue. This fact alone (if it is allowed as authentic) sufficiently warrants the antiquity of those writings, which M. d'Anquetil has brought into Europe, and translated into French.

[2] Hyde de Religione veterum Pers. c. 21.

[3] I have principally drawn this account from the Zendavesta of M. d'Anquetil, and the Sadder, subjoined to Dr. Hyde's treatise. It must, however, be confessed, that the studied obscurity of a prophet, the figurative style of the East, and the deceitful medium of a French or Latin ver-

The great and fundamental article of the system was the celebrated doctrine of the two principles; a bold and injudicious
attempt of Eastern philosophy to reconcile the existence of moral
and physical evil with the attributes of a beneficent Creator
and Governor of the world. The first and original Being, in
whom, or by whom, the universe exists, is denominated in the
writings of Zoroaster, *Time without bounds ;* but it must be confessed that this infinite substance seems rather a metaphysical
abstraction of the mind, than a real object endowed with self-
consciousness, or possessed of moral perfections.[1] From either
the blind or the intelligent operation of this infinite Time, which
bears but too near an affinity with the chaos of the Greeks, the
two secondary but active principles of the universe were from all
eternity produced, Ormusd and Ahriman, each of them possessed
of the powers of creation, but each disposed, by his invariable
nature, to exercise them with different designs. The principle
of good is eternally absorbed in light; the principle of evil
eternally buried in darkness. The wise benevolence of Ormusd
formed man capable of virtue, and abundantly provided his fair
habitation with the materials of happiness. By his vigilant
providence, the motion of the planets, the order of the seasons,
and the temperate mixture of the elements, are preserved. But
the malice of Ahriman has long since pierced *Ormusd's egg ;* or,
in other words, has violated the harmony of his works. Since
that fatal irruption the most minute articles of good and evil
are intimately intermingled and agitated together; the rankest
poisons spring up amidst the most salutary plants; deluges,
earthquakes, and conflagrations, attest the conflict of Nature,
and the little world of man is perpetually shaken by vice and
misfortune. Whilst the rest of human kind are led away captives
in the chains of their infernal enemy, the faithful Persian alone
reserves his religious adoration for his friend and protector
Ormusd, and fights under his banner of light, in the full confi-

sion, may have betrayed us into error and heresy in this abridgment of
Persian theology.
  [It is to be regretted (says Guizot) that Gibbon followed the Sadder,
which is certainly post-Mahometan. Hyde considered that it was written
not more than 200 years before his time.—O. S.]
  [1] [This is not correct. The doctrine of *Time without Bounds*, a translation of Zarvaneakarane, as the first or original principle from which
Ormuzd and Ahriman were created, is not found in the Zendavesta. It
was probably introduced through the Persian religion from Greek philosophy. In the Zendavesta the simple representation is that all the good
spirits are subject to Ormuzd, and all the evil ones to Ahriman. The
doctrine of *Time without Bounds* is first mentioned by Theodore of Mops-
uestia in A.D. 429.—O. S.]

dence that he shall, in the last day, share the glory of his triumph. At that decisive period, the enlightened wisdom of goodness will render the power of Ormusd superior to the furious malice of his rival. Ahriman and his followers, disarmed and subdued, will sink into their native darkness; and virtue will maintain the eternal peace and harmony of the universe.[1]

The theology of Zoroaster was darkly comprehended by foreigners, and even by the far greater number of his disciples; but the most careless observers were struck with the philosophic simplicity of the Persian worship. " That people," säys Herodotus,[2] " rejects the use of temples, of altars, and of statues, and smiles at the folly of those nations who imagine that the gods are sprung from, or bear any affinity with, the human nature. The tops of the highest mountains are the places chosen for sacrifices. Hymns and prayers are the principal worship; the Supreme God who fills the wide circle of Heaven is the object to whom they are addressed." Yet, at the same time, in the true spirit of a polytheist, he accuses them of adoring Earth, Water, Fire, the Winds, and the Sun and Moon. But the Persians of every age have denied the charge, and explained the equivocal conduct, which might appear to give a colour to it. The elements, and more particularly Fire, Light, and the Sun, whom they called Mithra, were the objects of their religious reverence, because they considered them as the purest symbols, the noblest productions, and the most powerful agents of the Divine Power and Nature.[3]

Every mode of religion, to make a deep and lasting impression on the human mind, must exercise our obedience, by enjoining practices of devotion; and must acquire our esteem, by incul-

---

[1] The modern Persees (and in some degree the Sadder) exalt Ormusd into the first and omnipotent cause, whilst they degrade Ahriman into an inferior but rebellious spirit. Their desire of pleasing the Mahometans may have contributed to refine their theological system.

[The fragments of the Zendavesta contain nothing respecting the final defeat of Ahriman, and the future happiness of the world. It is evident, however, from the Greek writers that this doctrine formed part of the Persian system of religion even at an early period.—O. S.]

[2] Herodotus, l. i. c. 131. But Dr. Prideaux thinks, with reason, that the use of temples was afterwards permitted in the Magian religion.

[The fire temples such as are now in use among the Parsees are first mentioned by Strabo (xv. p. 732). Pausanias, v. 27, § 5-6. At a later period (says Berosus) the Persians began to worship statues of the Gods in human form. The same writer relates that this custom was first introduced by Artaxerxes, son of Ochus.—O. S.]

[3] Hyde de Relig. Pers. c. 8. Notwithstanding all their distinctions and protestations, which seem sincere enough, their tyrants, the Mahometans, have constantly stigmatised them as idolatrous worshippers of the Fire.

ca:ing moral duties analogous to the dictates of our own hearts. The religion of Zoroaster was abundantly provided with the former, and possessed a sufficient portion of the latter. At the age of puberty, the faithful Persian was invested with a mysterious girdle, the badge of the divine protection, and from that moment all the actions of his life, even the most indifferent, or the most necessary, were sanctified by their peculiar prayers, ejaculations, or genuflexions; the omission of which, under any circumstances, was a grievous sin, not inferior in guilt to the violation of the moral duties. The moral duties, however, of justice, mercy, liberality, etc., were in their turn required of the disciple of Zoroaster, who wished to escape the persecution of Ahriman, and to live with Ormusd in a blissful eternity, where the degree of felicity will be exactly proportioned to the degree of virtue and piety.[1]

But there are some remarkable instances, in which Zoroaster lays aside the prophet, assumes the legislator, and discovers a liberal concern for private and public happiness, seldom to be found among the grovelling or visionary schemes of superstition. Fasting and celibacy, the common means of purchasing the Divine favour, he condemns with abhorrence, as a criminal rejection of the best gifts of Providence. The saint, in the Magian religion, is obliged to beget children, to plant useful trees, to destroy noxious animals, to convey water to the dry lands of Persia, and to work out his salvation by pursuing all the labours of agriculture. We may quote from the Zendavesta a wise and benevolent maxim, which compensates for many an absurdity. " He who sows the ground with care and diligence, acquires a greater stock of religious merit, than he could gain by the repetition of ten thousand prayers." [2] In the spring of every year a festival was celebrated, destined to represent the primitive equality, and the present connection, of mankind. The stately kings of Persia, exchanging their vain pomp for more genuine greatness, freely mingled with the humblest but most useful of their subjects. On that day the husbandmen were admitted, without distinction, to the table of the king, and his satraps. The monarch accepted their petitions, inquired into their grievances, and conversed with them on the most equal terms,

---

[1] See the Sadder, the smallest part of which consists of moral precepts. The ceremonies enjoined are infinite and trifling. Fifteen genuflexions, prayers, etc., were required whenever the devout Persian cut his nails or made water; or as often as he put on the sacred girdle. Sadder, Art. 14, 50, 60.

[2] Zendavesta, tom. i. p. 224, and Precis du Système de Zoroastre, tom. iii.

" From your labours," was he accustomed to say (and to say with
truth, if not with sincerity), " from your labours, we receive our
subsistence; you derive your tranquillity from our vigilance;
since, therefore, we are mutually necessary to each other, let
us live together like brothers in concord and love." [1] Such a
festival must indeed have degenerated, in a wealthy and despotic
empire, into a theatrical representation; but it was at least a
comedy well worthy of a royal audience, and which might sometimes imprint a salutary lesson on the mind of a young prince.

Had Zoroaster, in all his institutions, invariably supported
this exalted character, his name would deserve a place with those
of Numa and Confucius, and his system would be justly entitled
to all the applause which it has pleased some of our divines, and
even some of our philosophers, to bestow on it. But in that
motley composition, dictated by reason and passion, by enthusiasm and by selfish motives, some useful and sublime truths were
disgraced by a mixture of the most abject and dangerous superstition. The Magi, or sacerdotal order, were extremely numerous,
since, as we have already seen, fourscore thousand of them were
convened in a general council. Their forces were multiplied by
discipline. A regular hierarchy was diffused through all the
provinces of Persia; and the Archimagus, who resided at Balch,
was respected as the visible head of the church, and the lawful
successor of Zoroaster.[2] The property of the Magi was very
considerable. Besides the less invidious possession of a large
tract of the most fertile lands of Media,[3] they levied a general
tax on the fortunes and the industry of the Persians.[4] " Though
your good works, ' says the interested prophet, " exceed in
number the leaves of the trees, the drops of rain, the stars in the
heaven, or the sands on the sea-shore, they will all be unprofitable to you, unless they are accepted by the *destour*, or priest.
To obtain the acceptation of this guide to salvation, you must
faithfully pay him *tithes* of all you possess, of your goods, of
your lands, and of your money. If the destour be satisfied,

[1] Hyde de Religione Persarum, c. 19.
[2] Hyde de Religione Persarum, c. 28. Both Hyde and Prideaux affect
to apply to the Magian the terms consecrated to the Christian hierarchy.
[3] Ammian. Marcellin. xxiii. 6. He informs us (as far as we may credit
him) of two curious particulars; 1, that the Magi derived some of their
most secret doctrines from the Indian Brachmans; and 2, that they were
a tribe or family, as well as order.
[4] The divine institution of tithes exhibits a singular instance of conformity between the law of Zoroaster and that of Moses. Those who cannot
otherwise account for it, may suppose, if they please, that the Magi of the
latter times inserted so useful an interpolation into the writings of their
prophet.

your soul will escape hell tortures; you will secure praise in this
world and happiness in the next. For the destours are the
teachers of religion; they know all things, and they deliver all
men." [1]

These convenient maxims of reverence and implicit faith were
doubtless imprinted with care on the tender minds of youth;
since the Magi were the masters of education in Persia, and to
their hands the children even of the royal family were intrusted.[2]
The Persian priests, who were of a speculative genius, preserved
and investigated the secrets of Oriental philosophy; and acquired, either by superior knowledge or superior art, the reputation of being well versed in some occult sciences, which have
derived their appellation from the Magi.[3] Those of more active
dispositions mixed with the world in courts and cities; and it is
observed, that the administration of Artaxerxes was in a great
measure directed by the counsels of the sacerdotal order, whose
dignity, either from policy or devotion, that prince restored to
its ancient splendour.[4]

The first counsel of the Magi was agreeable to the unsociable
genius of their faith,[5] to the practice of ancient kings,[6] and even
to the example of their legislator, who had fallen a victim to a
religious war, excited by his own intolerant zeal.[7] By an edict
of Artaxerxes, the exercise of every worship, except that of
Zoroaster, was severely prohibited. The temples of the Parthians, and the statues of their deified monarchs, were thrown
down with ignominy.[8] The sword of Aristotle (such was the
name given by the Orientals to the polytheism and philosophy
of the Greeks) was easily broken;[9] the flames of persecution soon
reached the more stubborn Jews and Christians;[10] nor did they
spare the heretics of their own nation and religion. The majesty
of Ormusd, who was jealous of a rival, was seconded by the

[1] Sadder, Art. 8. [2] Plato in Alcibiad.
[3] Pliny (Hist. Natur. l. xxx. c. 1) observes, that magic held mankind by
the triple chain of religion, of physic, and of astronomy.
[4] Agathias, l. iv. p. 134.
[5] Mr. Hume, in the Natural History of Religion, remarks that the most
refined and philosophic sects are the most intolerant.
[6] Cicero de Legibus, ii. 10. Xerxes, by the advice of the Magi, destroyed
the temples of Greece.
[7] Hyde de Rel. Persar. c. 23, 24. D'Herbelot Bibliothèque Orientale
Zordusht. Life of Zoraster in tom. ii. of the Zendavesta.
[8] Compare Moses of Chorene, l. ii. c. 74 with Ammian. Marcellin. xxiii. 6.
Hereafter I shall make use of these passages.
[9] Rabbi Abraham in the Tarikh Schickard, p. 108, 109.
[10] Basnage Histoire des Juifs, l. viii. c. 3. Sozomen, l. ii. c. 1. Manes,
who suffered an ignominious death, may be deemed a Magian as well as a
Christian heretic.

despotism of Artaxerxes, who could not suffer a rebel; and the schismatics within his vast empire were soon reduced to the inconsiderable number of eighty thousand.[1] This spirit of persecution reflects dishonour on the religion of Zoroaster; but as it was not productive of any civil commotion, it served to strengthen the new monarchy, by uniting all the various inhabitants of Persia in the bands of religious zeal.

II. Artaxerxes, by his valour and conduct, had wrested the sceptre of the East from the ancient royal family of Parthia. There still remained the more difficult task of establishing, throughout the vast extent of Persia, a uniform and vigorous administration. The weak indulgence of the Arsacides had resigned to their sons and brothers the principal provinces, and the greatest offices of the kingdom, in the nature of hereditary possessions. The *vitaxæ*, or eighteen most powerful satraps, were permitted to assume the regal title; and the vain pride of the monarch was delighted with a nominal dominion over so many vassal kings. Even tribes of barbarians in their mountains, and the Greek cities of Upper Asia,[2] within their walls, scarcely acknowledged, or seldom obeyed, any superior; and the Parthian empire exhibited, under other names, a lively image of the feudal system [3] which has since prevailed in Europe. But the active victor, at the head of a numerous and disciplined army, visited in person every province of Persia. The defeat of the boldest rebels, and the reduction of the strongest fortifications,[4] diffused the terror of his arms, and prepared the way for the peaceful reception of his authority. An obstinate resistance was fatal to the chiefs; but their followers were treated with lenity.[5] A cheerful submission was rewarded with honours and riches; but the prudent Artaxerxes, suffering no person except

---

[1] Hyde de Religione Persar. c. 21.

[2] These colonies were extremely numerous. Seleucus Nicator founded thirty-nine cities, all named from himself, or some of his relations (Appian in Syriac. p. 124). The æra of Seleucus (still in use among the Eastern Christians) appears as late as the year 508, of Christ 196, on the medals of the Greek cities within the Parthian empire. Moyle, vol. i. p. 273, etc., and M. Freret, Mém. de l'Académie, tom. xix.

[3] The modern Persians distinguish that period as the dynasty of the kings of the nations. Plin. Hist. Nat. vi. 25.

[4] Eutychius (tom. i. p. 367, 371, 375) relates the siege of the island of Mesene in the Tigris, with some circumstances not unlike the story of Nisus and Scylla.

[5] Agathias, ii. 164. The princes of Segestan defended their independence during many years. As romances generally transport to an ancient period the events of their own time, it is not impossible that the fabulous exploits of Rustan prince of Segestan may have been grafted on this real history.

himself to assume the title of king, abolished every intermediate
power between the throne and the people. His kingdom, nearly
equal in extent to modern Persia, was, on every side, bounded
by the sea, or by great rivers; by the Euphrates, the Tigris, the
Araxes, the Oxus, and the Indus, by the Caspian Sea, and the
Gulf of Persia.[1] That country was computed to contain, in the
last century, five hundred and fifty-four cities, sixty thousand
villages, and about forty millions of souls.[2] If we compare the
administration of the house of Sassan with that of the house of
Sefi, the political influence of the Magian with that of the
Mahometan religion, we shall probably infer, that the kingdom
of Artaxerxes contained at least as great a number of cities,
villages, and inhabitants. But it must likewise be confessed,
that in every age the want of harbours on the sea-coast, and the
scarcity of fresh water in the inland provinces, have been very
unfavourable to the commerce and agriculture of the Persians;
who, in the calculation of their numbers, seem to have indulged
one of the meanest, though most common, articles of national
vanity.

As soon as the ambitious mind of Artaxerxes had triumphed
over the resistance of his vassals, he began to threaten the neighbouring states, who, during the long slumber of his predecessors,
had insulted Persia with impunity. He obtained some easy
victories over the wild Scythians and the effeminate Indians;
but the Romans were an enemy who, by their past injuries and
present power, deserved the utmost efforts of his arms. A forty
years' tranquillity, the fruit of valour and moderation, had succeeded the victories of Trajan. During the period that elapsed
from the accession of Marcus to the reign of Alexander, the
Roman and the Parthian empires were twice engaged in war;
and although the whole strength of the Arsacides contended with
a part only of the forces of Rome, the event was most commonly

---

[1] We can scarcely attribute to the Persian monarchy the sea-coast of
Gedrosia or Macran, which extends along the Indian Ocean from Cape Jast
(the promontory of Capella) to Cape Goadel. In the time of Alexander,
and probably many ages afterwards, it was thinly inhabited by a savage
people of Icthyophagi, or Fishermen, who knew no arts, who acknowledged
no master, and who were divided by inhospitable deserts from the rest of
the world. (Arrian de Reb. Indicis.) In the twelfth century, the little
town of Taiz (supposed by M. d'Anville to be the Tesa of Ptolemy) was
peopled and enriched by the resort of the Arabian merchants. (Geographie
Nubiens, p. 58; d'Anville Géographie Ancienne, tom. ii. p. 283.) In
the last age the whole country was divided between three princes, one
Mahometan and two Idolaters, who maintained their independence against
the successors of Shaw Abbas. (Voyages de Tavernier, part. i. l. v. p. 635).
[2] Chardin, tom. iii. c. 1, 2, 3.

in favour of the latter. Macrinus, indeed, prompted by his
precarious situation and pusillanimous temper, purchased a
peace at the expense of near two millions of our money;[1] but the
generals of Marcus, the emperor Severus, and his son, erected
many trophies in Armenia, Mesopotamia, and Assyria. Among
their exploits, the imperfect relation of which would have un-
seasonably interrupted the more important series of domestic
revolutions, we shall only mention the repeated calamities of
the two great cities of Seleucia and Ctesiphon.

Seleucia, on the western bank of the Tigris, about forty-five
miles to the north of ancient Babylon, was the capital of the
Macedonian conquests in Upper Asia.[2] Many ages after the fall
of their empire, Seleucia retained the genuine characters of a
Grecian colony, arts, military virtue, and the love of freedom.
The independent republic was governed by a senate of three
hundred nobles; the people consisted of six hundred thousand
citizens; the walls were strong, and as long as concord prevailed
among the several orders of the state, they viewed with contempt the power of the Parthian: but the madness of faction was
sometimes provoked to implore the dangerous aid of the common
enemy, who was posted almost at the gates of the colony.[3] The
Parthian monarchs, like the Mogul sovereigns of Hindostan,
delighted in the pastoral life of their Scythian ancestor; and the
Imperial camp was frequently pitched in the plain of Ctesiphon,
on the eastern bank of the Tigris, at the distance of only three
miles from Seleucia.[4] The innumerable attendants on luxury
and despotism resorted to the court, and the little village of
Ctesiphon insensibly swelled into a great city.[5] Under the reign
of Marcus, the Roman generals (A.D. 165) penetrated as far as
Ctesiphon and Seleucia. They were received as friends by the
Greek colony; they attacked as enemies the seat of the Parthian
kings; yet both cities experienced the same treatment. The
sack and conflagration of Seleucia, with the massacre of three

---

[1] Dion, l. xxviii. p. 1335.

[2] For the precise situation of Babylon, Seleucia, Ctesiphon, Modain, and
Bagdad, cities often confounded with each other, see an excellent Geographical Tract of M. d'Anville, in Mem. de l'Academie, tom. xxx.

[3] Tacit. Annal. xi. 42. Plin. Hist. Nat. vi. 26.

[4] This may be inferred from Strabo, l. xvi. p. 743.

[5] That most curious traveller Bernier, who followed the camp of Aureng-
zebe from Delhi to Cashmir, describes with great accuracy the immense
moving city. The guard of cavalry consisted of 35,000 men, that of infantry of 10,000. It was computed that the camp contained 150,000
horses, mules, and elephants; 50,000 camels, 50,000 oxen, and between
300,000 and 400,000 persons. Almost all Delhi followed the court, whose
magnificence supported its industry.

hundred thousand of the inhabitants, tarnished the glory of the
Roman triumph.[1] Seleucia, already exhausted by the neigh
bourhood of a too powerful rival, sunk under the fatal blow;
but Ctesiphon (A.D. 198), in about thirty-three years, had sufficiently recovered its strength to maintain an obstinate siege
against the emperor Severus. The city was, however, taken by
assault; the king, who defended it in person, escaped with
precipitation; an hundred thousand captives, and a rich booty,
rewarded the fatigues of the Roman soldiers.[2] Notwithstanding these misfortunes, Ctesiphon succeeded to Babylon and to
Seleucia, as one of the great capitals of the East. In summer,
the monarch of Persia enjoyed at Ecbatana the cool breezes of
the mountains of Media; but the mildness of the climate engaged
him to prefer Ctesiphon for his winter residence.

From these successful inroads, the Romans derived no real or
lasting benefit; nor did they attempt to preserve such distant
conquests, separated from the provinces of the empire by a
large tract of intermediate desert. The reduction of the kingdom of Osrhoene, was an acquisition of less splendour indeed,
but of a far more solid advantage. That little state occupied the
northern and most fertile part of Mesopotamia, between the
Euphrates and the Tigris. Edessa, its capital, was situated
about twenty miles beyond the former of those rivers; and the
inhabitants, since the time of Alexander, were a mixed race of
Greeks, Arabs, Syrians, and Armenians.[3] The feeble sovereigns
of Osrhoene, placed on the dangerous verge of two contending
empires, were attached from inclination to the Parthian cause;
but the superior power of Rome exacted from them a reluctant
homage, which is still attested by their medals. After the conclusion of the Parthian war under Marcus, it was judged prudent
to secure some substantial pledges of their doubtful fidelity.
Forts were constructed in several parts of the country, and a
Roman garrison was fixed in the strong town of Nisibis. During
the troubles that followed the death of Commodus, the princes

---

[1] Dion, l. lxxi. [c. 2] p. 1178. Hist. August. [Capit. Verro], p. 38.
Eutrop. viii. 10. Euseb. in Chronic. Quadratus (quoted in the Augustan
History) attempted to vindicate the Romans, by alleging that the citizens
of Seleucia had first violated their faith.

[2] Dion, l. lxxv. p. 1263. Herodian, l. iii. p. 120. Hist. August. [Spart.
Sever. c. 16], p. 70.

[3] The polished citizens of Antioch called those of Edessa mixed bar-
barians. It was, however, some praise, that of the three dialects of the
Syriac, the purest and most elegant (the Aramæan) was spoken at Edessa.
This remark of M. Bayer (Hist. Edess. p. 5) has borrowed from George of
Malatia, a Syrian writer.

of Osrhoene attempted to shake off the yoke; but the stern policy of Severus confirmed their dependence,[1] and the perfidy of Caracalla completed the easy conquest. Abgarus, the last king of Edessa, was (A.D. 216) sent in chains to Rome, his dominions reduced into a province, and his capital dignified with the rank of colony; and thus the Romans, about ten years before the fall of the Parthian monarchy, obtained a firm and permanent establishment beyond the Euphrates.[2]

Prudence as well as glory might have justified a war on the side of Artaxerxes, had his views been confined to the defence or the acquisition of a useful frontier. But the ambitious Persian openly avowed a far more extensive design of conquest; and (A.D. 230) he thought himself able to support his lofty pretensions by the arms of reason as well as by those of power. Cyrus, he alleged, had first subdued, and his successors had for a long time possessed, the whole extent of Asia, as far as the Propontis and the Ægean sea; the provinces of Caria and Ionia, under their empire, had been governed by Persian satraps, and all Egypt, to the confines of Æthiopia, had acknowledged their sovereignty.[3] Their rights had been suspended, but not destroyed, by a long usurpation; and as soon as he received the Persian diadem, which birth and successful valour had placed upon his head, the first great duty of his station called upon him to restore the ancient limits and splendour of the monarchy. The Great King, therefore (such was the haughty style of his embassies to the emperor Alexander), commanded the Romans instantly to depart from all the provinces of his ancestors, and, yielding to the Persians the empire of Asia, to content themselves with the undisturbed possession of Europe. This haughty mandate was delivered by four hundred of the tallest and most beautiful of the Persians; who, by their fine horses, splendid arms, and rich apparel, displayed the pride and greatness of their master.[4] Such an embassy was much less an offer of negotiation than a declaration of war. Both Alexander Severus and Artaxerxes, collecting

---

[1] Dion, l. lxxv. p. 1248, 1249, 1250. M. Bayer has neglected to use this most important passage.

[2] This kingdom, from Osrhoes, who gave a new name to the country, to the last Abgarus, had lasted 353 years. See the learned work of M. Bayer, Historia Osrhoena et Edessena.

[3] Xenophon, in the preface to the Cyropædia, gives a clear and magnificent idea of the extent of the empire of Cyrus. Herodotus (l. iii. c. 7-9, etc.) enters into a curious and particular description of the twenty great *Satrapies* into which the Persian empire was divided by Darius Hystaspes.

[4] Herodian, vi. 209, 212.

the military force of the Roman and Persian monarchies, resolved in this important contest to lead their armies in person.

If we credit what should seem the most authentic of all records, an oration, still extant, and delivered by the emperor himself to the senate, we must allow that the victory of Alexander Severus was not inferior to any of those formerly obtained over the Persians by the son of Philip. The army of the Great King consisted of one hundred and twenty thousand horse, clothed in complete armour of steel; of seven hundred elephants, with towers filled with archers on their backs; and of eighteen hundred chariots, armed with scythes. This formidable host, the like of which is not to be found in eastern history, and has scarcely been imagined in eastern romance,[1] was (A.D. 233) discomfited in a great battle, in which the Roman Alexander approved himself an intrepid soldier and a skilful general. The Great King fled before his valour; an immense booty, and the conquest of Mesopotamia, were the immediate fruits of this signal victory. Such are the circumstances of this ostentatious and improbable relation, dictated, as it too plainly appears, by the vanity of the monarch, adorned by the unblushing servility of his flatterers, and received without contradiction by a distant and obsequious senate.[2] Far from being inclined to believe that the arms of Alexander obtained any memorable advantage over the Persians, we are induced to suspect that all this blaze of imaginary glory was designed to conceal some real disgrace.

Our suspicions are confirmed by the authority of a contemporary historian, who mentions the virtues of Alexander with respect, and his faults with candour. He describes the judicious

[1] There were two hundred scythed chariots at the battle of Arbela, in the host of Darius. In the vast army of Tigranes, which was vanquished by Lucullus, seventeen thousand horse only were completely armed. Antiochus brought fifty-four elephants into the field against the Romans: by his frequent wars and negotiations with the princes of India, he had once collected an hundred and fifty of those great animals; but it may be questioned whether the most powerful monarch of Hindostan ever formed a line of battle of seven hundred elephants. Instead of three or four thousand elephants, which the Great Mogul was supposed to possess, Tavernier (Voyages, part ii. l. i. p. 198) discovered, by a more accurate inquiry, that he had only five hundred for his baggage, and eighty or ninety for the service of war. The Greeks have varied with regard to the number which Porus brought into the field: but Quintus Curtius (viii. 13), in this instance judicious and moderate, is contented with eighty-five elephants, distinguished by their size and strength. In Siam, where these animals are the most numerous and the most esteemed, eighteen elephants are allowed as a sufficient proportion for each of the nine brigades into which a just army is divided. The whole number, of one hundred and sixty-two elephants of war, may sometimes be doubled. Hist. des Voyages, tom. ix. p. 260.

[2] Hist. August. p. 133.

plan which had been formed for the conduct of the war. Three
Roman armies were destined to invade Persia at the same time,
and by different roads. But the operations of the campaign,
though wisely concerted, were not executed either with ability
or success. The first of these armies, as soon as it had entered
the marshy plains of Babylon, towards the artificial conflux of
the Euphrates and the Tigris,[1] was encompassed by the superior
numbers, and destroyed by the arrows, of the enemy. The
alliance of Chosroes, king of Armenia,[2] and the long tract of
mountainous country, in which the Persian cavalry was of little
service, opened a secure entrance into the heart of Media to the
second of the Roman armies. These brave troops laid waste the
adjacent provinces, and by several successful actions against
Artaxerxes, gave a faint colour to the emperor's vanity. But
the retreat of this victorious army was imprudent, or at least
unfortunate. In repassing the mountains great numbers of
soldiers perished by the badness of the roads, and the severity of
the winter season. It had been resolved, that whilst these two
great detachments penetrated into the opposite extremes of
the Persian dominions, the main body, under the command of
Alexander himself, should support their attack by invading the
centre of the kingdom. But the inexperienced youth, influenced
by his mother's counsels, and perhaps by his own fears, deserted
the bravest troops and the fairest prospect of victory; and after
consuming in Mesopotamia an inactive and inglorious summer,
he led back to Antioch an army diminished by sickness, and
provoked by disappointment. The behaviour of Artaxerxes had
been very different. Flying with rapidity from the hills of
Media to the marshes of the Euphrates, he had everywhere
opposed the invaders in person; and in either fortune had united
with the ablest conduct the most undaunted resolution. But in
several obstinate engagements against the veteran legions of
Rome, the Persian monarch had lost the flower of his troops.
Even his victories had weakened his power. The favourable
opportunities of the absence of Alexander, and of the confusions
that followed that emperor's death, presented themselves in
vain to his ambition. Instead of expelling the Romans,
as he pretended, from the continent of Asia, he found him-

---

[1] M. de Tillemont has already observed, that Herodian's geography is
somewhat confused.

[2] Moses of Chorene (Hist. Armen. l. ii. c. 71) illustrates this invasion of
Media, by asserting that Chosroes, king of Armenia, defeated Artaxerxes,
and pursued him to the confines of India. The exploits of Chosroes have
been magnified; and he acted as a dependent ally to the Romans.

self unable to wrest from their hands the little province of Mesopotamia.[1]

The reign of Artaxerxes, which from the last defeat of the Parthians (A.D. 240) lasted only fourteen years, forms a memorable era in the history of the East, and even in that of Rome. His character seems to have been marked by those bold and commanding features that generally distinguished the princes who conquer, from those who inherit, an empire. Till the last period of the Persian monarchy his code of laws was respected as the ground-work of their civil and religious policy.[2] Several of his sayings are preserved. One of them in particular discovers a deep insight into the constitution of government. "The authority of the prince," said Artaxerxes, "must be defended by a military force; that force can only be maintained by taxes; all taxes must, at last, fall upon agriculture; and agriculture can never flourish except under the protection of justice and moderation."[3] Artaxerxes bequeathed his new empire, and his ambitious designs against the Romans, to Sapor, a son not unworthy of his great father; but those designs were too extensive for the power of Persia, and served only to involve both nations in a long series of destructive wars and reciprocal calamities.

The Persians, long since civilised and corrupted, were very far from possessing the martial independence and the intrepid hardness, both of mind and body, which have rendered the northern barbarians masters of the world. The science of war, that constituted the more rational force of Greece and Rome, as it now does of Europe, never made any considerable progress in the East. Those disciplined evolutions which harmonise and animate a confused multitude were unknown to the Persians. They were equally unskilled in the arts of constructing, besieging, or defending regular fortifications. They trusted more to their courage than to their discipline. The infantry was a half-armed spiritless crowd of peasants, levied in haste by the allurements of plunder, and as easily dispersed by a victory as by a defeat. The monarch and his nobles transported into the camp the pride

---

[1] For the account of this war, see Herodian, l. vi. [cap. 5], p. 209, 212. The old abbreviators and modern compilers have blindly followed the Augustan History.

[2] Eutychius, tom. ii. p. 180, vers. Pocock. The great Chosroes Noushirwan sent the Code of Artaxerxes to all his satraps, as the invariable rule of their conduct.

[3] D'Herbelot Bibliothèque Orientale, au mot *Ardshir*. We may observe, that after an ancient period of fables, and a long interval of darkness, the modern histories of Persia begin to assume an air of truth with the dynasty of the Sassanides.

and luxury of the seraglio. Their military operations were impeded by a useless train of women, eunuchs, horses, and camels, and in the midst of a successful campaign the Persian host was often separated or destroyed by an unexpected famine.[1]

But the nobles of Persia, in the bosom of luxury and despotism, preserved a strong sense of personal gallantry and national honour. From the age of seven years they were taught to speak truth, to shoot with the bow, and to ride; and it was universally confessed, that in the two last of these arts they had made a more than common proficiency.[2] The most distinguished youth were educated under the monarch's eye, practised their exercises in the gate of his palace, and were severely trained up to the habits of temperance and obedience in their long and laborious parties of hunting. In every province the satrap maintained a like school of military virtue. The Persian nobles (so natural is the idea of feudal tenures) received from the king's bounty lands and houses, on the condition of their service in war. They were ready on the first summons to mount on horseback, with a martial and splendid train of followers, and to join the numerous bodies of guards, who were carefully selected from amongst the most robust slaves, and the bravest adventurers of Asia. These armies, both of light and of heavy cavalry, equally formidable by the impetuosity of their charge, and the rapidity of their motions, threatened, as an impending cloud, the eastern provinces of the declining empire of Rome.[3]

---

[1] Herodian, l. vi. p. 214. Ammianus Marcellinus, l. xxiii. c. 6. Some differences may be observed between the two historians, the natural effects of the changes produced by a century and a half.

[2] The Persians are still the most skilful horsemen, and their horses the finest, in the East.

[3] From Herodotus, Xenophon, Herodian, Ammianus, Chardin, etc., I have extracted such *probable* accounts of the Persian nobility, as seem either common to every age, or particular to that of the Sassanides.

GENEALOGICAL TABLE OF THE SASSANIDAN KINGS OF PERSIA

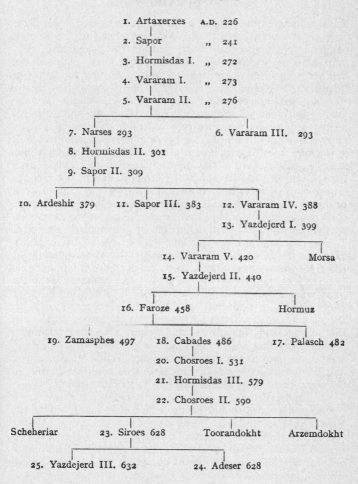

1. Artaxerxes   A.D. 226
2. Sapor   „   241
3. Hormisdas I.   „   272
4. Vararam I.   „   273
5. Vararam II.   „   276

7. Narses 293   6. Vararam III. 293

8. Hormisdas II. 301

9. Sapor II. 309

10. Ardeshir 379   11. Sapor III. 383   12. Vararam IV. 388

13. Yazdejerd I. 399

14. Vararam V. 420   Morsa

15. Yazdejerd II. 440

16. Faroze 458   Hormuz

19. Zamasphes 497   18. Cabades 486   17. Palasch 482

20. Chosroes I. 531

21. Hormisdas III. 579

22. Chosroes II. 590

Scheheriar   23. Siroes 628   Toorandokht   Arzemdokht

25. Yazdejerd III. 632   24. Adeser 628

CHAPTER IX

The State of Germany till the Invasion of the Barbarians, in the time of the Emperor Decius

THE government and religion of Persia have deserved some notice from their connection with the decline and fall of the Roman empire. We shall occasionally mention the Scythian or Sarmatian tribes, which, with their arms and horses, their flocks and herbs, their wives and families, wandered over the immense plains which spread themselves from the Caspian Sea to the Vistula, from the confines of Persia to those of Germany. But the warlike Germans, who first resisted, then invaded, and at length overturned, the western monarchy of Rome, will occupy a much more important place in this history, and possess a stronger, and, if we may use the expression, a more domestic, claim to our attention and regard. The most civilised nations of modern Europe issued from the woods of Germany, and in the rude institutions of those barbarians we may still distinguish the original principles of our present laws and manners. In their primitive state of simplicity and independence the Germans were surveyed by the discerning eye, and delineated by the masterly pencil, of Tacitus, the first of historians who applied the science of philosophy to the study of facts. The expressive conciseness of his descriptions has deserved to exercise the diligence of innumerable antiquarians, and to excite the genius and penetration of the philosophic historians of our own times. The subject, however various and important, has already been so frequently, so ably, and so successfully discussed, that it is now grown familiar to the reader, and difficult to the writer. We shall therefore content ourselves with observing, and indeed with repeating, some of the most important circumstances of climate, of manners, and of institutions, which rendered the wild barbarians of Germany such formidable enemies to the Roman power.

Ancient Germany, excluding from its independent limits the province westward of the Rhine, which had submitted to the Roman yoke, extended itself over a third part of Europe. Almost the whole of modern Germany, Denmark, Norway, Sweden, Finland, Livonia, Prussia, and the greater part of Poland, were peopled by the various tribes of one great nation, whose complexion, manners, and language denoted a common origin and preserved a striking resemblance. On the west, ancient Germany was divided by the Rhine from the Gallic, and on the south by the Danube from the Illyrian, provinces of the empire. A ridge of hills, rising from the Danube, and called the Carpathian mountains, covered Germany on the side of Dacia or Hungary. The eastern frontier was faintly marked by the mutual fears of the Germans and the Sarmatians, and was often confounded by the mixture of warring and confederating tribes of the two nations. In the remote darkness of the north, the ancients imperfectly descried a frozen ocean that lay beyond the Baltic Sea, and beyond the Peninsula, or islands,[1] of Scandinavia.

Some ingenious writers [2] have suspected that Europe was much colder formerly than it is at present; and the most ancient descriptions of the climate of Germany tend exceedingly to confirm their theory. The general complaints of intense frost, and eternal winter, are perhaps little to be regarded, since we have no method of reducing to the accurate standard of the thermometer the feelings or the expressions of an orator, born in the happier regions of Greece or Asia. But I shall select two remarkable circumstances of a less equivocal nature. 1. The great rivers which covered the Roman provinces, the Rhine and the Danube, were frequently frozen over, and capable of supporting the most enormous weights. The barbarians, who often chose that severe season for their inroads, transported, without apprehension or danger, their numerous armies, their cavalry, and their heavy waggons, over a vast and solid bridge of ice.[3] Modern ages have not presented an instance of a like phenomenon. 2. The reindeer, that useful animal, from whom the savage of the North derives the best comforts of his dreary life, is of a constitution that supports, and even requires, the most intense cold. He is found on the rock of Spitzberg, within ten degrees of the

---

[1] The modern philosophers of Sweden seem agreed that the waters of the Baltic gradually sink in a regular proportion, which they have ventured to estimate at half an inch every year. Twenty centuries ago, the flat country of Scandinavia must have been covered by the sea; while the high lands rose above the waters, as so many islands of various forms and dimensions. Such indeed is the notion given us by Mela, Pliny, and Tacitus, of the vast countries round the Baltic. See in the Bibliothèque Raisonée, tom. xl. and xlv. a large abstract of Dalin's History of Sweden, composed in the Swedish language.

[2] In particular, Hume, the Abbé du Bos, and M. Pelloutier, Hist. des Celtes, tom. i.

[3] Diodorus Siculus, l. v. p. 340, Edit. Wessel. Herodian, l. vi. p. 221. Jornandes, c. 55. On the banks of the Danube, the wine, when brought to table, was frequently frozen into great lumps, *frusta vini.* Ovid. Epist. ex Ponto, l. iv. 7, 9, 10. Virgil. Georgic. l. iii. 355. The fact is confirmed by a soldier and a philosopher, who had experienced the intense cold of Thrace. Xenophon, Anabasis, l. vii. p. 560. Edit. Hutchinson.

Pole; he seems to delight in the snows of Lapland and Siberia;
but at present he cannot subsist, much less multiply, in any
country to the south of the Baltic.[1] In the time of Cæsar, the
reindeer, as well as the elk and the wild bull, was a native of the
Hercynian forest, which then overshadowed a great part of
Germany and Poland.[2] The modern improvements sufficiently
explain the causes of the diminution of the cold. These immense
woods have been gradually cleared, which intercepted from the
earth the rays of the sun.[3] The morasses have been drained,
and, in proportion as the soil has been cultivated, the air has
become more temperate. Canada, at this day, is an exact
picture of ancient Germany. Although situated in the same
parallel with the finest provinces of France and England, that
country experiences the most rigorous cold. The reindeer are
very numerous, the ground is covered with deep and lasting
snow, and the great river of St. Lawrence is regularly frozen, in
a season when the waters of the Seine and the Thames are
usually free from ice.[4]

It is difficult to ascertain, and easy to exaggerate, the influence
of the climate of ancient Germany over the minds and bodies
of the natives. Many writers have supposed, and most have
allowed, though, as it should seem, without any adequate proof,
that the rigorous cold of the North was favourable to long life
and generative vigour, that the women were more fruitful,
and the human species more prolific, than in warmer or more
temperate climates.[5] We may assert, with greater confidence,
that the keen air of Germany formed the large and masculine
limbs of the natives, who were, in general, of a more lofty stature
than the people of the South,[6] gave them a kind of strength better
adapted to violent exertions than to patient labour, and inspired
them with constitutional bravery, which is the result of nerves
and spirits. The severity of a winter campaign, that chilled the
courage of the Roman troops, was scarcely felt by these hardy

[1] Buffon, Histoire Naturelle, tom. xii. p. 79, 116.
[2] Cæsar de Bell. Gallic. vi. 23, etc. The most inquisitive of the Germans
were ignorant of its utmost limits, although some of them had travelled in
it more than sixty days' journey.
[3] Cluverius (Germania Antiqua, l. iii. c. 47) investigates the small and
scattered remains of the Hercynian wood.
[4] Charlevoix, Histoire du Canada.
[5] Olaus Rudbeck asserts that the Swedish women often bear ten or
twelve children, and not uncommonly twenty or thirty; but the authority
of Rudbeck is much to be suspected.
[6] In hos artus, in hæc corpora, quæ miramur, excrescunt. Tacit. Germania, 3, 20. Cluver. l. i. c. 14.

children of the North,[1] who in their turn were unable to resist the summer heats, and dissolved away in languor and sickness under the beams of an Italian sun.[2]

There is not anywhere upon the globe a large tract of country which we have discovered destitute of inhabitants, or whose first population can be fixed with any degree of historical certainty. And yet, as the most philosophic minds can seldom refrain from investigating the infancy of great nations, our curiosity consumes itself in toilsome and disappointed efforts. When Tacitus considered the purity of the German blood, and the forbidding aspect of the country, he was disposed to pronounce those barbarians *Indigenæ*, or natives of the soil. We may allow with safety, and perhaps with truth, that ancient Germany was not originally peopled by any foreign colonies already formed into a political society;[3] but that the name and nation received their existence from the gradual union of some wandering savages of the Hercynian woods. To assert those savages to have been the spontaneous production of the earth which they inhabited would be a rash inference, condemned by religion and unwarranted by reason.

Such rational doubt is but ill-suited with the genius of popular vanity. Among the nations who have adopted the Mosaic history of the world, the ark of Noah has been of the same use as was formerly to the Greeks and Romans the siege of Troy. On a narrow basis of acknowledged truth an immense but rude superstructure of fable has been erected, and the " Wild Irishman,"[4]

---

[1] Plutarch. in Mario. The Cimbri, by way of amusement, often slid down mountains of snow on their broad shields.

[2] The Romans made war in all climates, and by their excellent discipline were in a great measure preserved in health and vigour. It may be remarked, that man is the only animal which can live and multiply in every country from the equator to the poles. The hog seems to approach the nearest to our species in that privilege.

[3] Tacit. German. c. 3. The emigration of the Gauls followed the course of the Danube, and discharged itself on Greece and Asia. Tacitus could discover only one inconsiderable tribe that retained any traces of a Gallic origin.

[The Gothini, whom Tacitus distinguishes from the Gothi, and whom he places behind the Marcomanni and Quadi (Tacit. German. c. 43). But the improbability of an isolated Gallic people in this district is very great, and it has therefore been conjectured that they spoke the Galician. Cf. Latham's Germania of Tacitus.—O. S.]

[4] [According to Dr. Keating the giant Partholanus, who was the son of Seara, the son of Esra, the son of Sru, the son of Framant, the son of Fathaclan, the son of Magog, the son of Japhet, the son of Noah, landed on the coast of Munster, the 14 day of May, in the year of the world 1978. Though he was successful in his great enterprise, the loose behaviour of his wife rendered his domestic life very unhappy, and provoked him to such a

as well as the Wild Tartar,[1] could point out the individual
son of Japhet, from whose loins his ancestors were lineally
descended. The last century abounded with antiquarians of
profound learning and easy faith, who by the dim light of legends
and traditions, of conjectures and etymologies, conducted the
great-grandchildren of Noah from the tower of Babel to the
extremities of the globe. Of these judicious critics, one of the
most entertaining was Olaus Rudbeck, professor in the University
of Upsal.[2] Whatever is celebrated, either in history or fable,
this zealous patriot ascribes to his country. From Sweden
(which formed so considerable a part of ancient Germany) the
Greeks themselves derived their alphabetical characters, their
astronomy, and their religion. Of that delightful region (for
such it appeared to the eyes of a native) the Atlantis of Plato,
the country of the Hyperboreans, the gardens of the Hesperides,
the Fortunate Islands, and even the Elysian Fields, were all
but faint and imperfect transcripts. A clime so profusely
favoured by Nature could not long remain desert after the
flood. The learned Rudbeck allows the family of Noah a few
years to multiply from eight to about twenty thousand persons.
He then disperses them into small colonies to replenish the earth
and to propagate the human species. The German or Swedish
detachment (which marched, if I am not mistaken, under the
command of Askenaz, the son of Gomer, the son of Japhet) distinguished itself by a more than common diligence in the prosecution of this great work. The northern hive cast its swarms over
the greatest part of Europe, Africa, and Asia; and (to use the
author's metaphor) the blood circulated from the extremities
to the heart.

But all this well-laboured system of German antiquities is
annihilated by a single fact, too well attested to admit of any
doubt, and of too decisive a nature to leave room for any reply.
The Germans, in the age of Tacitus, were unacquainted with the
use of letters; [3] and the use of letters is the principal circumstance

degree that he killed—her favourite greyhound. This, as the learned
historian observes, was the first instance of female falsehood and infidelity
ever known in Ireland.—O. S.]

[1] [Genealogical History of the Tartars by Abulghazi Bahudar, Khan.—
O. S.]

[2] His work, entitled Atlantica, is uncommonly scarce. Bayle has given
two most curious extracts from it. République des Lettres, Janvier et
Février, 1685.

[3] Tacit. Germ. ii. 19. Literarum secreta viri pariter ac fœminæ ignorant.
We may rest contented with this decisive authority, without entering into
the obscure disputes concerning the antiquity of the Runic characters.
The learned Celsius, a Swede, a scholar, and a philosopher, was of opinion,

that distinguishes a civilised people from a herd of savages incapable of knowledge or reflection. Without that artificial help,
the human memory soon dissipates or corrupts the ideas intrusted to her charge; and the nobler faculties of the mind, no
longer supplied with models or with materials, gradually forget
their powers; the judgment becomes feeble and lethargic, the
imagination languid or irregular. Fully to apprehend this
important truth, let us attempt, in an improved society, to
calculate the immense distance between the man of learning and
the *illiterate* peasant. The former, by reading and reflection,
multiplies his own experience, and lives in distant ages and remote
countries; whilst the latter, rooted to a single spot, and confined
to a few years of existence, surpasses, but very little, his fellow-
labourer the ox in the exercise of his mental faculties. The same,
and even a greater, difference will be found between nations than
between individuals; and we may safely pronounce that, without
some species of writing, no people has ever preserved the faithful
annals of their history, ever made any considerable progress in
the abstract sciences, or ever possessed, in any tolerable degree
of perfection, the useful and agreeable arts of life.

Of these arts, the ancient Germans were wretchedly destitute.
They passed their lives in a state of ignorance and poverty, which
it has pleased some declaimers to dignify with the appellation of
virtuous simplicity. Modern Germany is said to contain about
two thousand three hundred walled towns.[1] In a much wider
extent of country, the geographer Ptolemy could discover no
more than ninety places, which he decorates with the name of
cities;[2] though, according to our ideas, they would but ill deserve

that they were nothing more than the Roman letters, with the curves
changed into straight lines for the ease of engraving. See Pelloutier,
Histoire des Celtes, l. ii. c. 11. Dictionnaire Diplomatique, tom. i. p. 223.
We may add, that the oldest Runic inscriptions are supposed to be of the
third century, and the most ancient writer who mentions the Runic characters is Venantius Fortunatus (Carm. vii. 18), who lived towards the end
of the sixth century—
      Barbara fraxineis pingatur RUNA tabellis.
[The Runic characters have exercised the learning of Scandinavian
scholars as to their origin. Three theories have been mooted, the first, by
Schlözer, that the 16 Runic letters are corruptions of the Roman alphabet,
post-Christian in date; the second, that by Frederick Schlegel, that these
characters were left by the Phœnicians, preserved by the priestly castes and
employed for purposes of magic; the last theory supposes them to be Indo-
Teutonic, brought from the East ages before our era. Cf. *Foreign Quarterly
Review*, vol. ix. p. 438.—O. S.]
[1] Recherches Philosophiques sur les Américains, tom. iii. p. 228. The
author of that very curious work is, if I am not misinformed, a German by
birth.
[2] The Alexandrian Geographer is often criticised by the accurate
Cluverius.

that splendid title. We can only suppose them to have been rude fortifications, constructed in the centre of the woods, and designed to secure the women, children, and cattle, whilst the warriors of the tribe marched out to repel a sudden invasion.[1] But Tacitus asserts, as a well-known fact, that the Germans, in his time, had *no* cities;[2] and that they affected to despise the works of Roman industry as places of confinement rather than of security.[3] Their edifices were not even contiguous, or formed into regular villas;[4] each barbarian fixed his independent dwelling on the spot to which a plain, a wood, or a stream of fresh water had induced him to give the preference. Neither stone, nor brick, nor tiles, were employed in these slight habitations.[5] They were indeed no more than low huts of a circular figure, built of rough timber, thatched with straw, and pierced at the top to leave a free passage for the smoke. In the most inclement winter, the hardy German was satisfied with a scanty garment made of the skin of some animal. The nations who dwelt towards the North clothed themselves in furs; and the women manufactured for their own use a coarse kind of linen.[6] The game of various sorts, with which the forests of Germany were plentifully stocked, supplied its inhabitants with food and exercise.[7] Their monstrous herds of cattle, less remarkable indeed for their beauty than for their utility,[8] formed the principal object of their wealth. A small quantity of corn was the only produce exacted from the earth: the use of orchards or artificial meadows was unknown to the Germans; nor can we expect any improvements in agriculture from a people whose property every year experienced a general change by a new division of the arable lands, and who, in that strange operation, avoided disputes by suffering a great part of their territory to lie waste and without tillage.[9]

Gold, silver, and iron were extremely scarce in Germany. Its

---

[1] See Cæsar, and Whitaker's History of Manchester, vol. i.

[2] Tacit. Germ. 15.

[3] When the Germans cammanded the Ubii of Cologne to cast off the Roman yoke, and with their new freedom to resume their ancient manners, they insisted on the immediate demolition of the walls of the colony. " Postulamus a vobis, muros coloniæ, munimenta servitii detrahatis; etiam fera animalia, si clausa teneas, virtutis obliviscuntur." Tacit. Hist. iv. 64.

[4] The straggling villages of Silesia are several miles in length. Cluver. l. i. c. 13.

[5] One hundred and forty years after Tacitus, a few more regular structures were erected near the Rhine and Danube. Herodian, l. vii. p. 234.

[6] Tacit. Germ. 17.

[7] Tacit. Germ. 5.

[8] Cæsar de Bell. Gall. vi. 21.

[9] Tacit. Germ. 26. Cæsar, vi. 22.

barbarous inhabitants wanted both skill and patience to investigate those rich veins of silver, which have so liberally
rewarded the attention of the princes of Brunswick and Saxony.
Sweden, which now supplies Europe with iron, was equally
ignorant of its own riches; and the appearance of the arms of the
Germans furnished a sufficient proof how little iron they were
able to bestow on what they must have deemed the noblest
use of that metal. The various transactions of peace and war
had introduced some Roman coins (chiefly silver) among the
borderers of the Rhine and Danube; but the more distant tribes
were absolutely unacquainted with the use of money, carried
on their confined traffic by the exchange of commodities, and
prized their rude earthen vessels as of equal value with the silver
vases, the presents of Rome to their princes and ambassadors.[1]
To a mind capable of reflection, such leading facts convey more
instruction than a tedious detail of subordinate circumstances.
The value of money has been settled by general consent to express
our wants and our property, as letters were invented to express
our ideas; and both these institutions, by giving a more active
energy to the powers and passions of human nature, have contributed to multiply the objects they were designed to represent.
The use of gold and silver is in a great measure fictitious; but
it would be impossible to enumerate the important and various
services which agriculture, and all the arts, have received from
iron, when tempered and fashioned by the operation of fire and
the dexterous hand of man. Money, in a word, is the most
universal incitement, iron the most powerful instrument, of
human industry; and it is very difficult to conceive by what
means a people, neither actuated by the one nor seconded by
the other, could emerge from the grossest barbarism.[2]

If we contemplate a savage nation in any part of the globe, a
supine indolence and a carelessness of futurity will be found to
constitute their general character. In a civilised state, every
faculty of man is expanded and exercised; and the great chain
of mutual dependence connects and embraces the several
members of society. The most numerous portion of it is employed in constant and useful labour. The select few, placed
by fortune above that necessity, can, however, fill up their time
by the pursuits of interest or glory, by the improvement of their

---

[1] Tacit. Germ. 6.
[2] It is said that the Mexicans and Peruvians, without the use of either
money or iron, had made a very great progress in the arts. Those arts, and
the monuments they produced, have been strangely magnified. Recherches
sur les Américains, tom. ii. p. 153, etc.

estate or of their understanding, by the duties, the pleasures, and
even the follies of social life. The Germans were not possessed
of these varied resources. The care of the house and family, the
management of the land and cattle, were delegated to the old
and the infirm, to women and slaves. The lazy warrior, destitute
of every art that might employ his leisure hours, consumed his
days and nights in the animal gratifications of sleep and food.
And yet, by a wonderful diversity of Nature (according to the
remark of a writer who had pierced into its darkest recesses),
the same barbarians are by turns the most indolent and the most
restless of mankind. They delight in sloth, they detest tranquillity.[1] The languid soul, oppressed with its own weight,
anxiously required some new and powerful sensation; and war
and danger were the only amusements adequate to its fierce
temper. The sound that summoned the German to arms was
grateful to his ear. It roused him from his uncomfortable
lethargy, gave him an active pursuit, and, by strong exercise
of the body, and violent emotions of the mind, restored him to
a more lively sense of his existence. In the dull intervals of
peace, these barbarians were immoderately addicted to deep
gaming and excessive drinking; both of which, by different
means, the one by inflaming their passions, the other by extinguishing their reason, alike relieved them from the pain of thinking. They gloried in passing whole days and nights at table;
and the blood of friends and relations often stained their
numerous and drunken assemblies.[2] Their debts of honour (for
in that light they have transmitted to us those of play) they
discharged with the most romantic fidelity. The desperate
gamester, who had staked his person and liberty on a last throw
of the dice, patiently submitted to the decision of fortune, and
suffered himself to be bound, chastised, and sold into remote
slavery, by his weaker but more lucky antagonist.[3]

Strong beer, a liquor extracted with very little art from wheat
or barley, and *corrupted* (as it is strongly expressed by Tacitus)
into a certain semblance of wine, was sufficient for the gross
purposes of German debauchery. But those who had tasted
the rich wines of Italy, and afterwards of Gaul, sighed for that
more delicious species of intoxication. They attempted not,
however (as has since been executed with so much success), to
naturalise the vine on the banks of the Rhine and Danube; nor

[1] Tacit. Germ. 15.   [2] Tacit. Germ. 22, 23.
[3] Tacit. Germ. 24. The Germans might borrow the *arts* of play from the
Romans, but the *passion* is wonderfully inherent in the human species.

did they endeavour to procure by industry the materials of an
advantageous commerce. To solicit by labour what might be
ravished by arms was esteemed unworthy of the German spirit.[1]
The intemperate thirst of strong liquors often urged the barbarians to invade the provinces on which art or nature had
bestowed those much envied presents. The Tuscan who betrayed
his country to the Celtic nations attracted them into Italy by
the prospect of the rich fruits and delicious wines, the productions
of a happier climate.[2] And in the same manner the German
auxiliaries, invited into France during the civil wars of the sixteenth century, were allured by the promise of plenteous quarters
in the provinces of Champagne and Burgundy.[3] Drunkenness,
the most illiberal, but not the most dangerous, of *our* vices, was
sometimes capable, in a less civilised state of mankind, of
occasioning a battle, a war, or a revolution.

The climate of ancient Germany has been mollified, and the
soil fertilised, by the labour of ten centuries from the time of
Charlemagne. The same extent of ground which at present
maintains, in ease and plenty, a million of husbandmen and
artificers, was unable to supply an hundred thousand lazy
warriors with the simple necessaries of life.[4] The Germans
abandoned their immense forests to the exercise of hunting, employed in pasturage the most considerable part of their lands,
bestowed on the small remainder a rude and careless cultivation,
and then accused the scantiness and sterility of a country that
refused to maintain the multitude of its inhabitants. When the
return of famine severely admonished them of the importance of
the arts, the national distress was sometimes alleviated by the
emigration of a third, perhaps, or a fourth part of their youth.[5]
The possession and the enjoyment of property are the pledges
which bind a civilised people to an improved country. But the
Germans, who carried with them what they most valued, their
arms, their cattle, and their women, cheerfully abandoned the
vast silence of their woods for the unbounded hopes of plunder
and conquest. The innumerable swarms that issued, or seemed

---

[1] Tacit. Germ. 14.　　[2] Plutarch. in Camillo. T. Liv. v. 33.
[3] Dubos. Hist. de la Monar. Franç., 1. p. 193.
[4] The Helvetian nation, which issued from the country called Switzerland, contained, of every age and sex, 368,000 persons (Cæsar de Bell. Gall.
i. 29). At present, the number of people in the Pays de Vaud (a small
district on the banks of the Leman Lake, much more distinguished for
politeness than for industry) amounts to 112,591. See an excellent tract of
M. Muret, in the Memoires de la Societé de Bern.
[5] Paul Diaconus, c. 1, 2, 3. Machiavel, Davila, and the rest of Paul's
followers, represent these emigrations too much as regular and concerted
measures.

to issue, from the great storehouse of nations, were multiplied
by the fears of the vanquished and by the credulity of succeeding ages. And from facts thus exaggerated, an opinion was
gradually established, and has been supported by writers of distinguished reputation, that, in the age of Cæsar and Tacitus, the
inhabitants of the North were far more numerous than they are
in our days.[1] A more serious inquiry into the causes of population seems to have convinced modern philosophers of the falsehood, and indeed the impossibility, of the supposition. To the
names of Mariana and of Machiavel,[2] we can oppose the equal
names of Robertson and Hume.[3]

A warlike nation like the Germans, without either cities,
letters, arts, or money, found some compensation for this
savage state in the enjoyment of liberty. Their poverty secured
their freedom, since our desires and our possessions are the
strongest fetters of despotism. "Among the Suiones (says
Tacitus), riches are held in honour. They are *therefore* subject
to an absolute monarch, who, instead of intrusting his people
with the free use of arms, as is practised in the rest of Germany,
commits them to the safe custody not of a citizen, or even of a
freedman, but of a slave. The neighbours of the Suiones, the
Sitones, are sunk even below servitude; they obey a woman."[4]
In the mention of these exceptions, the great historian sufficiently acknowledges the general theory of government. We are
only at a loss to conceive by what means riches and despotism
could penetrate into a remote corner of the North, and extinguish the generous flame that blazed with such fierceness on the
frontier of the Roman provinces: or how the ancestors of those
Danes and Norwegians, so distinguished in latter ages by their
unconquered spirit, could thus tamely resign the great character
of German liberty.[5] Some tribes, however, on the coast of the

---

[1] Sir William Temple and Montesquieu have indulged, on this subject,
the usual liveliness of their fancy.

[2] Machiavel Hist. di Firenze, l. i. Mariana Hist. Hispan. l. v. c. 1.

[3] Robertson's Charles V. Hume's Political Essays.

[It is a wise observation of Malthus that these nations were not populous
in proportion to the land they occupied, but to the food they produced.
They were prolific from their pure morals, but their institutions were not
calculated to produce food.—O. S.]

[4] Tacit. German. 44, 45. Frenshemius (who dedicated his supplement
to Livy to Christina of Sweden) thinks proper to be very angry with the
Roman who expressed so very little reverence for Northern queens.

[5] May we not suspect that superstition was the parent of despotism?
The descendants of Odin (whose race was not extinct till the year 1060) are
said to have reigned in Sweden above a thousand years. The temple of
Upsal was the ancient seat of religion and empire. In the year 1153 I find
a singular law, prohibiting the use and profession of arms to any except the

Baltic, acknowledged the authority of kings, though without
relinquishing the rights of men;[1] but in the far greater part of
Germany, the form of government was a democracy tempered
indeed, and controlled, not so much by general and positive laws,
as by the occasional ascendant of birth or valour, of eloquence
or superstition.[2]

Civil governments, in their first institutions, are voluntary
associations for mutual defence. To obtain the desired end, it
is absolutely necessary that each individual should conceive
himself obliged to submit his private opinion and actions to the
judgment of the greater number of his associates. The German
tribes were contented with this rude but liberal outline of political
society. As soon as a youth, born of free parents, had attained
the age of manhood, he was introduced into the general council
of his countrymen, solemnly invested with a shield and spear,
and adopted as an equal and worthy member of the military
commonwealth. The assembly of the warriors of the tribe was
convened at stated seasons or on sudden emergencies. The
trial of public offences, the election of magistrates, and the great
business of peace and war, were determined by its independent
voice. Sometimes, indeed, these important questions were
previously considered and prepared in a more select council of
the principal chieftains.[3] The magistrates might deliberate and
persuade, the people only could resolve and execute; and the
resolutions of the Germans were for the most part hasty and
violent. Barbarians accustomed to place their freedom in gratifying the present passion, and their courage in overlooking all
future consequences, turned away with indignant contempt
from the remonstrance of justice and policy, and it was the
practice to signify by a hollow murmur their dislike of such
timid counsels. But whenever a more popular orator proposed
to vindicate the meanest citizen from either foreign or domestic
injury, whenever he called upon his fellow-countrymen to assert
the national honour, or to pursue some enterprise full of danger
and glory, a loud clashing of shields and spears expressed the
eager applause of the assembly. For the Germans always met
in arms, and it was constantly to be dreaded lest an irregular
multitude, inflamed with faction and strong liquors, should use

king's guards. Is it not probable that it was coloured by the pretence of
reviving an old institution? Dalling's History of Sweden in the Bibliothèque Raisonée, xl. xlv.
[1] Tacit. Germ. c. 43. [2] Tacit. Germ. c. 11, 12, 13, etc.
[3] Grotius changes an expression of Tacitus, *pertractantur* into *prætrac-
tantur*. The correction is equally just and ingenious.

those arms to enforce, as well as to declare, their furious resolves.
We may recollect how often the diets of Poland have been
polluted with blood, and the more numerous party has been
compelled to yield to the more violent and seditious.[1]

A general of the tribe was elected on occasions of danger;
and, if the danger was pressing and extensive, several tribes concurred in the choice of the same general. The bravest warrior
was named to lead his countrymen into the field, by his example
rather than by his commands. But this power, however limited,
was still invidious. It expired with the war, and in time of
peace the German tribes acknowledged not any supreme chief.[2]
Princes were, however, appointed in the general assembly, to
administer justice, or rather to compose differences,[3] in their
respective districts. In the choice of these magistrates as
much regard was shown to birth as to merit.[4] To each was
assigned, by the public, a guard and a council of an hundred
persons; and the first of the princes appears to have enjoyed a
pre-eminence of rank and honour which sometimes tempted the
Romans to compliment him with the regal title.[5]

The comparative view of the powers of the magistrates, in
two remarkable instances, is alone sufficient to represent the
whole system of German manners. The disposal of the landed
property within their district was absolutely vested in their
hands, and they distributed it every year according to a new
division.[6] At the same time they were not authorised to punish
with death, to imprison, or even to strike, a private citizen.[7]
A people thus jealous of their persons, and careless of their possessions, must have been totally destitute of industry and the
arts, but animated with a high sense of honour and independence.

The Germans respected only those duties which they imposed
on themselves. The most obscure soldier resisted with disdain
the authority of the magistrates. " The noblest youths blushed
not to be numbered among the faithful companions of some
renowned chief, to whom they devoted their arms and service.
A noble emulation prevailed among the companions to obtain
the first place in the esteem of their chief; amongst the chiefs, to
acquire the greatest number of valiant companions. To be ever

---

[1] Even in *our* ancient parliament, the barons often carried a question, not
so much by the number of votes, as by that of their armed followers.
[2] Cæsar de Bell. Gall. vi. 23.
[3] Minuunt controversias is a very happy expression of Cæsar's.
[4] Reges ex nobilitate, duces ex virtute sumunt. Tacit. Germ. 7.
[5] Cluver. Germ. Ant. l. i. c. 38.
[6] Cæsar, vi. 22. Tacit. Germ. 26.   [7] Tacit. Germ. 7.

surrounded by a band of select youths was the pride and strength of the chiefs, their ornament in peace, their defence in war. The glory of such distinguished heroes diffused itself beyond the narrow limits of their own tribe. Presents and embassies solicited their friendship, and the fame of their arms often ensured victory to the party which they espoused. In the hour of danger it was shameful for the chief to be surpassed in valour by his companions; shameful for the companions not to equal the valour of their chief. To survive his fall in battle was indelible infamy. To protect his person and to adorn his glory with the trophies of their own exploits were the most sacred of their duties. The chiefs combated for victory, the companions for the chief. The noblest warriors, whenever their native country was sunk in the laziness of peace, maintained their numerous bands in some distant scene of action, to exercise their restless spirit and to acquire renown by voluntary dangers. Gifts worthy of soldiers, the warlike steed, the bloody and ever victorious lance, were the rewards which the companions claimed from the liberality of their chief. The rude plenty of his hospitable board was the only pay that *he* could bestow or *they* would accept. War, rapine, and the free-will offerings of his friends, supplied the materials of this munificence." [1] This institution, however it might accidentally weaken the several republics, invigorated the general character of the Germans, and even ripened amongst them all the virtues of which barbarians are susceptible; the faith and valour, the hospitality and the courtesy, so conspicuous long afterwards in the ages of chivalry. The honourable gifts, bestowed by the chief on his brave companions, have been supposed, by an ingenious writer, to contain the first rudiments of the fiefs, distributed, after the conquest of the Roman provinces, by the barbarian lords among their vassals, with a similar duty of homage and military service.[2] These conditions are, however, very repugnant to the maxims of the ancient Germans, who delighted in mutual presents; but without either imposing, or accepting, the weight of obligations.[3]

" In the days of chivalry, or more properly of romance, all the men were brave, and all the women were chaste; " and notwithstanding the latter of these virtues is acquired and preserved with

---

[1] Tacit. Germ. 13, 14.

[2] Esprit des Loix, l. xxx. c. 5. The brilliant imagination of Montesquieu is corrected, however, by the dry cold reason of the Abbé de Mably. Observations sur l'Histoire de France, tom. i. p. 356.

[3] Gaudent muneribus, sed nec data imputant, nec acceptis obligantur. Tacit. Germ. c. 21.

much more difficulty than the former, it is ascribed, almost without exception, to the wives of the ancient Germans. Polygamy was not in use, except among the princes, and among them only for the sake of multiplying their alliances. Divorces were prohibited by manners rather than by laws. Adulteries were punished as rare and inexpiable crimes; nor was seduction justified by example and fashion.[1] We may easily discover that Tacitus indulges an honest pleasure in the contrast of barbarian virtue with the dissolute conduct of the Roman ladies; yet there are some striking circumstances that give an air of truth, or at least of probability, to the conjugal faith and chastity of the Germans.

Although the progress of civilisation has undoubtedly contributed to assuage the fiercer passions of human nature, it seems to have been less favourable to the virtue of chastity, whose most dangerous enemy is the softness of the mind. The refinements of life corrupt while they polish the intercourse of the sexes. The gross appetite of love becomes most dangerous when it is elevated, or rather, indeed, disguised by sentimental passion. The elegance of dress, of motion, and of manners gives a lustre to beauty, and inflames the senses through the imagination. Luxurious entertainments, midnight dances, and licentious spectacles, present at once temptation and opportunity to female frailty.[2] From such dangers the unpolished wives of the barbarians were secured by poverty, solitude, and the painful cares of a domestic life. The German huts, open on every side to the eye of indiscretion or jealousy, were a better safeguard of conjugal fidelity than the walls, the bolts, and the eunuchs of a Persian harem. To this reason, another may be added of a more honourable nature. The Germans treated their women with esteem and confidence, consulted them on every occasion of importance, and fondly believed that in their breasts resided a sanctity and wisdom more than human. Some of these interpreters of fate, such as Velleda, in the Batavian war, governed, in the name of the deity, the fiercest nations of Germany.[3] The rest of the sex, without being adored as goddesses, were respected as the free and equal companions of soldiers; associated even by the marriage ceremony to a life of toil, of danger, and of glory.[4]

[1] The adulteress was whipped through the village. Neither wealth nor beauty could inspire compassion, or procure her a second husband. Germ. c. 18, 19.

[2] Ovid considers the theatre as the best adapted to collect the beauties of Rome, and to melt them into tenderness and sensuality.

[3] Tacit. Hist. iv. 61, 65.

[4] The marriage present was yoke of oxen, horses, and arms. Germ. c. 18. Tacitus is somewhat too florid on the subject.

In their great invasions, the camps of the barbarians were filled with a multitude of women, who remained firm and undaunted amidst the sound of arms, the various forms of destruction, and the honourable wounds of their sons and husbands.[1] Fainting armies of Germans have more than once been driven back upon the enemy by the generous despair of the women who dreaded death much less than servitude. If the day was irrecoverably lost, they well knew how to deliver themselves and their children, with their own hands, from an insulting victor.[2] Heroines of such a cast may claim our admiration; but they were most assuredly neither lovely, nor very susceptible of love. Whilst they affected to emulate the stern virtues of *man*, they must have resigned that attractive softness in which principally consists the charm of *woman*. Conscious pride taught the German females to suppress every tender emotion that stood in competition with honour, and the first honour of the sex has ever been that of chastity. The sentiments and conduct of these high-spirited matrons may, at once, be considered as a cause, as an effect, and as a proof of the general character of the nation. Female courage, however it may be raised by fanaticism, or confirmed by habit, can be only a faint and imperfect imitation of the manly valour that distinguishes the age or country in which it may be found.

The religious system of the Germans (if the wild opinions of savages can deserve that name) was dictated by their wants, their fears, and their ignorance.[3] They adored the great visible objects and agents of nature, the Sun and the Moon, the Fire and the Earth; together with those imaginary deities, who were supposed to preside over the most important occupations of human life. They were persuaded that, by some ridiculous arts of divination, they could discover the will of the superior beings, and that human sacrifices were the most precious and acceptable offering to their altars. Some applause has been hastily bestowed on the sublime notion, entertained by that people, of the Deity, whom they neither confined within the walls of a temple, nor

---

[1] The change of *exigere* into *exugere* is a most excellent correction.

[2] Tacit. Germ. c. 7. Plutarch in Mario. Before the wives of the Teutones destroyed themselves and their children they had offered to surrender on condition that they should be received as the slaves of the vestal virgins.

[3] Tacitus has employed a few lines, and Cluverius one hundred and twenty-four pages, on this obscure subject. The former discovers in Germany the gods of Greece and Rome. The latter is positive, that under the emblems of the sun, the moon, and the fire, his pious ancestors worshipped the Trinity in unity.

represented by any human figure; but when we recollect that
the Germans were unskilled in architecture, and totally unacquainted with the art of sculpture, we shall readily assign the true
reason of a scruple which arose not so much from a superiority of
reason as from a want of ingenuity.   The only temples in Germany were dark and ancient groves, consecrated by the reverence
of succeeding generations.   Their secret gloom, the imagined
residence of an invisible power, by presenting no distinct object
of fear or worship, impressed the mind with a still deeper sense
of religious horror; [1] and the priests, rude and illiterate as they
were, had been taught by experience the use of every artifice
that could preserve and fortify impressions so well suited to their
own interest.

The same ignorance, which renders barbarians incapable of
conceiving or embracing the useful restraints of laws, exposes
them naked and unarmed to the blind terrors of superstition.
The German priests, improving this favourable temper of their
countrymen, had assumed a jurisdiction, even in temporal concerns, which the magistrate could not venture to exercise; and
the haughty warrior patiently submitted to the lash of correction,
when it was inflicted, not by any human power, but by the immediate order of the god of war. [2]   The defects of civil policy
were sometimes supplied by the interposition of ecclesiastical
authority.   The latter was constantly exerted to maintain
silence and decency in the popular assemblies; and was sometimes extended to a more enlarged concern for the national
welfare.   A solemn procession was occasionally celebrated in
the present countries of Mecklenburgh and Pomerania.   The
unknown symbol of the *Earth*, covered with a thick veil, was
placed on a carriage drawn by cows; and in this manner the
goddess, whose common residence was in the isle of Rugen,
visited several adjacent tribes of her worshippers.   During her
progress the sound of war was hushed, quarrels were suspended,
arms laid aside, and the restless Germans had an opportunity
of tasting the blessings of peace and harmony. [3]   The *truce of
God*, so often and so ineffectually proclaimed by the clergy of
the eleventh century, was an obvious imitation of this ancient
custom. [4]

But the influence of religion was far more powerful to inflame

---

[1] The sacred wood, described with such sublime horror by Lucan, was in
the neighbourhood of Marseilles; but there were many of the same kind in
Germany. [1]
[2] Tacit. Germania, c. 7.   [3] Tacit. Germania, c. 40.
[4] Robertson's Hist. of Charles V. vol. i. note 10.

than to moderate the fierce passions of the Germans. Interest
and fanaticism often prompted its ministers to sanctify the most
daring and the most unjust enterprises, by the approbation
of Heaven, and full assurances of success. The consecrated
standards, long revered in the groves of superstition, were placed
in the front of the battle; [1] and the hostile army was devoted with
dire execrations to the gods of war and of thunder.[2] In the
faith of soldiers (and such were the Germans) cowardice is the
most unpardonable of sins. A brave man was the worthy
favourite of their martial deities; the wretch, who had lost his
shield, was alike banished from the religious and the civil assemblies of his countrymen. Some tribes of the north seem to have
embraced the doctrine of transmigration,[3] others imagined a gross
paradise of immortal drunkenness.[4] All agreed that a life spent
in arms, and a glorious death in battle, were the best preparations
for a happy futurity either in this or in another world.

The immortality so vainly promised by the priests was in some
degree conferred by the bards. That singular order of men has
most deservedly attracted the notice of all who have attempted
to investigate the antiquities of the Celts, the Scandinavians, and
the Germans. Their genius and character, as well as the reverence paid to that important office, have been sufficiently illustrated. But we cannot so easily express, or even conceive, the
enthusiasm of arms and glory, which they kindled in the breast
of their audience. Among a polished people, a taste for poetry
is rather an amusement of the fancy than a passion of the soul.
And yet, when in calm retirement we peruse the combats
described by Homer or Tasso, we are insensibly seduced by the
fiction, and feel a momentary glow of martial ardour. But how
faint, how cold is the sensation which a peaceful mind can receive
from solitary study! It was in the hour of battle, or in the feast
of victory, that the bards celebrated the glory of heroes of ancient
days, the ancestors of those warlike chieftains who listened with
transport to their artless but animated strains. The view of
arms and of danger heightened the effect of the military song;
and the passions which it tended to excite, the desire of fame

---

[1] Tacit. Germ. c. 7. These standards were only the heads of wild beasts.
[2] Tacit. Annal. xiii. 57.
[3] Cæsar, Diodorus, and Lucan seem to ascribe this doctrine to the Gauls,
but M. Pelloutier (Histoire des Celtes, l. iii. c. 18) labours to reduce their
expressions to a more orthodox sense.
[4] Concerning this gross but alluring doctrine of the Edda, see Fable xx.
in the curious version of that book, published by M. Mallet, in his Introduction to the History of Denmark.

and the contempt of death, were the habitual sentiments of a German mind.[1]

Such was the situation, and such were the manners, of the ancient Germans. Their climate, their want of learning, of arts, and of laws, their notions of honour, of gallantry, and of religion, their sense of freedom, impatience of peace, and thirst of enterprise, all contributed to form a people of military heroes. And yet we find that, during more than two hundred and fifty years that elapsed from the defeat of Varus to the reign of Decius, these formidable barbarians made few considerable attempts, and not any material impression on the luxurious and enslaved provinces of the empire. Their progress was checked by their want of arms and discipline, and their fury was diverted by the intestine divisions of ancient Germany.

I. It has been observed, with ingenuity, and not without truth, that the command of iron soon gives a nation the command of gold. But the rude tribes of Germany, alike destitute of both those valuable metals, were reduced slowly to acquire, by their unassisted strength, the possession of the one as well as the other. The face of a German army displayed their poverty of iron. Swords, and the longer kind of lances, they could seldom use. Their *frameæ* (as they called them in their own language) were long spears headed with a sharp but narrow iron point, and which, as occasion required, they either darted from a distance or pushed in close onset. With this spear, and with a shield, their cavalry was contented. A multitude of darts, scattered [2] with incredible force, were an additional resource of the infantry. Their military dress, when they wore any, was nothing more than a loose mantle. A variety of colours was the only ornament of their wooden or osier shields. Few of the chiefs were distinguished by cuirasses, scarce any by helmets. Though the horses of Germany were neither beautiful, swift, nor practised

---

[1] Tacit. Germ. c. 3. Diodor. Sicul. l. v. Strabo, l. iv. p. 197. The classical reader may remember the rank of Demodocus in the Phæacian court, and the ardour infused by Tyrtæus into the fainting Spartans. Yet there is little probability that the Greeks and the Germans were the same people. Much learned trifling might be spared if our antiquarians would condescend to reflect, that similar manners will naturally be produced by similar situations.

[Besides these battle-songs, the Germans sang at their festal banquets and around the bodies of their slain heroes. King Theodoric, of the tribe of the Goths, killed in a battle against Attila, was honoured by song while he was being borne from the field. The same honour was paid to Attila's remains. The Germans had songs also at their weddings, but this was not so common, for their marriages were only purchases.—O. S.]

[2] Missilia spargunt, Tacit. Germ. c. 6. Either that historian used a vague expression, or he meant that they were thrown at random.

in the skilful evolutions of the Roman manege, several of the nations obtained renown by their cavalry; but, in general, the principal strength of the Germans consisted in their infantry,[1] which was drawn up in several deep columns, according to the distinction of tribes and families. Impatient of fatigue or delay, these half-armed warriors rushed to battle with dissonant shouts and disordered ranks; and sometimes, by the effort of native valour, prevailed over the constrained and more artificial bravery of the Roman mercenaries. But as the barbarians poured forth their whole souls on the first onset, they knew not how to rally or to retire. A repulse was a sure defeat; and a defeat was most commonly total destruction. When we recollect the complete armour of the Roman soldiers, their discipline, exercises, evolutions, fortified camps, and military engines, it appears a just matter of surprise how the naked and unassisted valour of the barbarians could dare to encounter in the field the strength of the legions, and the various troops of the auxiliaries which seconded their operations. The contest was too unequal, till the introduction of luxury had enervated the vigour, and a spirit of disobedience and sedition had relaxed the discipline, of the Roman armies. The introduction of barbarian auxiliaries into those armies was a measure attended with very obvious dangers, as it might gradually instruct the Germans in the arts of war and of policy. Although they were admitted in small numbers and with the strictest precaution, the example of Civilis was proper to convince the Romans that the danger was not imaginary, and that their precautions were not always sufficient.[2] During the civil wars that followed the death of Nero, that artful and intrepid Batavian, whom his enemies condescended to compare with Hannibal and Sertorius,[3] formed a great design of freedom and ambition. Eight Batavian cohorts, renowned in the wars of Britain and Italy, repaired to his standard. He introduced an army of Germans into Gaul, prevailed on the powerful cities of Treves and Langres to embrace his cause, defeated the legions, destroyed their fortified camps, and employed against the Romans the military knowledge which he had acquired in their service. When at length, after an obstinate struggle, he yielded to the power of the empire, Civilis

---

[1] It was their principal distinction from the Sarmatians, who generally fought on horseback.

[2] The relation of this enterprise occupies a great part of the fourth and fifth books of the History of Tacitus, and is more remarkable for its eloquence than perspicuity. Sir Henry Saville has observed several inaccuracies.

[3] Tacit. Hist. iv. 13: like them he had lost an eye.

secured himself and his country by an honourable treaty. The Batavians still continued to occupy the islands of the Rhine,[1] the allies not the servants of the Roman monarchy.

II. The strength of ancient Germany appears formidable when we consider the effects that might have been produced by its united effort. The wide extent of country might very possibly contain a million of warriors, as all who were of age to bear arms were of a temper to use them. But this fierce multitude, incapable of concerting or executing any plan of national greatness, was agitated by various and often hostile intentions. Germany was divided into more than forty independent states; and even in each state the union of the several tribes was extremely loose and precarious. The barbarians were easily provoked; they knew not how to forgive an injury, much less an insult; their resentments were bloody and implacable. The casual disputes that so frequently happened in their tumultuous parties of hunting or drinking were sufficient to inflame the minds of whole nations; the private feud of any considerable chieftains diffused itself among their followers and allies. To chastise the insolent, or to plunder the defenceless, were alike causes of war. The most formidable states of Germany affected to encompass their territories with a wide frontier of solitude and devastation. The awful distance preserved by their neighbours attested the terror of their arms, and in some measure defended them from the danger of unexpected incursions.[2]

" The Bructeri (it is Tacitus who now speaks) were totally exterminated by the neighbouring tribes,[3] provoked by their insolence, allured by the hopes of spoil, and perhaps inspired by the tutelar deities of the empire. Above sixty thousand barbarians were destroyed; not by the Roman arms, but in our sight, and for our entertainment. May the nations, enemies of Rome, ever preserve this enmity to each other! We have now attained the utmost verge of prosperity,[4] and have nothing left to demand of Fortune, except the discord of these barbarians." [5]

---

[1] It was contained between the two branches of the old Rhine, as they subsisted before the face of the country was changed by art and nature. Cluver. Germ. Antiq. l. iii. c. 30, 37.

[2] Cæsar de Bell. Gall. l. vi. 23.

[3] They are mentioned however in the fourth and fifth centuries by Nazarius, Ammianus, Claudian, etc., as a tribe of Franks. Cluver. Germ. Antiq. l. iii. c. xiii.

[4] *Urgentibus* is the common reading, but good sense, Lipsius, and some MSS. declare for *Vergentibus*.

[5] Tacit. Germania, c. 33. The pious Abbé de la Bleterie is very angry with Tacitus, talks of the devil who was a murderer from the beginning, etc., etc.

These sentiments, less worthy of the humanity than of the patriotism of Tacitus, express the invariable maxims of the policy of his countrymen. They deemed it a much safer expedient to divide than to combat the barbarians, from whose defeat they could derive neither honour nor advantage. The money and negotiations of Rome insinuated themselves into the heart of Germany; and every art of seduction was used with dignity to conciliate those nations whom their proximity to the Rhine or Danube might render the most useful friends as well as the most troublesome enemies. Chiefs of renown and power were flattered by the most trifling presents, which they received either as marks of distinction, or as the instruments of luxury. In civil dissensions, the weaker faction endeavoured to strengthen its interest by entering into secret connections with the governors of the frontier provinces. Every quarrel among the Germans was fomented by the intrigues of Rome; and every plan of union and public good was defeated by the stronger bias of private jealousy and interest.[1]

The general conspiracy which terrified the Romans under the reign of Marcus Antoninus comprehended almost all the nations of Germany, and even Sarmatia, from the mouth of the Rhine to that of the Danube.[2] It is impossible for us to determine whether this hasty confederation was formed by necessity, by reason, or by passion; but we may rest assured that the barbarians were neither allured by the indolence, nor provoked by the ambition, of the Roman monarch. This dangerous invasion required all the firmness and vigilance of Marcus. He fixed generals of ability in the several stations of attack, and assumed in person the conduct of the most important province on the Upper Danube. After a long and doubtful conflict, the spirit of the barbarians was subdued. The Quadi and the Marcomanni,[3] who had taken the lead in the war, were the most severely

---

[1] Many traces of this policy may be discovered in Tacitus and Dion: and many more may be inferred from the principles of human nature.

[2] Hist. August. p. 31. Ammian. Marcellin. l. xxxi. c. 5. Aurel. Victor. The emperor Marcus was reduced to sell the rich furniture of the palace, and to enlist slaves and robbers.

[3] The Marcomanni, a colony, who, from the banks of the Rhine, occupied Bohemia and Moravia, had once erected a great and formidable monarchy under their king Maroboduus. Strabo, l. vii. Vell. Pat. ii. 105. Tacit. Annal. ii. 63.

[*Marc-o-manni*—the men of the marches—a name given to different tribes on the different marches of Germany, and not to have been the name of the Saeve people. There were Marcomanni in the army of Ariovistus that fought against Cæsar (*De Bello Gallico*, i. 51), and they could not be the same as those. See Latham, Germania.—O. S.]

punished in its catastrophe. They were commanded to retire five miles [1] from their own banks of the Danube, and to deliver up the flower of the youth, who were immediately sent into Britain, a remote island, where they might be secure as hostages, and useful as soldiers.[2] On the frequent rebellions of the Quadi and Marcomanni, the irritated emperor resolved to reduce their country into the form of a province. His designs were disappointed by death. This formidable league, however, the only one that appears in the two first centuries of the Imperial history, was entirely dissipated, without leaving any traces behind in Germany.

In the course of this introductory chapter, we have confined ourselves to the general outlines of the manners of Germany, without attempting to describe or to distinguish the various tribes which filled the great country in the time of Cæsar, of Tacitus, or of Ptolemy. As the ancient, or as new tribes successively present themselves in the series of this history, we shall concisely mention their origin, their situation, and their particular character. Modern nations are fixed and permanent societies, connected among themselves by laws and government, bound to their native soil by arts and agriculture. The German tribes were voluntary and fluctuating associations of soldiers, almost of savages. The same territory often changed its inhabitants in the tide of conquest and emigration. The same communities, uniting in a plan of defence or invasion, bestowed a new title on their new confederacy. The dissolution of an ancient confederacy restored to the independent tribes their peculiar but long-forgotten appellation. A victorious state often communicated its own name to a vanquished people. Sometimes crowds of volunteers flocked from all parts to the standard of a favourite leader; his camp became their country, and some circumstance of the enterprise soon gave a common denomination to the mixed multitude. The distinctions of the ferocious invaders were perpetually varied by themselves, and confounded by the astonished subjects of the Roman empire.[3]

Wars, and the administration of public affairs, are the principal subjects of history; but the number of persons interested in these

----

[1] Wotton (Hist. of Rome, p. 166) increases the prohibition to ten times the distance. His reasoning is specious, but not conclusive. Five miles were sufficient for a fortified barrier.

[2] Dion, l. lxxi. and lxxii.

[3] See an excellent dissertation on the origin and migrations of nations, in the Mém. de l'Acad. des Inscript. tom. xviii. p. 48-71. It is seldom that the antiquarian and the philosopher are so happily blended.

busy scenes is very different according to the different condition
of mankind.   In great monarchies, millions of obedient subjects
pursue their useful occupations in peace and obscurity.   The
attention of the writer, as well as of the reader, is solely confined
to a court, a capital, a regular army, and the districts which
happen to be the occasional scene of military operations.   But
a state of freedom and barbarism, the season of civil commotions,
or the situation of petty republics,[1] raises almost every member
of the community into action, and consequently into notice.
The irregular divisions, and the restless motions, of the people
of Germany dazzle our imagination and seem to multiply their
numbers.   The profuse enumeration of kings and warriors of
armies and nations inclines us to forget that the same objects are
continually repeated under a variety of appellations, and that
the most splendid appellations have been frequently lavished
on the most inconsiderable objects.

CHAPTER X

The Emperors Decius, Gallus, Æmilianus, Valerian, and Gallienus—The
general Irruption of the Barbarians—The thirty Tyrants

FROM the great secular games celebrated by Philip to the death
of the emperor Gallienus there elapsed (A.D. 248-268) twenty
years of shame and misfortune.   During that calamitous period
every instant of time was marked, every province of the Roman
world was afflicted by barbarous invaders and military tyrants,
and the ruined empire seemed to approach the last and fatal
moment of its dissolution.   The confusion of the times, and the
scarcity of authentic memorials, oppose equal difficulties to the
historian, who attempts to preserve a clear and unbroken thread
of narration.   Surrounded with imperfect fragments, always
concise, often obscure, and sometimes contradictory, he is
reduced to collect, to compare, and to conjecture: and though
he ought never to place his conjectures in the rank of facts, yet
the knowledge of human nature, and of the sure operation of
its fierce and unrestrained passions, might, on some occasions,
supply the want of historical materials.

There is not, for instance, any difficulty in conceiving that the

---

[1] Should we suspect that Athens contained only 21,000 citizens, and
Sparta no more than 39,000?   See Hume and Wallace on the number of
mankind in ancient and modern times.

successive murders of so many emperors had loosened all the
ties of allegiance between the prince and people; that all the
generals of Philip were disposed to imitate the example of their
master; and that the caprice of armies, long since habituated to
frequent and violent revolutions, might any day raise to the
throne the most obscure of their fellow-soldiers. History can
only add that the rebellion against the emperor Philip broke
out in the summer of the year two hundred and forty-nine,
among the legions of Mæsia; and that a subaltern officer,[1] named
Marinus, was the object of their seditious choice. Philip was
alarmed. He dreaded lest the treason of the Mæsian army
should prove the first spark of a general conflagration. Distracted with the consciousness of his guilt and of his danger, he
communicated the intelligence to the senate. A gloomy silence
prevailed, the effect of fear, and perhaps of disaffection: till at
length Decius, one of the assembly, assuming a spirit worthy of
his noble extraction, ventured to discover more intrepidity than
the emperor seemed to possess. He treated the whole business
with contempt, as a hasty and inconsiderate tumult, and Philip's
rival as a phantom of royalty, who in a very few days would be
destroyed by the same inconstancy that had created him. The
speedy completion of the prophecy inspired Philip with a just
esteem for so able a counsellor: and Decius appeared to him the
only person capable of restoring peace and discipline to an army
whose tumultuous spirit did not immediately subside after the
murder of Marinus. Decius, who long resisted his own nomination, seems to have insinuated the danger of presenting a leader
of merit to the angry and apprehensive minds of the soldiers;
and his prediction was again confirmed by the event. The legion
of Mæsia forced their judge to become (A.D. 249) their accomplice.
They left him only the alternative of death or the purple. His
subsequent conduct, after that decisive measure, was unavoid-
able. He conducted or followed his army to the confines of
Italy, whither Philip, collecting all his force to repel the formidable competitor whom he had raised up, advanced to meet him.
The Imperial troops were superior in number; but the rebels
formed an army of veterans, commanded by an able and experienced leader.[2] Philip was either killed in the battle or put

---

[1] The expression used by Zosimus and Zonaras may signify that Marinus
commanded a centenary, a cohort, or a legion.
[2] His birth at Bubalia, a little village in Pannonia (Eutrop. ix. Victor in
Cæsarib. et epitom.), seems to contradict, unless it was merely accidental,
his supposed descent from the Decii. Six hundred years had bestowed
nobility on the Decii; but at the commencement of that period they were

to death a few days afterwards at Verona. His son and associate in the empire was massacred at Rome by the Prætorian guards; and the victorious Decius, with more favourable circumstances than the ambition of that age can usually plead, was universally acknowledged by the senate and provinces. It is reported that, immediately after his reluctant acceptance of the title of Augustus, he had assured Philip, by a private message, of his innocence and loyalty, solemnly protesting that, on his arrival in Italy, he would resign the imperial ornaments and return to the condition of an obedient subject. His professions might be sincere. But in the situation where fortune had placed him it was scarcely possible that he could either forgive or be forgiven.[1]

The emperor Decius had employed a few months in the works of peace and the administration of justice, when (A.D. 250) he was summoned to the banks of the Danube by the invasion of the GOTHS. This is the first considerable occasion in which history mentions that great people, who afterwards broke the Roman power, sacked the Capitol, and reigned in Gaul, Spain, and Italy. So memorable was the part which they acted in the subversion of the Western empire that the name of GOTHS is frequently but improperly used as a general appellation of rude and warlike barbarism.

In the beginning of the sixth century, and after the conquest of Italy, the Goths, in possession of present greatness, very naturally indulged themselves in the prospect of past and of future glory. They wished to preserve the memory of their ancestors, and to transmit to posterity their own achievements. The principal minister of the court of Ravenna, the learned Cassiodorus, gratified the inclination of the conquerors in a Gothic history, which consisted of twelve books, now reduced to the imperfect abridgment of Jornandes.[2] These writers passed with the most artful conciseness over the misfortunes of the nation, celebrated its successful valour, and adorned the triumph with many Asiatic trophies that more properly belonged to the people of Scythia. On the faith of ancient songs, the uncertain, but the only, memorials of barbarians, they

---

only Plebeians of merit, and among the first who shared the consulship with the haughty Patricians. Plebeiæ Deciorum animæ, etc. Juvenal, Sat. viii. 254. See the spirited speech of Decius, in Livy, x. 9, 10.

[1] Zosimus, l. i. [c. 22] p. 20. Zonaras, l. xii. p. 624.

[2] Prefaces of Cassiodorus and Jornandes: it is surprising that the latter should be omitted in the excellent edition published by Grotius, of the Gothic writers. [Jordanes, not Jornandes, is now the recognised spelling. —O. S.]

deduced the first origin of the Goths from the vast island, or peninsula, of Scandinavia.[1] That extreme country of the north was not unknown to the conquerors of Italy: the ties of ancient consanguinity had been strengthened by recent offices of friendship; and a Scandinavian king had cheerfully abdicated his savage greatness that he might pass the remainder of his days in the peaceful and polished court of Ravenna.[2] Many vestiges, which cannot be ascribed to the arts of popular vanity, attest the ancient residence of the Goths in the countries beyond the Baltic. From the time of the geographer Ptolemy, the southern part of Sweden seems to have continued in the possession of the less enterprising remnant of the nation, and a large territory is even at present divided into east and west Gothland. During the middle ages (from the ninth to the twelfth century), whilst Christianity was advancing with a slow progress into the north, the Goths and the Swedes composed two distinct and sometimes

[1] On the authority of Ablavius, Jornandes quotes some old Gothic chronicles in verse. De Reb. Geticis, c. 4.

[The alleged Scandinavian origin of the Goths has given rise to much discussion, and has been denied by several eminent modern scholars. The only reasons in favour of their Scandinavian origin are the testimony of Jordanes (not Jornandes as the name is oftentimes incorrectly spelt) and the existence of the name Gothland in Sweden. But the testimony of Jordanes contains at best only the tradition of the people respecting their origin, which (as Dr. William Smith says) is never of much value, and the mere fact of the existence of the name Gothland in Sweden is not sufficient to prove that this country was the aboriginal abode of the people. For example, Scotland, though named after the Scots, was not their original home, for they migrated from Ireland. When the Romans first saw the Goths in the reign of Caracalla, they dwelt in the land of the Getæ, and Jordanes, Procopius, and others thought the Goths to be the same as the Getæ of the earlier historians. But the Getæ are now admitted to have been Thracians. There are two theories on this subject, both trying to explain the singular circumstance that a people named Gothi should have migrated from Germany and settled among the Getæ. The first hypothesis is that of Grimm, who supposes that there was no migration of Goths, but that they had been settled on the Lower Danube from the beginning. But against this we have the objection of the early writers that the Getæ were Thracians, and the Thracians were certainly not Germans. The other hypothesis is that of Latham, who argues that the name Get or Goth was the general name given by the Slavonic nations to the Lithuanians. According to this theory, the Gothones at the mouth of the Vistula, mentioned by Tacitus and Ptolemy, are Lithuanians, and the Getæ belong to the same nation.

In Morris's English Accidence the name Gothic is regarded as the oldest and most primitive of the Teutonic dialects, being spoken by the Eastern and Western Goths, who originally lived near the Vistula, but migrated about the third century of the Christian era to the neighbourhood of the Danube and the Black Sea, and afterwards over-ran all the countries of Southern Europe.—O. S.]

[2] Jornandes, c. 3.

hostile members of the same monarchy.[1] The latter of these
two names has prevailed without extinguishing the former. The
Swedes, who might well be satisfied with their own fame in arms,
have in every age claimed the kindred glory of the Goths. In
a moment of discontent against the court of Rome, Charles the
Twelfth insinuated that his victorious troops were not degenerated from their brave ancestors who had already subdued the
mistress of the world.[2]

Till the end of the eleventh century, a celebrated temple subsisted at Upsal, the most considerable town of the Swedes and
Goths. It was enriched with the gold which the Scandinavians
had acquired in their piratical adventures, and sanctified by the
uncouth representations of the three principal deities, the god
of war, the goddess of generation, and the god of thunder. In
the general festival that was solemnised every ninth year, nine
animals of every species (without excepting the human) were
sacrificed, and their bleeding bodies suspended in the sacred
grove adjacent to the temple.[3] The only traces that now subsist
of this barbaric superstition are contained in the Edda, a system
of mythology compiled in Iceland about the thirteenth century,
and studied by the learned of Denmark and Sweden as the most
valuable remains of their ancient traditions.

Notwithstanding the mysterious obscurity of the Edda, we can
easily distinguish two persons confounded under the name of
Odin, the god of war, and the great legislator of Scandinavia.
The latter, the Mahomet of the north, instituted a religion
adapted to the climate and to the people. Numerous tribes on
either side of the Baltic were subdued by the invincible valour
of Odin, by his persuasive eloquence, and by the fame, which
he acquired, of a most skilful magician. The faith that he had
propagated during a long and prosperous life he confirmed by
a voluntary death. Apprehensive of the ignominious approach
of disease and infirmity, he resolved to expire as became a
warrior. In a solemn assembly of the Swedes and Goths, he
wounded himself in nine mortal places, hastening away (as he

---

[1] The Prolegomena of Grotius has some large extracts from Adam of
Bremen and Saxo Grammaticus. The former wrote in the year 1077, the
latter flourished about the year 1200.

[2] Voltaire, Hist. de Charles XII. l. iii. When the Austrians desired the aid
of the court of Rome against Gustavus Adolphus, they always represented
that conqueror as the lineal successor of Alaric. Harte's Hist. of Gustavus,
vol. ii. p. 123.

[3] Adam of Bremen in Grotii Prolegomenis, p. 104. The temple of
Upsal was destroyed by Ingo king of Sweden, who began his reign in the
year 1075, and about fourscore years afterwards a Christian cathedral was
erected on its ruins. Dalin's Hist. of Sweden, in Bibliothèque Raisonnée.

asserted with his dying voice) to prepare the feast of heroes in the palace of the god of war. [1]

The native and proper habitation of Odin is distinguished by the appellation of As-gard. The happy resemblance of that name with As-burg, or As-of,[2] words of a similar signification, has given rise to an historical system of so pleasing a contexture that we could almost wish to persuade ourselves of its truth. It is supposed that Odin was the chief of a tribe of barbarians which dwelt on the banks of the lake Mætois, till the fall of Mithridates and the arms of Pompey menaced the north with servitude. That Odin, yielding with indignant fury to a power which he was unable to resist, conducted his tribe from the frontiers of the Asiatic Sarmatia into Sweden, with the great design of forming, in that inaccessible retreat of freedom, a religion and a people which, in some remote age, might be subservient to his immortal revenge; when his invincible Goths, armed with martial fanaticism, should issue in numerous swarms from the neighbourhood of the Polar circle, to chastise the oppressors of mankind.[3]

If so many successive generations of Goths were capable of preserving a faint tradition of their Scandinavian origin, we must not expect, from such unlettered barbarians, any distinct account of the time and circumstances of their emigration. To cross the Baltic was an easy and natural attempt. The inhabitants of Sweden were masters of a sufficient number of large vessels, with oars,[4] and the distance is little more than one hundred miles from Carlscrona to the nearest ports of Pomerania and Prussia. Here, at length, we land on firm and historic ground. At least as early as the Christian era,[5] and as late as the age of the Antonines,[6] the Goths were established towards the mouth of the

[1] Mallet, Introd. à l'Hist. du Dannemarc.

[2] Mallet, c. iv. p. 55 has collected from Strabo, Pliny, Ptolemy, and Stephanus Byzantinus, the vestiges of such a city and people.

[3] This wonderful expedition of Odin, which, by deducing the enmity of the Goths and Romans from so memorable a cause, might supply the noble groundwork of an epic poem, cannot safely be received as authentic history. According to the obvious sense of the Edda, and the interpretation of the most skilful critics, As-gard, instead of denoting a real city of the Asiatic Sarmatia, is the fictitious appellation of the mystic abode of the gods, the Olympus of Scandinavia: from whence the prophet was supposed to descend, when he announced his new religion to the Gothic nations, who were already seated in the southern parts of Sweden.

[4] Tacit. Germ. c 44.

[5] Tacit. Annal. ii. 62. If we could yield a firm assent to the navigations of Pytheas of Marseilles, we must allow that the Goths had passed the Baltic at least three hundred years before Christ.

[6] Ptolemy, l. ii.

Vistula, and in that fertile province where the commercial cities
of Thorn, Elbing, Koningsberg, and Dantzic were long afterwards founded.[1] Westward of the Goths, the numerous tribes
of the Vandals were spread along the banks of the Oder, and the
sea-coast of Pomerania and Mecklenburg. A striking resemblance of manners, complexion, religion, and language, seemed
to indicate that the Vandals and the Goths were originally one
great people.[2] The latter appear to have been subdivided into
Ostrogoths, Visigoths, and Gepidæ.[3] The distinction among the
Vandals was more strongly marked by the independent names
of Heruli, Burgundians, Lombards, and a variety of other petty
states, many of which, in a future age, expanded themselves
into powerful monarchies.

In the age of the Antonines, the Goths were still seated in
Prussia. About the reign of Alexander Severus, the Roman

[1] By the German colonies who followed the arms of the Teutonic knights.
The conquest and conversion of Prussia were completed by those adventurers in the thirteenth century.

[2] Pliny (Hist. Natur. iv. 14) and Procopius (in Bell. Vandal. l. i. c. 1) agree
in this opinion. They lived in distant ages, and possessed different means
of investigating the truth.

[This statement may be questioned, notwithstanding the authority of
these writers, to which that of Tacitus may be added. But Tacitus and
others included many nations under the name " Germans " that were not
Germans, and the name " Vandals " is a strong presumption that they
were a Sclavonic and not a Germanic people. The Germans have always
called them " Wends " or " Vends," and it is not improbable the Vandals
may have been Slavonian Servians from Saxony and Silesia.—O. S.]

[3] The *Ostro* and *Visi*, the eastern and western Goths, obtained those
denominations from their original seats in Scandinavia. In all their
future marches and settlements they preserved, with their names, the same
relative situation. When they first departed from Sweden, the infant
colony was contained in three vessels. The third being a heavy sailer
lagged behind, and the crew, which afterwards swelled into a nation,
received from that circumstance the appellation of Gepidæ or Loiterers.
Jornandes, c. 17.

[The statement regarding the Ostro- and Visi-goths, which rests solely on
the authority of Jordanes, cannot be admitted, though we do not know
when they got the names, probably not till they were settled on the shores
of the Black Sea. The earliest trace of the name Visigoths is in Sidonius
Apollinaris, who uses *Vesus* as a simple name; in Cassiodorus we find
Vuisigothi, and in Jordanes Wesegothæ and Wesigothæ. The name of
the Ostrogoths occurs earlier, first in the form Austrogothi (Pollio Claud.
c. 6) and afterwards in that of Ostrogothi (Claudian in Eutrop. ii. 153).
Neither of these names occurs in Zosimus or Ammianus Marcellinus, both
of whom, however, make frequent mention of the Grutungi or Greutungi,
and the Thervingi or Tervingi: it is probable (says Dr. W. Smith) that
that Grutungi were the most illustrious tribe among the Ostrogoths, and
that the Thervingi occupied the same rank among the Visigoths. As to
the Gepidæ, it is uncertain whether they were Goths at all. Their seat was
the middle Danube in Dacia. The close political connection of the Gepidæ
with the Goths may have led to their being regarded as a branch of the
latter people.—O. S.]

province of Dacia had already experienced their proximity by
frequent and destructive inroads.[1] In this interval, therefore,
of about seventy years, we must place the second migration of
the Goths from the Baltic to the Euxine; but the cause that
produced it lies concealed among the various motives which
actuate the conduct of unsettled barbarians. Either a pestilence
or a famine, a victory or a defeat, an oracle of the gods or the
eloquence of a daring leader, were sufficient to impel the Gothic
arms on the milder climates of the south. Besides the influence
of a martial religion, the numbers and spirit of the Goths were
equal to the most dangerous adventures. The use of round
bucklers and short swords rendered them formidable in a close
engagement; the manly obedience which they yielded to hereditary kings gave uncommon union and stability to their councils;[2]
and the renowned Amala, the hero of that age, and the tenth
ancestor of Theodoric, king of Italy, enforced, by the ascendant
of personal merit, the prerogative of his birth, which he derived
from the *Anses*, or demigods of the Gothic nation.[3]

The fame of a great enterprise excited the bravest warriors
from all the Vandalic states of Germany, many of whom are seen
a few years afterwards combating under the common standard
of the Goths.[4] The first motions of the emigrants carried them
to the banks of the Prypec, a river universally conceived by the
ancients to be the southern branch of the Borysthenes.[5] The
windings of that great stream through the plains of Poland and
Russia gave a direction to their line of march, and a constant
supply of fresh water and pasturage to their numerous herds of
cattle. They followed the unknown course of the river, confident in their valour, and careless of whatever power might
oppose their progress. The Bastarnæ and the Venedi were the
first who presented themselves; and the flower of their youth,
either from choice or compulsion, increased the Gothic army.
The Bastarnæ dwelt on the northern side of the Carpathian

---

[1] Fragment of Peter Patricius in the Excerpta Legationum; and with
regard to its probable date, Tillemont, Hist. des Empereurs, tom. iii. p. 346.

[2] Omnium harum gentium insigne, rotunda scuta, breves gladii, et erga
reges obsequium. Tacit. Germania, c. 43. The Goths probably acquired
their iron by the commerce of amber.

[3] Jornandes, c. 13, 14.

[4] The Heruli, and the Uregundi or Burgundi, are particularly mentioned.
Mascou's History of the Germans, l. v. A passage in the Augustan History, p. 28, seems to allude to this great emigration. The Marcomannic
war was partly occasioned by the pressure of barbarous tribes, who fled
before the arms of more northern barbarians.

[5] D'Anville, Géographie Ancienne, and the third part of his incomparable map of Europe.

mountains; the immense tract of land that separated the Bastarnæ from the savages of Finland was possessed, or rather
wasted, by the Venedi;[1] we have some reason to believe that the
first of these nations, which distinguished itself in the Macedonian
war,[2] and was afterwards divided into the formidable tribes of
the Peucini, the Borani, the Carpi, etc., derived its origin from
the Germans. With better authority, a Sarmatian extraction
may be assigned to the Venedi, who rendered themselves so
famous in the middle ages.[3] But the confusion of blood and
manners on that doubtful frontier often perplexed the most
accurate observers.[4] As the Goths advanced near the Euxine
Sea, they encountered a purer race of Sarmatians, the Jazyges,
the Alani, and the Roxolani; and they were probably the first
Germans who saw the mouths of the Borysthenes and of the
Tanais. If we inquire into the characteristic marks of the people
of Germany and of Sarmatia, we shall discover that those two
great portions of human kind were principally distinguished by
fixed huts or movable tents, by a close dress or flowing garments,
by the marriage of one or of several wives, by a military force
consisting, for the most part, either of infantry or cavalry; and
above all by the use of the Teutonic or of the Sclavonian language;
the last of which has been diffused by conquest from the confines
of Italy to the neighbourhood of Japan.

The Goths were now in possession of the Ukraine, a country of
considerable extent and uncommon fertility, intersected with
navigable rivers, which, from either side, discharge themselves
into the Borysthenes; and interspersed with large and lofty
forests of oaks. The plenty of game and fish, the innumerable
bee-hives, deposited in the hollows of old trees, and in the cavities
of rocks, and forming, even in that rude age, a valuable branch
of commerce, the size of the cattle, the temperature of the air,
the aptness of the soil for every species of grain, and the
luxuriancy of the vegetation, all displayed the liberality of
Nature, and tempted the industry of man.[5] But the Goths withstood all these temptations, and still adhered to a life of idleness,
of poverty, and of rapine.

[1] Tacit. Germ. c. 46.
[2] Cluver. Germ. Antiq. l. iii. c. 43.
[3] The Venedi, the *Slavi*, and the Antes, were the three great tribes of the
same people. Jornandes, c. 24.
[4] Tacitus most assuredly deserves that title, and even his cautious suspense is a proof of his diligent inquiries.
[5] Genealogical History of the Tartars, p. 593. Bell (vol. ii. p. 379)
traversed the Ukraine in his journey from Petersburgh to Constantinople.
The modern face of the country is a just representation of the ancient,
since, in the hands of the Cossacks, it still remains in a state of nature.

The Scythian hordes, which, towards the east, bordered on the new settlements of the Goths, presented nothing to their arms except the doubtful chance of an unprofitable victory. But the prospect of the Roman territories was far more alluring; and the fields of Dacia were covered with rich harvests, sown by the hands of an industrious, and exposed to be gathered by those of a warlike, people. It is probable that the conquests of Trajan maintained by his successors, less for any real advantage than for ideal dignity, had contributed to weaken the empire on that side. The new and unsettled province of Dacia was neither strong enough to resist, nor rich enough to satiate, the rapaciousness of the barbarians. As long as the remote banks of the Dniester were considered as the boundary of the Roman power, the fortifications of the Lower Danube were more carelessly guarded, and the inhabitants of Mæsia lived in supine security, fondly conceiving themselves at an inaccessible distance from any barbarian invaders. The irruptions of the Goths, under the reign of Philip, fatally convinced them of their mistake. The king, or leader, of that fierce nation traversed with contempt the province of Dacia, and passed both the Dniester and the Danube without encountering any opposition capable of retarding his progress. The relaxed discipline of the Roman troops betrayed the most important posts where they were stationed, and the fear of deserved punishment induced great numbers of them to enlist under the Gothic standard. The various multitude of barbarians appeared, at length, under the walls of Marcianopolis, a city built by Trajan in honour of his sister, and at that time the capital of the second Mæsia.[1] The inhabitants consented to ransom their lives and property by the payment of a large sum of money, and the invaders retreated back into their deserts, animated, rather than satisfied, with the first success of their arms against an opulent but feeble country. Intelligence was soon transmitted to the emperor Decius that Cniva, king of the Goths, had passed the Danube a second time, with more considerable forces; that his numerous detachments scattered devastation over the province of Mæsia, whilst the main body of the army, consisting of seventy thousand Germans and Sarmatians, a force equal to the most daring achievements,

---

[1] In the sixteenth chapter of Jornandes, instead of *secundo* Mæsiam, we may venture to substitute *secundam*, the second Mæsia, of which Marcianopolis was certainly the capital (Hierocles de Provinciis, and Wesseling ad locum, p. 636 Itinerar.). It is surprising how this palpable error of the scribe could escape the judicious correction of Grotius.

required the presence of the Roman monarch, and the exertion of his military power.

Decius found (A.D. 250) the Goths engaged before Nicopolis, on the Jatrus, one of the many monuments of Trajan's victories.[1] On his approach they raised the siege, but with a design only of marching away to a conquest of greater importance, the siege of Philippopolis, a city of Thrace, founded by the father of Alexander, near the foot of mount Hæmus.[2] Decius followed them through a difficult country, and by forced marches; but when he imagined himself at a considerable distance from the rear of the Goths, Cniva turned with rapid fury on his pursuers. The camp of the Romans was surprised and pillaged, and, for the first time, their emperor fled in disorder before a troop of half-armed barbarians. After a long resistance, Philippopolis, destitute of succour, was taken by storm. A hundred thousand persons are reported to have been massacred in the sack of that great city.[3] Many prisoners of consequence became a valuable accession to the spoil; and Priscus, a brother of the late emperor Philip, blushed not to assume the purple under the protection of the barbarous enemies of Rome.[4] The time, however, consumed in that tedious siege enabled Decius to revive the courage, restore the discipline, and recruit the numbers of his troops. He intercepted several parties of Carpi, and other Germans, who were hastening to share the victory of their countrymen,[5] intrusted the passes of the mountains to officers of approved valour and fidelity;[6] repaired and strengthened the fortifications of the Danube, and exerted his utmost vigilance to oppose either the progress or the retreat of the Goths. Encouraged by the return of fortune, he anxiously waited for an opportunity to retrieve, by a great and decisive blow, his own glory and that of the Roman arms.[7]

[1] The place is still called Nicop. The little stream, on whose banks it stood, falls into the Danube. D'Anville, Geographie Ancienne, tom. i. p. 307.

[2] Stephan. Byzant. de Urbibus, p. 740. Wesseling Itinerar. p. 136. Zonaras, by an odd mistake, ascribes the foundation of Philippopolis to the immediate predecessor of Decius.

[3] Ammian. xxxi. 5.1 [4] Aurel. Victor [de Cæsar], c. 29.

[5] *Victoriæ Carpicæ*, on some medals of Decius, insinuate these advantages.

[6] Claudius (who afterwards reigned with so much glory) was posted in the pass of Thermopylæ with 200 Dardanians, 100 heavy and 160 light horse, 60 Cretan archers, and 1000 well armed recruits. See an original letter from the emperor to his officer, in the Augustan History, p. 200. [Trebell. Pollio in Claud. c. 16.]

[7] Jornandes, c. 16-18. Zosimus, l. i. [c. 22] p. 22. In the general account of this war, it is easy to discover the opposite prejudices of the Gothic and the Grecian writers. In carelessness alone they are alike.

At the same time when Decius was struggling with the violence of the tempest, his mind, calm and deliberate amidst the tumult of war, investigated the more general causes that, since the age of the Antonines, had so impetuously urged the decline of the Roman greatness. He soon discovered that it was impossible to replace that greatness on a permanent basis without restoring public virtue, ancient principles and manners, and the oppressed majesty of the laws. To execute this noble but arduous design, he first resolved to revive the obsolete officer of censor; an office which, as long as it had subsisted in its pristine integrity, had so much contributed to the perpetuity of the state,[1] till it was usurped and gradually neglected by the Cæsars.[2] Conscious that the favour of the sovereign may confer power, but that the esteem of the people can alone bestow authority, he submitted the choice of the censor to the unbiassed voice of the senate. By their unanimous votes, or rather acclamations, Valerian, who was afterwards emperor, and who then served with distinction in the army of Decius, was (A.D. 251, 27 Oct.) declared the most worthy of that exalted honour. As soon as the decree of the senate was transmitted to the emperor, he assembled a great council in his camp, and, before the investiture of the censor elect, he apprised him of the difficulty and importance of his great office. " Happy Valerian," said the prince to his distinguished subject, " happy in the general approbation of the senate and of the Roman republic! Accept the censorship of mankind; and judge of our manners. You will select those who deserve to continue members of the senate; you will restore the equestrian order to its ancient splendour; you will improve the revenue, yet moderate the public burdens. You will distinguish into regular classes the various and infinite multitude of citizens, and accurately review the military strength, the wealth, the virtue, and the resources of Rome. Your decisions shall obtain the force of laws. The army, the palace, the ministers of justice, and the great officers of the empire, are all subject to your tribunal. None are exempted, excepting only the ordinary consuls,[3] the prefect of the city, the king of the sacrifices, and

[1] Montesquieu, Grandeur et Decadence des Romains, c. viii. He illustrates the nature and use of the censorship with his usual ingenuity, and with uncommon precision.

[2] Vespasian and Titus were the last censors (Pliny, Hist. Natur. vii. 49. Censorinus de Die Natali). The modesty of Trajan refused an honour which he deserved, and his example became a law to the Antonines. Pliny's Panegyric, c. 45 and 60.

[3] Yet in spite of this exemption Pompey appeared before that tribunal during his consulship. The occasion indeed was equally singular and donourable. Plutarch in Pomp. [c. 22] p. 630.

(as long as she preserves her chastity inviolate) the eldest of the
vestal virgins. Even these few, who may not dread the severity,
will anxiously solicit the esteem, of the Roman censor." [1]

A magistrate, invested with such extensive powers, would have
appeared not so much the minister as the colleague of his sovereign.[2] Valerian justly dreaded an elevation so full of envy and
of suspicion. He modestly urged the alarming greatness of the
trust, his own insufficiency, and the incurable corruption of the
times. He artfully insinuated that the office of censor was
inseparable from the Imperial dignity, and that the feeble hands
of a subject were unequal to the support of such an immense
weight of cares and of power.[3] The approaching event of war
soon put an end to the prosecution of a project so specious but
so impracticable; and whilst it preserved Valerian from the
danger, saved the emperor Decius from the disappointment which
would most probably have attended it. A censor may maintain,
he can never restore, the morals of a state. It is impossible for
such a magistrate to exert his authority with benefit, or even
with effect, unless he is supported by a quick sense of honour and
virtue in the minds of the people, by a decent reverence for the
public opinion, and by a train of useful prejudices combating
on the side of national manners. In a period when these principles are annihilated, the censorial jurisdiction must either sink
into empty pageantry, or be converted into a partial instrument
of vexatious oppression.[4] It was easier to vanquish the Goths
than to eradicate the public vices; yet even in the first of these
enterprises Decius lost his army and his life.

The Goths were now, on every side, surrounded and pursued
by the Roman arms. The flower of their troops had perished
in the long siege of Philippopolis, and the exhausted country
could no longer afford subsistence for the remaining multitude
of licentious barbarians. Reduced to this extremity, the Goths
would gladly have purchased, by the surrender of all their booty
and prisoners, the permission of an undisturbed retreat. But
the emperor, confident of victory, and resolving, by the chastisement of these invaders, to strike a salutary terror into the nations
of the North, refused to listen to any terms of accommodation.
The high-spirited barbarians preferred death to slavery. An

[1] Original speech, in the Augustan Hist. p. 173, 174 [Treb. Poll. c. 2].
[2] This transaction might deceive Zonaras, who supposes that Valerian
was actually declared the colleague of Decius, l. xii. p. 625.
[3] Hist. August. p. 174 [Treb. Poll. l. c.]. The emperor's reply is omitted.
[4] Such as the attempts of Augustus towards a reformation of manners.
Tacit. Annal. iii. 24.

obscure town of Mæsia, called Forum Terebronii,[1] was the scene
of the battle. The Gothic army was drawn up in three lines,
and, either from choice or accident, the front of the third line
was covered by a morass. In the beginning of the action, the
son of Decius, a youth of the fairest hopes, and already associated
to the honours of the purple, was slain by an arrow, in the sight
of his afflicted father; who, summoning all his fortitude, admonished the dismayed troops that the loss of a single soldier
was of little importance to the republic.[2] The conflict was
terrible; it was the combat of despair against grief and rage.
The first line of the Goths at length gave way in disorder; the
second, advancing to sustain it, shared its fate; and the third
only remained entire, prepared to dispute the passage of the
morass, which was imprudently attempted by the presumption
of the enemy. "Here the fortune of the day turned, and all
things became adverse to the Romans: the place deep with ooze,
sinking under those who stood, slippery to such as advanced;
their armour heavy, the waters deep; nor could they wield, in
that uneasy situation, their weighty javelins. The barbarians, on
the contrary, were enured to encounters in the bogs, their persons
tall, their spears long, such as could wound at a distance."[3] In
this morass the Roman army, after an ineffectual struggle, was
irrecoverably lost; nor could the body of the emperor ever be
found.[4] Such was the fate of Decius, in the fiftieth year of his
age; an accomplished prince, active in war, and affable in peace;[5]
who, together with his son, has deserved to be compared, both in
life and death, with the brightest examples of ancient virtue.[6]

This fatal blow humbled, for a very little time, the insolence
of the legions. They appear to have patiently expected, and
submissively obeyed, the decree of the senate, which regulated
the succession to the throne. From a just regard for the memory
of Decius, the Imperial title was (A.D. 251, Dec.) conferred on

[1] Tillemont, Histoire des Empereurs, tom. iii. p. 598. As Zosimus and
some of his followers mistake the Danube for the Tanais, they place the
field of battle in the plains of Scythia.
[2] Aurelius Victor allows two distinct actions for the deaths of the two
Decii; but I have preferred the account of Jornandes.
[3] I have ventured to copy from Tacitus (Annal. i. 64) the picture of a
similar engagement between a Roman army and a German tribe.
[4] Jornandes, c. 18. Zosimus, l. i. [c. 23] p. 22. Zonaras, l. xii. [c. 20]
p. 627. Aurelius Victor. [Epitome c. 29].
[5] The Decii were killed before the end of the year two hundred and fifty
one, since the new princes took possession of the consulship on the ensuing
calends of January.
[6] Hist. August. p. 223 [Vopisc. Aur. c. 42] gives them a very honourable
place among the small number of good emperors who reigned between
Augustus and Diocletian.

Hostilianus, his only surviving son; but an equal rank, with
more effectual power, was granted to Gallus, whose experience
and ability seemed equal to the great trust of guardian to the
young prince and the distressed empire.[1] The first care of the
new emperor was to deliver the Illyrian provinces from the
intolerable weight of the victorious Goths. He (A.D. 252) consented to leave in their hands the rich fruits of their invasion, an
immense booty, and, what was still more disgraceful, a great
number of prisoners of the highest merit and quality. He
plentifully supplied their camp with every conveniency that
could assuage their angry spirits, or facilitate their so much
wished-for departure; and he even promised to pay them annually
a large sum of gold, on condition they should never afterwards
infest the Roman territories by their incursions.[2]

In the age of the Scipios, the most opulent kings of the earth,
who courted the protection of the victorious commonwealth,
were gratified with such trifling presents as could only derive a
value from the hand that bestowed them; an ivory chair, a
coarse garment of purple, an inconsiderable piece of plate, or a
quantity of copper coin.[3] After the wealth of nations had
centred in Rome, the emperors displayed their greatness, and
even their policy, by the regular exercise of a steady and
moderate liberality towards the allies of the state. They
relieved the poverty of the barbarians, honoured their merit,
and recompensed their fidelity. These voluntary marks of
bounty were understood to flow not from the fears, but merely
from the generosity or the gratitude of the Romans; and whilst
presents and subsidies were liberally distributed among friends
and suppliants, they were sternly refused to such as claimed
them as a debt.[4] But this stipulation of an annual payment to
a victorious enemy appeared without disguise in the light of an
ignominious tribute; the minds of the Romans were not yet
accustomed to accept such unequal laws from a tribe of barbarians;
and the prince, who by a necessary concession had probably
saved his country, became the object of the general contempt
and aversion. The death of Hostilianus, though it happened in

---

[1] Hæc ubi Patres comperere . . . decernunt. Victor in Cæsaribus [c. 30].
[2] Zonaras, l. xii. [c. 21] p. 628.
[3] A *Sella*, a *Toga*, and a golden *Patera* of five pounds weight, were accepted with joy and gratitude by the wealthy king of Egypt (Livy, xxvii. 4).
Quina Millia Æris, a weight of copper in value about eighteen pounds
sterling, was the usual present made to foreign ambassadors (Livy, xxxi. 9).
[4] See the firmness of a Roman general so late as the time of Alexander
Severus, in the Excerpta Legationum, p. 25, edit. Louvre.

the midst of a raging pestilence, was interpreted as the personal crime of Gallus;[1] and even the defeat of the late emperor was ascribed by the voice of suspicion to the perfidious counsels of his hated successor.[2] The tranquillity which the empire enjoyed during the first year of his administration[3] served rather to inflame than to appease the public discontent; and, as soon as the apprehensions of war were removed, the infamy of the peace was more deeply and more sensibly felt.

But the Romans were irritated to a still higher degree when they discovered that they had not even secured their repose, though at the expense of their honour. The dangerous secret of the wealth and weakness of the empire had been revealed to the world. New swarms of barbarians, encouraged (A.D. 253) by the success, and not conceiving themselves bound by the obligation, of their brethren, spread devastation through the Illyrian provinces, and terror as far as the gates of Rome. The defence of the monarchy, which seemed abandoned by the pusillanimous emperor, was assumed by Æmilianus, governor of Pannonia and Mæsia; who rallied the scattered forces, and revived the fainting spirits of the troops. The barbarians were unexpectedly attacked, routed, chased, and pursued beyond the Danube. The victorious leader distributed as a donative the money collected for the tribute, and the acclamations of the soldiers proclaimed him emperor on the field of battle.[4] Gallus, who, careless of the general welfare, indulged himself in the pleasures of Italy, was almost in the same instant informed of the success of the revolt and of the rapid approach of his aspiring lieutenant. He advanced to meet him as far as the plains of Spoleto. When the armies came in sight of each other, the soldiers of Gallus compared the ignominious conduct of their sovereign with the glory of his rival. They admired the valour of Æmilianus; they were attracted by his liberality, for he offered a considerable increase of pay to all deserters.[5] The murder of Gallus, and of his son Volusianus, put an end to the civil war; and the senate (A.D. 253, May) gave a legal sanction to the rights of conquest. The letters of Æmilianus to that assembly displayed a mixture of moderation and vanity. He assured them that he should resign to their wisdom the civil administration;

---

[1] Jornandes, c. 19, and Victor in Cæsaribus.
[2] These improbable accusations are alleged by Zosimus, l. i. p. 23, 24.
[3] Jornandes, c. 19. The Gothic writer at least observed the peace which his victorious countrymen had sworn to Gallus.
[4] Zosimus, l. i. p. 25, 26.
[5] Victor in Cæsaribus, [c. 30].

and, contenting himself with the quality of their general, would in a short time assert the glory of Rome, and deliver the empire from all the barbarians both of the North and of the East.[1] His pride was flattered by the applause of the senate; and medals are still extant representing him with the name and attributes of Hercules the Victor and of Mars the Avenger.[2]

If the new monarch possessed the abilities, he wanted the time necessary to fulfil these splendid promises. Less than four months intervened between his victory and his fall.[3] He had vanquished Gallus: he sunk under the weight of a competitor more formidable than Gallus. That unfortunate prince had sent Valerian, already distinguished by the honourable title of censor, to bring the legions of Gaul and Germany to his aid.[4] Valerian executed that commission with zeal and fidelity; and as he arrived too late to save his sovereign, he resolved to revenge him. The troops of Æmilianus, who still lay encamped in the plains of Spoleto, were awed by the sanctity of his character, but much more by the superior strength of his army; and as they were now become as incapable of personal attachment as they had always been of constitutional principle, they (A.D. 253, Aug.) readily imbrued their hands in the blood of a prince who had so lately been the object of their partial choice. The guilt was theirs, but the advantage of it was Valerian's; who obtained the possession of the throne by the means indeed of a civil war, but with a degree of innocence singular in that age of revolutions; since he owned neither gratitude nor allegiance to his predecessor whom he dethroned.

Valerian was about sixty years of age[5] when he was invested with the purple, not by the caprice of the populace, or the clamours of the army, but by the unanimous voice of the Roman world. In his gradual ascent through the honours of the state, he had deserved the favour of virtuous princes, and had declared himself the enemy of tyrants.[6] His noble birth, his mild but unblemished manners, his learning, prudence, and experience, were revered by the senate and people; and if mankind (accord-

---

[1] Zonaras, l. xii. p. 628. [2] Banduri Numismata, p. 94.
[3] Eutropius, l. ix. c. 6 says tertio mense. Eusebius omits this emperor.
[4] Zosimus, l. i. p. 28. Eutropius and Victor station Valerian's army in Rhætia.
[5] He was about seventy at the time of his accession, or, as it is more probable, of his death. Hist. August. p. 173. Tillemont, Hist. des Empereurs, tom. iii. p. 893, note 1.
[6] Inimicus Tyrannorum. Hist. August. p. 173. In the glorious struggle of the senate against Maximin, Valerian acted a very spirited part. Hist. August. p. 156.

ing to the observation of an ancient writer) had been left at liberty to choose a master, their choice would most assuredly have fallen on Valerian.[1] Perhaps the merit of this emperor was inadequate to his reputation; perhaps his abilities, or at least his spirit, were affected by the languor and coldness of old age. The consciousness of his decline engaged him to share the throne with a younger and more active associate:[2] the emergency of the times demanded a general no less than a prince; and the experience of the Roman censor might have directed him where to bestow the Imperial purple, as the reward of military merit. But instead of making a judicious choice, which would have confirmed his reign and endeared his memory, Valerian, consulting only the dictates of affection or vanity, immediately invested with the supreme honours his son Gallienus, a youth whose effeminate vices had been hitherto concealed by the obscurity of a private station. The joint government of the father and the son subsisted about seven, and the sole administration of Gallienus continued about eight years (A.D. 253–268). But the whole period was one uninterrupted series of confusion and calamity. As the Roman empire was at the same time, and on every side, attacked by the blind fury of foreign invaders, and the wild ambition of domestic usurpers, we shall consult order and perspicuity by pursuing not so much the doubtful arrangement of dates as the more natural distribution of subjects. The most dangerous enemies of Rome, during the reigns of Valerian and Gallienus, were, 1. The Franks; 2. The Alemanni; 3. The Goths; and 4. The Persians. Under these general appellations we may comprehend the adventures of less considerable tribes, whose obscure and uncouth names would only serve to oppress the memory and perplex the attention of the reader.

I. As the posterity of the Franks compose one of the greatest and most enlightened nations of Europe, the powers of learning and ingenuity have been exhausted in the discovery of their unlettered ancestors. To the tales of credulity have succeeded the systems of fancy. Every passage has been sifted, every spot has been surveyed, that might possibly reveal some faint traces of their origin. It has been supposed that Pannonia,[3] that Gaul,

[1] According to the distinction of Victor, he seems to have received the title of *Imperator* from the army, and that of Augustus from the senate.

[2] From Victor and from the medals, Tillemont (tom. iii. p. 710) very justly infers that Gallienus was associated to the empire about the month of August of the year 253.

[3] Various systems have been formed to explain a difficult passage in Gregory of Tours, l. i. c. 9.

that the northern parts of Germany,[1] gave birth to that celebrated colony of warriors. At length the most rational critics,
rejecting the fictitious emigrations of ideal conquerors, have
acquiesced in a sentiment whose simplicity persuades us of its
truth.[2] They suppose that, about the year two hundred and
forty,[3] a new confederacy was formed under the name of Franks,
by the old inhabitants of the Lower Rhine and the Weser. The
present circle of Westphalia, the Landgraviate of Hesse, and the
duchies of Brunswick and Luneburg, were the ancient seat of
the Chauci, who, in their inaccessible morasses, defied the Roman
arms;[4] of the Cherusci, proud of the fame of Arminius; of the
Catti, formidable by their firm and intrepid infantry; and of
several other tribes of inferior power and renown.[5] The love of
liberty was the ruling passion of these Germans; the enjoyment
of it their best treasure; the word that expressed that enjoyment the most pleasing to their ear. They deserved, they
assumed, they maintained the honourable epithet of Franks or
Freemen; which concealed, though it did not extinguish, the
peculiar names of the several states of the confederacy.[6] Tacit
consent, and mutual advantage, dictated the first laws of the
union; it was gradually cemented by habit and experience.
The league of the Franks may admit of some comparison with
the Helvetic body; in which every canton, retaining its independent sovereignty, consults with its brethren in the common
cause, without acknowledging the authority of any supreme
head or representative assembly.[7] But the principle of the

---

[1] The Geographer of Ravenna, l. 11, by mentioning *Mauringania* on the
confines of Denmark, as the ancient seat of the Franks, gave birth to an
ingenious system of Leibnitz.

[2] Cluver. Germania Antiqua, l. iii. c. 20. M. Freret, in the Memoires des
l'Academie des Inscriptions, tom. xviii.

[3] Most probably under the reign of Gordian, from an accidental circumstance fully canvassed by Tillemont, tom. iii. p. 710, 1181.

[4] Plin. Hist. Natur. xvi. 1. The panegyrists frequently allude to the
morasses of the Franks.

[5] Tacit. Germania, c. 30, 37.

[6] In a subsequent period, most of those old names are occasionally mentioned. See some vestiges of them in Cluver. Germ. Antiq. l. iii.

[The term Frank, like that of Marcomanni, was probably applied to several
confederacies on the Roman frontier, which called themselves by this name
in opposition to their fellow-Germans in the Decumates agri, who were subject to Rome. Hence Dr. Latham thinks that instead of assuming migration to account for names, such as the Franks of France, the Franks of
Franconia, and the like, we may simply suppose them to be Franks of a
different division of the Frankish name. See Latham's Germania of
Tacitus. Later writers have divided them into the Salian or Lower
Rhine Franks, and the Ripuarian or Middle Rhine.—O. S.]

[7] Simler de Republica Helvet. cum notis Fuselin.

two confederacies was extremely different. A peace of two hundred years has rewarded the wise and honest policy of the Swiss. An inconstant spirit, the thirst of rapine, and a disregard to the most solemn treaties, disgraced the character of the Franks.

The Romans had long experienced the daring valour of the people of Lower Germany. The union of their strength threatened Gaul with a more formidable invasion, and required the presence of Gallienus, the heir and colleague of imperial power.[1] Whilst that prince, and his infant son Salonius, displayed, in the court of Treves, the majesty of the empire, its armies were ably conducted by their general Posthumus, who, though he afterwards betrayed the family of Valerian, was ever faithful for the great interest of the monarchy. The treacherous language of panegyrics and medals darkly announces a long series of victories. Trophies and titles attest (if such evidence can attest) the fame of Posthumus, who is repeatedly styled The conqueror of the Germans, and the saviour of Gaul.[2]

But a single fact, the only one indeed of which we have any distinct knowledge, erases, in a great measure, these monuments of vanity and adulation. The Rhine, though dignified with the title of Safeguard of the provinces, was an imperfect barrier against the daring spirit of enterprise with which the Franks were actuated. Their rapid devastations stretched from the river to the foot of the Pyrenees: nor were they stopped by those mountains. Spain, which had never dreaded, was unable to resist, the inroads of the Germans. During twelve years, the greatest part of the reign of Gallienus, that opulent country was the theatre of unequal and destructive hostilities. Tarragona, the flourishing capital of a peaceful province, was sacked and almost destroyed,[3] and so late as the days of Orosius, who wrote in the fifth century, wretched cottages, scattered amidst the ruins of magnificent cities, still recorded the rage of the barbarians.[4] When the exhausted country no longer supplied a variety of plunder, the Franks seized on some vessels in the ports

---

[1] Zosimus, l. i. p. 27.

[2] M. de Brequigny (Mém. de l'Acad. tom. xxx.) has given us a very curious life of Posthumus. A series of the Augustan History from Medals and Inscriptions has been more than once planned, and is still much wanted.

[3] Aurel. Victor, c. 33. Instead of *Pæne direpto*, both the sense and the expression require *deleto*; though, indeed, for different reasons, it is alike difficult to correct the text of a best, and of the worst, writers.

[4] In the time of Ausonius (the end of the fouth century) Herda or Lerida was in a very ruinous state, which probably was the consequence of this invasion. Aus. ep. 25, 8.

of Spain,[1] and transported themselves into Mauritania. The distant province was astonished with the fury of these barbarians, who seemed to fall from a new world, as their name, manners, and complexion were equally unknown on the coast of Africa.[2]

II. In that part of Upper Saxony beyond the Elbe, which is at present called the Marquisate of Lusace, there existed, in ancient times, a sacred wood, the awful seat of the superstition of the Suevi. None were permitted to enter the holy precincts without confessing, by their servile bonds and suppliant posture, the immediate presence of the sovereign Deity.[3] Patriotism contributed as well as devotion to consecrate the Sonnenwald, or wood of the Semnones.[4] It was universally believed that the nation had received its first existence on that sacred spot. At stated periods, the numerous tribes who gloried in the Suevic blood resorted thither by their ambassadors; and the memory of their common extraction was perpetuated by barbaric rites and human sacrifices. The wide extended name of Suevi filled the interior countries of Germany from the banks of the Oder to those of the Danube. They were distinguished from the other Germans by their peculiar mode of dressing their long hair, which they gathered into a rude knot on the crown of the head; and they delighted in an ornament that showed their ranks more lofty and terrible in the eyes of the enemy.[5] Jealous as the Germans were of military renown, they all confessed the superior valour of the Suevi; and the tribes of the Usipetes and Tencteri, who, with a vast army, encountered the dictator Cæsar, declared that they esteemed it not a disgrace to have fled before a people to whose arms the immortal gods themselves were unequal.[6]

In the reign of the emperor Caracalla, an innumerable swarm of Suevi appeared on the banks of the Mein, and in the neighbourhood of the Roman provinces, in quest either of food, of plunder, or of glory.[7] The hasty army of volunteers gradually coalesced into a great and permanent nation, and as it was composed from so many different tribes, assumed the name of

---

[1] Valesius is therefore mistaken in supposing that the Franks had invaded Spain by sea.
[2] Aurel. Victor. Eutrop. ix. 6.
[3] Tacit. Germania, 38.
[4] Cluver. Germ. Antiq. iii. 25.
[5] Sic Suevi a cateri Germanus, sic suevorum ingenui, a Servis separantur—A proud separation.
[6] Cæsar in Bello Gallico, iv. 7.
[7] Victor in Caracal. [c. 21]. Dion Cassius, lxvii. [c. 13] p. 1350.

Alemanni, or *All-men ;* to denote at once their various lineage
and their common bravery.[1] The latter was soon felt by the
Romans in many a hostile inroad. The Alemanni fought
chiefly on horseback; but their cavalry was rendered still more
formidable by a mixture of light infantry, selected from the
bravest and most active of the youth, whom frequent exercise
had enured to accompany the horsemen in the longest march,
the most rapid charge, or the most precipitate retreat.[2]

This warlike people of Germans had been astonished by the
immense preparations of Alexander Severus, they were dismayed by the arms of his successor, a barbarian equal in valour
and fierceness to themselves. But still hovering on the frontiers
of the empire, they increased the general disorder that ensued
after the death of Decius. They inflicted severe wounds on the
rich provinces of Gaul; they were the first who removed the
veil that covered the feeble majesty of Italy. A numerous body
of the Alemanni penetrated across the Danube, and through the
Rhætian Alps, into the plains of Lombardy, advanced as far as
Ravenna, and displayed the victorious banners of barbarians
almost in sight of Rome.[3] The insult and the danger rekindled
in the senate some sparks of their ancient virtue. Both the
emperors were engaged in far distant wars, Valerian in the East
and Gallienus on the Rhine. All the hopes and resources of the
Romans were in themselves. In this emergency, the senators
resumed the defence of the republic, drew out the Prætorian
guards, who had been left to garrison the capital, and filled up
their numbers by enlisting into the public service the stoutest
and most willing of the Plebeians. The Alemanni, astonished
with the sudden appearance of an army more numerous than
their own, retired into Germany laden with spoil; and their
retreat was esteemed as a victory by the unwarlike Romans.[4]

When Gallienus received the intelligence that his capital was
delivered from the barbarians, he was much less delighted than
alarmed with the courage of the senate, since it might one day
prompt them to rescue the public from domestic tyranny as well
as from foreign invasion. His timid ingratitude was published
to his subjects in an edict which prohibited the senators from

---

[1] This etymology (far different from those which amuse the fancy of the
learned) is preserved by Asinius Quadratus, an original historian, quoted
by Agathias, i. c. 5.
[2] The Suevi engaged Cæsar in this manner, and the manœuvre deserved
the approbation of the conqueror (Bell. Gall. i. 48.)
[3] Hist. August. p. 215, 216. [Vopis. Aurel. c. 18, 21]. Dexippus in the
Excerpta Legationum. p. 8. Hieronym. Chron. Orosius, vii. 22.
[4] Zosimus, l. i. p. 34.

exercising any military employment, and even from approaching the camps of the legions. But his fears were groundless.
The rich and luxurious nobles, sinking into their natural character, accepted, as a favour, this disgraceful exemption from
military service; and as long as they were indulged in the
enjoyment of their baths, their theatres, and their villas, they
cheerfully resigned the more dangerous cares of empire to the
rough hands of peasants and soldiers.[1]

Another invasion of the Alemanni, of a more formidable aspect,
but more glorious event, is mentioned by a writer of the lower
empire. Three hundred thousand of that warlike people are said
to have been vanquished, in a battle near Milan, by Gallienus in
person at the head of only ten thousand Romans.[2] We may,
however, with great probability, ascribe this incredible victory
either to the credulity of the historian or to some exaggerated
exploits of one of the emperor's lieutenants. It was by arms
of a very different nature that Gallienus endeavoured to protect Italy from the fury of the Germans. He espoused Pipa, the
daughter of a king of the Marcomanni, a Suevic tribe, which
was often confounded with the Alemanni in their wars and
conquests.[3] To the father, as the price of his alliance, he
granted an ample settlement in Pannonia. The native charms
of unpolished beauty seem to have fixed the daughter in the
affections of the inconstant emperor, and the bonds of policy
were more firmly connected by those of love. But the haughty
prejudice of Rome still refused the name of marriage to the profane mixture of a citizen and a barbarian; and has stigmatised
the German princess with the opprobrious title of concubine of
Gallienus.[4]

III. We have already traced the emigration of the Goths from
Scandinavia, or at least from Prussia, to the mouth of the
Borysthenes, and have followed their victorious arms from the
Borysthenes to the Danube. Under the reigns of Valerian and
Gallienus, the frontier of the last-mentioned river was perpetually infested by the inroads of Germans and Sarmatians; but it
was defended by the Romans with more than usual firmness and
success. The provinces that were the seat of war recruited the
armies of Rome with an inexhaustible supply of hardy soldiers;

---

[1] Aurel. Victor in Gallieno et Probo. His complaints breathe an uncommon spirit of freedom.

[2] Zonaras, l. xii. p. 631.

[3] One of the Victors calls him King of the Marcomanni; the other, of the
Germans.

[4] Tillemont, Hist. des Empereurs, tom. iii. p. 398, etc.

and more than one of these Illyrian peasants attained the station
and displayed the abilities of a general. Though flying parties
of the barbarians, who incessantly hovered on the banks of the
Danube, penetrated sometimes to the confines of Italy and Macedonia; their progress was commonly checked, or their return
intercepted, by the Imperial lieutenants.[1] But the great stream
of the Gothic hostilities was diverted into a very different channel.
The Goths, in their new settlement of the Ukraine, soon became
masters of the northern coast of the Euxine: to the south of that
inland sea were situated the soft and wealthy provinces of Asia
Minor, which possessed all that could attract, and nothing that
could resist, a barbarian conqueror.

The banks of the Borysthenes are only sixty miles distant from
the narrow entrance [2] of the peninsula of Crim Tartary, known
to the ancients under the name of Chersonesus Taurica.[3] On
that inhospitable shore, Euripides, embellishing with exquisite
art the tales of antiquity, has placed the scene of one of his most
affecting tragedies.[4] The bloody sacrifices of Diana, the arrival
of Orestes and Pylades, and the triumph of virtue and religion
over savage fierceness, serve to represent an historical truth,
that the Tauri, the original inhabitants of the peninsula, were,
in some degree, reclaimed from their brutal manners by a
gradual intercourse with the Grecian colonies which settled along
the maritime coast. The little kingdom of Bosphorus, whose
capital was situated on the Straits, through which the Mæotis
communicates itself to the Euxine, was composed of degenerate
Greeks and half-civilised barbarians. It subsisted, as an independent state, from the time of the Peloponnesian war,[5] was at
last swallowed up by the ambition of Mithridates,[6] and, with
the rest of his dominions, sunk under the weight of the Roman
arms. From the reign of Augustus,[7] the kings of Bosphorus
were the humble, but not useless, allies of the empire. By
presents, by arms, and by a slight fortification drawn across the
Isthmus, they effectually guarded against the roving plunderers

[1] See Lives of Claudius, Aurelian, and Probus, in the Augustan History.
[2] It is about half a league in breadth. Genealogical History of the
Tartars. p. 598.
[3] M. de Peyssonel, who had been French consul at Caffa, in his Observations sur les Peuples Barbares, qui ont habité les bords du Danube.
[4] Euripides in Iphigenia in Taurid.
[5] Strabo, l. vii. p. 309. The first kings of Bosphorus were the allies of
Athens.
[6] Appian in Mithridat.
[7] It was reduced by the arms of Agrippa. Orosius, vi. 21. Eutropius,
vii. 9. The Romans once advanced within three days' march of the
Tanais. Tacit. Annal. xii. 17.

of Sarmatia the access of a country which, from its peculiar
situation and convenient harbours, commanded the Euxine Sea
and Asia Minor.[1] As long as the sceptre was possessed by a
lineal succession of kings, they acquitted themselves of their
important charge with vigilance and success.   Domestic factions,
and the fears, or private interest, of obscure usurpers, who
seized on the vacant throne, admitted the Goths into the heart
of Bosphorus. With the acquisition of a superfluous waste of
fertile soil, the conquerors obtained the command of a naval
force, sufficient to transport their armies to the coast of Asia.[2]
The ships used in the navigation of the Euxine were of a very
singular construction. They were slight flat-bottomed barks
framed of timber only, without the least mixture of iron, and
occasionally covered with a shelving roof on the appearance
of a tempest.[3] In these floating houses, the Goths carelessly
trusted themselves to the mercy of an unknown sea, under
the conduct of sailors pressed into the service, and whose skill
and fidelity were equally suspicious. But the hopes of plunder
had banished every idea of danger, and a natural fearlessness of
temper supplied in their minds the more rational confidence
which is the just result of knowledge and experience. Warriors
of such a daring spirit must have often murmured against the
cowardice of their guides, who required the strongest assurances
of a settled calm before they would venture to embark; and
would scarcely ever be tempted to lose sight of the land. Such,
at least, is the practice of the modern Turks,[4] and they are
probably not inferior in the art of nagivation to the ancient
inhabitants of Bosphorus.

The fleet of the Goths, leaving the coast of Circassia on the
left hand, first appeared before Pityus,[5] the utmost limits of the
Roman provinces; a city provided with a convenient port and
fortified with a strong wall. Here they met with a resistance
more obstinate than they had reason to expect from the feeble
garrison of a distant fortress. They were repulsed; and their
disappointment seemed to diminish the terror of the Gothic

---

[1] See the Toxaris of Lucian, if we credit the sincerity and the virtues of
the Scythian, who relates a great war of his nation against the kings of
Bosphorus.

[2] Zosimus, l. i. p. 28.

[3] Strabo, l. xi.   Tacit. Hist. iii. 47.—They were called *Camaræ*.

[4] See a very natural picture of the Euxine navigation, in the sixteenth
letter of Tournefort.

[5] Arrian places the frontier garrison at Dioscurias, or Sebastopolis, forty-
four miles to the east of Pityus.   The garrison of Phasis consisted in his
time of only four hundred foot.   Periplus of the Euxine.

name. As long as Successianus, an officer of superior rank and
merit, defended that frontier, all their efforts were ineffectual;
but as soon as he was removed by Valerian to a more honourable
but less important station, they resumed the attack of Pityus;
and, by the destruction of that city, obliterated the memory of
their former disgrace.[1]

Circling round the eastern extremity of the Euxine Sea, the
navigation from Pityus to Trebizond is about three hundred
miles.[2] The course of the Goths carried them in sight of the
country of Colchis, so famous by the expedition of the Argonauts,
and they even attempted, though 'without success, to pillage a
rich temple at the mouth of the river Phasis. Trebizond, celebrated in the retreat of the Ten Thousand as an ancient colony
of Greeks,[3] derived its wealth and splendour from the munificence of the emperor Hadrian, who had constructed an artificial
port on a coast left destitute by nature of secure harbours.[4] The
city was large and populous; a double enclosure of walls seemed
to defy the fury of the Goths, and the usual garrison had been
strengthened by a reinforcement of ten thousand men. But
there are not any advantages capable of supplying the absence
of discipline and vigilance. The numerous garrison of Trebizond, dissolved in riot and luxury, disdained to guard their
impregnable fortifications. The Goths soon discovered the
supine negligence of the besieged, erected a lofty pile of fascines,
ascended the walls in the silence of the night, and entered the
defenceless city sword in hand. A general massacre of the
people ensued, whilst the affrighted soldiers escaped through
the opposite gates of the town. The most holy temples, and the
most splendid edifices, were involved in a common destruction.
The booty that fell into the hands of the Goths was immense:
the wealth of the adjacent countries had been deposited in Trebizond, as in a secure place of refuge. The number of captives
was incredible, as the victorious barbarians ranged without
opposition through the extensive province of Pontus.[5] The rich
spoils of Trebizond filled a great fleet of ships that had been
found in the port. The robust youth of the sea-coast were
chained to the oar; and the Goths, satisfied with the success of

---

[1] Zosimus, l. i. p. 30.

[2] Arrian (in Periplo Maris Euxin. p. 130) calls the distance 2610 stadia.

[3] Xenophon. Anabasis, l. iv. [c. 8, 22] p. 348.

[4] Arrian, p. 129. The general observation is Tournefort's.

[5] Epistle of Gregory Thaumaturgus, bishop of Neo-Cæsarea, quoted by
Mascon, v. 37.

their first naval expedition, returned in triumph to their new establishments in the kingdom of Bosphorus.[1]

The second expedition of the Goths was undertaken with greater powers of men and ships; but they steered a different course, and, disdaining the exhausted provinces of Pontus, followed the western coast of the Euxine, passed before the wide mouths of the Borysthenes, the Dniester, and the Danube, and increasing their fleet by the capture of a great number of fishing barks, they approached the narrow outlet through which the Euxine Sea pours its waters into the Mediterranean, and divides the continents of Europe and Asia. The garrison of Chalcedon was encamped near the temple of Jupiter Urius, on a promontory that commanded the entrance of the Strait; and so dreaded were the invasions of the barbarians, that this body of troops surpassed in number the Gothic army. But it was in numbers alone that they surpassed it. They deserted with precipitation their advantageous post, and abandoned the town of Chalcedon, most plentifully stored with arms and money, to the discretion of the conquerors. Whilst they hesitated whether they should prefer the sea or land, Europe or Asia, for the scene of their hostilities, a perfidious fugitive pointed out Nicomedia, once the capital of the kings of Bithynia, as a rich and easy conquest. He guided the march, which was only sixty miles from the camp of Chalcedon,[2] directed the resistless attack, and partook of the booty; for the Goths had learned sufficient policy to reward the traitor whom they detested. Nice, Prusa, Apamæa, Cius, cities that had sometimes rivalled, or imitated, the splendour of Nicomedia, were involved in the same calamity, which, in a few weeks, raged without control through the whole province of Bithynia. Three hundred years of peace, enjoyed by the soft inhabitants of Asia, had abolished the exercise of arms and removed the apprehension of danger. The ancient walls were suffered to moulder away, and all the revenue of the most opulent cities was reserved for the construction of baths, temples, and theatres.[3]

When the city of Cyzicus withstood the utmost effort of Mithridates,[4] it was distinguished by wise laws, a naval power of two hundred galleys, and three arsenals; of arms, of military engines,

---

[1] Zosimus, l. i. [c. 33] p. 32, 33.
[2] Itiner. Hierosolym. p. 572. Wesseling.
[3] Zosimus, l. i. [c. 35] p. 32, 33.
[4] He besieged the place with 40u galleys, 150,000 foot, and a numerous cavalry. Plutarch in Lucul. [c. 9]. Appian in Mithridat. Cicero pro Lege Maniliâ, c. 8.

and of corn.¹ It was still the seat of wealth and luxury; but of its ancient strength nothing remained except the situation, in a little island of the Propontis, connected with the continent of Asia only by two bridges. From the recent sack of Prusa, the Goths advanced within eighteen miles ² of the city, which they had devoted to destruction; but the ruin of Cyzicus was delayed by a fortunate accident. The season was rainy; and the lake Apolloniates, the reservoir of all the springs of Mount Olympus, rose to an uncommon height. The little river of Rhyndacus, which issues from the lake, swelled into a broad and rapid stream, and stopped the progress of the Goths. Their retreat to the maritime city of Heraclea, where the fleet had probably been stationed, was attended by a long train of waggons, laden with the spoils of Bithynia, and was marked by the flames of Nice and Nicomedia, which they wantonly burnt.³ Some obscure hints are mentioned of a doubtful combat that secured their retreat.⁴ But even a complete victory would have been of little moment, as the approach of the autumnal equinox summoned them to hasten their return. To navigate the Euxine before the month of May, or after that of September, is esteemed by the modern Turks the most unquestionable instance of rashness and folly.⁵

When we are informed that the third fleet, equipped by the Goths in the ports of Bosphorus, consisted of five hundred sail of ships,⁶ our ready imagination instantly computes and multiplies the formidable armament; but as we are assured, by the judicious Strabo,⁷ that the piratical vessels used by the barbarians of Pontus and the Lesser Scythia were not capable of containing more than twenty-five or thirty men, we may safely affirm that fifteen thousand warriors, at the most, embarked in this great expedition. Impatient of the limits of the Euxine, they steered their destructive course from the Cimmerian to the Thracian Bosphorus. When they had almost gained the middle of the Straits, they were suddenly driven back to the entrance of them, till a favourable wind springing up the next day carried them in a few hours into the placid sea, or rather lake, of the Propontis.

¹ Strabo, l. xii. p. 573.
² Pocock's Description of the East, l. ii. c. 23, 24.
³ Zosimus, l. i. [c. 35] p. 33.
⁴ Syncellus tells an unintelligible story of Prince *Odenathus*, who defeated the Goths, and who was killed by Prince *Odenathus* [p. 382, ed. Paris].
⁵ Voyages de Chardin, tom. i. p. 45. He sailed with the Turks from Constantinople to Caffa.
⁶ Syncellus (p. 382) speaks of this expedition as undertaken by the Heruli.
⁷ Strabo, l. xi. p. 495.

Their landing on the little island of Cyzicus was attended with
the ruin of that ancient and noble city. From thence issuing
again through the narrow passage of the Hellespont, they pursued
their winding navigation amidst the numerous islands scattered
over the Archipelago, or the Ægean Sea. The assistance of
captives and deserters must have been very necessary to pilot
their vessels and to direct their various incursions, as well on
the coast of Greece as on that of Asia. At length the Gothic
fleet anchored in the port of Piræus, five miles distant from
Athens,[1] which had attempted to make some preparations for a
vigorous defence. Cleodamus, one of the engineers employed
by the emperor's orders to fortify the maritime cities against the
Goths, had already begun to repair the ancient walls fallen to
decay since the time of Sylla. The efforts of his skill were ineffectual, and the barbarians became masters of the native seat
of the muses and the arts. But while the conquerors abandoned
themselves to the licence of plunder and intemperance, their
fleet, that lay with a slender guard in the harbour of Piræus, was
unexpectedly attacked by the brave Dexippus, who, flying with
the engineer Cleodamus from the sack of Athens, collected a hasty
band of volunteers, peasants as well as soldiers, and in some
measure avenged the calamities of his country.[2]

But this exploit, whatever lustre it might shed on the declining
age of Athens, served rather to irritate than to subdue the undaunted spirit of the northern invaders. A general conflagration
blazed out at the same time in every district of Greece. Thebes
and Argos, Corinth and Sparta, which had formerly waged such
memorable wars against each other, were now unable to bring
an army into the field, or even to defend their ruined fortifications. The rage of war, both by land and by sea, spread from
the eastern point of Sunium to the western coast of Epirus. The
Goths had already advanced within sight of Italy, when the
approach of such imminent danger awakened the indolent
Gallienus from his dream of pleasure. The emperor appeared
in arms; and his presence seems to have checked the ardour,
and to have divided the strength, of the enemy. Naulobatus, a
chief of the Heruli, accepted an honourable capitulation, entered

---

[1] Plin. Hist. Natur. iii. 7.
[2] Hist. August. p. 181. Victor, c. 33. Orosius, vii. 42. Zosimus, l. i.
[c. 39] p. 35. Zonaras, l. xii. [c. 26] 635. Syncellus, p. 382 [vol. i. p. 717, ed.
Bonn]. It is not without some attention, that we can explain and conciliate their imperfect hints. We can still discover some traces of the
partiality of Dexippus, in the relation of his own and his countrymen's
exploits.

with a large body of his countrymen into the service of Rome,
and was invested with the ornaments of the consular dignity,
which had never before been profaned by the hands of a barbarian.[1] Great numbers of the Goths, disgusted with the perils
and hardships of a tedious voyage, broke into Mæsia, with a
design of forcing their way over the Danube to their settlements in the Ukraine. The wild attempt would have proved
inevitable destruction if the discord of the Roman generals had
not opened to the barbarians the means of an escape.[2] The
small remainder of this destroying host returned on board their
vessels; and measuring back their way through the Hellespont
and the Bosphorus, ravaged in their passage the shores of Troy,
whose fame, immortalised by Homer, will probably survive the
memory of the Gothic conquests. As soon as they found themselves in safety within the basin of the Euxine, they landed at
Anchialus in Thrace, near the foot of Mount Hæmus; and, after
all their toils, indulged themselves in the use of those pleasant
and salutary hot baths. What remained of the voyage was a
short and easy navigation.[3] Such was the various fate of this
third and greatest of their naval enterprises. It may seem difficult to conceive how the original body of fifteen thousand
warriors could sustain the losses and divisions of so bold an
adventure. But as their numbers were gradually wasted by
the sword, by shipwrecks, and by the influence of a warm
climate, they were perpetually renewed by troops of banditti
and deserters, who flocked to the standard of plunder, and by a
crowd of fugitive slaves, often of German or Sarmatian extraction, who eagerly seized the glorious opportunity of freedom
and revenge. In these expeditions, the Gothic nation claimed a
superior share of honour and danger; but the tribes that fought
under the Gothic banners are sometimes distinguished and sometimes confounded in the imperfect histories of that age; and as
the barbarian fleets seemed to issue from the mouth of the
Tanais, the vague but familiar appellation of Scythians was
frequently bestowed on the mixed multitude.[4]

In the general calamities of mankind the death of an indi-

---

[1] Syncellus, p. 382. This body of Heruli was for a long time faithful and
famous.

[2] Claudius, who commanded on the Danube, thought with propriety and
acted with spirit. His colleague was jealous of his fame. Hist. August.
p. 181.

[3] Jornandes, c. 20.

[4] Zosimus and the Greeks (as the author of the Philopatris) give the
name of Scythians to those whom Jornandes, and the Latin writers, constantly represent as Goths.

vidual, however exalted, the ruin of an edifice, however famous, are passed over with careless inattention. Yet we cannot forget that the temple of Diana at Ephesus, after having risen with increasing splendour from seven repeated misfortunes,[1] was finally burnt by the Goths in their third naval invasion. The arts of Greece, and the wealth of Asia, had conspired to erect that sacred and magnificent structure. It was supported by an hundred and twenty-seven marble columns of the Ionic order. They were the gifts of devout monarchs, and each was sixty feet high. The altar was adorned with the masterly sculptures of Praxiteles, who had, perhaps, selected from the favourite legends of the place the birth of the divine children of Latona, the concealment of Apollo after the slaughter of the Cyclops, and the clemency of Bacchus to the vanquished Amazons.[2] Yet the length of the temple of Ephesus was only four hundred and twenty-five feet, about two-thirds of the measure of the church of St. Peter's at Rome.[3] In the other dimensions it was still more inferior to that sublime production of modern architecture. The spreading arms of a Christian cross require a much greater breadth than the oblong temples of the Pagans; and the boldest artists of antiquity would have been startled at the proposal of raising in the air a dome of the size and proportions of the Pantheon. The temple of Diana was, however, admired as one of the wonders of the world. Successive empires, the Persian, the Macedonian, and the Roman, had revered its sanctity and enriched its splendour.[4] But the rude savages of the Baltic were destitute of a taste for the elegant arts, and they despised the ideal terrors of a foreign superstition.[5]

Another circumstance is related of these invasions, which might deserve our notice, were it not justly to be suspected as the fanciful conceit of a recent sophist. We are told that in the sack of Athens the Goths had collected all the libraries, and were on the point of setting fire to this funeral pile of Grecian learning, had not one of their chiefs, of more refined policy than his

---

[1] Hist. August. p. 178. Jornandes, c. 20.

[2] Strabo, l. xiv. p. 640. Vitruvius, l. i. c. 1, præfat. l. vii. Tacit. Annal. iii. 61. Plin. Hist. Nat. xxxvi. 14.

[3] The length of St. Peter's is 840 Roman palms; each palm is very little short of nine English inches. Greaves's Miscellanies, vol. i. p. 233; On the Roman foot.

[4] The policy, however, of the Romans induced them to abridge the extent of the sanctuary or asylum, which by successive privileges had spread itself two stadia round the temple. Strabo, l. xiv. p. 641. Tacit. Annal. iii. 60, etc.

[5] They offered no sacrifices to the Grecian gods. Epistol. Gregor. Thaumat.

brethren, dissuaded them from the design; by the profound
observation that as long as the Greeks were addicted to the
study of books, they would never apply themselves to the
exercise of arms.[1] The sagacious counsellor (should the truth
of the fact be admitted) reasoned like an ignorant barbarian.
In the most polite and powerful nations, genius of every kind
has displayed itself about the same period; and the age of science
has generally been the age of military virtue and success.

IV. The new sovereigns of Persia, Artaxerxes and his son
Sapor, had triumphed over the house of Arsaces. Of the many
princes of that ancient race, Chosroes, king of Armenia, had alone
preserved both his life and his independence. He defended himself by the natural strength of his country; by the perpetual
resort of fugitives and malcontents; by the alliance of the
Romans, and, above all, by his own courage. Invincible in
arms, during a thirty years' war, he was at length assassinated
by the emissaries of Sapor, king of Persia. The patriotic satraps
of Armenia, who asserted the freedom and dignity of the crown,
implored the protection of Rome in favour of Tiridates the lawful
heir. But the son of Chosroes was an infant, the allies were
at a distance, and the Persian monarch advanced towards the
frontier at the head of an irresistible force. Young Tiridates,
the future hope of his country, was saved by the fidelity of a
servant, and Armenia continued above twenty-seven years a
reluctant province of the great monarchy of Persia.[2] Elated
with this easy conquest, and presuming on the distresses or the
degeneracy of the Romans, Sapor obliged the strong garrisons of
Carrhæ and Nisibis[3] to surrender, and spread devastation and
terror on either side of the Euphrates.

The loss of an important frontier, the ruin of a faithful and
natural ally, and the rapid success of Sapor's ambition, affected
Rome with a deep sense of the insult as well as of the danger.
Valerian flattered himself that the vigilance of his lieutenants
would sufficiently provide for the safety of the Rhine and of the
Danube; but he resolved, notwithstanding his advanced age,

[1] Zonaras, l. xii. p. 635. Such an anecdote was perfectly suited to the
taste of Montaigne. He makes use of it in his agreeable Essay on Pedantry,
l. i. c. 24.

[2] Moses Chorenensis, l. ii. c. 71, 73, 74. Zonaras, l. xii. p. 628. The
authentic relation of the Armenian historian serves to rectify the confused
account of the Greek. The latter talks of the children of Tiridates, who
at that time was himself an infant.

[3] [Nisibis was taken by a miracle, say Persian writers: the wall fell like
that of Jericho in answer to the prayers of the army. Cf. Malcolm's
Persia.—O. S.]

to march in person to the defence of the Euphrates. During
his progress through Asia Minor, the naval enterprises of the
Goths were suspended, and the afflicted province enjoyed a
transient and fallacious calm. He passed the Euphrates, encountered the Persian monarch near the walls of Edessa, was
(A.D. 260) vanquished and taken prisoner by Sapor. The particulars of this great event are darkly and imperfectly represented; yet by the glimmering light which is afforded us, we may
discover a long series of imprudence, of error, and of deserved
misfortunes on the side of the Roman emperor. He reposed an
implicit confidence in Macrinus, his Prætorian præfect.[1] That
worthless minister rendered his master formidable only to the
oppressed subjects, and contemptible to the enemies of Rome.
By his weak or wicked counsels, the Imperial army was betrayed
into a situation where valour and military skill were equally
unavailing.[2] The vigorous attempt of the Romans to cut their
way through the Persian host was repulsed with great slaughter;[3]
and Sapor, who encompassed the camp with superior numbers,
patiently waited till the increasing rage of famine and pestilence
had ensured his victory. The licentious murmurs of the legions
soon accused Valerian as the cause of their calamities; their
seditious clamours demanded an instant capitulation. An in-
mense sum of gold was offered to purchase the permission of a
disgraceful retreat. But the Persian, conscious of his superiority,
refused the money with disdain; and detaining the deputies,
advanced in order of battle to the foot of the Roman rampart,
and insisted on a personal conference with the emperor. Valerian
was reduced to the necessity of intrusting his life and dignity to
the faith of an enemy. The interview ended as it was natural to
expect. The emperor was made a prisoner, and his astonished
troops laid down their arms.[4] In such a moment of triumph,
the pride and policy of Sapor prompted him to fill the vacant
throne with a successor entirely dependent on his pleasure.
Cyriades, an obscure fugitive of Antioch, stained with every
vice, was chosen to dishonour the Roman purple; and the will
of the Persian victor could not fail of being ratified by the
acclamations, however reluctant, of the captive army.[5]

[1] Hist. August. p. 191. As Macrinus was an enemy to the Christians,
they charged him with being a magician.
[2] Zosimus, l. i. p. 33.
[3] Victor. in Cæsar. Eutropius, ix. 7.
[4] Zosimus, l. i. p. 33. Zonaras, l. xii. p. 630. Peter Patricius in the
Excerpta Legat. p. 20.
[5] Hist. August. p. 185. The reign of Cyriades appears in that collection
prior to the death of Valerian; but I have preferred a probable series of
events to the doubtful chronology of a most inaccurate writer.

The Imperial slave was eager to secure the favour of his master by an act of treason to his native country. He conducted Sapor over the Euphrates, and by the way of Chalcis to the metropolis of the East. So rapid were the motions of the Persian cavalry that, if we may credit a very judicious historian,[1] the city of Antioch was surprised when the idle multitude was fondly gazing on the amusements of the theatre. The splendid buildings of Antioch, private as well as public, were either pillaged or destroyed; and the numerous inhabitants were put to the sword, or led away into captivity.[2] The tide of devastation was stopped for a moment by the resolution of the high priest of Emesa. Arrayed in his sacerdotal robes, he appeared at the head of a great body of fanatic peasants, armed only with slings, and defended his god and his property from the sacrilegious hands of the followers of Zoroaster.[3] But the ruin of Tarsus, and many other cities, furnishes a melancholy proof that, except in this single instance, the conquest of Syria and Cilicia scarcely interrupted the progress of the Persian arms. The advantages of the narrow passes of mount Taurus were abandoned, in which an invader, whose principal force consisted in his cavalry, would have been engaged in a very unequal combat: and Sapor was permitted to form the siege of Cæsarea, the capital of Cappadocia; a city, though of the second rank, which was supposed to contain four hundred thousand inhabitants. Demosthenes commanded in the place, not so much by the commission of the emperor, as in the voluntary defence of his country. For a long time he deferred its fate; and, when at last Cæsarea was betrayed by the perfidy of a physician, he cut his way through the Persians, who had been ordered to exert their utmost diligence to take him alive. This heroic chief escaped the power of a foe, who might either have honoured or punished his obstinate valour; but many thousands of his fellow-citizens were involved in a general massacre, and Sapor is accused of treating his prisoners with wanton and unrelenting cruelty.[4] Much should undoubtedly be allowed for national animosity, much for humbled pride and impotent revenge; yet, upon the whole, it is certain that the

---

[1] The sack of Antioch, anticipated by some historians, is assigned, by the decisive testimony of Ammianus Marcellinus, to the reign of Gallienus, xxiii. 5.

[2] Zosimus, l. i. [c. 36] p. 35.

[3] John Malala, tom. i. p. 391 [ed. Oxon.; p. 127, ed. Ven.; p. 296, ed. Bonn]. He corrupts this probable event by some fabulous circumstances.

[4] Zonaras, l. xii. p. 630. Deep valleys were filled up with the slain. Crowds of prisoners were driven to water like beasts, and many perished for want of food.

same prince, who, in Armenia, had displayed the mild aspect of a legislator, showed himself to the Romans under the stern features of a conqueror. He despaired of making any permanent establishment in the empire, and sought only to leave behind him a wasted desert, whilst he transported into Persia the people and the treasures of the provinces.[1]

At the time when the East trembled at the name of Sapor, he received a present not unworthy of the greatest kings; a long train of camels laden with the most rare and valuable merchandises. The rich offering was accompanied with an epistle, respectful but not servile, from Odenathus, one of the noblest and most opulent senators of Palmyra. " Who is this Odenathus " (said the haughty victor, and he commanded that the presents should be cast into the Euphrates), " that he thus insolently presumes to write to his lord? If he entertains a hope of mitigating his punishment let him fall prostrate before the foot of our throne with his hands bound behind his back. Should he hesitate, swift destruction shall be poured on his head, on his whole race, and on his country." [2] The desperate extremity to which the Palmyrenian was reduced called into action all the latent powers of his soul. He met Sapor; but he met him in arms. Infusing his own spirit into a little army collected from the villages of Syria [3] and the tents of the desert,[4] he hovered round the Persian host, harassed their retreat, carried off part of the treasure, and, what was dearer than any treasure, several of the women of the Great King; who was at last obliged to repass the Euphrates with some marks of haste and confusion.[5] By this exploit, Odenathus laid the foundations of his future fame and fortunes. The majesty of Rome, oppressed by a Persian, was protected by a Syrian or Arab of Palmyra.

The voice of history, which is often little more than the organ of hatred or flattery, reproaches Sapor with a proud abuse of the rights of conquest. We are told that Valerian, in chains, but invested with the Imperial purple, was exposed to the multitude, a constant spectacle of fallen greatness; and that whenever the

---

[1] Zosimus, l. i. p. 25, asserts that Sapor, had he not preferred spoil to conquest, might have remained master of Asia.

[2] Peter Patricius in Excerpt. Leg. p. 29.

[3] Syrorum agrestium manû. Sextus Rufus, c. 23. Rufus Victor, the Augustan History (p. 192), and several inscriptions agree in making Odenathus a citizen of Palmyra.

[4] He possessed so powerful an interest among the wandering tribes, that Procopius (Bellersic, l. ii. c. 5) and John Malala (tom. i. p. 391) style him prince of the Saracens.

[5] Peter Patricius, p. 25.

Persian monarch mounted on horseback, he placed his foot on the neck of a Roman emperor. Notwithstanding all the remonstrances of his allies, who repeatedly advised him to remember the vicissitude of fortune, to dread the returning power of Rome, and to make his illustrious captive the pledge of peace, not the object of insult, Sapor still remained inflexible. When Valerian sunk under the weight of shame and grief, his skin, stuffed with straw, and formed into the likeness of a human figure, was preserved for ages in the most celebrated temple of Persia; a more real monument of triumph than the fancied trophies of brass and marble so often erected by Roman vanity.[1] The tale is moral and pathetic, but the truth of it may very fairly be called in question. The letters still extant from the princes of the East to Sapor are manifest forgeries;[2] nor is it natural to suppose that a jealous monarch should, even in the person of a rival, thus publicly degrade the majesty of kings. Whatever treatment the unfortunate Valerian might experience in Persia, it is at least certain that the only emperor of Rome who had ever fallen into the hands of the enemy languished away his life in hopeless captivity.

The emperor Gallienus, who had long supported with impatience the censorial severity of his father and colleague, received the intelligence of his misfortunes with secret pleasure and avowed indifference. " I knew that my father was a mortal," said he, " and since he has acted as becomes a brave man, I am satisfied." Whilst Rome lamented the fate of her sovereign, the savage coldness of his son was extolled by the servile courtiers as the perfect firmness of a hero and a stoic.[3] It is difficult to paint the light, the various, the inconstant character of Gallienus, which he displayed without constraint, as soon as he became sole possessor of the empire. In every art that he attempted his lively genius enabled him to succeed; and as his genius was destitute of judgment, he attempted every art except the important ones of war and government. He was a master of several curious but useless sciences, a ready orator and

---

[1] The pagan writers lament, the Christian insult, the misfortunes of Valerian. Their various testimonies are accurately collected by Tillemont, tom. iii. p. 739, etc. So little has been preserved of eastern history before Mahomet, that the modern Persians are totally ignorant of the victory of Sapor, an event so glorious to their nation. Bibliothèque Orientale.

[2] One of these epistles is from Artavasdes, king of Armenia: since Armenia was then a province in Persia, the king, the kingdom, and the epistle, must be fictitious.

[3] See his Life in the Augustan History.

elegant poet,[1] a skilful gardener, an excellent cook, and most contemptible prince. When the great emergencies of the state required his presence and attention, he was engaged in conversation with the philosopher Plotinus,[2] wasting his time in trifling or licentious pleasures, preparing his initiation to the Grecian mysteries, or soliciting a place in the Areopagus of Athens. His profuse magnificence insulted the general poverty; the solemn ridicule of his triumphs impressed a deeper sense of the public disgrace.[3] The repeated intelligence of invasions, defeats, and rebellions, he received with a careless smile; and singling out, with affected contempt, some particular production of the lost province, he carelessly asked whether Rome must be ruined unless it was supplied with linen from Egypt and Arras cloth from Gaul? There were, however, a few short moments in the life of Gallienus when, exasperated by some recent injury, he suddenly appeared the intrepid soldier and the cruel tyrant; till satiated with blood, or fatigued by resistance, he insensibly sunk into the natural mildness and indolence of his character.[4]

At a time when the reins of government were held with so loose a hand, it is not surprising that a crowd of usurpers should start up in every province of the empire against the son of Valerian. It was probably some ingenious fancy, of comparing the thirty tyrants of Rome with the thirty tyrants of Athens,

[1] There is still extant a very pretty Epithalamium, composed by Gallienus for the nuptials of his nephews:—

> Ite ait, O Juvenes, pariter sudate medullis
> Omnibus, inter vos; non murmura vestra columbæ,
> Brachia non hederæ, non vincant oscula conchæ.

[2] He was on the point of giving Plotinus a ruined city of Campania, to try the experiment of realising Plato's Republic. Life of Plotinus, by Porphyry, in Fabricius's Biblioth. Græc. l. iv.

[3] A medal which bears the head of Gallienus has perplexed the antiquarians by its legend and reverse; the former *Galliena Augusta*, the latter *Ubique Pax*. M. Spanheim supposes that the coin was struck by some of the enemies of Gallienus, and was designed as a severe satire on that effeminate prince. But as the use of irony may seem unworthy of the gravity of the Roman mint, M. de Vallemont has deduced from a passage of Trebellius Pollio (Hist. August. p. 198) an ingenious and natural solution. *Galliena* was first cousin to the emperor. By delivering Africa from the usurper Celsus, she deserved the title of Augusta. On a medal in the French king's collection, we read a similar inscription of *Faustina Augusta* round the head of Marcus Aurelius. With regard to the *Ubique Pax*, it is easily explained by the vanity of Gallienus, who seized, perhaps, the occasion of some momentary calm. Nouvelles de la République des Lettres, Janvier 1700, p. 21-34.

[4] This singular character has, I believe, been fairly transmitted to us. The reign of his immediate successor was short and busy; and the historians who wrote before the elevation of the family of Constantine could not have the most remote interest to misrepresent the character of Gallienus.

that induced the writers of the Augustan History to select that
celebrated number, which has been gradually received into a
popular appellation.[1]   But in every light the parallel is idle and
defective.   What resemblance can we discover between a council
of thirty persons, the united oppressors of a single city, and an
uncertain list of independent rivals, who rose and fell in irregular
succession through the extent of a vast empire?   Nor can the
number of thirty be completed, unless we include in the account
the women and children who were honoured with the Imperial
title.   The reign of Gallienus, distracted as it was, produced
only nineteen pretenders to the throne; Cyriades, Macrianus,
Balista, Odenathus, and Zenobia in the east; in Gaul, and the
western provinces, Posthumus, Lollianus, Victorinus and his
mother Victoria, Marius, and Tetricus.   In Illyricum and the
confines of the Danube, Ingenuus, Regillianus, and Aureolus;
in Pontus,[2] Saturninus; in Isauria, Trebellianus; Piso in Thessaly;
Valens in Achaia; Æmilianus in Egypt; and Celsus in Africa.
To illustrate the obscure monuments of the life and death of
each individual would prove a laborious task, alike barren of instruction and of amusement.   We may content ourselves with
investigating some general characters that most strongly mark
the condition of the times and the manners of the men, their
pretensions, their motives, their fate, and the destructive consequences of their usurpation.[3]

It is sufficiently known that the odious appellation of *Tyrant*
was often employed by the ancients to express the illegal seizure
of supreme power, without any reference to the abuse of it.
Several of the pretenders, who raised the standard of rebellion
against the emperor Gallienus, were shining models of virtue,
and almost all possessed a considerable share of vigour and ability.
Their merit had recommended them to the favour of Valerian,
and gradually promoted them to the most important commands
of the empire.   The generals, who assumed the title of Augustus,
were either respected by their troops for their able conduct and
severe discipline, or admired for valour and success in war, or
beloved for frankness and generosity.   The field of victory was
often the scene of their election; and even the armourer Marius,
the most contemptible of all the candidates for the purple, was
distinguished however by intrepid courage, matchless strength,

---

[1] Pollio expresses the most minute anxiety to complete the number.
[2] The place of his reign is somewhat doubtful: but there *was* a tyrant in
Pontus, and we are acquainted with the seat of all the others.
[3] Tillemont, tom. iii. p. 1163, reckons them somewhat differently.

and blunt honesty.[1]   His mean and recent trade cast indeed an
air of ridicule on his elevation; but his birth could not be more
obscure than was that of the greater part of his rivals, who were
born of peasants and inlisted in the army as private soldiers.
In times of confusion, every active genius finds the place
assigned him by Nature: in a general state of war, military merit
is the road to glory and to greatness.   Of the nineteen tyrants,
Tetricus only was a senator; Piso alone was a noble.   The blood
of Numa, through twenty-eight successive generations, ran in
the veins of Calphurnius Piso,[2] who, by female alliances, claimed
a right of exhibiting, in his house, the images of Crassus and of
the great Pompey.[3]   His ancestors had been repeatedly dignified with all the honours which the commonwealth could bestow;
and of all the ancient families of Rome, the Calphurnian alone
had survived the tyranny of the Cæsars.   The personal qualities
of Piso added new lustre to his race.   The usurper Valens, by
whose order he was killed, confessed, with deep remorse, that
even an enemy ought to have respected the sanctity of Piso;
and although he died in arms against Gallienus, the senate, with
the emperor's generous permission, decreed the triumphal ornaments to the memory of so virtuous a rebel.[4]

The lieutenants of Valerian were grateful to the father, whom
they esteemed.   They disdained to serve the luxurious indolence
of his unworthy son.   The throne of the Roman world was unsupported by any principle of loyalty; and treason against such
a prince might easily be considered as patriotism to the state.
Yet if we examine with candour the conduct of these usurpers,
it will appear that they were much oftener driven into rebellion
by their fears than urged to it by their ambition.   They dreaded
the cruel suspicions of Gallienus; they equally dreaded the
capricious violence of their troops.   If the dangerous favour of
the army had imprudently declared them deserving of the
purple, they were marked for sure destruction; and even

---

[1] Speech of Marius, in the Augustan History, p. 197.   [Pollio. xxx.
Tyranni de Mario.]   The accidental identity of names was the only circumstance that could tempt Pollio to imitate Sallust.

[2] Vos, O Pompilius sanguis; is Horace's address to the Pisos.   Art. Poet.
v. 292, with Dacier's and Sanadon's notes.

[3] Tacit. Annal. xv. 48.   Hist. i. 15.   In the former of these passages we
may venture to change *paterna* into *materna*.   In every generation from
Augustus to Alexander Severus, one or more Pisos appear as consuls.   A
Piso was deemed worthy of the throne by Augustus (Tacit. Annal. i. 13).
A second headed a formidable conspiracy against Nero; and a third was
adopted, and declared Cæsar by Galba.

[4] Hist. August. p. 195.   The senate, in a moment of enthusiasm, seems
to have presumed on the approbation of Gallienus.

prudence would counsel them to secure a short enjoyment of empire, and rather to try the fortune of war than to expect the hand of an executioner. When the clamour of the soldiers invested the reluctant victims with the ensigns of sovereign authority, they sometimes mourned in secret their approaching fate. " You have lost," said Saturninus on the day of his elevation, " you have lost a useful commander, and you have made a very wretched emperor." [1]

The apprehensions of Saturninus were justified by the repeated experience of revolutions. Of the nineteen tyrants who started up under the reign of Gallienus, there was not one who enjoyed a life of peace or a natural death. As soon as they were invested with the bloody purple, they inspired their adherents with the same fears and ambition which had occasioned their own revolt. Encompassed with domestic conspiracy, military sedition, and civil war, they trembled on the edge of precipices, in which, after a longer or shorter term of anxiety, they were inevitably lost. The precarious monarchs received, however, such honours as the flattery of their respective armies and provinces could bestow; but their claim, founded on rebellion, could never obtain the sanction of law or history. Italy, Rome, and the senate constantly adhered to the cause of Gallienus, and he alone was considered as the sovereign of the empire. That prince condescended indeed to acknowledge the victorious arms of Odenathus, who deserved the honourable distinction, by the respectful conduct which he always maintained towards the son of Valerian. With the general applause of the Romans, and the consent of Gallienus, the senate conferred the title of Augustus on the brave Palmyrenian; and seemed to intrust him with the government of the East, which he already possessed, in so independent a manner, that, like a private succession, he bequeathed it to his illustrious widow Zenobia. [2]

The rapid and perpetual transitions from the cottage to the throne, and from the throne to the grave, might have amused an indifferent philosopher; were it possible for a philosopher to remain indifferent amidst the general calamities of human kind. The election of these precarious emperors, their power and their death, were equally destructive to their subjects and adherents. The price of their fatal elevation was instantly discharged to the troops, by an immense donative, drawn from the bowels of

[1] Hist. August. p. 196.
[2] The association of the brave Palmyrenian was the most popular act of the whole reign of Gallienus. Hist. August. p. 180.

the exhausted people. However virtuous was their character, however pure their intentions, they found themselves reduced to the hard necessity of supporting their usurpation by frequent acts of rapine and cruelty. When they fell, they involved armies and provinces in their fall. There is still extant a most savage mandate from Gallienus to one of his ministers, after the suppression of Ingenuus, who had assumed the purple in Illyricum. " It is not enough," says that soft but inhuman prince, " that you exterminate such as have appeared in arms: the chance of battle might have served me as effectually. The male sex of every age must be extirpated; provided that, in the execution of the children and old men, you can contrive means to save our reputation. Let every one die who has dropped an expression, who has entertained a thought against me, against *me*, the son of Valerian, the father and brother of so many princes.[1] Remember that Ingenuus was made emperor: tear, kill, hew in pieces. I write to you with my own hand, and would inspire you with my own feelings." [2] Whilst the public forces of the state were dissipated in private quarrels, the defenceless provinces lay exposed to every invader. The bravest usurpers were compelled, by the perplexity of their situation, to conclude ignominious treaties with the common enemy, to purchase with oppressive tributes the neutrality or services of the barbarians, and to introduce hostile and independent nations into the heart of the Roman monarchy.[3]

Such were the barbarians, and such the tyrants, who, under the reigns of Valerian and Gallienus, dismembered the provinces, and reduced the empire to the lowest pitch of disgrace and ruin, from whence it seemed impossible that it should ever emerge. As far as the barrenness of materials would permit, we have attempted to trace, with order and perspicuity, the general events of that calamitous period. There still remain some particular facts; I. The disorders of Sicily; II. The tumults of Alexandria; and, III. The rebellion of the Isaurians, which may serve to reflect a strong light on the horrid picture.

---

[1] Gallienus had given the titles of Cæsar and Augustus to his son Saloninus, slain at Cologne by the usurper Posthumus. A second son of Gallienus succeeded to the name and rank of his elder brother. Valerian, the brother of Gallienus, was also associated to the empire: several other brothers, sisters, nephews, and nieces of the emperor, formed a very numerous royal family. Tillemont, tom. iii. and M. de Brequigny in the Mémoires de l'Académie, tom. xxxii. p. 262.

[2] Hist. August. p. 188.

[3] Regillianus had some bands of Roxolani in his service. Posthumus a body of Franks. It was perhaps in the character of auxiliaries that the latter introduced themselves into Spain.

I. Whenever numerous troops of banditti, multiplied by success and impunity, publicly defy, instead of eluding the justice of their country, we may safely infer that the excessive weakness of the government is felt and abused by the lowest ranks of the community. The situation of Sicily preserved it from the barbarians; nor could the disarmed province have supported an usurper. The sufferings of that once flourishing and still fertile island were inflicted by baser hands. A licentious crown of slaves and peasants reigned for a while over the plundered country, and renewed the memory of the servile wars of more ancient times.[1] Devastations, of which the husbandman was either the victim or the accomplice, must have ruined the agriculture of Sicily; and as the principal estates were the property of the opulent senators of Rome, who often enclosed within a farm the territory of an old republic, it is not improbable that this private injury might affect the capital more deeply than all the conquests of the Goths or the Persians.

II. The foundation of Alexandria was a noble design, at once conceived and executed by the son of Philip. The beautiful and regular form of that great city, second only to Rome itself, comprehended a circumference of fifteen miles;[2] it was peopled by three hundred thousand free inhabitants, besides at least an equal number of slaves.[3] The lucrative trade of Arabia and India flowed through the port of Alexandria to the capital and provinces of the empire. Idleness was unknown. Some were employed in blowing of glass, others in weaving of linen, others again manufacturing the papyrus. Either sex, and every age, was engaged in the pursuits of industry, nor did even the blind or the lame want occupations suited to their condition.[4] But the people of Alexandria, a various mixture of nations, united the vanity and inconstancy of the Greeks with the superstition and obstinacy of the Egyptians. The most trifling occasion, a transient scarcity of flesh or lentils, the neglect of an accustomed salutation, a mistake of precedency in the public baths, or a religious dispute,[5] were at any time sufficient to kindle a sedition among that vast multitude, whose resentments were furious and implacable.[6] After the captivity of Valerian and the in-

---

[1] The Augustan History, p. 177, calls it *servile bellum*. Diodor. Sicul. l. xxxiv.

[2] Plin. Hist. Natur. v. 10.

[3] Diodor. Sicul. l. xvii. [c. 52] p. 590. Edit. Wesseling.

[4] See a very curious letter of Hadrian in Aug. Hist. [Vopis. Sat. c. 8] p. 245.

[5] Such as the sacrilegious murder of a divine cat. Diodor Sicul. l. i. [c. 83].

[6] Hist. August. p. 195. This long and terrible sedition was first occasioned by a dispute between a soldier and a townsman about a pair of shoes.

solence of his son had relaxed the authority of the laws, the Alexandrians abandoned themselves to the ungoverned rage of their passions, and their unhappy country was the theatre of a civil war, which continued (with a few short and suspicious truces) above twelve years.[1] All intercourse was cut off between the several quarters of the afflicted city, every street was polluted with blood, every building of strength converted into a citadel; nor did the tumults subside, till a considerable part of Alexandria was irretrievably ruined. The spacious and magnificent district of Bruchion, with its palaces and museum, the residence of the kings and philosophers of Egypt, is described above a century afterwards as already reduced to its present state of dreary solitude.[2]

III. The obscure rebellion of Trebellianus, who assumed the purple in Isauria, a petty province of Asia Minor, was attended with strange and memorable consequences. The pageant of royalty was soon destroyed by an officer of Gallienus; but his followers, despairing of mercy, resolved to shake off their allegiance, not only to the emperor, but to the empire, and suddenly returned to the savage manners, from which they had never perfectly been reclaimed. Their craggy rocks, a branch of the wide-extended Taurus, protected their inaccessible retreat. The tillage of some fertile valleys[3] supplied them with necessaries, and a habit of rapine with the luxuries of life. In the heart of the Roman monarchy, the Isaurians long continued a nation of wild barbarians. Succeeding princes, unable to reduce them to obedience either by arms or policy, were compelled to acknowledge their weakness by surrounding the hostile and independent spot with a strong chain of fortifications,[4] which often proved insufficient to restrain the incursions of these domestic foes. The Isaurians, gradually extending their territory to the sea-coast, subdued the western and mountainous part of Cilicia, formerly the nest of those daring pirates, against whom the republic had once been obliged to exert its utmost force, under the conduct of the great Pompey.[5]

Our habits of thinking so fondly connect the order of the universe with the fate of man, that this gloomy period of history has been decorated with inundations, earthquakes, uncommon

---

[1] Dionysius apud Euseb. Hist. Eccl. v. vii. p. 21. Ammian. xxii. 16.
[2] Scaliger, Animadver. ad Euseb. Chron. p. 258. Three dissertations of M. Bonamy in the Mem. de l'Academie, tom. ix.
[3] Strabo, l. xii. p. 569.
[4] Hist. August. p. 197 [xxiv. 25].
[5] See Cellarius, Georg. Antiq. tom. ii. p. 137, upon the limits of Isaurai.

meteors, preternatural darkness, and a crowd of prodigies fictitious or exaggerated.[1] But a long and general famine was a calamity of a more serious kind. It was the inevitable consequence of rapine and oppression, which extirpated the produce of the present, and the hope of future harvests. Famine is almost always followed by epidemical diseases, the effect of scanty and unwholesome food. Other causes must however have contributed to the furious plague, which, from the year two hundred and fifty to the year two hundred and sixty-five, raged without interruption in every province, every city, and almost every family, of the Roman empire. During some time five thousand persons died daily in Rome; and many towns, that had escaped the hands of the barbarians, were entirely depopulated.[2]

We have the knowledge of a very curious circumstance, of some use perhaps in the melancholy calculation of human calamities. An exact register was kept at Alexandria, of all the citizens entitled to receive the distribution of corn. It was found that the ancient number of those comprised between the ages of forty and seventy had been equal to the whole sum of claimants, from fourteen to fourscore years of age, who remained alive after the reign of Gallienus.[3] Applying this authentic fact to the most correct tables of mortality, it evidently proves that above half the people of Alexandria had perished; and could we venture to extend the analogy to the other provinces, we might suspect that war, pestilence, and famine had consumed, in a few years, the moiety of the human species.[4]

---

[1] Hist. August. p. 177 [xxiii. 5].

[2] Hist. August. p. 177. Zosimus, l. i. p. 24, 26. Zonaras, l. xii. p. 623. Euseb. Chronicon. Victor in Epitom. Victor in Cæsar [c. 33]. Eutropius, ix. 5. Orosius, vii. 21.

[3] Euseb. Hist. Eccles. vii. 21. The fact is taken from the Letters of Dionysius, who, in the time of those troubles, was bishop of Alexandria.

[4] In a great number of parishes 11,000 persons were found between fourteen and eighty: 5305 between forty and seventy. See Buffon, Histoire Naturelle, tom. ii. p. 500.

CHAPTER XI

Reign of Claudius—Defeat of the Goths—Victories, Triumph, and
Death of Aurelian

UNDER the deplorable reigns of Valerian and Gallienus the empire
was oppressed and almost destroyed by the soldiers, the tyrants,
and the barbarians. It was saved by a series of great princes,
who derived their obscure origin from the martial provinces of
Illyricum. Within a period of about thirty years, Claudius,
Aurelian, Probus, Diocletian and his colleagues, triumphed over
the foreign and domestic enemies of the state, re-established,
with the military discipline, the strength of the frontiers, and
deserved the glorious title of Restorers of the Roman world.

The removal of an effeminate tyrant made way for a succession
of heroes. The indignation of the people imputed all their
calamities to Gallienus, and the far greater part were, indeed,
the consequence of his dissolute manners and careless administration. He was even destitute of a sense of honour, which
so frequently supplies the absence of public virtue; and as long
as he was permitted to enjoy the possession of Italy, a victory
of the barbarians, the loss of a province, or the rebellion of a
general, seldom disturbed the tranquil course of his pleasures.
At length a considerable army, stationed on the Upper Danube,
invested with the Imperial purple their leader Aureolus, who,
disdaining a confined and barren reign over the mountains of
Rhætia, passed the Alps, occupied Milan, threatened Rome, and
challenged Gallienus to dispute in the field the sovereignty of
Italy. The emperor, provoked by the insult, and alarmed by
the instant danger, suddenly exerted that latent vigour which
sometimes broke through the indolence of his temper. Forcing
himself from the luxury of the palace, he appeared in arms at
the head of his legions, and advanced beyond the Po to encounter
his competitor. The corrupted name of Pontirolo [1] still preserves the memory of a bridge over the Adda, which, during the
action, must have proved an object of the utmost importance
to both armies. The Rhætian usurper, after receiving a total

---

[1] *Pons Aureoli*, thirteen miles from Bergamo, and thirty-two from Milan.
See Cluver. Italia Antiq. tom. i. p. 245. Near this place, in the year 1703,
the obstinate battle of Cassano was fought between the French and
Austrians. The excellent relation of the Chevalier de Folard, who was
present, gives a very distinct idea of the ground. See Polybe de Folard,
tom. iii. p. 223-248.

defeat and a dangerous wound, retired into Milan. The siege
of that great city was immediately formed; the walls were
battered with every engine in use among the ancients; and
Aureolus, doubtful of his internal strength and hopeless of
foreign succours, already anticipated the fatal consequences of
unsuccessful rebellion.

His last resource was an attempt to seduce the loyalty of the
besiegers. He scattered libels through their camp, inviting the
troops to desert an unworthy master, who sacrificed the public
happiness to his luxury, and the lives of his most valuable
subjects to the slightest suspicions. The arts of Aureolus diffused
fears and discontent among the principal officers of his rival.
A conspiracy was formed by Heraclianus, the Prætorian præfect,
by Marcian, a general of rank and reputation, and by Cecrops,
who commanded a numerous body of Dalmatian guards. The
death of Gallienus was resolved, and, notwithstanding their
desire of first terminating the siege of Milan, the extreme danger
which accompanied every moment's delay obliged them to hasten
the execution of their daring purpose. At a late hour of the
night, but while the emperor still protracted the pleasures of
the table, an alarm was suddenly given that Aureolus, at the
head of all his forces, had made a desperate sally from the town;
Gallienus, who was never deficient in personal bravery, started
from his silken coach, and, without allowing himself time either
to put on his armour or to assemble his guards, he mounted on
horseback and rode full speed towards the supposed place of
the attack. Encompassed by his declared or concealed enemies,
he soon, amidst the nocturnal tumult, received a mortal dart
from an uncertain hand. Before he expired, a patriotic sentiment rising in the mind of Gallienus induced him to name a
deserving successor, and it was his last request that the Imperial
ornaments should be delivered to Claudius, who then commanded
a detached army in the neighbourhood of Pavia. The report at
least was diligently propagated, and the order cheerfully obeyed
by the conspirators, who had already agreed to place Claudius
on the throne. On the first news of the emperor's death the
troops expressed some suspicion and resentment, till the one was
removed and the other assuaged by a donative of twenty pieces
of gold to each soldier. They then ratified the election and
acknowledged the merit of their new sovereign.[1]

[1] On the death of Gallienus, see Trebellius Pollio in Hist. August. p. 181.
[Gallieni II., c. 14.] Zosimus, l. i. [c. 40] p. 37. Zonaras, l. xii. [c. 25]
p. 634 [ed. Paris; p. 602, ed. Bonn]. Eutrop. ix. 8. Aurelius Victor in
Epitom. [c. 33.] Victor in Cæsar. [c. 33.] I have compared and blended

The obscurity which covered the origin of Claudius, though it was afterwards embellished by some flattering fictions,[1] sufficiently betrays the meanness of his birth. We can only discover that he was a native of one of the provinces bordering on the Danube, that his youth was spent in arms, and that his modest valour attracted the favour and confidence of Decius. The senate and people already considered him as an excellent officer, equal to the most important trusts, and censured the inattention of Valerian, who suffered him to remain in the subordinate station of a tribune. But it was not long before that emperor distinguished the merit of Claudius, by declaring him general and chief of the Illyrian frontier, with the command of all the troops in Thrace, Mæsia, Dacia, Pannonia, and Dalmatia, the appointments of the præfect of Egypt, the establishment of the proconsul of Africa, and the sure prospect of the consulship. By his victories over the Goths he deserved from the senate the honour of a statue, and excited the jealous apprehensions of Gallienus. It was impossible that a soldier could esteem so dissolute a sovereign, nor is it easy to conceal a just contempt. Some unguarded expressions which dropped from Claudius were officiously transmitted to the royal ear. The emperor's answer to an officer of confidence describes in very lively colours his own character and that of the times. " There is not anything capable of giving me more serious concern than the intelligence contained in your last despatch,[2] that some malicious suggestions have indisposed towards us the mind of our friend and *parent* Claudius. As you regard your allegiance, use every means to appease his resentment, but conduct your negotiation with secrecy; let it not reach the knowledge of the Dacian troops; they are already provoked, and it might inflame their fury. I myself have sent him some presents: be it your care that he accept them with pleasure. Above all, let him not suspect that I am made acquainted with his imprudence. The fear of my anger might urge him to desperate counsels." [3] The presents which accom-

them all, but have chiefly followed Aurelius Victor, who seems to have had the best memoirs.

[1] Some supposed him, oddly enough, to be a bastard of the younger Gordian. Others took advantage of the province of Dardania to deduce his origin from Dardanus and the ancient kings of Troy. [His full name was Marcus Aurelius Claudius.—O. S.]

[2] *Notoria*, a periodical and official despatch which the emperors received from the *frumentarii*, or agents dispersed through the provinces. Of these we may speak hereafter.

[3] Hist. August. p. 208. [Pollio, Claud. c. 17.] Gallienus describes the plate, vestments, etc., like a man who loved and understood those splendid trifles.

panied this humble epistle, in which the monarch solicited a
reconciliation with his discontented subject, consisted of a considerable sum of money, a splendid wardrobe, and a valuable
service of silver and gold plate. By such arts Gallienus softened
the indignation and dispelled the fears of his Illyrian general,
and during the remainder of that reign the formidable sword of
Claudius was always drawn in the cause of a master whom he
despised. At last, indeed, he received from the conspirators
the bloody purple of Gallienus; but he had been absent from
their camp and counsels; and however he might applaud the
deed, we may candidly presume that he was innocent of the
knowledge of it.[1] When Claudius ascended the throne he was
about fifty-four years of age.

The siege of Milan was still continued, and Aureolus soon discovered that the success of his artifices had only raised up a more
determined adversary. He attempted to negotiate with Claudius
a treaty of alliance and partition. "Tell him," replied the intrepid emperor, "that such proposals should have been made
to Gallienus; he, perhaps, might have listened to them with
patience, and accepted a colleague as despicable as himself." [2]
This stern refusal, and a last unsuccessful effort, obliged Aureolus
to yield the city and himself to the discretion of the conqueror.
The judgment of the army pronounced him worthy of death,
and Claudius, after a feeble resistance, consented to the execution
of the sentence. Nor was the zeal of the senate less ardent in
the cause of their new sovereign. They ratified, perhaps with
a sincere transport of zeal, the election of Claudius; and as
his predecessor had shown himself the personal enemy of their
order, they exercised, under the name of justice, a severe revenge
against his friends and family. The senate was permitted to
discharge the ungrateful office of punishment, and the emperor
reserved for himself the pleasure and merit of obtaining by his
intercession a general act of indemnity.[3]

Such ostentatious clemency discovers less of the real character
of Claudius than a trifling circumstance in which he seems to

---

[1] Julian (Orat. i. p. 6) affirms that Claudius acquired the empire in a just
and even holy manner. But we may distrust the partiality cf a kinsman.
[2] Hist. August. p. 203. [Pollio, Claud. c. 5.] There are some trifling
differences concerning the circumstances of the last defeat and death of
Aureolus.
[3] Aurelius Victor in Gallien. [De Cæsar. c. 33.] The people loudly
prayed for the damnation of Gallienus. The senate decreed that his relations and servants should be thrown down headlong from the Gemonian
stairs. An obnoxious officer of the revenue had his eyes torn out whilst
under examination.

have consulted only the dictates of his heart. The frequent
rebellions of the provinces had involved almost every person in
the guilt of treason, almost every estate in the case of confiscation; and Gallienus often displayed his liberality by distributing
among his officers the property of his subjects. On the accession
of Claudius, an old woman threw herself at his feet and complained
that a general of the late emperor had obtained an arbitrary
grant of her patrimony. This general was Claudius himself,
who had not entirely escaped the contagion of the times. The
emperor blushed at the reproach, but deserved the confidence
which she had reposed in his equity. The confession of his fault
was accompanied with immediate and ample restitution.[1]

In the arduous task which Claudius had undertaken of restoring the empire to its ancient splendour, it was first necessary to
revive among his troops a sense of order and obedience. With
the authority of a veteran commander, he represented to them
that the relaxation of discipline had introduced a long train of
disorders, the effects of which were at length experienced by the
soldiers themselves; that a people ruined by oppression, and
indolent from despair, could no longer supply a numerous army
with the means of luxury, or even of subsistence; that the danger
of each individual had increased with the despotism of the military order, since princes who tremble on the throne will guard
their safety by the instant sacrifice of every obnoxious subject.
The emperor expatiated on the mischiefs of a lawless caprice,
which the soldiers could only gratify at the expense of their own
blood, as their seditious elections had so frequently been followed
by civil wars, which consumed the flower of the legions either in
the field of battle or in the cruel abuse of victory. He painted
in the most lively colours the exhausted state of the treasury,
the desolation of the provinces, the disgrace of the Roman name,
and the insolent triumph of rapacious barbarians. It was
against those barbarians, he declared, that he intended to point
the first effort of their arms. Tetricus might reign for a while
over the West, and even Zenobia might preserve the dominion
of the East.[2] These usurpers were his personal adversaries, nor
could he think of indulging any private resentment till he had
saved an empire whose impending ruin would, unless it was
timely prevented, crush both the army and the people.

[1] Zonaras, l. xii. [c. 26] p. 635 [ed. Paris; p. 604, ed. Bonn].
[2] Zonaras on this occasion mentions Posthumus; but the registers of
the senate (Hist. August. p. 203. [Pollio. Claud. c. 4]) prove that Tetricus
was already emperor of the western provinces.

The various nations of Germany and Sarmatia who fought under the Gothic standard had already collected an armament more formidable than any which had yet issued from the Euxine. On the banks of the Dniester, one of the great rivers that discharge themselves into that sea, they constructed a fleet of two thousand, or even of six thousand vessels; [1] numbers which, however incredible they may seem, would have been insufficient to transport their pretended army of three hundred and twenty thousand barbarians. Whatever might be the real strength of the Goths, the vigour and success of the expedition were not adequate to the greatness of the preparations. In their passage through the Bosphorus the unskilful pilots were overpowered by the violence of the current; and while the multitude of their ships were crowded in a narrow channel, many were dashed against each other or against the shore. The barbarians made several descents on the coasts both of Europe and Asia; but the open country was already plundered, and they were repulsed with shame and loss from the fortified cities which they assaulted. A spirit of discouragement and division arose in the fleet, and some of their chiefs sailed away towards the islands of Crete and Cyprus; but the main body, pursuing a more steady course, anchored at length near the foot of Mount Athos, and assaulted the city of Thessalonica, the wealthy capital of all the Macedonian provinces. Their attacks, in which they displayed a fierce but artless bravery, were soon interrupted by the rapid approach of Claudius, hastening to a scene of action that deserved the presence of a warlike prince at the head of the remaining powers of the empire. Impatient for battle, the Goths immediately broke up their camp, relinquished the siege of Thessalonica, left their navy at the foot of Mount Athos, traversed the hills of Macedonia, and pressed forwards to engage the last defence of Italy.

We still possess an original letter addressed by Claudius to the senate and people on this memorable occasion. " Conscript fathers," says the emperor, " know that three hundred and twenty thousand Goths have invaded the Roman territory. If I vanquish them, your gratitude will reward my services. Should I fall, remember that I am the successor of Gallienus. The whole republic is fatigued and exhausted. We shall fight after Valerian, after Ingenuus, Regillianus, Lollianus, Posthumus, Celsus, and a thousand others, whom a just contempt for

---

[1] The Augustan History mentions the smaller, Zonaras the larger, number; the lively fancy of Montesquieu induced him to prefer the latter.

Gallienus provoked into rebellion. We are in want of darts, of spears, and of shields. The strength of the empire, Gaul, and Spain, are usurped by Tetricus; and we blush to acknowledge that the archers of the East serve under the banners of Zenobia. Whatever we shall perform will be sufficiently great." [1] The melancholy firmness of this epistle announces a hero careless of his fate, conscious of his danger, but still deriving a well-grounded hope from the resources of his own mind.

The event surpassed his own expectations and those of the world. By the most signal victories he delivered the empire from this host of barbarians, and was distinguished by posterity under the glorious appellation of the Gothic Claudius. The imperfect historians of an irregular war [2] do not enable us to describe the order and circumstances of his exploits; but, if we could be indulged in the allusion, we might distribute into three acts this memorable tragedy. I. The decisive battle was fought near Naissus, a city of Dardania. The legions at first gave way, oppressed by numbers and dismayed by misfortunes. Their ruin was inevitable, had not the abilities of their emperor prepared a seasonable relief. A large detachment, rising out of the secret and difficult passes of the mountains, which by his order they had occupied, suddenly assailed the rear of the victorious Goths. The favourable instant was improved by the activity of Claudius. He revived the courage of his troops, restored their ranks, and pressed the barbarians on every side. Fifty thousand men are reported to have been slain in the battle of Naissus. Several large bodies of barbarians, covering their retreat with a movable fortification of waggons, retired, or rather escaped, from the field of slaughter. II. We may presume that some insurmountable difficulty—the fatigue, perhaps, or the disobedience, of the conquerors—prevented Claudius from completing in one day the destruction of the Goths. The war was diffused over the provinces of Mæsia, Thrace, and Macedonia, and its operations drawn out into a variety of marches, surprises, and tumultuary engagements, as well by sea as by land. When the Romans suffered any loss, it was commonly occasioned by their own cowardice or rashness; but the superior talents of the emperor, his perfect knowledge of the country, and his judicious choice of measures as well as officers, assured on

---

[1] Trebell. Pollio in Hist. August. p. 204 [Claud. c. 7].
[2] Hist. August. in Claud. Aurelian. et Prob. Zosimus, l. i. [c. 42–46] p. 38–42. Zonaras, l. xii. [c. 26], p. 636 [ed. Paris; p. 605, ed. Bonn]. Aurel. Victor in Epitom. Victor Junior in Cæsar. Eutrop. ix. 8. Euseb. in Chron. [An. CCLXXI.]

most occasions the success of his arms. The immense booty, the fruit of so many victories, consisted for the greater part of cattle and slaves. A select body of the Gothic youth was received among the Imperial troops; the remainder was sold into servitude; and so considerable was the number of female captives that every soldier obtained as his share two or three women. A circumstance from which we may conclude that the invaders entertained some designs of settlement as well as of plunder; since even in a naval expedition they were accompanied by their families. III. The loss of their fleet, which was either taken or sunk, had intercepted the retreat of the Goths. A vast circle of Roman posts, distributed with skill, supported with firmness, and gradually closing towards a common centre, forced the barbarians into the most inaccessible parts of Mount Hæmus, where they found a safe refuge, but a very scanty subsistence. During the course of a rigorous winter, in which they were besieged by the emperor's troops, famine and pestilence, desertion and the sword, continually diminished the imprisoned multitude. On the return of spring nothing appeared in arms except a hardy and desperate band, the remnant of that mighty host which had embarked at the mouth of the Dniester.

The pestilence which swept away such numbers of the barbarians at length proved fatal to their conqueror. After a short but glorious reign of two years, Claudius expired at Sirmium, amidst the tears and acclamations of his subjects. In his last illness he convened the principal officers of the state and army, and in their presence recommended Aurelian,[1] one of his generals, as the most deserving of the throne, and the best qualified to execute the great design which he himself had been permitted only to undertake. The virtues of Claudius, his valour, affability, justice, and temperance, his love of fame and of his country, place him in that short list of emperors who added lustre to the Roman purple. Those virtues, however, were celebrated with peculiar zeal and complacency by the courtly writers of the age of Constantine, who was the great-grandson of Crispus, the elder brother of Claudius. The voice of flattery was soon taught to repeat that the gods, who so hastily had snatched Claudius from the earth, rewarded his merit and piety by the perpetual establishment of the empire in his family.[2]

---

[1] According to Zonaras (l. xii. [c 26] p. 636 [ed. Par.; p. 605, ed. Bonn]) Claudius, before his death, invested him with the purple; but this singular fact is rather contradicted than confirmed by other writers.

[2] See the Life of Claudius by Pollio, and the Orations of Mamertinus,

Notwithstanding these oracles, the greatness of the Flavian family (a name which it had pleased them to assume) was deferred above twenty years, and the elevation of Claudius occasioned the immediate ruin of his brother Quintilius, who possessed not sufficient moderation or courage to descend into the private station to which the patriotism of the late emperor had condemned him. Without delay or reflection he assumed the purple at Aquileia, where he commanded a considerable force; and though his reign lasted only seventeen days, he had time to obtain the sanction of the senate and to experience a mutiny of the troops. As soon as he was informed that the great army of the Danube had invested the well-known valour of Aurelian with Imperial power, he sunk under the fame and merit of his rival; and, ordering his veins to be opened, prudently withdrew himself from the unequal contest.[1]

The general design of this work will not permit us minutely to relate the actions of every emperor after he ascended the throne, much less to deduce the various fortunes of his private life. We shall only observe that the father of Aurelian was a peasant of the territory of Sirmium, who occupied a small farm, the property of Aurelius, a rich senator. His warlike son enlisted in the troops as a common soldier, successively rose to the rank of a centurion, a tribune, the præfect of a legion, the inspector of the camp, the general, or, as it was then called, the duke of a frontier; and at length, during the Gothic war, exercised the important office of commander-in-chief of the cavalry. In every station he distinguished himself by matchless valour,[2] rigid discipline, and successful conduct. He was invested with the consulship by the emperor Valerian, who styles him, in the pompous language of that age, the deliverer of Illyricum, the restorer of Gaul, and the rival of the Scipios. At the recommendation of Valerian, a senator of the highest rank and merit, Ulpius Crinitus, whose blood was derived from the same source as that of Trajan, adopted the Pannonian peasant, gave him his daughter in

---

Eumenius, and Julian. See likewise the Cæsars of Julian, p. 313. In Julian it was not adulation, but superstition and vanity.

[1] Zosimus, l. i. [c. 47] p. 42. Pollio (Hist. August. p. 206 [Claud. c. 12]) allows him virtues, and says, that, like Pertinax, he was killed by the licentious soldiers. According to Dexippus, he died of a disease.

[2] Theoclius (as quoted in the Augustan History, p. 211 [Vopisc. Aurel. c. 6]) affirms that in one day he killed with his own hand forty-eight Sarmatians, and in several subsequent engagements nine hundred and fifty. This heroic valour was admired by the soldiers, and celebrated in their rude songs, the burden of which was *mille, mille, mille, occidit.*

marriage, and relieved with his ample fortune the honourable poverty which Aurelian had preserved inviolate.[1]

The reign of Aurelian lasted only four years and about nine months; but every instant of that short period was filled by some memorable achievement. He put an end to the Gothic war, chastised the Germans who invaded Italy, recovered Gaul, Spain, and Britain out of the hands of Tetricus, and destroyed the proud monarchy which Zenobia had erected in the East on the ruins of the afflicted empire.

It was the rigid attention of Aurelian even to the minutest articles of discipline which bestowed such uninterrupted success on his arms. His military regulations are contained in a very concise epistle to one of his inferior officers, who is commanded to enforce them, as he wishes to become a tribune, or as he is desirous to live. Gaming, drinking, and the arts of divination were severely prohibited. Aurelian expected that his soldiers should be modest, frugal, and laborious; that their armour should be constantly kept bright, their weapons sharp, their clothing and horses ready for immediate service; that they should live in their quarters with chastity and sobriety, without damaging the corn-fields, without stealing even a sheep, a fowl, or a bunch of grapes, without exacting from their landlords either salt, or oil, or wood. " The public allowance," continues the emperor, " is sufficient for their support; their wealth should be collected from the spoil of the enemy, not from the tears of the provincials." [2] A single instance will serve to display the rigour, and even cruelty, of Aurelian. One of the soldiers had seduced the wife of his host. The guilty wretch was fastened to two trees forcibly drawn towards each other, and his limbs were torn asunder by their sudden separation. A few such examples impressed a salutary consternation. The punishments of Aurelian were terrible; but he had seldom occasion to punish more than once the same offence. His own conduct gave a sanction to his laws, and the seditious legions dreaded a chief who had learned to obey, and who was worthy to command.

The death of Claudius had revived the fainting spirit of the

[1] Acholius (ap. Hist. August. p. 213 [Vopisc. Aurel. c. 13]) describes the ceremony of the adoption, as it was performed at Byzantium, in the presence of the emperor and his great officers.

[2] Hist. August. p. 211 [Vopisc. Aurel. c. 7]. This laconic epistle is truly the work of a soldier; it abounds with military phrases and words, some of which cannot be understood without difficulty. *Ferramenta samiata* is well explained by Salmasius. The former of the words means all weapons of offence, and is contrasted with *Arma*, defensive armour. The latter signifies keen and well sharpened.

Goths. The troops which guarded the passes of Mount Hæmus
and the banks of the Danube had been drawn away by the
apprehension of a civil war; and it seems probable that the
remaining body of the Gothic and Vandalic tribes embraced
the favourable opportunity, abandoned their settlements of the
Ukraine, traversed the rivers, and swelled with new multitudes
the destroying host of their countrymen. Their united numbers
were at length encountered by Aurelian, and the bloody and
doubtful conflict ended only with the approach of night.[1] Exhausted by so many calamities, which they had mutually endured
and inflicted during a twenty years' war, the Goths and the
Romans consented to a lasting and beneficial treaty. It was
earnestly solicited by the barbarians, and cheerfully ratified by
the legions, to whose suffrage the prudence of Aurelian referred
the decision of that important question. The Gothic nation
engaged to supply the armies of Rome with a body of two thousand auxiliaries, consisting entirely of cavalry, and stipulated
in return an undisturbed retreat, with a regular market as far
as the Danube, provided by the emperor's care, but at their own
expense. The treaty was observed with such religious fidelity
that, when a party of five hundred men straggled from the camp
in quest of plunder, the king or general of the barbarians commanded that the guilty leader should be apprehended and shot
to death with darts, as a victim devoted to the sanctity of their
engagements. It is, however, not unlikely that the precaution
of Aurelian, who had exacted as hostages the sons and daughters
of the Gothic chiefs, contributed something to this pacific temper.
The youths he trained in the exercise of arms, and near his own
person; to the damsels he gave a liberal and Roman education,
and, by bestowing them in marriage on some of his principal
officers, gradually introduced between the two nations the closest
and most endearing connections.[2]

But the most important condition of peace was understood
rather than expressed in the treaty. Aurelian withdrew the
Roman forces from Dacia, and tacitly relinquished that great
province to the Goths and Vandals.[3] His manly judgment convinced him of the solid advantages, and taught him to despise

---

[1] Zosimus, l. i. [c. 48, p. 43] p. 45.

[2] Dexippus (ap. Excerpta Legat. p. 12 [ed. Paris; p. 8, ed Ven.; p. 19,
ed. Bonn]) relates the whole transaction under the name of Vandals.
Aurelian married one of the Gothic ladies to his general Bonosus, who was
able to drink with the Goths and discover their secrets. Hist. August.
p. 247. [Vopisc. Bonosus, c. 15.]

[3] Hist. August. p. 222. [Vopisc. Aurel. c. 39.] Eutrop. ix. 15 [c. 9].
Sextus Rufus, c. 8. Lactantius de Mortibus Persecutorum, c. 9.

the seeming disgrace, of thus contracting the frontiers of the monarchy. The Dacian subjects, removed from those distant possessions which they were unable to cultivate or defend, added strength and populousness to the southern side of the Danube. A fertile territory, which the repetition of barbarous inroads had changed into a desert, was yielded to their industry, and a new province of Dacia still preserved the memory of Trajan's conquests. The old country of that name detained, however, a considerable number of its inhabitants, who dreaded exile more than a Gothic master.[1] These degenerate Romans continued to serve the empire, whose allegiance they had renounced, by introducing among their conquerors the first notions of agriculture, the useful arts, and the conveniences of civilised life. An intercourse of commerce and language was gradually established between the opposite banks of the Danube; and, after Dacia became an independent state, it often proved the firmest barrier of the empire against the invasions of the savages of the North. A sense of interest attached these more settled barbarians to the alliance of Rome, and a permanent interest very frequently ripens into sincere and useful friendship. This various colony, which filled the ancient province, and was insensibly blended into one great people, still acknowledged the superior renown and authority of the Gothic tribe, and claimed the fancied honour of a Scandinavian origin. At the same time the lucky, though accidental, resemblance of the name of Getæ infused among the credulous Goths a vain persuasion that, in a remote age, their own ancestors, already seated in the Dacian provinces, had received the instructions of Zamolxis, and checked the victorious arms of Sesostris and Darius.[2]

While the vigorous and moderate conduct of Aurelian restored the Illyrian frontier, the nation of the Alemanni[3] violated the

---

[1] The Wallachians still preserve many traces of the Latin language, and have boasted, in every age, of their Roman descent. They are surrounded by, but not mixed with, the barbarians. See a Memoir of M. d'Anville on ancient Dacia, in the Academy of Inscriptions, tom. xxx.

[The Wallachian language not only preserves many traces of the Latin language, but is derived from it, like the Italian, Spanish, Portuguese, and French. The " new province of Dacia " mentioned by Gibbon, was called " Dacia Aureliani," and was the district south of the Danube lying between Upper and Lower Mœsia.—O. S.]

[2] See the first chapter of Jornandes. The Vandals, however (c. 22), maintained a short independence between the rivers Marisia and Grissia (Maros and Keres [Körösz]), which fell into the Theiss.

[3] Dexippus, p. 7-12 [ed. Paris; p. 5, sqq. ed. Ven.; p. 11, sqq. ed. Bonn]. Zosimus, I. i. [c. 49] p. 43. Vopiscus in Aurelian. in Hist. August. However these historians differ in names (Alemanni, Juthungi, and Marcomanni), it is evident that they mean the same people and the same war; but it requires some care to conciliate and explain them.

conditions of peace which either Gallienus had purchased, or
Claudius had imposed, and, inflamed by their impatient youth,
suddenly flew to arms. Forty thousand horse appeared in the
field,[1] and the numbers of the infantry doubled those of the
cavalry.[2] The first objects of their avarice were a few cities of
the Rhætian frontier; but their hopes soon rising with success,
the rapid march of the Alemanni traced a line of devastation
from the Danube to the Po.[3]

The emperor was almost at the same time informed of the
irruption, and of the retreat, of the barbarians. Collecting an
active body of troops, he marched with silence and celerity along
the skirts of the Hercynian forest; and the Alemanni, laden with
the spoils of Italy, arrived at the Danube, without suspecting
that on the opposite bank, and in an advantageous post, a Roman
army lay concealed and prepared to intercept their return.
Aurelian indulged the fatal security of the barbarians, and permitted about half their forces to pass the river without disturbance and without precaution. Their situation and astonishment
gave him an easy victory; his skilful conduct improved the
advantage. Disposing the legions in a semicircular form, he
advanced the two horns of the crescent across the Danube, and,
wheeling them on a sudden towards the centre, enclosed the
rear of the German host. The dismayed barbarians, on whatsoever side they cast their eyes, beheld with despair a wasted
country, a deep and rapid stream, a victorious and implacable
enemy.

Reduced to this distressed condition, the Alemanni no longer
disdained to sue for peace. Aurelian received their ambassadors
at the head of his camp, and with every circumstance of martial
pomp that could display the greatness and discipline of Rome.
The legions stood to their arms in well-ordered ranks and awful
silence. The principal commanders, distinguished by the ensigns
of their rank, appeared on horseback on either side of the Imperial
throne. Behind the throne the consecrated images of the emperor
and his predecessors,[4] the golden eagles, and the various titles

---

[1] Cantoclarus, with his usual accuracy, chooses to translate three hundred
thousand; his version is equally repugnant to sense and to grammar.

[2] We may remark, as an instance of bad taste, that Dexippus applies to
the light infantry of the Alemanni the technical terms proper only to the
Grecian phalanx.

[3] In Dexippus we at present read Rhodanus: M. de Valois very judiciously alters the word to Eridanus. [Niebuhr, in his edition of Dexippus
p. 19, ed. Bonn), keeps Rhodanus.—O. S.]

[4] The emperor Claudius was certainly of the number; but we are ignorant
how far this mark of respect was extended; if to Cæsar and Augustus, it
must have produced a very awful spectacle; a long line of the masters of
the world.

of the legions, engraved in letters of gold, were exalted in the
air on lofty pikes covered with silver. When Aurelian assumed
his seat, his manly grace and majestic figure [1] taught the barbarians to revere the person as well as the purple of their conqueror. The ambassadors fell prostrate on the ground in silence.
They were commanded to rise, and permitted to speak. By the
assistance of interpreters they extenuated their perfidy, magnified
their exploits, expatiated on the vicissitudes of fortune and the
advantages of peace, and, with an ill-timed confidence, demanded
a large subsidy as the price of the alliance which they offered
to the Romans. The answer of the emperor was stern and imperious. He treated their offer with contempt, and their demand
with indignation; reproached the barbarians that they were as
ignorant of the arts of war as of the laws of peace; and finally
dismissed them with the choice only of submitting to his uncon-
ditioned mercy, or awaiting the utmost severity of his resentment. [2] Aurelian had resigned a distant province to the Goths;
but it was dangerous to trust or to pardon these perfidious barbarians, whose formidable power kept Italy itself in perpetual
alarms.

Immediately after this conference it should seem that some
unexpected emergency required the emperor's presence in Pannonia. He devolved on his lieutenants the care of finishing the
destruction of the Alemanni, either by the sword, or by the surer
operation of famine. But an active despair has often triumphed
over the indolent assurance of success. The barbarians, finding
it impossible to traverse the Danube and the Roman camp,
broke through the posts in their rear, which were more feebly
or less carefully guarded; and with incredible diligence, but by
a different road, returned towards the mountains of Italy. [3]
Aurelian, who considered the war as totally extinguished, received the mortifying intelligence of the escape of the Alemanni,
and of the ravage which they already committed in the territory
of Milan. The legions were commanded to follow, with as much
expedition as those heavy bodies were capable of exerting, the
rapid flight of an enemy, whose infantry and cavalry moved with
almost equal swiftness. A few days afterwards the emperor
himself marched to the relief of Italy, at the head of a chosen
body of auxiliaries (among whom were the hostages and cavalry

[1] Vopiscus in Hist. August. p. 210.   [Aurel. c. 6.]
[2] Dexippus gives them a subtle and prolix oration, worthy of a Grecian
sophist.
[3] Hist. August. p. 215.   [Vopisc. Aurel. c. 18.]

of the Vandals), and of all the Prætorian guards who had served in the wars on the Danube.[1]

As the light troops of the Alemanni had spread themselves from the Alps to the Apennine, the incessant vigilance of Aurelian and his officers was exercised in the discovery, the attack, and the pursuit of the numerous detachments. Notwithstanding this desultory war, three considerable battles are mentioned, in which the principal force of both armies was obstinately engaged.[2] The success was various. In the first, fought near Placentia, the Romans received so severe a blow that, according to the expression of a writer extremely partial to Aurelian, the immediate dissolution of the empire was apprehended.[3] The crafty barbarians, who had lined the woods, suddenly attacked the legions in the dusk of the evening, and, it is most probable, after the fatigue and disorder of a long march. The fury of their charge was irresistible; but at length, after a dreadful slaughter, the patient firmness of the emperor rallied his troops, and restored, in some degree, the honour of his arms. The second battle was fought near Fano in Umbria; on the spot which, five hundred years before, had been fatal to the brother of Hannibal.[4] Thus far the successful Germans had advanced along the Æmilian and Flaminian way, with a design of sacking the defenceless mistress of the world. But Aurelian, who, watchful for the safety of Rome, still hung on their rear, found in this place the decisive moment of giving them a total and irretrievable defeat.[5] The flying remnant of their host was exterminated in a third and last battle near Pavia; and Italy was delivered from the inroads of the Alemanni.

Fear has been the original parent of superstition, and every new calamity urges trembling mortals to deprecate the wrath of their invisible enemies. Though the best hope of the republic was in the valour and conduct of Aurelian, yet such was the public consternation, when the barbarians were hourly expected at the gates of Rome, that, by a decree of the senate, the Sibyl-line books were consulted. Even the emperor himself, from a motive either of religion or of policy, recommended this salutary

---

[1] Dexippus, p. 12 [ed. Paris; p. 8, ed. Ven.; p. 21, ed. Bonn].
[2] Victor Junior in Aurelian [Epit. 35, 2].
[3] Vopiscus in Hist. August. p. 216. [Aurel. c. 21.]
[4] The little river, or rather torrent, of Metaurus, near Fano, has been immortalised by finding such an historian as Livy, and such a poet as Horace.
[5] It is recorded by an inscription found at Pesaro. See Gruter, cclxxvi. 3.

measure, chided the tardiness of the senate,[1] and offered to supply whatever expense, whatever animals, whatever captives of any nation, the gods should require. Notwithstanding this liberal offer, it does not appear that any human victims expiated with their blood the sins of the Roman people. The Sibylline books enjoined ceremonies of a more harmless nature—processions of priests in white robes, attended by a chorus of youths and virgins; lustrations of the city and adjacent country; and sacrifices, whose powerful influence disabled the barbarians from passing the mystic ground on which they had been celebrated. However puerile in themselves, these superstitious arts were subservient to the success of the war; and if, in the decisive battle of Fano, the Alemanni fancied they saw an army of spectres combating on the side of Aurelian, he received a real and effectual aid from this imaginary reinforcement.[2]

But whatever confidence might be placed in ideal ramparts, the experience of the past, and the dread of the future, induced the Romans to construct fortifications of a grosser and more substantial kind. The seven hills of Rome had been surrounded, by the successors of Romulus, with an ancient wall of more than thirteen miles.[3] The vast enclosure may seem disproportioned to the strength and numbers of the infant state. But it was necessary to secure an ample extent of pasture and arable land against the frequent and sudden incursions of the tribes of Latium, the perpetual enemies of the republic. With the pro-

---

[1] One should imagine, he said, that you were assembled in a Christian church, not in the temple of all the gods.

[2] Vopiscus, in Hist. August. p. 215, 216 [Aurel. c. 18, *sqq.*], gives a long account of these ceremonies from the registers of the senate.

[3] Plin. Hist. Natur. iii. 5 [§ 9]. To confirm our idea, we may observe that for a long time Mount Cælius was a grove of oaks, and Mount Viminal was overrun with osiers; that in the fourth century the Aventine was a vacant and solitary retirement; that till the time of Augustus the Esquiline was an unwholesome burying-ground; and that the numerous inequalities remarked by the ancients in the Quirinal sufficiently prove that it was not covered with buildings. Of the seven hills, the Capitoline and Palatine only, with the adjacent valleys, were the primitive habitation of the Roman people. But this subject would require a dissertation.
[The statement of Pliny referred to would be startling were it read in what may be called the accepted sense of the passage, because the walls of Servius Tullius did not exceed seven miles, and no new walls were built round the city till the time of Aurelian. But the explanation given by Bunsen of this passage in Pliny is beyond doubt the true one, and has been accepted by the best modern scholars. The city had long outgrown its original limits, and the fourteen regions into which it was divided by Augustus embraced a considerable space outside the city walls. Bunsen therefore supposes that the measurement of Pliny refers to the circumference of the city as marked by its ancient walls. Both Dr. W. Smith and Professor Bury support this view.—O. S.]

gress of Roman greatness, the city and its inhabitants gradually
increased, filled up the vacant space, pierced through the useless
walls, covered the field of Mars, and, on every side, followed
the public highways in long and beautiful suburbs.[1] The extent
of the new walls, erected by Aurelian, and finished in the reign
of Probus, was magnified by popular estimation to near fifty,[2]
but is reduced by accurate measurement to about twenty-one
miles.[3] It was a great but a melancholy labour, since the defence
of the capital betrayed the decline of the monarchy. The
Romans of a more prosperous age, who trusted to the arms of
the legions the safety of the frontier camps,[4] were very far from
entertaining a suspicion that it would ever become necessary to
fortify the seat of empire against the inroads of the barbarians.[5]

The victory of Claudius over the Goths, and the success of
Aurelian against the Alemanni, had already restored to the arms
of Rome their ancient superiority over the barbarous nations
of the North. To chastise domestic tyrants, and to reunite the
dismembered parts of the empire, was a task reserved for the
second of those warlike emperors. Though he was acknowledged
by the senate and people, the frontiers of Italy, Africa, Illyricum,
and Thrace, confined the limits of his reign. Gaul, Spain, and
Britain, Egypt, Syria, and Asia Minor, were still possessed by
two rebels, who alone, out of so numerous a list, had hitherto
escaped the dangers of their situation; and to complete the
ignominy of Rome, these rival thrones had been usurped by
women.

A rapid succession of monarchs had arisen and fallen in the
provinces of Gaul. The rigid virtues of Posthumus served only
to hasten his destruction. After suppressing a competitor who
had assumed the purple at Mentz, he refused to gratify his
troops with the plunder of the rebellious city; and, in the
seventh year of his reign, became the victim of their disap-

---

[1] Exspatiantia tecta multas addidere urbes, is the expression of Pliny.
[2] Hist. August. p. 222. [Vopisc. Aurel. c. 39.] Both Lipsius and Isaac
Vossius have eagerly embraced this measure.
[3] See Nardini, Roma Antica, l. i. c. 8.
[This estimate of twenty-one miles is excessive. The walls which surround the city of Rome to-day (says Dr. W. Smith) are, with the exception
of the part beyond the Tiber, essentially the same as those of Aurelian.
Now these walls measure only between twelve and thirteen miles. Cf.
Becker de Romæ veteris Muris, p. 109, also Jordan. Topographie der Stadt
Rom. im Alterthum, I. p. 340, *sqq.*—O. S.]
[4] Tacit. Hist. iv. 23.
[5] For Aurelian's walls, see Vopiscus in Hist. August. p. 216, 222. [Aurel.
c. 21 and 39.] Zosimus, l. i. [c. 49] p. 43. Eutropius, ix. 15 [9]. Aurel.
Victor in Aurelian. Victor Junior in Aurelian. Euseb. Hieronym. et
Idatius in Chronic.

pointed avarice.[1] The death of Victorinus, his friend and associate, was occasioned by a less worthy cause. The shining accomplishments [2] of that prince were stained by a licentious passion, which he indulged in acts of violence, with too little regard to the laws of society, or even to those of love.[3] He was slain at Cologne, by a conspiracy of jealous husbands, whose revenge would have appeared more justifiable had they spared the innocence of his son. After the murder of so many valiant princes, it is somewhat remarkable that a female for a long time controlled the fierce legions of Gaul, and still more singular that she was the mother of the unfortunate Victorinus. The arts and treasures of Victoria enabled her successively to place Marius and Tetricus on the throne, and to reign with a manly vigour under the name of those dependent emperors. Money of copper, of silver, and of gold, was coined in her name, she assumed the titles of Augusta and Mother of the Camps: her power ended only with her life; but her life was perhaps shortened by the ingratitude of Tetricus.[4]

When, at the instigation of his ambitious patroness, Tetricus assumed the ensigns of royalty, he was governor of the peaceful province of Aquitaine, an employment suited to his character and education. He reigned four or five years over Gaul, Spain, and Britain, the slave and sovereign of a licentious army, whom he dreaded, and by whom he was despised. The valour and fortune of Aurelian at length opened the prospect of a deliverance. He ventured to disclose his melancholy situation, and conjured the emperor to hasten to the relief of his unhappy rival. Had this secret correspondence reached the ears of the soldiers, it would most probably have cost Tetricus his life; nor could he resign the sceptre of the West without committing an act of treason against himself. He affected the appearances of a civil war, led his forces into the field against Aurelian, posted them

[1] His competitor was Lollianus, or Ælianus, if, indeed, these names mean the same person. See Tillemont, tom. iii. p. 1177.

[2] The character of this prince by Julius Aterianus (ap. Hist. August. p. 187 [Pollio, xxx. Tyranni, c. 5]) is worth transcribing, as it seems fair and impartial. Victorino, qui post Junium Posthumum Gallias rexit, neminem existimo præferendum; non in virtute Trajanum; non Antoninum in clementia: non in gravitate Nervam: non in gubernando ærario Vespasianum; non in censura totius vitæ ac severitate militari Pertinacem vel Severum. Sed omnia hæc libido et cupiditas voluptatis mulierariæ sic perdidit, ut nemo audeat virtutes ejus in literas mittere quem constat omnium judicio meruisse puniri.

[3] He ravished the wife of Attitianus, an *actuary*, or army agent. Hist. August. p. 186. [Pollio, l. c.] Aurel. Victor in Aurelian.

[4] Pollio assigns her an article among the thirty tyrants. Hist. August. p. 200. [xxx. Tyranni, c. 30.]

in the most disadvantageous manner, betrayed his own counsels to the enemy, and with a few chosen friends deserted in the beginning of the action. The rebel legions, though disordered and dismayed by the unexpected treachery of their chief, defended themselves with desperate valour, till they were cut in pieces almost to a man, in this bloody and memorable battle, which was fought near Châlons in Champagne.[1] The retreat of the irregular auxiliaries, Franks and Batavians,[2] whom the conqueror soon compelled or persuaded to repass the Rhine, restored the general tranquillity, and the power of Aurelian was acknowledged from the wall of Antoninus to the Columns of Hercules.

As early as the reign of Claudius, the city of Autun, alone and unassisted, had ventured to declare against the legions of Gaul. After a siege of seven months they stormed and plundered that unfortunate city, already wasted by famine.[3] Lyons, on the contrary, had resisted with obstinate disaffection the arms of Aurelian. We read of the punishment of Lyons,[4] but there is not any mention of the rewards of Autun. Such, indeed, is the policy of civil war: severely to remember injuries, and to forget the most important services. Revenge is profitable, gratitude is expensive.

Aurelian had no sooner secured the person and provinces of Tetricus than he turned his arms against Zenobia, the celebrated queen of Palmyra and the East. Modern Europe has produced several illustrious women who have sustained with glory the weight of empire; nor is our own age destitute of such distinguished characters. But if we except the doubtful achievements of Semiramis, Zenobia is perhaps the only female whose superior genius broke through the servile indolence imposed on her sex by the climate and manners of Asia.[5] She claimed her descent

---

[1] Pollio in Hist. August. p. 196. [xxx. Tyranni, c. 23.] Vopiscus in Hist. August. p. 220. [Aurel. c. 32.] The two Victors, in the lives of Gallienus and Aurelian. Eutrop. ix. 13 [c. 9]. Euseb. in Chron. Of all these writers, only the two last (but with strong probability) place the fall of Tetricus before that of Zenobia. M. de Boze (in the Academy of Inscriptions, tom. xxx.) does not wish, and Tillemont (tom. iii. p. 1189) does not dare, to follow them. I have been fairer than the one, and bolder than the other. [Clinton places the fall of Tetricus after that of Zenobia, in 274.—S.]

[2] Victor Junior in Aurelian. Eumenius mentions *Batavicæ ;* some critics, without any reason, would fain alter the word to *Bagaudicæ.*

[3] Eumen. in Vet. Panegyr. iv. 8.

[4] Vopiscus in Hist. August. p. 246 [in Proculo, c. 13]. Autun was not restored till the reign of Diocletian. See Eumenius de restaurandis scholis.

[5] Almost everything that is said of the manners of Odenathus and Zenobia is taken from their Lives in the Augustan History, by Trebellius Pollio: see p. 192, 198 [xxx. Tyranni, c. 14 and 29].

from the Macedonian kings of Egypt, equalled in beauty her ancestor Cleopatra, and far surpassed that princess in chastity [1] and valour. Zenobia was esteemed the most lovely as well as the most heroic of her sex. She was of a dark complexion (for in speaking of a lady these trifles become important). Her teeth were of a pearly whiteness, and her large black eyes sparkled with uncommon fire, tempered by the most attractive sweetness. Her voice was strong and harmonious. Her manly understanding was strengthened and adorned by study. She was not ignorant of the Latin tongue, but possessed in equal perfection the Greek, the Syriac, and the Egyptian languages. She had drawn up for her own use an epitome of oriental history, and familiarly compared the beauties of Homer and Plato under the tuition of the sublime Longinus.

This accomplished woman gave her hand to Odenathus, who, from a private station, raised himself to the dominion of the East. She soon became the friend and companion of a hero. In the intervals of war Odenathus passionately delighted in the exercise of hunting; he pursued with ardour the wild beasts of the desert, lions, panthers, and bears; and the ardour of Zenobia in that dangerous amusement was not inferior to his own. She had inured her constitution to fatigue, disdained the use of a covered carriage, generally appeared on horseback in a military habit, and sometimes marched several miles on foot at the head of the troops. The success of Odenathus was in a great measure ascribed to her incomparable prudence and fortitude. Their splendid victories over the Great King, whom they twice pursued as far as the gates of Ctesiphon, laid the foundations of their united fame and power. The armies which they commanded, and the provinces which they had saved, acknowledged not any other sovereigns than their invincible chiefs. The senate and people of Rome revered a stranger who had avenged their captive emperor, and even the insensible son of Valerian accepted Odenathus for his legitimate colleague.

After a successful expedition against the Gothic plunderers of Asia, the Palmyrenian prince returned to the city of Emesa in Syria. Invincible in war, he was there cut off by domestic treason, and his favourite amusement of hunting was the cause, or at least the occasion, of his death. [2] His nephew, Mæonius,

---

[1] She never admitted her husband's embraces but for the sake of posterity. If her hopes were baffled, in the ensuing *month* she reiterated the experiment.

[2] Hist. August. p. 192, 193. [Pollio, xxx. Tyranni, c. 14.] Zosimus, l. i. [c. 39] p. 36. Zonaras, l. xii. [c. 24] p. 633 [ed. Paris; p. 600, ed. Bonn].

presumed to dart his javelin before that of his uncle; and, though admonished of his error, repeated the same insolence. As a monarch, and as a sportsman, Odenathus was provoked, took away his horse, a mark of ignominy among the barbarians, and chastised the rash youth by a short confinement. The offence was soon forgot, but the punishment was remembered; and Mæonius, with a few daring associates, assassinated his uncle in the midst of a great entertainment. Herod, the son of Odenathus, though not of Zenobia, a young man of a soft and effeminate temper,[1] was killed with his father. But Mæonius obtained only the pleasure of revenge by this bloody deed. He had scarcely time to assume the title of Augustus before he was sacrificed by Zenobia to the memory of her husband.[2]

With the assistance of his most faithful friends, she immediately filled the vacant throne, and governed with manly counsels Palmyra, Syria, and the East, above five years. By the death of Odenathus, that authority was at an end which the senate had granted him only as a personal distinction; but his martial widow, disdaining both the senate and Gallienus, obliged one of the Roman generals who was sent against her to retreat into Europe, with the loss of his army and his reputation.[3] Instead of the little passions which so frequently perplex a female reign, the steady administration of Zenobia was guided by the most judicious maxims of policy. If it was expedient to pardon, she could calm her resentment; if it was necessary to punish, she could impose silence on the voice of pity. Her strict economy was accused of avarice; yet on every proper occasion she appeared magnificent and liberal. The neighbouring states of Arabia, Armenia, and Persia, dreaded her enmity, and solicited her alliance. To the dominions of Odenathus, which extended from the Euphrates to the frontiers of Bithynia, his widow added the inheritance of her ancestors, the populous and fertile kingdom of Egypt.[4] The emperor Claudius acknow-

The last is clear and probable, the others confused and inconsistent. The text of Syncellus, if not corrupt, is absolute nonsense.

[1] Odenathus and Zenobia often sent him, from the spoils of the enemy, presents of gems and toys, which he received with infinite delight.

[2] Some very unjust suspicions have been cast on Zenobia, as if she was accessory to her husband's death.

[3] Hist. August. p. 180, 181. [Pollio, Gallieni II. c. 13.]

[4] See in Hist. August. p. 198 [Pollio, xxx. Tyranni, c. 29], Aurelian's testimony to her merit; and for the conquest of Egypt, Zosimus, l. i. [c. 44] p. 39, 40.

[There must be some mistake here: Claudius during his reign was always represented on the medals of Alexandria as emperor and ruler of Egypt. If Zenobia possessed any power in Egypt it could only have been

ledged her merit, and was content that, while *he* pursued the
Gothic war, *she* should assert the dignity of the empire in the
East. The conduct, however, of Zenobia was attended with
some ambiguity; nor is it unlikely that she had conceived the
design of erecting an independent and hostile monarchy. She
blended with the popular manners of Roman princes the stately
pomp of the courts of Asia, and exacted from her subjects the
same adoration that was paid to the successors of Cyrus. She
bestowed on her three sons [1] a Latin education, and often showed
them to the troops adorned with the Imperial purple. For
herself she reserved the diadem, with the splendid but doubtful
title of Queen of the East.

When Aurelian passed over into Asia, against an adversary
whose sex alone could render her an object of contempt, his
presence restored obedience to the province of Bithynia, already
shaken by the arms and intrigues of Zenobia.[2] Advancing at
the head of his legions, he accepted the submission of Ancyra,
and was admitted into Tyana, after an obstinate siege, by the
help of a perfidious citizen. The generous though fierce temper
of Aurelian abandoned the traitor to the rage of the soldiers: a
superstitious reverence induced him to treat with lenity the
countrymen of Apollonius the philosopher.[3] Antioch was deserted on his approach, till the emperor, by his salutary edicts,
recalled the fugitives, and granted a general pardon to all who,
from necessity rather than choice, had been engaged in the
service of the Palmyrenian queen. The unexpected mildness of
such a conduct reconciled the minds of the Syrians, and, as far
as the gates of Emesa, the wishes of the people seconded the
terror of his arms.[4]

at the beginning of the reign of Aurelian. The explanation advanced by
Guizot is at least feasible that perhaps Zenobia had administered Egypt
in the name of Claudius, and emboldened by his death had subjected it to
her own power.—O. S.]

[1] Timolaus, Herennianus, and Vabalathus. It is supposed that the two
former were already dead before the war. On the last, Aurelian bestowed
a small province of Armenia, with the title of King; several of his medals
are still extant. See Tillemont, tom. iii. p. 1190.

[2] Zosimus, l. i. [c. 50] p. 44.
[Of the three sons of Zenobia it is probable that the first two, Timolaus
and Herennianus, were dead before the war between Zenobia and Aurelian.
Vopiscus asserts that at first, after the death of her husband, Zenobia ruled
as the regent for her son.—O. S.]

[3] Vopiscus (in Hist. August. p. 217 [Aurel. c. 23, *seq.*]) gives us an
authentic letter, and a doubtful vision, of Aurelian. Apollonius of Tyana
was born about the same time as Jesus Christ. His life (that of the former)
is related in so fabulous a manner by his disciples, that we are at a loss to
discover whether he was a sage, an impostor, or a fanatic.

[4] Zosimus, l. i. [c. 54] p. 46.

Zenobia would have ill deserved her reputation had she indolently permitted the emperor of the West to approach within an hundred miles of her capital. The fate of the East was decided in two great battles; so similar in almost every circumstance, that we can scarcely distinguish them from each other, except by observing that the first was fought near Antioch,[1] and the second near Emesa.[2] In both the queen of Palmyra animated the armies by her presence, and devolved the execution of her orders on Zabdas, who had already signalised his military talents by the conquest of Egypt. The numerous forces of Zenobia consisted for the most part of light archers, and of heavy cavalry clothed in complete steel. The Moorish and Illyrian horse of Aurelian were unable to sustain the ponderous charge of their antagonists. They fled in real or affected disorder, engaged the Palmyrenians in a laborious pursuit, harassed them by a desultory combat, and at length discomfited this impenetrable but unwieldy body of cavalry. The light infantry, in the meantime, when they had exhausted their quivers, remaining without protection against a closer onset, exposed their naked sides to the swords of the legions. Aurelian had chosen these veteran troops who were usually stationed on the Upper Danube, and whose valour had been severely tried in the Alemannic war.[3] After the defeat of Emesa, Zenobia found it impossible to collect a third army. As far as the frontier of Egypt, the nations subject to her empire had joined the standard of the conqueror, who detached Probus, the bravest of his generals, to possess himself of the Egyptian provinces. Palmyra was the last resource of the widow of Odenathus. She retired within the walls of her capital, made every preparation for a vigorous resistance, and declared, with the intrepidity of a heroine, that the last moment of her reign and of her life should be the same.

Amid the barren deserts of Arabia a few cultivated spots rise like islands out of the sandy ocean. Even the name of Tadmor, or Palmyra, by its signification in the Syriac as well as in the Latin language, denoted the multitude of palm-trees which afforded shade and verdure to that temperate region. The air was pure, and the soil, watered by some invaluable springs, was

---

[1] At a place called Immæ. Eutropius, Sextus Rufus, and Jerome mention only this first battle.

[2] Vopiscus, in Hist. August. p. 217 [Aurel. c. 25], mentions only the second.

[3] Zosimus, l. i. [c. 50, sqq.] p. 44-48. His account of the two battles is clear and circumstantial.

capable of producing fruits as well as corn. A place possessed
of such singular advantages, and situated at a convenient distance [1] between the Gulf of Persia and the Mediterranean, was
soon frequented by the caravans which conveyed to the nations
of Europe a considerable part of the rich commodities of India.
Palmyra insensibly increased into an opulent and independent
city, and, connecting the Roman and the Parthian monarchies
by the mutual benefits of commerce, was suffered to observe an
humble neutrality, till at length, after the victories of Trajan,
the little republic sunk into the bosom of Rome, and flourished
more than one hundred and fifty years in the subordinate though
honourable rank of a colony. It was during that peaceful period,
if we may judge from a few remaining inscriptions, that the
wealthy Palmyrenians constructed those temples, palaces, and
porticos of Grecian architecture, whose ruins, scattered over an
extent of several miles, have deserved the curiosity of our
travellers. The elevation of Odenathus and Zenobia appeared to
reflect new splendour on their country, and Palmyra, for a while,
stood forth the rival of Rome; but the competition was fatal,
and ages of prosperity were sacrificed to a moment of glory.[2]

In his march over the sandy desert between Emesa and
Palmyra, the emperor Aurelian was perpetually harassed by
the Arabs; nor could he always defend his army, and especially
his baggage, from those flying troops of active and daring robbers,
who watched the moment of surprise, and eluded the slow pursuit of the legions. The siege of Palmyra was an object far more
difficult and important, and the emperor, who, with incessant
vigour, pressed the attacks in person, was himself wounded with
a dart. " The Roman people," says Aurelian, in an original
letter, " speak with contempt of the war which I am waging
against a woman. They are ignorant both of the character and
of the power of Zenobia. It is impossible to enumerate her

----

[1] It was five hundred and thirty-seven miles from Seleucia, and two
hundred and three from the nearest coast of Syria, according to the reckoning of Pliny, who, in a few words (Hist. Natur. v. 25), gives an excellent
description of Palmyra.
[Tadmor or Palmyra was probably at a very early period the connecting
link between the commerce of Tyre and Babylon. It was built by Solomon
as a commercial station. See 1 Kings, ix. 18 and 2 Chronicles, viii. 14:
" Tadmor in the wilderness." Cf. Dr. Kelman's " Palmyra " (1908).—O. S.]
[2] Some English travellers from Aleppo *discovered* the ruins of Palmyra
about the end of the last century. Our curiosity has since been gratified
in a more splendid manner by Messieurs Wood and Dawkins. For the
history of Palmyra we may consult the masterly dissertation of Dr. Halley
in the Philosophical Transactions: Lowthorp's Abridgment, vol. iii. p.
518. [Cf. also among recent works that of Dr. John Kelman, 1908.—O. S.]

warlike preparations, of stones, of arrows, and of every species
of missile weapons. Every part of the walls is provided with two
or three *balistæ*, and artificial fires are thrown from her military
engines. The fear of punishment has armed her with a desperate
courage. Yet still I trust in the protecting deities of Rome,
who have hitherto been favourable to all my undertakings." [1]
Doubtful, however, of the protection of the gods, and of the
event of the siege, Aurelian judged it more prudent to offer
terms of an advantageous capitulation; to the queen, a splendid
retreat; to the citizens, their ancient privileges. His proposals
were obstinately rejected, and the refusal was accompanied with
insult.

The firmness of Zenobia was supported by the hope that in a
very short time famine would compel the Roman army to repass
the desert; and by the reasonable expectation that the kings of
the East, and particularly the Persian monarch, would arm in
the defence of their most natural ally. But fortune and the perseverance of Aurelian overcame every obstacle. The death of
Sapor, which happened about this time,[2] distracted the councils
of Persia, and the inconsiderable succours that attempted to
relieve Palmyra were easily intercepted either by the arms or the
liberality of the emperor. From every part of Syria a regular
succession of convoys safely arrived in the camp, which was
increased by the return of Probus with his victorious troops
from the conquest of Egypt. It was then that Zenobia resolved
to fly. She mounted the fleetest of her dromedaries,[3] and had
already reached the banks of the Euphrates, about sixty miles
from Palmyra, when she was overtaken by the pursuit of
Aurelian's light horse, seized and brought back a captive to the
feet of the emperor. Her capital soon afterwards surrendered,
and was treated with unexpected lenity. The arms, horses, and
camels, with an immense treasure of gold, silver, silk, and
precious stones, were all delivered to the conqueror, who, leaving
only a garrison of six hundred archers, returned to Emesa, and
employed some time in the distribution of rewards and punish-

---

[1] Vopiscus in Hist. August. p. 218. [Aurel. c. 26.]

[2] From a very doubtful chronology I have endeavoured to extract the
most probable date.

[3] Hist. August. p. 218. [Vopisc. Aurel. c. 28.] Zosimus, l. i. [c. 55] p.
50. Though the camel is a heavy beast of burden, the dromedary, which
is either of the same or of a kindred species, is used by the natives of Asia
and Africa on all occasions which require celerity. The Arabs affirm that
he will run over as much ground in one day as their fleetest horses can
perform in eight or ten. See Buffon, Hist. Naturelle, tom. xi. p. 222; and
Shaw's Travels, p. 167.

ments at the end of so memorable a war, which restored to the
obedience of Rome those provinces that had renounced their
allegiance since the captivity of Valerian.

When the Syrian queen was brought into the presence of
Aurelian, he sternly asked her, How she had presumed to rise in
arms against the emperors of Rome? The answer of Zenobia
was a prudent mixture of respect and firmness. " Because I
disdained to consider as Roman emperors an Aureolus or a
Gallienus. You alone I acknowledge as my conqueror and my
sovereign." [1] But as female fortitude is commonly artificial,
so it is seldom steady or consistent. The courage of Zenobia
deserted her in the hour of trial; she trembled at the angry
clamours of the soldiers, who called aloud for her immediate
execution, forgot the generous despair of Cleopatra, which she
had proposed as her model, and ignominiously purchased life
by the sacrifice of her fame and her friends. It was to their
counsels, which governed the weakness of her sex, that she
imputed the guilt of her obstinate resistance; it was on their
heads that she directed the vengeance of the cruel Aurelian.
The fame of Longinus, who was included among the numerous
and perhaps innocent victims of her fear, will survive that of
the queen who betrayed, or the tyrant who condemned him.
Genius and learning were incapable of moving a fierce unlettered
soldier, but they had served to elevate and harmonise the soul of
Longinus. Without uttering a complaint, he calmly followed
the executioner, pitying his unhappy mistress, and bestowing
comfort on his afflicted friends.[2]

Returning from the conquest of the East, Aurelian had
already crossed the Straits which divide Europe from Asia,
when he was provoked by the intelligence that the Palmyre-
nians had massacred the governor and garrison which he had
left among them, and again erected the standard of revolt.
Without a moment's deliberation, he once more turned his face
towards Syria. Antioch was alarmed by his rapid approach, and
the helpless city of Palmyra felt the irresistible weight of his
resentment. We have a letter of Aurelian himself, in which he
acknowledges [3] that old men, women, children, and peasants,
had been involved in that dreadful execution, which should have
been confined to armed rebellion; and although his principal
concern seems directed to the re-establishment of a temple of

---

[1] Pollio in Hist. August. p. 199. [xxx. Tyranni, de Zenobia, c. 29.]
[2] Vopiscus in Hist. August. p. 219. [Aurel. c. 30.]   Zosimus, l. i. [c. 56,
p. 49] p. 51.
[3] Hist. August. p. 219. [Vopisc. Aurel. c. 31.]

the Sun, he discovers some pity for the remnant of the Palmyre-nians, to whom he grants the permission of rebuilding and inhabiting their city. But it is easier to destroy than to restore. The seat of commerce, of arts, and of Zenobia, gradually sunk into an obscure town, a trifling fortress, and at length a miserable village. The present citizens of Palmyra, consisting of thirty or forty families, have erected their mud-cottages within the spacious court of a magnificent temple.

Another and a last labour still awaited the indefatigable Aurelian; to suppress a dangerous though obscure rebel, who, during the revolt of Palmyra, had arisen on the banks of the Nile. Firmus, the friend and ally, as he proudly styled himself, of Odenathus and Zenobia, was no more than a wealthy merchant of Egypt. In the course of his trade to India he had formed very intimate connections with the Saracens and the Blemmyes, whose situation, on either coast of the Red Sea, gave them an easy introduction into the Upper Egypt. The Egyptians he inflamed with the hope of freedom, and, at the head of their furious multitude, broken into the city of Alexandria, where he assumed the Imperial purple, coined money, published edicts, and raised an army, which, as he vainly boasted, he was capable of main-taining from the sole profits of his paper trade. Such troops were a feeble defence against the approach of Aurelian; and it seems almost unnecessary to relate that Firmus was routed, taken, tortured, and put to death.[1] Aurelian might now con-gratulate the senate, the people, and himself, that, in little more than three years, he had restored universal peace and order to the Roman world.

Since the foundation of Rome no general had more nobly de-served a triumph than Aurelian; nor was a triumph ever cele-brated with superior pride and magnificence.[2] The pomp was opened by twenty elephants, four royal tigers, and above two hundred of the most curious animals from every climate of the North, the East, and the South. They were followed by sixteen hundred gladiators, devoted to the cruel amusement of the amphitheatre. The wealth of Asia, the arms and ensigns of so many conquered nations, and the magnificent plate and ward-

[1] See Vopiscus in Hist. August. p. 220, 242. [Aurel. c. 32; Firmus, c. 2.] As an instance of luxury, it is observed that he had glass windows. He was remarkable for his strength and appetite, his courage and dexterity. From the letter of Aurelian we may justly infer that Firmus was the last of the rebels, and consequently that Tetricus was already suppressed.

[2] See the triumph of Aurelian, described by Vopiscus. He relates the particulars with his usual minuteness; and on this occasion they *happen* to be interesting. Hist. August. p. 220. [Vopisc. Aurel. c. 33, *seq.*]

robe of the Syrian queen, were disposed in exact symmetry or artful disorder. The ambassadors of the most remote parts of the earth, of Æthiopia, Arabia, Persia, Bactriana, India, and China, all remarkable by their rich or singular dresses, displayed the fame and power of the Roman emperor, who exposed likewise to the public view the presents that he had received, and particularly a great number of crowns of gold, the offerings of grateful cities. The victories of Aurelian were attested by the long train of captives who reluctantly attended his triumph— Goths, Vandals, Sarmatians, Alemanni, Franks, Gauls, Syrians, and Egyptians. Each people was distinguished by its peculiar inscription, and the title of Amazons was bestowed on ten martial heroines of the Gothic nation who had been taken in arms.[1] But every eye, disregarding the crowd of captives, was fixed on the emperor Tetricus and the queen of the East. The former, as well as his son, whom he had created Augustus, was dressed in Gallic trousers,[2] a saffron tunic, and a robe of purple. The beauteous figure of Zenobia was confined by fetters of gold; a slave supported the gold chain which encircled her neck, and she almost fainted under the intolerable weight of jewels. She preceded on foot the magnificent chariot in which she once hoped to enter the gates of Rome. It was followed by two other chariots, still more sumptuous, of Odenathus and of the Persian monarch. The triumphal car of Aurelian (it had formerly been used by a Gothic king) was drawn, on this memorable occasion, either by four stags or by four elephants.[3] The most illustrious of the senate, the people, and the army closed the solemn procession. Unfeigned joy, wonder, and gratitude swelled the acclamations of the multitude; but the satisfaction of the senate was clouded by the appearance of Tetricus; nor could they suppress a rising murmur that the haughty emperor should thus expose to public ignominy the person of a Roman and a magistrate.[4]

[1] Among barbarous nations women have often combated by the side of their husbands. But it is *almost* impossible that a society of Amazons should ever have existed either in the old or new world.

[2] The use of *braccæ*, breeches, or trousers, was still considered in Italy as a Gallic and barbarian fashion. The Romans, however, had made great advances towards it. To encircle the legs and thighs with *fasciæ*, or bands, was understood, in the time of Pompey and Horace, to be a proof of ill health or effeminacy. In the age of Trajan the custom was confined to the rich and luxurious. It gradually was adopted by the meanest of the people. See a very curious note of Casaubon, ad. Sueton. in August. c. 82.

[3] Most probably the former; the latter, seen on the medals of Aurelian, only denote (according to the learned Cardinal Norris) an oriental victory.

[4] The expression of Calpurnius (Eclog. i. 50), Nullos ducet *captiva* triumphos, as applied to Rome, contains a very manifest allusion and censure.

But, however in the treatment of his unfortunate rivals Aurelian might indulge his pride, he behaved towards them with a generous clemency which was seldom exercised by the ancient conquerors. Princes who, without success, had defended their throne or freedom, were frequently strangled in prison as soon as the triumphal pomp ascended the Capitol. These usurpers, whom their defeat had convicted of the crime of treason, were permitted to spend their lives in affluence and honourable repose. The emperor presented Zenobia with an elegant villa at Tibur or Tivoli, about twenty miles from the capital; the Syrian queen insensibly sunk into a Roman matron, her daughters married into noble families, and her race was not yet extinct in the fifth century.[1] Tetricus and his son were reinstated in their rank and fortunes. They erected on the Cælian hill a magnificent palace, and, as soon as it was finished invited Aurelian to supper. On his entrance he was agreeably surprised with a picture which represented their singular history. They were delineated offering to the emperor a civic crown and the sceptre of Gaul, and again receiving at his hands the ornaments of the senatorial dignity. The father was afterwards invested with the government of Lucania,[2] and Aurelian, who soon admitted the abdicated monarch to his friendship and conversation, familiarly asked him, Whether it were not more desirable to administer a province of Italy than to reign beyond the Alps? The son long continued a respectable member of the senate; nor was there any one of the Roman nobility more esteemed by Aurelian, as well as by his successors.[3]

So long and so various was the pomp of Aurelian's triumph, that, although it opened with the dawn of day, the slow majesty of the procession ascended not the Capitol before the ninth hour; and it was already dark when the emperor returned to the palace. The festival was protracted by theatrical representations, the games of the circus, the hunting of wild beasts, combats of gladiators, and naval engagements. Liberal donatives were distributed to the army and people, and several institutions, agreeable or beneficial to the city, contributed to perpetuate the glory of Aurelian. A considerable portion of his oriental spoils

---

[1] Vopiscus in Hist. August. p. 199. [xxx. Tyranni, Zenobia, c. 29.] Hieronym. in Chron. Prosper in Chron. Baronius supposes that Zenobius, bishop of Florence in the time of St. Ambrose, was of her family.

[2] Vopisc. in Hist. August. p. 222. [Aurel. c 39.] Eutropius, ix. 13 [9]. Victor junior. But Pollio, in Hist. August. p. 196 [xxx. Tyranni de Tetrico, sen. c. 23], says that Tetricus was made corrector of all Italy.

[3] Hist. August. p. 197. [Vopisc. xxx. Tyranni, de Tetrico jun. c. 24.]

was consecrated to the gods of Rome; the Capitol, and every other temple, glittered with the offerings of his ostentatious piety; and the temple of the Sun alone received above fifteen thousand pounds of gold.[1] This last was a magnificent structure, erected by the emperor on the side of the Quirinal hill, and dedicated, soon after the triumph, to that deity whom Aurelian adored as the parent of his life and fortunes. His mother had been an inferior priestess in a chapel of the Sun; a peculiar devotion to the god of Light was a sentiment which the fortunate peasant imbibed in his infancy; and every step of his elevation, every victory of his reign, fortified superstition by gratitude.[2]

The arms of Aurelian had vanquished the foreign and domestic foes of the republic. We are assured that, by his salutary rigour, crimes and factions, mischievous arts and pernicious connivance, the luxuriant growth of a feeble and oppressive government, were eradicated throughout the Roman world.[3] But if we attentively reflect how much swifter is the progress of corruption than its cure, and if we remember that the years abandoned to public disorders exceeded the months allotted to the martial reign of Aurelian, we must confess that a few short intervals of peace were insufficient for the arduous work of reformation. Even his attempt to restore the integrity of the coin was opposed by a formidable insurrection. The emperor's vexation breaks out in one of his private letters: " Surely," says he, " the gods have decreed that my life should be a perpetual warfare. A sedition within the walls has just now given birth to a very serious civil war. The workmen of the mint, at the instigation of Felicissimus, a slave to whom I had intrusted an employment in the finances, have risen in rebellion. They are at length suppressed; but seven thousand of my soldiers have been slain in the contest, of those troops whose ordinary station is in Dacia and the camps along the Danube." [4] Other writers, who confirm the same fact, add likewise, that it happened soon after Aurelian's triumph; that the decisive engagement was fought on the Cælian hill;

---

[1] Vopiscus in Hist. August. 222. [Aurel. c. 39.] Zosimus, l. i. [c. 61, p. 53] p. 56. He placed in it the images of Belus and of the Sun, which he had brought from Palmyra. It was dedicated in the fourth year of his reign (Euseb. in Chron. [an. CCLXXV.]), but was most assuredly begun immediately on his accession.

[2] See in the Augustan History, p. 210 [Vopisc. Aurel. c. 5], the omens of his fortune. His devotion to the sun appears in his letters, on his medals, and is mentioned in the Cæsars of Julian. Commentaire de Spanheim, p. 109.

[3] Vopiscus in Hist. August. p. 221. [Aurel. c. 37.]

[4] Hist. August. p. 222. [Vopisc. Aurel. c. 38.] Aurelian calls these soldiers *Hiberi, Riparienses, Castriani,* and *Dacisci.*

that the workmen of the mint had adulterated the coin; and
that the emperor restored the public credit, by delivering out
good money in exchange for the bad, which the people were
commanded to bring into the treasury.[1]

We might content ourselves with relating this extraordinary
transaction, but we cannot dissemble how much, in its present
form, it appears to us inconsistent and incredible. The debase-
ment of the coin is indeed well suited to the administration of
Gallienus; nor is it unlikely that the instruments of the corruption might dread the inflexible justice of Aurelian. But the
guilt, as well as the profit, must have been confined to a few;
nor is it easy to conceive by what arts they could arm a people
whom they had injured against a monarch whom they had
betrayed. We might naturally expect that such miscreants
should have shared the public detestation with the informers and
the other ministers of oppression; and that the reformation of
the coin should have been an action equally popular with the
destruction of those obsolete accounts which, by the emperor's
order, were burnt in the forum of Trajan.[2] In an age when the
principles of commerce were so imperfectly understood, the most
desirable end might perhaps be effected by harsh and injudicious
means; but a temporary grievance of such a nature can scarcely
excite and support a serious civil war. The repetition of intolerable taxes, imposed either on the land or on the necessaries of
life, may at last provoke those who will not, or who cannot,
relinquish their country. But the case is far otherwise in every
operation which, by whatsoever expedients, restores the just
value of money. The transient evil is soon obliterated by the
permanent benefit, the loss is divided among multitudes; and
if a few wealthy individuals experience a sensible diminution of
treasure, with their riches they at the same time lose the degree
of weight and importance which they derived from the possession of them. However Aurelian might choose to disguise the
real cause of the insurrection, his reformation of the coin could
furnish only a faint pretence to a party already powerful and
discontented. Rome, though deprived of freedom, was distracted by faction. The people, towards whom the emperor,
himself a plebeian, always expressed a peculiar fondness, lived
in perpetual dissension with the senate, the equestrian order,

---

[1] Zosimus, l. i. [c. 61, p. 53] p. 56. Eutropius, ix. 14 [9]. Aurel. Victor.
[de Cæsar. 35.]

[2] Hist. August. p. 222. [Vopisc. Aurel. c. 39.] Aurel. Victor. [de
Cæsar. 35.]

and the Prætorian guards.[1] Nothing less than the firm though secret conspiracy of those orders, of the authority of the first, the wealth of the second, and the arms of the third, could have displayed a strength capable of contending in battle with the veteran legions of the Danube, which, under the conduct of a martial sovereign, had achieved the conquest of the West and of the East.

Whatever was the cause or the object of this rebellion, imputed with so little probability to the workmen of the mint, Aurelian used his victory with unrelenting rigour.[2] He was naturally of a severe disposition. A peasant and a soldier, his nerves yielded not easily to the impressions of sympathy, and he could sustain without emotion the sight of tortures and death. Trained from his earliest youth in the exercise of arms, he set too small a value on the life of a citizen, chastised by military execution the slightest offences, and transferred the stern discipline of the camp into the civil administration of the laws. His love of justice often became a blind and furious passion; and, whenever he deemed his own or the public safety endangered, he disregarded the rules of evidence and the proportion of punishments. The unprovoked rebellion with which the Romans rewarded his services exasperated his haughty spirit. The noblest families of the capital were involved in the guilt or suspicion of this dark conspiracy. A hasty spirit of revenge urged the bloody prosecution, and it proved fatal to one of the nephews of the emperor. The executioners (if we may use the expression of a contemporary poet) were fatigued, the prisons were crowded, and the unhappy senate lamented the death or absence of its most illustrious members.[3] Nor was the pride of Aurelian less offensive to that assembly than his cruelty. Ignorant or impatient of the restraints of civil institutions, he disdained to hold his power by any other title than that of the sword, and governed by right of conquest an empire which he had saved and subdued.[4]

It was observed by one of the most sagacious of the Roman

---

[1] It already raged before Aurelian's return from Egypt. See Vopiscus, who quotes an original letter. Hist. August. p. 244. [Vopisc. Firmus, c. 5.]

[2] Vopiscus in Hist. August. p. 222. [Aurel. c. 39.] The two Victors. Eutropius, ix. 14 [9]. Zosimus (l. i. p. 43) mentions only three senators, and places their death before the eastern war.

[3] Nulla catenati feralis pompa senatûs
   Carnificum lassabit opus; nec carcere pleno
   Infelix raros numerabit curia Patres. Calpurn. Eclog. i. 60.

[4] According to the younger Victor [Epitome, c. 35], he sometimes wore the diadem. *Deus* and *Dominus* appear on his medals.

princes, that the talents of his predecessor Aurelian were better suited to the command of an army than to the government of an empire.[1] Conscious of the character in which nature and experience had enabled him to excel, he again took the field a few months after his triumph. It was expedient to exercise the restless temper of the legions in some foreign war, and the Persian monarch, exulting in the shame of Valerian, still braved with impunity the offended majesty of Rome. At the head of an army, less formidable by its numbers than by its discipline and valour, the emperor advanced as far as the Straits which divide Europe from Asia. He there experienced that the most absolute power is a weak defence against the effects of despair. He had threatened one of his secretaries who was accused of extortion, and it was known that he seldom threatened in vain. The last hope which remained for the criminal was to involve some of the principal officers of the army in his danger, or at least in his fears. Artfully counterfeiting his master's hand, he showed them, in a long and bloody list, their own names devoted to death. Without suspecting or examining the fraud, they resolved to secure their lives by the murder of the emperor. On his march, between Byzantium and Heraclea, Aurelian was suddenly attacked by the conspirators, whose stations gave them a right to surround his person, and, after a short resistance, fell by the hand of Mucapor, a general whom he had always loved and trusted. He died regretted by the army, detested by the senate, but universally acknowledged as a warlike and fortunate prince, the useful though severe reformer of a degenerate state.[2]

CHAPTER XII

Conduct of the Army and Senate after the Death of Aurelian—Reigns of Tacitus, Probus, Carus and his Sons

SUCH was the unhappy condition of the Roman emperors, that, whatever might be their conduct, their fate was commonly the same. A life of pleasure or virtue, of severity or mildness, of indolence or glory, alike led to an untimely grave; and almost every reign is closed by the same disgusting repetition of

[1] It was the observation of Diocletian. See Vopiscus in Hist. August. p. 224. [Aurel. c 44.]

[2] Vopiscus in Hist. August. p. 221. [Aurel. c. 35, *seq.*] Zosimus, l. i [c. 62] p. 57. Eutrop. ix. 15 [9]. The two Victors.

treason and murder. The death of Aurelian, however, is remarkable by its extraordinary consequences. The legions admired, lamented, and revenged their victorious chief. The artifice of his perfidious secretary was discovered and punished. The deluded conspirators attended the funeral of their injured sovereign with sincere or well-feigned contrition, and submitted to the unanimous resolution of the military order, which was signified by the following epistle: " The brave and fortunate armies to the senate and people of Rome.—The crime of one man, and the error of many, have deprived us of the late emperor Aurelian. May it please you, venerable lords and fathers! to place him in the number of the gods, and to appoint a successor whom your judgment shall declare worthy of the Imperial purple! None of those whose guilt or misfortune have contributed to our loss shall ever reign over us." [1]   The Roman senators heard, without surprise, that another emperor had been assassinated in his camp; they secretly rejoiced in the fall of Aurelian; but the modest and dutiful address of the legions, when it was communicated in full assembly by the consul, diffused the most pleasing astonishment. Such honours as fear and perhaps esteem could extort they liberally poured forth on the memory of their deceased sovereign. Such acknowledgments as gratitude could inspire they returned to the faithful armies of the republic, who entertained so just a sense of the legal authority of the senate in the choice of an emperor. Yet, notwithstanding this flattering appeal, the most prudent of the assembly declined exposing their safety and dignity to the caprice of an armed multitude. The strength of the legions was, indeed, a pledge of their sincerity, since those who may command are seldom reduced to the necessity of dissembling; but could it naturally be expected that a hasty repentance would correct the inveterate habits of fourscore years? Should the soldiers relapse into their accustomed seditions, their insolence might disgrace the majesty of the senate and prove fatal to the object of its choice. Motives like these dictated a decree by which the election of a new emperor was referred to the suffrage of the military order.

The contention that ensued is one of the best attested but most improbable events in the history of mankind.[2] The troops, as

[1] Vopiscus in Hist. August. p. 222. [Aurel. c. 41.] Aurelius Victor mentions a formal deputation from the troops to the senate.

[2] Vopiscus, our principal authority, wrote at Rome sixteen years only after the death of Aurelian; and, besides the recent notoriety of the facts, constantly draws his materials from the Journals of the Senate and the original papers of the Ulpian library. Zosimus and Zonaras appear as

if satiated with the exercise of power, again conjured the senate
to invest one of its own body with the Imperial purple. The
senate still persisted in its refusal; the army in its request. The
reciprocal offer was pressed and rejected at least three times, and,
whilst the obstinate modesty of either party was resolved to
receive a master from the hands of the other, eight months insensibly elapsed; an amazing period of tranquil anarchy, during
which the Roman world remained without a sovereign, without
an usurper, and without a sedition. The generals and magistrates appointed by Aurelian continued to execute their ordinary
functions; and it is observed that a proconsul of Asia was the
only considerable person removed from his office in the whole
course of the interregnum.

An event somewhat similar but much less authentic is supposed
to have happened after the death of Romulus, who, in his life and
character, bore some affinity with Aurelian. The throne was
vacant during twelve months till the election of a Sabine philosopher, and the public peace was guarded in the same manner
by the union of the several orders of the state. But, in the time
of Numa and Romulus, the arms of the people were controlled
by the authority of the Patricians; and the balance of freedom
was easily preserved in a small and virtuous community.[1] The
decline of the Roman state, far different from its infancy, was
attended with every circumstance that could banish from an
interregnum the prospect of obedience and harmony: an immense and tumultuous capital, a wide extent of empire, the servile
equality of despotism, an army of four hundred thousand mercenaries, and the experience of frequent revolutions. Yet, notwithstanding all these temptations, the discipline and memory
of Aurelian still restrained the seditious temper of the troops, as
well as the fatal ambition of their leaders. The flower of the
legions maintained their stations on the banks of the Bosphorus,
ignorant of this transaction as they were in general of the Roman constitution.

[The date given in Vopiscus is " III. Non Febr." (Aurel. c. 41); but as it
is in opposition to the statements of other authorities, which make the interregnum between the death of Aurelian and the elevation of Tacitus only
six months, not eight as Gibbon says, Clinton proposed to read: " III.
Non. Apr." in place of " III. Non. Febr.," which would place the death of
Aurelian at the end of March. Tacitus was elected on 25th September,
and during the interregnum Severina, the widow of Aurelian, was acknowledged as empress at Alexandria, since her Alexandrian coins bear only
the years 6 and 7, and Aurelian died in the sixth year of his reign.—O. S.]

[1] Liv. i. 17. Dionys. Halicarn, l. ii. [c. 57] p. 115. Plutarch in Numa
[c. 2], p. 60. The first of these writers relates the story like an orator, the
second like a lawyer, and the third like a moralist, and none of them probably without some intermixture of fable.

and the Imperial standard awed the less powerful camps of Rome and of the provinces. A generous though transient enthusiasm seemed to animate the military order; and we may hope that a few real patriots cultivated the returning friendship of the army and the senate as the only expedient capable of restoring the republic to its ancient beauty and vigour.

On the twenty-fifth of September, near eight months after the murder of Aurelian, the consul convoked an assembly of the senate, and reported the doubtful and dangerous situation of the empire. He slightly insinuated that the precarious loyalty of the soldiers depended on the chance of every hour and of every accident; but he represented, with the most convincing eloquence, the various dangers that might attend any farther delay in the choice of an emperor. Intelligence, he said, was already received that the ,Germans had passed the Rhine and occupied some of the strongest and most opulent cities of Gaul. The ambition of the Persian king kept the East in perpetual alarms; Egypt, Africa, and Illyricum were exposed to foreign and domestic arms; and the levity of Syria would prefer even a female sceptre to the sanctity of the Roman laws. The consul then, addressing himself to Tacitus, the first of the senators,[1] required his opinion on the important subject of a proper candidate for the vacant throne.

If we can prefer personal merit to accidental greatness, we shall esteem the birth of Tacitus more truly noble than that of kings. He claimed his descent from the philosophic historian whose writings will instruct the last generations of mankind.[2] The senator Tacitus was then seventy-five years of age.[3] The long period of his innocent life was adorned with wealth and honours. He had twice been invested with the consular dignity,[4] and enjoyed with elegance and sobriety his ample patrimony of between two and three millions sterling.[5] The experience of so

---

[1] Vopiscus (in Hist. August. p. 227 [Tacit, c. 4] calls him " primæ sententiæ consularis; " and soon afterwards *Princeps senatûs*. It is natural to suppose that the monarchs of Rome, disdaining that humble title, resigned it to the most ancient of the senators.

[2] The only objection to this genealogy is, that the historian was named Cornelius, the emperor Claudius. But under the Lower Empire surnames were extremely various and uncertain.

[3] Zonaras, l. xii. [c. 28] p. 637 [ed. Paris; p. 608, ed. Bonn]. The Alexandrian Chronicle, by an obvious mistake, transfers that age to Aurelian.

[4] In the year 273 he was ordinary consul. But he must have been Suffectus many years before, and most probably under Valerian.

[5] *Bis millies octingenties.* Vopiscus in Hist. August. p. 229. [Tacit. c. 10.] This sum, according to the old standard, was equivalent to eight hundred and forty thousand Roman pounds of silver, each of the value of three pounds sterling. But in the age of Tacitus the coin had lost much of its weight and purity.

many princes, whom he had esteemed or endured, from the vain
follies of Elagabalus to the useful rigour of Aurelian, taught him
to form a just estimate of the duties, the dangers, and the temptations of their sublime station.   From the assiduous study of his
immortal ancestor he derived the knowledge of the Roman constitution and of human nature.[1]   The voice of the people had
already named Tacitus as the citizen the most worthy of empire.
The ungrateful rumour reached his ears, and induced him to
seek the retirement of one of his villas in Campania.   He had
passed two months in the delightful privacy of Baiæ, when he
reluctantly obeyed the summons of the consul to resume his
honourable place in the senate, and to assist the republic with
his counsels on this important occasion.

He arose to speak, when, from every quarter of the house, he
was saluted with the names of Augustus and Emperor. " Tacitus
Augustus, the gods preserve thee! we choose thee for our sovereign, to thy care we intrust the republic and the world.   Accept
the empire from the authority of the senate.   It is due to thy
rank, to thy conduct, to thy manners."   As soon as the tumult
of acclamations subsided, Tacitus attempted to decline the
dangerous honour, and to express his wonder that they should
elect his age and infirmities to succeed the martial vigour of
Aurelian.   " Are these limbs, conscript fathers! fitted to sustain
the weight of armour, or to practise the exercises of the camp?
The variety of climates, and the hardships of a military life,
would soon oppress a feeble constitution, which subsists only by
the most tender management.   My exhausted strength scarcely
enables me to discharge the duty of a senator; how insufficient
would it prove to the arduous labours of war and government!
Can you hope that the legions will respect a weak old man,
whose days have been spent in the shade of peace and retirement?
Can you desire that I should ever find reason to regret the
favourable opinion of the senate? " [2]

The reluctance of Tacitus, and it might possibly be sincere,
was encountered by the affectionate obstinacy of the senate.
Five hundred voices repeated at once, in eloquent confusion,
that the greatest of the Roman princes, Numa, Trajan, Hadrian,

---

[1] After his accession he gave orders that ten copies of the historian
should be annually transcribed and placed in the public libraries.   The
Roman libraries have long since perished, and the most valuable part of
Tacitus was preserved in a single MS., and discovered in a monastery of
Westphalia.   See Bayle, Dictionnaire, Art. *Tacite*, and Lipsius ad Annal.
ii. 9.
[2] Vopiscus in Hist. August. p. 227.   [Tacit. c. 4.]

and the Antonines, had ascended the throne in a very advanced
season of life; that the mind, not the body, a sovereign, not a
soldier, was the object of their choice; and that they expected
from him no more than to guide by his wisdom the valour of
the legions.   These pressing though tumultuary instances were
seconded by a more regular oration of Metius Falconius, the
next on the consular bench to Tacitus himself.   He reminded
the assembly of the evils which Rome had endured from the
vices of headstrong and capricious youths, congratulated them
on the election of a virtuous and experienced senator, and with
a manly, though perhaps a selfish, freedom, exhorted Tacitus
to remember the reasons of his elevation, and to seek a successor,
not in his own family, but in the republic.   The speech of Falconius was enforced by a general acclamation.   The emperor
elect submitted to the authority of his country, and received the
voluntary homage of his equals.   The judgment of the senate
was confirmed by the consent of the Roman people and of the
Prætorian guards.[1]

The administration of Tacitus was not unworthy of his life and
principles.   A grateful servant of the senate, he considered that
national council as the author, and himself as the subject, of the
laws.[2]   He studied to heal the wounds which Imperial pride,
civil discord, and military violence had inflicted on the constitution, and to restore, at least, the image of the ancient republic
as it had been preserved by the policy of Augustus and the virtues
of Trajan and the Antonines.   It may not be useless to recapitu-
late some of the most important prerogatives which the senate
appeared to have regained by the election of Tacitus.[3]   1. To
invest one of their body, under the title of emperor, with the
general command of the armies and the government of the
frontier provinces.   2. To determine the list, or, as it was then
styled, the College of Consuls.   They were twelve in number,
who, in successive pairs, each during the space of two months,
filled the year, and represented the dignity of that ancient office.
The authority of the senate, in the nomination of the consuls,
was exercised with such independent freedom, that no regard

---

[1] Hist. August. p. 228 [ib. c. 7].   Tacitus addressed the Prætorians by
the appellation of *sanctissimi milites*, and the people by that of *sacratissimi
Quirites*.
[2] In his manumissions he never exceeded the number of an hundred, as
limited by the Caninian law, which was enacted under Augustus, and at
length repealed by Justinian.   See Casaubon ad locum Vopisci.
[3] See the Lives of Tacitus, Florianus, and Probus, in the Augustan
History; we may be well assured that whatever the soldier gave the
senator had already given.

was paid to an irregular request of the emperor in favour of his
brother Florianus. "The senate," exclaimed Tacitus, with the
honest transport of a patriot, "understand the character of a
prince whom they have chosen." 3. To appoint the proconsuls
and presidents of the provinces, and to confer on all the magistrates their civil jurisdiction. 4. To receive appeals through
the intermediate office of the præfect of the city from all the
tribunals of the empire. 5. To give force and validity, by their
decrees, to such as they should approve of the emperor's edicts.
6. To these several branches of authority we may add some inspection over the finances, since, even in the stern reign of
Aurelian, it was in their power to divert a part of the revenue
from the public service.[1]

Circular epistles were sent, without delay, to all the principal
cities of the empire—Treves, Milan, Aquileia, Thessalonica,
Corinth, Athens, Antioch, Alexandria, and Carthage—to claim
their obedience, and to inform them of the happy revolution
which had restored the Roman senate to its ancient dignity.
Two of these epistles are still extant. We likewise possess two
very singular fragments of the private correspondence of the
senators on this occasion. They discover the most excessive
joy and the most unbounded hopes. "Cast away your indolence,"
it is thus that one of the senators addresses his friend, " emerge
from your retirements of Baiæ and Puteoli. Give yourself to
the city, to the senate. Rome flourishes, the whole republic
flourishes. Thanks to the Roman army, to an army truly
Roman, at length we have recovered our just authority, the end
of all our desires. We hear appeals, we appoint proconsuls,
we create emperors; perhaps, too, we may restrain them—to
the wise a word is sufficient." [2] These lofty expectations were,
however, soon disappointed; nor, indeed, was it possible that
the armies and the provinces should long obey the luxurious and
unwarlike nobles of Rome. On the slightest touch the unsupported fabric of their pride and power fell to the ground. The
expiring senate displayed a sudden lustre, blazed for a moment,
and was extinguished for ever.

All that had yet passed at Rome was no more than a theatrical
representation, unless it was ratified by the more substantial
power of the legions. Leaving the senators to enjoy their dream

---

[1] Vopiscus in Hist. August. p. 216. [Aurel. c. 20.] The passage is perfectly clear, yet both Casaubon and Salmasius wish to correct it.
[2] Vopiscus in Hist. August. p. 230, 232, 233. [Florian. c. 5 and 6.] The
senators celebrated the happy restoration with hetacombs and public
rejoicings.

of freedom and ambition, Tacitus proceeded to the Thracian camp, and was there, by the Prætorian præfect, presented to the assembled troops as the prince whom they themselves had demanded, and whom the senate had bestowed. As soon as the præfect was silent the emperor addressed himself to the soldiers with eloquence and propriety. He gratified their avarice by a liberal distribution of treasure under the names of pay and donative. He engaged their esteem by a spirited declaration that, although his age might disable him from the performance of military exploits, his counsels should never be unworthy of a Roman general, the successor of the brave Aurelian.[1]

Whilst the deceased emperor was making preparations for a second expedition into the East, he had negotiated with the Alani, a Scythian people, who pitched their tents in the neighbourhood of the lake Mæotis. Those barbarians, allured by presents and subsidies, had promised to invade Persia with a numerous body of light cavalry. They were faithful to their engagements; but when they arrived on the Roman frontier Aurelian was already dead, the design of the Persian war was at least suspended, and the generals who, during the interregnum, exercised a doubtful authority, were unprepared either to receive or to oppose them. Provoked by such treatment, which they considered as trifling and perfidious, the Alani had recourse to their own valour for their payment and revenge; and as they moved with the usual swiftness of Tartars, they had soon spread themselves over the provinces of Pontus, Cappadocia, Cilicia, and Galatia. The legions who, from the opposite shores of the Bosphorus, could almost distinguish the flames of the cities and villages, impatiently urged their general to lead them against the invaders. The conduct of Tacitus was suitable to his age and station. He convinced the barbarians of the faith, as well as of the power, of the empire. Great numbers of the Alani, appeased by the punctual discharge of the engagements which Aurelian had contracted with them, relinquished their booty and captives, and quietly retreated to their own deserts beyond the Phasis. Against the remainder, who refused peace, the Roman emperor waged, in person, a successful war. Seconded by an army of brave and experienced veterans, in a few weeks he delivered the provinces of Asia from the terror of the Scythian invasion.[2]

---

[1] Hist. August. p. 228. [Vopisc. Tacit. c. 8.]
[2] Vopiscus in Hist. August. p. 230. [Tacit. c. 13.] Zosimus, l. i. [c. 63] p. 57. Zonaras, l. xii. [c. 28] p. 637 [ed. Paris; p. 608, ed. Bonn]. Two passages in the Life of Probus (p. 236, 238 [Vopisc. Probus, c. 8 and 12])

But the glory and life of Tacitus were of short duration. Transported in the depth of winter from the soft retirement of Campania to the foot of Mount Caucasus, he sunk under the unaccustomed hardships of a military life. The fatigues of the body were aggravated by the cares of the mind. For a while the angry and selfish passions of the soldiers had been suspended by the enthusiasm of public virtue. They soon broke out with redoubled violence, and raged in the camp, and even in the tent of the aged emperor. His mild and amiable character served only to inspire contempt, and he was incessantly tormented with factions which he could not assuage, and by demands which it was impossible to satisfy. Whatever flattering expectations he had conceived of reconciling the public disorders, Tacitus soon was convinced that the licentiousness of the army disdained the feeble restraint of laws, and his last hour was hastened by anguish and disappointment. It may be doubtful whether the soldiers imbrued their hands in the blood of this innocent prince.[1] It is certain that their insolence was the cause of his death. He expired at Tyana in Cappadocia, after a reign of only six months and about twenty days.[2]

The eyes of Tacitus were scarcely closed before his brother Florianus showed himself unworthy to reign by the hasty usurpation of the purple, without expecting the approbation of the senate. The reverence for the Roman constitution, which yet influenced the camp and the provinces, was sufficiently strong to dispose them to censure, but not to provoke them to oppose, the precipitate ambition of Florianus. The discontent would have evaporated in idle murmurs, had not the general of the East, the heroic Probus, boldly declared himself the avenger of the senate. The contest, however, was still unequal; nor could the most able leader, at the head of the effeminate troops of Egypt and Syria, encounter, with any hopes of victory, the legions of Europe, whose irresistible strength appeared to support the brother of Tacitus. But the fortune and activity of Probus triumphed over every obstacle. The hardy veterans of

convince me that these Scythian invaders of Pontus were Alani. If we may believe Zosimus (l. i. [c. 64] p. 58), Florianus pursued them as far as the Cimmerian Bosphorus. But he had scarcely time for so long and difficult an expedition.

[1] Eutropius [9, c. 10] and Aurelius Victor [c. 36] only say that he died; Victor Junior adds, that it was of a fever. Zosimus [i. 63, p. 55] and Zonaras [xii. c. 28] affirm that he was killed by the soldiers. Vopiscus [Tacit. c. 13] mentions both accounts, and seems to hesitate. Yet surely these jarring opinions are easily reconciled.

[2] According to the two Victors, he reigned exactly two hundred days.

his rival, accustomed to cold climates, sickened and consumed away in the sultry heats of Cilicia, where the summer proved remarkably unwholesome. Their numbers were diminished by frequent desertion, the passes of the mountains were feebly defended; Tarsus opened its gates; and the soldiers of Florianus, when they had permitted him to enjoy the Imperial title about three months, delivered the empire from civil war by the easy sacrifice of a prince whom they despised.[1]

The perpetual revolutions of the throne had so perfectly erased every notion of hereditary right, that the family of an unfortunate emperor was incapable of exciting the jealousy of his successors. The children of Tacitus and Florianus were permitted to descend into a private station, and to mingle with the general mass of the people. Their poverty indeed became an additional safeguard to their innocence. When Tacitus was elected by the senate he resigned his ample patrimony to the public service,[2] an act of generosity specious in appearance, but which evidently disclosed his intention of transmitting the empire to his descendants. The only consolation of their fallen state was the remembrance of transient greatness, and a distant hope, the child of a flattering prophecy, that, at the end of a thousand years, a monarch of the race of Tacitus should arise, the protector of the senate, the restorer of Rome, and the conqueror of the whole earth.[3]

The peasants of Illyricum, who had already given Claudius and Aurelian to the sinking empire, had an equal right to glory in the elevation of Probus.[4] Above twenty years before, the emperor Valerian, with his usual penetration, had discovered the rising merit of the young soldier, on whom he conferred the rank of tribune long before the age prescribed by the military regulations. The tribune soon justified his choice by a victory over a great body of Sarmatians, in which he saved the life of a near relation of Valerian; and deserved to receive from the emperor's hand the

---

[1] Hist. August. p. 231. [Vopiscus, Florian. c. 1.] Zosimus, l. i. [c. 64, p. 56] p. 58, 59. Zonaras, l. xii. [c. 29, p. 609] p. 637. Aurelius Victor [de Cæsar. c. 37] says that Probus assumed the empire in Illyricum; an opinion which (though adopted by a very learned man) would throw that period of history into inextricable confusion.

[2] Hist. August. p. 229. [Vopisc. Tacit. c. 10.]

[3] He was to send judges to the Parthians, Persians, and Sarmatians, a president to Taprobana, and a proconsul to the Roman island (supposed by Casaubon and Salmasius to mean Britain). Such a history as mine (says Vopiscus with proper modesty) will not subsist a thousand years to expose or justify the prediction.

[4] For the private life of Probus, see Vopiscus in Hist. August. p. 234-237. [Probus, c. 3, sqq.]

collars, bracelets, spears, and banners, the mural and the civic crown, and all the honourable rewards reserved by ancient Rome for successful valour. The third, and afterwards the tenth, legion were intrusted to the command of Probus, who, in every step of his promotion, showed himself superior to the station which he filled. Africa and Pontus, the Rhine, the Danube, the Euphrates, and the Nile, by turns afforded him the most splendid occasions of displaying his personal prowess and his conduct in war. Aurelian was indebted to him for the conquest of Egypt, and still more indebted for the honest courage with which he often checked the cruelty of his master. Tacitus, who desired by the abilities of his generals to supply his own deficiency of military talents, named him commander-in-chief of all the eastern provinces, with five times the usual salary, the promise of the consulship, and the hope of a triumph. When Probus ascended the Imperial throne he was about forty-four years of age;[1] in the full possession of his fame, of the love of the army, and of a mature vigour of mind and body.

His acknowledged merit, and the success of his arms against Florianus, left him without an enemy or a competitor. Yet, if we may credit his own professions, very far from being desirous of the empire, he had accepted it with the most sincere reluctance. "But it is no longer in my power," says Probus in a private letter, "to lay down a title so full of envy and of danger. I must continue to personate the character which the soldiers have imposed upon me."[2] His dutiful address to the senate displayed the sentiments, or at least the language, of a Roman patriot: "When you elected one of your order, conscript fathers! to succeed the emperor Aurelian, you acted in a manner suitable to your justice and wisdom. For you are the legal sovereigns of the world, and the power which you derive from your ancestors will descend to your posterity. Happy would it have been if Florianus, instead of usurping the purple of his brother, like a private inheritance, had expected what your majesty might determine, either in his favour, or in that of any other person. The prudent soldiers have punished his rashness. To me they have offered the title of Augustus; but I submit to your clemency my pretensions and my merits."[3] When this

---

[1] According to the Alexandrian chronicle, he was fifty at the time of his death.

[2] The letter was addressed to the Prætorian præfect, whom (on condition of his good behaviour) he promised to continue in his great office. See Hist. August. p. 237. [Vopisc. Probus, c. 10.]

[3] Vopiscus in Hist. August. p. 237 [in Probo, c. 11]. The date of the letter is assuredly faulty. Instead of *Non. Februar.* we may read *Non. August.*

respectful epistle was read by the consul, the senators were unable
to disguise their satisfaction that Probus should condescend thus
humbly to solicit a sceptre which he already possessed. They
celebrated with the warmest gratitude his virtues, his exploits,
and above all his moderation. A decree immediately passed,
without a dissenting voice, to ratify the election of the eastern
armies, and to confer on their chief all the several branches of the
Imperial dignity: the names of Cæsar and Augustus, the title of
Father of his country, the right of making in the same day three
motions in the senate,[1] the office of Pontifex Maximus, the
tribunitian power, and the proconsular command; a mode of
investiture which, though it seemed to multiply the authority of
the emperor, expressed the constitution of the ancient republic.
The reign of Probus corresponded with this fair beginning. The
senate was permitted to direct the civil administration of the
empire. Their faithful general asserted the honour of the Roman
arms, and often laid at their feet crowns of gold and barbaric
trophies, the fruits of his numerous victories.[2] Yet, whilst
he gratified their vanity, he must secretly have despised their
indolence and weakness. Though it was every moment in their
power to repeal the disgraceful edict of Gallienus, the proud
successors of the Scipios patiently acquiesced in their exclusion
from all military employments. They soon experienced that
those who refuse the sword must renounce the sceptre.

The strength of Aurelian had crushed on every side the enemies
of Rome. After his death they seemed to revive with an
increase of fury and of numbers. They were again vanquished
by the active vigour of Probus, who, in a short reign of about
six years,[3] equalled the fame of ancient heroes, and restored
peace and order to every province of the Roman world. The
dangerous frontier of Rhætia he so firmly secured that he left it
without the suspicion of an enemy. He broke the wandering
power of the Sarmatian tribes, and by the terror of his arms compelled those barbarians to relinquish their spoil. The Gothic
nation courted the alliance of so warlike an emperor.[4] He

---

[1] Hist. August. p. 238. [Vopisc. *ib.* c. 12.] It is odd that the senate
should treat Probus less favourably than Marcus Antoninus. That prince
had received, even before the death of Pius, *Jus quintæ relationis*. See
Capitolin. in Hist. August. p. 24 [in M. Anton. c. 6].

[2] See the dutiful letter of Probus to the senate after his German victories.
Hist. August. p. 239. [Vopisc. Prob. c. 15.]

[3] The date and duration of the reign of Probus are very correctly ascertained by Cardinal Noris in his learned work, De Epochis Syro-Macedonum,
p. 96-105. A passage of Eusebius connects the second year of Probus with
the eras of several of the Syrian cities.

[4] Vopiscus in Hist. August. p. 239. [Prob. c. 16.]

attacked the Isaurians in their mountains, besieged and took
several of their strongest castles,[1] and flattered himselt that
he had for ever suppressed a domestic foe whose independence
so deeply wounded the majesty of the empire. The troubles
excited by the usurper Firmus in the Upper Egypt had never
been perfectly appeased, and the cities of Ptolemais and Coptos,
fortified by the alliance of the Blemmyes, still maintained an
obscure rebellion. The chastisement of those cities, and of their
auxiliaries the savages of the South, is said to have alarmed the
court of Persia,[2] and the Great King sued in vain for the friendship of Probus. Most of the exploits which distinguished his
reign were achieved by the personal valour and conduct of the
emperor, insomuch that the writer of his Life expresses some
amazement how, in so short a time, a single man could be present
in so many distant wars. The remaining actions he intrusted to
the care of his lieutenants, the judicious choice of whom forms
no inconsiderable part of his glory. Carus, Diocletian, Maximian, Constantius, Galerius, Asclepiodatus, Annibalianus, and
a crowd of other chiefs, who afterwards ascended or supported
the throne, were trained to arms in the severe school of Aurelian
and Probus.[3]

But the most important service which Probus rendered to the
republic was the deliverance of Gaul, and the recovery of seventy
flourishing cities oppressed by the barbarians of Germany, who,
since the death of Aurelian, had ravaged that great province
with impunity.[4] Among the various multitude of those fierce
invaders, we may distinguish, with some degree of clearness,
three great armies, or rather nations, successively vanquished
by the valour of Probus. He drove back the Franks into their
morasses; a descriptive circumstance from whence we may infer
that the confederacy known by the manly appellation of *Free*
already occupied the flat maritime country, intersected and
almost overflown by the stagnating waters of the Rhine, and that
several tribes of the Frisians and Batavians had acceded to their
alliance. He vanquished the Burgundians, a considerable people

---

[1] Zosimus (l. i. [c. 69, *sqq.*] p. 62-65) tells us a very long and trifling story
of Lydius the Isaurian robber.

[2] Zosim. l. i. [c. 7] p. 65. Vopiscus in Hist. August. p. 239, 240. [Prob
c. 17.] But it seems incredible that the defeat of the savages of Æthiopia
could affect the Persian monarch.

[3] Besides these well-known chiefs, several others are named by Vopiscus
(Hist. August. p. 241 [Prob. c. 22]), whose actions have not reached our
knowledge.

[4] See the Cæsars of Julian [p. 314], and Hist. August. p. 238, 240, 241
[Vopisc. Prob. c. 13, c. 18, *sqq.*]

of the Vandalic race. They had wandered in quest of booty
from the banks of the Oder to those of the Seine. They esteemed
themselves sufficiently fortunate to purchase, by the restitution
of all their booty, the permission of an undisturbed retreat.
They attempted to elude that article of the treaty. Their
punishment was immediate and terrible.[1] But of all the
invaders of Gaul, the most formidable were the Lygians, a
distant people who reigned over a wide domain on the frontiers
of Poland and Silesia.[2] In the Lygian nation the Arii held the
first rank by their numbers and fierceness. " The Arii " (it is
thus that they are described by the energy of Tacitus) " study
to improve by art and circumstances the innate terrors of their
barbarism. Their shields are black, their bodies are painted
black. They choose for the combat the darkest hour of the
night. Their host advances, covered as it were with a funeral
shade;[3] nor do they often find an enemy capable of sustaining
so strange and infernal an aspect. Of all our senses, the eyes
are the first vanquished in battle." [4] Yet the arms and discipline of the Romans easily discomfited these horrid phantoms.
The Lygii were defeated in a general engagement, and Semno,
the most renowned of their chiefs, fell alive into the hands of
Probus. That prudent emperor, unwilling to reduce a brave
people to despair, granted them an honourable capitulation,
and permitted them to return in safety to their native country.
But the losses which they suffered in the march, the battle, and
the retreat, broke the power of the nation: nor is the Lygian
name ever repeated in the history either of Germany or of the
empire. The deliverance of Gaul is reported to have cost the
lives of four hundred thousand of the invaders; a work of labour
to the Romans, and of expense to the emperor, who gave a piece

---

[1] Zosimus, l. i. [c. 68] p. 62. Hist. August. p. 238. [Vopisc. Probus, c.
13, 14.] But the latter supposes the punishment inflicted with the consent
of their kings: if so, it was partial, like the offence.

[2] See Cluver. Germania Antiqua, l. iii. Ptolemy places in their country
the city of Calisia, probably Calish in Silesia.
[In all probability the Burgundians were a German people, whereas the
Vandals were of Slavonic extraction. The Lyggi or Lygii seems to have
the generic name of the Slavonians on the Vistula. They are thought to
be the same people as those called Lekhs by Nestor, the Russian chronicler
of the twelfth century. The Lekhs or Letts are the ancestors of the Poles,
the Lettic division of the great Slavonic family comprehending the
Lithuanian, the Old Prussian, and the Lettish, the language of Courland
and Livonia.—O. S.]

[3] Feralis umbra is the expression of Tacitus: it is surely a very bold one.
[The words of Tacitus are " umbrâ feralis exercitus terrorem inferunt."
Gibbon is here mistaken, " umbrâ " being in the ablative case.—O. S.]

[4] Tacit. Germania (c. 43.)

of gold for the head of every barbarian.[1] But as the fame of warriors is built on the destruction of human kind, we may naturally suspect that the sanguinary account was multiplied by the avarice of the soldiers, and accepted without any very severe examination by the liberal vanity of Probus.

Since the expedition of Maximin, the Roman generals had confined their ambition to a defensive war against the nations of Germany, who perpetually pressed on the frontiers of the empire. The more daring Probus pursued his Gallic victories, passed the Rhine, and displayed his invincible eagles on the banks of the Elbe and the Neckar. He was fully convinced that nothing could reconcile the minds of the barbarians to peace, unless they experienced in their own country the calamities of war. Germany, exhausted by the ill success of the last emigration, was astonished by his presence. Nine of the most considerable princes repaired to his camp, and fell prostrate at his feet. Such a treaty was humbly received by the Germans as it pleased the conqueror to dictate. He exacted a strict restitution of the effects and captives which they had carried away from the provinces; and obliged their own magistrates to punish the more obstinate robbers who presumed to detain any part of the spoil. A considerable tribute of corn, cattle, and horses, the only wealth of barbarians, was reserved for the use of the garrisons which Probus established on the limits of their territory. He even entertained some thoughts of compelling the Germans to relinquish the exercise of arms, and to trust their differences to the justice, their safety to the power, of Rome. To accomplish these salutary ends, the constant residence of an Imperial governor, supported by a numerous army, was indispensably requisite. Probus therefore judged it more expedient to defer the execution of so great a design; which was indeed rather of specious than solid utility.[2] Had Germany been reduced into the state of a province, the Romans, with immense labour and expense, would have acquired only a more extensive boundary to defend against the fiercer and more active barbarians of Scythia.

Instead of reducing the warlike natives of Germany to the condition of subjects, Probus contented himself with the humble expedient of raising a bulwark against their inroads. The

---

[1] Vopiscus in Hist. August. p. 238 [Prob. c. 14.]

[2] Hist. August. p. 238, 239. [Vopisc. Probus, c. 14, *sqq.*] Vopiscus quotes a letter [c. 15] from the emperor to the senate, in which he mentions his design of reducing Germany into a province.

country which now forms the circle of Swabia had been left
desert in the age of Augustus by the emigration of its ancient
inhabitants.[1] The fertility of the soil soon attracted a new
colony from the adjacent provinces of Gaul. Crowds of adventurers, of a roving temper and of desperate fortunes, occupied
the doubtful possession, and acknowledged, by the payment of
tithes, the majesty of the empire.[2] To protect these new subjects, a line of frontier garrisons was gradually extended from
the Rhine to the Danube. About the reign of Hadrian, when
that mode of defence began to be practised, these garrisons were
connected and covered by a strong entrenchment of trees and
palisades. In the place of so rude a bulwark, the emperor
Probus constructed a stone wall of a considerable height and
strengthened it by towers at convenient distances. From the
neighbourhood of Neustadt and Ratisbon on the Danube, it
stretched across hills, valleys, rivers, and morasses, as far as
Wimpfen on the Neckar, and at length terminated on the banks
of the Rhine, after a winding course of near two hundred miles.[3]
This important barrier, uniting the two mighty streams that
protected the provinces of Europe, seemed to fill up the vacant
space through which the barbarians, and particularly the
Alemanni, could penetrate with the greatest facility into the
heart of the empire. But the experience of the world, from
China to Britain, has exposed the vain attempt of fortifying any
extensive tract of country.[4] An active enemy, who can select
and vary his points of attack, must in the end discover some
feeble spot, or some unguarded moment. The strength, as well
as the attention, of the defenders is divided; and such are the
blind effects of terror on the firmest troops that a line broken in
a single place is almost instantly deserted. The fate of the wall
which Probus erected may confirm the general observation.
Within a few years after his death it was overthrown by the

---

[1] Strabo, l. vii. [p. 290]. According to Velleius Paterculus (ii. 108, 109),
Maroboduus led his Marcomanni into Bohemia: Cluverius (German.
Antiq. iii. 8) proves that it was from Swabia.

[2] These settlers, from the payment of tithes, were denominated Decumates. Tacit. Germania, c. 29.

[3] See notes de l'Abbé de la Bléterie à la Germanie de Tacite, p. 183. His
account of the wall is chiefly borrowed (as he says himself) from the Alsatia
Illustrata of Schœpflin.

[4] See Recherches sur les Chinois et les Egyptiens, tom. ii. p. 81-102.
The anonymous author is well acquainted with the globe in general, and
with Germany in particular: with regard to the latter, he quotes a work
of M. Hanselman; but he seems to confound the wall of Probus, designed
against the Alemanni, with the fortification of the Mattiaci, constructed
in the neighbourhood of Frankfort against the Catti.

Alemanni. Its scattered ruins, universally ascribed to the
power of the Dæmon, now serve only to excite the wonder of
the Swabian peasant.

Among the useful conditions of peace imposed by Probus
on the vanquished nations of Germany was the obligation of
supplying the Roman army with sixteen thousand recruits, the
bravest and most robust of their youth. The emperor dispersed
them through all the provinces, and distributed this dangerous
reinforcement, in small bands of fifty or sixty each, among the
national troops; judiciously observing that the aid which the
republic derived from the barbarians should be felt but not seen.[1]
Their aid was now become necessary. The feeble elegance of
Italy and the internal provinces could no longer support the
weight of arms. The hardy frontier of the Rhine and Danube
still produced minds and bodies equal to the labours of the
camp; but a perpetual series of wars had gradually diminished
their numbers. The infrequency of marriage, and the ruin of
agriculture, affected the principles of population, and not only
destroyed the strength of the present, but intercepted the hope
of future generations. The wisdom of Probus embraced a
great and beneficial plan of replenishing the exhausted frontiers
by new colonies of captive or fugitive barbarians, on whom he
bestowed lands, cattle, instruments of husbandry, and every
encouragement that might engage them to educate a race of
soldiers for the service of the republic. Into Britain, and most
probably into Cambridgeshire,[2] he transported a considerable
body of Vandals. The impossibility of an escape reconciled
them to their situation, and in the subsequent troubles of that
island they approved themselves the most faithful servants of
the state.[3] Great numbers of Franks and Gepidæ were settled
on the banks of the Danube and the Rhine. An hundred thousand Bastarnæ, expelled from their own country, cheerfully
accepted an establishment in Thrace, and soon imbibed the
manners and sentiments of Roman subjects.[4] But the expectations of Probus were too often disappointed. The impatience
and idleness of the barbarians could ill brook the slow labours of

[1] He distributed about fifty or sixty barbarians to a *Numerus*, as it was
then called, a corps with whose established number we are not exactly
acquainted.

[2] Camden's Britannia, Introduction, p. 136; but he speaks from a very
doubtful conjecture.

[3] Zosimus, l. i. [c. 68] p. 62. According to Vopiscus, another body of
Vandals was less faithful.

[4] Hist. August. p. 240. [Vopisc. Probus, c. 18.] They were probably
expelled by the Goths. Zosim. l. i. [c. 71] p. 66.

agriculture. Their unconquerable love of freedom, rising against despotism, provoked them into hasty rebellions, alike fatal to themselves and to the provinces,[1] nor could these artificial supplies, however repeated by succeeding emperors, restore the important limit of Gaul and Illyricum to its ancient and native vigour.

Of all the barbarians who abandoned their new settlements, and disturbed the public tranquillity, a very small number returned to their own country. For a short season they might wander in arms through the empire, but in the end they were surely destroyed by the power of a warlike emperor. The successful rashness of a party of Franks was attended, however, with such memorable consequences that it ought not to be passed unnoticed. They had been established by Probus on the sea-coast of Pontus, with a view of strengthening the frontier against the inroads of the Alani. A fleet stationed in one of the harbours of the Euxine fell into the hands of the Franks; and they resolved, through unknown seas, to explore their way from the mouth of the Phasis to that of the Rhine. They easily escaped through the Bosphorus and the Hellespont, and, cruising along the Mediterranean, indulged their appetite for revenge and plunder by frequent descents on the unsuspecting shores of Asia, Greece, and Africa. The opulent city of Syracuse, in whose port the navies of Athens and Carthage had formerly been sunk, was sacked by a handful of barbarians, who massacred the greatest part of the trembling inhabitants. From the island of Sicily the Franks proceeded to the Columns of Hercules, trusted themselves to the ocean, coasted round Spain and Gaul, and, steering their triumphant course through the British Channel, at length finished their surprising voyage by landing in safety on the Batavian or Frisian shores.[2] The example of their success, instructing their countrymen to conceive the advantages and to despise the dangers of the sea, pointed out to their enterprising spirit a new road to wealth and glory.

Notwithstanding the vigilance and activity of Probus, it was almost impossible that he could at once contain in obedience every part of his wide-extended dominions. The barbarians who broke their chains had seized the favourable opportunity of a domestic war. When the emperor marched to the relief of Gaul, he devolved the command of the East on Saturninus. That general, a man of merit and experience, was driven into

[1] Hist. August. p. 240. [Vopisc. l. c.]
[2] Panegyr. Vet. v. 18. Zosimus, l. i. [c. 71] p. 66.

rebellion by the absence of his sovereign, the levity of the Alexandrian people, the pressing instances of his friends, and his own
fears; but from the moment of his elevation he never entertained
a hope of empire or even of life. " Alas ! " he said, " the republic
has lost a useful servant, and the rashness of an hour has destroyed
the services of many years. You know not," continued he,
" the misery of sovereign power: a sword is perpetually suspended over our head. We dread our very guards, we distrust
our companions. The choice of action or of repose is no longer
in our. disposition, nor is there any age, or character, or conduct,
that can protect us from the censure of envy. In thus exalting
me to the throne, you have doomed me to a life of cares, and to
an untimely fate. The only consolation which remains is the
assurance that I shall not fall alone." [1] But as the former part
of his prediction was verified by the victory, so the latter was
disappointed by the clemency, of Probus. That amiable prince
attempted even to save the unhappy Saturninus from the fury
of the soldiers. He had more than once solicited the usurper
himself to place some confidence in the mercy of a sovereign who
so highly esteemed his character that he had punished as a
malicious informer the first who related the improbable news of
his defection.[2] Saturninus might perhaps have embraced the
generous offer had he not been restrained by the obstinate distrust of his adherents. Their guilt was deeper, and their hopes
more sanguine, than those of their experienced leader.

The revolt of Saturninus was scarcely extinguished in the
East before new troubles were excited in the West by the
rebellion of Bonosus and Proculus in Gaul. The most distinguished merit of those two officers was their respective prowess,
of the one in the combats of Bacchus, of the other in those of
Venus,[3] yet neither of them were destitute of courage and
capacity, and both sustained with honour the august character
which the fear of punishment had engaged them to assume, till
they sunk at length beneath the superior genius of Probus. He

---

[1] Vopiscus in Hist. August. p. 245, 246 [in Saturnino, c. 10]. The unfortunate orator had studied rhetoric at Carthage; and was therefore more
probably a Moor (Zosim. l. i. [c. 66] p. 60) than a Gaul, as Vopiscus calls
him.

[2] Zonaras, l. xii. [c. 29] p. 638 [ed. Par.; p. 609, ed. Bonn.]

[3] A very surprising instance is recorded of the prowess of Proculus. He
had taken one hundred Sarmatian virgins. The rest of the story he must
relate in his own language: Ex his unâ nocte decem inivi; omnes tamen,
quod in me erat, mulieres intra dies quindecim reddidi. Vopiscus in Hist.
August. p. 246 [in Proculo, 12].

used the victory with his accustomed moderation, and spared the fortunes as well as the lives of their innocent families.[1]

The arms of Probus had now suppressed all the foreign and domestic enemies of the state. His mild but steady administration confirmed the re-establishemnt of the public tranquillity; nor was there left in the provinces a hostile barbarian, a tyrant, or even a robber, to revive the memory of past disorders. It was time that the emperor should revisit Rome, and celebrate his own glory and the general happiness. The triumph due to the valour of Probus was conducted with a magnificence suitable to his fortune; and the people, who had so lately admired the trophies of Aurelian, gazed with equal pleasure on those of his heroic successor.[2] We cannot on this occasion forget the desperate courage of about fourscore gladiators, reserved, with near six hundred others, for the inhuman sports of the amphitheatre. Disdaining to shed their blood for the amusement of the populace, they killed their keepers, broke from the place of their confinement, and filled the streets of Rome with blood and confusion. After an obstinate resistance, they were overpowered and cut in pieces by the regular forces; but they obtained at least an honourable death, and the satisfaction of a just revenge.[3]

The military discipline which reigned in the camps of Probus was less cruel than that of Aurelian, but it was equally rigid and exact. The latter had punished the irregularities of the soldiers with unrelenting severity, the former prevented them by employing the legions in constant and useful labours. When Probus commanded in Egypt, he executed many considerable works for the splendour and benefit of that rich country. The navigation of the Nile, so important to Rome itself, was improved; and temples, bridges, porticoes, and palaces, were constructed by the hands of the soldiers, who acted by turns as architects, as engineers, and as husbandmen.[4] It was reported of Hannibal that, in order to preserve his troops from the dangerous temptations of idleness, he had obliged them to form large plantations of olive-trees along the coast of Africa.[5] From

---

[1] Proculus, who was a native of Albengue on the Genoese coast, armed two thousand of his own slaves. His riches were great, but they were acquired by robbery. It was afterwards a saying of his family, sibi non placere esse vel principes vel latrones. Vopiscus in Hist. August. p. 247 [in Proculo, 13].

[2] Hist. August. p. 240. [Vopisc. in Probo, c. 19.]

[3] Zosim. l. i. [c. 71] p. 66.

[4] Hist. August. p. 236. [Vopisc. in Probo, c. 9.]

[5] Aurel. Victor. in Prob. [De Cæsar. c. 37.] But the policy of Hannibal, unnoticed by any more ancient writer, is irreconcilable with the history of

a similar principle, Probus exercised his legions in covering with
rich vineyards the hills of Gaul and Pannonia, and two consider
able spots are described which were entirely dug and planted
by military labour.[1] One of these, known under the name of
Mount Alma, was situated near Sirmium, the country where
Probus was born, for which he ever retained a partial affection,
and whose gratitude he endeavoured to secure, by converting
into tillage a large and unhealthy tract of marshy ground. An
army thus employed constituted perhaps the most useful as
well as the bravest portion of Roman subjects.

But, in the prosecution of a favourite scheme, the best of men,
satisfied with the rectitude of their intentions, are subject to
forget the bounds of moderation; nor did Probus himself
sufficiently consult the patience and disposition of his fierce
legionaries.[2] The dangers of the military profession seem only
to be compensated by a life of pleasure and idleness; but if
the duties of the soldier are incessantly aggravated by the
labours of the peasant, he will at last sink under the intolerable
burden or shake it off with indignation. The imprudence of
Probus is said to have inflamed the discontent of his troops.
More attentive to the interests of mankind than to those of the
army, he expressed the vain hope that, by the establishment
of universal peace, he should soon abolish the necessity of a
standing and mercenary force.[3] The unguarded expression
proved fatal to him. In one of the hottest days of summer,
as he severely urged the unwholesome labour of draining the
marshes of Sirmium, the soldiers, impatient of fatigue, on a
sudden threw down their tools, grasped their arms, and broke
out into a furious mutiny. The emperor, conscious of his
danger, took refuge in a lofty tower constructed for the purpose
of surveying the progress of the work.[4] The tower was instantly
forced, and a thousand swords were plunged at once into the
bosom of the unfortunate Probus. The rage of the troops sub-

his life. He left Africa when he was nine years old, returned to it when
he was forty-five, and immediately lost his army in the decisive battle of
Zama. Livius, xxx. 35.

[1] Hist. August. p. 240. [Vopisc. Probus, c. 18.] Eutrop. ix. 17 [7].
Aurel. Victor. in Prob. Victor Junior. He revoked the prohibition of
Domitian, and granted a general permission of planting vines to the Gauls,
the Britons, and the Pannonians.

[2] Julian [Cæsares, p. 314] bestows a severe, and indeed excessive, censure
on the rigour of Probus, who, as he thinks, almost deserved his fate.

[3] Vopiscus in Hist. August. p. 241 [in Probo, c. 20]. He lavishes on this
idle hope a large stock of very foolish eloquence.

[4] Turris ferrata. It seems to have been a movable tower, and cased
with iron.

sided as soon as it had been gratified. They then lamented
their fatal rashness, forgot the severity of the emperor whom
they had massacred, and hastened to perpetuate, by an honourable monument, the memory of his virtues and victories.[1]

When the legions had indulged their grief and repentance for
the death of Probus, their unanimous consent declared Carus,
his Prætorian præfect, the most deserving of the Imperial throne.
Every circumstance that relates to this prince appears of a mixed
and doubtful nature. He gloried in the title of Roman Citizen;
and affected to compare the purity of *his* blood with the foreign,
and even barbarous, origin of the preceding emperors; yet the
most inquisitive of his contemporaries, very far from admitting
his claim, have variously deduced his own birth, or that of his
parents, from Illyricum, from Gaul, or from Africa.[2] Though a
soldier, he had received a learned education; though a senator,
he was invested with the first dignity of the army; and in an
age when the civil and military professions began to be irrecoverably separated from each other, they were united in the
person of Carus. Notwithstanding the severe justice which he
exercised against the assassins of Probus, to whose favour and
esteem he was highly indebted, he could not escape the suspicion
of being accessory to a deed from whence he derived the principal
advantage. He enjoyed, at least before his elevation, an acknowledged character of virtue and abilities; [3] but his austere temper
insensibly degenerated into moroseness and cruelty; and the
imperfect writers of his life almost hesitate whether they shall
not rank him in the number of Roman tyrants.[4] When Carus
assumed the purple he was about sixty years of age, and his two
sons, Carinus and Numerian, had already attained the season of
manhood.[5]

---

[1] [Hic] Probus, et vere probus situs est; Victor omnium gentium Barbararum: victor etiam tyrannorum. [Vopisc. Prob. c. 21.]

[2] Yet all this may be conciliated. He was born at Narbonne in Illyricum,
confounded by Eutropius with the more famous city of that name in Gaul.
His father might be an African, and his mother a noble Roman. Carus
himself was educated in the capital. See Scaliger, Animadversion, ad
Euseb. Chron. p. 241.

[3] Probus had requested of the senate an equestrian statue and a marble
palace, at the public expense, as a just recompense of the singular merit of
Carus. Vopiscus in Hist. August. p. 249 [in Caro, c. 6].

[4] Vopiscus in Hist. August. p. 242, 249 [in Probo, c. 24; in Caro, c. 3].
Julian excludes the emperor Carus and both his sons from the banquet of
the Cæsars.

[5] John Malala, tom. i. p. 401 [ed. Oxon.; p. 129, ed. Ven.; p. 303, ed.
Bonn]. But the authority of that ignorant Greek is very slight. He
ridiculously derives from Carus the city of Carrhæ and the province of
Caria, the latter of which is mentioned by Homer.

The authority of the senate expired with Probus; nor was the repentance of the soldiers displayed by the same dutiful regard for the civil power which they had testified after the unfortunate death of Aurelian. The election of Carus was decided without expecting the approbation of the senate, and the new emperor contented himself with announcing, in a cold and stately epistle, that he had ascended the vacant throne.[1] A behaviour so very opposite to that of his amiable predecessor afforded no favourable presage of the new reign: and the Romans, deprived of power and freedom, asserted their privilege of licentious murmurs.[2] The voice of congratulation and flattery was not however silent; and we may still peruse, with pleasure and contempt, an eclogue which was composed on the accession of the emperor Carus. Two shepherds, avoiding the noontide heat, retire into the cave of Faunus. On a spreading beech they discover some recent characters. The rural deity had described, in prophetic verses, the felicity promised to the empire under the reign of so great a prince. Faunus hails the approach of that hero, who, receiving on his shoulders the sinking weight of the Roman world, shall extinguish war and faction, and once again restore the innocence and security of the golden age.[3]

It is more than probable that these elegant trifles never reached the ears of a veteran general who, with the consent of the legions, was preparing to execute the long-suspended design of the Persian war. Before his departure for this distant expedition, Carus conferred on his two sons, Carinus and Numerian, the title of Cæsar, and, investing the former with almost an equal share of the Imperial power, directed the young prince first to suppress some troubles which had arisen in Gaul, and afterwards to fix the seat of his residence at Rome, and to assume the government of the Western provinces.[4] The safety of Illyricum was confirmed by a memorable defeat of the Sarmatians; sixteen thousand of those barbarians remained on the field of battle, and the number of captives amounted to twenty thousand. The old emperor, animated with the fame and prospect of victory, pursued his march, in the midst of winter, through the countries of Thrace and Asia Minor, and at length, with his younger son

---

[1] Hist. August. p. 249. [Vopisc. Carus, c. 5.] Carus congratulated the senate that one of their own order was made emperor.

[2] Hist. August. p. 242. [Vopisc. Probus, c. 24.]

[3] See the first eclogue of Calphurnius. The design of it is preferred by Fontenelle to that of Virgil's Pollio. See tom. iii. p. 148.

[4] Hist. August. p. 250. [Vopisc. Carus, c. 7.] Eutropius, ix. 18 [12]. Pagi, Annal.

Numerian, arrived on the confines of the Persian monarchy.
There, encamping on the summit of a lofty mountain, he pointed
out to his troops the opulence and luxury of the enemy whom
they were about to invade.

The successor of Artaxerxes, Varanes, or Bahram, though he
had subdued the Segestans, one of the most warlike nations of
Upper Asia,[1] was alarmed at the approach of the Romans, and
endeavoured to retard their progress by a negotiation of peace.
His ambassadors entered the camp about sunset, at the time
when the troops were satisfying their hunger with a frugal repast.
The Persians expressed their desire of being introduced to the
presence of the Roman emperor. They were at length conducted
to a soldier who was seated on the grass. A piece of stale bacon
and a few hard peas composed his supper. A coarse woollen
garment of purple was the only circumstance that announced
his dignity. The conference was conducted with the same disregard of courtly elegance. Carus, taking off a cap which he
wore to conceal his baldness, assured the ambassadors that,
unless their master acknowledged the superiority of Rome, he
would speedily render Persia as naked of trees as his own head
was destitute of hair.[2] Notwithstanding some traces of art and
preparation, we may discover in this scene the manners of Carus,
and the severe simplicity which the martial princes who succeeded Gallienus had already restored in the Roman camps.
The ministers of the Great King trembled and retired.

The threats of Carus were not without effect. He ravaged
Mesopotamia, cut in pieces whatever opposed his passage, made
himself master of the great cities of Seleucia and Ctesiphon
(which seem to have surrendered without resistance), and carried
his victorious arms beyond the Tigris.[3] He had seized the favourable moment for an invasion. The Persian councils were distracted by domestic factions, and the greater part of their forces
were detained on the frontiers of India. Rome and the East
received with transport the news of such important advantages.

---

[1] Agathias, l. iv. p. 135 [ed. Paris; p. 94, ed. Ven.; c. 24, p. 261, ed
Bonn]. We find one of his sayings in the Bibliothèque Orientale of M.
d'Herbelot. "The definition of humanity includes all other virtues."
[Gibbon here is in error, for Varanes or Bahram was not the successor of
Artaxerxes. Three monarchs had intervened, Sapor (Shahpour), Hor-
misdas (Hormooz), Varanes or Baharam the First.—O. S.]

[2] Synesius tells this story of Carinus; and it is much more natural to
understand it of Carus than (as Petavius and Tillemont choose to do) of
Probus.

[3] Vopiscus in Hist. August. p. 250. [Vopisc. Carus, c. 8.] Eutropius,
ix. 18 [12]. The two Victors.

Flattery and hope painted in the most lively colours the fall of Persia, the conquest of Arabia, the submission of Egypt, and a lasting deliverance from the inroads of the Scythian nations.[1] But the reign of Carus was destined to expose the vanity of predictions. They were scarcely uttered before they were contradicted by his death; an event attended with such ambiguous circumstances that it may be related in a letter from his own secretary to the præfect of the city. " Carus," says he, " our dearest emperor, was confined by sickness to his bed, when a furious tempest arose in the camp. The darkness which overspread the sky was so thick that we could no longer distinguish each other; and the incessant flashes of lightning took from us the knowledge of all that passed in the general confusion. Immediately after the most violent clap of thunder we heard a sudden cry that the emperor was dead; and it soon appeared that his chamberlains, in a rage of grief, had set fire to the royal pavilion, a circumstance which gave rise to the report that Carus was killed by lightning. But, as far as we have been able to investigate the truth, his death was the natural effect of his disorder." [2]

The vacancy of the throne was not productive of any disturbance. The ambition of the aspiring generals was checked by their mutual fears; and young Numerian, with his absent brother Carinus, were unanimously acknowledged as Roman emperors. The public expected that the successor of Carus would pursue his father's footsteps, and, without allowing the Persians to recover from their consternation, would advance sword in hand to the palaces of Susa and Ecbatana.[3] But the legions, however strong in numbers and discipline, were dismayed by the most abject superstition. Notwithstanding all the arts that were practised to disguise the manner of the late emperor's death, it was found impossible to remove the opinion of the multitude, and the power of opinion is irresistible. Places or persons struck with lightning were considered by the ancients

[1] To the Persian victory of Carus, I refer the dialogue of the *Philopatris*, which has so long been an object of dispute among the learned. But to explain and justify my opinion would require a dissertation.
[Niebuhr in vol. xi. of the Byzantine Historians has assigned the Philopatris to the tenth century and to the reign of Nicephorus Phocas. Milman thinks that this occurrence took place in the devastation of the island by the Gothic pirates during the reign of Claudius.—O. S.]
[2] Hist. August. p. 250. [Vopisc. Carus, c. 8.] Yet Eutropius, Festus, Rufus, the two Victors, Jerome, Sidonius Apollinaris, Syncellus, and Zonaras, all ascribe the death of Carus to lightning.
[3] See Nemesian. Cynegeticon, v. 71, etc.

with pious horror, as singularly devoted to the wrath of Heaven.[1]
An oracle was remembered which marked the river Tigris as the
fatal boundary of the Roman arms. The troops, terrified with
the fate of Carus and with their own danger, called aloud on young
Numerian to obey the will of the gods, and to lead them away
from this inauspicious scene of war. The feeble emperor was
unable to subdue their obstinate prejudice, and the Persians
wondered at the unexpected retreat of a victorious enemy.[2]

The intelligence of the mysterious fate of the late emperor was
soon carried from the frontiers of Persia to Rome; and the
senate, as well as the provinces, congratulated the accession of
the sons of Carus. These fortunate youths were strangers, however, to that conscious superiority, either of birth or of merit,
which can alone render the possession of a throne easy, and as it
were natural. Born and educated in a private station, the
election of their father raised them at once to the rank of princes;
and his death, which happened about sixteen months afterwards,
left them the unexpected legacy of a vast empire. To sustain
with temper this rapid elevation, an uncommon share of virtue
and prudence was requisite; and Carinus, the elder of the
brothers, was more than commonly deficient in those qualities.
In the Gallic war he discovered some degree of personal courage;[3]
but from the moment of his arrival at Rome he abandoned himself to the luxury of the capital, and to the abuse of his fortune.
He was soft, yet cruel; devoted to pleasure, but destitute of
taste; and, though exquisitely susceptible of vanity, indifferent
to the public esteem. In the course of a few months he successively married and divorced nine wives, most of whom he left
pregnant; and, notwithstanding this legal inconstancy, found
time to indulge such a variety of irregular appetites as brought
dishonour on himself and on the noblest houses of Rome. He
beheld with inveterate hatred all those who might remember
his former obscurity, or censure his present conduct. He
banished or put to death the friends and counsellors whom his
father had placed about him to guide his inexperienced youth;
and he persecuted with the meanest revenge his schoolfellows
and companions who had not sufficiently respected the latent
majesty of the emperor. With the senators Carinus affected a

[1] See Festus and his commentators, on the word *Scribonianum*. *Places*
struck by lightning were surrounded with a wall; *things* were buried with
mysterious ceremony.
[2] Vopiscus in Hist. August. p. 250. [Carus, c. 9.] Aurelius Victor
seems to believe the prediction, and to approve the retreat.
[3] Nemesian. Cynegeticon, v. 69. He was a contemporary, but a poet.

lofty and regal demeanour, frequently declaring that he designed to distribute their estates among the populace of Rome. From the dregs of that populace he selected his favourites, and even his ministers. The palace, and even the Imperial table, was filled with singers, dancers, prostitutes, and all the various retinue of vice and folly. One of his doorkeepers [1] he intrusted with the government of the city. In the room of the Prætorian præfect, whom he put to death, Carinus substituted one of the ministers of his looser pleasures. Another, who possessed the same or even a more infamous title to favour, was invested with the consulship. A confidential secretary, who had acquired uncommon skill in the art of forgery, delivered the indolent emperor, with his own consent, from the irksome duty of signing his name.

When the emperor Carus undertook the Persian war, he was induced, by motives of affection as well as policy, to secure the fortunes of his family by leaving in the hands of his eldest son the armies and provinces of the West. The intelligence which he soon received of the conduct of Carinus filled him with shame and regret; nor had he concealed his resolution of satisfying the republic by a severe act of justice, and of adopting, in the place of an unworthy son, the brave and virtuous Constantius, who at that time was governor of Dalmatia. But the elevation of Constantius was for a while deferred; and as soon as the father's death had released Carinus from the control of fear or decency, he displayed to the Romans the extravagancies of Elagabalus, aggravated by the cruelty of Domitian. [2]

The only merit of the administration of Carinus that history could record, or poetry celebrate, was the uncommon splendour with which, in his own and his brother's name, he exhibited the Roman games of the theatre, the circus, and the amphitheatre. More than twenty years afterwards, when the courtiers of Diocletian represented to their frugal sovereign the fame and popularity of his munificent predecessor, he acknowledged that the reign of Carinus had indeed been a reign of pleasure. [3] But

---

[1] *Cancellarius.* This word, so humble in its origin, has by a singular fortune risen into the title of the first great office of state in the monarchies of Europe. See Casaubon and Salmasius, ad Hist. August. p. 253. [Vopisc. Carinus, c. 15.]

[2] Vopiscus in Hist. August. p. 253, 254 [*id. ib.* c. 15, 16]. Eutropius, ix. 19 [13]. Victor Junior. The reign of Diocletian indeed was so long and prosperous, that it must have been very unfavourable to the reputation of Carinus.

[3] Vopiscus in Hist. August. p. 254 [in Carino, 19]. He calls him Carus, but the sense is sufficiently obvious, and the words were often confounded.

this vain prodigality, which the prudence of Diocletian might justly despise, was enjoyed with surprise and transport by the Roman people. The oldest of the citizens, recollecting the spectacles of former days, the triumphal pomp of Probus or Aurelian, and the secular games of the emperor Philip, acknowledged that they were all surpassed by the superior magnificence of Carinus.[1]

The spectacles of Carinus may therefore be best illustrated by the observation of some particulars which history has condescended to relate concerning those of his predecessors. If we confine ourselves solely to the hunting of wild beasts, however we may censure the vanity of the design or the cruelty of the execution, we are obliged to confess that neither before nor since the time of the Romans so much art and expense have ever been lavished for the amusement of the people.[2] By the order of Probus, a great quantity of large trees, torn up by the roots, were transplanted into the midst of the circus. The spacious and shady forest was immediately filled with a thousand ostriches, a thousand stags, a thousand fallow-deer, and a thousand wild boars; and all this variety of game was abandoned to the riotous impetuosity of the multitude. The tragedy of the succeeding day consisted in the massacre of an hundred lions, an equal number of lionesses, two hundred leopards, and three hundred bears.[3] The collection prepared by the younger Gordian for his triumph, and which his successor exhibited in the secular games, was less remarkable by the number than by the singularity of the animals. Twenty zebras displayed their elegant forms and variegated beauty to the eyes of the Roman people.[4] Ten elks, and as many camelopards, the loftiest and most harmless creatures that wander over the plains of Sarmatia and Æthiopia, were contrasted with thirty African hyænas and ten Indian tigers, the most implacable savages of the torrid zone. The unoffending strength with which Nature has endowed the greater quadrupeds was admired in the rhinoceros, the hippopotamus of the Nile,[5] and a majestic troop of thirty-two

---

[1] See Calphurnius, Eclog. vii. 43. We may observe that the spectacles of Probus were still recent, and that the poet is seconded by the historian.

[2] The philosopher Montaigne (Essais, l. iii. 6) gives a very just and lively view of Roman magnificence in these spectacles.

[3] Vopiscus in Hist. August. p. 240. [Probus, c. 19.]

[4] They are called *Onagri ;* but the number is too inconsiderable for mere wild asses. Cuper (de Elephantis Exercitat. ii. 7) has proved from Oppian, Dion, and an anonymous Greek, that zebras had been seen at Rome. They were brought from some island of the ocean, perhaps Madagascar.

[5] Carinus gave an hippopotamus (see Calphurn. Eclog. vii. 66). In the

elephants.[1] While the populace gazed with stupid wonder on the splendid show, the naturalist might indeed observe the figure and properties of so many different species, transported from every part of the ancient world into the amphitheatre of Rome. But this accidental benefit which science might derive from folly is surely insufficient to justify such a wanton abuse of the public riches. There occurs, however, a single instance in the first Punic war in which the senate wisely connected this amusement of the multitude with the interest of the state. A considerable number of elephants, taken in the defeat of the Carthaginian army, were driven through the circus by a few slaves, armed only with blunt javelins.[2] The useful spectacle served to impress the Roman soldier with a just contempt for those unwieldy animals; and he no longer dreaded to encounter them in the ranks of war.

The hunting or exhibition of wild beasts was conducted with a magnificence suitable to a people who styled themselves the masters of the world; nor was the edifice appropriated to that entertainment less expressive of Roman greatness. Posterity admires, and will long admire, the awful remains of the amphitheatre of Titus, which so well deserved the epithet of Colossal.[3] It was a building of an elliptic figure, five hundred and sixty-four feet in length, and four hundred and sixty-seven in breadth, founded on fourscore arches, and rising, with four successive orders of architecture, to the height of one hundred and forty feet.[4] The outside of the edifice was encrusted with marble and decorated with statues. The slopes of the vast concave, which formed the inside, were filled and surrounded with sixty or eighty rows of seats, of marble likewise, covered with cushions, and capable of receiving with ease above four-score thousand spectators.[5] Sixty-four *vomitories* (for by that name the doors were

latter spectacles I do not recollect any crocodiles, of which Augustus once exhibited thirty-six. Dion Cassius, l. lv. [c. 10] p. 781.

[1] Capitolin. in Hist. August. p. 164, 165. [Gordian. III. c. 33.] We are not acquainted with the animals which he calls *archeleontes*; some read *argoleontes*, others *agrioleontes*: both corrections are very nugatory.

[2] Plin. Hist. Natur. viii. 6, from the annals of Piso.

[3] See Maffei, Verona Illustrata, p. iv. l. i. c. 2.

[4] Maffei, l. ii. c. 2. The height was very much exaggerated by the ancients. It reached almost to the heavens, according to Calpurnius (Eclog. vii. 23); and surpassed the ken of human sight, according to Ammianus Marcellinus (xvi. 10). Yet how trifling to the great pyramid of Egypt, which rises 500 feet perpendicular! [The height was 157 feet. See Smith's Dict. of Antiq. p. 86.—S.]

[5] According to different copies of Victor, we read 77,000 or 87,000 spectators; but Maffei (l. ii. c. 12) finds room on the open seats for no more than 34,000. The remainder were contained in the upper covered galleries.

very aptly distinguished) poured forth the immense multitude; and the entrances, passages, and staircases were contrived with such exquisite skill, that each person, whether of the senatorial, the equestrian, or the plebeian order, arrived at his destined place without trouble or confusion.[1] Nothing was omitted which, in any respect, could be subservient to the convenience and pleasure of the spectators. They were protected from the sun and rain by an ample canopy, occasionally drawn over their heads. The air was continually refreshed by the playing of fountains, and profusely impregnated by the grateful scent of aromatics. In the centre of the edifice, the *arena*, or stage, was strewed with the finest sand, and successively assumed the most different forms. At one moment it seemed to rise out of the earth, like the garden of the Hesperides, and was afterwards broken into the rocks and caverns of Thrace. The subterraneous pipes conveyed an inexhaustible supply of water; and what had just before appeared a level plain might be suddenly converted into a wide lake, covered with armed vessels, and replenished with the monsters of the deep.[2] In the decoration of these scenes the Roman emperors displayed their wealth and liberality; and we read on various occasions that the whole furniture of the amphitheatre consisted either of silver, or of gold, or of amber.[3] The poet who describes the games of Carinus, in the character of a shepherd attracted to the capital by the fame of their magnificence, affirms that the nets designed as a defence against the wild beasts were of gold wire; that the porticoes were gilded; and that the *belt* or circle which divided the several ranks of spectators from each other was studded with a precious mosaic of beautiful stones.[4]

In the midst of this glittering pageantry, the emperor Carinus, secure of his fortune, enjoyed the acclamations of the people, the flattery of his courtiers, and the songs of the poets, who, for want of a more essential merit, were reduced to celebrate the divine graces of his person.[5] In the same hour, but at the dis-

---

[1] See Maffei, l. ii. c. 5-12. He treats the very difficult subject with all possible clearness, and like an architect as well as an antiquarian.

[2] Calphurn. Eclog. vii. 64-73. These lines are curious, and the whole eclogue has been of infinite use to Maffei. Calphurnius, as well as Martial (see his first book), was a poet; but when they described the amphitheatre, they both wrote from their own senses, and to those of the Romans.

[3] Consult Plin. Hist. Natur. xxxiii. 16, xxxvii. 11.

[4]   Balteus en gemmis, en inclita porticus auro
          Certatim radiant, etc. Calphurn. vii. [v. 47.]

[5] Et Martis vultus et Apollinis esse putavi, says Calphurnius [Ecl. vii. 83]; but John Malala, who had perhaps seen pictures of Carinus, describes him as thick, short, and white, tom. i. p. 403.

tance of nine hundred miles from Rome, his brother expired; and a sudden revolution transferred into the hands of a stranger the sceptre of the house of Carus.[1]

The sons of Carus never saw each other after their father's death. The arrangements which their new situation required were probably deferred till the return of the younger brother to Rome, where a triumph was decreed to the young emperors for the glorious success of the Persian war.[2] It is uncertain whether they intended to divide between them the administration or the provinces of the empire; but it is very unlikely that their union would have proved of any long duration. The jealousy of power must have been inflamed by the opposition of characters. In the most corrupt of times Carinus was unworthy to live: Numerian deserved to reign in a happier period. His affable manners and gentle virtues secured him, as soon as they became known, the regard and affections of the public. He possessed the elegant accomplishments of a poet and orator, which dignify as well as adorn the humblest and the most exalted station. His eloquence, however it was applauded by the senate, was formed not so much on the model of Cicero as on that of the modern declaimers; but in an age very far from being destitute of poetical merit, he contended for the prize with the most celebrated of his contemporaries, and still remained the friend of his rivals; a circumstance which evinces either the goodness of his heart, or the superiority of his genius.[3] But the talents of Numerian were rather of the contemplative than of the active kind. When his father's elevation reluctantly forced him from the shade of retirement, neither his temper nor his pursuits had qualified him for the command of armies. His constitution was destroyed by the hardships of the Persian war; and he had contracted, from the heat of the climate,[4] such a weakness in his eyes, as obliged him, in the course of a long retreat, to confine himself to the solitude and darkness of a tent or litter. The administration of all affairs, civil as well as military, was de-

---

[1] With regard to the time when these Roman games were celebrated, Scaliger, Salmasius, and Cuper have given themselves a great deal of trouble to perplex a very clear subject.

[2] Nemesianus (in the Cynegeticon [v. 80, *sqq.*]) seems to anticipate in his fancy that auspicious day.

[3] He won all the crowns from Nemesianus, with whom he vied in didactic poetry. The senate erected a statue to the son of Carus, with a very ambiguous inscription, " To the most powerful of orators." See Vopiscus in Hist. August. p. 251. [Numerian. c. 11.]

[4] A more natural cause, at least, than that assigned by Vopiscus (Hist. August. p. 251 [Numerian. c. 12]), incessantly weeping for his father's death.

volved on Arrius Aper, the Prætorian præfect, who, to the power
of his important office, added the honour of being father-in-law
to Numerian. The Imperial pavilion was strictly guarded by
his most trusty adherents; and during many days Aper delivered to the army the supposed mandates of their invisible
sovereign.[1]

It was not till eight months after the death of Carus that the
Roman army, returning by slow marches from the banks of the
Tigris, arrived on those of the Thracian Bosphorus. The
legions halted at Chalcedon in Asia, while the court passed over
to Heraclea, on the European side of the Propontis.[2] But a
report soon circulated through the camp, at first in secret
whispers, and at length in loud clamours, of the emperor's death,
and of the presumption of his ambitious minister, who still
exercised the sovereign power in the name of a prince who was
no more. The impatience of the soldiers could not long support
a state of suspense. With rude curiosity they broke into the
imperial tent, and discovered only the corpse of Numerian.[3]
The gradual decline of his health might have induced them to
believe that his death was natural; but the concealment was
interpreted as an evidence of guilt, and the measures which Aper
had taken to secure his election became the immediate occasion
of his ruin. Yet, even in the transport of their rage and grief,
the troops observed a regular proceeding, which proves how
firmly discipline had been re-established by the martial successors of Gallienus. A general assembly of the army was
appointed to be held at Chalcedon, whither Aper was transported
in chains, as a prisoner and a criminal. A vacant tribunal was
erected in the midst of the camp, and the generals and tribunes
formed a great military council. They soon announced to
the multitude that their choice had fallen on Diocletian, commander of the domestics or body-guards, as the person the most
capable of revenging and succeeding their beloved emperor.
The future fortunes of the candidate depended on the chance or
conduct of the present hour. Conscious that the station which
he had filled exposed him to some suspicions, Diocletian ascended
the tribunal, and, raising his eyes towards the Sun, made a

---

[1] In the Persian war Aper was suspected of a design to betray Carus.
Hist. August. p. 250. [Vopiscus, Carus, c. 8.]

[2] We are obliged to the Alexandrian Chronicle, p. 274, for the knowledge
of the time and place where Diocletian was elected emperor.

[3] Hist. August. p. 251. [Vopisc. Numer. c. 12.] Eutrop. ix. 88 [c. 12].
Hieronym. in Chron. According to these *judicious* writers, the death of
Numerian was discovered by the stench of his dead body. Could no
aromatics be found in the Imperial household?

solemn profession of his own innocence, in the presence of that all-seeing Deity.[1] Then, assuming the tone of a sovereign and a judge, he commanded that Aper should be brought in chains to the foot of the tribunal. "This man," said he, "is the murderer of Numerian;" and without giving him time to enter on a dangerous justification, drew his sword, and buried it in the breast of the unfortunate præfect. A charge supported by such decisive proof was admitted without contradiction, and the legions, with repeated acclamations, acknowledged the justice and authority of the emperor Diocletian.[2]

Before we enter upon the memorable reign of that prince, it will be proper to punish and dismiss the unworthy brother of Numerian. Carinus possessed arms and treasures sufficient to support his legal title to the empire. But his personal vices over-balanced every advantage of birth and situation. The most faithful servants of the father despised the incapacity, and dreaded the cruel arrogance of the son. The hearts of the people were engaged in favour of his rival, and even the senate was inclined to prefer an usurper to a tyrant. The arts of Dio-cletian inflamed the general discontent; and the winter was employed in secret intrigues and open preparations for a civil war. In the spring the forces of the East and of the West encountered each other in the plains of Margus, a small city of Mæsia, in the neighbourhood of the Danube.[3] The troops, so lately returned from the Persian war, had acquired their glory at the expense of health and numbers, nor were they in a con-dition to contend with the unexhausted strength of the legions of Europe. Their ranks were broken, and, for a moment, Dio-cletian despaired of the purple and of life. But the advantage which Carinus had obtained by the valour of his soldiers he quickly lost by the infidelity of his officers. A tribune, whose wife he had seduced, seized the opportunity of revenge, and by a single blow extinguished civil discord in the blood of the adulterer.[4]

---

[1] Aurel. Victor. [De Cæsar c. 39.] Eutropius, ix. 20 [c. 13]. Hieronym. in Chron.

[2] Vopiscus in Hist. August. p. 252. [Numer. c. 13.] The reason why Diocletian killed *Aper* (a wild boar) was founded on a prophecy and a pun, as foolish as they are well known. [Vopisc. l. c.]

[3] Eutropius [lib. ix. c. 13] marks its situation very accurately; it was between the Mons Aureus and Viminiacum. M. d'Anville (Géographie Ancienne, tom. i. p. 304) places Margus at Kastolatz in Servia, a little below Belgrade and Semendria.

[4] Hist. August. p. 254. [Vopisc. Carin. c. 17.] Eutropius, ix. 20 [13]. Aurelius Victor. Victor in Epitome.

CHAPTER XIII

The Reign of Diocletian and his Three Associates, Maximian, Galerius, and Constantius—General Re-establishment of Order and Tranquillity—The Persian War, Victory, and Triumph—The new Form of Administration—Abdication and Retirement of Diocletian and Maximian

As the reign of Diocletian was more illustrious than that of any of his predecessors, so was his birth more abject and obscure. The strong claims of merit and of violence had frequently superseded the ideal prerogatives of nobility; but a distinct line of separation was hitherto preserved between the free and the servile part of mankind. The parents of Diocletian had been slaves in the house of Anulinus, a Roman senator; nor was he himself distinguished by any other name than that which he derived from a small town in Dalmatia, from whence his mother deduced her origin.[1] It is, however, probable that his father obtained the freedom of the family, and that he soon acquired an office of scribe, which was commonly exercised by persons of his condition.[2] Favourable oracles, or rather the consciousness of superior merit, prompted his aspiring son to pursue the profession of arms and the hopes of fortune; and it would be extremely curious to observe the gradation of arts and accidents which enabled him in the end to fulfil those oracles, and to display that merit to the world. Diocletian was successively promoted to the government of Mæsia, the honours of the consulship, and the important command of the guards of the palace. He distinguished his abilities in the Persian war; and after the death of Numerian, the slave, by the confession and judgment of his rivals, was declared the most worthy of the Imperial throne. The malice of religious zeal, whilst it arraigns the savage fierceness of his colleague Maximian, has affected to cast suspicions on the personal courage of the emperor Diocletian.[3] It would not

---

[1] Eutrop. ix. 19 [13]. Victor in Epitome [c. 39]. The town seems to have been properly called Doclia, from a small tribe of Illyrians (see Cellarius, Geograph. Antiqua, tom. i. p. 393); and the original name of the fortunate slave was probably Docles; he first lengthened it to the Grecian harmony of Diocles, and at length to the Roman majesty of Diocletianus. He likewise assumed the Patrician n..me of Valerius, and it is usually given him by Aurelius Victor.

[2] See Dacier on the sixth satire of the second book of Horace. Cornel. Nepos, in Vit. Eumen. c. 1.

[3] Lactantius (or whoever was the author of the little treatise De Mortibus Persecutorum) accuses Diocletian of *timidity* in two places, c. 7, 8. In chap. 9 he says of him, " erat in omni tumultu meticulosus et animi disjectus."

be easy to persuade us of the cowardice of a soldier of fortune
who acquired and preserved the esteem of the legions, as well
as the favour of so many warlike princes. Yet even calumny
is sagacious enough to discover and to attack the most vulner-
able part. The valour of Diocletian was never found inadequate
to his duty, or to the occasion; but he appears not to have
possessed the daring and generous spirit of a hero, who courts
danger and fame, disdains artifice, and boldly challenges the
allegiance of his equals. His abilities were useful rather than
splendid—a vigorous mind improved by the experience and study
of mankind; dexterity and application in business; a judicious
mixture of liberality and economy, of mildness and rigour; profound dissimulation under the disguise of military frankness;
steadiness to pursue his ends; flexibility to vary his means; and,
above all, the great art of submitting his own passions, as well
as those of others, to the interest of his ambition, and of colouring
his ambition with the most specious pretences of justice and
public utility. Like Augustus, Diocletian may be considered
as the founder of a new empire. Like the adopted son of Cæsar,
he was distinguished as a statesman rather than as a warrior;
nor did either of those princes employ force, whenever their
purpose could be effected by policy.

The victory of Diocletian was remarkable for its singular mildness. A people accustomed to applaud the clemency of the
conqueror, if the usual punishments of death, exile, and confiscation were inflicted with any degree of temper and equity, beheld,
with the most pleasing astonishment, a civil war, the flames of
which were extinguished in the field of battle. Diocletian received into his confidence Aristobulus, the principal minister of
the house of Carus, respected the lives, the fortunes, and the
dignity of his adversaries, and even continued in their respective
stations the greater number of the servants of Carinus.[1] It is
not improbable that motives of prudence might assist the
humanity of the artful Dalmatian: of these servants, many had
purchased his favour by secret treachery; in others, he esteemed
their grateful fidelity to an unfortunate master. The discerning
judgment of Aurelian, of Probus, and of Carus, had filled the
several departments of the state and army with officers of
approved merit, whose removal would have injured the public
service, without promoting the interest of the successor. Such

[1] In this encomium Aurelius Victor seems to convey a just, though in-
direct, censure of the cruelty of Constantius. It appears from the Fasti
that Aristobulus remained præfect of the city, and that he ended with
Diocletian the consulship which he had commenced with Carinus.

a conduct, however, displayed to the Roman world the fairest
prospect of the new reign, and the emperor affected to confirm
this favourable prepossession by declaring that, among all the
virtues of his predecessors, he was the most ambitious of imitating the humane philosophy of Marcus Antoninus.[1]

The first considerable action of his reign seemed to evince his
sincerity as well as his moderation. After the example of Marcus,
he gave himself a colleague in the person of Maximian, on whom
he bestowed at first the title of Cæsar, and afterwards that of
Augustus.[2] But the motives of his conduct, as well as the object
of his choice, were of a very different nature from those of his
admired predecessor. By investing a luxurious youth with the
honours of the purple, Marcus had discharged a debt of private
gratitude, at the expense, indeed, of the happiness of the state.
By associating a friend and a fellow-soldier to the favours of
government, Diocletian, in a time of public danger, provided
for the defence both of the East and of the West. Maximian
was born a peasant, and, like Aurelian, in the territory of
Sirmium. Ignorant of letters,[3] careless of laws, the rusticity
of his appearance and manners still betrayed in the most elevated
fortune the meanness of his extraction. War was the only art
which he professed. In a long course of service he had distinguished himself on every frontier of the empire; and though his
military talents were formed to obey rather than to command,
though, perhaps, he never attained the skill of a consummate
general, he was capable, by his valour, constancy, and experience,
of executing the most arduous undertakings. Nor were the vices
of Maximian less useful to his benefactor. Insensible to pity,
and fearless of consequences, he was the ready instrument of
every act of cruelty which the policy of that artful prince might
at once suggest and disclaim. As soon as a bloody sacrifice had
been offered to prudence or to revenge, Diocletian, by his seasonable intercession, saved the remaining few whom he had never

---

[1] Aurelius Victor styles Diocletian " Parentem potius quam Dominum."
[De Cæsar. 39.] See Hist. August. p. 30. [Capitol. M. Anton. Phil. c. 19.]

[2] The question of the time when Maximian received the honours of
Cæsar and Augustus has divided modern critics and given occasion to a
great deal of learned wrangling. I have followed M. de Tillemont (Histoire
des Empereurs, tom. iv. p. 500-505), who has weighed the several reasons
and difficulties with his scrupulous accuracy.

[3] In an oration delivered before him (Panegyr. Vet. i. 8) Mamertinus
expresses a doubt whether his hero, in imitating the conduct of Hannibal
and Scipio, had ever heard of their names. From thence we may fairly
infer that Maximian was more desirous of being considered as a soldier
than as a man of letters: and it is in this manner that we can often translate the language of flattery into that of truth.

designed to punish, gently censured the severity of his stern
colleague, and enjoyed the comparison of a golden and an iron
age, which was universally applied to their opposite maxims of
government. Notwithstanding the difference of their characters,
the two emperors maintained, on the throne, that friendship
which they had contracted in a private station. The haughty
turbulent spirit of Maximian, so fatal afterwards to himself and
to the public peace, was accustomed to respect the genius of
Diocletian, and confessed the ascendant of reason over brutal
violence.[1] From a motive either of pride or superstition, the
two emperors assumed the titles, the one of Jovius, the other of
Herculius. Whilst the motion of the world (such was the
language of their venal orators) was maintained by the all-
seeing wisdom of Jupiter, the invincible arm of Hercules purged
the earth from monsters and tyrants.[2]

But even the omnipotence of Jovius and Herculius was insufficient to sustain the weight of the public administration.
The prudence of Diocletian discovered that the empire, assailed
on every side by the barbarians, required on every side the
presence of a great army and of an emperor. With this view,
he resolved once more to divide his unwieldy power, and, with
the inferior title of *Cæsars*, to confer on two generals of approved
merit an equal share of the sovereign authority.[3] Galerius, surnamed Armentarius, from his original profession of a herdsman,
and Constantius, who from his pale complexion had acquired the
denomination of Chlorus,[4] were the two persons invested with
the second honours of the Imperial purple. In describing the
country, extraction, and manners of Herculius, we have already
delineated those of Galerius, who was often, and not improperly,
styled the younger Maximian, though, in many instances both
of virtue and ability, he appears to have possessed a manifest
superiority over the elder. The birth of Constantius was less
obscure than that of his colleagues. Eutropius, his father, was

[1] Lactantius de M. P. c. 8. Aurelius Victor [de Cæsar. c. 39]. As
among the Panegyrics we find orations pronounced in praise of Maximian,
and others which flatter his adversaries at his expense, we derive some
knowledge from the contrast.
[2] See the second and third Panegyrics, particularly iii. [ii.] 3, 10, 14; but
it would be tedious to copy the diffuse and affected expressions of their
false eloquence. With regard to the titles, consult Aurel. Victor, Lactantius de M. P. c. 52. Spanheim de Usu Numismatum, etc. Dissertat. xii. 8.
[3] Aurelius Victor. Victor in Epitome. Eutrop. ix. 22 [14]. Lactant.
de M. P. c. 7. Hieronym. in Chron.
[4] It is only among the modern Greeks that Tillemont can discover his
appellation of Chlorus. Any remarkable degree of paleness seems inconsistent with the *rubor* mentioned in Panegyric v 19.

one of the most considerable nobles of Dardania, and his mother was the niece of the emperor Claudius.[1] Although the youth of Constantius had been spent in arms, he was endowed with a mild and amiable disposition, and the popular voice had long since acknowledged him worthy of the rank which he at last attained. To strengthen the bonds of political, by those of domestic, union, each of the emperors assumed the character of a father to one of the Cæsars, Diocletian to Galerius, and Maximian to Constantius; and each, obliging them to repudiate their former wives, bestowed his daughter in marriage on his adopted son.[2] These four princes distributed among themselves the wide extent of the Roman empire. The defence of Gaul, Spain,[3] and Britain was intrusted to Constantius: Galerius was stationed on the banks of the Danube, as the safeguard of the Illyrian provinces. Italy and Africa were considered as the department of Maximian; and for his peculiar portion Diocletian reserved Thrace, Egypt, and the rich countries of Asia. Every one was sovereign within his own jurisdiction; but their united authority extended over the whole monarchy, and each of them was prepared to assist his colleagues with his counsels or presence. The Cæsars, in their exalted rank, revered the majesty of the emperors, and the three younger princes invariably acknowledged, by their gratitude and obedience, the common parent of their fortunes. The suspicious jealousy of power found not any place among them; and the singular happiness of their union has been compared to a chorus of music, whose harmony was regulated and maintained by the skilful hand of the first artist.[4]

This important measure was not carried into execution till about six years after the association of Maximian, and that interval of time had not been destitute of memorable incidents. But we have preferred, for the sake of perspicuity, first to describe the more perfect form of Diocletian's government, and afterwards to relate the actions of his reign, following rather the natural order of the events than the dates of a very doubtful chronology.

[1] Julian, the grandson of Constantius, boasts that his family was derived from the warlike Mæsians. Misopogon, p. 348. The Dardanians dwelt on the edge of Mæsia.

[2] Galerius married Valeria, the daughter of Diocletian; if we speak with strictness, Theodora, the wife of Constantius, was daughter only to the wife of Maximian. Spanheim, Dissertat. xi. 2.

[3] This division agrees with that of the four præfectures; yet there is some reason to doubt whether Spain was not a province of Maximian. See Tillemont, tom. iv. p. 517.

[4] Julian in Cæsarib. p. 315. Spanheim's notes to the French translation, p. 122.

The first exploit of Maximian, though it is mentioned in a few
words by our imperfect writers, deserves, from its singularity,
to be recorded in a history of human manners. He suppressed
the peasants of Gaul, who, under the appellation of Bagaudæ,[1]
had risen in a general insurrection; very similar to those which
in the fourteenth century successively afflicted both France and
England.[2] It should seem that very many of those institutions,
referred by an easy solution to the feudal system, are derived
from the Celtic barbarians. When Cæsar subdued the Gauls,
that great nation was already divided into three orders of
men; the clergy, the nobility, and the common people. The first
governed by superstition, the second by arms, but the third
and last was not of any weight or account in their public councils.
It was very natural for the plebeians, oppressed by debt or
apprehensive of injuries, to implore the protection of some powerful chief, who acquired over their persons and property the same
absolute rights as, among the Greeks and Romans, a master
exercised over his slaves.[3] The greatest part of the nation was
gradually reduced into a state of servitude; compelled to perpetual labour on the estates of the Gallic nobles, and confined
to the soil, either by the real weight of fetters, or by the no less
cruel and forcible restraints of the laws. During the long series
of troubles which agitated Gaul, from the reign of Gallienus to
that of Diocletian, the condition of those servile peasants was
peculiarly miserable; and they experienced at once the com-
plicated tyranny of their masters, of the barbarians, of the
soldiers, and of the officers of the revenue.[4]

Their patience was at last provoked into despair. On every
side they rose in multitudes, armed with rustic weapons, and
with irresistible fury. The ploughman became a foot soldier,
the shepherd mounted on horseback, the deserted villages and
open towns were abandoned to the flames, and the ravages of
the peasants equalled those of the fiercest barbarians.[5] They
asserted the natural rights of men, but they asserted those

[1] The general name of *Bagaudæ* (in the signification of Rebels) continued
till the fifth century in Gaul. Some critics derive it from a Celtic word,
Bagad, a tumultuous assembly. Scaliger ad Euseb. Du Cange Glossar.
[Compare S. Turner, Anglo-Sax. History, i. 214.—M.]
[2] Chronique de Froissart, vol. i. c. 182, ii. 73, 79. The *naïveté* of his
story is lost in our best modern writers.
[3] Cæsar de Bell. Gallic. vi. 13. Orgetorix, the Helvetian, could arm for
his defence a body of ten thousand slaves.
[4] Their oppression and misery are acknowledged by Eumenius (Panegyr.
vi. 8), Gallias efferatas injuriis.
[5] Panegyr. Vet. ii. 4. Aurelius Victor [de Cæsar. c. 39].

rights with the most savage cruelty. The Gallic nobles, justly
dreading their revenge, either took refuge in the fortified cities,
or fled from the wild scene of anarchy. The peasants reigned
without control; and two of their most daring leaders had the
folly and rashness to assume the Imperial ornaments.[1] Their
power soon expired at the approach of the legions. The strength
of union and discipline obtained an easy victory over a licentious
and divided multitude.[2] A severe retaliation was inflicted on
the peasants who were found in arms: the affrighted remnant
returned to their respective habitations, and their unsuccessful
effort for freedom served only to confirm their slavery. So
strong and uniform is the current of popular passions, that we
might almost venture, from very scanty materials, to relate the
particulars of this war; but we are not disposed to believe that
the principal leaders, Ælianus and Amandus, were Christians,[3]
or to insinuate that the rebellion, as it happened in the time of
Luther, was occasioned by the abuse of those benevolent principles of Christianity which inculcate the natural freedom of
mankind.

Maximian had no sooner recovered Gaul from the hands of the
peasants, than he lost Britain by the usurpation of Carausius.
Ever since the rash but successful enterprise of the Franks under
the reign of Probus, their daring countrymen had constructed
squadrons of light brigantines, in which they incessantly ravaged
the provinces adjacent to the ocean.[4] To repel their desultory
incursions, it was found necessary to create a naval power; and
the judicious measure was prosecuted with prudence and vigour.
Gessoriacum, or Boulogne, in the strai.s of the British Channel,
was chosen by the emperor for the station of the Roman fleet;
and the command of it was intrusted to Carausius, a Menapian
of the meanest origin,[5] but who had long signalised his skill as

[1] Ælianus and Amandus. We have medals coined by them. Goltzius
in Thes. R. A. p. 117, 121.

[2] Levibus prœliis domuit. Eutrop. ix. 20 [13].

[3] The fact rests indeed on very slight authority, a Life of St. Babolinus,
which is probably of the seventh century. See Duchesne Scriptores Rer.
Francicar. tom. i. p. 662.

[4] Aurelius Victor [de Cæsar. c. 39] calls them Germans. Eutropius (ix.
21 [13]) gives them the name of Saxons. But Eutropius lived in the
ensuing century, and seems to use the language of his own times.

[Eutropius speaks both of Franks and of Saxons. The name of Saxons
occurs in the second century, and there seems no reason to question the
statement of Eutropius.—O. S.]

[5] The three expressions of Eutropius [ix. 13], Aurelius Victor [de Cæsar.
39], and Eumenius, " vilissime natus," " Bataviæ alumnus," and " Mena-
piæ civis," give us a very doubtful account of the birth of Carausius. Dr.
Stukely however (Hist. of Carausius, p. 62), chooses to make him a native

a pilot and his valour as a soldier. The integrity of the new
admiral corresponded not with his abilities. When the German
pirates sailed from their own harbours he connived at their
passage, but he diligently intercepted their return, and appropriated to his own use an ample share of the spoil which they had
acquired The wealth of Carausius was, on this occasion, very
justly considered as an evidence of his guilt; and Maximian
had already given orders for his death. But the crafty Menapian
foresaw and prevented the severity of the emperor. By his
liberality he had attached to his fortunes the fleet which he commanded, and secured the barbarians in his interest. From the
port of Boulogne he sailed over to Britain, persuaded the legions
and the auxiliaries which guarded that island to embrace his
party, and boldly assuming, with the Imperial purple, the title
of Augustus, defied the justice and the arms of his injured
sovereign.[1]

When Britain was thus dismembered from the empire its
importance was sensibly felt and its loss sincerely lamented.
The Romans celebrated, and perhaps magnified, the extent of
that noble island, provided on every side with convenient
harbours; the temperature of the climate, and the fertility of
the soil, alike adapted for the production of corn or of vines;
the valuable minerals with which it abounded; its rich pastures
covered with innumerable flocks, and its woods free from wild
beasts or venomous serpents. Above all, they regretted the
large amount of the revenue of Britain, whilst they confessed
that such a province well deserved to become the seat of an
independent monarchy.[2] During the space of seven years it was
possessed by Carausius; and fortune continued propitious to a
rebellion supported with courage and ability. The British
emperor defended the frontiers of his dominions against the
Caledonians of the North, invited from the continent a great

---

of St. David's and a prince of the blood royal of Britain. The former idea
he had found in Richard of Cirencester, p. 44.

[Carausius was of German origin, and when planning his rising appears
to have thought it likely that he would receive assistance from the Germans
already settled in Britain. Cf. Kemble, the Saxons in England, vol. i. p.
12. Carausius was slain in A.D. 293, not 294 as stated by Gibbon. See
Clinton, Fasti Romani, vol. i. p. 334.—O. S.]

[1] Panegyr. v. 12. Britain at this time was secure, and slightly guarded.
[2] Panegyr. Vet. v. 11, vii. 9. The orator Eumenius wished to exalt the
glory of the hero (Constantius) with the importance of the conquest.
Notwithstanding our laudable partiality for our native country, it is difficult to conceive that, in the beginning of the fourth century, England deserved *all* these commendations. A century and a half before it hardly
paid its own establishment. See Appian in Procem.

number of skilful artists, and displayed, on a variety of coins that are still extant, his taste and opulence. Born on the confines of the Franks, he courted the friendship of that formidable people by the flattering imitation of their dress and manners. The bravest of their youths he enlisted among his land or sea forces; and, in return for their useful alliance, he communicated to the barbarians the dangerous knowledge of military and naval arts. Carausius still preserved the possession of Boulogne and the adjacent country. His fleets rode triumphant in the channel, commanded the mouths of the Siene and of the Rhine, ravaged the coasts of the ocean, and diffused beyond the Columns of Hercules the terror of his name. Under his command, Britain, destined in a future age to obtain the empire of the sea, already assumed its natural and respectable station of a maritime power.[1]

By seizing the fleet of Boulogne, Carausius had deprived his master of the means of pursuit and revenge. And when, after a vast expense of time and labour, a new armament was launched into the water,[2] the Imperial troops, unaccustomed to that element, were easily baffled and defeated by the veteran sailors of the usurper. This disappointed effort was soon productive of a treaty of peace. Diocletian and his colleague, who justly dreaded the enterprising spirit of Carausius, resigned to him the sovereignty of Britain, and reluctantly admitted their perfidious servant to a participation of the Imperial honours.[3] But the adoption of the two Cæsars restored new vigour to the Roman arms; and while the Rhine was guarded by the presence of Maximian, his brave associate Constantius assumed the conduct of the British war. His first enterprise was against the important place of Boulogne. A stupendous mole, raised across the entrance of the harbour, intercepted all hopes of relief. The town surrendered after an obstinate defence; and a considerable part of the naval strength of Carausius fell into the hands of the

---

[1] As a great number of medals of Carausius are still preserved, he is become a very favourite object of antiquarian curiosity, and every circumstance of his life and actions has been investigated with sagacious accuracy. Dr. Stukely in particular has devoted a large volume to the British emperor. I have used his materials, and rejected most of his fanciful conjectures.

[2] When Mamertinus pronounced his first panegyric the naval preparations of Maximian were completed; and the orator presaged an assured victory. His silence in the second panegyric might alone inform us that the expedition had not succeeded.

[3] Aurelius Victor, Eutropius, and the medals (Pax Augg.), inform us of this temporary reconciliation; though I will not presume (as Dr. Stukely has done, Medallic History of Carausius, p. 86, etc.) to insert the identical articles of the treaty.

besiegers. During the three years which Constantius employed
in preparing a fleet adequate to the conquest of Britain, he
secured the coast of Gaul, invaded the country of the Franks, and
deprived the usurper of the assistance of those powerful
allies.

Before the preparations were finished, Constantius received the
intelligence of the tyrant's death, and it was considered as a sure
presage of the approaching victory. The servants of Carausius
imitated the example of treason which he had given. He was
murdered by his first minister Allectus, and the assassin succeeded
to his power and to his danger. But he possessed not equal
abilities either to exercise the one or to repel the other. He
beheld with anxious terror the opposite shores of the continent,
already filled with arms, with troops, and with vessels; for Constantius had very prudently divided his forces, that he might
likewise divide the attention and resistance of the enemy. The
attack was at length made by the principal squadron, which,
under the command of the præfect Asclepiodotus, an officer of
distinguished merit, had been assembled in the mouth of the
Seine. So imperfect in those times was the art of navigation,
that orators have celebrated the daring courage of the Romans,
who ventured to set sail with a side-wind, and on a stormy day.
The weather proved favourable to their enterprise. Under the
cover of a thick fog they escaped the fleet of Allectus, which had
been stationed off the Isle of Wight to receive them, landed in
safety on some part of the western coast, and convinced the
Britons that a superiority of naval strength will not always
protect their country from a foreign invasion. Asclepiodotus
had no sooner disembarked the imperial troops than he set fire
to his ships; and, as the expedition proved fortunate, his heroic
conduct was universally admired. The usurper had posted himself near London, to expect the formidable attack of Constantius,
who commanded in person the fleet of Boulogne; but the descent
of a new enemy required his immediate presence in the West.
He performed this long march in so precipitate a manner that
he encountered the whole force of the præfect with a small body
of harassed and disheartened troops. The engagement was soon
terminated by the total defeat and death of Allectus; a single
battle, as it has often happened, decided the fate of this great
island; and when Constantius landed on the shores of Kent, he
found them covered with obedient subjects. Their acclamations were loud and unanimous; and the virtues of the conqueror
may induce us to believe that they sincerely rejoiced in a revolu-

tion which, after a separation of ten years, restored Britain to the body of the Roman empire.[1]

Britain had none but domestic enemies to dread; and as long as the governors preserved their fidelity, and the troops their discipline, the incursions of the naked savages of Scotland or Ireland could never materially affect the safety of the province. The peace of the continent, and the defence of the principal rivers which bounded the empire, were objects of far greater difficulty and importance. The policy of Diocletian, which inspired the councils of his associates, provided for the public tranquillity, by encouraging a spirit of dissension among the barbarians, and by strengthening the fortifications of the Roman limit. In the East he fixed a line of camps from Egypt to the Persian dominions, and, for every camp, he instituted an adequate number of stationary troops, commanded by their respective officers, and supplied with every kind of arms, from the new arsenals which he had formed at Antioch, Emesa, and Damascus.[2] Nor was the precaution of the emperor less watchful against the well-known valour of the barbarians of Europe. From the mouth of the Rhine to that of the Danube, the ancient camps, towns, and citadel were diligently re-established, and, in the most exposed places, new ones were skilfully constructed; the strictest vigilance was introduced among the garrisons of the frontier, and every expedient was practised that could render the long chain of fortifications firm and impenetrable.[3] A barrier so respectable was seldom violated, and the barbarians often turned against each other their disappointed rage. The Goths, the Vandals, the Gepidæ, the Burgundians, the Alemanni, wasted each other's strength by destructive hostilities: and whosoever vanquished, they vanquished the enemies of Rome. The subjects of Diocletian enjoyed the bloody spectacle, and congratulated each other that the mischiefs of civil war were now experienced only by the barbarians.[4]

[1] With regard to the recovery of Britain, we obtain a few hints from Aurelius Victor and Eutropius.

[2] John Malala, in Chron. Antiochen. tom. i. p. 408, 409 [ed. Oxon.; p. 132, ed. Ven.; p. 308, ed. Bonn].

[3] Zosim. l. i. p. 3 [l. ii. c. 34]. That partial historian seems to celebrate the vigilance of Diocletian, with a design of exposing the negligence of Constantine; we may, however, listen to an orator: " Nam quid ego alarum et cohortium castra percenseam, toto Rheni et Istri et Euphratis limite restituta." Panegyr. Vet. iv. 18.

[4] Ruunt omnes in sanguinem suum populi, quibus non contigit esse Romanis, obstinatæque feritatis pœnas nunc sponte persolvunt. Panegyr. Vet. iii. 16. Mamertinus illustrates the fact by the example of almost all the nations of the world.

Notwithstanding the policy of Diocletian, it was impossible to maintain an equal and undisturbed tranquillity during a reign of twenty years, and along a frontier of many hundred miles. Sometimes the barbarians suspended their domestic animosities, and the relaxed vigilance of the garrisons sometimes gave a passage to their strength or dexterity. Whenever the provinces were invaded, Diocletian conducted himself with that calm dignity which he always affected or possessed; reserved his presence for such occasions as were worthy of his interposition, never exposed his person or reputation to any unnecessary danger, ensured his success by every means that prudence could suggest, and displayed, with ostentation, the consequences of his victory. In wars of a more difficult nature, and more doubtful event, he employed the rough valour of Maximian; and that faithful soldier was content to ascribe his own victories to the wise counsels and auspicious influence of his benefactor. But after the adoption of the two Cæsars, the emperors, themselves retiring to a less laborious scene of action, devolved on their adopted sons the defence of the Danube and of the Rhine. The vigilant Galerius was never reduced to the necessity of vanquishing an army of barbarians on the Roman territory.[1] The brave and active Constantius delivered Gaul from a very furious inroad of the Alemanni; and his victories of Langres and Vindonissa appear to have been actions of considerable danger and merit. As he traversed the open country with a feeble guard, he was encompassed on a sudden by the superior multitude of the enemy. He retreated with difficulty towards Langres; but, in the general consternation, the citizens refused to open their gates, and the wounded prince was drawn up the wall by the means of a rope. But, on the news of his distress, the Roman troops hastened from all sides to his relief, and before the evening he had satisfied his honour and revenge by the slaughter of six thousand Alemanni.[2] From the monuments of those times the obscure traces of several other victories over the barbarians of Sarmatia and Germany might possibly be collected; but the tedious search would not be rewarded either with amusement or with instruction.

The conduct which the emperor Probus had adopted in the

[1] He complained, though not with the strictest truth, " Jam fluxisse annos quindecim in quibus, in Illyrico, ad ripam Danubii relegatus cum gentibus barbaris luctaret." Lactant. de M. P. c. 18.
[2] In the Greek text of Eusebius we read six thousand, a number which I have preferred to the sixty thousand of Jerome, Orosius, Eutropius, and his Greek translator Pæanius.

disposal of the vanquished was imitated by Diocletian and his associates. The captive barbarians, exchanging death for slavery, were distributed among the provincials, and assigned to those districts (in Gaul, the territories of Amiens, Beauvais, Cambray, Treves, Langres, and Troyes, are particularly specified) [1] which had been depopulated by the calamities of war. They were usefully employed as shepherds and husbandmen, but were denied the exercise of arms, except when it was found expedient to enrol them in the military service. Nor did the emperors refuse the property of lands, with a less servile tenure, to such of the barbarians as solicited the protection of Rome. They granted a settlement to several colonies of the Carpi, the Bastarnæ, and the Sarmatians; and, by a dangerous indulgence, permitted them in some measure to retain their national manners and independence.[2] Among the provincials it was a subject of flattering exultation that the barbarian, so lately an object of terror, now cultivated their lands, drove their cattle to the neighbouring fair, and contributed by his labour to the public plenty. They congratulated their masters on the powerful accession of subjects and soldiers; but they forgot to observe that multitudes of secret enemies, insolent from favour, or desperate from oppression, were introduced into the heart of the empire.[3]

While the Cæsars exercised their valour on the banks of the Rhine and Danube, the presence of the emperors was required on the southern confines of the Roman world. From the Nile to Mount Atlas Africa was in arms. A confederacy of five Moorish nations issued from their deserts to invade the peaceful provinces.[4] Julian had assumed the purple at Carthage.[5] Achilleus at Alexandria, and even the Blemmyes, renewed, or rather continued, their incursions into the Upper Egypt.

---

[1] Panegyr. Vet. vii. 21.

[2] There was a settlement of the Sarmatians in the neighbourhood of Treves, which seems to have been deserted by those lazy barbarians; Ausonius speaks of them in his Mosella [v. 5, sqq.]:—

> Unde iter ingrediens nemorosa per avia solum,
> Et nulla humani spectans vestigia cultus;
> .   .   .   .
> Arvaque Sauromatum nuper metata colonis;

There was a town of the Carpi in the Lower Mæsia.

[3] See the rhetorical exultation of Eumenius. Panegyr. vii. 9.

[4] Scaliger (Animadvers. ad Euseb. p. 243) decides, in his usual manner, that the Quinquegentiani, or five African nations, were the five great cities, the Pentapolis of the inoffensive province of Cyrene.

[5] After his defeat Julian stabbed himself with a dagger, and immediately leaped into the flames. Victor in Epitome [c. 39].

Scarcely any circumstances have been preserved of the exploits of Maximian in the western parts of Africa; but it appears, by the event, that the progress of his arms was rapid and decisive, that he vanquished the fiercest barbarians of Mauritania, and that he removed them from the mountains, whose inaccessible strength had inspired their inhabitants with a lawless confidence, and habituated them to a life of rapine and violence.[1] Diocletian, of his side, opened the campaign in Egypt by the siege of Alexandria, cut off the aqueducts which conveyed the waters of the Nile into every quarter of that immense city,[2] and, rendering his camp impregnable to the sallies of the besieged multitude, he pushed his reiterated attacks with caution and vigour. After a siege of eight months, Alexandria, wasted by the sword and by fire, implored the clemency of the conqueror, but it experienced the full extent of his severity. Many thousands of the citizens perished in a promiscuous slaughter, and there were few obnoxious persons in Egypt who escaped a sentence either of death or at least of exile.[3] The fate of Busiris and of Coptos was still more melancholy than that of Alexandria; those proud cities, the former distinguished by its antiquity, the latter enriched by the passage of the Indian trade, were utterly destroyed by the arms and by the severe order of Diocletian.[4] The character of the Egyptian nation, insensible to kindness, but extremely susceptible of fear, could alone justify this excessive rigour. The seditions of Alexandria had often affected the tranquillity and subsistence of Rome itself. Since the usurpation of Firmus, the province of Upper Egypt, incessantly relapsing into rebellion, had embraced the alliance of the savages of Æthiopia. The number of the Blemmyes, scattered between the island of Meroe and the Red Sea, was very inconsiderable, their disposition was unwarlike, their weapons rude and inoffensive.[5] Yet in the public disorders these barbarians, whom antiquity, shocked with the deformity of their figure, had almost

---

[1] Tu ferocissimos Mauritaniæ populos inaccessis montium jugis et naturali munitione fidentes, expugnasti, recepisti, transtulisti. Panegyr. Vet. vi. 8.

[2] See the description of Alexandria in Hirtius de Bell. Alexandrin, c. 5.

[3] Eutrop. ix. 24 [15]. Orosius, vii. 25. John Malala in Chron. Antioch. p. 409, 410 [ed. Oxon.; p. 132, ed. Ven.; p. 309, ed. Bonn]. Yet Eumenius assures us that Egypt was pacified by the clemency of Diocletian.

[4] Eusebius (in Chron. [An. CCXCIII.]) places their destruction several years sooner, and at a time when Egypt itself was in a state of rebellion against the Romans.

[5] Strabo, l. xvii. p. 819. Pomponius Mela, l. i. c. 4. His words are curious: " Intra, si credere libet, vix homines magisque semiferi; Ægipanes, et Blemmyes, et " Satyri."

excluded from the human species, presumed to rank themselves among the enemies of Rome.[1] Such had been the unworthy allies of the Egyptians; and while the attention of the state was engaged in more serious wars, their vexatious inroads might again harass the repose of the province. With a view of opposing to the Blemmyes a suitable adversary, Diocletian persuaded the Nobatæ, or people of Nubia, to remove from their ancient habitations in the deserts of Libya, and resigned to them an extensive but unprofitable territory above Syene and the cataracts of the Nile, with the stipulation that they should ever respect and guard the frontier of the empire. The treaty long subsisted; and till the establishment of Christianity introduced stricter notions of religious worship, it was annually ratified by a solemn sacrifice in the isle of Elephantine, in which the Romans, as well as the barbarians, adored the same visible or invisible powers of the universe.[2]

At the same time that Diocletian chastised the past crimes of the Egyptians, he provided for their future safety and happiness by many wise regulations, which were confirmed and enforced under the succeeding reigns.[3] One very remarkable edict which he published, instead of being condemned as the effect of jealous tyranny, deserves to be applauded as an act of prudence and humanity. He caused a diligent inquiry to be made " for all the ancient books which treated of the admirable art of making gold and silver, and without pity committed them to the flames; apprehensive, as we are assured, lest the opulence of the Egyptians should inspire them with confidence to rebel against the empire." [4] But if Diocletian had been convinced of the reality of that valuable art, far from extinguishing the memory, he would have converted the operation of it to the benefit of the public revenue. It is much more likely that his good sense discovered to him the folly of such magnificent pretensions, and that he was desirous of preserving the reason and fortunes of his subjects from the mischievous pursuit. It may be remarked that these ancient books, so liberally ascribed to Pythagoras, to Solomon, or to Hermes, were the pious frauds of more recent

[1] Ausus sese inserere fortunæ et provocare arma Romana.
[2] See Procopius de Bell. Persic. l. i. c. 19.
[In the island of Philæ (Elephantina) the rites of Paganism continued to be practised down to the sixth century, when the edict of Theodosius was promulgated.—O. S.]
[3] He fixed the public allowance of corn for the people of Alexandria at two millions of *medimni*; about four hundred thousand quarters. Chron. Paschal. p. 276. Procop. Hist. Arcan. c. 26.
[4] John Antioch. in Excerp. Valesian. p. 834. Suidas in Diocletian.

adepts. The Greeks were inattentive either to the use or to the abuse of chemistry. In that immense register, where Pliny has deposited the discoveries, the arts, and the errors of mankind, there is not the least mention of the transmutation of metals; and the persecution of Diocletian is the first authentic event in the history of alchymy. The conquest of Egypt by the Arabs diffused that vain science over the globe. Congenial to the avarice of the human heart, it was studied in China as in Europe, with equal eagerness and with equal success. The darkness of the middle ages ensured a favourable reception to every tale of wonder, and the revival of learning gave new vigour to hope, and suggested more specious arts of deception. Philosophy, with the aid of experience, has at length banished the study of alchymy; and the present age, however desirous of riches, is content to seek them by the humbler means of commerce and industry.[1]

The reduction of Egypt was immediately followed by the Persian war. It was reserved for the reign of Diocletian to vanquish that powerful nation, and to extort a confession from the successors of Artaxerxes of the superior majesty of the Roman empire.

We have observed, under the reign of Valerian, that Armenia was subdued by the perfidy and the arms of the Persians, and that, after the assassination of Chosroes, his son Tiridates, the infant heir of the monarchy, was saved by the fidelity of his friends, and educated under the protection of the emperors. Tiridates derived from his exile such advantages as he could never have obtained on the throne of Armenia; the early knowledge of adversity, of mankind, and of the Roman discipline. He signalised his youth by deeds of valour, and displayed a matchless dexterity, as well as strength, in every martial exercise, and even in the less honourable contests of the Olympian games.[2] Those qualities were more nobly exerted in the defence of his benefactor Licinius.[3] That officer, in the sedition which

---

[1] See a short history and confutation of Alchymy, in the works of that philosophical compiler, La Mothe le Vayer, tom. i. p. 327-353.

[2] See the education and strength of Tiridates in the Armenian history of Moses of Chorene, l. ii. c. 76. He could seize two wild bulls by the horns and break them off with his hands.

[3] If we give credit to the younger Victor [Epit. 41], who supposes that in the year 323 Licinius was only sixty years of age, he could scarcely be the same person as the patron of Tiridates; but we know from much better authority (Euseb. Hist. Ecclesiast. l. x. c. 8) that Licinius was at that time in the last period of old age: sixteen years before, he is represented with grey hairs and as the contemporary of Galerius. See Lactant. c. 32. Licinius was probably born about the year 250.

occasioned the death of Probus, was exposed to the most
imminent danger, and the enraged soldiers were forcing their
way into his tent when they were checked by the single arm
of the Armenian prince. The gratitude of Tiridates contributed
soon afterwards to his restoration. Licinius was in every
station the friend and companion of Galerius, and the merit of
Galerius, long before he was raised to the dignity of Cæsar, had
been known and esteemed by Diocletian. In the third year of
that emperor's reign, Tiridates was invested with the kingdom of
Armenia. The justice of the measure was not less evident than
its expediency. It was time to rescue from the usurpation of the
Persian monarch an important territory, which, since the reign of
Nero, had been always granted under the protection of the
empire to a younger branch of the house of Arsaces.[1]

When Tiridates appeared on the frontiers of Armenia, he was
received with an unfeigned transport of joy and loyalty. During
twenty-six years the country had experienced the real and
imaginary hardships of a foreign yoke. The Persian monarchs
adorned their new conquest with magnificent buildings; but
those monuments had been erected at the expense of the people,
and were abhorred as badges of slavery. The apprehension of
a revolt had inspired the most rigorous precautions: oppression
had been aggravated by insult, and the consciousness of the
public hatred had been productive of every measure that could
render it still more implacable. We have already remarked
the intolerant spirit of the Magian religion. The statues of the
deified kings of Armenia, and the sacred images of the sun and
moon, were broke in pieces by the zeal of the conqueror; and
the perpetual fire of Ormuzd was kindled and preserved upon an
altar erected on the summit of Mount Bagavan.[2] It was natural
that a people exasperated by so many injuries should arm with
zeal in the cause of their independence, their religion, and their
hereditary sovereign. The torrent bore down every obstacle,
and the Persian garrisons retreated before its fury. The nobles
of Armenia flew to the standard of Tiridates, all alleging their
past merit, offering their future service, and soliciting from the
new king those honours and rewards from which they had been
excluded with disdain under the foreign government.[3] The

---

[1] See the sixty-second and sixty-third books of Dion Cassius [l. lxiii. c. 5].
[2] Moses of Chorene, Hist. Armen. l. ii. c. 74. The statues had been
erected by Valarsaces, who reigned in Armenia about 130 years before
Christ, and was the first king of the family of Arsaces (see Moses, Hist.
Armen. l. ii. 2, 3). The deification of the Arsacides is mentioned by Justin
(xli. 5) and by Ammianus Marcellinus (xxiii. 6).
[3] The Armenian nobility was numerous and powerful. Moses mentions

command of the army was bestowed on Artavasdes, whose father
had saved the infancy of Tiridates, and whose family had been
massacred for that generous action. The brother of Artavasdes
obtained the government of a province. One of the first military dignities was conferred on the satrap Otas, a man of singular
temperance and fortitude, who presented to the king his sister [1]
and a considerable treasure, both of which, in a sequestered
fortress, Otas had preserved from violation. Among the Armenian nobles appeared an ally whose fortunes are too remarkable to pass unnoticed. His name was Mamgo, his origin was
Scythian, and the horde which acknowledged his authority had
encamped a very few years before on the skirts of the Chinese
empire,[2] which at that time extended as far as the neighbourhood of Sogdiana.[3] Having incurred the displeasure of his
master, Mamgo, with his followers, retired to the banks of the
Oxus, and implored the protection of Sapor. The emperor of
China claimed the fugitive, and alleged the rights of sovereignty.
The Persian monarch pleaded the laws of hospitality, and with
some difficulty avoided a war by the promise that he would
banish Mamgo to the uttermost parts of the West, a punishment,
as he described it, not less dreadful than death itself. Armenia

many families which were distinguished under the reign of Valarsaces (l. ii.
7), and which still subsisted in his own time, about the middle of the fifth
century. See the preface of his editors.
  [1] She was named Chosroiduchta, and had not the *os patulum* like other
women. (Hist. Armen. l. ii. c. 79.) I do not understand the expression.
  [2] In the Armenian History (l. ii. 78), as well as in the Geography (p. 367),
China is called Zenia, or Zenastan. It is characterised by the production
of silk, by the opulence of the natives, and by their love of peace, above all
the other nations of the earth.
  [Mamgo belonged to the Imperial race of Han, which had filled the throne
of China for 400 years. Dethroned by the usurping race of Wei, Mamgo
found a hospitable reception in Persia in the reign of Ardeschir. The
emperor of China having demanded the surrender of the fugitive and his
partisans. Sapor, then king, threatened with war both by Rome and China,
counselled Mamgo to retire into Armenia. To the Chinese ambassador
he said: " I have expelled him from my dominions, I have banished him
to the extremity of the earth, where the sun sets. I have dismissed
him to certain death."—O. S.]
  [3] Vou-ti, the first emperor of the seventh dynasty, who then reigned in
China, had political transactions with Fergana, a province of Sogdiana,
and is said to have received a Roman embassy (Histoire des Huns, tom. i.
p. 38). In those ages the Chinese kept a garrison at Kashgar, and one of their
generals, about the time of Trajan, marched as far as the Caspian Sea.
With regard to the intercourse between China and the western countries, a
curious memoir of M. de Guignes may be consulted, in the Académie des
Inscriptions, tom. xxii. p. 355.
  [The Chinese annals mention, under the ninth year of Yan-hi (A.D. 166),
an embassy which arrived from Ta-thsin, being sent by a prince named
An-thun, who can be no other than Marcus Aurelius Antoninus, who then
ruled in Rome. The embassy came by Jynan or Tonquin.—O. S.]

was chosen for the place of exile, and a large district was assigned
to the Scythian horde, on which they might feed their flocks and
herds, and remove their encampment from one place to another,
according to the different seasons of the year. They were employed to repel the invasion of Tiridates; but their leader, after
weighing the obligations and injuries which he had received from
the Persian monarch, resolved to abandon his party. The Armenian prince, who was well acquainted with the merit as well
as power of Mamgo, treated him with distinguished respect;
and, by admitting him into his confidence, acquired a brave
and faithful servant, who contributed very effectually to his
restoration.[1]

For a while fortune appeared to favour the enterprising valour
of Tiridates. He not only expelled the enemies of his family
and country from the whole extent of Armenia, but in the prosecution of his revenge he carried his arms, or at least his incursions,
into the heart of Assyria. The historian who has preserved the
name of Tiridates from oblivion, celebrates, with a degree of
national enthusiasm, his personal prowess; and, in the true
spirit of eastern romance, describes the giants and the elephants
that fell beneath his invincible arm. It is from other information that we discover the distracted state of the Persian
monarchy, to which the king of Armenia was indebted for some
part of his advantages. The throne was disputed by the
ambition of contending brothers; and Hormuz, after exerting
without success the strength of his own party, had recourse to
the dangerous assistance of the barbarians who inhabited the
banks of the Caspian Sea.[2] The civil war was, however, soon
terminated, either by a victory or by a reconciliation; and
Narses, who was universally acknowledged as king of Persia,
directed his whole force against the foreign enemy. The contest
then became too unequal: nor was the valour of the hero able to
withstand the power of the monarch. Tiridates, a second time
expelled from the throne of Armenia, once more took refuge
in the court of the emperors. Narses soon re-established his
authority over the revolted province; and, loudly complaining

---

[1] See Hist. Armen. l. ii. c. 81.
[2] Ipsos Persas ipsumque Regem ascitis Sacis, et Rufiis, et Gellis, petit
frater Ormies. Panegyric. Vet. iii. [ii.] 17. The Sacæ were a nation of
wandering Scythians, who encamped towards the sources of the Oxus and
the Jaxartes. The Gelli were the inhabitants of Ghilan, along the Caspian
Sea, and who so long, under the name of Dilemites, infested the Persian
monarchy. See D'Herbelot, Bibliothèque Orientale.

of the protection afforded by the Romans to rebels and fugitives, aspired to the conquest of the East.[1]

Neither prudence nor honour could permit the emperors to forsake the cause of the Armenian king, and it was resolved to exert the force of the empire in the Persian war. Diocletian, with the calm dignity which he constantly assumed, fixed his own station in the city of Antioch, from whence he prepared and directed the military operations.[2] The conduct of the legions was intrusted to the intrepid valour of Galerius, who, for that important purpose, was removed from the banks of the Danube to those of the Euphrates. The armies soon encountered each other in the plains of Mesopotamia, and two battles were fought with various and doubtful success: but the third engagement was of a more decisive nature; and the Roman army received a total overthrow, which is attributed to the rashness of Galerius, who, with an inconsiderable body of troops, attacked the innumerable host of the Persians.[3] But the consideration of the country that was the scene of action may suggest another reason for his defeat. The same ground on which Galerius was vanquished had been rendered memorable by the death of Crassus and the slaughter of ten legions. It was a plain of more than sixty miles, which extended from the hills of Carrhæ to the Euphrates; a smooth and barren surface of sandy desert, without a hillock, without a tree, and without a spring of fresh water.[4] The steady infantry of the Romans, fainting with heat and thirst, could neither hope for victory if they preserved their ranks, nor break their ranks without exposing themselves to the most imminent danger. In this situation they were gradually encompassed by the superior numbers, harassed by the rapid evolutions and destroyed by the arrows of the barbarian cavalry. The king of Armenia had signalised his valour in the battle, and acquired personal glory by the public misfortune. He was pursued as far as the Euphrates; his horse was wounded, and it

[1] Moses of Chorene takes no notice of this second revolution, which I have been obliged to collect from a passage of Ammianus Marcellinus (l. xxiii. c. 5). Lactantius speaks of the ambition of Narses: "Concitatus domesticis exemplis avi sui Saporis ad occupandum orientem magnis copiis inhiabat." De Mort. Persecut. c. 9.

[2] We may readily believe that Lactantius ascribes to cowardice the conduct of Diocletian. Julian, in his oration, says that he remained with all the forces of the empire; a very hyperbolical expression.

[3] Our five abbreviators, Eutropius, Festus, the two Victors, and Orosius, all relate the last and great battle; but Orosius is the only one who speaks of the two former.

[4] The nature of the country is finely described by Plutarch, in the Life of Crassus; and by Xenophon, in the first book of the Anabasis.

appeared impossible for him to escape the victorious enemy. In this extremity Tiridates embraced the only refuge which he saw before him: he dismounted and plunged into the stream. His armour was heavy, the river very deep, and at those parts at least half a mile in breadth;[1] yet such was his strength and dexterity, that he reached in safety the opposite bank.[2] With regard to the Roman general, we are ignorant of the circumstances of his escape; but when he returned to Antioch, Diocletian received him, not with the tenderness of a friend and colleague, but with the indignation of an offended sovereign. The haughtiest of men, clothed in his purple, but humbled by the sense of his fault and misfortune, was obliged to follow the emperor's chariot above a mile on foot, and to exhibit, before the whole court, the spectacle of his disgrace.[3]

As soon as Diocletian had indulged his private resentment, and asserted the majesty of supreme power, he yielded to the submissive entreaties of the Cæsar, and permitted him to retrieve his own honour, as well as that of the Roman arms. In the room of the unwarlike troops of Asia, which had most probably served in the first expedition, a second army was drawn from the veterans and new levies of the Illyrian frontier, and a considerable body of Gothic auxiliaries were taken into the Imperial pay.[4] At the head of a chosen army of twenty-five thousand men Galerius again passed the Euphrates; but, instead of exposing his legions in the open plains of Mesopotamia, he advanced through the mountains of Armenia, where he found the inhabitants devoted to his cause, and the country as favourable to the operations of infantry as it was inconvenient for the motions of cavalry.[5] Adversity had confirmed the Roman discipline, while the barbarians, elated by success, were become so negligent and remiss that, in the moment when they least expected it, they were surprised by the active conduct of Galerius, who, attended only by two horsemen, had with his own eyes secretly examined the state and position of their camp. A sur-

---

[1] See Foster's Dissertation in the second volume of the translation of the Anabasis by Spelman; which I will venture to recommend as one of the best versions extant.

[2] Hist. Armen. l. ii. c. 76. I have transferred this exploit of Tiridates from an imaginary defeat to the real one of Galerius.

[3] Ammian. Marcellin. l. xiv. [c. 11.] The mile, in the hands of Eutropius (ix. 24 [15]), of Festus (c. 25), and of Orosius (vii. 25), easily increased to *several* miles.

[4] Aurelius Victor. Jornandes de Rebus Geticis, c. 21.

[5] Aurelius Victor [de Cæsar. c. 39] says, " Per Armeniam in hostes contendit, quæ ferme sola, seu facilior vincendi via est." He followed the conduct of Trajan and the idea of Julius Cæsar.

prise, especially in the night-time, was for the most part fatal to a Persian army. "Their horses were tied, and generally shackled, to prevent their running away; and if an alarm happened, a Persian had his housing to fix, his horse to bridle, and his corselet to put on, before he could mount." [1] On this occasion the impetuous attack of Galerius spread disorder and dismay over the camp of the barbarians. A slight resistance was followed by a dreadful carnage, and in the general confusion the wounded monarch (for Narses commanded his armies in person) fled towards the deserts of Media. His sumptuous tents, and those of his satraps, afforded an immense booty to the conqueror; and an incident is mentioned which proves the rustic but martial ignorance of the legions in the elegant superfluities of life. A bag of shining leather, filled with pearls, fell into the hands of a private soldier; he carefully preserved the bag, but he threw away its contents, judging that whatever was of no use could not possibly be of any value. [2] The principal loss of Narses was of a much more affecting nature. Several of his wives, his sisters, and children, who had attended the army, were made captives in the defeat. But though the character of Galerius had in general very little affinity with that of Alexander, he imitated, after his victory, the amiable behaviour of the Macedonian towards the family of Darius. The wives and children of Narses were protected from violence and rapine, conveyed to a place of safety, and treated with every mark of respect and tenderness that was due from a generous enemy to their age, their sex, and their royal dignity. [3]

While the East anxiously expected the decision of this great contest, the emperor Diocletian, having assembled in Syria a strong army of observation, displayed from a distance the resources of the Roman power, and reserved himself for any future emergency of the war. On the intelligence of the victory he condescended to advance towards the frontier, with a view of moderating, by his presence and counsels, the pride of Galerius. The interview of the Roman princes at Nisibis was accompanied with every expression of respect on one side, and of esteem on the other. It was in that city that they soon afterwards gave

---

[1] Xenophon's Anabasis, l. iii. [c. 4, § 35.] For that reason the Persian cavalry encamped sixty stadia from the enemy.

[2] The story is told by Ammianus, l. xxii. Instead of *saccum* some read *scutum*.

[3] The Persians confessed the Roman superiority in morals as well as in arms. Eutrop. ix. 24. But this respect and gratitude of enemies is very seldom to be found in their own accounts.

audience to the ambassador of the Great King.[1] The power, or at least the spirit, of Narses had been broken by his last defeat; and he considered an immediate peace as the only means that could stop the progress of the Roman arms. He despatched Apharban, a servant who possessed his favour and confidence, with a commission to negotiate a treaty, or rather to receive whatever conditions the conqueror should impose. Apharban opened the conference by expressing his master's gratitude for the generous treatment of his family, and by soliciting the liberty of those illustrious captives. He celebrated the valour of Galerius, without degrading the reputation of Narses, and thought it no dishonour to confess the superiority of the victorious Cæsar over a monarch who had surpassed in glory all the princes of his race. Notwithstanding the justice of the Persian cause, he was empowered to submit the present differences to the decision of the emperors themselves; convinced as he was that, in the midst of prosperity, they would not be unmindful of the vicissitudes of fortune. Apharban concluded his discourse in the style of Eastern allegory, by observing that the Roman and Persian monarchies were the two eyes of the world, which would remain imperfect and mutilated if either of them should be put out.

" It well becomes the Persians," replied Galerius, with a transport of fury which seemed to convulse his whole frame, " it well becomes the Persians to expatiate on the vicissitudes of fortune, and calmly to read us lectures on the virtues of moderation. Let them remember their own *moderation* towards the unhappy Valerian. They vanquished him by fraud, they treated him with indignity. They detained him till the last moment of his life in shameful captivity, and after his death they exposed his body to perpetual ignominy." Softening, however, his tone, Galerius insinuated to the ambassador that it had never been the practice of the Romans to trample on a prostrate enemy; and that, on this occasion, they should consult their own dignity rather than the Persian merit. He dismissed Apharban with a hope that Narses would soon be informed on what conditions he might obtain, from the clemency of the emperors, a lasting peace and the restoration of his wives and children. In this conference we may discover the fierce passions

---

[1] The account of the negotiation is taken from the fragments of Peter the Patrician, in the Excerpta Legationum published in the Byzantine Collection. Peter lived under Justinian; but it is very evident, by the nature of his materials, that they are drawn from the most authentic and respectable writers.

of Galerius, as well as his deference to the superior wisdom and
authority of Diocletian. The ambition of the former grasped
at the conquest of the East, and had proposed to reduce Persia
into the state of a province. The prudence of the latter, who
adhered to the moderate policy of Augustus and the Antonines,
embraced the favourable opportunity of terminating a successful war by an honourable and advantageous peace.[1]

In pursuance of their promise, the emperors soon afterwards
appointed Sicorius Probus, one of their secretaries, to acquaint
the Persian court with their final resolution. As the minister
of peace, he was received with every mark of politeness and
friendship; but, under the pretence of allowing him the necessary
repose after so long a journey, the audience of Probus was deferred from day to day, and he attended the slow motions of the
king, till at length he was admitted to his presence, near the
river Asprudus, in Media. The secret motive of Narses in this
delay had been to collect such a military force as might enable
him, though sincerely desirous of peace, to negotiate with the
greater weight and dignity. Three persons only assisted at this
important conference, the minister Apharban, the præfect of the
guards, and an officer who had commanded on the Armenian
frontier.[2] The first condition proposed by the ambassador is not
at present of a very intelligible nature; that the city of Nisibis
might be established for the place of mutual exchange, or, as we
should formerly have termed it, for the staple of trade, between
the two empires. There is no difficulty in conceiving the intention of the Roman princes to improve their revenue by some
restraints upon commerce; but as Nisibis was situated within
their own dominions, and as they were masters both of the
imports and exports, it should seem that such restraints were the
objects of an internal law, rather than of a foreign treaty. To
render them more effectual, some stipulations were probably
required on the side of the king of Persia, which appeared so
very repugnant either to his interest or to his dignity that Narses
could not be persuaded to subscribe them. As this was the only
article to which he refused his consent, it was no longer insisted
on; and the emperors either suffered the trade to flow in its

---

[1] Adeo victor (says Aurelius [de Cæsar. c. 39]) ut ni Valerius, cujus nutu
omnia gerebantur, abnuisset, Romani fasces in provinciam novam ferrentur.
Verum pars terrárum tamen nobis utilior quæsita.

[2] He had been governor of Sumium (Pet. Patricius in Excerpt. Legat.
p. 30) [ed. Paris; p. 21, ed. Ven.; p. 135, ed. Bonn]. This province seems
to be mentioned by Moses of Chorene (Geograph. p. 360), and lay to the
east of Mount Ararat.

natural channels, or contented themselves with such restrictions as it depended on their own authority to establish.

As soon as this difficulty was removed, a solemn peace was concluded and ratified between the two nations. The conditions of a treaty so glorious to the empire, and so necessary to Persia, may deserve a more peculiar attention, as the history of Rome presents very few transactions of a similar nature; most of her wars having either been terminated by absolute conquest, or waged against barbarians ignorant of the use of letters. I. The Aboras, or, as it is called by Xenophon, the Araxes, was fixed as the boundary between the two monarchies.[1] That river, which rose near the Tigris, was increased, a few miles below Nisibis, by the little stream of the Mygdonius, passed under the walls of Singara, and fell into the Euphrates at Circesium, a frontier town which, by the care of Diocletian, was very strongly fortified.[2] Mesopotamia, the object of so many wars, was ceded to the empire; and the Persians, by this treaty, renounced all pretensions to that great province. II. They relinquished to the Romans five provinces beyond the Tigris.[3] Their situation

[1] By an error of the geographer Ptolemy, the position of Singara is removed from the Aboras to the Tigris, which may have produced the mistake of Peter in assigning the latter river for the boundary instead of the former. The line of the Roman frontier traversed, but never followed, the course of the Tigris.

[Dr. William Smith indicates several errors in this note. The course of the Aboras or Aborrhas, the Araxes of Xenophon (Anab. i. 4, 19), more usually called Chaboras, the Habor or Chebar of the Samaritan captivity, and the modern Khabar was traced by Layard, and was found to rise not near the Tigris, but far to the West, in the direction of Harran, at a place called Ras-al-Ain (the head of the spring). Thence it flows in a general south-easterly direction to the hill Koukab, where it receives the Mydonius, now called the Jerujer, upon which Nisibis was situated, and which rises near the Tigris. After its union with the Mygdonius, the Chaboras flows in a southerly direction and falls into the Euphrates at Circesium.—O. S.]

[2] Procopius de Ædificiis, l. ii. c. 6.

[3] Three of the provinces, Zabdicene, Arzanene, and Carduene, are allowed on all sides. But instead of the other two, Peter (in Excerpt. Leg. p. 30) inserts Rehimene and Sophene. I have preferred Ammianus (l. xxv. 7), because it might be proved that Sophene was never in the hands of the Persians, either before the reign of Diocletian or after that of Jovian. For want of correct maps, like those of M. d'Anville, almost all the moderns, with Tillemont and Valesius at their head, have imagined that it was in respect to Persia, and not to Rome, that the five provinces were situate beyond the Tigris.

[On this point where Gibbon is notoriously in error, Milman says these provinces do not appear to have ever been an integral part of the Roman empire. Roman garrisons replaced those of Persia, but the sovereignty remained in the hands of the feudatory princes of Armenia. Prof. Bury adds *in loc :* " Intilene and Moxoene are the same. Peter gives Intelene and Sophene, Ammianus Moxoene and Rehimene. Thus the question is between Rehimene and Sophene.—O. S.]

formed a very useful barrier, and their natural strength was soon improved by art and military skill. Four of these, to the north of the river, were districts of obscure fame and inconsiderable extent—Intiline, Zabdicene, Arzanene, and Moxoene; but on the east of the Tigris the empire acquired the large and mountainous territory of Carduene, the ancient seat of the Carduchians, who preserved for many ages their manly freedom in the heart of the despotic monarchies of Asia. The ten thousand Greeks traversed their country after a painful march, or rather engagement, of seven days; and it is confessed by their leader, in his incomparable relation of the retreat, that they suffered more from the arrows of the Carduchians than from the power of the Great King.[1] Their posterity, the Curds, with very little alteration either of name or manners, acknowledged the nominal sovereignty of the Turkish sultan. III. It is almost needless to observe that Tiridates, the faithful ally of Rome, was restored to the throne of his fathers, and that the rights of the Imperial supremacy were fully asserted and secured. The limits of Armenia were extended as far as the fortress of Sintha in Media, and this increase of dominion was not so much an act of liberality as of justice. Of the provinces already mentioned beyond the Tigris, the four first had been dismembered by the Parthians from the crown of Armenia;[2] and when the Romans acquired the possession of them, they stipulated, at the expense of the usurpers, an ample compensation, which invested their ally with the extensive and fertile country of Atropatene. Its principal city, in the same situation perhaps as the modern Tauris, was frequently honoured with the residence of Tiridates; and as it sometimes bore the name of Ecbatana, he imitated, in the buildings and fortifications, the splendid capital of the Medes.[3] IV. The country of Iberia was barren, its inhabitants rude and savage. But they were accustomed to the use of arms, and they separated from the empire by barbarians much fiercer and more formidable than themselves. The narrow defiles of Mount Caucasus were in their hands, and it was in their choice either to admit or to exclude the wandering tribes of Sarmatia, whenever a rapacious spirit urged them to penetrate into the richer

[1] Xenophon's Anabasis, l. iv. [c. 3 init.] Their bows were three cubits in length, their arrows two; they rolled down stones that were each a waggon-load. The Greeks found a great many villages in that rude country.

[2] According to Eutropius (vi. 9, as the text is represented by the best MSS.), the city of Tigranocerta was in Arzanene. The names and situation of the other three may be faintly traced.

[3] Compare Herodotus, l. i. c. 98, with Moses Chorenens. Hist. Armen. l. ii. c. 84, and the map of Armenia given by his editors.

climates of the South.[1] The nomination of the kings of Iberia, which was resigned by the Persian monarch to the emperors, contributed to the strength and security of the Roman power in Asia.[2] The East enjoyed a profound tranquillity during forty years; and the treaty between the rival monarchies was strictly observed till the death of Tiridates; when a new generation, animated with different views and different passions, succeeded to the government of the world; and the grandson of Narses undertook a long and memorable war against the princes of the house of Constantine.

The arduous work of rescuing the distressed empire from tyrants and barbarians had now been completely achieved by a succession of Illyrian peasants. As soon as Diocletian entered into the twentieth year of his reign, he celebrated that memorable era, as well as the success of his arms, by the pomp of a Roman triumph.[3] Maximian, the equal partner of his power, was his only companion in the glory of that day. The two Cæsars had fought and conquered, but the merit of their exploits was ascribed, according to the rigour of ancient maxims, to the auspicious influence of their fathers and emperors.[4] The triumph of Diocletian and Maximian was less magnificent, perhaps, than those of Aurelian and Probus, but it was dignified by several circumstances of superior fame and good fortune. Africa and Britain, the Rhine, the Danube, and the Nile, furnished their respective trophies; but the most distinguished ornament was of a more singular nature, a Persian victory followed by an important conquest. The representations of rivers, mountains, and provinces were carried before the Imperial car. The images of the captive wives, the sisters, and the children of the Great King afforded a new and grateful spectacle to the vanity of the people.[5] In the

[1] Hiberi, locorum potentes, Caspiâ viâ Sarmatam in Armenios raptim effundunt. Tacit. Annal. vi. 33. See Strabon. Geograph. l. xi. p. 500.
[2] Peter Patricius (in Excerpt. Leg. p. 30 [ed. Paris; p. 21, ed. Ven.; p. 135, ed. Bonn]) is the only writer who mentions the Iberian article of the treaty.
[3] Euseb. in Chron. Pagi ad annum. Till the discovery of the treatise De Mortibus Persecutorum, it was not certain that the triumph and the Vicennalia were celebrated at the same time.
[Clinton, on the authority of Hieronymus and Prosper, places the triumph in A. D. 302, the year before the Vicennalia; though on the other hand, as Bury points out, Preuss agrees with Gibbon. Though the Vicennalia were celebrated Nov. 20, that day was not the anniversary of the accession of Diocletian, for he began to reign Sept. 17, A.D. 284.—O.S.]
[4] At the time of the Vicennalia, Galerius seems to have kept his station on the Danube. See Lactant. de M. P. c. 38.
[5] Eutropius (ix. 27 [16]) mentions them as a part of the triumph. As the *persons* had been restored to Narses, nothing more than their *images* could be exhibited.

eyes of posterity this triumph is remarkable by a distinction of a less honourable kind. It was the last that Rome ever beheld. Soon after this period the emperors ceased to vanquish, and Rome ceased to be the capital of the empire.

The spot on which Rome was founded had been consecrated by ancient ceremonies and imaginary miracles. The presence of some god, or the memory of some hero, seemed to animate every part of the city, and the empire of the world had been promised to the Capitol.[1] The native Romans felt and confessed the power of this agreeable illusion. It was derived from their ancestors, had grown up with their earliest habits of life, and was protected, in some measure, by the opinion of political utility. The form and the seat of government were intimately blended together, nor was it esteemed possible to transport the one without destroying the other.[2] But the sovereignty of the capital was gradually annihilated in the extent of conquest; the provinces rose to the same level, and the vanquished nations acquired the name and privileges, without imbibing the partial affections, of Romans. During a long period, however, the remains of the ancient constitution and the influence of custom preserved the dignity of Rome. The emperors, though perhaps of African or Illyrian extraction, respected their adopted country as the seat of their power and the centre of their extensive dominions. The emergencies of war very frequently required their presence on the frontiers; but Diocletian and Maximian were the first Roman princes who fixed, in time of peace, their ordinary residence in the provinces; and their conduct, however it might be suggested by private motives, was justified by very specious considerations of policy. The court of the emperor of the West was, for the most part, established at Milan, whose situation, at the foot of the Alps, appeared far more convenient than that of Rome, for the important purpose of watching the motions of the barbarians of Germany. Milan soon assumed the splendour of an Imperial city. The houses are described as numerous and well built; the manners of the people as polished and liberal. A circus, a theatre, a mint, a palace, baths, which bore the name of their founder Maximian; porticoes adorned

---

[1] Livy gives us a speech of Camillus on that subject (v. 51-54), full of eloquence and sensibility, in opposition to a design of removing the seat of government from Rome to the neighbouring city of Veii.

[2] Julius Cæsar was reproached with the intention of removing the empire to Ilium or Alexandria. See Sueton. in Cæsar. c. 79. According to the ingenious conjecture of Le Fèvre and Dacier, the third ode of the third book of Horace was intended to divert Augustus from the execution of a similar design.

with statues, and a double circumference of walls, contributed to the beauty of the new capital; nor did it seem oppressed even by the proximity of Rome.[1] To rival the majesty of Rome was the ambition likewise of Diocletian, who employed his leisure and the wealth of the East in the embellishment of Nicomedia, a city placed on the verge of Europe and Asia, almost at an equal distance between the Danube and the Euphrates. By the taste of the monarch, and at the expense of the people, Nicomedia acquired, in the space of a few years, a degree of magnificence which might appear to have required the labour of ages, and became inferior only to Rome, Alexandria, and Antioch in extent or populousness.[2] The life of Diocletian and Maximian was a life of action, and a considerable portion of it was spent in camps, or in their long and frequent marches; but whenever the public business allowed them any relaxation, they seem to have retired with pleasure to their favourite residences of Nicomedia and Milan. Till Diocletian, in the twentieth year of his reign, celebrated his Roman triumph, it is extremely doubtful whether he ever visited the ancient capital of the empire. Even on that memorable occasion his stay did not exceed two months. Disgusted with the licentious familiarity of the people, he quitted Rome with precipitation thirteen days before it was expected that he should have appeared in the senate invested with the ensigns of the consular dignity.[3]

The dislike expressed by Diocletian towards Rome and Roman freedom was not the effect of momentary caprice, but the result

---

[1] See Aurelius Victor [de Cæsar. c. 39], who likewise mentions the buildings erected by Maximian at Carthage, probably during the Moorish war. We shall insert some verses of Ausonius de Clar. Urb. v.:—

> Et Mediolani mira omnia: copia rerum;
> Innumeræ cultæque domus; facunda virorum
> Ingenia, et mores læti: tum duplice muro
> Amplificata loci species; populique voluptas
> Circus; et inclusi moles cuneata Theatri;
> Templa, Palatinæque arces, opulensque Moneta,
> Et regio *Herculei* celebris sub honore lavacri.
> Cunctaque marmoreis ornata Peristyla signis;
> Mœniaque in valli formam circumdata labro,
> Omnia quæ magnis operum velut æmula formis
> Excellunt: nec juncta premit vicinia Romæ.

[2] Lactant. de M. P. c. 17. Libanius, Orat. vi. p. 203 [ed. Morell. Paris, 1627].

[3] Lactant. de M. P. c. 17. On a similar occasion, Ammianus mentions the *dicacitas plebis* as not very agreeable to an Imperial ear. (See l. xvi. c. 10.)

[Gibbon here falls into serious error. Ammianus just says the opposite to what is here represented. the precise words being—he is speaking of Constantius—" dicacitate plebis oblectabatur."—O. S.]

of the most artful policy. That crafty prince had framed a new
system of Imperial government, which was afterwards completed by the family of Constantine; and as the image of the
old constitution was religiously preserved in the senate, he
resolved to deprive that order of its small remains of power and
consideration. We may recollect, about eight years before the
elevation of Diocletian, the transient greatness and the ambitious
hopes of the Roman senate. As long as that enthusiasm prevailed, many of the nobles imprudently displayed their zeal in
the cause of freedom; and after the successors of Probus had
withdrawn their countenance from the republican party, the
senators were unable to disguise their impotent resentment. As
the sovereign of Italy, Maximian was intrusted with the care of
extinguishing this troublesome rather than dangerous spirit,
and the task was perfectly suited to his cruel temper. The
most illustrious members of the senate, whom Diocletian always
affected to esteem, were involved, by his colleague, in the accusation of imaginary plots; and the possession of an elegant villa,
or a well-cultivated estate, was interpreted as a convincing
evidence of guilt.[1] The camp of the Prætorians, which had so
long oppressed, began to protect, the majesty of Rome; and
as those haughty troops were conscious of the decline of their
power, they were naturally disposed to unite their strength with
the authority of the senate. By the prudent measures of Diocletian, the numbers of the Prætorians were insensibly reduced,
their privileges abolished,[2] and their place supplied by two
faithful legions of Illyricum, who, under the new titles of Jovians
and Herculians, were appointed to perform the service of the
Imperial guards.[3] But the most fatal though secret wound
which the senate received from the hands of Diocletian and
Maximian was inflicted by the inevitable operation of their
absence. As long as the emperors resided at Rome, that
assembly might be oppressed, but it could scarcely be neglected.
The successors of Augustus exercised the power of dictating
whatever laws their wisdom or caprice might suggest; but those

---

[1] Lactantius accuses Maximian of destroying fictis criminationibus
lumina senatûs (de M. P. c. 8). Aurelius Victor speaks very doubtfully of
the faith of Diocletian towards his friends.

[2] Truncatæ vires urbis, imminuto prætoriarum cohortium atque in armis
vulgi numero. Aurelius Victor [de Cæsar. c. 39]. Lactantius attributes
to Galerius the prosecution of the same plan (c. 26).

[3] They were old corps stationed in Illyricum; and, according to the
ancient establishment, they each consisted of six thousand men. They
had acquired much reputation by the use of the *plumbatæ*, or darts loaded
with lead. Each soldier carried five of these, which he darted from a considerable distance with great strength and dexterity. See Vegetius, i. 17.

laws were ratified by the sanction of the senate. The model of ancient freedom was preserved in its deliberations and decrees; and wise princes, who respected the prejudices of the Roman people, were in some measure obliged to assume the language and behaviour suitable to the general and first magistrate of the republic. In the armies and in the provinces they displayed the dignity of monarchs; and when they fixed their residence at a distance from the capital, they for ever laid aside the dissimulation which Augustus had recommended to his successors. In the exercise of the legislative as well as the executive power, the sovereign advised with his ministers, instead of consulting the great council of the nation. The name of the senate was mentioned with honour till the last period of the empire; the vanity of its members were still flattered with honorary distinctions;[1] but the assembly which had so long been the source, and so long the instrument of power, was respectfully suffered to sink into oblivion. The senate of Rome, losing all connection with the Imperial court and the actual constitution, was left a venerable but useless monument of antiquity on the Capitoline hill.

When the Roman princes had lost sight of the senate and of their ancient capital, they easily forgot the origin and nature of their legal power. The civil offices of consul, of proconsul, of censor, and of tribune, by the union of which it had been formed, betrayed to the people its republican extraction. Those modest titles were laid aside;[2] and if they still distinguished their high station by the appellation of Emperor, or IMPERATOR, that word was understood in a new and more dignified sense, and no longer denoted the general of the Roman armies, but the sovereign of the Roman world. The name of Emperor, which was at first of a military nature, was associated with another of a more servile kind. The epithet of DOMINUS, or Lord, in its primitive signification, was expressive not of the authority of a prince over his subjects, or of a commander over his soldiers, but of the despotic power of a master over his domestic slaves.[3] Viewing it in that odious light, it had been rejected with abhorrence by

---

[1] See the Theodosian Code, 1. vi. tit. ii. with Godefroy's commentary.

[2] See the 12th dissertation in Spanheim's excellent work de Usu Numismatum. From medals, inscriptions, and historians, he examines every title separately, and traces it from Augustus to the moment of its disappearing.

[3] Pliny (in Panegyr. c. 3, 55, etc.) speaks of *Dominus* with execration, as synonymous to Tyrant, and opposite to Prince. And the same Pliny regularly gives that title (in the tenth book of the epistles) to his friend rather than master, the virtuous Trajan. This strange contradiction puzzles the commentators who think, and the translators who can write.

the first Cæsars. Their resistance insensibly became more feeble,
and the name less odious; till at length the style of *our Lord and
Emperor* was not only bestowed by flattery, but was regularly
admitted into the laws and public monuments. Such lofty
epithets were sufficient to elate and satisfy the most excessive
vanity ; and if the successors of Diocletian still declined the title
of King, it seems to have been the effect not so much of their
moderation as of their delicacy. Wherever the Latin tongue
was in use (and it was the language of government throughout
the empire), the Imperial title, as it was peculiar to themselves,
conveyed a more respectable idea than the name of king, which
they must have shared with an hundred barbarian chieftains;
or which, at the best, they could derive only from Romulus, or
from Tarquin. But the sentiments of the East were very different
from those of the West. From the earliest period of history, the
sovereigns of Asia had been celebrated in the Greek language by
the title of BASILEUS, or King; and since it was considered as the
first distinction among men, it was soon employed by the servile
provincials of the East in their humble addresses to the Roman
throne.[1] Even the attributes, or at least the titles, of the
DIVINITY were usurped by Diocletian and Maximian, who transmitted them to a succession of Christian emperors.[2] Such extravagant compliments, however, soon lose their impiety by

---

[1] Synesius de Regno, edit. Petav. p. 15. I am indebted for this quotation
to the Abbé de la Blétérie.

[2] See Van Dale de Consecratione, p. 354, etc. It was customary for the
emperors to mention (in the preamble of laws) their *numen, sacred majesty,
divine oracles, etc.* According to Tillemont, Gregory Nazianzen complains
most bitterly of the profanation, especially when it was practised by an
Arian emperor.

[In the time of the republic (says Milman, quoting Hegewisch) when the
consuls, the prætors, and the other magistrates appeared in public to perform the functions of their office, their dignity was announced both by the
symbols which use had consecrated and the brilliant cortege by which they
were accompanied. But this dignity belonged to the office, not to the
individual, the pomp belonged to the magistrate, not to the man. . . .
The consul followed in the comitia by all the senate, the prætors, the
ædiles, the lictors, the apparitors, and the heralds, on re-entering his house
was served only by his freedmen and his slaves. The first emperors went
no farther. Tiberius had, for his personal attendance, only a moderate
number of slaves and a few freedmen (Tacit. Annal. iv. 7). But in proportion as the republican forms disappeared one after another, the inclination of the emperors to envelope themselves with personal pomp displayed
itself more and more. The magnificence and the ceremonial of the East
were entirely introduced by Diocletian, and were consecrated by Constantine to the Imperial use. Thenceforth the palace, the court, the table, all
the personal attendance, distinguished the emperor from his subjects still
more than his superior dignity. The organisation which Diocletian gave
to his new court attached less honour and distinction to rank than to
services performed towards the members of the Imperial family.—O. S.]

losing their meaning; and when the ear is once accustomed to the sound, they are heard with indifference as vague though excessive professions of respect.

From the time of Augustus to that of Diocletian, the Roman princes, conversing in a familiar manner among their fellow-citizens, were saluted only with the same respect that was usually paid to senators and magistrates. Their principal distinction was the Imperial or military robe of purple; whilst the senatorial garment was marked by a broad, and the equestrian by a narrow, band or stripe of the same honourable colour. The pride, or rather the policy, of Diocletian, engaged that artful prince to introduce the stately magnificence of the court of Persia.[1] He ventured to assume the diadem, an ornament detested by the Romans as the odious ensign of royalty, and the use of which had been considered as the most desperate act of the madness of Caligula. It was no more than a broad white fillet set with pearls, which encircled the emperor's head. The sumptuous robes of Diocletian and his successors were of silk and gold; and it is remarked with indignation that even their shoes were studded with the most precious gems. The access to their sacred person was every day rendered more difficult by the institution of new forms and ceremonies. The avenues of the palace were strictly guarded by the various *schools*, as they began to be called, of domestic officers. The interior apartments were intrusted to the jealous vigilance of the eunuchs; the increase of whose numbers and influence was the most infallible symptom of the progress of despotism. When a subject was at length admitted to the Imperial presence, he was obliged, whatever might be his rank, to fall prostrate on the ground, and to adore, according to the eastern fashion, the divinity of his lord and master.[2] Diocletian was a man of sense, who, in the course of private as well as public life, had formed a just estimate both of himself and of mankind: nor is it easy to conceive that in substituting the manners of Persia to those of Rome he was seriously actuated by so mean a principle as that of vanity. He flattered himself that an ostentation of splendour and luxury would subdue the imagination of the multitude; that the monarch would be less exposed to the rude licence of the people and the soldiers, as his person was secluded from the public view; and

---

[1] See Spanheim de Usu Numismat. Dissert. xii.
[2] Aurelius Victor. Eutropius, ix. 26 [16]. It appears by the Panegyrists that the Romans were soon reconciled to the name and ceremony of adoration.

that habits of submission would insensibly be productive of sentiments of veneration. Like the modesty affected by Augustus,
the state maintained by Diocletian was a theatrical representation; but it must be confessed that, of the two comedies, the
former was of a much more liberal and manly character than
the latter. It was the aim of the one to disguise, and the object
of the other to display, the unbounded power which the emperors
possessed over the Roman world.

Ostentation was the first principle of the new system instituted
by Diocletian. The second was division. He divided the
empire, the provinces, and every branch of the civil as well
as military administration. He multiplied the wheels of the
machine of government, and rendered its operations less rapid
but more secure. Whatever advantages and whatever defects
might attend these innovations, they must be ascribed in a very
great degree to the first inventor; but as the new frame of policy
was gradually improved and completed by succeeding princes,
it will be more satisfactory to delay the consideration of it till
the season of its full maturity and perfection.[1] Reserving, therefore, for the reign of Constantine a more exact picture of the
new empire, we shall content ourselves with describing the
principal and decisive outline, as it was traced by the hand of
Diocletian. He had associated three colleagues in the exercise
of the supreme power; and as he was convinced that the abilities
of a single man were inadequate to the public defence, he considered the joint administration of four princes not as a temporary expedient, but as a fundamental law of the constitution.
It was his intention that the two elder princes should be distinguished by the use of the diadem and the title of *Augusti*;
that, as affection or esteem might direct their choice, they should
regularly call to their assistance two subordinate colleagues;
and that the *Cæsars*, rising in their turn to the first rank, should
supply an uninterrupted succession of emperors. The empire
was divided into four parts. The East and Italy were the most
honourable, the Danube and the Rhine the most laborious
stations. The former claimed the presence of the *Augusti*, the
latter were intrusted to the administration of the *Cæsars*. The
strength of the legions was in the hands of the four partners of
sovereignty, and the despair of successively vanquishing four

---

[1] The innovations introduced by Diocletian are chiefly deduced, 1st,
from some very strong passages in Lactantius; and, secondly, from the
new and various offices which, in the Theodosian code, appear *already*
established in the beginning of the reign of Constantine.

formidable rivals might intimidate the ambition of an aspiring general. In their civil government the emperors were supposed to exercise the undivided power of the monarch, and their edicts, inscribed with their joint names, were received in all the provinces as promulgated by their mutual councils and authority. Notwithstanding these precautions, the political union of the Roman world was gradually dissolved, and a principle of division was introduced, which, in the course of a few years, occasioned the perpetual separation of the eastern and western empires.

The system of Diocletian was accompanied with another very material disadvantage, which cannot even at present be totally overlooked; a more expensive establishment, and consequently an increase of taxes, and the oppression of the people. Instead of a modest family of slaves and freedmen, such as had contented the simple greatness of Augustus and Trajan, three or four magnificent courts were established in the various parts of the empire, and as many Roman *kings* contended with each other and with the Persian monarch for the vain superiority of pomp and luxury. The number of ministers, of magistrates, of officers, and of servants, who filled the different departments of the state, was multiplied beyond the example of former times; and (if we may borrow the warm expression of a contemporary), " when the proportion of those who received exceeded the proportion of those who contributed, the provinces were oppressed by the weight of tributes." [1]   From this period to the extinction of the empire, it would be easy to deduce an uninterrupted series of clamours and complaints. According to his religion and situation, each writer chooses either Diocletian, or Constantine, or Valens, or Theodosius, for the object of his invectives; but they unanimously agree in representing the burden of the public impositions, and particularly the land-tax and capitation, as the intolerable and increasing grievance of their own times. From such a concurrence, an impartial historian, who is obliged to extract truth from satire, as well as from panegyric, will be inclined to divide the blame among the princes whom they accuse, and to ascribe their exactions much less to their personal vices than to the uniform system of their administration. The emperor Diocletian was indeed the author of that system; but during his reign the growing evil was confined within the bounds of modesty and discretion, and he deserves the reproach of establishing pernicious precedents, rather than of exercising actual oppression.[1] It may be added, that his revenues were managed with prudent economy; and that, after all the current expenses were discharged, there still remained in the Imperial treasury an ample provision either for judicious liberality or for any emergency of the state.

It was in the twenty-first year of his reign that Diocletian executed his memorable resolution of abdicating the empire; an action more naturally to have been expected from the elder or the younger Antoninus than from a prince who had never practised the lessons of philosophy either in the attainment or in the use of supreme power. Diocletian acquired the glory of giving to the world the first example of a resignation [2] which has not been very frequently imitated by succeeding monarchs. The parallel of Charles the Fifth, however, will naturally offer itself to our mind, not only since the eloquence of a modern historian has rendered that name so familiar to an English reader, but from the very striking resemblance between the characters of the two emperors, whose political abilities were superior to their military genius, and whose specious virtues were much less the effect of nature than of art. The abdication of Charles appears to have been hastened by the vicissitude of fortune; and the disappointment of his favourite schemes urged him to relinquish a power which he found inadequate to his ambition. But the reign of Diocletian had flowed with a tide of uninterrupted success; nor was it till after he had vanquished all his enemies, and accomplished all his designs, that he seems to have enter-

[1] Indicta lex nova quæ sane illorum temporum modestiâ tolerabilis, in perniciem processit. Aurel. Victor [de Cæsar. c. 39]; who has treated the character of Diocletian with good sense, though in bad Latin.

[The most curious document which has come to light since the publication of Gibbon's History is the edict of Diocletian published from an inscription found at Eskihissâr (Stratoniceia), by Col. Leake. This edict, according to Milman, was issued in the name of the four Cæsars, Diocletian, Maximian, Constantius, and Galerius. It fixed a maximum of prices throughout the empire for all the necessaries and commodities of life. The preamble insists with great vehemence on the extortion and inhumanity of the merchants and vendors. Among the articles of which the maximum value is assessed are oil, salt, honey, butcher's meat, poultry, game, fish, vegetables, fruit, the wages of labourers and artisans, schoolmasters and orators, clothes, skins, boots and shoes, harness, timber, corn, wine, and beer (zythus). The depreciation in the value of money or the rise in the price of commodities had been so great during the last century that butcher's meat, which in the second century was two denarii the pound, was now fixed at a maximum of eight. An excellent edition of the edict has been published with a commentary by Mommsen, who shows that it was issued in A. D. 301. Cf. Finlay's Hist. of Greece, vol. i. Appendix 1.—O. S.]

[2] Solus omnium, post conditum Romanum Imperium, qui ex tanto fastigio sponte ad privatæ vitæ statum civilitatemque remearet. Eutrop. ix. 28 [16].

tained any serious thoughts of resigning the empire. Neither
Charles nor Diocletian were arrived at a very advanced period of
life; since the one was only fifty-five, and the other was no more
than fifty-nine years of age; but the active life of those princes,
their wars and journeys, the cares of royalty, and their application to business, had already impaired their constitution, and
brought on the infirmities of a premature old age.[1]

Notwithstanding the severity of a very cold and rainy winter,
Diocletian left Italy soon after the ceremony of his triumph,
and began his progress towards the East round the circuit of the
Illyrian provinces. From the inclemency of the weather and the
fatigue of the journey, he soon contracted a slow illness; and
though he made easy marches, and was generally carried in a
close litter, his disorder, before he arrived at Nicomedia, about
the end of the summer, was become very serious and alarming.
During the whole winter he was confined to his palace; his
danger inspired a general and unaffected concern; but the people
could only judge of the various alterations of his health from
the joy or consternation which they discovered in the counten-
ances and behaviour of his attendants. The rumour of his
death was for some time universally believed, and it was supposed to be concealed with a view to prevent the troubles that
might have happened during the absence of the Cæsar Galerius.
At length, however, on the first of March, Diocletian once more
appeared in public, but so pale and emaciated that he could
scarcely have been recognised by those to whom his person was
the most familiar. It was time to put an end to the painful
struggle, which he had sustained during more than a year,
between the care of his health and that of his dignity. The
former required indulgence and relaxation, the latter compelled
him to direct, from the bed of sickness, the administration of a
great empire. He resolved to pass the remainder of his days in
honourable repose, to place his glory beyond the reach of fortune,
and to relinquish the theatre of the world to his younger and
more active associates.[2]

The ceremony of his abdication was performed in a spacious
plain, about three miles from Nicomedia. The emperor ascended

[1] The particulars of the journey and illness are taken from Lactantius
(c. 17), who may *sometimes* be admitted as an evidence of public facts,
though very seldom of private anecdotes.

[2] Aurelius Victor [de Cæsar. c. 39] ascribes the abdication, which had
been so variously accounted for, to two causes: first, Diocletian's contempt of ambition; and secondly, His apprehension of impending troubles.
One of the panegyrists (vi. [v.] 9) mentions the age and infirmities of Diocletian as a very natural reason for his retirement.

a lofty throne, and, in a speech full of reason and dignity, declared his intention, both to the people and to the soldiers who
were assembled on this extraordinary occasion. As soon as he
had divested himself of the purple, he withdrew from the gazing
multitude, and, traversing the city in a covered chariot, proceeded without delay to the favourite retirement which he had
chosen in his native country of Dalmatia. On the same day,
which was the first of May,[1] Maximian, as it had been previously
concerted, made his resignation of the Imperial dignity at Milan.
Even in the splendour of the Roman triumph, Diocletian had
meditated his design of abdicating the government. As he
wished to secure the obedience of Maximian, he exacted from
him either a general assurance that he would submit his actions
to the authority of his benefactor, or a particular promise that
he would descend from the throne whenever he should receive
the advice and the example. This engagement, though it was
confirmed by the solemnity of an oath before the altar of the
Capitoline Jupiter,[2] would have proved a feeble restraint on the
fierce temper of Maximian, whose passion was the love of power,
and who neither desired present tranquillity nor future reputation. But he yielded, however reluctantly, to the ascendant
which his wiser colleague had acquired over him, and retired
immediately after his abdication to a villa in Lucania, where it
was almost impossible that such an impatient spirit could find
any lasting tranquillity.

Diocletian, who, from a servile origin, had raised himself to
the throne, passed the nine last years of his life in a private
condition. Reason had dictated, and content seems to have
accompanied, his retreat, in which he enjoyed for a long time the
respect of those princes to whom he had resigned the possession
of the world.[3] It is seldom that minds long exercised in business
have formed any habits of conversing with themselves, and in
the loss of power they principally regret the want of occupation.
The amusements of letters and of devotion, which afford so many
resources in solitude, were incapable of fixing the attention of
Diocletian; but he had preserved, or at least he soon recovered,

[1] The difficulties as well as mistakes attending the dates both of the year
and of the day of Diocletian's abdication are perfectly cleared up by Tillemont, Hist. des Empereurs, tom. iv. p. 525, note 19, and by Pagi ad annum.

[2] See Panegyr. Veter. vi. [v.] 9. The oration was pronounced after
Maximian had reassumed the purple.

[3] Eumenius pays him a very fine compliment: " At enim divinum illum
virum, qui primus imperium et participavit et posuit, consilii et facti sui
non poenitet; nec amisisse se putat quod sponte transcripsit. Felix
beatusque vere quem vestra, tantorum principum, colunt obsequia
privatum." Panegyr. Vet. vii. [vi.] 15.

a taste for the most innocent as well as natural pleasures, and his leisure hours were sufficiently employed in building, planting, and gardening. His answer to Maximian is deservedly celebrated. He was solicited by that restless old man to reassume the reins of government and the Imperial purple. He rejected the temptation with a smile of pity, calmly observing that, if he could show Maximian the cabbages which he had planted with his own hands at Salona, he should no longer be urged to relinquish the enjoyment of happiness for the pursuit of power.[1] In his conversations with his friends he frequently acknowledged that of all arts the most difficult was the art of reigning; and he expressed himself on that favourite topic with a degree of warmth which could be the result only of experience. " How often," was he accustomed to say, " is it the interest of four or five ministers to combine together to deceive their sovereign! Secluded from mankind by his exalted dignity, the truth is concealed from his knowledge; he can see only with their eyes, he hears nothing but their misrepresentations. He confers the most important offices upon vice and weakness, and disgraces the most virtuous and deserving among his subjects. By such infamous arts," added Diocletian, " the best and wisest princes are sold to the venal corruption of their courtiers." [2] A just estimate of greatness, and the assurance of immortal fame, improve our relish for the pleasures of retirement; but the Roman emperor had filled too important a character in the world to enjoy without alloy the comforts and security of a private condition. It was impossible that he could remain ignorant of the troubles which afflicted the empire after his abdication. It was impossible that he could be indifferent to their consequences. Fear, sorrow, and discontent sometimes pursued him into the solitude of Salona. His tenderness, or at least his pride, was deeply wounded by the misfortunes of his wife and daughter; and the last moments of Diocletian were embittered by some affronts, which Licinius and Constantine might have spared the father of so many emperors, and the first author of their own fortune. A report, though of a very doubtful nature, has reached our times that he prudently withdrew himself from their power by a voluntary death.[3]

[1] We are obliged to the younger Victor [Epit. c. 39] for this celebrated bon mot. Eutropius [l. ix. c. 16] mentions the thing in a more general manner.

[2] Hist. August. p. 223, 224. [Vopisc. Aurel. c. 43.] Vopiscus had learned this conversation from his father.

[3] The younger Victor [Epit. c. 39] slightly mentions the report. But as

Before we dismiss the consideration of the life and character of Diocletian, we may for a moment direct our view to the place of his retirement. Salona, a principal city of his native province of Dalmatia, was near two hundred Roman miles (according to the measurement of the public highways) from Aquileia and the confines of Italy, and about two hundred and seventy from Sirmium, the usual residence of the emperors whenever they visited the Illyrian frontier.[1] A miserable village still preserves the name of Salona; but so late as the sixteenth century the remains of a theatre, and a confused prospect of broken arches and marble columns, continued to attest its ancient splendour.[2] About six or seven miles from the city Diocletian constructed a magnificent palace, and we may infer, from the greatness of the work, how long he had meditated his design of abdicating the empire. The choice of a spot which united all that could contribute either to health or to luxury did not require the partiality of a native. " The soil was dry and fertile, the air is pure and wholesome, and, though extremely hot during the summer months, this country seldom feels those sultry and noxious winds to which the coasts of Istria and some parts of Italy are exposed. The views from the palace are no less beautiful than the soil and climate were inviting. Towards the west lies the fertile shore that stretches along the Adriatic, in which a number of small islands are scattered in such a manner as to give this part of the sea the appearance of a great lake. On the north side lies the bay, which led to the ancient city of Salona; and the country beyond it, appearing in sight, forms a proper contrast to that more extensive prospect of water which the Adriatic presents both to the south and to the east. Towards the north the view is terminated by high and irregular mountains, situated at a proper distance, and in many places covered with villages, woods, and vineyards."[3]

Diocletian had disobliged a powerful and successful party, his memory has been loaded with every crime and misfortune. It has been affirmed that he died raving mad, that he was condemned as a criminal by the Roman senate, etc.

[1] See the Itiner. p. 269, 272, edit. Wessel.

[2] The Abate Fortis, in his Viaggio in Dalmazia, p. 43 (printed at Venice in the year 1774, in two small volumes in quarto), quotes a MS. account of the antiquities of Salona, composed by Giambattista Giustiniani about the middle of the sixteenth century.

[3] Adam's Antiquities of Diocletian's Palace at Spalatro, p. 6. We may add a circumstance or two from the Abate Fortis: the little stream of the Hyader, mentioned by Lucan, produces most exquisite trout, which a sagacious writer, perhaps a monk, supposes to have been one of the principal reasons that determined Diocletian in the choice of his retirement. Fortis, p. 45. The same author (p. 38) observes that a taste for agriculture

Though Constantine, from a very obvious prejudice, affects to mention the palace of Diocletian with contempt,[1] yet one of their successors, who could only see it in a neglected and mutilated state, celebrates its magnificence in terms of the highest admiration.[2] It covered an extent of ground consisting of between nine and ten English acres. The form was quadrangular, flanked with sixteen towers. Two of the sides were near six hundred, and the other two near seven hundred, feet in length. The whole was constructed of a beautiful free-stone, extracted from the neighbouring quarries of Trau, or Tragutium, and very little inferior to marble itself. Four streets, intersecting each other at right angles, divided the several parts of this great edifice, and the approach to the principal apartment was from a very stately entrance, which is still denominated the Golden Gate. The approach was terminated by a *peristylium* of granite columns, on one side of which we discover the square temple of Æsculapius, on the other the octagon temple of Jupiter. The latter of those deities Diocletian revered as the patron of his fortunes, the former as the protector of his health. By comparing the present remains with the precepts of Vitruvius, the several parts of the building, the baths, bedchamber, the *atrium*, the *basilica*, and the Cyzicene, Corinthian, and Egyptian halls have been described with some degree of precision, or at least of probability. Their forms were various, their proportions just, but they were all attended with two imperfections, very repugnant to our modern notions of taste and conveniency. These stately rooms had neither windows nor chimneys. They were lighted from the top (for the building seems to have consisted of no more than one story), and they received their heat by the help of pipes that were conveyed along the walls. The range of principal apartments was protected towards the south-west by a portico five hundred and seventeen feet long, which must have formed a very noble and delightful walk, when the beauties of painting and sculpture were added to those of the prospect.

Had this magnificent edifice remained in a solitary country, it would have been exposed to the ravages of time; but it might, perhaps, have escaped the rapacious industry of man. The

is reviving at Spalatro; and that an experimental farm has lately been established near the city by a society of gentlemen.

[1] Constantin. Orat. ad Cœtum Sanct. c. 25. In this sermon, the emperor, or the bishop who composed it for him, affects to relate the miserable end of all the persecutors of the church.

[2] Constantin. Porphyr. de Statu Imper. p. 86 [ed. Paris; vol. iii. p. 125, ed. Bonn].

village of Aspalathus,[1] and, long afterwards, the provincial town
of Spalatro, have grown out of its ruins. The Golden Gate now
opens into the market-place. St. John the Baptist has usurped
the honours of Æsculapius; and the temple of Jupiter, under the
protection of the Virgin, is converted into the cathedral church.
For this account of Diocletian's palace we are principally indebted to an ingenious artist of our own time and country, whom
a very liberal curiosity carried into the heart of Dalmatia.[2] But
there is room to suspect that the elegance of his designs and
engraving has somewhat flattered the objects which it was their
purpose to represent. We are informed by a more recent and
very judicious traveller that the awful ruins of Spalatro are not
less expressive of the decline of the arts than of the greatness
of the Roman empire in the time of Diocletian.[3] If such was
indeed the state of architecture, we must naturally believe that
painting and sculpture had experienced a still more sensible
decay. The practice of architecture is directed by a few general
and even mechanical rules. But sculpture, and, above all,
painting, propose to themselves the imitation not only of the
forms of nature, but of the characters and passions of the human
soul. In those sublime arts the dexterity of the hand is of little
avail unless it is animated by fancy and guided by the most
correct taste and observation.

It is almost unnecessary to remark that the civil distractions
of the empire, the licence of the soldiers, the inroads of the barbarians, and the progress of despotism, had proved very unfavourable to genius, and even to learning. The succession of
Illyrian princes restored the empire without restoring the
sciences. Their military education was not calculated to inspire
them with the love of letters; and even the mind of Diocletian,
however active and capacious in business, was totally uninformed
by study or speculation. The professions of law and physic are
of such common use and certain profit that they will always
secure a sufficient number of practitioners endowed with a
reasonable degree of abilities and knowledge; but it does not

---

[1] D'Anville, Géographie Ancienne, tom. i. p. 162.

[2] Messieurs Adam and Clerisseau, attended by two draughtsmen, visited
Spalatro in the month of July, 1757. The magnificent work which their
journey produced was published in London seven years afterwards.

[3] I shall quote the words of the Abbate Fortis. " E'bastevolmente nota
agli amatori dell' Architettura, e dell' Antichità, l'opera del Signor ADAMS,
che a donato molto a que' superbi vestigi coll' abituale eleganza del suo
toccalapis e del bulino. In generale la rozzezza del scalpello, e'l cattivo
gusto del secolo vi gareggiano colla magnificenza del fabricato." See
Viaggio in Dalmazia, p. 40.

appear that the students in those two faculties appeal to any celebrated masters who have flourished within that period. The voice of poetry was silent. History was reduced to dry and confused abridgments, alike destitute of amusement and instruction. A languid and affected eloquence was still retained in the pay and service of the emperors, who encouraged not any arts except those which contributed to the gratification of their pride or the defence of their power.[1]

The declining age of learning and of mankind is marked, however, by the rise and rapid progress of the new Platonists. The school of Alexandria silenced those of Athens; and the ancient sects enrolled themselves under the banners of the more fashionable teachers, who recommended their system by the novelty of their method and the austerity of their manners. Several of these masters—Ammonius, Plotinus, Amelius, and Porphyry[2] —were men of profound thought and intense application; but, by mistaking the true object of philosophy, their labours contributed much less to improve than to corrupt the human understanding. The knowledge that is suited to our situation and powers, the whole compass of moral, natural, and mathematical science, was neglected by the new Platonists; whilst they exhausted their strength in the verbal disputes of metaphysics, attempted to explore the secrets of the invisible world, and studied to reconcile Aristotle with Plato, on subjects of which both these philosophers were as ignorant as the rest of mankind. Consuming their reason in these deep but unsubstantial meditations, their minds were exposed to illusions of fancy. They flattered themselves that they possessed the secret of disengaging the soul from its corporeal prison; claimed a familiar intercourse with dæmons and spirits; and, by a very singular revolution, converted the study of philosophy into that of magic. The ancient sages had derided the popular superstition; after disguising its extravagance by the thin pretence of allegory, the disciples of Plotinus and Porphyry became its most zealous

---

[1] The orator Eumenius was secretary to the emperors Maximian and Constantius, and Professor of Rhetoric in the college of Autun. His salary was six hundred thousand sesterces, which, according to the lowest computation of that age, must have exceeded three thousand pounds a year. He generously requested the permission of employing it in rebuilding the college. See his Oration De Restaurandis Scholis [c. 11]; which, though not exempt from vanity, may atone for his panegyrics.

[2] Porphyry died about the time of Diocletian's abdication. The life of his master Plotinus, which he composed, will give us the most complete idea of the genius of the sect and the manners of its professors. This very curious piece is inserted in Fabricius, Bibliotheca Græca, tom. iv. p. 88-148.

defenders. As they agreed with the Christians in a few mysterious points of faith, they attacked the remainder of their theological system with all the fury of civil war. The new Platonists would scarcely deserve a place in the history of science, but in that of the church the mention of them will very frequently occur.

CHAPTER XIV

Troubles after the Abdication of Diocletian—Death of Constantius—
Elevation of Constantine and Maxentius—Six Emperors at the same
Time—Death of Maximian and Galerius—Victories of Constantine
over Maxentius and Licinius—Reunion of the Empire under the
Authority of Constantine

THE balance of power established by Diocletian subsisted no longer than while it was sustained by the firm and dexterous hand of the founder. It required such a fortunate mixture of different tempers and abilities as could scarcely be found, or even expected, a second time; two emperors without jealousy, two Cæsars without ambition and the same general interest invariably pursued by four independent princes. The abdication of Diocletian and Maximian was succeeded by eighteen years of discord and confusion. The empire was afflicted by five civil wars; and the remainder of the time was not so much a state of tranquillity as a suspension of arms between several hostile monarchs, who, viewing each other with an eye of fear and hatred, strove to increase their respective forces at the expense of their subjects.

As soon as Diocletian and Maximian had resigned the purple, their station, according to the rules of the new constitution, was filled by the two Cæsars, Constantius and Galerius, who immediately assumed the title of Augustus.[1] The honours of seniority and precedence were allowed to the former of those princes, and he continued under a new appellation to administer his ancient department of Gaul, Spain, and Britain. The government of those ample provinces was sufficient to exercise his talents and to satisfy his ambition. Clemency, temperance, and moderation distinguished the amiable character of Constantius, and his fortunate subjects had frequently occasion to compare the virtues

[1] M. de Montesquieu (Considérations sur la Grandeur et la Décadence des Romains, c. 17) supposes, on the authority of Orosius and Eusebius, that, on this occasion, the empire, for the first time, was *really* divided into two parts. It is difficult, however, to discover in what respect the plan of Galerius differed from that of Diocletian.

of their sovereign with the passions of Maximian, and even with the arts of Diocletian.[1] Instead of imitating their eastern pride and magnificence, Constantius preserved the modesty of a Roman -prince. He declared, with unaffected sincerity, that his most valued treasure was in the hearts of his people; and that, whenever the dignity of the throne or the danger of the state required any extraordinary supply, he could depend with confidence on their gratitude and liberality.[2] The provincials of Gaul, Spain, and Britain, sensible of his worth, and of their own happiness, reflected with anxiety on the declining health of the emperor Constantius, and the tender age of his numerous family, the issue of his second marriage with the daughter of Maximian.

The stern temper of Galerius was cast in a very different mould; and while he commanded the esteem of his subjects, he seldom condescended to solicit their affections. His fame in arms, and, above all, the success of the Persian war, had elated his haughty mind, which was naturally impatient of a superior, or even of an equal. If it were possible to rely on the partial testimony of an injudicious writer, we might ascribe the abdication of Diocletian to the menaces of Galerius, and relate the particulars of a *private* conversation between the two princes, in which the former discovered as much pusillanimity as the latter displayed ingratitude and arrogance.[3] But these obscure anecdotes are sufficiently refuted by an impartial view of the character and conduct of Diocletian. Whatever might otherwise have been his intentions,

---

[1] Hic non modo amabilis, sed etiam venerabilis Gallis fuit; præcipue quòd Diocletiani suspectam prudentiam, et Maximiani sanguinariam violentiam imperio ejus evaserant. Eutrop. Breviar. x. i.

[2] Divitiis Provincialium (mel. *provinciarum*) ac privatorum studens, fisci commoda non admodum affectans; ducensque melius publicas opes a privatis haberi, quam intra unum claustrum reservari. Id. ibid. He carried this maxim so far, that, whenever he gave an entertainment, he was obliged to borrow a service of plate.

[3] Lactantius de Mort. Persecutor. c. 18. Were the particulars of this conference more consistent with truth and decency, we might still ask how they came to the knowledge of an obscure rhetorician? But there are many historians who put us in mind of the admirable saying of the great Condé to Cardinal de Retz: " Ces coquins nous font parler et agir comme ils auroient fait eux-mêmes à notre place."

[This attack upon Lactantius (as Guizot says) is quite unfounded. Lactantius was so far from having been an obscure rhetorician, that he had taught rhetoric publicly and with the greatest success first in Africa and afterwards in Nicomedia. His reputation obtained him the esteem of Constantine, who invited him to his court, and entrusted to him the education of his son Crispus. Further on, Dr. W. Smith adds it ought to be borne in mind that the authorship of the treatise De Mortibus Persecutorum is uncertain, and cannot be ascribed without grave doubts to Lactantius.—O. S.]

if he had apprehended any danger from the violence of Galerius,
his good sense would have instructed him to prevent the ignominious contest; and as he had held the sceptre with glory, he
would have resigned it without disgrace.

After the elevation of Constantius and Galerius to the rank of
Augusti, two new *Cæsars* were required to supply their place,
and to complete the system of the Imperial government.   Diocletian was sincerely desirous of withdrawing himself from the
world; he considered Galerius, who had married his daughter,
as the firmest support of his family and of the empire; and he
consented, without reluctance, that his successor should assume
the merit as well as the envy of the important nomination.   It
was fixed without consulting the interest or inclination of the
princes of the West.   Each of them had a son who was arrived at
the age of manhood, and who might have been deemed the most
natural candidates for the vacant honour.   But the impotent
resentment of Maximian was no longer to be dreaded; and the
moderate Constantius, though he might despise the dangers, was
humanely apprehensive of the calamities, of civil war.   The two
persons whom Galerius promoted to the rank of Cæsar were much
better suited to serve the views of his ambition; and their principal recommendation seems to have consisted in the want of
merit or personal consequence.   The first of these was Daza, or,
as he was afterwards called, Maximin, whose mother was the
sister of Galerius.[1]   The inexperienced youth still betrayed by
his manners and language his rustic education, when, to his own
astonishment, as well as that of the world, he was invested by
Diocletian with the purple, exalted to the dignity of Cæsar, and
intrusted with the sovereign command of Egypt and Syria.[2]
At the same time Severus, a faithful servant, addicted to pleasure
but not incapable of business, was sent to Milan to receive from
the reluctant hands of Maximian the Cæsarian ornaments and

---

[1] The following table shows the connection between the above-mentioned
persons:—

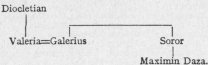

Diocletian

Valeria=Galerius   Soror

Maximin Daza.

See Clinton, Fast. Rom. vol. ii. p. 72.
[2] Sublatus nuper a pecoribus et silvis (says Lactantius de M. P. c. 19)
statim Scutarius, continuo Protector, mox Tribunus, postridie Cæsar,
accepit Orientem.   Aurelius Victor is too liberal in giving him the whole
portion of Diocletian.

the possession of Italy and Africa.[1] According to the forms of
the constitution, Severus acknowledged the supremacy of the
western emperor; but he was absolutely devoted to the commands of his benefactor Galerius, who, reserving to himself the
intermediate countries from the confines of Italy to those of
Syria, firmly established his power over three-fourths of the
monarchy. In the full confidence that the approaching death
of Constantius would leave him sole master of the Roman world,
we are assured that he had arranged in his mind a long succession
of future princes, and that he meditated his own retreat from
public life after he should have accomplished a glorious reign of
about twenty years.[2]

But, within less than eighteen months, two unexpected revolutions overturned the ambitious schemes of Galerius. The hopes
of uniting the western provinces to his empire were disappointed
by the elevation of Constantine; whilst Italy and Africa were
lost by the successful revolt of Maxentius.

I. The fame of Constantine has rendered posterity attentive
to the most minute circumstances of his life and actions. The
place of his birth, as well as the condition of his mother Helena,
have been the subject not only of literary but of national disputes.
Notwithstanding the recent tradition which assigns for her father
a British king,[3] we are obliged to confess that Helena was the
daughter of an innkeeper; but at the same time we may defend
the legality of her marriage against those who have represented
her as the concubine of Constantius.[4] The great Constantine
was most probably born at Naissus, in Dacia;[5] and it is not

---

[1] His diligence and fidelity are acknowledged even by Lactantius, de
M.P. c. 18.

[2] These schemes, however, rest only on the very doubtful authority of
Lactantius de M. P. c. 20.

[3] This tradition, unknown to the contemporaries of Constantine, was invented in the darkness of monasteries, was embellished by Jeffrey of Mon-
mouth and the writers of the twelfth century, has been defended by our
antiquarians of the last age, and is seriously related in the ponderous
History of England compiled by Mr. Carte (vol. i. p. 147). He transports,
however, the kingdom of Coil, the imaginary father of Helena, from Essex
to the wall of Antoninus.

[4] Eutropius (x. 2) expresses, in a few words, the real truth, and the occasion of the error, " *ex obscuriori matrimonio* ejus filius." Zosimus (l. ii.
[c. 8] p. 78) eagerly seized the most unfavourable report, and is followed
by Orosius (vii. 25), whose authority is oddly enough overlooked by the
indefatigable but partial Tillemont. By insisting on the divorce of
Helena, Diocletian acknowledged her marriage.

[5] There are three opinions with regard to the place of Constantine's birth.
1. Our English antiquarians were used to dwell with rapture on the words
of his panegyrist, " Britannias illic oriendo nobiles fecisti." But this celebrated passage may be referred with as much propriety to the accession
as to the nativity of Constantine. 2. Some of the modern Greeks have

surprising that, in a family and province distinguished only by
the profession of arms, the youth should discover very little inclination to improve his mind by the acquisition of knowledge.[1]
He was about eighteen years of age when his father was promoted
to the rank of Cæsar; but that fortunate event was attended
with his mother's divorce; and the splendour of an Imperial
alliance reduced the son of Helena to a state of disgrace and
humiliation. Instead of following Constantius in the West, he
remained in the service of Diocletian, signalising his valour in
the wars of Egypt and Persia, and gradually rose to the honourable station of a tribune of the first order. The figure of
Constantine was tall and majestic; he was dexterous in all his
exercises, intrepid in war, affable in peace; in his whole conduct
the active spirit of youth was tempered by habitual prudence;
and while his mind was engrossed by ambition, he appeared cold
and insensible to the allurements of pleasure. The favour of the
people and soldiers, who had named him as a worthy candidate
for the rank of Cæsar, served only to exasperate the jealousy of
Galerius; and though prudence might restrain him from exercising any open violence, an absolute monarch is seldom at a loss
how to execute a sure and secret revenge.[2] Every hour increased
the danger of Constantine and the anxiety of his father, who, by
repeated letters, expressed the warmest desire of embracing his
son. For some time the policy of Galerius supplied him with
delays and excuses, but it was impossible long to refuse so natural
a request of his associate without maintaining his refusal by

ascribed the honour of his birth to Drepanum, a town on the gulf of Nicomedia (Cellarius, tom. ii. p. 174), which Constantine dignified with the
name of Helenopolis, and Justinian adorned with many splendid buildings
(Procop. de Edificiis, v. 2). It is indeed probable enough that Helena's
father kept an inn at Drepanum, and that Constantius might lodge there
when he returned from a Persian embassy in the reign of Aurelian. But
in the wandering life of a soldier, the place of his marriage, and the places
where his children are born, have very little connection with each other.
3. The claim of Naissus is supported by the anonymous writer, published
at the end of Ammianus, p. 710 [vol. ii. p. 295, ed. Bip.], and who in general
copied very good materials: and it is confirmed by Julius Firmicus (de
Astrologia, l. i. c. 4), who flourished under the reign of Constantine himself.
Some objections have been raised against the integrity of the text, and the
application of the passage, of Firmicus; but the former is established by
the best MSS., and the latter is very ably defended by Lipsius de Magnitudine Romana, l. iv. c. 11, et Supplement.

[1] Literis minus instructus. Anonym. ad Ammian. p. 710.

[2] Galerius, or perhaps his own courage, exposed him to single combat
with a Sarmatian (Anonym. p. 710), and with a monstrous lion. See
Praxagoras apud Photium, p. 63. Praxagoras, an Athenian philosopher,
had written a life of Constantine in two books, which are now lost. He
was a contemporary.

arms. The permission of the journey was reluctantly granted, and, whatever precautions the emperor might have taken to intercept a return, the consequences of which he with so much reason apprehended, they were effectually disappointed by the incredible diligence of Constantine.[1] Leaving the palace of Nicomedia in the night, he travelled post through Bithynia, Thrace, Dacia, Pannonia, Italy, and, amidst the joyful acclamations of the people, reached the port of Boulogne in the very moment when his father was preparing to embark for Britain.[2]

The British expedition, and an easy victory over the barbarians of Caledonia, were the last exploits of the reign of Constantius. He ended his life in the Imperial palace of York, fifteen months after he had received the title of Augustus, and almost fourteen years and a half after he had been promoted to the rank of Cæsar. His death was immediately succeeded by the elevation of Constantine. The ideas of inheritance and succession are so very familiar that the generality of mankind consider them as founded not only in reason but in nature itself. Our imagination readily transfers the same principles from private property to public dominion: and whenever a virtuous father leaves behind him a son whose merit seems to justify the esteem, or even the hopes, of the people, the joint influence of prejudice and of affection operates with irresistible weight. The flower of the western armies had followed Constantius into Britain, and the national troops were reinforced by a numerous body of Alemanni, who obeyed the orders of Crocus, one of their hereditary chieftains.[3] The opinion of their own importance, and the assurance that Britain, Gaul, and Spain would acquiesce in their nomination, were diligently inculcated to the legions by the adherents of Constantine. The soldiers were asked whether they could hesitate a moment between the honour of placing at their head the worthy son of their beloved emperor and the ignominy of tamely expecting the arrival of some obscure stranger, on

---

[1] Zosimus, l. ii. [c. 8] p. 78, 79. Lactantius de M. P. c. 24. The former tells a very foolish story, that Constantine caused all the post-horses which he had used to be hamstrung. Such a bloody execution, without preventing a pursuit, would have scattered suspicions, and might have stopped his journey.

[2] Anonym. p. 710. Panegyr. Veter. vii. 7. But Zosimus, l. ii. [c. 9] p. 79, Eusebius de Vit. Constant. l. i. c. 21, and Lactantius de M. P. c. 24, suppose, with less accuracy, that he found his father on his death-bed.

[3] Cunctis qui aderant annitentibus, sed præcipue Croco (alii Eroco) [Erich?] Alemannorum Rege, auxiliâ gratiâ Constantium comitato, imperium capit. Victor Junior, c. 41. This is perhaps the first instance of a barbarian king who assisted the Roman arms with an independent body of his own subjects. The practice grew familiar, and at last became fatal.

whom it might please the sovereign of Asia to bestow the armies and provinces of the West? It was insinuated to them that gratitude and liberality held a distinguished place among the virtues of Constantine; nor did that artful prince show himself to the troops till they were prepared to salute him with the names of Augustus and Emperor. The throne was the object of his desires; and had he been less actuated by ambition, it was his only means of safety. He was well acquainted with the character and sentiments of Galerius, and sufficiently apprised that, if he wished to live, he must determine to reign. The decent, and even obstinate, resistance which he chose to affect [1] was contrived to justify his usurpation; nor did he yield to the acclamations of the army till he had provided the proper materials for a letter, which he immediately despatched to the emperor of the East. Constantine informed him of the melancholy event of his father's death, modestly asserted his natural claim to the succession, and respectfully lamented that the affectionate violence of his troops had not permitted him to solicit the Imperial purple in the regular and constitutional manner. The first emotions of Galerius were those of surprise, disappointment, and rage; and, as he could seldom restrain his passions, he loudly threatened that he would commit to the flames both the letter and the messenger. But his resentment insensibly subsided; and when he recollected the doubtful chance of war, when he had weighed the character and strength of his adversary, he consented to embrace the honourable accommodation which the prudence of Constantine had left open to him. Without either condemning or ratifying the choice of the British army, Galerius accepted the son of his deceased colleague as the sovereign of the provinces beyond the Alps; but he gave him only the title of Cæsar, and the fourth rank among the Roman princes, whilst he conferred the vacant place of Augustus on his favourite Severus. The apparent harmony of the empire was still preserved, and Constantine, who already possessed the substance, expected, without impatience, an opportunity of obtaining the honours of supreme power.[2]

The children of Constantius by his second marriage were six in number, three of either sex, and whose Imperial descent might have solicited a preference over the meaner extraction

---

[1] His panegyrist Eumenius (vii. 8) ventures to affirm, in the presence of Constantine, that he put spurs to his horse, and tried, but in vain, to escape from the hands of his soldiers.

[2] Lactantius de M. P. c. 25. Eumenius (vii. 8) gives a rhetorical turn to the whole transaction.

of the son of Helena. But Constantine was in the thirty-second year of his age, in the full vigour both of mind and body, at the time when the eldest of his brothers could not possibly be more than thirteen years old. His claim of superior merit had been allowed and ratified by the dying emperor.[1] In his last moments Constantius bequeathed to his eldest son the care of the safety, as well as greatness, of the family; conjuring him to assume both the authority and the sentiments of a father with regard to the children of Theodora. Their liberal education, advantageous marriages, the secure dignity of their lives, and the first honours of the state with which they were invested, attest the fraternal affection of Constantine; and, as those princes possessed a mild and grateful disposition, they submitted without reluctance to the superiority of his genius and fortune.[2]

II. The ambitious spirit of Galerius was scarcely reconciled to the disappointment of his views upon the Gallic provinces before the unexpected loss of Italy wounded his pride as well as power in a still more sensible part. The long absence of the emperors had filled Rome with discontent and indignation; and the people gradually discovered that the preference given to Nicomedia and Milan was not to be ascribed to the particular inclination of Diocletian, but to the permanent form of government which he had instituted. It was in vain that, a few months after his abdication, his successors dedicated, under his name, those magnificent baths whose ruins still supply the ground as well as the materials for so many churches and convents.[3] The tranquillity of those elegant recesses of ease and luxury was disturbed by the impatient murmurs of the Romans, and a report was insensibly circulated that the sums expended in erecting those buildings would soon be required at their hands. About that

---

[1] The choice of Constantine by his dying father, which is warranted by reason, and insinuated by Eumenius, seems to be confirmed by the most unexceptionable authority, the concurring evidence of Lactantius (de M. P. c. 24) and of Libanius (Oratio i.), of Eusebius (in Vit. Constantin. l. i. c. 21) and of Julian (Oratio i. [p. 7]).

[2] Of the three sisters of Constantine, Constantia married the emperor Licinius, Anastasia the Cæsar Bassianus, and Eutropia the consul Nepotianus. The three brothers were, Dalmatius, Julius Constantius, and Annibalianus, of whom we shall have occasion to speak hereafter.

[3] See Gruter Inscrip. p. 178. The six princes are all mentioned, Diocletian and Maximian as the senior Augusti, and fathers of the emperors. They jointly dedicate, for the use of *their own* Romans, this magnificent edifice. The architects have delineated the ruins of these *Thermæ*; and the antiquarians, particularly Donatus and Nardini, have ascertained the ground which they covered. One of the great rooms is now the Carthusian church; and even one of the porter's lodges is sufficient to form another church, which belongs to the Feuillans.

time the avarice of Galerius, or perhaps the exigencies of the
state, had induced him to make a very strict and rigorous inquisition into the property of his subjects for the purpose of a
general taxation, both on their lands and on their persons. A
very minute survey appears to have been taken of their real
estates; and, wherever there was the slightest suspicion of concealment, torture was very freely employed to obtain a sincere
declaration of their personal wealth.[1] The privileges which had
exalted Italy above the rank of the provinces were no longer
regarded: and the officers of the revenue already began to number
the Roman people, and to settle the proportion of the new taxes.
Even when the spirit of freedom had been utterly extinguished,
the tamest subjects have sometimes ventured to resist an un-
precedented invasion of their property; but on this occasion the
injury was aggravated by the insult, and the sense of private
interest was quickened by that of national honour. The conquest of Macedonia, as we have already observed, had delivered
the Roman people from the weight of personal taxes. Though
they had experienced every form of despotism, they had now
enjoyed that exemption near five hundred years; nor could
they patiently brook the insolence of an Illyrian peasant, who,
from his distant residence in Asia, presumed to number Rome
among the tributary cities of his empire.[2] The rising fury of the
people was encouraged by the authority, or at least the connivance, of the senate; and the feeble remains of the Prætorian
guards, who had reason to apprehend their own dissolution,
embraced so honourable a pretence, and declared their readiness
to draw their swords in the service of their oppressed country.
It was the wish, and it soon became the hope, of every citizen
that, after expelling from Italy their foreign tyrants, they should
elect a prince who, by the place of his residence, and by his
maxims of government, might once more deserve the title of
Roman emperor. The name, as well as the situation of Maxentius, determined in his favour the popular enthusiasm.

Maxentius was the son of the emperor Maximian, and he
had married the daughter of Galerius. His birth and alliance
seemed to offer him the fairest promise of succeeding to the

[1] See Lactantius de M. P. c. 26, 31.

[2] [Notwithstanding the discontent of the people, the system of taxation
which had prevailed in the provinces was now permanently established in
Rome and all throughout Italy. There was, therefore, according to
Aurelius Victor (De Cæsar c. 39), one uniform system of taxation throughout the Roman empire, the only exceptions being those towns which had
the *jus Italicum*, this name continuing to be employed, although no longer
appropriate, since Italy had ceased to possess any special rights.—O. S.]

empire; but his vices and incapacity procured him the same
exclusion from the dignity of Cæsar which Constantine had
deserved by a dangerous superiority of merit. The policy of
Galerius preferred such associates as would never disgrace the
choice, nor dispute the commands, of their benefactor. An
obscure stranger was therefore raised to the throne of Italy, and
the son of the late emperor of the West was left to enjoy the
luxury of a private fortune in a villa a few miles distant from the
capital. The gloomy passions of his soul, shame, vexation, and
rage, were inflamed by envy on the news of Constantine's success; but the hopes of Maxentius revived with the public discontent, and he was easily persuaded to unite his personal injury
and pretensions with the cause of the Roman people. Two
Prætorian tribunes and a commissary of provisions undertook
the management of the conspiracy; and, as every order of men
was actuated by the same spirit, the immediate event was neither
doubtful nor difficult. The præfect of the city and a few magistrates, who maintained their fidelity to Severus, were massacred
by the guards; and Maxentius, invested with the Imperial
ornaments, was acknowledged, by the applauding senate and
people, as the protector of the Roman freedom and dignity. It
is uncertain whether Maximian was previously acquainted with
the conspiracy; but as soon as the standard of rebellion was
erected at Rome, the old emperor broke from the retirement
where the authority of Diocletian had condemned him to pass a
life of melancholy solitude, and concealed his returning ambition
under the disguise of paternal tenderness. At the request of his
son and of the senate he condescended to reassume the purple.
His ancient dignity, his experience, and his fame in arms added
strength as well as reputation to the party of Maxentius.[1]

According to the advice, or rather the orders, of his colleague,
the emperor Severus immediately hastened to Rome, in the full
confidence that, by his unexpected celerity, he should easily
suppress the tumult of an unwarlike populace, commanded by
a licentious youth. But he found on his arrival the gates of the
city shut against him, the walls filled with men and arms, an
experienced general at the head of the rebels, and his own troops
without spirit or affection. A large body of Moors deserted to
the enemy, allured by the promise of a large donative; and, if

[1] The sixth Panegyric represents the conduct of Maximian in the most
favourable light; and the ambiguous expression of Aurelius Victor [de
Cæsar. c. 40], "retractante diu," may signify either that he contrived, or
that he opposed, the conspiracy. See Zosimus, l. ii. [c. 9] p. 79, and
Lactantius de M. P. c 26.

it be true that they had been levied by Maximian in his African war, preferring the natural feelings of gratitude to the artificial ties of allegiance. Anulinus, the Prætorian præfect, declared himself in favour of Maxentius, and drew after him the most considerable part of the troops accustomed to obey his commands. Rome, according to the expression of an orator, recalled her armies; and the unfortunate Severus, destitute of force and of counsel, retired, or rather fled, with precipitation to Ravenna. Here he might for some time have been safe. The fortifications of Ravenna were able to resist the attempts, and the morasses that surrounded the town were sufficient to prevent the approach, of the Italian army. Thesea, which Severus commanded with a powerful fleet, secured him an inexhaustible supply of provisions, and gave a free entrance to the legions which, on the return of spring, would advance to his assistance from Illyricum and the East. Maximian, who conducted the siege in person, was soon convinced that he might waste his time and his army in the fruitless enterprise, and that he had nothing to hope either from force or famine. With an art more suitable to the character of Diocletian than to his own, he directed his attack not so much against the walls of Ravenna as against the mind of Severus. The treachery which he had experienced disposed that unhappy prince to distrust the most sincere of his friends and adherents. The emissaries of Maximian easily persuaded his credulity that a conspiracy was formed to betray the town, and prevailed upon his fears not to expose himself to the discretion of an irritated conqueror, but to accept the faith of an honourable capitulation. He was at first received with humanity and treated with respect. Maximian conducted the captive emperor to Rome, and gave him the most solemn assurances that he had secured his life by the resignation of the purple. But Severus could obtain only an easy death and an Imperial funeral. When the sentence was signified to him, the manner of executing it was left to his own choice; he preferred the favourite mode of the ancients, that of opening his veins; and, as soon as he expired, his body was carried to the sepulchre which had been constructed for the family of Gallienus.[1]

Though the characters of Constantine and Maxentius had very little affinity with each other, their situation and interest were the same, and prudence seemed to require that they should

[1] The circumstances of this war, and the death of Severus, are very doubtfully and variously told in our ancient fragments (see Tillemont, Hist. des Empereurs, tom. iv. part. i. p. 555). I have endeavoured to extract from them a consistent and probable narration.

unite their forces against the common enemy. Notwithstanding the superiority of his age and dignity, the indefatigable Maximian passed the Alps, and, courting a personal interview with the sovereign of Gaul, carried with him his daughter Fausta as the pledge of the new alliance. The marriage was celebrated at Arles with every circumstance of magnificence; and the ancient colleague of Diocletian, who again asserted his claim to the Western empire, conferred on his son-in-law and ally the title of Augustus. By consenting to receive that honour from Maximian, Constantine seemed to embrace the cause of Rome and of the senate; but his professions were ambiguous, and his assistance slow and ineffectual. He considered with attention the approaching contest between the masters of Italy and the emperor of the East, and was prepared to consult his own safety or ambition in the event of the war.[1]

The importance of the occasion called for the presence and abilities of Galerius. At the head of a powerful army collected from Illyricum and the East, he entered Italy, resolved to revenge the death of Severus and to chastise the rebellious Romans; or, as he expressed his intentions, in the furious language of a barbarian, to extirpate the senate, and to destroy the people by the sword. But the skill of Maximian had concerted a prudent system of defence. The invader found every place hostile, fortified, and inaccessible; and though he forced his way as far as Narni, within sixty miles of Rome, his dominion in Italy was confined to the narrow limits of his camp. Sensible of the increasing difficulties of his enterprise, the haughty Galerius made the first advances towards a reconciliation, and despatched two of his most considerable officers to tempt the Roman princes by the offer of a conference, and the declaration of his paternal regard for Maxentius, who might obtain much more from his liberality than he could hope from the doubtful chance of war.[2] The offers of Galerius were rejected with firmness, his perfidious friendship refused with contempt, and it was not long before he discovered that unless he provided for his safety by a timely retreat, he had some reason to apprehend the fate of Severus. The wealth which the Romans defended against his rapacious

[1] The sixth Panegyric was pronounced to celebrate the elevation of Constantine; but the prudent orator avoids the mention either of Galerius or of Maxentius. He introduces only one slight allusion to the actual troubles, and to the majesty of Rome.

[2] With regard to this negotiation, see the fragments of an anonymous historian, published by Valesius at the end of his edition of Ammianus Marcellinus, p. 711. These fragments have furnished us with several curious, and, as it should seem, authentic anecdotes.

tyranny they freely contributed for his destruction. The name of Maximian, the popular arts of his son, the secret distribution of large sums, and the promise of still more liberal rewards, checked the ardour and corrupted the fidelity of the Illyrian legions; and when Galerius at length gave the signal of the retreat, it was with some difficulty that he could prevail on his veterans not to desert a banner which had so often conducted them to victory and honour. A contemporary writer assigns two other causes for the failure of the expedition; but they are both of such a nature that a cautious historian will scarcely venture to adopt them. We are told that Galerius, who had formed a very imperfect notion of the greatness of Rome by the cities of the East with which he was acquainted, found his forces inadequate to the siege of that immense capital. But the extent of a city serves only to render it more accessible to the enemy: Rome had long since been accustomed to submit on the approach of a conqueror; nor could the temporary enthusiasm of the people have long contended against the discipline and valour of the legions. We are likewise informed that the legions themselves were struck with horror and remorse, and that those pious sons of the republic refused to violate the sanctity of their venerable parent.[1] But when we recollect with how much ease, in the more ancient civil wars, the zeal of party and the habits of military obedience had converted the native citizens of Rome into her most implacable enemies, we shall be inclined to distrust this extreme delicacy of strangers and barbarians who had never beheld Italy till they entered it in a hostile manner. Had they not been restrained by motives of a more interested nature, they would probably have answered Galerius in the words of Cæsar's veterans: " If our general wishes to lead us to the banks of the Tiber, we are prepared to trace out his camp. Whatsoever walls he has determined to level with the ground, our hands are ready to work the engines: nor shall we hesitate, should the name of the devoted city be Rome itself." These are indeed the expressions of a poet; but of a poet who has been distinguished, and even censured, for his strict adherence to the truth of history.[2]

---

[1] Lactantius de M. P. c. 27. The former of these reasons is probably taken from Virgil's Shepherd: " Illam . . . ego huic nostræ similem, Melibœe, putavi, etc." Lactantius delights in these poetical allusions.

[2] Castra super Tusci si ponere Tybridis undas (*jubeas*)
Hesperios audax veniam metator in agros.
Tu quoscunque voles in planum effundere muros,
His aries actus disperget saxa lacertis;
Illa licet penitus tolli quam jusseris urbem
Roma sit.   Lucan. Pharsal. i. 381.

The legions of Galerius exhibited a very melancholy proof of their disposition by the ravages which they committed in their retreat. They murdered, they ravished, they plundered, they drove away the flocks and herds of the Italians; they burnt the villages through which they passed, and they endeavoured to destroy the country which it had not been in their power to subdue. During the whole march Maxentius hung on their rear, but he very prudently declined a general engagement with those brave and desperate veterans. His father had undertaken a second journey into Gaul, with the hope of persuading Constantine, who had assembled an army on the frontier, to join the pursuit, and to complete the victory. But the actions of Constantine were guided by reason, and not by resentment. He persisted in the wise resolution of maintaining a balance of power in the divided empire, and he no longer hated Galerius when that aspiring prince had ceased to be an object of terror.[1]

The mind of Galerius was the most susceptible of the sterner passions, but it was not, however, incapable of a sincere and lasting friendship. Licinius, whose manners as well as character were not unlike his own, seems to have engaged both his affection and esteem. Their intimacy had commenced in the happier period, perhaps, of their youth and obscurity. It had been cemented by the freedom and dangers of a military life; they had advanced almost by equal steps through the successive honours of the service; and as soon as Galerius was invested with the Imperial dignity, he seems to have conceived the design of raising his companion to the same rank with himself. During the short period of his prosperity, he considered the rank of Cæsar as unworthy of the age and merit of Licinius, and rather chose to reserve for him the place of Constantius, and the empire of the West. While the emperor was employed in the Italian war, he intrusted his friend with the defence of the Danube; and immediately after his return from that unfortunate expedition he invested Licinius with the vacant purple of Severus, resigning to his immediate command the provinces of Illyricum.[2] The news of his promotion was no sooner carried into the East, than Maximin, who governed, or rather oppressed,

---

[1] Lactantius de M. P. c. 27. Zosim. l. ii. [c. 10] p. 82. The latter insinuates that Constantine, in his interview with Maximian, had promised to declare war against Galerius.

[2] M. de Tillemont (Hist. des Empereurs, tom. iv. part. i. p. 559) has proved that Licinius, without passing through the intermediate rank of Cæsar, was declared Augustus, the 11th of November, A.D. 307, after the return of Galerius from Italy.

the countries of Egypt and Syria, betrayed his envy and discontent, disdained the inferior name of Cæsar, and, notwithstanding
the prayers as well as arguments of Galerius, exacted, almost by
violence, the equal title of Augustus.[1] For the first, and indeed
for the last time, the Roman world was administered by six
emperors. In the West, Constantine and Maxentius affected to
reverence their father Maximian. In the East, Licinius and
Maximin honoured with more real consideration their benefactor Galerius. The opposition of interest, and the memory of
a recent war, divided the empire into two great hostile powers;
but their mutual fears produced an apparent tranquillity, and
even a feigned reconciliation, till the death of the elder princes,
of Maximian, and more particularly of Galerius, gave a new
direction to the views and passions of their surviving associates.

When Maximian had reluctantly abdicated the empire, the
venal orators of the times applauded his philosophic moderation.
When his ambition excited, or at least encouraged, a civil war,
they returned thanks to his generous patriotism, and gently
censured that love of ease and retirement which had withdrawn
him from the public service.[2] But it was impossible that minds
like those of Maximian and his son could long possess in harmony
an undivided power. Maxentius considered himself as the legal
sovereign of Italy, elected by the Roman senate and people; nor
would he endure the control of his father, who arrogantly
declared that by *his* name and abilities the rash youth had been
established on the throne. The cause was solemnly pleaded
before the Prætorian guards; and those troops, who dreaded
the severity of the old emperor, espoused the party of Maxentius.[3]
The life and freedom of Maximian were, however, respected, and
he retired from Italy into Illyricum, affecting to lament his past
conduct, and secretly contriving new mischiefs. But Galerius,
who was well acquainted with his character, soon obliged him
to leave his dominions, and the last refuge of the disappointed

---

[1] Lactantius de M. P. c. 32. When Galerius declared Licinius Augustus
with himself, he tried to satisfy his younger associates, by inventing for
Constantine and *Maximin* (not *Maxentius*, see Baluze, p. 81) the new title
of sons of the Augusti. But when Maximin acquainted him that he had
been saluted Augustus by the army, Galerius was obliged to acknowledge
him, as well as Constantine, as equal associates in the Imperial dignity.

[2] See Panegyr. Vet. vi. [v.] 9. Audi doloris nostri liberam vocem, etc.
The whole passage is imagined with artful flattery, and expressed with an
easy flow of eloquence.

[3] Lactantius de M. P. c. 28. Zosim. l. ii. [c. 11] p. 82. A report was
spread that Maxentius was the son of some obscure Syrian, and had been
substituted by the wife of Maximian as her own child. See Aurelius Victor
[Epit. 40], Anonym. Valesian. [§ 12], and Panegyr. Vet. ix. 3, 4.

Maximian was the court of his son-in-law Constantine.[1] He was received with respect by that artful prince, and with the appearance of filial tenderness by the empress Fausta. That he might remove every suspicion, he resigned the Imperial purple a second time,[2] professing himself at length convinced of the vanity of greatness and ambition. Had he persevered in this resolution, he might have ended his life with less dignity, indeed, than in his first retirement, yet, however, with comfort and reputation. But the near prospect of a throne brought back to his remembrance the state from whence he was fallen, and he resolved, by a desperate effort, either to reign or to perish. An incursion of the Franks had summoned Constantine, with a part of his army, to the banks of the Rhine; the remainder of the troops were stationed in the southern provinces of Gaul, which lay exposed to the enterprises of the Italian emperor, and a considerable treasure was deposited in the city of Arles. Maximian either craftily invented, or hastily credited, a vain report of the death of Constantine. Without hesitation he ascended the throne, seized the treasure, and, scattering it with his accustomed profusion among the soldiers, endeavoured to awake in their minds the memory of his ancient dignity and exploits. Before he could establish his authority, or finish the negotiation which he appears to have entered into with his son Maxentius, the celerity of Constantine defeated all his hopes. On the first news of his perfidy and ingratitude, that prince returned by rapid marches from the Rhine to the Saone, embarked on the last-mentioned river at Châlons, and, at Lyons trusting himself to the rapidity of the Rhone, arrived at the gates of Arles with a military force which it was impossible for Maximian to resist, and which scarcely permitted him to take refuge in the neighbouring city of Marseilles. The narrow neck of land which joined that place to the continent was fortified against the besiegers, whilst the sea was open, either for the escape of Maximian, or for the succours of Maxentius, if the latter should choose to disguise his invasion of Gaul under the honourable pretence of defending a distressed, or, as he might allege, an injured father. Apprehensive of the fatal consequences of delay,

---

[1] Ab urbe pulsum, ab Italia fugatum, ab Illyrico repudiatum, tuis provinciis, tuis copiis, tuo palatio recepisti. Eumen. in Panegyr. Vet. vii. [vi.] 14.

[2] Lactantius de M. P. c. 29. Yet after the resignation of the purple, Constantine still continued to Maximian the pomp and honours of the Imperial dignity; and on all public occasions gave the right-hand place to his father-in-law. Panegyr. Vet. viii. 15.

Constantine gave orders for an immediate assault; but the scaling-ladders were found too short for the height of the walls, and Marseilles might have sustained as long a siege as it formerly did against the arms of Cæsar, if the garrison, conscious either of their fault or of their danger, had not purchased their pardon by delivering up the city and the person of Maximian. A secret but irrevocable sentence of death was pronounced against the usurper; he obtained only the same favour which he had indulged to Severus, and it was published to the world that, oppressed by the remorse of his repeated crimes, he strangled himself with his own hands. After he had lost the assistance, and disdained the moderate counsels, of Diocletian, the second period of his active life was a series of public calamities and personal mortifications, which were terminated, in about three years, by an ignominious death. He deserved his fate; but we should find more reason to applaud the humanity of Constantine if he had spared an old man, the benefactor of his father and the father of his wife. During the whole of this melancholy transaction, it appears that Fausta sacrificed the sentiments of nature to her conjugal duties.[1]

The last years of Galerius were less shameful and unfortunate; and though he had filled with more glory the subordinate station of Cæsar than the superior rank of Augustus, he preserved, till the moment of his death, the first place among the princes of the Roman world. He survived his retreat from Italy about four years; and, wisely relinquishing his views of universal empire, he devoted the remainder of his life to the enjoyment of pleasure and to the execution of some works of public utility, among which we may distinguish the discharging into the Danube the superfluous waters of the lake Pelso, and the cutting down the immense forests that encompassed it: an operation worthy of a monarch, since it gave an extensive country to the agriculture of his Pannonian subjects.[2] His death was occasioned by a

[1] Zosim. l. ii. [c. 11] p. 82. Eumenius in Panegyr. Vet. vii. 16-21. The latter of these has undoubtedly represented the whole affair in the most favourable light for his sovereign. Yet even from this partial narrative we may conclude that the repeated clemency of Constantine, and the reiterated treasons of Maximian, as they are described by Lactantius (de M. P. c. 29, 30), and copied by the moderns, are destitute of any historical foundation.

[2] Aurelius Victor, c. 40. But that lake was situated on the upper Pannonia, near the borders of Noricum; and the province of Valeria (a name which the wife of Galerius gave to the drained country) undoubtedly lay between the Drave and the Danube (Sextus Rufus, c. 8). I should therefore suspect that Victor has confounded the lake Pelso with the Volocean marshes, or, as they are now called, the lake Sabaton. It is placed in the

very painful and lingering disorder. His body, swelled by an intemperate course of life to an unwieldy corpulence, was covered with ulcers, and devoured by innumerable swarms of those insects who have given their name to a most loathsome disease; [1] but as Galerius had offended a very zealous and powerful party among his subjects, his sufferings, instead of exciting their compassion, have been celebrated as the visible effects of divine justice. [2] He had no sooner expired in his palace of Nicomedia than the two emperors, who were indebted for their purple to his favour, began to collect their forces, with the intention either of disputing or of dividing the dominions which he had left without a master. They were persuaded, however, to desist from the former design, and to agree in the latter. The provinces of Asia fell to the share of Maximin, and those of Europe augmented the portion of Licinius. The Hellespont and the Thracian Bosphorus formed their mutual boundary, and the banks of those narrow seas, which flowed in the midst of the Roman world, were covered with soldiers, with arms, and with fortifications. The deaths of Maximian and of Galerius reduced the number of emperors to four. The sense of their true interest soon connected Licinius and Constantine; a secret alliance was concluded between Maximin and Maxentius, and their unhappy subjects expected with terror the bloody consequences of their inevitable dissensions, which were no longer restrained by the fear or the respect which they had entertained for Galerius. [3]

Among so many crimes and misfortunes, occasioned by the passions of the Roman princes, there is some pleasure in discovering a single action which may be ascribed to their virtue. In the sixth year of his reign Constantine visited the city of Autun, and generously remitted the arrears of tribute, reducing at the same time the proportion of their assessment from twenty-five to eighteen thousand heads, subject to the real and personal capitation. [4] Yet even this indulgence affords the most un-

heart of Valeria, and its present extent is not less than twelve Hungarian miles (about seventy English) in length, and two in breadth. See Severini Pannonia, l. i. c. 9.

[1] Lactantius (de M. P. c. 33) and Eusebius (l. viii. c. 16) describe the symptoms and progress of his disorder with singular accuracy and apparent pleasure. [See *Merivale*, note on page 261—O. S.]

[2] If any (like the late Dr. Jortin, Remarks on Ecclesiastical History, vol. ii. p. 307-356) still delight in recording the wonderful deaths of the persecutors, I would recommend to their perusal an admirable passage of Grotius (Hist. l. vii. p. 332) concerning the last illness of Philip II. of Spain.

[3] See Eusebius, l. ix. 6, 10. Lactantius de M. P. c. 36. Zosimus is less exact, and evidently confounds Maximian with Maximin.

[4] See the eighth Panegyr., in which Eumenius displays, in the presence of Constantine, the misery and the gratitude of the city of Autun.

questionable proof of the public misery. This tax was so extremely oppressive, either in itself or in the mode of collecting
it, that, whilst the revenue was increased by extortion, it was
diminished by despair: a considerable part of the territory of
Autun was left uncultivated; and great numbers of the provincials rather chose to live as exiles and outlaws than to support
the weight of civil society. It is but too probable that the
bountiful emperor relieved, by a partial act of liberality, one
among the many evils which he had caused by his general
maxims of administration. But even those maxims were less
the effect of choice than of necessity. And if we except the
death of Maximian, the reign of Constantine in Gaul seems to
have been the most innocent and even virtuous period of his
life. The provinces were protected by his presence from the
inroads of the barbarians, who either dreaded or experienced his
active valour. After a signal victory over the Franks and
Alemanni, several of their princes were exposed by his order
to the wild beasts in the amphitheatre of Treves, and the people
seem to have enjoyed the spectacle, without discovering, in
such a treatment of royal captives, anything that was repugnant
to the laws of nations or of humanity.[1]

The virtues of Constantine were rendered more illustrious by
the vices of Maxentius. Whilst the Gallic provinces enjoyed as
much happiness as the condition of the times was capable of
receiving, Italy and Africa groaned under the dominion of a
tyrant as contemptible as he was odious. The zeal of flattery and
faction has indeed too frequently sacrificed the reputation of the
vanquished to the glory of their successful rivals; but even those
writers who have revealed, with the most freedom and pleasure,
the faults of Constantine, unanimously confess that Maxentius
was cruel, rapacious, and profligate.[2] He had the good fortune
to suppress a slight rebellion in Africa. The governor and a few
adherents had been guilty; the province suffered for their crime.
The flourishing cities of Cirtha and Carthage, and the whole
extent of that fertile country, were wasted by fire and sword.
The abuse of victory was followed by the abuse of law and justice.
A formidable army of sycophants and delators invaded Africa;
the rich and the noble were easily convicted of a connection with

---

[1] Eutropius x. 2. Panegyr. Veter. vii. 10, 11, 12. A great number of
the French youth were likewise exposed to the same cruel and ignominious
death.

[2] Julian excludes Maxentius from the banquet of the Cæsars with abhorrence and contempt; and Zosimus (l. ii. [c. 14] p. 85) accuses him of every
kind of cruelty and profligacy.

the rebels; and those among them who experienced the emperor's
clemency were only punished by the confiscation of their estates.[1]
So signal a victory was celebrated by a magnificent triumph,
and Maxentius exposed to the eyes of the people the spoils and
captives of a Roman province. The state of the capital was no
less deserving of compassion than that of Africa. The wealth of
Rome supplied an inexhaustible fund for his vain and prodigal
expenses, and the ministers of his revenue were skilled in the
arts of rapine. It was under his reign that the method of exacting a *free gift* from the senators was first invented; and as the
sum was insensibly increased, the pretences of levying it, a
victory, a birth, a marriage, or an Imperial consulship, were
proportionably multiplied.[2] Maxentius had imbibed the same
implacable aversion to the senate which had characterised most
of the former tyrants of Rome; nor was it possible for his ungrateful temper to forgive the generous fidelity which had raised
him to the throne and supported him against all his enemies.
The lives of the senators were exposed to his jealous suspicions,
the dishonour of their wives and daughters heightened the gratification of his sensual passions.[3] It may be presumed that an
Imperial lover was seldom reduced to sigh in vain; but whenever
persuasion proved ineffectual, he had recourse to violence; and
there remains *one* memorable example of a noble matron who
preserved her chastity by a voluntary death. The soldiers were
the only order of men whom he appeared to respect, or studied
to please. He filled Rome and Italy with armed troops, connived at their tumults, suffered them with impunity to plunder,
and even to massacre, the defenceless people; [4] and indulging
them in the same licentiousness which their emperor enjoyed,
Maxentius often bestowed on his military favourites the splendid
villa, or the beautiful wife, of a senator. A prince, of such a
character, alike incapable of governing either in peace or in
war, might purchase the support, but he could never obtain the

---

[1] Zosimus, l. ii. [c. 14] p. 83-85. Aurelius Victor. [Cæsar. 40.]
[2] The passage of Aurelius Victor [l. c.] should be read in the following
manner: Primus instituto pessimo, *munerum* specie, Patres *Oratoresque*
pecuniam conferre prodigenti sibi cogeret.
[3] Panegyr. Vet. ix. 3.   Euseb. Hist. Eccles. viii. 14, et in Vit. Constant. i.
33, 34. Rufinus, c. 17. The virtuous matron, who stabbed herself to escape
the violence of Maxentius, was a Christian, wife to the præfect of the city, and
her name was Sophronia.   It still remains a question among the casuists,
Whether, on such occasions, suicide is justifiable?
[4] Prætorianis cædem vulgi quondam annuerit, is the vague expression of
Aurelius Victor. [Cæsar. 40.] See more particular, though somewhat
different, accounts of a tumult and massacre which happened at Rome, in
Eusebius (l. viii. c. 14), and in Zosimus (l. ii. [c. 13] p. 84).

esteem, of the army. Yet his pride was equal to his other vices. Whilst he passed his indolent life, either within the walls of his palace or in the neighbouring gardens of Sallust, he was repeatedly heard to declare that *he alone* was emperor, and that the other princes were no more than his lieutenants, on whom he had devolved the defence of the frontier provinces, that he might enjoy without interruption the elegant luxury of the capital. Rome, which had so long regretted the absence, lamented, during the six years of his reign, the presence of her sovereign.[1]

Though Constantine might view the conduct of Maxentius with abhorrence, and the situation of the Romans with compassion, we have no reason to presume that he would have taken up arms to punish the one or to relieve the other. But the tyrant of Italy rashly ventured to provoke a formidable enemy whose ambition had been hitherto restrained by considerations of prudence rather than by principles of justice.[2] After the death of Maximian, his titles, according to the established custom, had been erased, and his statues thrown down with ignominy. His son, who had persecuted and deserted him when alive, affected to display the most pious regard for his memory, and gave orders that a similar treatment should be immediately inflicted on all the statues that had been erected in Italy and Africa to the honour of Constantine. That wise prince, who sincerely wished to decline a war, with the difficulty and importance of which he was sufficiently acquainted, at first dissembled the insult, and sought for redress by the milder expedients of negotiation, till he was convinced that the hostile and ambitious designs of the Italian emperor made it necessary for him to arm in his own defence. Maxentius, who openly avowed his pretentions to the whole monarchy of the West, had already prepared a very considerable force to invade the Gallic provinces on the side of Rhætia; and though he could not expect any assistance from Licinius, he was flattered with the hope that the legions of Illyricum, allured by his presents and promises, would desert the standard of that prince, and unanimously declare themselves

---

[1] See in the Panegyrics (ix. 14) a lively description of the indolence and vain pride of Maxentius. In another place [*ib.* c. 3] the orator observes that the riches which Rome had accumulated in a period of 1060 years were lavished by the tyrant on his mercenary bands; redemptis ad civile latrocinium manibus ingesserat.

[2] After the victory of Constantine it was universally allowed that the motive of delivering the republic from a detested tyrant would, at any time, have justified his expedition into Italy. Euseb. in Vit. Constantin. 1 i. c. 26. Panegyr. Vet. ix. 2.

his soldiers and subjects.[1]　Constantine no longer hesitated.
He had deliberated with caution, he acted with vigour.　He
gave a private audience to the ambassadors who, in the name of
the senate and people, conjured him to deliver Rome from a
detested tyrant; and, without regarding the timid remonstrances
of his council, he resolved to prevent the enemy, and to carry
the war into the heart of Italy.[2]

The enterprise was as full of danger as of glory; and the
unsuccessful event of two former invasions was sufficient to inspire the most serious apprehensions.　The veteran troops, who
revered the name of Maximian, had embraced in both those wars
the party of his son, and were now restrained by a sense of honour,
as well as of interest, from entertaining an idea of a second desertion.　Maxentius, who considered the Prætorian guards as the
firmest defence of his throne, had increased them to their ancient
establishment; and they composed, including the rest of the
Italians who were enlisted into his service, a formidable body
of fourscore thousand men.　Forty thousand Moors and Cartha-
ginians had been raised since the reduction of Africa.　Even
Sicily furnished its proportion of troops; and the armies of
Maxentius amounted to one hundred and seventy thousand foot
and eighteen thousand horse.　The wealth of Italy supplied the
expenses of the war; and the adjacent provinces were exhausted
to form immense magazines of corn and every other kind of
provisions.

The whole force of Constantine consisted of ninety thousand
foot and eight thousand horse;[3] and as the defence of the Rhine
required an extraordinary attention during the absence of the
emperor, it was not in his power to employ above half his troops
in the Italian expedition, unless he sacrificed the public safety
to his private quarrel.[4]　At the head of about forty thousand

---

[1] Zosimus, l. ii. [c. 14] p. 84, 85.　Nazarius in Panegyr. x. 7-13.

[2] See Panegyr. Vet. ix. [viii.] 2.　Omnibus fere tuis Comitibus et Ducibus
non solum tacite mussantibus, sed etiam aperte timentibus; contra con-
silia hominum, contra Haruspicum monita, ipse per temet liberandæ urbis
tempus venisse sentires.　The embassy of the Romans is mentioned only
by Zonaras (l. xiii. [c. 1]), and by Cedrenus (in Compend. Hist. p. 270 [ed.
Paris; vol. i. p. 474, ed. Bonn]); but those modern Greeks had the opportunity of consulting many writers which have since been lost, among which
we may reckon the Life of Constantine by Praxagoras.　Photius (p. 63)
has made a short extract from that historical work.

[3] Zosimus (l. ii. [c. 15] p. 86) has given us this curious account of the
forces on both sides.　He makes no mention of any naval armaments,
though we are assured (Panegyr. Vet. ix. 25) that the war was carried on
by sea as well as by land; and that the fleet of Constantine took possession
of Sardinia, Corsica, and the ports of Italy.

[4] Panegyr. Vet. ix. 3.　It is not surprising that the orator should diminish

soldiers, he marched to encounter an enemy whose numbers were
at least four times superior to his own. But the armies of Rome,
placed at a secure distance from danger, were enervated by
indulgence and luxury. Habituated to the baths and theatres
of Rome, they took the field with reluctance, and were chiefly
composed of veterans who had almost forgotten, or of new levies
who had never acquired, the use of arms and the practice of war.
The hardy legions of Gaul had long defended the frontiers of
the empire against the barbarians of the North; and in the performance of that laborious service their valour was exercised
and their discipline confirmed. There appeared the same difference between the leaders as between the armies. Caprice or
flattery had tempted Maxentius with the hopes of conquest;
but these aspiring hopes soon gave way to the habits of pleasure
and the consciousness of his inexperience. The intrepid mind
of Constantine had been trained from his earliest youth to war,
to action, and to military command.

When Hannibal marched from Gaul into Italy, he was obliged
first to discover and then to open a way over mountains, and
through savage nations that had never yielded a passage to a
regular army.[1] The Alps were then guarded by nature, they are
now fortified by art. Citadels, constructed with no less skill
than labour and expense, command every avenue into the plain,
and on that side render Italy almost inaccessible to the enemies
of the king of Sardinia.[2] But in the course of the intermediate
period, the generals who have attempted the passage have seldom
experienced any difficulty or resistance. In the age of Constantine the peasants of the mountains were civilised and obedient
subjects; the country was plentifully stocked with provisions,
and the stupendous highways which the Romans had carried
over the Alps opened several communications between Gaul
and Italy.[3] Constantine preferred the road of the Cottian Alps,

the numbers with which his sovereign achieved the conquest of Italy; but
it appears somewhat singular that he should esteem the tyrant's army at no
more than 100,000 men.

[1] The three principal passages of the Alps between Gaul and Italy are
those of Mount St. Bernard, Mount Cenis, and Mount Genevre. Tradition,
and a resemblance of names (*Alpes Penninæ*), had assigned the first of
these for the march of Hannibal (see Simler de Alpibus). The Chevalier
de Folard (Polyb. tom. iv.) and M. d'Anville have led him over Mount
Genevre. But notwithstanding the authority of an experienced officer
and a learned geographer, the pretensions of Mount Cenis are supported in
a specious, not to say a convincing manner, by M. Grosley, Observations
sur l'Italie, tom. i. p. 40, etc.

[2] La Brunette near Suse, Demont, Exiles, Fenestrelles, Coni, etc.

[3] See Ammian. Marcellin. xv. 10. His description of the roads over the
Alps is clear, lively and accurate.

or, as it is now called, of Mount Cenis, and led his troops with such active diligence, that he descended into the plain of Piedmont before the court of Maxentius had received any certain intelligence of his departure from the banks of the Rhine. The city of Susa, however, which is situated at the foot of Mount Cenis, was surrounded with walls, and provided with a garrison sufficiently numerous to check the progress of an invader; but the impatience of Constantine's troops disdained the tedious forms of a siege. The same day that they appeared before Susa they applied fire to the gates and ladders to the walls; and mounting to the assault amidst a shower of stones and arrows, they entered the place sword in hand, and cut in pieces the greatest part of the garrison. The flames were extinguished by the care of Constantine, and the remains of Susa preserved from total destruction. About forty miles from thence a more severe contest awaited him. A numerous army of Italians was assembled, under the lieutenants of Maxentius, in the plains of Turin. Its principal strength consisted in a species of heavy cavalry, which the Romans, since the decline of their discipline, had borrowed from the nations of the East. The horses, as well as the men, were clothed in complete armour, the joints of which were artfully adapted to the motions of their bodies. The aspect of this cavalry was formidable, their weight almost irresistible; and as, on this occasion, their generals had drawn them up in a compact column or wedge, with a sharp point, and with spreading flanks, they flattered themselves that they should easily break and trample down the army of Constantine. They might, perhaps, have succeeded in their design, had not their experienced adversary embraced the same method of defence which in similar circumstances had been practised by Aurelian. The skilful evolutions of Constantine divided and baffled this massy column of cavalry. The troops of Maxentius fled in confusion towards Turin; and as the gates of the city were shut against them, very few escaped the sword of the victorious pursuers. By this important service Turin deserved to experience the clemency and even favour of the conqueror. He made his entry into the Imperial palace of Milan, and almost all the cities of Italy between the Alps and the Po not only acknowledged the power, but embraced with zeal the party of Constantine.[1]

From Milan to Rome, the Æmilian and Flaminian highways

---

[1] Zosimus as well as Eusebius hasten from the passage of the Alps to the decisive action near Rome. We must apply to the two Panegyrics for the intermediate actions of Constantine.

offered an easy march of about four hundred miles; but though Constantine was impatient to encounter the tyrant, he prudently directed his operations against another army of Italians, who, by their strength and position, might either oppose his progress, or, in case of a misfortune, might intercept his retreat. Ruricius Pompeianus, a general distinguished by his valour and ability, had under his command the city of Verona, and all the troops that were stationed in the province of Venetia. As soon as he was informed that Constantine was advancing towards him, he detached a large body of cavalry, which was defeated in an engagement near Brescia, and pursued by the Gallic legions as far as the gates of Verona. The necessity, the importance, and the difficulties of the siege of Verona, immediately presented themselves to the sagacious mind of Constantine.[1] The city was accessible only by a narrow peninsula towards the west, as the other three sides were surrounded by the Adige, a rapid river, which covered the province of Venetia, from whence the besieged derived an inexhaustible supply of men and provisions. It was not without great difficulty, and after several fruitless attempts, that Constantine found means to pass the river at some distance above the city, and in a place where the torrent was less violent. He then encompassed Verona with strong lines, pushed his attacks with prudent vigour, and repelled a desperate sally of Pompeianus. That intrepid general, when he had used every means of defence that the strength of the place or that of the garrison could afford, secretly escaped from Verona, anxious not for his own but for the public safety. With indefatigable diligence he soon collected an army sufficient either to meet Constantine in the field, or to attack him if he obstinately remained within his lines. The emperor, attentive to the motions, and informed of the approach of so formidable an enemy, left a part of his legions to continue the operations of the siege, whilst, at the head of those troops on whose valour and fidelity he more particularly depended, he advanced in person to engage the general of Maxentius. The army of Gaul was drawn up in two lines, according to the usual practice of war; but their experienced leader, perceiving that the numbers of the Italians far exceeded his own, suddenly changed his disposition, and, reducing the

[1] The Marquis Maffei has examined the siege and battle of Verona with that degree of attention and accuracy which was due to a memorable action that happened in his native country. The fortifications of that city, constructed by Gallienus, were less extensive than the modern walls, and the amphitheatre was not included within their circumference. See Verona Illustrata, part. i. p. 142, 150.

second, extended the front of his first line to a just proportion
with that of the enemy. Such evolutions, which only veteran
troops can execute without confusion in a moment of danger,
commonly prove decisive; but as this engagement began towards
the close of the day, and was contested with great obstinacy
during the whole night, there was less room for the conduct of
the generals than for the courage of the soldiers. The return of
light displayed the victory of Constantine, and a field of carnage
covered with many thousands of the vanquished Italians. Their
general, Pompeianus, was found among the slain; Verona immediately surrendered at discretion, and the garrison was made
prisoners of war.[1] When the officers of the victorious army congratulated their master on this important success, they ventured
to add some respectful complaints, of such a nature, however,
as the most jealous monarchs will listen to without displeasure.
They represented to Constantine that, not contented with per-
forming all the duties of a commander, he had exposed his own
person with an excess of valour which almost degenerated into
rashness; and they conjured him for the future to pay more
regard to the preservation of a life in which the safety of Rome
and of the empire was involved.[2]

While Constantine signalised his conduct and valour in the
field, the sovereign of Italy appeared insensible of the calamities and danger of a civil war which raged in the heart of his
dominions. Pleasure was still the only business of Maxentius.
Concealing, or at least attempting to conceal, from the public
knowledge the misfortunes of his arms,[3] he indulged himself
in a vain confidence, which deferred the remedies of the approaching evil without deferring the evil itself.[4] The rapid progress
of Constantine [5] was scarcely sufficient to awaken him from this
fatal security; he flattered himself that his well-known liberality
and the majesty of the Roman name, which had already delivered
him from two invasions, would dissipate with the same facility
the rebellious army of Gaul. The officers of experience and

---

[1] They wanted chains for so great a multitude of captives; and the
whole council was at a loss; but the sagacious conqueror imagined the
happy expedient of converting into fetters the swords of the vanquished.
Panegyr. Vet. ix. 9.

[2] Panegyr. Vet. ix. 10.

[3] Literas calamitatum suarum indices supprimebat. Panegyr. Vet. ix.
15.

[4] Remedia malorum potius quam mala differebat, is the fine censure
which Tacitus passes on the supine indolence of Vitellius.

[5] The Marquis Maffei has made it extremely probable that Constantine
was still at Verona, the 1st of September, A.D. 312, and that the memorable
era of the Indictions was dated from his conquest of the Cisalpine Gaul.

ability who had served under the banners of Maximian were
at length compelled to inform his effeminate son of the imminent
danger to which he was reduced; and, with a freedom that at
once surprised and convinced him, to urge the necessity of preventing his ruin by a vigorous exertion of his remaining power.
The resources of Maxentius, both of men and money, were still
considerable. The Prætorian guards felt how strongly their own
interest and safety were connected with his cause; and a third
army was soon collected, more numerous than those which had
been lost in the battles of Turin and Verona. It was far from
the intention of the emperor to lead his troops in person. A
stranger to the exercises of war, he trembled at the apprehension
of so dangerous a contest; and, as fear is commonly superstitious,
he listened with melancholy attention to the rumours of omens
and presages which seemed to menace his life and empire. Shame
at length supplied the place of courage, and forced him to take
the field. He was unable to sustain the contempt of the Roman
people. The circus resounded with their indignant clamours,
and they tumultuously besieged the gates of the palace, reproach-
ing the pusillanimity of their indolent sovereign, and celebrating
the heroic spirit of Constantine.[1] Before Maxentius left Rome
he consulted the Sibylline books. The guardians of these ancient
oracles were as well versed in the arts of this world as they were
ignorant of the secrets of fate; and they returned him a very
prudent answer, which might adapt itself to the event, and secure
their reputation, whatever should be the chance of arms.[2]

The celerity of Constantine's march has been compared to the
rapid conquest of Italy by the first of the Cæsars; nor is the
flattering parallel repugnant to the truth of history, since no
more than fifty-eight days elapsed between the surrender of
Verona and the final decision of the war. Constantine had always
apprehended that the tyrant would consult the dictates of fear,
and perhaps of prudence; and that, instead of risking his last
hopes in a general engagement, he would shut himself up within
the walls of Rome. His ample magazines secured him against
the danger of famine; and as the situation of Constantine admitted not of delay, he might have been reduced to the sad
necessity of destroying with fire and sword the Imperial city, the
noblest reward of his victory, and the deliverance of which had

---

[1] See Panegyr. Vet. xi. 16 [ix. 14 ?]. Lactantius de M. P. c. 44.
[2] Illo die hostem Romanorum esse periturum. [Lact. l. c.] The vanquished prince became of course the enemy of Rome.

been the motive, or rather indeed the pretence, of the civil war.[1]
It was with equal surprise and pleasure that, on his arrival at a
place called Saxa Rubra, about nine miles from Rome,[2] he discovered the army of Maxentius prepared to give him battle.[3]
Their long front filled a very spacious plain, and their deep array
reached to the banks of the Tiber, which covered their rear, and
forbade their retreat. We are informed, and we may believe,
that Constantine disposed his troops with consummate skill,
and that he chose for himself the post of honour and danger.
Distinguished by the splendour of his arms, he charged in person
the cavalry of his rival; and his irresistible attack determined
the fortune of the day. The cavalry of Maxentius was principally composed either of unwieldy cuirassiers or of light Moors
and Numidians. They yielded to the vigour of the Gallic horse,
which possessed more activity than the one, more firmness than
the other. The defeat of the two wings left the infantry without
any protection on its flanks, and the undisciplined Italians fled
without reluctance from the standard of a tyrant whom they
had always hated, and whom they no longer feared. The Prætorians, conscious that their offences were beyond the reach of
mercy, were animated by revenge and despair. Notwithstanding
their repeated efforts, those brave veterans were unable to recover the victory; they obtained, however, an honourable death;
and it was observed that their bodies covered the same ground
which had been occupied by their ranks.[4] The confusion then
became general, and the dismayed troops of Maxentius, pursued
by an implacable enemy, rushed by thousands into the deep
and rapid stream of the Tiber. The emperor himself attempted
to escape back into the city over the Milvian bridge, but the
crowds which pressed together through that narrow passage
forced him into the river, where he was immediately drowned
by the weight of his armour.[5] His body, which had sunk very

[1] See Panegyr. Vet. ix. 16, x. 27. The former of these orators magnifies
the hoards of corn which Maxentius had collected from Africa and the
islands. And yet, if there is any truth in the scarcity mentioned by Eusebius (in Vit. Constantin. l. i. c. 36), the Imperial granaries must have been
open only to the soldiers.

[2] Maxentius . . . tandem urbe in *Saxa Rubra*, millia ferme novem æger-
rime progressus. Aurelius Victor. [de Cæsar. 40.] See Cellarius Geograph.
Antiq. tom. i. p. 463. Saxa Rubra was in the neighbourhood of the
Cremera, a trifling rivulet, illustrated by the valour and glorious death of
the three hundred Fabii.

[3] The post which Maxentius had taken, with the Tiber in his rear, is very
clearly described by the two Panegyrists, ix. 16, x. 28.

[4] Exceptis latrocinii illius primis auctoribus, qui desperatâ veniâ, locum
quem pugnæ sumpserant texere corporibus. Panegyr. Vet. ix. 17.

[5] A very idle rumour soon prevailed, that Maxentius, who had not taken

deep into the mud, was found with some difficulty the next day.
The sight of his head, when it was exposed to the eyes of the
people, convinced them of their deliverance, and admonished
them to receive with acclamations of loyalty and gratitude the
fortunate Constantine, who thus achieved by his valour and
ability the most splendid enterprise of his life.[1]

In the use of victory Constantine neither deserved the praise
of clemency nor incurred the censure of immoderate rigour.[2]
He inflicted the same treatment to which a defeat would have
exposed his own person and family, put to death the two sons of
the tyrant, and carefully extirpated his whole race. The most
distinguished adherents of Maxentius must have expected to
share his fate, as they had shared his prosperity and his crimes;
but when the Roman people loudly demanded a greater number
of victims, the conqueror resisted, with firmness and humanity,
those servile clamours, which were dictated by flattery as well
as by resentment. Informers were punished and discouraged;
the innocent who had suffered under the late tyranny were
recalled from exile, and restored to their estates. A general
act of oblivion quieted the minds and settled the property of the
people both in Italy and in Africa.[3] The first time that Constantine honoured the senate with his presence he recapitulated

any precaution for his own retreat, had contrived a very artful snare to
destroy the army of the pursuers; but that the wooden bridge, which was
to have been loosened on the approach of Constantine, unluckily broke
down under the weight of the flying Italians. M. de Tillemont (Hist. des
Empereurs, tom. iv. part i. p. 576) very seriously examines whether, in
contradiction to common sense, the testimony of Eusebius and Zosimus
ought to prevail over the silence of Lactantius, Nazarius, and the anonymous but contemporary orator who composed the ninth Panegyric.

[Manso (Beylage vi.) examines the question, and adduces two manifest
allusions to the bridge from the Life of Constantine by Praxagoras, and
from Libanius. Is it not very probable, he asks, that the bridge in question was thrown over the river to facilitate the advance and to secure the
retreat of Maxentius? In case of defeat orders were given for destroying
it to check the pursuit; it broke down accidentally, or in the confusion
was destroyed, as has not infrequently been the case, before the proper
time.—O. S.]

[1] Zosimus, l. ii. [c. 15, sq.] p. 86-88, and the two Panegyrics, the former
of which was pronounced a few months afterwards, afford the clearest
notion of this great battle. Lactantius, Eusebius, and even the Epitomes,
supply several useful hints.

[2] Zosimus, the enemy of Constantine, allows (l. ii. [c. 17] p. 88) that only
a few of the friends of Maxentius were put to death; but we may remark
the expressive passage of Nazarius (Panegyr. Vet. x. 6): Omnibus qui labe-
factari statum ejus poterant cum stirpe deletis. The other orator (Panegyr.
Vet. ix. 20, 21) contents himself with observing that Constantine, when he
entered Rome, did not imitate the cruel massacres of Cinna, of Marius, or
of Sylla.

[3] See the two Panegyrics, and the laws of this and the ensuing year, in
the Theodosian Code.

his own services and exploits in a modest oration, assured that
illustrious order of his sincere regard, and promised to re-
establish its ancient dignity and privileges. The grateful senate
repaid these unmeaning professions by the empty titles of honour
which it was yet in their power to bestow; and, without presuming to ratify the authority of Constantine, they passed a
decree to assign him the first rank among the three *Augusti* who
governed the Roman world.[1] Games and festivals were instituted to preserve the fame of his victory, and several edifices,
raised at the expense of Maxentius, were dedicated to the honour
of his successful rival. The triumphal arch of Constantine still
remains a melancholy proof of the decline of the arts, and a
singular testimony of the meanest vanity. As it was not possible
to find in the capital of the empire a sculptor who was capable
of adorning that public monument, the arch of Trajan, without
any respect either for his memory or for the rules of propriety,
was stripped of its most elegant figures. The difference of times
and persons, of actions and characters, was totally disregarded.
The Parthian captives appear prostrate at the feet of a prince
who never carried his arms beyond the Euphrates; and curious
antiquarians can still discover the head of Trajan on the trophies
of Constantine. The new ornaments which it was necessary
to introduce between the vacancies of ancient sculpture are
executed in the rudest and most unskilful manner.[2]

The final abolition of the Prætorian guards was a measure of
prudence as well as of revenge. Those haughty troops, whose
numbers and privileges had been restored, and even augmented,
by Maxentius, were for ever suppressed by Constantine. Their
fortified camp was destroyed, and the few Prætorians who had
escaped the fury of the sword were dispersed among the legions
and banished to the frontiers of the empire, where they might be
serviceable without again becoming dangerous.[3] By suppressing the troops which were usually stationed in Rome, Constantine
gave the fatal blow to the dignity of the senate and people, and

---

[1] Panegyr. Vet. ix. 20. Lactantius de M. P. c. 44. Maximin, who was
confessedly the eldest Cæsar, claimed, with some show of reason, the first
rank among the Augusti.

[2] Adhuc cuncta opera quæ magnifice construxerat, urbis fanum, atque
basilicam, Flavii meritis patres sacravere. Aurelius Victor. [de Cæsar. 40.]
With regard to the theft of Trajan's trophies, consult Flaminius Vacca,
apud Montfaucon, Diarium Italicum, p. 250, and l'Antiquité Expliquée of
the latter, tom. iv. p. 171.

[3] Prætoriæ legiones ac subsidia factionibus aptiora quam urbi Romæ,
sublata penitus; simul arma atque usus indumenti militaris. Aurelius
Victor. [l. c.] Zosimus (l. ii. [c. 17] p. 89) mentions this fact as an historian,
and it is very pompously celebrated in the ninth Panegyric.

the disarmed capital was exposed, without protection, to the insults or neglect of its distant master. We may observe that, in this last effort to preserve their expiring freedom, the Romans, from the apprehension of a tribute, had raised Maxentius to the throne. He exacted that tribute from the senate under the name of a free gift. They implored the assistance of Constantine. He vanquished the tyrant, and converted the free gift into a perpetual tax. The senators, according to the declaration which was required of their property, were divided into several classes. The most opulent paid annually eight pounds of gold, the next class paid four, the last two, and those whose poverty might have claimed an exemption were assessed, however, at seven pieces of gold. Besides the regular members of the senate, their sons, their descendants, and even their relations, enjoyed the vain privileges and supported the heavy burdens of the senatorial order; nor will it any longer excite our surprise that Constantine should be attentive to increase the number of persons who were included under so useful a description.[1] After the defeat of Maxentius the victorious emperor passed no more than two or three months in Rome, which he visited twice during the remainder of his life to celebrate the solemn festivals of the tenth and of the twentieth years of his reign. Constantine was almost perpetually in motion, to exercise the legions or to inspect the state of the provinces. Treves, Milan, Aquileia, Sirmium, Naissus, and Thessalonica were the occasional places of his residence till he founded a NEW ROME on the confines of Europe and Asia.[2]

Before Constantine marched into Italy he had secured the friendship, or at least the neutrality, of Licinius, the Illyrian emperor. He had promised his sister Constantia in marriage to that prince; but the celebration of the nuptials was deferred till after the conclusion of the war, and the interview of the two emperors at Milan, which was appointed for that purpose, appeared to cement the union of their families and interests.[3]

---

[1] Ex omnibus provinciis optimates viros Curiæ tuæ pigneraveris; ut Senatûs dignitas . . . ex totius Orbis flore consisteret. Nazarius in Panegyr. Vet. x. [ix.] 35. The word *pigneraveris* might almost seem maliciously chosen. Concerning the senatorial tax, see Zosimus, l. ii. [c. 38] p. 115; the second title of the sixth book of the Theodosian Code, with Godefroy's Commentary; and Mémoires de l'Académie des Inscriptions, tom. xxviii. p. 726.

[2] From the Theodosian Code we may now begin to trace the motions of the emperors; but the dates both of time and place have frequently been altered by the carelessness of transcribers.

[3] Zosimus (l. ii. [c. 17] p. 89) observes, that before the war the sister of Constantine had been betrothed to Licinius. According to the younger

In the midst of the public festivity they were suddenly obliged to take leave of each other. An inroad of the Franks summoned Constantine to the Rhine, and the hostile approach of the sovereign of Asia demanded the immediate presence of Licinius. Maximin had been the secret ally of Maxentius, and, without being discouraged by his fate, he resolved to try the fortune of a civil war. He moved out of Syria, towards the frontiers of Bithynia, in the depth of winter. The season was severe and tempestuous; great numbers of men as well as horses perished in the snow; and as the roads were broken up by incessant rains, he was obliged to leave behind him a considerable part of the heavy baggage, which was unable to follow the rapidity of his forced marches. By this extraordinary effort of diligence, he arrived, with a harassed but formidable army, on the banks of the Thracian Bosphorus before the lieutenants of Licinius were apprised of his hostile intentions. Byzantium surrendered to the power of Maximin after a siege of eleven days. He was detained some days under the walls of Heraclea; and he had no sooner taken possession of that city than he was alarmed by the intelligence that Licinius had pitched his camp at the distance of only eighteen miles. After a fruitless negotiation, in which the two princes attempted to seduce the fidelity of each other's adherents, they had recourse to arms. The emperor of the East commanded a disciplined and veteran army of above seventy thousand men; and Licinius, who had collected about thirty thousand Illyrians, was at first oppressed by the superiority of numbers. His military skill and the firmness of his troops restored the day and obtained a decisive victory. The incredible speed which Maximin exerted in his flight is much more celebrated than his prowess in the battle. Twenty-four hours afterwards he was seen pale, trembling, and without his Imperial ornaments, at Nicomedia, one hundred and sixty miles from the place of his defeat. The wealth of Asia was yet unexhausted; and though the flower of his veterans had fallen in the late action, he had still power, if he could obtain time, to draw very numerous levies from Syria and Egypt. But he survived his misfortune only three or four months. His death, which happened at Tarsus, was variously ascribed to despair, to poison, and to the divine justice. As Maximin was alike destitute of

Victor [Epit. c. 39], Diocletian was invited to the nuptials; but having ventured to plead his age and infirmities, he received a second letter filled with reproaches for his supposed partiality to the cause of Maxentius and Maximin.

abilities and of virtue, he was lamented neither by the people nor
by the soldiers. The provinces of the East, delivered from the
terrors of civil war, cheerfully acknowledged the authority of
Licinius.[1]

The vanquished emperor left behind him two children, a boy
of about eight, and a girl of about seven, years old. Their
inoffensive age might have excited compassion; but the compassion of Licinius was a very feeble resource, nor did it restrain
him from *extinguishing* the name and memory of his adversary.
The death of Severianus will admit of less excuse, as it was
dictated neither by revenge nor by policy. The conqueror had
never received any injury from the father of that unhappy youth,
and the short and obscure reign of Severus, in a distant part
of the empire, was already forgotten. But the execution of
Candidianus was an act of the blackest cruelty and ingratitude.
He was the natural son of Galerius, the friend and benefactor of
Licinius. The prudent father had judged him too young to sustain the weight of a diadem; but he hoped that, under the protection of princes who were indebted to his favour for the
Imperial purple, Candidianus might pass a secure and honourable
life. He was now advancing towards the twentieth year of his
age, and the royalty of his birth, though unsupported either by
merit or ambition, was sufficient to exasperate the jealous mind
of Licinius.[2] To these innocent and illustrious victims of his
tyranny we must add the wife and daughter of the emperor
Diocletian. When that prince conferred on Galerius the title of
Cæsar, he had given him in marriage his daughter Valeria, whose
melancholy adventures might furnish a very singular subject for
tragedy. She had fulfilled and even surpassed the duties of a
wife. As she had not any children herself, she condescended to
adopt the illegitimate son of her husband, and invariably displayed towards the unhappy Candidianus the tenderness and
anxiety of a real mother. After the death of Galerius, her ample
possessions provoked the avarice, and her personal attractions
excited the desires, of his successor, Maximin.[3] He had a wife

---

[1] Zosimus mentions the defeat and death of Maximin as ordinary events;
but Lactantius expatiates on them (de M. P. c. 45-50), ascribing them to
the miraculous interposition of Heaven. Licinius at that time was one of
the protectors of the church.

[2] Lactantius de M. P. c. 50. Aurelius Victor touches on the different
conduct of Licinius, and of Constantine, in the use of victory.

[3] The sensual appetites of Maximin were gratified at the expense of his
subjects. His eunuchs, who forced away wives and virgins, examined
their naked charms with anxious curiosity, lest any part of their body
should be found unworthy of the royal embraces. Coyness and disdain

still alive; but divorce was permitted by the Roman law, and the fierce passions of the tyrant demanded an immediate gratification. The answer of Valeria was such as became the daughter and widow of emperors; but it was tempered by the prudence which her defenceless condition compelled her to observe. She represented to the persons whom Maximin had employed on this occasion, "that, even if honour could permit a woman of her character and dignity to entertain a thought of second nuptials, decency at least must forbid her to listen to his addresses at a time when the ashes of her husband and his benefactor were still warm, and while the sorrows of her mind were still expressed by her mourning garments. She ventured to declare that she could place very little confidence in the professions of a man whose cruel inconstancy was capable of repudiating a faithful and affectionate wife." [1] On this repulse, the love of Maximin was converted into fury; and as witnesses and judges were always at his disposal, it was easy for him to cover his fury with an appearance of legal proceedings, and to assault the reputation as well as the happiness of Valeria. Her estates were confiscated, her eunuchs and domestics devoted to the most inhuman tortures; and several innocent and respectable matrons, who were honoured with her friendship, suffered death, on a false accusation of adultery. The empress herself, together with her mother Prisca, was condemned to exile; and as they were ignominiously hurried from place to place before they were confined to a sequestered village in the deserts of Syria, they exposed their shame and distress to the provinces of the East, which, during thirty years, had respected their august dignity. Diocletian made several ineffectual efforts to alleviate the misfortunes of his daughter; and, as the last return that he expected for the Imperial purple which he had conferred upon Maximin, he entreated that Valeria might be permitted to share his retirement of Salona, and to close the eyes of her afflicted father.[2] He entreated; but as he could no longer threaten, his prayers were received with coldness and disdain; and the pride of Maximin was gratified in treating Diocletian as a suppliant, and

were considered as treason, and the obstinate fair one was condemned to be drowned. A custom was gradually introduced that no person should marry a wife without the permission of the emperor, "ut ipse in omnibus nuptiis præguistator esset." Lactantius de M. P. c. 38.

[1] Lactantius de M. P. c. 39.

[2] Diocletian at last sent cognatum suum, quendam militarem ac potentem virum, to intercede in favour of his daughter (Lactantius de M. P. c. 41). We are not sufficiently acquainted with the history of these times to point out the person who was employed.

his daughter as a criminal. The death of Maximin seemed to
assure the empresses of a favourable alteration in their fortune.
The public disorders relaxed the vigilance of their guard, and
they easily found means to escape from the place of their exile,
and to repair, though with some precaution, and in disguise, to
the court of Licinius. His behaviour, in the first days of his
reign, and the honourable reception which he gave to young
Candidianus, inspired Valeria with a secret satisfaction, both
on her own account, and on that of her adopted son. But these
grateful prospects were soon succeeded by horror and astonishment; and the bloody executions which stained the palace of
Nicomedia sufficiently convinced her that the throne of Maximin
was filled by a tyrant more inhuman than himself. Valeria consulted her safety by a hasty flight, and, still accompanied by
her mother Prisca, they wandered above fifteen months [1] through
the provinces, concealed in the disguise of plebeian habits. They
were at length discovered at Thessalonica; and as the sentence
of their death was already pronounced, they were immediately
beheaded, and their bodies thrown into the sea. The people
gazed on the melancholy spectacle; but their grief and indignation were suppressed by the terrors of a military guard. Such
was the unworthy fate of the wife and daughter of Diocletian.
We lament their misfortunes, we cannot discover their crimes;
and whatever idea we may justly entertain of the cruelty of
Licinius, it remains a matter of surprise that he was not contented with some more secret and decent method of revenge.[2]

The Roman world was now divided between Constantine and
Licinius, the former of whom was master of the West, and the
latter of the East. It might perhaps have been expected that
the conquerors, fatigued with civil war, and connected by a
private as well as public alliance, would have renounced, or at
least would have suspended, any farther designs of ambition.
And yet a year had scarcely elapsed after the death of Maximin,
before the victorious emperors turned their arms against each
other. The genius, the success, and the aspiring temper of

---

[1] Valeria quoque per varias provincias quindecim mensibus plebeio cultû
pervagata. Lactantius de M. P. c. 51. There is some doubt whether we
should compute the fifteen months from the moment of her exile, or from
that of her escape. The expression of *pervagata* seems to denote the
latter; but in that case we must suppose that the treatise of Lactantius
was written after the first civil war between Licinius and Constantine.
See Cuper, p. 254.

[2] Ita illis pudicitia et conditio exitio fuit. Lactantius de M. P. c. 51.
He relates the misfortunes of the innocent wife and daughter of Diocletian
with a very natural mixture of pity and exultation.

Constantine, may seem to mark him out as the aggressor; but
the perfidious character of Licinius justifies the most unfavourable suspicions, and by the faint light which history reflects on
this transaction [1] we may discover a conspiracy fomented by his
arts against the authority of his colleague. Constantine had
lately given his sister Anastasia in marriage to Bassianus, a
man of a considerable family and fortune, and had elevated his
new kinsman to the rank of Cæsar. According to the system of
government instituted by Diocletian, Italy, and perhaps Africa,
were designed for his department in the empire. But the performance of the promised favour was either attended with so
much delay, or accompanied with so many unequal conditions,
that the fidelity of Bassianus was alienated rather than secured
by the honourable distinction which he had obtained. His
nomination had been ratified by the consent of Licinius; and
that artful prince, by the means of his emissaries, soon contrived
to enter into a secret and dangerous correspondence with the new
Cæsar, to irritate his discontents, and to urge him to the rash
enterprise of extorting by violence what he might in vain solicit
from the justice of Constantine. But the vigilant emperor discovered the conspiracy before it was ripe for execution; and,
after solemnly renouncing the alliance of Bassianus, despoiled
him of the purple, and inflicted the deserved punishment on his
treason and ingratitude. The haughty refusal of Licinius, when
he was required to deliver up the criminals who had taken refuge
in his dominions, confirmed the suspicions already entertained
of his perfidy; and the indignities offered at Æmona, on the
frontiers of Italy, to the statues of Constantine, became the
signal of discord between the two princes.[2]

The first battle was fought near Cibalis, a city of Pannonia,
situated on the river Save, about fifty miles above Sirmium.[3]

---

[1] The curious reader who consults the Valesian Fragment, p. 713, will
probably accuse me of giving a bold and licentious paraphrase; but if he
considers it with attention, he will acknowledge that my interpretation is
probable and consistent.

[2] The situation of Æmona, or, as it is now called, Laybach, in Carniola
(d'Anville, Géographie Ancienne, tom. i. p. 187), may suggest a conjecture.
As it lay to the north-east of the Julian Alps, that important territory
became a natural object of dispute between the sovereigns of Italy and of
Illyricum.

[3] Cibalis or Cibalæ (whose name is still preserved in the obscure ruins of
Swilei) was situated about fifty miles from Sirmium, the capital of Illyricum,
and about one hundred from Taurunum, or Belgrade, and the conflux of
the Danube and the Save. The Roman garrisons and cities on those rivers
are finely illustrated by M. d'Anville, in a memoir inserted in l'Académie
des Inscriptions, tom. xxviii.

From the inconsiderable forces which in this important contest two such powerful monarchs brought into the field, it may be inferred that the one was suddenly provoked, and that the other was unexpectedly surprised. The emperor of the West had only twenty thousand, and the sovereign of the East no more than five-and-thirty thousand, men. The inferiority of number was, however, compensated by the advantage of the ground. Constantine had taken post in a defile about half a mile in breadth, between a steep hill and a deep morass, and in that situation he steadily expected and repulsed the first attack of the enemy. He pursued his success and advanced into the plain. But the veteran legions of Illyricum rallied under the standard of a leader who had been trained to arms in the school of Probus and Diocletian. The missile weapons on both sides were soon exhausted; the two armies, with equal valour, rushed to a closer engagement of swords and spears, and the doubtful contest had already lasted from the dawn of the day to a late hour of the evening, when the right wing, which Constantine led in person, made a vigorous and decisive charge. The judicious retreat of Licinius saved the remainder of his troops from a total defeat; but when he computed his loss, which amounted to more than twenty thousand men, he thought it unsafe to pass the night in the presence of an active and victorious enemy. Abandoning his camp and magazines, he marched away with secrecy and diligence at the head of the greatest part of his cavalry, and was soon removed beyond the danger of a pursuit. His diligence preserved his wife, his son, and his treasures, which he had deposited at Sirmium. Licinius passed through that city, and, breaking down the bridge on the Save, hastened to collect a new army in Dacia and Thrace. In his flight he bestowed the precarious title of Cæsar on Valens, his general of the Illyrian frontier.[1]

The plain of Mardia in Thrace was the theatre of a second battle no less obstinate and bloody than the former. The troops on both sides displayed the same valour and discipline; and the victory was once more decided by the superior abilities of Constantine, who directed a body of five thousand men to gain an advantageous height, from whence, during the heat of the action, they attacked the rear of the enemy, and made a very considerable slaughter. The troops of Licinius, however, presenting a double front, still maintained their ground till the

[1] Zosimus (l. ii. [c. 18] p. 90, 91) gives a very particular account of this battle; but the descriptions of Zosimus are rhetorical rather than military.

approach of night put an end to the combat, and secured their
retreat towards the mountains of Macedonia.[1] The loss of two
battles, and of his bravest veterans, reduced the fierce spirit of
Licinius to sue for peace. His ambassador, Mistrianus, was
admitted to the audience of Constantine: he expatiated on the
common topics of moderation and humanity, which are so
familiar to the eloquence of the vanquished; represented in the
most insinuating language that the event of the war was still
doubtful, whilst its inevitable calamities were alike pernicious to
both the contending parties; and declared that he was authorised
to propose a lasting and honourable peace in the name of the
two emperors his masters. Constantine received the mention
of Valens with indignation and contempt. " It was not for such
a purpose," he sternly replied, " that we have advanced from
the shores of the western ocean in an uninterrupted course of
combats and victories, that, after rejecting an ungrateful kinsman, we should accept for our colleague a contemptible slave.
The abdication of Valens is the first article of the treaty." [2] It
was necessary to accept this humiliating condition; and the
unhappy Valens, after a reign of a few days, was deprived of the
purple and of his life. As soon as this obstacle was removed,
the tranquillity of the Roman world was easily restored. The
successive defeats of Licinius had ruined his forces, but they had
displayed his courage and abilities. His situation was almost
desperate, but the efforts of despair are sometimes formidable,
and the good sense of Constantine preferred a great and certain
advantage to a third trial of the chance of arms. He consented
to leave his rival, or, as he again styled Licinius, his friend and
brother, in the possession of Thrace, Asia Minor, Syria, and
Egypt; but the provinces of Pannonia, Dalmatia, Dacia, Macedonia, and Greece were yielded to the Western empire, and the
dominions of Constantine now extended from the confines of
Caledonia to the extremity of Peloponnesus. It was stipulated
by the same treaty that three royal youths, the sons of the
emperors, should be called to the hopes of the succession.

[1] Zosimus, l. ii. [c. 19] p. 92, 93. Anonym. Valesian. p. 713. The
Epitomes furnish some circumstances; but they frequently confound the
two wars between Licinius and Constantine.
[2] Petrus Patricius in Excerpt. Legat. p. 27 [ed. Paris; p. 19, ed. Ven.;
p. 129, ed. Bonn]. If it should be thought that γάμβρος signifies more properly
a son-in-law, we might conjecture that Constantine, assuming the name as
well as the duties of a father, had adopted his younger brothers and sisters,
the children of Theodora. But in the best authors γάμβρος sometimes
signifies a husband, sometimes a father-in-law, and sometimes a kinsman
in general. See Spanheim Observat. ad Julian. Orat. i. p. 72.

Crispus and the young Constantine were soon afterwards declared
Cæsars in the West, while the younger Licinius was invested
with the same dignity in the East. In this double proportion
of honours, the conqueror asserted the superiority of his arms and
power.[1]

The reconciliation of Constantine and Licinius, though it was
embittered by resentment and jealousy, by the remembrance
of recent injuries, and by the apprehension of future dangers,
maintained, however, above eight years, the tranquillity of
the Roman world. As a very regular series of the Imperial
laws commences about this period, it would not be difficult to
transcribe the civil regulations which employed the leisure of
Constantine. But the most important of his institutions are
intimately connected with the new system of policy and religion,
which was not perfectly established till the last and peaceful
years of his reign. There are many of his laws which, as far as
they concern the rights and property of individuals, and the
practice of the bar, are more properly referred to the private than
to the public jurisprudence of the empire; and he published many
edicts of so local and temporary a nature that they would ill
deserve the notice of a general history. Two laws, however,
may be selected from the crowd; the one for its importance, the
other for its singularity; the former for its remarkable benevolence, the latter for its excessive severity. 1. The horrid practice,
so familiar to the ancients, of exposing or murdering their new-
born infants, was become every day more frequent in the provinces, and especially in Italy. It was the effect of distress;
and the distress was principally occasioned by the intolerable
burden of taxes, and by the vexatious as well as cruel prosecu-
tions of the officers of the revenue against their insolvent debtors.
The less opulent or less industrious part of mankind, instead of
rejoicing in an increase of family, deemed it an act of paternal
tenderness to release their children from the impending miseries
of a life which they themselves were unable to support. The
humanity of Constantine, moved, perhaps, by some recent and
extraordinary instances of despair, engaged him to address an

---

[1] Zosimus, l. ii. [c. 20] p. 93. Anonym. Valesian. p. 713. Eutropius, x.
4. Aurelius Victor, Euseb. in Chron. [An. CCCXVIII.] Sozomen, l. i.
c. 2. Four of these writers affirm that the promotion of the Cæsars was an
article of the treaty. It is however certain that the younger Constantine
and Licinius were not yet born; and it is highly probable that the promotion was made the 1st of March, A.D. 317. The treaty had probably stipulated that the two Cæsars might be created by the western, and one only
by the eastern emperor; but each of them reserved to himself the choice of
the persons.

edict to all the cities of Italy, and afterwards of Africa, directing immediate and sufficient relief to be given to those parents who should produce before the magistrates the children whom their own poverty would not allow them to educate. But the promise was too liberal, and the provision too vague, to effect any general or permanent benefit.[1] The law, though it may merit some praise, served rather to display than to alleviate the public distress. It still remains an authentic monument to contradict and confound those venal orators who were too well satisfied with their own situation to discover either vice or misery under the government of a generous sovereign.[2] 2. The laws of Constantine against rapes were dictated with very little indulgence for the most amiable weaknesses of human nature; since the description of that crime was applied not only to the brutal violence which compelled, but even to the gentle seduction which might persuade, an unmarried woman, under the age of twenty-five, to leave the house of her parents. " The successful ravisher was punished with death; and as if simple death was inadequate to the enormity of his guilt, he was either burnt alive, or torn in pieces by wild beasts in the amphitheatre. The virgin's declaration that she had been carried away with her own consent, instead of saving her lover, exposed her to share his fate. The duty of a public prosecution was intrusted to the parents of the guilty or unfortunate maid; and if the sentiments of nature prevailed on them to dissemble the injury, and to repair by a subsequent marriage the honour of their family, they were themselves punished by exile and confiscation. The slaves, whether male or female, who were convicted of having been accessary to the rape or seduction, were burnt alive, or put to death by the ingenious torture of pouring down their throats a quantity of melted lead. As the crime was of a public kind, the accusation was permitted even to strangers. The commencement of the action was not limited to any term of years, and the consequences of the sentence were extended to the innocent offspring of such an irregular union." [3] But whenever the offence inspires less horror than the punishment, the rigour of penal law is obliged to give way to the common feelings of mankind. The most

---

[1] Codex Theodosian. l. xi. tit. 27, tom. iv. p. 188, with Godefroy's observations. See likewise, l. v. tit. 7, 8.

[2] Omnia foris placida, domi prospera, annonæ ubertate, fructuum copiâ, etc. Panegyr. Vet. x. 38. This oration of Nazarius was pronounced on the day of the Quinquennalia of the Cæsars, the 1st of March, A.D. 321.

[3] See the edict of Constantine, addressed to the Roman people, in the Theodosian Code, l. ix. tit. 24, tom. iii. p. 189.

odious parts of this edict were softened or repealed in the subsequent reigns; [1] and even Constantine himself very frequently
alleviated, by partial acts of mercy, the stern temper of his
general institutions. Such, indeed, was the singular humour of
that emperor, who showed himself as indulgent, and even remiss,
in the execution of his laws, as he was severe, and even cruel, in
the enacting of them. It is scarcely possible to observe a more
decisive symptom of weakness, either in the character of the
prince, or in the constitution of the government.[2]

The civil administration was sometimes interrupted by the
military defence of the empire. Crispus, a youth of the most
amiable character, who had received with the title of Cæsar the
command of the Rhine, distinguished his conduct as well as
valour in several victories over the Franks and Alemanni, and
taught the barbarians of that frontier to dread the eldest son of
Constantine, and the grandson of Constantius.[3] The emperor
himself had assumed the more difficult and important province
of the Danube. The Goths, who in the time of Claudius and
Aurelian had felt the weight of the Roman arms, respected the
power of the empire, even in the midst of its intestine divisions.
But the strength of that warlike nation was now restored by a
peace of near fifty years; a new generation had arisen, who no
longer remembered the misfortunes of ancient days: the Sarmatians of the lake Mæotis followed the Gothic standard either
as subjects or as allies, and their united force was poured upon
the countries of Illyricum. Campona, Margus, and Bononia,
appear to have been the scenes of several memorable sieges and
battles; [4] and though Constantine encountered a very obstinate

[1] His son very fairly assigns the true reason of the repeal, "Ne sub specie
atrocioris judicii aliqua in ulciscendo crimine dilatio nasceretur." Cod.
Theod. tom. iii. p. 193.

[2] Eusebius (in Vitâ Constant. l. iii. c. 1) chooses to affirm that in the
reign of this hero the sword of justice hung idle in the hands of the magistrates. Eusebius himself (l. iv. c. 29, 54) and the Theodosian Code will
inform us that this excessive lenity was not owing to the want either of
atrocious criminals or of penal laws.

[3] Nazarius in Panegyr. Vet. x. [36.] The victory of Crispus over the
Alemanni is expressed on some medals.

[Other medals are extant, the scripts on which commemorate the success
of Constantine over the Sarmatians and other barbarous nations, *Sarmatia
Devicta, Victoria Gothica, Debellatori Gentium Barbararum, Exuperator
Omnium Gentium.*—O. S.]

[4] See Zosimus, l. ii. [c. 21] p. 93, 94; though the narrative of that historian is neither clear nor consistent. The Panegyric of Optatianus (c. 32)
mentions the alliance of the Sarmatians with the Carpi and Getæ, and
points out the several fields of battle. It is supposed that the Sarmatian
games, celebrated in the month of November, derived their origin from
the success of this war.

resistance, he prevailed at length in the contest, and the Goths were compelled to purchase an ignominious retreat by restoring the booty and prisoners which they had taken. Nor was this advantage sufficient to satisfy the indignation of the emperor. He resolved to chastise as well as to repulse the insolent barbarians who had dared to invade the territories of Rome. At the head of his legions he passed the Danube, after repairing the bridge which had been constructed by Trajan, penetrated into the strongest recesses of Dacia,[1] and, when he had inflicted a severe revenge, condescended to give peace to the suppliant Goths, on condition that, as often as they were required, they should supply his armies with a body of forty thousand soldiers.[2] Exploits like these were no doubt honourable to Constantine and beneficial to the state; but it may surely be questioned whether they can justify the exaggerated assertion of Eusebius, that ALL SCYTHIA, as far as the extremity of the North, divided as it was into so many names and nations of the most various and savage manners, had been added by his victorious arms to the Roman empire.[3]

In this exalted state of glory it was impossible that Constantine should any longer endure a partner in the empire. Confiding in the superiority of his genius and military power, he determined, without any previous injury, to exert them for the destruction of Licinius, whose advanced age and unpopular vices seemed to offer a very easy conquest.[4] But the old emperor, awakened by the approaching danger, deceived the expectations of his friends as well as of his enemies. Calling forth that spirit and those abilities by which he had deserved the friendship of Galerius and the Imperial purple, he prepared himself for the contest, collected the forces of the East, and soon filled the plains of Hadrianople with his troops, and the Straits of the Hellespont

---

[1] In the Cæsars of Julian (p. 329. Commentaire de Spanheim, p. 252). Constantine boasts that he had recovered the province (Dacia) which Trajan had subdued. But it is insinuated by Silenus that the conquests of Constantine were like the gardens of Adonis, which fade and wither almost the moment they appear.

[2] Jornandes de Rebus Geticis, c. 21. I know not whether we may entirely depend on his authority. Such an alliance has a very recent air, and scarcely is suited to the maxims of the beginning of the fourth century.

[3] Eusebius in Vit. Constantin. l. i. c. 8. This passage, however, is taken from a general declamation on the greatness of Constantine, and not from any particular account of the Gothic war.

[4] Constantinus tamen, vir ingens, et omnia efficere nitens quæ animo præparasset, simul principatum totius orbis affectans, Licinio bellum intulit. Eutropius, x. 5 [4]. Zosimus, l. ii. [c. 18] p. 89. The reasons which they have assigned for the first civil war may, with more propriety, be applied to the second.

with his fleet. The army consisted of one hundred and fifty
thousand foot and fifteen thousand horse; and as the cavalry
was drawn, for the most part, from Phrygia and Cappadocia, we
may conceive a more favourable opinion of the beauty of the
horses than of the courage and dexterity of their riders. The
fleet was composed of three hundred and fifty galleys of three
ranks of oars. An hundred and thirty of these were furnished
by Egypt and the adjacent coast of Africa. An hundred and
ten sailed from the ports of Phœnicia and the isle of Cyprus;
and the maritime countries of Bithynia, Ionia, and Caria were
likewise obliged to provide an hundred and ten galleys. The
troops of Constantine were ordered to rendezvous at Thessalonica; they amounted to above an hundred and twenty thousand horse and foot.[1] Their emperor was satisfied with their
martial appearance, and his army contained more soldiers,
though fewer men, than that of his eastern competitor. The
legions of Constantine were levied in the warlike provinces of
Europe; action had confirmed their discipline, victory had
elevated their hopes, and there were among them a great number
of veterans, who, after seventeen glorious campaigns under the
same leader, prepared themselves to deserve an honourable dis-
mission by a last effort of their valour.[2] But the naval preparations of Constantine were in every respect much inferior to those
of Licinius. The maritime cities of Greece sent their respective
quotas of men and ships to the celebrated harbour of Piræus,
and their united forces consisted of no more than two hundred
small vessels; a very feeble armament, if it is compared with
those formidable fleets which were equipped and maintained by
the republic of Athens during the Peloponnesian war.[3] Since
Italy was no longer the seat of government, the naval establishments of Misenum and Ravenna had been gradually neglected;
and as the shipping and mariners of the empire were supported
by commerce rather than by war, it was natural that they should
the most abound in the industrious provinces of Egypt and Asia.
It is only surprising that the eastern emperor, who possessed so

---

[1] Zosimus, l. ii. [c. 22] p. 94, 95.
[2] Constantine was very attentive to the privileges and comforts of his
fellow-veterans (Conveterani), as he now began to style them. See the
Theodosian Code, l. vii. tit. 10, tom. ii. p. 419, 429.
[3] Whilst the Athenians maintained the empire of the sea, their fleet consisted of three, and afterwards of four, hundred galleys of three ranks of
oars, all completely equipped and ready for immediate service. The
arsenal in the port of Piræus had cost the republic a thousand talents,
about two hundred and sixteen thousand pounds. See Thucydides de Bel.
Pelopon. l. ii. c. 13; and Meursius de Fortuna Attica, c. 19.

great a superiority at sea, should have neglected the opportunity
of carrying an offensive war into the centre of his rival's
dominions.

Instead of embracing such an active resolution, which might
have changed the whole face of the war, the prudent Licinius
expected the approach of his rival in a camp near Hadrianople,
which he had fortified with an anxious care that betrayed his
apprehension of the event. Constantine directed his march
from Thessalonica towards that part of Thrace, till he found himself stopped by the broad and rapid stream of the Hebrus, and
discovered the numerous army of Licinius, which filled the steep
ascent of the hill, from the river to the city of Hadrianople.
Many days were spent in doubtful and distant skirmishes; but
at length the obstacles of the passage and of the attack were
removed by the intrepid conduct of Constantine. In this place
we might relate a wonderful exploit of Constantine, which,
though it can scarcely be paralleled either in poetry or romance,
is celebrated, not by a venal orator devoted to his fortune, but
by an historian, the partial enemy of his fame. We are assured
that the valiant emperor threw himself into the river Hebrus
accompanied only by *twelve* horsemen, and that by the effort or
terror of his invincible arm, he broke, slaughtered, and put to
flight a host of an hundred and fifty thousand men. The credulity
of Zosimus prevailed so strongly over his passion that, among
the events of the memorable battle of Hadrianople, he seems to
have selected and embellished, not the most important, but the
most marvellous. The valour and danger of Constantine are
attested by a slight wound which he received in the thigh; but
it may be discovered, even from an imperfect narration, and
perhaps a corrupted text, that the victory was obtained no less by
the conduct of the general than by the courage of the hero; that
a body of five thousand archers marched round to occupy a thick
wood in the rear of the enemy, whose attention was diverted by
the construction of a bridge; and that Licinius, perplexed by so
many artful evolutions, was reluctantly drawn from his advantageous post to combat on equal ground in the plain. The
contest was no longer equal. His confused multitude of new
levies was easily vanquished by the experienced veterans of the
West. Thirty-four thousand men are reported to have been
slain. The fortified camp of Licinius was taken by assault the
evening of the battle; the greater part of the fugitives, who had
retired to the mountains, surrendered themselves the next day
to the discretion of the conqueror; and his rival, who could no

longer keep the field, confined himself within the walls of Byzantium.[1]

The siege of Byzantium, which was immediately undertaken by Constantine, was attended with great labour and uncertainty. In the late civil wars, the fortifications of that place, so justly considered as the key of Europe and Asia, had been repaired and strengthened; and as long as Licinius remained master of the sea, the garrison was much less exposed to the danger of famine than the army of the besiegers. The naval commanders of Constantine were summoned to his camp, and received his positive orders to force the passage of the Hellespont, as the fleet of Licinius, instead of seeking and destroying their feeble enemy, continued inactive in those narrow straits, where its superiority of numbers was of little use or advantage. Crispus, the emperor's eldest son, was intrusted with the execution of this daring enterprise, which he performed with so much courage and success, that he deserved the esteem, and most probably excited the jealousy, of his father. The engagement lasted two days; and in the evening of the first, the contending fleets, after a considerable and mutual loss, retired into their respective harbours of Europe and Asia. The second day about noon a strong south wind[2] sprang up, which carried the vessels of Crispus against the enemy; and as the casual advantage was improved by his skilful intrepidity, he soon obtained a complete victory. An hundred and thirty vessels were destroyed, five thousand men were slain, and Amandus, the admiral of the Asiatic fleet, escaped with the utmost difficulty to the shores of Chalcedon. As soon as the Hellespont was open, a plentiful convoy of provisions flowed into the camp of Constantine, who had already advanced the operations of the siege. He constructed artificial mounds of earth of an equal height with the ramparts of Byzantium. The lofty towers which were erected on that foundation galled the besieged with large stones and darts from the military engines, and the battering rams had shaken the walls in several places.

[1] Zosimus, l. ii. [c. 22] p. 95, 96. This great battle is described in the Valesian fragment (p. 714) [ad fin. Amm. Marcell. vol. ii. p. 300, ed. Bip.] in a clear though concise manner. "Licinius vero circum Hadrianopolin maximo exercitu latera ardui montis impleverat; illuc toto agmine Constantinus inflexit. Cum bellum terrâ marique traheretur, quamvis per arduum suis nitentibus, attamen disciplinâ militari et felicitate, Constantinus Licinii confusum et sine ordine agentem vicit exercitum; leviter femore sauciatus."

[2] Zosimus, l. ii. [c. 24] p. 97, 98. The current always sets out of the Hellespont; and when it is assisted by a north wind, no vessel can attempt the passage. A south wind renders the force of the current almost imperceptible. See Tournefort's Voyage au Levant. Let. xi.

If Licinius persisted much longer in the defence, he exposed
himself to be involved in the ruin of the place.   Before he was
surrounded, he prudently removed his person and treasures to
Chalcedon in Asia; and as he was always desirous of associating
companions to the hopes and dangers of his fortune, he now
bestowed the title of Cæsar on Martinianus, who exercised one
of the most important offices of the empire.[1]

Such were still the resources, and such the abilities, of Licinius
that, after so many successive defeats, he collect.d in Bithynia
a new army of fifty or sixty thousand men, while the activity
of Constantine was employed in the siege of Byzantium.   The
vigilant emperor did not, however, neglect the last struggles
of his antagonist.   A considerable part of his victorious army
was transported over the Bosphorus in small vessels, and the
decisive engagement was fought soon after their landing on the
heights of Chrysopolis, or, as it is now called, of Scutari.   The
troops of Licinius, though they were lately raised, ill armed, and
worse disciplined, made head against their conquerors with
fruitless but desperate valour, till a total defeat, and the slaughter
of five-and-twenty thousand men, irretrievably determined the
fate of their leader.[2]   He retired to Nicomedia, rather with the
view of gaining some time for negotiation than with the hope of
any effectual defence.   Constantia, his wife, and the sister of
Constantine, interceded with her brother in favour of her husband,
and obtained from his policy, rather than from his compassion, a
solemn promise, confirmed by an oath, that after the sacrifice
of Martinianus, and the resignation of the purple, Licinius himself should be permitted to pass the remainder of his life in peace
and affluence.   The behaviour of Constantia, and her relation to
the contending parties, naturally recalls the remembrance of that
virtuous matron who was the sister of Augustus and the wife of
Antony.   But the temper of mankind was altered, and it was no
longer esteemed infamous for a Roman to survive his honour
and independence.   Licinius solicited and accepted the pardon
of his offences, laid himself and his purple at the feet of his *lord*
and *master*, was raised from the ground with insulting pity, was
admitted the same day to the imperial banquet, and soon after-

[1] Aurelius Victor. [de Cæsar. c. 41.]   Zosimus, l. ii. [c. 25] p. 93.   According to the latter, Martinianus was Magister Officiorum (he uses the
Latin appellation in Greek).   Some medals seem to intimate that during
his short reign he received the title of Augustus.

[2] Eusebius (in Vitâ Constantin. l. ii. c. 16, 17) ascribes this decisive
victory to the pious prayers of the emperor.   The Valesian fragment
(p. 714) [Amm. Marcell. vol. ii. p. 301, ed. Bip.] mentions a body of Gothic
auxiliaries, under their chief Aliquaca, who adhered to the party of Licinius.

wards was sent away to Thessalonica, which had been chosen
for the place of his confinement.[1] His confinement was soon
terminated by death, and it is doubtful whether a tumult of the
soldiers, or a decree of the senate, was suggested as the motive
for his execution. According to the rules of tyranny, he was
accused of forming a conspiracy, and of holding a treasonable
correspondence with the barbarians; but as he was never convicted, either by his own conduct or by any legal evidence, we
may perhaps be allowed, from his weakness, to presume his
innocence.[2] The memory of Licinius was branded with infamy,
his statues were thrown down, and by a hasty edict, of such mischievous tendency that it was almost immediately corrected,
all his laws and all the judicial proceedings of his reign were at
once abolished.[3] By this victory of Constantine the Roman
world was again united under the authority of one emperor,
thirty-seven years after Diocletian had divided his power and
provinces with his associate Maximian.

The successive steps of the elevation of Constantine, from his
first assuming the purple at York, to the resignation of Licinius
at Nicomedia, have been related with some minuteness and
precision, not only as the events are in themselves both interesting and important, but still more as they contributed to the
decline of the empire by the expense of blood and treasure, and
by the perpetual increase, as well of the taxes as of the military
establishment. The foundation of Constantinople, and the
establishment of the Christian religion, were the immediate and
memorable consequences of this revolution.

[1] Zosimus, l. ii. [c. 28] p. 102. Victor Junior in Epitome. [c. 41.]
Anonym. Valesian, p. 714.
[2] Contra religionem sacramenti Thessalonicæ privatus occisus est.
Eutropius, x. 6 [4]; and his evidence is confirmed by Jerome (in Chronic.),
as well as by Zosimus, l. ii. [c. 28] p. 102. The Valesian writer is the only
one who mentions the soldiers, and it is Zonaras alone who calls in the
assistance of the senate. Eusebius prudently slides over this delicate
transaction. But Sozomen, a century afterwards, ventures to assert the
treasonable practices of Licinius.
[3] See the Theodosian Code, l. xv. tit. 15, tom. v. p. 404, 405. These
edicts of Constantine betray a degree of passion and precipitancy very unbecoming the character of a lawgiver.

CHAPTER XV

The Progress of the Christian Religion, and the Sentiments, Manners, Numbers, and Condition of the Primitive Christians

A CANDID but rational inquiry into the progress and establish-ment of Christianity may be considered as a very essential part of the history of the Roman empire. While that great body was invaded by open violence, or undermined by slow decay, a pure and humble religion gently insinuated itself into the minds of men, grew up in silence and obscurity, derived new vigour from opposition, and finally erected the triumphant banner of the Cross on the ruins of the Capitol. Nor was the influence of Christianity confined to the period or to the limits of the Roman empire. After a revolution of thirteen or fourteen centuries, that religion is still professed by the nations of Europe, the most distinguished portion of human kind in arts and learning as well as in arms. By the industry and zeal of the Europeans it has been widely diffused to the most distant shores of Asia and Africa; and by the means of their colonies has been firmly estab-lished from Canada to Chili, in a world unknown to the ancients.

But this inquiry, however useful or entertaining, is attended with two peculiar difficulties. The scanty and suspicious materials of ecclesiastical history seldom enable us to dispel the dark cloud that hangs over the first age of the church. The great law of impartiality too often obliges us to reveal the imperfec-tions of the uninspired teachers and believers of the Gospel; and, to a careless observer, *their* faults may seem to cast a shade on the faith which they professed. But the scandal of the pious Christian, and the fallacious triumph of the Infidel, should cease as soon as they recollect not only *by whom*, but likewise *to whom*, the Divine Revelation was given. The theologian may indulge the pleasing task of describing Religion as she descended from Heaven, arrayed in her native purity. A more melancholy duty is imposed on the historian. He must discover the inevitable mixture of error and corruption which she contracted in a long residence upon earth, among a weak and degenerate race of beings.[1]

[1] [Sir James Mackintosh, in his " Life," says of these famous chapters xv. and xvi. that they might be endorsed by a Christian writer, and the causes assigned for the diffusion of Christianity be safely accepted by any Christian author with some change in the language and manner. Milman says that the art of Gibbon, or at least the unfair impression produced by those two

Our curiosity is naturally prompted to inquire by what means the Christian faith obtained so remarkable a victory over the established religions of the earth. To this inquiry an obvious but satisfactory answer may be returned; that it was owing to the convincing evidence of the doctrine itself, and to the ruling providence of its great Author. But as truth and reason seldom find so favourable a reception in the world, and as the wisdom of Providence frequently condescends to use the passions of the human heart, and the general circumstances of mankind, as instruments to execute its purpose, we may still be permitted, though with becoming submission, to ask, not indeed what were the first, but what were the secondary causes of the rapid growth of the Christian church? It will, perhaps, appear that it was most effectually favoured and assisted by the five following causes:—I. The inflexible, and, if we may use the expression, the intolerant zeal of the Christians, derived, it is true, from the Jewish religion, but purified from the narrow and unsocial spirit which, instead of inviting, had deterred the Gentiles from embracing the law of Moses. II. The doctrine of a future life, improved by every additional circumstance which could give weight and efficacy to that important truth. III. The miraculous powers ascribed to the primitive church. IV. The pure and austere morals of the Christians. V. The union and discipline of the Christian republic, which gradually formed an independent and increasing state in the heart of the Roman empire.

I. We have already described the religious harmony of the ancient world, and the facility with which the most different and even hostile nations embraced, or at least respected, each other's superstitions. A single people refused to join in the common intercourse of mankind. The Jews, who, under the Assyrian and Persian monarchies, had languished for many ages the most despised portion of their slaves,[1] emerged from obscurity

memorable chapters consists in confounding together in one indistinguishable mass the origin and apostolic propagation of the Christian religion with its later progress. The main question, the divine origin of the religion, is dexterously eluded or speciously conceded, his plan enabling him to commence his account in most parts below apostolic times, and it is only by the strength of the dark colouring with which he has brought out the failings and the follies of succeeding ages, that a shadow of doubt or suspicion is thrown back on the primitive period of Christianity. Divest this whole passage of the latent sarcasm betrayed by the subsequent tone of the whole disquisition, and it might commence a Christian history, written in the most Christian spirit of candour.—O. S.]

[1] Dum Assyrios penes, Medosque, et Persas Oriens fuit, despectissima pars servientium. Tacit. Hist. v. 8. Herodotus, who visited Asia whilst

under the successors of Alexander; and as they multiplied to a surprising degree in the East, and afterwards in the West, they soon excited the curiosity and wonder of other nations.[1] The sullen obstinacy with which they maintained their peculiar rites and unsocial manners seemed to mark them out a distinct species of men, who boldly professed, or who faintly disguised, their implacable hatred to the rest of human-kind.[2] Neither the violence of Antiochus, nor the arts of Herod, nor the example of the circumjacent nations, could ever persuade the Jews to associate with the institutions of Moses the elegant mythology of the Greeks.[3] According to the maxims of universal toleration, the Romans protected a superstition which they despised.[4] The polite Augustus condescended to give orders that sacrifices should be offered for his prosperity in the temple of Jerusalem;[5] while the meanest of the posterity of Abraham, who should have paid the same homage to the Jupiter of the Capitol, would have

it obeyed the last of those empires, slightly mentions the Syrians of Palestine, who, according to their own confession, had received from Egypt the rite of circumcision. See l. ii. c. 104.

[1] Diodorus Siculus, l. xl. [Eclog. 1. vol. ii. p. 542, ed. Wesseling.] Dion Cassius, l. xxxvii. [c. 16] p. 121. Tacit. Hist. v. 1-9. Justin, xxxvi. 2, 3.

[2] Tradidit arcano quæcunque volumine Moses:
    Non monstrare vias eadem nisi sacra colenti,
    Quæsitum ad fontem solos deducere verpos.
        [Juvenal, Sat. xiv. 102.]

The letter of this law is not to be found in the present volume of Moses. But the wise, the humane Maimonides openly teaches that, if an idolater fall into the water, a Jew ought not to save him from instant death. See Basnage, Histoire des Juifs, l. vi. c. 28 [l. v. c. 24].

[It is diametrically opposed to its spirit and to its letter; see among other passages, Deut. x. 18, 19, " God . . . loveth the stranger in giving him food and raiment: love ye therefore the stranger, for ye were strangers in the land of Egypt." Juvenal is a satirist, whose strong expression can hardly be received as historic evidence, and he wrote after the horrible cruelties of the Romans which, during and after the war, might give some cause for the complete isolation of the Jew from the rest of the world. The Jew was a bigot, but his religion was not the only source of his bigotry. After how many centuries of mutual wrong and hatred, which had still further estranged the Jew from mankind, did Maimonides write?—O. S.]

[3] A Jewish sect, which indulged themselves in a sort of occasional conformity, derived from Herod, by whose example and authority they had been seduced, the name of Herodians. But their numbers were so inconsiderable, and their duration so short, that Josephus has not thought them worthy of his notice. See Prideaux's Connection, vol. ii. p. 285.

[The Herodians were probably more of a political party than a religious sect, though Gibbon is most likely right as to their usual conformity.—O. S.]

[4] Cicero pro Flacco, c. 28.

[5] Philo de Legatione. Augustus left a foundation for a perpetual sacrifice. Yet he approved of the neglect which his grandson Caius expressed towards the temple of Jerusalem. See Sueton. in August. c. 93, and Casaubon's notes on that passage.

been an object of abhorrence to himself and to his brethren. But the moderation of the conquerors was insufficient to appease the jealous prejudices of their subjects, who were alarmed and scandalised at the ensigns of paganism, which necessarily introduced themselves into a Roman province.[1] The mad attempt of Caligula to place his own statue in the temple of Jerusalem was defeated by the unanimous resolution of a people who dreaded death much less than such an idolatrous profanation.[2] Their attachment to the law of Moses was equal to their detestation of foreign religions. The current of zeal and devotion, as it was contracted into a narrow channel, ran with the strength, and sometimes with the fury, of a torrent.

This inflexible perseverance, which appeared so odious or so ridiculous to the ancient world, assumes a more awful character, since Providence has deigned to reveal to us the mysterious history of the chosen people. But the devout and even scrupulous attachment to the Mosaic religion, so conspicuous among the Jews who lived under the second temple, becomes still more surprising if it is compared with the stubborn incredulity of their forefathers. When the law was given in thunder from Mount Sinai; when the tides of the ocean and the course of the planets were suspended for the convenience of the Israelites; and when temporal rewards and punishments were the immediate consequences of their piety or disobedience, they perpetually relapsed into rebellion against the visible majesty of their Divine King, placed the idols of the nations in the sanctuary of Jehovah, and imitated every fantastic ceremony that was practised in the tents of the Arabs, or in the cities of Phœnicia.[3] As the protection of Heaven was deservedly withdrawn from the ungrateful race, their faith acquired a proportionable degree of vigour and purity. The contemporaries of Moses and Joshua had beheld with careless indifference the

[1] See in particular, Joseph. Antiquit. xvii. 6, xviii. 3; and De Bel. Judaic. i. 33, and ii. 9, edit. Havercamp.
[This was during the governorship of Pontius Pilate (Hist. of Jews, ii 156. Probably, in part to avoid this collision, the Roman governor in general resided at Cæsarea.—O. S.]

[2] Jussi a Caio Cesare, effigiem ejus in templo locare, arma potius sumpsere. Tacit. Hist. v. 9. Philo and Josephus give a very circumstantial, but a very rhetorical, account of this transaction, which exceedingly perplexed the governor of Syria. At the first mention of this idolatrous proposal king Agrippa fainted away, and did not recover his senses until the third day.

[3] For the enumeration of the Syrian and Arabian deities, it may be observed that Milton has comprised in one hundred and thirty very beautiful lines the two large and learned syntagmas which Selden had composed on that abstruse subject.

most amazing miracles. Under the pressure of every calamity,
the belief of those miracles has preserved the Jews of a later
period from the universal contagion of idolatry; and in contradiction to every known principle of the human mind, that
singular people seems to have yielded a stronger and more ready
assent to the traditions of their remote ancestors than to the
evidence of their own senses.[1]

The Jewish religion was admirably fitted for defence, but it
was never designed for conquest; and it seems probable that
the number of proselytes was never much superior to that of
apostates. The divine promises were originally made, and the
distinguishing rite of circumcision was enjoined, to a single family.
When the posterity of Abraham had multiplied like the sands of
the sea, the Deity, from whose mouth they received a system of
laws and ceremonies, declared himself the proper and as it were
the national God of Israel; and with the most jealous care
separated his favourite people from the rest of mankind. The
conquest of the land of Canaan was accompanied with so many
wonderful and with so many bloody circumstances, that the
victorious Jews were left in a state of irreconcilable hostility
with all their neighbours. They had been commanded to
extirpate some of the most idolatrous tribes, and the execution
of the Divine will had seldom been retarded by the weakness of
humanity. With the other nations they were forbidden to contract any marriages or alliances; and the prohibition of receiving
them into the congregation, which in some cases was perpetual,
almost always extended to the third, to the seventh, or even

---

[1] " How long will this people provoke me? and how long will it be ere
they *believe* me, for all the *signs* which I have shown among them? "
(Numbers xiv. 11.) It would be easy, but it would be unbecoming, to
justify the complaint of the Deity from the whole tenor of the Mosaic
history.

[In regard to this, Milman says that among a rude and barbarous people
religious impressions are easily made and as soon effaced. The ignorance
which multiplies imaginary wonders would weaken or destroy the effect of
real miracle. At the period of Jewish history referred to in the passage in
Numbers their fear predominated over their faith—the fears of an unwarlike people just rescued from debasing slavery, and commanded to attack
a fierce, well-armed, gigantic, and far more numerous race—the inhabitants
of Canaan. As to the frequent apostacy of the Jews, for many centuries
subsequent to their departure from Egypt their religion was at that time
beyond their state of civilisation. Nor is it uncommon for a people to
cling with passionate attachment to that of which, at first, they did not
understand the value. Patriotism and natural pride will contend even to
death for political rights which at first were forced on a reluctant people.
The Christian may with justice retort that the great sign of his religion,
the Resurrection of Jesus, was most ardently believed and most resolutely
asserted by the eye-witnesses of the fact.—O. S.]

to the tenth generation. The obligation of preaching to the
Gentiles the faith of Moses had never been inculcated as a precept of the law, nor were the Jews inclined to impose it on
themselves as a voluntary duty.

In the admission of new citizens that unsocial people was
actuated by the selfish vanity of the Greeks rather than by the
generous policy of Rome. The descendants of Abraham were
flattered by the opinion that they alone were the heirs of the
covenant, and they were apprehensive of diminishing the value
of their inheritance by sharing it too easily with the strangers of
the earth. A larger acquaintance with mankind extended their
knowledge without correcting their prejudices; and whenever
the God of Israel acquired any new votaries, he was much more
indebted to the inconstant humour of polytheism than to the
active zeal of his own missionaries.[1] The religion of Moses seems
to be instituted for a particular country as well as for a single
nation; and if a strict obedience had been paid to the order that
every male, three times in the year, should present himself before
the Lord Jehovah, it would have been impossible that the Jews
could ever have spread themselves beyond the narrow limits of
the promised land.[2] That obstacle was indeed removed by the
destruction of the temple of Jerusalem; but the most considerable part of the Jewish religion was involved in its destruction;
and the Pagans, who had long wondered at the strange report of
an empty sanctuary,[3] were at a loss to discover what could be
the object, or what could be the instruments, of a worship which
was destitute of temples and of altars, of priests and of sacrifices.
Yet even in their fallen state, the Jews, still asserting their lofty
and exclusive privileges, shunned, instead of courting, the
society of strangers. They still insisted with inflexible rigour on
those parts of the law which it was in their power to practise.
Their peculiar distinctions of days, of meats, and a variety of
trivial though burdensome observances, were so many objects
of disgust and aversion for the other nations, to whose habits and
prejudices they were diametrically opposite. The painful and

---

[1] All that relates to the Jewish proselytes has been very ably treated by
Basnage, Hist. des Juifs, l. v. c. 6, 7.

[2] See Exod. xxxiv. 23, Deut. xvi. 16, the commentators, and a very sensible note in the Universal History, vol. i. p. 603, edit. fol.

[3] When Pompey, using or abusing the right of conquest, entered into the
Holy of Holies, it was observed with amazement, " Nullâ intus Deûm
effigie, vacuam sedem et inania arcana." Tacit. Hist. v. 9. It was a
popular saying, with regard to the Jews,

Nil præter nubes et cœli numen adorant.

even dangerous rite of circumcision was alone capable of repelling a willing proselyte from the door of the synagogue.[1]

Under these circumstances, Christianity offered itself to the world, armed with the strength of the Mosaic law, and delivered from the weight of its fetters. An exclusive zeal for the truth of religion and the unity of God was as carefully inculcated in the new as in the ancient system: and whatever was now revealed to mankind concerning the nature and designs of the Supreme Being was fitted to increase their reverence for that mysterious doctrine. The divine authority of Moses and the prophets was admitted, and even established, as the firmest basis of Christianity. From the beginning of the world an uninterrupted series of predictions had announced and prepared the long-expected coming of the Messiah, who, in compliance with the gross apprehensions of the Jews, had been more frequently represented under the character of a King and Conqueror, than under that of a Prophet, a Martyr, and the Son of God. By his expiatory sacrifice the imperfect sacrifices of the temple were at once consummated and abolished. The ceremonial law, which consisted only of types and figures, was succeeded by a pure and spiritual worship, equally adapted to all climates, as well as to every condition of mankind; and to the initiation of blood, was substituted a more harmless initiation of water. The promise of divine favour, instead of being partially confined to the posterity of Abraham, was universally proposed to the freeman and the slave, to the Greek and to the barbarian, to the Jew and to the Gentile. Every privilege that could raise the proselyte from earth to heaven, that could exalt his devotion, secure his happiness, or even gratify that secret pride which, under the semblance of devotion, insinuates itself into the human heart, was still reserved for the members of the Christian church; but at the same time all mankind was permitted, and even solicited, to accept the glorious distinction, which was not only proffered as a favour, but imposed as an obligation. It became the most sacred duty of a new convert to diffuse among his friends and relations the inestimable blessing which he had received, and to warn them against a refusal that would be severely punished as a criminal disobedience to the will of a benevolent but all-powerful Deity.

The enfranchisement of the church from the bonds of the

[1] A second kind of circumcision was inflicted on a Samaritan or Egyptian proselyte. The sullen indifference of the Talmudists, with respect to the conversion of strangers, may be seen in Basnage, Histoire des Juifs, l. v. c. 6.

synagogue was a work, however, of some time and of some difficulty. The Jewish converts, who acknowledged Jesus in the character of the Messiah foretold by their ancient oracles, respected him as a prophetic teacher of virtue and religion; but they obstinately adhered to the ceremonies of their ancestors, and were desirous of imposing them on the Gentiles, who continually augmented the number of believers. These Judaising Christians seem to have argued with some degree of plausibility from the Divine origin of the Mosaic law, and from the immutable perfections of its great Author. They affirmed, *that*, if the Being who is the same through all eternity had designed to abolish those sacred rites which had served to distinguish his chosen people, the repeal of them would have been no less clear and solemn than their first promulgation: *that*, instead of those frequent declarations which either suppose or assert the perpetuity of the Mosaic religion, it would have been represented as a provisionary scheme intended to last only till the coming of the Messiah, who should instruct mankind in a more perfect mode of faith and of worship: [1] *that* the Messiah himself, and his disciples who conversed with him on earth, instead of authorising by their example the most minute observances of the Mosaic law, [2] would have published to the world the abolition of those useless and obsolete ceremonies, without suffering Christianity to remain during so many years obscurely confounded among the sects of the Jewish church. Arguments like these appear to have been used in the defence of the expiring cause of the Mosaic law; but the industry of our learned divines has abundantly explained the ambiguous language of the Old Testament, and the ambiguous conduct of the apostolic teachers. It was proper gradually to unfold the system of the Gospel, and to pronounce with the utmost caution and tenderness a sentence of condemnation so repugnant to the inclination and prejudices of the believing Jews.

The history of the church of Jerusalem affords a lively proof of the necessity of those precautions, and of the deep impression which the Jewish religion had made on the minds of its sectaries.

[1] These arguments were urged with great ingenuity by the Jew Orobio, and refuted with equal ingenuity and candour by the Christian Limborch. See the Amica Collatio (it well deserves that name), or account of the dispute between them.

[2] Jesus . . . circumcisus erat; cibis utebatur Judaicis; vestitû simili; purgatos scabie mittebat ad sacerdotes; Paschata et alios dies festos religiosè observabat: si quos sanavit sabbatho, ostendit non tantum ex lege, sed et ex receptis sententiis, talia opera sabbatho non interdicta. Grotius de Veritate Religionis Christianæ, l. v. c. 7. A little afterwards (c. 12) he expatiates on the condescension of the apostles.

The first fifteen bishops of Jerusalem were all circumcised Jews; and the congregation over which they presided united the law of Moses with the doctrine of Christ.[1] It was natural that the primitive tradition of a church which was founded only forty days after the death of Christ, and was governed almost as many years under the immediate inspection of his apostle, should be received as the standard of orthodoxy.[2] The distant churches very frequently appealed to the authority of their venerable Parent, and relieved her distresses by a liberal contribution of alms. But when numerous and opulent societies were established in the great cities of the empire, in Antioch, Alexandria, Ephesus, Corinth, and Rome, the reverence which Jerusalem had inspired to all the Christian colonies insensibly diminished. The Jewish converts, or, as they were afterwards called, the Nazarenes, who had laid the foundations of the church, soon found themselves overwhelmed by the increasing multitudes that from all the various religions of polytheism enlisted under the banner of Christ: and the Gentiles, who, with the approbation of their peculiar apostle, had rejected the intolerable weight of Mosaic ceremonies, at length refused to their more scrupulous brethren the same toleration which at first they had humbly solicited for their own practice. The ruin of the temple, of the city, and of the public religion of the Jews, was severely felt by the Nazarenes; as in their manners, though not in their faith, they maintained so intimate a connection with their impious countrymen, whose misfortunes were attributed by the Pagans to the contempt, and more justly ascribed by the Christians to the wrath, of the Supreme Deity. The Nazarenes retired from the ruins of Jerusalem to the little town of Pella beyond the Jordan, where that ancient church languished above sixty years in solitude and obscurity.[3] They still enjoyed the comfort of making frequent and devout visits to the *Holy City*, and the hope of being one day restored to those seats which both nature and religion taught them to love as well as to revere. But at length, under the reign of Hadrian, the desperate fanaticism of the Jews

---

[1] Pæne omnes Christum Deum sub legis observatione credebant. Sulpicius Severus, ii. 31. See Eusebius, Hist. Ecclesiast. l. iv. c. 5.

[2] Mosheim de Rebus Christianis ante Constantinum Magnum, p. 153. In this masterly performance, which I shall often have occasion to quote, he enters much more fully into the state of the primitive church than he has an opportunity of doing in his General History.

[3] Eusebius, l iii. c. 5. Le Clerc, Hist. Ecclesiast. p. 605. During this occasional absence, the bishop and church of Pella still retained the title of Jerusalem. In the same manner, the Roman pontiffs resided seventy years at Avignon; and the patriarchs of Alexandria have long since transferred their episcopal seat to Cairo.

filled up the measure of their calamities; and the Romans, exasperated by their repeated rebellions, exercised the rights of victory with unusual rigour. The emperor founded, under the name of Ælia Capitolina, a new city on Mount Sion,[1] to which he gave the privileges of a colony; and denouncing the severest penalties against any of the Jewish people who should dare to approach its precincts, he fixed a vigilant garrison of a Roman cohort to enforce the execution of his orders. The Nazarenes had only one way left to escape the common proscription, and the force of truth was on this occasion assisted by the influence of temporal advantages. They elected Marcus for their bishop, a prelate of the race of the Gentiles, and most probably a native either of Italy or of some of the Latin provinces. At his persuasion the most considerable part of the congregation renounced the Mosaic law, in the practice of which they had persevered above a century. By this sacrifice of their habits and prejudices they purchased a free admission into the colony of Hadrian, and more firmly cemented their union with the Catholic church.[2]

When the name and honours of the church of Jerusalem had been restored to Mount Sion, the crimes of heresy and schism were imputed to the obscure remnant of the Nazarenes which refused to accompany their Latin bishop. They still preserved their former habitation of Pella, spread themselves into the villages adjacent to Damascus, and formed an inconsiderable church in the city of Berœa, or, as it is now called, of Aleppo, in Syria.[3] The name of Nazarenes was deemed too honourable for those Christian Jews, and they soon received, from the supposed poverty of their understanding, as well as of their condition, the contemptuous epithet of Ebionites.[4] In a few years after the

[1] Dion Cassius, l. lxix. [c. 12.] The exile of the Jewish nation from Jerusalem is attested by Aristo of Pella (apud Euseb. l. iv. c. 6), and is mentioned by several ecclesiastical writers; though some of them too hastily extend this interdiction to the whole country of Palestine.

[2] Eusebius, l. iv. c. 6. Sulpicius Severus, ii. 31. By comparing their unsatisfactory accounts, Mosheim (p. 327, etc.) has drawn out a very distinct representation of the circumstances and motives of this revolution.

[3] Le Clerc (Hist. Ecclesiast. p. 477, 535) seems to have collected from Eusebius, Jerome, Epiphanius, and other writers, all the principal circumstances that relate to the Nazarenes or Ebionites. The nature of their opinions soon divided them into a stricter and a milder sect; and there is some reason to conjecture that the family of Jesus Christ remained members, at least, of the latter and more moderate party.

[4] Some writers have been pleased to create an Ebion, the imaginary author of their sect and name. But we can more safely rely on the learned Eusebius than on the vehement Tertullian, or the credulous Epiphanius. According to Le Clerc, the Hebrew word *Ebjonim* may be translated into Latin by that of *Pauperes*. See Hist. Ecclesiast. p. 477.

return of the church of Jerusalem, it became a matter of doubt
and controversy whether a man who sincerely acknowledged
Jesus as the Messiah, but who still continued to observe the law
of Moses, could possibly hope for salvation. The humane
temper of Justin Martyr inclined him to answer this question in
the affirmative; and though he expressed himself with the most
guarded diffidence, he ventured to determine in favour of such
an imperfect Christian, if he were content to practise the Mosaic
ceremonies without pretending to assert their general use or
necessity. But when Justin was pressed to declare the sentiment of the church, he confessed that there were very many
among the orthodox Christians who not only excluded their
Judaising brethren from the hope of salvation, but who declined
any intercourse with them in the common offices of friendship,
hospitality, and social life.[1] The more rigorous opinion prevailed, as it was natural to expect, over the milder; and an
eternal bar of separation was fixed between the disciples of
Moses and those of Christ. The unfortunate Ebionites, rejected
from one religion as apostates, and from the other as heretics,
found themselves compelled to assume a more decided character;
and although some traces of that obsolete sect may be discovered as late as the fourth century, they insensibly melted
away either into the church or the synagogue.[2]

While the orthodox church preserved a just medium between

[1] See the very curious Dialogue of Justin Martyr with the Jew Tryphon.
The conference between them was held at Ephesus, in the reign of Antoninus Pius, and about twenty years after the return of the church of Pella
to Jerusalem. For this date consult the accurate note of Tillemont,
Mémoires Ecclésiastiques, tom. ii. p. 511.

[Justin Martyr makes an important distinction which Gibbon has
neglected to notice, viz., that there were some who were not content with
observing the Mosaic law themselves, but enforced the same observance
as necessary to salvation upon the heathen converts, and refused all social
intercourse with them if they did not conform to the law. Justin Martyr
himself freely admits those who kept the law themselves to Christian
communion, though he acknowledges that *some*, but not the Church as a
whole, thought otherwise. The former by some are considered the
Nazarenes, the latter the Ebionites.—O. S.]

[2] Of all the systems of Christianity, that of Abyssinia is the only one
which still adheres to the Mosaic rites (Geddes's Church History of Æthiopia,
and Dissertations de La Grand sur la Relation du P. Lobo). The eunuch
of the queen Candace might suggest some suspicions; but as we are assured
(Socrates, i. 19; Sozomen, ii. 24; Ludolphus, p. 281) that the Æthiopians
were not converted till the fourth century, it is more reasonable to believe
that they respected the sabbath, and distinguished the forbidden meats, in
imitation of the Jews, who, in a very early period, were seated on both sides
of the Red Sea. Circumcision had been practised by the most ancient
Æthiopians, from motives of health and cleanliness, which seem to be explained in the Recherches Philosophiques sur les Américans, tom. ii. p. 117.

excessive veneration and improper contempt for the law of Moses, the various heretics deviated into equal but opposite extremes of error and extravagance. From the acknowledged truth of the Jewish religion, the Ebionites had concluded that it could never be abolished. From its supposed imperfections, the Gnostics as hastily inferred that it never was instituted by the wisdom of the Deity. There are some objections against the authority of Moses and the prophets which too readily present themselves to the sceptical mind; though they can only be derived from our ignorance of remote antiquity, and from our incapacity to form an adequate judgment of the Divine economy. These objections were eagerly embraced and as petulantly urged by the vain science of the Gnostics.[1] As those heretics were, for the most part, averse to the pleasures of sense, they morosely arraigned the polygamy of the patriarchs, the gallantries of David, and the seraglio of Solomon. The conquest of the land of Canaan, and the extirpation of the unsuspecting natives, they were at a loss how to reconcile with the common notions of humanity and justice. But when they recollected the sanguinary list of murders, of executions, and of massacres, which stain almost every page of the Jewish annals, they acknowledged that the barbarians of Palestine had exercised as much compassion towards their idolatrous enemies as they had ever shown to their friends or countrymen.[2] Passing from the sectaries of the law itself, they asserted that it was impossible that a religion which consisted only of bloody sacrifices and trifling ceremonies, and whose rewards as well as punishments were all of a carnal and temporal nature, could inspire the love of virtue, or restrain the impetuosity of passion. The Mosaic account of the creation and fall of man was treated with profane derision by the Gnostics, who would not listen with patience to the repose of the Deity after six days' labour, to the rib of Adam, the garden of Eden, the trees of life and of knowledge, the speaking serpent, the forbidden fruit, and the condemnation pronounced against human

---

[1] Beausobre, Histoire du Manichéisme, l. i. c. 3, has stated their objections, particularly those of Faustus, the adversary of Augustin, with the most learned impartiality.

[2] Apud ipsos fides obstinata, misericordia in promptû: adversus omnes alios hostile odium. Tacit. Hist. v. 5. Surely Tacitus had seen the Jews with too favourable an eye. The perusal of Josephus must have destroyed the antithesis.

[Few writers have suspected Tacitus of partiality towards the Jews. The whole later history of the Jews illustrates their strong feelings of humanity to their brethren, and their hostility to the rest of mankind.— O. S.]

kind for the venial offence of their first progenitors.[1] The God
of Israel was impiously represented by the Gnostics as a being
liable to passion and to error, capricious in his favour, implacable
in his resentment, meanly jealous of his superstitious worship,
and confining his partial providence to a single people, and to this
transitory life.   In such a character they could discover none of
the features of the wise and omnipotent Father of the universe.[2]
They allowed that the religion of the Jews was somewhat less
criminal than the idolatry of the Gentiles: but it was their fundamental doctrine that the Christ whom they adored as the first
and brightest emanation of the Deity appeared upon earth to
rescue mankind from their various errors, and to reveal a *new*
system of truth and perfection.   The most learned of the fathers,
by a very singular condescension, have imprudently admitted
the sophistry of the Gnostics.   Acknowledging that the literal
sense is repugnant to every principle of faith as well as reason,
they deem themselves secure and invulnerable behind the ample
veil of allegory, which they carefully spread over every tender
part of the Mosaic dispensation.[3]

It has been remarked with more ingenuity than truth that the
virgin purity of the church was never violated by schism or
heresy before the reign of Trajan or Hadrian, about one hundred
years after the death of Christ.[4]   We may observe with much
more propriety that, during that period, the disciples of the
Messiah were indulged in a freer latitude both of faith and
practice than has ever been allowed in succeeding ages.   As the
terms of communion were insensibly narrowed, and the spiritual
authority of the prevailing party was exercised with increasing
severity, many of its most respectable adherents, who were called
upon to renounce, were provoked to assert their private opinions,
to pursue the consequences of their mistaken principles, and
openly to erect the standard of rebellion against the unity of the
church.   The Gnostics were distinguished as the most polite,
the most learned, and the most wealthy of the Christian name;
and that general appellation, which expressed a superiority of

[1] Dr. Burnet (Archæologia, l. ii. c. 7) has discussed the first chapters of
Genesis with too much wit and freedom.

[2] The milder Gnostics considered Jehovah, the Creator, as a Being of a
mixed nature between God and the Dæmon.   Others confounded him
with the evil principle.   Consult the second century of the general history
of Mosheim, which gives a very distinct, though concise, account of their
strange opinions on this subject.

[3] See Beausobre, Hist. du Manichéisme, l. i. c. 4.   Origen and St.
Augustin were among the allegorists.

[4] Hegesippus, ap. Euseb, l. iii. 32; iv. 22.   Clemens Alexandrin. Stromat.
vii. 17.

knowledge, was either assumed by their own pride, or ironically bestowed by the envy of their adversaries. They were almost without exception of the race of the Gentiles, and their principal founders seem to have been natives of Syria or Egypt, where the warmth of the climate disposes both the mind and the body to indolent and contemplative devotion. The Gnostics blended with the faith of Christ many sublime but obscure tenets, which they derived from oriental philosophy, and even from the religion of Zoroaster, concerning the eternity of matter, the existence of two principles, and the mysterious hierarchy of the invisible world.[1] As soon as they launched out into that vast abyss, they delivered themselves to the guidance of a disordered imagination; and as the paths of error are various and infinite, the Gnostics were imperceptibly divided into more than fifty particular sects,[2] of whom the most celebrated appear to have been the Basilidians, the Valentinians, the Marcionites, and, in a still later period, the Manichæans. Each of these sects could boast of its bishops and congregations, of its doctors and martyrs;[3] and, instead of the Four Gospels adopted by the church, the heretics produced a multitude of histories, in which the actions and discourses of Christ and of his apostles were adapted to their respective tenets.[4] The success of the Gnostics was rapid and extensive.[5] They covered Asia and Egypt, established them-

---

[1] In the account of the Gnostics of the second and third centuries, Mosheim is ingenious and candid; Le Clerc dull, but exact; Beausobre almost always an apologist; and it is much to be feared that the primitive fathers are very frequently calumniators.

[For the best accounts of Gnosticism see *Histoire du Gnosticisme* by M. Matter, also R. A. Lipsius, *Quellen Kritik des Epiphanios*, with the article on Gnosticism in Ersch and Gruber's Encyclopædia by the same writer.—O. S.]

[2] See the catalogues of Irenæus and Epiphanius. It must indeed be allowed that those writers were inclined to multiply the number of sects which opposed the *unity* of the church.

[3] Eusebius, l. iv. c. 15. Sozomen, l. ii. c. 32. See in Bayle, in the article of *Marcion*, a curious detail of a dispute on that subject. It should seem that some of the Gnostics (the Basilidians) declined, and even refused, the honour of martyrdom. Their reasons were singular and abstruse. See Mosheim, p. 539.

[4] See a very remarkable passage of Origen (Proem. ad Lucam.). That indefatigable writer, who had consumed his life in the study of the Scriptures, relies for their authenticity on the inspired authority of the church. It was impossible that the Gnostics could receive our present Gospels, many parts of which (particularly in the resurrection of Christ) are directly, and as it might seem designedly, pointed against their favourite tenets. It is therefore somewhat singular that Ignatius (Epist. ad Smyrn. Patr. Apostol. tom. ii. p. 34) should choose to employ a vague and doubtful tradition, instead of quoting the certain testimony of the evangelists.

[5] Faciunt favos et vespæ; faciunt ecclesias et Marcionitæ, is the strong expression of Tertullian, which I am obliged to quote from memory. [Adv.

selves in Rome, and sometimes penetrated into the provinces of
the West.   For the most part they arose in the second century,
flourished during the third, and were suppressed in the fourth or
fifth, by the prevalence of more fashionable controversies, and
by the superior ascendant of the reigning power.   Though they
constantly disturbed the peace, and frequently disgraced the
name of religion, they contributed to assist rather than to retard
the progress of Christianity.   The Gentile converts, whose
strongest objections and prejudices were directed against the
law of Moses, could find admission into many Christian societies,
which required not from their untutored mind any belief of an
antecedent revelation.   Their faith was insensibly fortified and
enlarged, and the church was ultimately benefited by the conquests of its most inveterate enemies.[1]

But whatever difference of opinion might subsist between
the Orthodox, the Ebionites, and the Gnostics, concerning the
divinity or the obligation of the Mosaic law, they were all equally
animated by the same exclusive zeal, and by the same abhorrence for idolatry, which had distinguished the Jews from the
other nations of the ancient world.   The philosopher, who considered the system of polytheism as a composition of human
fraud and error, could disguise a smile of contempt under the
mask of devotion, without apprehending that either the mockery
or the compliance would expose him to the resentment of any
invisible, or, as he conceived them, imaginary powers.   But the
established religions of Paganism were seen by the primitive
Christians in a much more odious and formidable light.   It was
the universal sentiment both of the church and of heretics, that
the dæmons were the authors, the patrons, and the objects of
idolatry.[2]   Those rebellious spirits who had been degraded from
the rank of angels, and cast down into the infernal pit, were still
permitted to roam upon earth, to torment the bodies and to
seduce the minds of sinful men.   The dæmons soon discovered
and abused the natural propensity of the human heart towards
devotion, and, artfully withdrawing the adoration of mankind
from their Creator, they usurped the place and honours of the

Marcion. iv. 5.]   In the time of Epiphanius (advers. Hæreses, p. 302 [ed.
Paris, 1622]) the Marcionites were very numerous in Italy, Syria, Egypt,
Arabia, and Persia.

[1] Augustin is a memorable instance of this gradual progress from reason
to faith.   He was, during several years, engaged in the Manichæan sect.

[2] The unanimous sentiment of the primitive church is very clearly explained by Justin Martyr, Apolog. Major [c. 25, p. 59. ed. Bened.];   by
Athenagoras, Legat. c. 22, etc.;   and by Lactantius, Institut. Divin. ii.
14-19.

Supreme Deity. By the success of their malicious contrivances, they at once gratified their own vanity and revenge, and obtained the only comfort of which they were yet susceptible, the hope of involving the human species in the participation of their guilt and misery. It was confessed, or at least it was imagined, that they had distributed among themselves the most important characters of polytheism, one dæmon assuming the name and attributes of Jupiter, another of Æsculapius, a third of Venus, and a fourth perhaps of Apollo;[1] and that, by the advantage of their long experience and aërial nature, they were enabled to execute, with sufficient skill and dignity, the parts which they had undertaken. They lurked in the temples, instituted festivals and sacrifices, invented fables, pronounced oracles, and were frequently allowed to perform miracles. The Christians, who, by the interposition of evil spirits, could so readily explain every præternatural appearance, were disposed and even desirous to admit the most extravagant fictions of the Pagan mythology. But the belief of the Christian was accompanied with horror. The most trifling mark of respect to the national worship he considered as a direct homage yielded to the dæmon, and as an act of rebellion against the majesty of God.

In consequence of this opinion, it was the first but arduous duty of a Christian to preserve himself pure and undefiled by the practice of idolatry. The religion of the nations was not merely a speculative doctrine professed in the schools or preached in the temples. The innumerable deities and rites of polytheism were closely interwoven with every circumstance of business or pleasure, of public or of private life; and it seemed impossible to escape the observance of them, without, at the same time, renouncing the commerce of mankind, and all the offices and amusements of society.[2] The important transactions of peace and war were prepared or concluded by solemn sacrifices, in which the magistrate, the senator, and the soldier were obliged to preside or to participate.[3] The public spectacles were an essential part of the cheerful devotion of the Pagans, and the gods were supposed to accept, as the most grateful offering, the

[1] Tertullian (Apolog. c. 23) alleges the confession of the dæmons themselves as often as they were tormented by the Christian exorcists.

[2] Tertullian has written a most severe treatise against idolatry, to caution his brethren against the hourly danger of incurring that guilt. Recogita silvam, et quantæ latitant spinæ. De Coronâ Militis. c. 10.

[3] The Roman senate was always held in a temple or consecrated place (Aulus Gellius, xiv. 7). Before they entered on business, every senator dropped some wine and frankincense on the altar. Sueton. in August. c. 35.

games that the prince and people celebrated in honour of their peculiar festivals.[1] The Christian, who with pious horror avoided the abomination of the circus or the theatre, found himself encompassed with infernal snares in every convivial entertainment, as often as his friends, invoking the hospitable deities, poured out libations to each other's happiness.[2] When the bride, struggling with well-affected reluctance, was forced in hymenæal pomp over the threshold of her new habitation,[3] or when the sad procession of the dead slowly moved towards the funeral pile,[4] the Christian, on these interesting occasions, was compelled to desert the persons who were the dearest to him, rather than contract the guilt inherent to those impious ceremonies. Every art and every trade that was in the least concerned in the framing or adorning of idols was polluted by the stain of idolatry;[5] a severe sentence, since it devoted to eternal misery the far greater part of the community which is employed in the exercise of liberal or mechanic professions. If we cast our eyes over the numerous remains of antiquity, we shall perceive that, besides the immediate representations of the gods and the holy instruments of their worship, the elegant forms and agreeable fictions consecrated by the imagination of the Greeks were introduced as the richest ornaments of the houses, the dress, and the furniture of the Pagans.[6] Even the arts of music and painting, of eloquence and poetry, flowed from the same impure origin. In the style of the fathers, Apollo and the Muses were the organs of the infernal spirit; Homer and Virgil were the most eminent of his servants; and the beautiful mythology which pervades and animates the compositions of their genius

[1] See Tertullian, De Spectaculis. This severe reformer shows no more indulgence to a tragedy of Euripides than to a combat of gladiators. The dress of the actors particularly offends him. By the use of the lofty buskin they impiously strive to add a cubit to their stature: c. 23.

[2] The ancient practice of concluding the entertainment with libations may be found in every classic. Socrates and Seneca, in their last moments, made a noble application of this custom. Postremo stagnum calidæ aquæ introiit, respergens proximos servorum, additâ voce, libare se liquorem illum Jovi Liberatori. Tacit. Annal. xv. 64.

[3] See the elegant but idolatrous hymn of Catullus on the nuptials of Manlius and Julia. O Hymen, Hymenæe Iö! Quis huic Deo comparfor ausit?

[4] The ancient funerals (in those of Misenus and Pallas) are no less accurately described by Virgil than they are illustrated by his commentator Servius. The pile itself was an altar, the flames were fed with the blood of victims, and all the assistants were sprinkled with lustral water.

[5] Tertullian de Idololatria, c. 11.

[6] See every part of Montfaucon's Antiquities. Even the reverses of the Greek and Roman coins were frequently of an idolatrous nature. Here, indeed, the scruples of the Christian were suspended by a stronger passion.

is destined to celebrate the glory of the dæmons. Even the
common language of Greece and Rome abounded with familiar
but impious expressions, which the imprudent Christian might
too carelessly utter, or too patiently hear.[1]

The dangerous temptations which on every side lurked in
ambush to surprise the unguarded believer assailed him with
redoubled violence on the days of solemn festivals. So artfully
were they framed and disposed throughout the year, that superstition always wore the appearance of pleasure, and often of
virtue.[2] Some of the most sacred festivals in the Roman ritual
were destined to salute the new calends of January with vows
of public and private felicity; to indulge the pious remembrance
of the dead and living; to ascertain the inviolable bounds of
property; to hail, on the return of spring, the genial powers of
fecundity; to perpetuate the two memorable eras of Rome, the
foundation of the city, and that of the republic; and to restore,
during the humane licence of the Saturnalia, the primitive equality
of mankind. Some idea may be conceived of the abhorrence of
the Christians for such impious ceremonies, by the scrupulous
delicacy which they displayed on a much less alarming occasion.
On days of general festivity it was the custom of the ancients to
adorn their doors with lamps and with branches of laurel, and to
crown their heads with a garland of flowers. This innocent and
elegant practice might perhaps have been tolerated as a mere
civil institution. But it most unluckily happened that the doors
were under the protection of the household gods, that the laurel
was sacred to the lover of Daphne, and that garlands of flowers,
though frequently worn as a symbol either of joy or mourning,
had been dedicated in their first origin to the service of superstition. The trembling Christians, who were persuaded in this
instance to comply with the fashion of their country and the
commands of the magistrate, laboured under the most gloomy
apprehensions, from the reproaches of their own conscience, the
censures of the church, and the denunciations of divine vengeance.[3]

[1] Tertullian de Idololatria, c. 20, 21, 22. If a Pagan friend (on the occasion perhaps of sneezing) used the familiar expression of " Jupiter bless
you," the Christian was obliged to protest against the divinity of Jupiter.

[2] Consult the most laboured work of Ovid, his imperfect *Fasti*. He
finished no more than the first six months of the year. The compilation
of Macrobius is called the *Saturnalia*, but it is only a small part of the first
book that bears any relation to the title.

[3] Tertullian has composed a defence, or rather panegyric, of the rash
action of a Christian soldier, who, by throwing away his crown of laurel,
had exposed himself and his brethren to the most imminent danger. By
the mention of the *emperors* (Severus and Caracalla) it is evident, notwith-

Such was the anxious diligence which was required to guard the chastity of the Gospel from the infectious breath of idolatry. The superstitious observances of public or private rites were carelessly practised, from education and habit, by the followers of the established religion. But as often as they occurred, they afforded the Christians an opportunity of declaring and confirming their zealous opposition. By these frequent protestations their attachment to the faith was continually fortified; and in proportion to the increase of zeal, they combated with the more ardour and success in the holy war which they had undertaken against the empire of the dæmons.

II. The writings of Cicero [1] represent in the most lively colours the ignorance, the errors, and the uncertainty of the ancient philosophers with regard to the immortality of the soul. When they are desirous of arming their disciples against the fear of death, they inculcate, as an obvious though melancholy position, that the fatal stroke of our dissolution releases us from the calamities of life; and that those can no longer suffer who no longer exist. Yet there were a few sages of Greece and Rome who had conceived a more exalted, and, in some respects, a juster idea of human nature, though it must be confessed that, in the sublime inquiry, their reason had been often guided by their imagination, and that their imagination had been prompted by their vanity. When they viewed with complacency the extent of their own mental powers, when they exercised the various faculties of memory, of fancy, and of judgment, in the most profound speculations or the most important labours, and when they reflected on the desire of fame, which transported them into future ages, far beyond the bounds of death and of the grave, they were unwilling to confound themselves with the beasts of the field, or to suppose that a being, for whose dignity they entertained the most sincere admiration, could be limited to a spot of earth, and to a few years of duration. With this favourable prepossession they summoned to their aid the science, or rather the language, of Metaphysics. They soon discovered that, as none of the properties of matter will apply to the operations of the mind, the human soul must consequently be a

standing the wishes of M. de Tillemont, that Tertullian composed his treatise De Coronâ long before he was engaged in the errors of the Montanists. See Mémoires Ecclésiastiques, tom. iii. p. 384.

[1] In particular, the first book of the Tusculan Questions, and the treatise De Senectute, and the Somnium Scipionis, contain, in the most beautiful language, everything that Grecian philosophy or Roman good sense could possibly suggest on this dark but important object.

substance distinct from the body, pure, simple, and spiritual, incapable of dissolution, and susceptible of a much higher degree of virtue and happiness after the release from its corporeal prison. From these specious and noble principles the philosophers who trod in the footsteps of Plato deduced a very unjustifiable conclusion, since they asserted, not only the future immortality, but the past eternity of the human soul, which they were too apt to consider as a portion of the infinite and self-existing spirit which pervades and sustains the universe.[1] A doctrine thus removed beyond the senses and the experience of mankind might serve to amuse the leisure of a philosophic mind; or, in the silence of solitude, it might sometimes impart a ray of comfort to desponding virtue; but the faint impression which had been received in the schools was soon obliterated by the commerce and business of active life. We are sufficiently acquainted with the eminent persons who flourished in the age of Cicero and of the first Cæsars, with their actions, their characters, and their motives, to be assured that their conduct in this life was never regulated by any serious conviction of the rewards or punishments of a future state. At the bar and in the senate of Rome the ablest orators were not apprehensive of giving offence to their hearers by exposing that doctrine as an idle and extravagant opinion, which was rejected with contempt by every man of a liberal education and understanding.[2]

Since therefore the most sublime efforts of philosophy can extend no farther than feebly to point out the desire, the hope, or, at most, the probability of a future state, there is nothing, except a divine revelation that can ascertain the existence and describe the condition of the invisible country which is destined to receive the souls of men after their separation from the body. But we may perceive several defects inherent to the popular religions of Greece and Rome which rendered them very unequal to so arduous a task. 1. The general system of their mythology was unsupported by any solid proofs; and the wisest among the Pagans had already disclaimed its usurped authority. 2. The description of the infernal regions had been abandoned to the

---

[1] The pre-existence of human souls, so far at least as that doctrine is compatible with religion, was adopted by many of the Greek and Latin fathers. See Beausobre, Hist. du Manichéisme, l. vi. c. 4.

[2] See Cicero pro Cluent. c. 61. Cæsar ap. Sallust. de Bell. Catilin. c. 51. Juvenal. Satir. ii. 149.

Esse aliquid manes, et subterranea regna,
. . . . . .
Nec pueri credunt, nisi qui nondum ære lavantur.

fancy of painters and of poets, who peopled them with so many phantoms and monsters who dispensed their rewards and punishments with so little equity, that a solemn truth, the most congenial to the human heart, was oppressed and disgraced by the absurd mixture of the wildest fictions.[1] 3. The doctrine of a future state was scarcely considered among the devout polytheists of Greece and Rome as a fundamental article of faith. The providence of the gods, as it related to public communities rather than to private individuals, was principally displayed on the visible theatre of the present world. The petitions which were offered on the altars of Jupiter or Apollo expressed the anxiety of their worshippers for temporal happiness, and their ignorance or indifference concerning a future life.[2] The important truth of the immortality of the soul was inculcated with more diligence as well as success in India, in Assyria, in Egypt, and in Gaul; and since we cannot attribute such a difference to the superior knowledge of the barbarians, we must ascribe it to the influence of an established priesthood, which employed the motives of virtue as the instrument of ambition.[3]

We might naturally expect that a principle so essential to religion would have been revealed in the clearest terms to the chosen people of Palestine, and that it might safely have been intrusted to the hereditary priesthood of Aaron. It is incumbent on us to adore the mysterious dispensations of Providence,[4] when

[1] The eleventh book of the Odyssey gives a very dreary and incoherent account of the infernal shades. Pindar and Virgil have embellished the picture; but even those poets, though more correct than their great model, are guilty of very strange inconsistencies. See Bayle, Responses aux Questions d'un Provincial, part iii. c. 22.

[2] See the sixteenth epistle of the first book of Horace, the thirteenth Satire of Juvenal, and the second Satire of Persius: these popular discourses express the sentiment and language of the multitude.

[3] If we confine ourselves to the Gauls, we may observe that they intrusted not only their lives, but even their money, to the security of another world. Vetus ille mos Gallorum occurrit (says Valerius Maximus, l. ii. c. 6, § 10) quos, memoria proditum est, pecunias mutuas, quæ his apud inferos redderentur, dare solitos. The same custom is more darkly insinuated by Mela, l. iii. c. 2. It is almost needless to add that the profits of trade hold a just proportion to the credit of the merchant, and that the Druids derived from their holy profession a character of responsibility which could scarcely be claimed by any other order of men.

[4] The right reverend author of the Divine Legation of Moses assigns a very curious reason for the omission, and most ingeniously retorts it on the unbelievers.

[The hypothesis of Warburton regarding this remarkable fact of the silence of Moses regarding the immortality is that Moses deliberately excluded it from his system, in order to keep the Israelites from imagining themselves gods. It is fanciful, and can scarcely be regarded as any but an intellectual tour de force. Modern writers have endeavoured to account in various ways for the silence of Moses on the immortality of the soul.

we discover that the doctrine of the immortality of the soul is omitted in the law of Moses; it is darkly insinuated by the prophets; and during the long period which elapsed between the Egyptian and the Babylonian servitudes, the hopes as well as fears of the Jews appear to have been confined within the narrow compass of the present life.[1] After Cyrus had permitted the exiled nation to return into the promised land, and after Ezra had restored the ancient records of their religion, two celebrated sects, the Sadducees and the Pharisees, insensibly arose at Jerusalem.[2] The former, selected from the more opulent and

Michaelis says, " Moses wrote as a historian and a law-giver; he regulated the ecclesiastical discipline rather than the religious belief of the people, and the sanctions of the law being temporal, he had no occasion, and as a civil legislator could not with propriety threaten punishments in another world." M. Guizot considers that in the state of civilisation at the time of the legislator, this doctrine, becoming popular among the Jews, would necessarily have given birth to a multitude of idolatrous superstitions which he wished to prevent.

His primary object was to establish a firm theocracy, to make his people the conservators of the doctrine of the Divine Unity, the basis upon which Christianity was hereafter to rest. He carefully excluded everything which could obscure or weaken that doctrine. Other nations had strangely abused their notions on the immortality of the soul; Moses wished to prevent this abuse, hence he forbade the Jews from consulting necromancers (those who evoke the spirits of the dead—Deut. xviii. 11). Those who reflect on the state of the Pagans and the Jews, and on the facility with which idolatry crept in on every side, will not be astonished that Moses has not developed a doctrine, of which the influence might be more pernicious than useful to his people.

Moses as well from the intimations scattered in his writings, the passage relating to the translation of Enoch (Gen. v. 24), the prohibition of necromancy (Michaelis believes him to be the author of the Book of Job, though this theory is generally rejected; other learned writers considering this book to be coeval with and known to Moses) as from his long residence in Egypt, and his acquaintance with Egyptian wisdom, could not be ignorant of the doctrine of the immortality of the soul. But this doctrine, if popularly known among the Jews, must have been purely Egyptian, and, as so, intimately connected with the whole religious system of the country. It was no doubt moulded up with the tenet of the transmigration of the soul, perhaps with notions analagous to the Emanation system of India, in which the human soul was an efflux from, indeed a part of, the Deity. The Mosaic religion drew a wide and impassable interval between the Creator and created things and beings: in this it differed from all the Egyptian and all the Eastern religions. As then the immortality of the soul was thus inseparably blended with those foreign religions which were altogether to be effaced from the minds of the people, and by no means necessary for the establishment of the theocracy, Moses maintained silence on this point, and a purer notion of it was left to be developed at a more favourable period in the history of man.—O. S.]

[1] See Le Clerc (Prolegomena ad Hist. Ecclesiast. sect. 1, c. 8). His authority seems to carry the greater weight, as he has written a learned and judicious commentary on the books of the Old Testament.

[2] Joseph. Antiquitat. l. xiii. c. 10 [§ 5, sq.]; De Bell. Jud. ii. 8 [§ 2]. According to the most natural interpretation of his words, the Sadducees admitted only the Pentateuch; but it has pleased some modern critics to

distinguished ranks of society, were strictly attached to the literal sense of the Mosaic law, and they piously rejected the immortality of the soul as an opinion that received no countenance from the divine book, which they revered as the only rule of their faith. To the authority of Scripture the Pharisees added that of tradition, and they accepted, under the name of traditions, several speculative tenets from the philosophy or religion of the eastern nations. The doctrines of fate or predestination, of angels and spirits, and of a future state of rewards and punishments, were in the number of these new articles of belief; and as the Pharisees, by the austerity of their manners, had drawn into their party the body of the Jewish people, the immortality of the soul became the prevailing sentiment of the synagogue under the reign of the Asmonæan princes and pontiffs. The temper of the Jews was incapable of contenting itself with such a cold and languid assent as might satisfy the mind of a Polytheist; and as soon as they admitted the idea of a future state, they embraced it with the zeal which has always formed the characteristic of the nation. Their zeal, however, added nothing to its evidence, or even probability; and it was still necessary that the doctrine of life and immortality, which had been dictated by nature, approved by reason, and received by superstition, should obtain the sanction of divine truth from the authority and example of Christ.

When the promise of eternal happiness was proposed to mankind on condition of adopting the faith, and of observing the precepts, of the Gospel, it is no wonder that so advantageous an offer should have been accepted by great numbers of every religion, of every rank, and of every province in the Roman empire. The ancient Christians were animated by a contempt for their present existence, and by a just confidence of immortality, of which the doubtful and imperfect faith of modern ages cannot give us any adequate notion. In the primitive church the influence of truth was very powerfully strengthened by an opinion which, however it may deserve respect for its usefulness and antiquity, has not been found agreeable to experience. It was universally believed that the end of the world, and the kingdom of heaven, were at hand. The near approach of this wonderful event had been predicted by the apostles; the tradition of it was preserved by their earliest disciples, and those who

---

add the Prophets to their creed, and to suppose that they contented themselves with rejecting the traditions of the Pharisees. Dr. Jortin has argued that point in his Remarks on Ecclesiastical History, vol. ii. p. 103.

understood in their literal sense the discourses of Christ himself
were obliged to expect the second and glorious coming of the
Son of Man in the clouds, before that generation was totally
extinguished which had beheld his humble condition upon earth,
and which might still be witness of the calamities of the Jews
under Vespasian or Hadrian. The revolution of seventeen centuries has instructed us not to press too closely the mysterious
language of prophecy and revelation; but as long as, for wise
purposes, this error was permitted to subsist in the church, it
was productive of the most salutary effects on the faith and
practice of Christians, who lived in the awful expectation of that
moment when the globe itself, and all the various race of mankind,
should tremble at the appearance of their divine Judge.[1]

The ancient and popular doctrine of the Millennium was intimately connected with the second coming of Christ. As the
works of the creation had been finished in six days, their duration
in their present state, according to a tradition which was attributed to the prophet Elijah, was fixed to six thousand years.[2]
By the same analogy it was inferred that this long period of
labour and contention, which was now almost elapsed,[3] would

---

[1] This expectation was countenanced by the twenty-fourth chapter of
St. Matthew, and by the first epistle of St. Paul to the Thessalonians.
Erasmus removes the difficulty by the help of allegory and metaphor; and
the learned Grotius ventures to insinuate, that, for wise purposes, the
pious deception was permitted to take place.

[Some theologians (says Guizot) explain it without the use either of
allegory or pious deception. They say that Jesus Christ, after having
proclaimed the ruin of Jerusalem and of the Temple, speaks of his Second
Advent, and of the signs which were to precede it; but those who believed
that the moment was near deceived themselves as to the sense of two words,
an error which still exists in our versions of the Gospel of Matthew, xxiv.
29, 34. In verse 29 we read, " Immediately after the tribulation of these
days shall the sun be darkened." The Greek word εὐθέως signifies " all
at once," " suddenly," but not " immediately: " so that it signifies only
the sudden appearance of the signs which Jesus Christ announces, not the
shortness of the interval which was to separate them from the " days of
tribulation " of which he was speaking. Also in verse 34 we read, " This
generation shall not pass till all these things shall be fulfilled." Jesus,
speaking to his disciples, uses these words, ἡ γενεὰ αὕτη, which has been
rendered " this generation," but which means " this race of my disciples,"
viz. the race of Christians shall remain until his coming.—O. S.]

[2] See Burnet's Sacred Theory, part iii. c. 5. This tradition may be
traced as high as the author of the Epistle of Barnabas, who wrote in the
first century, and who seems to have been half a Jew.

[3] The primitive church of Antioch computed almost 6000 years from the
creation of the world to the birth of Christ. Africanus, Lactantius, and
the Greek church have reduced that number to 5500, and Eusebius has
contented himself with 5200 years. These calculations were formed on
the Septuagint, which was universally received during the six first centuries.
The authority of the Vulgate and of the Hebrew text has determined the

be succeeded by a joyful Sabbath of a thousand years; and that Christ, with the triumphant band of the saints and the elect who had escaped death, or who had been miraculously revived, would reign upon earth till the time appointed for the last and general resurrection. So pleasing was this hope to the mind of believers, that the *New Jerusalem*, the seat of this blissful kingdom, was quickly adorned with all the gayest colours of the imagination. A felicity consisting only of pure and spiritual pleasure would have appeared too refined for its inhabitants, who were still supposed to possess their human nature and senses. A garden of Eden, with the amusements of the pastoral life, was no longer suited to the advanced state of society which prevailed under the Roman empire. A city was therefore erected of gold and precious stones, and a supernatural plenty of corn and wine was bestowed on the adjacent territory; in the free enjoyment of whose spontaneous productions the happy and benevolent people was never to be restrained by any jealous laws of exclusive property.[1] The assurance of such a Millennium was carefully inculcated by a succession of fathers from Justin Martyr[2] and Irenæus, who conversed with the immediate disciples of the apostles, down to Lactantius, who was preceptor to the son of Constantine.[3] Though it might not be universally received, it appears to have been the reigning sentiment of the orthodox believers; and it seems so well adapted to the desires and apprehensions of mankind, that it must have contributed in a very considerable degree to the progress of the Christian faith. But when the edifice of the church was almost completed, the temporary support was laid aside. The doctrine of Christ's

moderns, Protestants as well as Catholics, to prefer a period of about 4000 years; though, in the study of profane antiquity, they often find themselves straitened by those narrow limits.

[1] Most of these pictures were borrowed from a misrepresentation of Isaiah, Daniel, and the Apocalypse. One of the grossest images may be found in Irenæus (l. v. [c. 23] p. 455 [ed. Oxon. 1702]), the disciple of Papias, who had seen the apostle St. John.

[2] See the second dialogue of Justin with Tryphon, and the seventh book of Lactantius. It is unnecessary to allege all the intermediate fathers, as the fact is not disputed. Yet the curious reader may consult Daillè de Usu Patrum, l. ii. c. 4.

[3] The testimony of Justin of his own faith and that of his orthodox brethren, in the doctrine of a Millennium, is delivered in the clearest and most solemn manner (Dialog. cum Tryphonte Jud. p. 177, 178, edit. Benedictin.). If in the beginning of this important passage there is anything like an inconsistency, we may impute it, as we think proper, either to the author or to his transcribers.

[The millennium is described in what once stood as the Forty-first Article of the Church of England (see Collier, Eccles. Hist. for Article of Edward VI.) as " a fable of Jewish dotage."—O. S.]

reign upon earth was at first treated as a profound allegory, was
considered by degrees as a doubtful and useless opinion, and was
at length rejected as the absurd invention of heresy and fanaticism.[1] A mysterious prophecy, which still forms a part of the
sacred canon, but which was thought to favour the exploded
sentiment, has very narrowly escaped the proscription of the
church.[2]

Whilst the happiness and glory of a temporal reign were
promised to the disciples of Christ, the most dreadful calamities
were denounced against an unbelieving world. The edification
of the new Jerusalem was to advance by equal steps with the
destruction of the mystic Babylon; and as long as the emperors
who reigned before Constantine persisted in the profession of
idolatry, the epithet of Babylon was applied to the city and to
the empire of Rome. A regular series was prepared of all the
moral and physical evils which can afflict a flourishing nation;
intestine discord, and the invasion of the fiercest barbarians
from the unknown regions of the North; pestilence and famine,
comets and eclipses, earthquakes and inundations.[3] All these
were only so many preparatory and alarming signs of the great
catastrophe of Rome, when the country of the Scipios and Cæsars
should be consumed by a flame from Heaven, and the city of the
seven hills, with her palaces, her temples, and her triumphal
arches, should be buried in a vast lake of fire and brimstone. It

[1] Dupin, Bibliothèque Ecclésiastique, tom. i. p. 223, tom. ii. p. 366, and
Mosheim, p. 720; though the latter of these learned divines is not altogether
candid on this occasion.

[2] In the council of Laodicea (about the year 360) the Apocalypse was
tacitly excluded from the sacred canon by the same churches of Asia to
which it is addressed; and we may learn from the complaint of Sulpicius
Severus that their sentence had been ratified by the greater number of
Christians of his time. From what causes then is the Apocalypse at
present so generally received by the Greek, the Roman, and the Protestant
churches? The following ones may be assigned:—1. The Greeks were
subdued by the authority of an impostor, who, in the sixth century,
assumed the character of Dionysius the Areopagite. 2. A just apprehension that the grammarians might become more important than the theologians engaged the council of Trent to fix the seal of their infallibility on
all the books of Scripture contained in the Latin Vulgate, in the number of
which the Apocalypse was fortunately included (Fr. Paolo, Istoria del
Concilio Tridentino, l. ii.). 3. The advantage of turning those mysterious
prophecies against the See of Rome inspired the Protestants with uncommon veneration for so useful an ally. See the ingenious and elegant
discourses of the present bishop of Lichfield on that unpromising subject.

[The exclusion of the Apocalypse (says Milman) is not improbably
assigned to its obvious unfitness to be read in churches. In this connection Lactantius believed that the Apocalypse foretold that a great Asiatic
empire was to arise on the ruins of Rome.—O. S.]

[3] Lactantius (Institut. Divin. vii. 15, etc.) relates the dismal tale of
uturity with great spirit and eloquence.

might, however, afford some consolation to Roman vanity, that
the period of their empire would be that of the world itself;
which, as it had once perished by the element of water, was
destined to experience a second and a speedy destruction from
the element of fire.   In the opinion of a general conflagration
the faith of the Christian very happily coincided with the tradition of the East, the philosophy of the Stoics, and the analogy
of Nature; and even the country which, from religious motives,
had been chosen for the origin and principal scene of the conflagration, was the best adapted for that purpose by natural and
physical causes—by its deep caverns, beds of sulphur, and
numerous volcanoes, of which those of Ætna, of Vesuvius, and
of Lipari exhibit a very imperfect representation.   The calmest
and most intrepid sceptic could not refuse to acknowledge that
the destruction of the present system of the world by fire was
in itself extremely probable.   The Christian, who founded his
belief much less on the fallacious arguments of reason than on
the authority of tradition and the interpretation of Scripture,
expected it with terror and confidence as a certain and approaching event; and as his mind was perpetually filled with the solemn
idea, he considered every disaster that happened to the empire
as an infallible symptom of an expiring world.[1]

The condemnation of the wisest and most virtuous of the
Pagans, on account of their ignorance or disbelief of the divine
truth, seems to offend the reason and the humanity of the
present age.[2]   But the primitive church, whose faith was of a
much firmer consistence, delivered over, without hesitation, to
eternal torture the far greater part of the human species.   A
charitable hope might perhaps be indulged in favour of Socrates,
or some other sages of antiquity, who had consulted the light of
reason before that of the Gospel had arisen.[3]   But it was unani-

[1] On this subject every reader of taste will be entertained with the third
part of Burnet's Sacred Theory.   He blends philosophy, Scripture, and
tradition, into one magnificent system; in the description of which he
displays a strength of fancy not inferior to that of Milton himself.

[2] And yet, whatever may be the language of individuals, it is still the
public doctrine of all the Christian churches; nor can even our own refuse
to admit the conclusions which must be drawn from the eighth and the
eighteenth of her Articles.   The Jansenists, who have so diligently studied
the works of the fathers, maintain this sentiment with distinguished zeal;
and the learned M. de Tillemont never dismisses a virtuous emperor without pronouncing his damnation.   Zuinglius is perhaps the only leader of
a party who has ever adopted the milder sentiment, and he gave no less
offence to the Lutherans than to the Catholics.   See Bossuet, Histoire des
Variations des Eglises Protestantes, l. ii. c. 19-22.

[3] Justin and Clemens of Alexandria allow that some of the philosophers
were instructed by the Logos; confounding its double signification of the
human reason and of the Divine Word.

mously affirmed that those who, since the birth or the death of Christ, had obstinately persisted in the worship of the dæmons, neither deserved nor could expect a pardon from the irritated justice of the Deity. These rigid sentiments, which had been unknown to the ancient world, appear to have infused a spirit of bitterness into a system of love and harmony. The ties of blood and friendship were frequently torn asunder by the difference of religious faith; and the Christians, who, in this world, found themselves oppressed by the power of the Pagans, were sometimes seduced by resentment and spiritual pride to delight in the prospect of their future triumph. " You are fond of spectacles," exclaims the stern Tertullian, " expect the greatest of all spectacles, the last and eternal judgment of the universe. How shall I admire, how laugh, how rejoice, how exult, when I behold so many proud monarchs, and fancied gods, groaning in the lowest abyss of darkness; so many magistrates, who persecuted the name of the Lord, liquefying in fiercer fires than they ever kindled against the Christians; so many sage philosophers blushing in red-hot flames with their deluded scholars; so many celebrated poets trembling before the tribunal, not of Minos, but of Christ; so many tragedians, more tuneful in the expression of their own sufferings; so many dancers—" But the humanity of the reader will permit me to draw a veil over the rest of this infernal description, which the zealous African pursues in a long variety of affected and unfeeling witticisms.[1]

Doubtless there were many among the primitive Christians of a temper more suitable to the meekness and charity of their profession. There were many who felt a sincere compassion for the danger of their friends and countrymen, and who exerted the most benevolent zeal to save them from the impending destruction. The careless Polytheist, assailed by new and unexpected terrors, against which neither his priests nor his philosophers could afford him any certain protection, was very frequently terrified and subdued by the menace of eternal tortures. His fears might assist the progress of his faith and reason; and if he could once persuade himself to suspect that the Christian religion might possibly be true, it became an easy task

---

[1] Tertullian, de Spectaculis, c. 30. In order to ascertain the degree of authority which the zealous African had acquired, it may be sufficient to allege the testimony of Cyprian, the doctor and guide of all the western churches (see Prudent. Hym. xiii. 100). As often as he applied himself to his daily study of the writings of Tertullian, he was accustomed to say " Da mihi magistrum; Give me my master." (Hieronym. de Viris Illustribus, tom. i. p. 284 [c. 53, tom. ii. p. 878, ed. Vallars.]).

to convince him that it was the safest and most prudent party that he could possibly embrace.

III. The supernatural gifts, which even in this life were ascribed to the Christians above the rest of mankind, must have conduced to their own comfort, and very frequently to the conviction of infidels. Besides the occasional prodigies, which might sometimes be effected by the immediate interposition of the Deity when he suspended the laws of Nature for the service of religion, the Christian church, from the time of the apostles and their first disciples,[1] has claimed an uninterrupted succession of miraculous powers, the gift of tongues, of vision, and of prophecy, the power of expelling dæmons, of healing the sick, and of raising the dead. The knowledge of foreign languages was frequently communicated to the contemporaries of Irenæus, though Irenæus himself was left to struggle with the difficulties of a barbarous dialect whilst he preached the Gospel to the natives of Gaul.[2] The divine inspiration, whether it was conveyed in the form of a waking or of a sleeping vision, is described as a favour very liberally bestowed on all ranks of the faithful, on women as on elders, on boys as well as upon bishops. When their devout minds were sufficiently prepared by a course of prayer, of fasting, and of vigils, to receive the extraordinary impulse, they were transported out of their senses, and delivered in ecstasy what was inspired, being mere organs of the Holy Spirit, just as a pipe or flute is of him who blows into it.[3] We may add that the design of these visions was, for the most part, either to disclose the future history, or to guide the present administration, of the church. The expulsion of the dæmons from the bodies of those unhappy persons whom they had been permitted to torment was considered as a signal though ordinary triumph of religion, and is repeatedly alleged by the ancient apologists as the most convincing evidence of the truth of Christianity. The awful ceremony was usually performed in a public manner, and in the presence of a great number of spec-

---

[1] Notwithstanding the evasions of Dr. Middleton, it is impossible to overlook the clear traces of visions and inspiration which may be found in the apostolic fathers.

[2] Irenæus adv. Hæres. Proem. p. 3.   Dr. Middleton (Free Inquiry, p. 96, etc.) observes that, as this pretension of all others was the most difficult to support by art, it was the soonest given up.   The observation suits his hypothesis.

[3] Athenagoras in Legatione.   Justin Martyr, Cohort. ad Gentes.   Tertullian advers. Marcionem, l. iv.   These descriptions are not very unlike the prophetic fury for which Cicero (de Divinat. ii. 54) expresses so little reverence.

tators; the patient was relieved by the power or skill of the
exorcist, and the vanquished dæmon was heard to confess that
he was one of the fabled gods of antiquity, who had impiously
usurped the adoration of mankind.[1] But the miraculous cure
of diseases of the most inveterate or even preternatural kind can
no longer occasion any surprise, when we recollect that in the
days of Irenæus, about the end of the second century, the resurrection of the dead was very far from being esteemed an uncommon event; that the miracle was frequently performed on
necessary occasions, by great fasting and the joint supplication
of the church of the place, and that the persons thus restored to
their prayers had lived afterwards among them many years.[2]
At such a period, when faith could boast of so many wonderful
victories over death, it seems difficult to account for the scepticism
of those philosophers who still rejected and derided the doctrine
of the resurrection. A noble Grecian had rested on this important ground the whole controversy, and promised Theophilus,
bishop of Antioch, that, if he could be gratified with the sight of
a single person who had been actually raised from the dead, he
would immediately embrace the Christian religion. It is somewhat remarkable that the prelate of the first eastern church,
however anxious for the conversion of his friend, thought proper
to decline this fair and reasonable challenge.[3]

The miracles of the primitive church, after obtaining the sanction of ages, have been lately attacked in a very free and ingenious inquiry;[4] which, though it has met with the most
favourable reception from the public, appears to have excited a
general scandal among the divines of our own as well as of the
other Protestant churches of Europe.[5] Our different sentiments
on this subject will be much less influenced by any particular
arguments than by our habits of study and reflection, and, above
all, by the degree of the evidence which we have accustomed

---

[1] Tertullian (Apolog. c. 23) throws out a bold defiance to the Pagan
magistrates. Of the primitive miracles, the power of exorcising is the only
one which has been assumed by Protestants.

[2] Irenæus adv. Hæreses, l. ii. c. 56, 57, l. v. c. 6. Mr. Dodwell (Dissertat.
ad Irenæum, ii. 42) concludes that the second century was still more fertile
n miracles than the first.

[3] Theophilus ad Autolycum, l. i. p. 345, edit. Benedictin. Paris, 1742
[p. 35, ed. Oxon. 1684].

[4] Dr. Middleton sent out his Introduction in the year 1747, published his
Free Inquiry in 1749, and before his death, which happened in 1750, he
had prepared a vindication of it against his numerous adversaries.

[5] The university of Oxford conferred degrees on his opponents. From
the indignation of Mosheim (p. 221) we may discover the sentiments of the
Lutheran divines.

ourselves to require for the proof of a miraculous event. The
duty of an historian does not call upon him to interpose his
private judgment in this nice and important controversy; but
he ought not to dissemble the difficulty of adopting such a
theory as may reconcile the interest of religion with that of
reason, of making a proper application of that theory, and of
defining with precision the limits of that happy period, exempt
from error and from deceit, to which we might be disposed to
extend the gift of supernatural powers. From the first of the
fathers to the last of the popes, a succession of bishops, of saints,
of martyrs, and of miracles, is continued without interruption;
and the progress of superstition was so gradual and almost
imperceptible, that we know not in what particular link we
should break the chain of tradition. Every age bears testimony
to the wonderful events by which it was distinguished, and its
testimony appears no less weighty and respectable than that of
the preceding generation, till we are insensibly led on to accuse
our own inconsistency if, in the eighth or in the twelfth century,
we deny to the venerable Bede, or to the holy Bernard, the same
degree of confidence which, in the second century, we had so
liberally granted to Justin or to Irenæus.[1]   If the truth of any of
those miracles is appreciated by their apparent use and propriety, every age had unbelievers to convince, heretics to confute,
and idolatrous nations to convert; and sufficient motives might
always be produced to justify the interposition of Heaven.   And
yet, since every friend to revelation is persuaded of the reality,
and every reasonable man is convinced of the cessation, of
miraculous powers, it is evident that there must have been *some
period* in which they were either suddenly or gradually withdrawn
from the Christian church.   Whatever era is chosen for that
purpose, the death of the apostles, the conversion of the Roman
empire, or the extinction of the Arian heresy,[2] the insensibility
of the Christians who lived at that time will equally afford a just
matter of surprise.   They still supported their pretensions after
they had lost their power.   Credulity performed the office of

[1] It may seem somewhat remarkable that Bernard of Clairvaux, who
records so many miracles of his friend St. Malachi, never takes any notice
of his own, which, in their turn, however, are carefully related by his companions and disciples.   In the long series of ecclesiastical history, does there
exist a single instance of a saint asserting that he himself possessed the
gift of miracles?
[2] The conversion of Constantine is the era which is most usually fixed by
Protestants.   The more rational divines are unwilling to admit the
miracles of the fourth, whilst the more credulous are unwilling to reject
those of the fifth century.

faith; fanaticism was permitted to assume the language of inspiration, and the effects of accident or contrivance were ascribed to supernatural causes. The recent experience of genuine miracles should have instructed the Christian world in the ways of Providence, and habituated their eye (if we may use a very inadequate expression) to the style of the Divine artist. Should the most skilful painter of modern Italy presume to decorate his feeble imitations with the name of Raphael or of Correggio, the insolent fraud would be soon discovered and indignantly rejected.

Whatever opinion may be entertained of the miracles of the primitive church since the time of the apostles, this unresisting softness of temper, so conspicuous among the believers of the second and third centuries, proved of some accidental benefit to the cause of truth and religion. In modern times, a latent and even involuntary scepticism adheres to the most pious dispositions. Their admission of supernatural truths is much less an active consent than a cold and passive acquiescence. Accustomed long since to observe and to respect the invariable order of Nature, our reason, or at least our imagination, is not sufficiently prepared to sustain the visible action of the Deity. But in the first ages of Christianity the situation of mankind was extremely different. The most curious, or the most credulous, among the Pagans were often persuaded to enter into a society which asserted an actual claim of miraculous powers. The primitive Christians perpetually trod on mystic ground, and their minds were exercised by the habits of believing the most extraordinary events. They felt, or they fancied, that on every side they were incessantly assaulted by dæmons, comforted by visions, instructed by prophecy, and surprisingly delivered from danger, sickness, and from death itself, by the supplications of the church. The real or imaginary prodigies, of which they so frequently conceived themselves to be the objects, the instruments, or the spectators, very happily disposed them to adopt with the same ease, but with far greater justice, the authentic wonders of the evangelic history; and thus miracles that exceeded not the measure of their own experience inspired them with the most lively assurance of mysteries which were acknowledged to surpass the limits of their understanding. It is this deep impression of supernatural truths which has been so much celebrated under the name of faith; a state of mind described as the surest pledge of the Divine favour and of future felicity, and recommended as the first or perhaps the only merit of a

Christian. According to the more rigid doctors, the moral virtues, which may be equally practised by infidels, are destitute of any value or efficacy in the work of our justification.

IV. But the primitive Christian demonstrated his faith by his virtues; and it was very justly supposed that the Divine persuasion, which enlightened or subdued the understanding, must at the same time purify the heart and direct the actions of the believer. The first apologists of Christianity who justify the innocence of their brethren, and the writers of a later period who celebrate the sanctity of their ancestors, display, in the most lively colours, the reformation of manners which was introduced into the world by the preaching of the Gospel. As it is my intention to remark only such human causes as were permitted to second the influence of revelation, I shall slightly mention two motives which might naturally render the lives of the primitive Christians much purer and more austere than those of their Pagan contemporaries or their degenerate successors— repentance for their past sins, and the laudable desire of supporting the reputation of the society in which they were engaged.

It is a very ancient reproach, suggested by the ignorance or the malice of infidelity, that the Christians allured into their party the most atrocious criminals, who, as soon as they were touched by a sense of remorse, were easily persuaded to wash away, in the water of baptism, the guilt of their past conduct, for which the temples of the gods refused to grant them any expiation. But this reproach, when it is cleared from misre-presentation, contributes as much to the honour as it did to the increase of the church.[1] The friends of Christianity may acknow-ledge without a blush that many of the most eminent saints had been before their baptism the most abandoned sinners. Those persons who in the world had followed, though in an imperfect manner, the dictates of benevolence and propriety, derived such a calm satisfaction from the opinion of their own rectitude as rendered them much less susceptible of the sudden emotions of shame, of grief, and of terror, which have given birth to so many wonderful conversions. After the example of their Divine Master, the missionaries of the Gospel disdained not the society of men, and especially of women, oppressed by the consciousness, and very often by the effects, of their vices. As they emerged from sin and superstition to the glorious hope of immortality, they resolved to devote themselves to a life, not only of virtue,

---

[1] The imputations of Celsus and Julian, with the defence of the fathers, are very fairly stated by Spanheim, Commentaire sur les Césars de Julian, p. 468.

but of penitence. The desire of perfection became the ruling
passion of their soul; and it is well known that, while reason
embraces a cold mediocrity, our passions hurry us with rapid
violence over the space which lies between the most opposite
extremes.

When the new converts had been enrolled in the number of the
faithful, and were admitted to the sacraments of the church,
they found themselves restrained from relapsing into their past
disorders by another consideration of a less spiritual but of a very
innocent and respectable nature. Any particular society that
has departed from the great body of the nation, or the religion
to which it belonged, immediately becomes the object of universal as well as invidious observation. In proportion to the
smallness of its numbers, the character of the society may be
affected by the virtue and vices of the persons who compose it;
and every member is engaged to watch with the most vigilant
attention over his own behaviour, and over that of his brethren,
since, as he must expect to incur a part of the common disgrace,
he may hope to enjoy a share of the common reputation. When
the Christians of Bithynia were brought before the tribunal of
the younger Pliny, they assured the proconsul that, far from
being engaged in any unlawful conspiracy, they were bound by
a solemn obligation to abstain from the commission of those
crimes which disturb the private or public peace of society, from
theft, robbery, adultery, perjury, and fraud.[1] Near a century
afterwards, Tertullian with an honest pride could boast that
very few Christians had suffered by the hand of the executioner,
except on account of their religion.[2] Their serious and sequestered life, averse to the gay luxury of the age, inured them to
chastity, temperance, economy, and all the sober and domestic
virtues. As the greater number were of some trade or profession, it was incumbent on them, by the strictest integrity and
the fairest dealing, to remove the suspicions which the profane
are too apt to conceive against the appearances of sanctity.
The contempt of the world exercised them in the habits of
humility, meekness, and patience. The more they were persecuted, the more closely they adhered to each other. Their
mutual charity and unsuspecting confidence has been remarked
by infidels, and was too often abused by perfidious friends.[3]

---

[1] Plin. Epist. x. 97.

[2] Tertullian, Apolog. c. 44. He adds, however, with some degree of hesitation, " Aut si [et] aliud, jam non Christianus."

[3] The philosopher Peregrinus (of whose life and death Lucian has left us
so entertaining an account) imposed, for a long time, on the credulous
simplicity of the Christians of Asia.

It is a very honourable circumstance for the morals of the primitive Christians, that even their faults, or rather errors, were derived from an excess of virtue. The bishops and doctors of the church, whose evidence attests, and whose authority might influence, the professions, the principles, and even the practice of their contemporaries, had studied the Scriptures with less skill than devotion; and they often received in the most literal sense those rigid precepts of Christ and the apostles to which the prudence of succeeding commentators has applied a looser and more figurative mode of interpretation. Ambitious to exalt the perfection of the Gospel above the wisdom of philosophy, the zealous fathers have carried the duties of self-mortification, of purity, and of patience, to a height which it is scarcely possible to attain, and much less to preserve, in our present state of weakness and corruption. A doctrine so extraordinary and so sublime must inevitably command the veneration of the people; but it was ill calculated to obtain the suffrage of those worldly philosophers who, in the conduct of this transitory life, consult only the feelings of nature and the interest of society.[1]

There are two very natural propensities which we may distinguish in the most virtuous and liberal dispositions, the love of pleasure and the love of action. If the former is refined by art and learning, improved by the charms of social intercourse, and corrected by a just regard to economy, to health, and to reputation, it is productive of the greatest part of the happiness of private life. The love of action is a principle of a much stronger and more doubtful nature. It often leads to anger, to ambition, and to revenge; but when it is guided by the sense of propriety and benevolence, it becomes the parent of every virtue, and, if those virtues are accompanied with equal abilities, a family, a state, or an empire may be indebted for their safety and prosperity to the undaunted courage of a single man. To the love of pleasure we may therefore ascribe most of the agreeable, to the love of action we may attribute most of the useful and respectable, qualifications. The character in which both the one and the other should be united and harmonised would seem to constitute the most perfect idea of human nature. The insensible and inactive disposition, which should be supposed alike destitute of both, would be rejected, by the common consent of mankind, as utterly incapable of procuring any happiness to the individual, or any public benefit to the world. But it was

[1] See a very judicious treatise of Barbeyrac sur la Morale des Pères.

not in *this* world that the primitive Christians were desirous of making themselves either agreeable or useful.

The acquisition of knowledge, the exercise of our reason or fancy, and the cheerful flow of unguarded conversation, may employ the leisure of a liberal mind. Such amusements, however, were rejected with abhorrence, or admitted with the utmost caution, by the severity of the fathers, who despised all knowledge that was not useful to salvation, and who considered all levity of discourse as a criminal abuse of the gift of speech. In our present state of existence the body is so inseparably connected with the soul, that it seems to be our interest to taste, with innocence and moderation, the enjoyments of which that faithful companion is susceptible. Very different was the reasoning of our devout predecessors; vainly aspiring to imitate the perfection of angels, they disdained, or they affected to disdain, every earthly and corporeal delight.[1] Some of our senses indeed are necessary for our preservation, others for our subsistence, and others again for our information; and thus far it was impossible to reject the use of them. The first sensation of pleasure was marked as the first moment of their abuse. The unfeeling candidate for heaven was instructed, not only to resist the grosser allurements of the taste or smell, but even to shut his ears against the profane harmony of sounds, and to view with indifference the most finished productions of human art. Gay apparel, magnificent houses, and elegant furniture were supposed to unite the double guilt of pride and of sensuality: a simple and mortified appearance was more suitable to the Christian who was certain of his sins and doubtful of his salvation. In their censures of luxury the fathers are extremely minute and circumstantial;[2] and among the various articles which excite their pious indignation, we may enumerate false hair, garments of any colour except white, instruments of music, vases of gold or silver, downy pillows (as Jacob reposed his head on a stone), white bread, foreign wines, public salutations, the use of warm baths, and the practice of shaving the beard, which, according to the expression of Tertullian, is a lie against our own faces, and an impious attempt to improve the works of the Creator.[3] When Christianity was introduced among the rich

---

[1] Lactant. Institut. Divin. l. vi. c. 20, 21, 22.

[2] Consult a work of Clemens of Alexandria, entitled The Pædagogue, which contains the rudiments of ethics, as they were taught in the most celebrated of the Christian schools.

[3] Tertullian, de Spectaculis, c. 23. Clemens Alexandrin, Pædagog. l. iii. c. 8.

and the polite, the observation of these singular laws was left, as it would be at present, to the few who were ambitious of superior sanctity. But it is always easy, as well as agreeable, for the inferior ranks of mankind to claim a merit from the contempt of that pomp and pleasure which fortune has placed beyond their reach. The virtue of the primitive Christians, like that of the first Romans, was very frequently guarded by poverty and ignorance.

The chaste severity of the fathers in whatever related to the commerce of the two sexes flowed from the same principle—their abhorrence of every enjoyment which might gratify the sensual and degrade the spiritual nature of man. It was their favourite opinion, that if Adam had preserved his obedience to the Creator, he would have lived for ever in a state of virgin purity, and that some harmless mode of vegetation might have peopled paradise with a race of innocent and immortal beings.[1] The use of marriage was permitted only to his fallen posterity, as a necessary expedient to continue the human species, and as a restraint, however imperfect, on the natural licentiousness of desire. The hesitation of the orthodox casuists on this interesting subject betrays the perplexity of men unwilling to approve an institution which they were compelled to tolerate.[2] The enumeration of the very whimsical laws which they most circumstantially imposed on the marriage-bed would force a smile from the young and a blush from the fair. It was their unanimous sentiment that a first marriage was adequate to all the purposes of nature and of society. The sensual connection was refined into a resemblance of the mystic union of Christ with his church, and was pronounced to be indissoluble either by divorce or by death. The practice of second nuptials was branded with the name of a legal adultery; and the persons who were guilty of so scandalous an offence against Christian purity were soon excluded from the honours, and even from the alms, of the church.[3] Since desire was imputed as a crime, and marriage was tolerated as a defect, it was consistent with the same principles to consider a state of celibacy as the nearest approach to the Divine perfection. It was with the utmost difficulty that ancient Rome could support the institution of six vestals;[4] but

[1] Beausobre, Hist. Critique du Manichéisme, l. vii. c. 3. Justin, Gregory of Nyssa, Augustin, etc., strongly inclined to this opinion.

[2] Some of the Gnostic heretics were more consistent; they rejected the use of marriage.

[3] See a chain of tradition, from Justin Martyr to Jerome, in the Morale des Pères, c. iv. 6-26.

[4] See a very curious Dissertation on the Vestals, in the Mémoires de

the primitive church was filled with a great number of persons
of either sex who had devoted themselves to the profession of
perpetual chastity.[1] A few of these, among whom we may
reckon the learned Origen, judged it the most prudent to disarm
the tempter.[2] Some were insensible and some were invincible
against the assaults of the flesh. Disdaining an ignominious
flight, the virgins of the warm climate of Africa encountered the
enemy in the closest engagement; they permitted priests and
deacons to share their bed, and gloried amidst the flames in their
unsullied purity. But insulted Nature sometimes vindicated
her rights, and this new species of martyrdom served only to
introduce a new scandal into the church.[3] Among the Christian
ascetics, however (a name which they soon acquired from their
painful exercise), many, as they were less presumptuous, were
probably more successful. The loss of sensual pleasure was
supplied and compensated by spiritual pride. Even the multitude of Pagans were inclined to estimate the merit of the sacrifice
by its apparent difficulty; and it was in the praise of these chaste
spouses of Christ that the fathers have poured forth the troubled
stream of their eloquence.[4] Such are the early traces of monastic
principles and institutions, which, in a subsequent age, have
counterbalanced all the temporal advantages of Christianity.[5]

The Christians were not less averse to the business than to the
pleasures of this world. The defence of our persons and property they knew not how to reconcile with the patient doctrine
which enjoined an unlimited forgiveness of past injuries, and
commanded them to invite the repetition of fresh insults. Their

l'Académie des Inscriptions, tom. iv. p. 161-227. Notwithstanding the
honours and rewards which were bestowed on those virgins, it was difficult
to procure a sufficient number; nor could the dread of the most horrible
death always restrain their incontinence.

[1] Cupiditatem procreandi aut unam scimus aut nullam. Minucius Felix,
c. 31. Justin. Apolog. Major. Athenagoras in Legat. c. 28. Tertullian
de Cultu Femin. l. ii.

[2] Eusebius, l. vi. 8. Before the fame of Origen had excited envy and
persecution, this extraordinary action was rather admired than censured.
As it was his general practice to allegorise Scripture, it seems unfortunate
that, in this instance only, he should have adopted the literal sense.

[3] Cyprian. Epist. 4, and Dodwell, Dissertat. Cyprianic. iii. Something
like this rash attempt was long afterwards imputed to the founder of the
order of Fontevrault. Bayle has amused himself and his readers on that
very delicate subject.

[4] Dupin (Bibliothèque Ecclésiastique, tom. i. p. 195) gives a particular
account of the dialogue of the ten virgins, as it was composed by Methodius,
bishop of Tyre. The praises of virginity are excessive.

[5] The Ascetics (as early as the second century) made a public profession
of mortifying their bodies, and of abstaining from the use of flesh and wine.
Mosheim, p. 310.

simplicity was offended by the use of oaths, by the pomp of
magistracy, and by the active contention of public life; nor
could their humane ignorance be convinced that it was lawful on
any occasion to shed the blood of our fellow-creatures, either by
the sword of justice or by that of war, even though their criminal
or hostile attempts should threaten the peace and safety of the
whole community.[1] It was acknowledged that, under a less
perfect law, the powers of the Jewish constitution had been
exercised, with the approbation of Heaven, by inspired prophets
and by anointed kings. The Christians felt and confessed that
such institutions might be necessary for the present system of
the world, and they cheerfully submitted to the authority of
their Pagan governors. But while they inculcated the maxims
of passive obedience, they refused to take any active part in the
civil administration or the military defence of the empire.
Some indulgence might perhaps be allowed to those persons
who, before their conversion, were already engaged in such
violent and sanguinary occupations;[2] but it was impossible
that the Christians, without renouncing a more sacred duty,
could assume the character of soldiers, of magistrates, or of
princes.[3] This indolent, or even criminal disregard to the public
welfare, exposed them to the contempt and reproaches of the
Pagans, who very frequently asked, what must be the fate of
the empire, attacked on every side by the barbarians, if all mankind should adopt the pusillanimous sentiments of the new
sect?[4] To this insulting question the Christian apologists re-

[1] See the Morale des Pères. The same patient principles have been
revived since the Reformation by the Socinians, the modern Anabaptists,
and the Quakers. Barclay, the Apologist of the Quakers, has protected
his brethren by the authority of the primitive Christians; p. 542-549.
[2] Tertullian, Apolog. c. 21; De Idololatriâ, c. 17, 18. Origen contra
Celsum, l. v. p. 253 [c. 33, tom. i. p. 602, ed. Bened.], l. vii. p. 349 [c. 26,
p. 712], l. viii. p. 423-428 [c. 68 sq. p. 793 sq.].
[3] Tertullian (de Coronâ Militis, c. 11) suggested to them the expedient of
deserting; a counsel which, if it had been generally known, was not very
proper to conciliate the favour of the emperors towards the Christian sect.
[There is nothing which ought to astonish us (says Guizot) in the refusal
of the primitive Christians to take part in public affairs. As Christians
they could not enter into the senate, which, according to Gibbon himself,
always assembled in a temple or consecrated place, and where each senator
before he took his seat made a libation of a few drops of wine and burnt
incense on the altar; as Christians they could not assist at festivals and
banquets, which always terminated with libations, and finally, as the innumerable deities and rites of polytheism were closely interwoven with
every circumstance of public and private life, the Christian could not
participate in them without incurring the guilt of impiety.—O. S.]
[4] As well as we can judge from the mutilated representation of Origen
(l. viii. p. 423 [c. 73, tom. i. p. 796, ed. Bened.]), his adversary, Celsus,
had urged his objection with great force and candour.

turned obscure and ambiguous answers, as they were unwilling to reveal the secret cause of their security; the expectation that, before the conversion of mankind was accomplished, war, government, the Roman empire, and the world itself, would be no more. It may be observed that, in this instance likewise, the situation of the first Christians coincided very happily with their religious scruples, and that their aversion to an active life contributed rather to excuse them from the service than to exclude them from the honours of the state and army.

V. But the human character, however it may be exalted or depressed by a temporary enthusiasm, will return by degrees to its proper and natural level, and will resume those passions that seem the most adapted to its present condition. The primitive Christians were dead to the business and pleasures of the world; but their love of action, which could never be entirely extinguished, soon revived, and found a new occupation in the government of the church. A separate society, which attacked the established religion of the empire, was obliged to adopt some form of internal policy, and to appoint a sufficient number of ministers, intrusted not only with the spiritual functions, but even with the temporal direction of the Christian commonwealth. The safety of the society, its honour, its aggrandisement, were productive, even in the most pious minds, of a spirit of patriotism, such as the first of the Romans had felt for the republic, and sometimes of a similar indifference in the use of whatever means might probably conduce to so desirable an end. The ambition of raising themselves or their friends to the honours and offices of the church was disguised by the laudable intention of devoting to the public benefit the power and consideration which, for that purpose only, it became their duty to solicit. In the exercise of their functions they were frequently called upon to detect the errors of heresy or the arts of faction, to oppose the designs of perfidious brethren, to stigmatise their characters with deserved infamy, and to expel them from the bosom of a society whose peace and happiness they had attempted to disturb. The ecclesiastical governors of the Christians were taught to unite the wisdom of the serpent with the innocence of the dove; but as the former was refined, so the latter was insensibly corrupted, by the habits of government. In the church as well as in the world, the persons who were placed in any public station rendered themselves considerable by their eloquence and firmness, by their knowledge of mankind, and by their dexterity in business; and while they concealed from others, and perhaps from themselves, the secret motives of their conduct, they too frequently relapsed into all the turbulent passions of active life, which were tinctured with an additional degree of bitterness and obstinacy from the infusion of spiritual zeal.

The government of the church has often been the subject, as well as the prize, of religious contention. The hostile disputants of Rome, of Paris, of Oxford, and of Geneva, have alike struggled to reduce the primitive and apostolic model [1] to the respective standards of their own policy. The few who have pursued this inquiry with more candour and impartiality are of opinion [2] that the apostles declined the office of legislation, and rather chose to endure some partial scandals and divisions, than to exclude the Christians of a future age from the liberty of varying their forms of ecclesiastical government according to the changes of times and circumstances. The scheme of policy which, under their approbation, was adopted for the use of the first century, may be discovered from the practice of Jerusalem, of Ephesus, or of Corinth. The societies which were instituted in the cities of the Roman empire were united only by the ties of faith and charity. Independence and equality formed the basis of their internal constitution. The want of discipline and human learning was supplied by the occasional assistance of the *prophets*,[3] who were called to that function without distinction of age, of sex, or of natural abilities, and who, as often as they felt the divine impulse, poured forth the effusions of the Spirit in the assembly of the faithful. But these extraordinary gifts were frequently abused or misapplied by the prophetic teachers. They displayed them at an improper season, presumptuously disturbed the service of the assembly, and by their pride or mistaken zeal they introduced, particularly into the apostolic church of Corinth, a long and melancholy train of disorders.[4] As the institution of prophets became useless, and even pernicious, their powers were withdrawn, and their office abolished.

The public functions of religion were solely intrusted to the established ministers of the church, the *bishops* and the

[1] The aristocratical party in France, as well as in England, has strenuously maintained the divine origin of bishops. But the Calvinistical presbyters were impatient of a superior; and the Roman Pontiff refused to acknowledge an equal. See Fra Paolo.

[2] In the history of the Christian hierarchy, I have, for the most part, followed the learned and candid Mosheim.

[3] For the prophets of the primitive church, see Mosheim, Dissertationes ad Hist. Eccles. pertinentes, tom. ii. p. 132-208.

[4] See the epistles of St. Paul, and of Clemens, to the Corinthians.

presbyters; two appellations which, in their first origin, appear to
have distinguished the same office and the same order of persons.
The name of Presbyter was expressive of their age, or rather of
their gravity and wisdom. The title of Bishop denoted their
inspection over the faith and manners of the Christians who
were committed to their pastoral care. In proportion to the
respective numbers of the faithful, a larger or smaller number
of these *episcopal presbyters* guided each infant congregation
with equal authority and with united counsels.[1]

But the most perfect equality of freedom requires the directing
hand of a superior magistrate: and the order of public deliberations soon introduces the office of a president, invested at least
with the authority of collecting the sentiments, and of executing
the resolutions, of the assembly. A regard for the public tranquillity, which would so frequently have been interrupted by
annual or by occasional elections, induced the primitive Christians to constitute an honourable and perpetual magistracy,
and to choose one of the wisest and most holy among their
presbyters to execute, during his life, the duties of their ecclesiastical governor. It was under these circumstances that the
lofty title of Bishop began to raise itself above the humble
appellation of Presbyter; and while the latter remained the
most natural distinction for the members of every Christian
senate, the former was appropriated to the dignity of its new
president.[2] The advantages of this episcopal form of government, which appears to have been introduced before the end of
the first century,[3] were so obvious, and so important for the
future greatness, as well as the present peace, of Christianity,
that it was adopted without delay by all the societies which were
already scattered over the empire, had acquired in a very early
period the sanction of antiquity,[4] and is still revered by the
most powerful churches, both of the East and of the West, as a

[1] Hooker's Ecclesiastical Polity, l. vii.
[2] See Jerome ad Titum, c. i. and Epistol. 85 (in the Benedictine edition,
101) [Ep. 146, ed. Vallars. tom. i. p. 1074], and the elaborate apology of
Blondel, pro sententiâ Hieronymi. The ancient state, as it is described by
Jerome, of the bishop and presbyters of Alexandria, receives a remarkable
confirmation from the patriarch Eutychius (Annal. tom. i. p. 330, Vers.
Pocock); whose testimony I know not how to reject, in spite of all the
objections of the learned Pearson in his Vindiciæ Ignatianæ, part i. c. 11.
[3] See the introduction to the Apocalypse. Bishops, under the name of
angels, were already instituted in the seven cities of Asia. And yet the
epistle of Clemens (which is probably of as ancient a date) does not lead us
to discover any traces of episcopacy either at Corinth or Rome.
[4] Nulla Ecclesia sine Episcopo, has been a fact as well as a maxim since
the time of Tertullian and Irenæus.

primitive and even as a divine establishment.[1] It is needless to
observe that the pious and humble presbyters who were first
dignified with the episcopal title could not possess, and would
probably have rejected, the power and pomp which now en-
circles the tiara of the Roman pontiff, or the mitre of a German
prelate. But we may define in a few words the narrow limits of
their original jurisdiction, which was chiefly of a spiritual, though
in some instances of a temporal nature.[2] It consisted in the
administration of the sacraments and discipline of the church,
the superintendency of religious ceremonies, which imperceptibly
increased in number and variety, the consecration of ecclesiastical ministers, to whom the bishop assigned their respective
functions, the management of the public fund, and the determination of all such differences as the faithful were unwilling to
expose before the tribunal of an idolatrous judge. These powers,
during a short period, were exercised according to the advice of
the presbyteral college, and with the consent and approbation of
the assembly of Christians. The primitive bishops were considered only as the first of their equals, and the honourable
servants of a free people. Whenever the episcopal chair became
vacant by death, a new president was chosen among the presbyters by the suffrage of the whole congregation, every member
of which supposed himself invested with a sacred and sacerdotal
character.[3]

Such was the mild and equal constitution by which the Christians were governed more than an hundred years after the death
of the apostles. Every society formed within itself a separate
and independent republic; and although the most distant of

---

[1] After we have passed the difficulties of the first century, we find the
episcopal government universally established, till it was interrupted by
the republican genius of the Swiss and German reformers.

[2] See Mosheim in the first and second centuries. Ignatius (ad Smyrnæos,
c. 8, etc.) is fond of exalting the episcopal dignity. Le Clerc (Hist. Eccles.
p. 569) very bluntly censures his conduct. Mosheim, with a more critical
judgment (p. 161), suspects the purity even of the smaller epistles.

[3] Nonne et Laici sacerdotes sumus? Tertullian, Exhort. ad Castitat.
c. 7. As the human heart is still the same, several of the observations
which Mr. Hume has made on Enthusiasm (Essays, vol. i. p. 76, quarto
edit.) may be applied even to real inspiration.

[The synods were not the first means taken by the insulated churches to
enter into communion and to assume a corporate character. The *dioceses*
were first formed by the union of several country churches with a church
in a city; many churches in one city uniting among themselves, or joining
a more considerable church because metropolitan. The dioceses were not
formed before the beginning of the second century: before that time the
Christian had not sufficient churches to stand in need of that union. The
provincial synods did not commence till towards the middle of the third
century.—O. S.]

these little states maintained a mutual as well as friendly intercourse of letters and deputations, the Christian world was not
yet connected by any supreme authority or legislative assembly.
As the numbers of the faithful were gradually multiplied, they
discovered the advantages that might result from a closer union
of their interest and designs. Towards the end of the second
century, the churches of Greece and Asia adopted the useful
institutions of provincial synods, and they may justly be supposed to have borrowed the model of a representative council
from the celebrated examples of their own country, the Amphic-
tyons, the Achæan league, or the assemblies of the Ionian cities.
It was soon established as a custom and as a law, that the bishops
of the independent churches should meet in the capital of the
province at the stated periods of spring and autumn. Their
deliberations were assisted by the advice of a few distinguished
presbysters, and moderated by the presence of a listening multitude.[1] Their decrees, which were styled Canons, regulated
every important controversy of faith and discipline; and it was
natural to believe that a liberal effusion of the Holy Spirit would
be poured on the united assembly of the delegates of the Christian people. The institution of synods was so well suited to
private ambition and to public interest, that in the space of a
few years it was received throughout the whole empire. A
regular correspondence was established between the provincial
councils, which mutually communicated and approved their
respective proceedings; and the catholic church soon assumed
the form, and acquired the strength, of a great fœderative
republic.[2]

As the legislative authority of the particular churches was
insensibly superseded by the use of councils, the bishops obtained
by their alliance a much larger share of executive and arbitrary
power; and as soon as they were connected by a sense of their
common interest, they were enabled to attack, with united
vigour, the original rights of their clergy and people. The prelates of the third century imperceptibly changed the language of
exhortation into that of command, scattered the seeds of future
usurpations, and supplied, by Scripture allegories and declama-

[1] Acta Concil. Carthag. apud Cyprian. edit. Fell, p. 158. This council
was composed of eighty-seven bishops from the provinces of Mauritania,
Numidia, and Africa; some presbyters and deacons assisted at the assembly;
præsente plebis maximâ parte.
[2] Aguntur præterea per Græcias illas, certis in locis concilia, etc. Tertullian de Jejuniis, c. 13. The African mentions it as a recent and foreign
institution. The coalition of the Christian churches is very ably explained
by Mosheim, p. 164-170.

tory rhetoric, their deficiency of force and of reason. They exalted the unity and power of the church, as it was represented in the EPISCOPAL OFFICE, of which every bishop enjoyed an equal and undivided portion.[1] Princes and magistrates, it was often repeated, might boast an earthly claim to a transitory dominion: it was the episcopal authority alone which was derived from the Deity, and extended itself over this and over another world. The bishops were the vicegerents of Christ, the successors of the apostles, and the mystic substitutes of the high priest of the Mosaic law. Their exclusive privilege of conferring the sacerdotal character invaded the freedom both of clerical and of popular elections: and if, in the administration of the church, they still consulted the judgment of the presbyters or the inclination of the people, they most carefully inculcated the merit of such a voluntary condescension. The bishops acknowledged the supreme authority which resided in the assembly of their brethren; but in the government of his peculiar diocese each of them exacted from his *flock* the same implicit obedience as if that favourite metaphor had been literally just, and as if the shepherd had been of a more exalted nature than that of his sheep.[2] This obedience, however, was not imposed without some efforts on one side, and some resistance on the other. The democratical part of the constitution was, in many places, very warmly supported by the zealous or interested opposition of the inferior clergy. But their patriotism received the ignominious epithets of faction and schism, and the episcopal cause was indebted for its rapid progress to the labours of many active prelates, who, like Cyprian of Carthage, could reconcile the arts of the most ambitious statesman with the Christian virtues which seem adapted to the character of a saint and martyr.[3]

The same causes which at first had destroyed the equality of the presbyters introduced among the bishops a pre-eminence of rank, and from thence a superiority of jurisdiction. As often as in the spring and autumn they met in provincial synod, the difference of personal merit and reputation was very sensibly

---

[1] Cyprian, in his admired treatise De Unitate Ecclesiæ, p. 75-86 [p. 108, ed. Oxon.].

[2] We may appeal to the whole tenor of Cyprian's conduct, of his doctrine, and of his epistles. Le Clerc, in a short Life of Cyprian (Bibliothèque Universelle, tom. xii. p. 207-378), has laid him open with great freedom and accuracy.

[3] If Novatus, Felicissimus, etc., whom the bishop of Carthage expelled from his church, and from Africa, were not the most detestable monsters of wickedness, the zeal of Cyprian must occasionally have prevailed over his veracity. For a very just account of these obscure quarrels, see Mosheim, p. 497-512.

felt among the members of the assembly, and the multitude was governed by the wisdom and eloquence of the few. But the order of public proceedings required a more regular and less invidious distinction; the office of perpetual presidents in the councils of each province was conferred on the bishops of the principal city; and these aspiring prelates, who soon acquired the lofty titles of Metropolitans and Primates, secretly prepared themselves to usurp over their episcopal brethren the same authority which the bishops had so lately assumed above the college of presbyters.[1] Nor was it long before an emulation of pre-eminence and power prevailed among the Metropolitans themselves, each of them affecting to display, in the most pompous terms, the temporal honours and advantages of the city over which he presided; the numbers and opulence of the Christians who were subject to their pastoral care; the saints and martyrs who had arisen among them; and the purity with which they preserved the tradition of the faith as it had been transmitted through a series of orthodox bishops from the apostle or the apostolic disciple to whom the foundation of their church was ascribed.[2] From every cause, either of a civil or of an ecclesiastical nature, it was easy to foresee that Rome must enjoy the respect, and would soon claim the obedience, of the provinces. The society of the faithful bore a just proportion to the capital of the empire; and the Roman church was the greatest, the most numerous, and, in regard to the West, the most ancient of all the Christian establishments, many of which had received their religion from the pious labours of her missionaries. Instead of *one* apostolic founder, the utmost boast of Antioch, of Ephesus, or of Corinth, the banks of the Tiber were supposed to have been honoured with the preaching and martyrdom of the *two* most eminent among the apostles;[3] and the bishops of Rome very prudently claimed the inheritance of whatsoever prerogatives were attributed either to the person or to the office of St. Peter.[4]

---

[1] Mosheim, p. 269, 574. Dupin, Antiquæ Eccles. Disciplin. p. 19, 20.

[2] Tertullian, in a distinct treatise, has pleaded against the heretics the right of prescription, as it was held by the apostolic churches.

[3] The journey of St. Peter to Rome is mentioned by most of the ancients (see Eusebius. ii. 25), maintained by all the Catholics, allowed by some Protestants (see Pearson and Dodwell de Success. Episcop. Roman.), but has been vigorously attacked by Spanheim (Miscellanea Sacra, iii. 3). According to father Hardouin, the monks of the thirteenth century, who composed the Æneid, represented St. Peter under the allegorical character of the Trojan hero.

[4] It is in French only that the famous allusion to St. Peter's name is exact. Tu es *Pierre*, et sur cette *pierre*.—The same is imperfect in Greek, Latin, Italian, etc., and totally unintelligible in our Teutonic languages.

The bishops of Italy and of the provinces were disposed to allow them a primacy of order and association (such was their very accurate expression) in the Christian aristocracy.[1] But the power of a monarch was rejected with abhorrence, and the aspiring genius of Rome experienced from the nations of Asia and Africa a more vigorous resistance to her spiritual than she had formerly done to her temporal dominion. The patriotic Cyprian, who ruled with the most absolute sway the church of Carthage and the provincial synods, opposed with resolution and success the ambition of the Roman pontiff, artfully connected his own cause with that of the eastern bishops, and, like Hannibal, sought out new allies in the heart of Asia.[2] If this Punic war was carried on without any effusion of blood, it was owing much less to the moderation than to the weakness of the contending prelates. Invectives and excommunications were *their* only weapons; and these, during the progress of the whole controversy, they hurled against each other with equal fury and devotion. The hard necessity of censuring either a pope or a saint and martyr distresses the modern Catholics whenever they are obliged to relate the particulars of a dispute in which the champions of religion indulged such passions as seem much more adapted to the senate or to the camp.[3]

The progress of the ecclesiastical authority gave birth to the memorable distinction of the laity and of the clergy, which had been unknown to the Greeks and Romans.[4] The former of these appellations comprehended the body of the Christian people; the latter, according to the signification of the word, was appropriated to the chosen portion that had been set apart for the service of religion; a celebrated order of men which has furnished the most important, though not always the most edifying, subjects for modern history. Their mutual hostilities sometimes disturbed the peace of the infant church, but their zeal and activity were united in the common cause, and the love

[1] Irenæus adv. Hæreses, iii. 3; Tertullian de Præscription, c. 36; and Cyprian Epistol. 27, 55, 71, 75. Le Clerc (Hist. Eccles. p. 764) and Mosheim (p. 258, 578) labour in the interpretation of these passages. But the loose and rhetorical style of the fathers often appears favourable to the pretensions of Rome.

[2] See the sharp epistle from Firmilianus, bishop of Cæsarea, to Stephen, bishop of Rome, ap. Cyprian. Epistol. 75.

[3] Concerning this dispute of the re-baptism of heretics, see the epistles of Cyprian, and the seventh book of Eusebius.

[4] For the origin of these words, see Mosheim, p. 141. Spanheim, Hist. Ecclesiast. p. 633. The distinction of *Clerus* and *Laicus* was established before the time of Tertullian.

of power, which (under the most artful disguises) could insinuate itself into the breasts of bishops and martyrs, animated them to increase the number of their subjects, and to enlarge the limits of the Christian empire. They were destitute of any temporal force, and they were for a long time discouraged and oppressed, rather than assisted, by the civil magistrate; but they had acquired, and they employed within their own society, the two most efficacious instruments of government, rewards and punishments; the former derived from the pious liberality, the latter from the devout apprehensions, of the faithful.

I. The community of goods, which had so agreeably amused the imagination of Plato,[1] and which subsisted in some degree among the austere sect of the Essenians,[2] was adopted for a short time in the primitive church. The fervour of the first proselytes prompted them to sell those worldly possessions which they despised, to lay the price of them at the feet of the apostles, and to content themselves with receiving an equal share out of the general distribution.[3] The progress of the Christian religion relaxed, and gradually abolished, this generous institution, which, in hands less pure than those of the apostles, would too soon have been corrupted and abused by the returning selfishness of human nature; and the converts who embraced the new religion were permitted to retain the possession of their patrimony, to receive legacies and inheritances, and to increase their separate property by all the lawful means of trade and industry. Instead of an absolute sacrifice, a moderate proportion was accepted by the ministers of the Gospel; and in their weekly or monthly assemblies every believer, according to the exigency of the occasion, and the measure of his wealth and piety, presented his voluntary offering for the use of the common fund.[4] Nothing, however inconsiderable, was refused; but it was diligently inculcated that, in the article of tithes, the Mosaic law was still of divine obligation; and that, since the Jews, under a less perfect discipline, had been commanded to pay a tenth part of all that they possessed, it would become the disciples of Christ

---

[1] The community instituted by Plato is more perfect than that which Sir Thomas More had imagined for his Utopia. The community of women, and that of temporal goods, may be considered as inseparable parts of the same system.

[2] Joseph Antiquitat. xviii. 2 [c. 1, § 5, ed. Oxon. 1720]. Philo, de Vit. Contemplativ.

[3] See the Acts of the Apostles, c. 2, 4, 5, with Grotius's Commentary. Mosheim, in a particular dissertation, attacks the common opinion with very inconclusive arguments.

[4] Justin Martyr, Apolog. Major, c. 89. Tertullian, Apolog. c. 39.

to distinguish themselves by a superior degree of liberality,[1]
and to acquire some merit by resigning a superfluous treasure,
which must so soon be annihilated with the world itself.[2]   It is
almost unnecessary to observe that the revenue of each particular
church, which was of so uncertain and fluctuating a nature, must
have varied with the poverty or the opulence of the faithful,
as they were dispersed in obscure villages, or collected in the
great cities of the empire.   In the time of the emperor Decius
it was the opinion of the magistrates that the Christians of Rome
were possessed of very considerable wealth, that vessels of gold
and silver were used in their religious worship, and that many
among their proselytes had sold their lands and houses to increase
the public riches of the sect, at the expense, indeed, of their
unfortunate children, who found themselves beggars because
their parents had been saints.[3]   We should listen with distrust
to the suspicions of strangers and enemies; on this occasion, however, they receive a very specious and probable colour from the
two following circumstances, the only ones that have reached our
knowledge which define any precise sums or convey any distinct
idea.   Almost at the same period the bishop of Carthage, from
a society less opulent than that of Rome, collected an hundred

---

[1] Irenæus ad Hæres. l. iv. c. 26, 34.   Origen in Num. Hom. 11.   Cyprian
de Unitat. Eccles. Constitut. Apostol. l. ii. c. 34, 35, with the notes of
Cotelerius.   The Constitutions introduce this divine precept by declaring
that priests are as much above kings as the soul is above the body.   Among
the tithable articles, they enumerate corn, wine, oil, and wool.   On this
interesting subject, consult Prideaux's History of Tithes, and Fra Paolo
delle Materie Beneficiarie; two writers of a very different character.

[2] The same opinion, which prevailed about the year one thousand, was
productive of the same effects.   Most of the donations express their
motive, "appropinquante mundi fine."   See Mosheim's General History
of the Church, vol. i. p. 457.

[3]   Tum summa cura est fratribus
          (Ut sermo testatur loquax)
          Offerre fundis venditis,
          Sestertiorum millia.
          Addicta avorum prædia
          Fœdis sub auctionibus,
          Successor exheres gemit,
          Sanctis egens parentibus.
          Hæc occuluntur abditis
          Ecclesiarum in angulis.
          Et summa pietas creditur
          Nudare dulces liberos.
               Prudent. περὶ στεφάνων.   Hymn 2 [v. 73, sqq.].

The subsequent conduct of the deacon Laurence only proves how proper a
use was made of the wealth of the Roman church; it was undoubtedly
very considerable; but Fra Paolo (c. 3) appears to exaggerate when he
supposes that the successors of Commodus were urged to persecute the
Christians by their own avarice, or that of their Prætorian præfects.

thousand sesterces (above eight hundred and fifty pounds sterling), on a sudden call of charity to redeem the brethren of Numidia, who had been carried away captives by the barbarians of the desert.[1] About an hundred years before the reign of Decius the Roman church had received, in a single donation, the sum of two hundred thousand sesterces from a stranger of Pontus, who proposed to fix his residence in the capital.[2] These oblations, for the most part, were made in money; nor was the society of Christians either desirous or capable of acquiring, to any considerable degree, the incumbrance of landed property. It had been provided by several laws, which were enacted with the same design as our statutes of mortmain, that no real estates should be given or bequeathed to any corporate body without either a special privilege or a particular dispensation from the emperor or from the senate;[3] who were seldom disposed to grant them in favour of a sect, at first the object of their contempt, and at last of their fears and jealousy. A transaction, however, is related under the reign of Alexander Severus, which discovers that the restraint was sometimes eluded or suspended, and that the Christians were permitted to claim and to possess lands within the limits of Rome itself.[4] The progress of Christianity, and the civil confusion of the empire, contributed to relax the severity of the laws; and, before the close of the third century, many considerable estates were bestowed on the opulent churches of Rome, Milan, Carthage, Antioch, Alexandria, and the other great cities of Italy and the provinces.

The bishop was the natural steward of the church; the public stock was intrusted to his care without account or control; the presbyters were confined to their spiritual functions, and the more dependent order of deacons was solely employed in the management and distribution of the ecclesiastical revenue.[5] If we may give credit to the vehement declamations of Cyprian, there were too many among his African brethren who, in the execution of their charge, violated every precept, not only of evangelic perfection, but even of moral virtue. By some of these

---

[1] Cyprian, Epistol. 62.

[2] Tertullian de Præscriptione, c. 30.

[3] Diocletian gave a rescript, which is only a declaration of the old law:—
"Collegium, si nullo speciali privilegio subnixum sit, hæreditatem capere non posse, dubium non est." Fra Paolo (c. 4) thinks that these regulations had been much neglected since the reign of Valerian.

[4] Hist. August. p. 131. [Lampr. Alex. Sever. c. 49.] The ground had been public; and was now disputed between the society of Christians and that of butchers.

[5] Constitut. Apostol. ii. 35.

unfaithful stewards the riches of the church were lavished in
sensual pleasures; by others they were perverted to the purposes
of private gain, of fraudulent purchases, and of rapacious usury.[1]
But as long as the contributions of the Christian people were
free and unconstrained, the abuse of their confidence could not
be very frequent, and the general uses to which their liberality
was applied reflected honour on the religious society. A decent
portion was reserved for the maintenance of the bishop and his
clergy; a sufficient sum was allotted for the expenses of the
public worship, of which the feasts of love, the *agapæ*, as they
were called, constituted a very pleasing part. The whole remainder was the sacred patrimony of the poor. According to
the discretion of the bishop, it was distributed to support widows
and orphans, the lame, the sick, and the aged of the community;
to comfort strangers and pilgrims, and to alleviate the misfortunes of prisoners and captives, more especially when their
sufferings had been occasioned by their firm attachment to the
cause of religion.[2] A generous intercourse of charity united the
most distant provinces, and the smaller congregations were
cheerfully assisted by the alms of their more opulent brethren.[3]
Such an institution, which paid less regard to the merit than to
the distress of the object, very materially conduced to the progress of Christianity. The pagans, who were actuated by a
sense of humanity, while they derided the doctrines, acknowledged the benevolence, of the new sect.[4] The prospect of immediate relief and of future protection allured into its hospitable
bosom many of those unhappy persons whom the neglect of the
world would have abandoned to the miseries of want, of sickness,
and of old age. There is some reason likewise to believe that
great numbers of infants who, according to the inhuman practice
of the times, had been exposed by their parents, were frequently
rescued from death, baptised, educated, and maintained by the
piety of the Christians, and at the expense of the public treasure.[5]

[1] Cyprian de Lapsis, p. 89 [p. 126, ed. Oxon.].   Epistol. 65.   The charge
is confirmed by the 19th and 20th canon of the council of Illiberis.
[2] See the apologies of Justin, Tertullian, etc.
[3] The wealth and liberality of the Romans to their most distant brethren
is gratefully celebrated by Dionysius of Corinth, ap. Euseb. l. iv. c. 23.
[4] See Lucian in Peregrin. [c. 13.]   Julian (Epist. 49) seems mortified
that the Christian charity maintains not only their own, but likewise the
heathen poor.
[5] Such, at least, has been the laudable conduct of more modern missionaries, under the same circumstances.   Above three thousand new-born
infants are annually exposed in the streets of Pekin.   See Le Comte,
Mémoires sur la Chine, and the Recherches sur les Chinois et les Egyptiens,
tom. i. p. 61.

II. It is the undoubted right of every society to exclude from its communion and benefits such among its members as reject or violate those regulations which have been established by general consent. In the exercise of this power the censures of the Christian church were chiefly directed against scandalous sinners, and particularly those who were guilty of murder, of fraud, or of incontinence; against the authors, or the followers, of any heretical opinions which had been condemned by the judgment of the episcopal order; and against those unhappy persons who, whether from choice or from compulsion, had polluted themselves after their baptism by any act of idolatrous worship. The consequences of excommunication were of a temporal as well as a spiritual nature. The Christian against whom it was pronounced was deprived of any part in the oblations of the faithful. The ties both of religious and of private friendship were dissolved: he found himself a profane object of abhorrence to the persons whom he the most esteemed, or by whom he had been the most tenderly beloved; and as far as an expulsion from a respectable society could imprint on his character a mark of disgrace, he was shunned or suspected by the generality of mankind. The situation of these unfortunate exiles was in itself very painful and melancholy; but, as it usually happens, their apprehensions far exceeded their sufferings. The benefits of the Christian communion were those of eternal life; nor could they erase from their minds the awful opinion that to those ecclesiastical governors by whom they were condemned the Deity had committed the keys of Hell and of Paradise. The heretics, indeed, who might be supported by the consciousness of their intentions, and by the flattering hope that they alone had discovered the true path of salvation, endeavoured to regain, in their separate assemblies, those comforts, temporal as well as spiritual, which they no longer derived from the great society of Christians. But almost all those who had reluctantly yielded to the power of vice or idolatry were sensible of their fallen condition, and anxiously desirous of being restored to the benefits of the Christian communion.

With regard to the treatment of these penitents, two opposite opinions, the one of justice, the other of mercy, divided the primitive church. The more rigid and inflexible casuists refused them for ever, and without exception, the meanest place in the holy community which they had disgraced or deserted; and leaving them to the remorse of a guilty conscience, indulged them only with a faint ray of hope that the contrition of their life and death might possibly be accepted by the Supreme Being.[1] A milder sentiment was embraced, in practice as well as in theory, by the purest and most respectable of the Christian churches.[2] The gates of reconciliation and of heaven were seldom shut against the returning penitent; but a severe and solemn form of discipline was instituted, which, while it served to expiate his crime, might powerfully deter the spectators from the imitation of his example. Humbled by a public confession, emaciated by fasting, and clothed in sackcloth, the penitent lay prostrate at the door of the assembly, imploring with tears the pardon cf his offences, and soliciting the prayers of the faithful.[3] If the fault was of a very heinous nature, whole years of penance were esteemed an inadequate satisfaction to the Divine justice; and it was always by slow and painful gradations that the sinner, the heretic, or the apostate was readmitted into the bosom of the church. A sentence of perpetual excommunication was, however, reserved for some crimes of an extraordinary magnitude, and particularly for the inexcusable relapses of those penitents who had already experienced and abused the clemency of their ecclesiastical superiors. According to the circumstances or the number of the guilty, the exercise of the Christian discipline was varied by the discretion of the bishops. The councils of Ancyra and Illiberis were held about the same time, the one in Galatia, the other in Spain; but their respective canons, which are still extant, seem to breathe a very different spirit. The Galatian, who after his baptism had repeatedly sacrificed to idols, might obtain his pardon by a penance of seven years; and if he had seduced others to imitate his example, only three years more were added to the term of his exile. But the unhappy Spaniard who had committed the same offence was deprived of the hope of reconciliation even in the article of death; and his idolatry was placed at the head of a list of seventeen other crimes, against which a sentence no less terrible was pronounced. Among these we may distinguish the inexpiable guilt of calumniating a bishop, a presbyter, or even a deacon.[4]

[1] The Montanists and the Novatians, who adhered to this opinion with the greatest rigour and obstinacy, found *themselves* at last in the number of excommunicated heretics. See the learned and copious Moshiem, Secul. ii. and iii.

[2] Dionysius ap. Euseb. iv. 23. Cyprian, de Lapsis.

[3] Cave's Primitive Christianity, part iii. c. 5. The admirers of antiquity regret the loss of this public penance.

[4] See in Dupin, Bibliothèque Ecclésiastique, tom. ii. p. 304-313, a short but rational exposition of the canons of those councils which were assembled in the first moments of tranquillity after the persecution of Dio-

The well-tempered mixture of liberality and rigour, the judicious dispensation of rewards and punishments, according to the maxims of policy as well as justice, constituted the *human* strength of the church. The bishops, whose paternal care extended itself to the government of both worlds, were sensible of the importance of these prerogatives; and, covering their ambition with the fair pretence of the love of order, they were jealous of any rival in the exercise of a discipline so necessary to prevent the desertion of those troops which had enlisted themselves under the banner of the Cross, and whose numbers every day became more considerable. From the imperious declamations of Cyprian we should naturally conclude that the doctrines of excommunication and penance formed the most essential part of religion; and that it was much less dangerous for the disciples of Christ to neglect the observance of the moral duties than to despise the censures and authority of their bishops. Sometimes we might imagine that we were listening to the voice of Moses, when he commanded the earth to open, and to swallow up, in consuming flames, the rebellious race which refused obedience to the priesthood of Aaron; and we should sometimes suppose that we heard a Roman consul asserting the majesty of the republic, and declaring his inflexible resolution to enforce the rigour of the laws. " If such irregularities are suffered with impunity " (it is thus that the bishop of Carthage chides the lenity of his colleague), " if such irregularities are suffered, there is an end of EPISCOPAL VIGOUR; [1] an end of the sublime and divine power of governing the Church; an end of Christianity itself." Cyprian had renounced those temporal honours which it is probable he would never have obtained; but the acquisition of such absolute command over the consciences and understanding of a congregation, however obscure or despised by the world, is more truly grateful to the pride of the human heart than the possession of the most despotic power imposed by arms and conquest on a reluctant people.

In the course of this important, though perhaps tedious, inquiry, I have attempted to display the secondary causes which so efficaciously assisted the truth of the Christian religion. If among these causes we have discovered any artificial ornaments, any accidental circumstances, or any mixture of error and passion,

cletian. This persecution had been much less severely felt in Spain than in Galatia; a difference which may, in some measure, account for the contrast of their regulations.

[1] Cyprian Epist. 69 [59].

it cannot appear surprising that mankind should be the most sensibly affected by such motives as were suited to their imperfect nature. It was by the aid of these causes—exclusive zeal, the immediate expectation of another world, the claim of miracles, the practice of rigid virtue, and the constitution of the primitive church—that Christianity spread itself with so much success in the Roman empire. To the first of these the Christians were indebted for their invincible valour, which disdained to capitulate with the enemy whom they were resolved to vanquish. The three succeeding causes supplied their valour with the most formidable arms. The last of these causes united their courage, directed their arms, and gave their efforts that irresistible weight which even a small band of well-trained and intrepid volunteers has so often possessed over an undisciplined multitude, ignorant of the subject and careless of the event of the war. In the various religions of Polytheism, some wandering fanatics of Egypt and Syria, who addressed themselves to the credulous superstition of the populace, were perhaps the only order of priests [1] that derived their whole support and credit from their sacerdotal profession, and were very deeply affected by a personal concern for the safety or prosperity of their tutelar deities. The ministers of Polytheism, both in Rome and in the provinces, were, for the most part, men of a noble birth and of an affluent fortune, who received, as an honourable distinction, the care of a celebrated temple or of a public sacrifice, exhibited, very frequently at their own expense, the sacred games,[2] and with cold indifference performed the ancient rites, according to the laws and fashion of their country. As they were engaged in the ordinary occupations of life, their zeal and devotion were seldom animated by a sense of interest, or by the habits of an ecclesiastical character. Confined to their respective temples and cities, they remained without any connection of discipline or government; and whilst they acknowledged the supreme jurisdiction of the senate, of the college of pontiffs, and of the emperor, those civil magistrates contented themselves with the easy task of

[1] The arts, the manners, and the vices of the priests of the Syrian goddess are very humorously described by Apuleius, in the eighth book of his Metamorphoses.

[2] The office of Asiarch was of this nature, and it is frequently mentioned in Aristides, the Inscriptions, etc. It was annual and elective. None but the vainest citizens could desire the honour; none but the most wealthy could support the expense. See in the Patres Apostol. tom. ii. p. 200 [Epist. Eccl. Smyrn. de Martyrio Polycarpi, c. 12], with how much indifference Philip the Asiarch conducted himself in the martyrdom of Polycarp. There were likewise Bithyniarchs, Lyciarchs, etc.

maintaining in peace and dignity the general worship of mankind. We have already seen how various, how loose, and how uncertain were the religious sentiments of Polytheists. They were abandoned, almost without control, to the natural workings of a superstitious fancy. The accidental circumstances of their life and situation determined the object as well as the degree of their devotion; and as long as their adoration was successively prostituted to a thousand deities, it was scarcely possible that their hearts could be susceptible of a very sincere or lively passion for any of them.

When Christianity appeared in the world, even these faint and imperfect impressions had lost much of their original power. Human reason, which by its unassisted strength is incapable of perceiving the mysteries of faith, had already obtained an easy triumph over the folly of Paganism; and when Tertullian or Lactantius employ their labours in exposing its falsehood and extravagance, they are obliged to transcribe the eloquence of Cicero or the wit of Lucian. The contagion of these sceptical writings had been diffused far beyond the number of their readers. The fashion of incredulity was communicated from the philosopher to the man of pleasure or business, from the noble to the plebeian, and from the master to the menial slave who waited at his table, and who eagerly listened to the freedom of his conversation. On public occasions the philosophic part of mankind affected to treat with respect and decency the religious institutions of their country, but their secret contempt penetrated through the thin and awkward disguise; and even the people, when they discovered that their deities were rejected and derided by those whose rank or understanding they were accustomed to reverence, were filled with doubts and apprehensions concerning the truth of those doctrines to which they had yielded the most implicit belief. The decline of ancient prejudice exposed a very numerous portion of human kind to the danger of a painful and comfortless situation. A state of scepticism and suspense may amuse a few inquisitive minds. But the practice of superstition is so congenial to the multitude that, if they are forcibly awakened, they still regret the loss of their pleasing vision. Their love of the marvellous and supernatural, their curiosity with regard to future events, and their strong propensity to extend their hopes and fears beyond the limits of the visible world, were the principal causes which favoured the establishment of Polytheism. So urgent on the vulgar is the necessity of believing, that the fall of any system of mythology will most probably be succeeded by the introduction of some other mode of superstition. Some deities of a more recent and fashionable cast might soon have occupied the deserted temples of Jupiter and Apollo, if, in the decisive moment, the wisdom of Providence had not interposed a genuine revelation fitted to inspire the most rational esteem and conviction, whilst, at the same time, it was adorned with all that could attract the curiosity, the wonder, and the veneration of the people. In their actual disposition, as many were almost disengaged from their artificial prejudices, but equally susceptible and desirous of a devout attachment, an object much less deserving would have been sufficient to fill the vacant place in their hearts, and to gratify the uncertain eagerness of their passions. Those who are inclined to pursue this reflection, instead of viewing with astonishment the rapid progress of Christianity, will perhaps be surprised that its success was not still more rapid and still more universal.

It has been observed, with truth as well as propriety, that the conquests of Rome prepared and facilitated those of Christianity. In the second chapter of this work we have attempted to explain in what manner the most civilised provinces of Europe, Asia, and Africa were united under the dominion of one sovereign, and gradually connected by the most intimate ties of laws, of manners, and of language. The Jews of Palestine, who had fondly expected a temporal deliverer, gave so cold a reception to the miracles of the divine prophet, that it was found unnecessary to publish, or at least to preserve, any Hebrew gospel.[1] The authentic histories of the actions of Christ were composed in the Greek language, at a considerable distance from Jerusalem, and after the Gentile converts were grown extremely numerous.[2] As soon as those histories were translated into the Latin tongue they were perfectly intelligible to all the subjects of Rome, excepting only to the peasants of Syria and Egypt, for whose benefit particular versions were afterwards made. The public highways, which had been constructed for the use of the legions, opened an easy passage for the Christian missionaries from Damascus to Corinth, and from Italy to the extremity of Spain or Britain; nor did those spiritual conquerors encounter any of

---

[1] The modern critics are not disposed to believe what the fathers almost unanimously assert, that St. Matthew composed a Hebrew gospel, of which only the Greek translation is extant. It seems, however, dangerous to reject their testimony.

[2] Under the reigns of Nero and Domitian, and in the cities of Alexandria, Antioch, Rome, and Ephesus. See Mill, Prolegomena ad. Nov. Testament, and Dr. Lardner's fair and extensive collection, vol xv.

the obstacles which usually retard or prevent the introduction of a foreign religion into a distant country. There is the strongest reason to believe that before the reigns of Diocletian and Constantine the faith of Christ had been preached in every province, and in all the great cities of the empire; but the foundation of the several congregations, the numbers of the faithful who composed them, and their proportion to the unbelieving multitude, are now buried in obscurity or disguised by fiction and declamation. Such imperfect circumstances, however, as have reached our knowledge concerning the increase of the Christian name in Asia and Greece, in Egypt, in Italy, and in the West, we shall now proceed to relate, without neglecting the real or imaginary acquisitions which lay beyond the frontiers of the Roman empire.

The rich provinces that extend from the Euphrates to the Ionian sea were the principal theatre on which the apostle of the Gentiles displayed his zeal and piety. The seeds of the Gospel, which he had scattered in a fertile soil, were diligently cultivated by his disciples; and it should seem that, during the two first centuries, the most considerable body of Christians was contained within those limits. Among the societies which were instituted in Syria, none were more ancient or more illustrious than those of Damascus, of Berœa or Aleppo, and of Antioch. The prophetic introduction of the Apocalypse has described and immortalised the seven churches of Asia—Ephesus, Smyrna, Pergamus, Thyatira,[1] Sardes, Laodicea, and Philadelphia; and their colonies were soon diffused over that populous country. In a very early period, the islands of Cyprus and Crete, the provinces of Thrace and Macedonia, gave a favourable reception to the new religion; and Christian republics were soon founded in the cities of Corinth, of Sparta, and of Athens.[2] The antiquity of the Greek and Asiatic churches allowed a sufficient space of time for their increase and multiplication; and even the swarms of Gnostics and other heretics serve to display the flourishing condition of the orthodox church, since the appellation of heretics has always been applied to the less numerous party. To these domestic testimonies we may add the confession, the complaints, and the apprehensions of the Gentiles themselves. From the

---

[1] The Alogians (Epiphanius de Hæres. 51 [p. 455, ed. Paris, 1622]) disputed the genuineness of the Apocalypse, because the church of Thyatira was not yet founded. Epiphanius, who allows the fact, extricates himself from the difficulty by ingeniously supposing that St. John wrote in the spirit of prophecy. See Abauzit, Discours sur l'Apocalypse.

[2] The epistles of Ignatius and Dionysius (ap. Euseb. iv. 23) point out many churches in Asia and Greece. That of Athens seems to have been one of the least flourishing.

writings of Lucian, a philosopher who had studied mankind, and who describes their manners in the most lively colours, we may learn that, under the reign of Commodus, his native country of Pontus was filled with Epicureans and *Christians*.[1] Within fourscore years after the death of Christ,[2] the humane Pliny laments the magnitude of the evil which he vainly attempted to eradicate. In his very curious epistle to the emperor Trajan he affirms that the temples were almost deserted, that the sacred victims scarcely found any purchasers, and that the superstition had not only infected the cities, but had even spread itself into the villages and the open country of Pontus and Bithynia.[3]

Without descending into a minute scrutiny of the expressions or of the motives of those writers who either celebrate or lament the progress of Christianity in the East, it may in general be observed that none of them have left us any grounds from whence a just estimate might be formed of the real numbers of the faithful in those provinces. One circumstance, however, has been fortunately preserved, which seems to cast a more distinct light on this obscure but interesting subject. Under the reign of Theodosius, after Christianity had enjoyed, during more than sixty years, the sunshine of Imperial favour, the ancient and illustrious church of Antioch consisted of one hundred thousand persons, three thousand of whom were supported out of the public oblations.[4] The splendour and dignity of the queen of the East, the acknowledged populousness of Cæsarea, Seleucia, and Alexandria, and the destruction of two hundred and fifty thousand souls in the earthquake which afflicted Antioch under the elder Justin,[5] are so many convincing proofs that the whole number of its inhabitants was not less than half a million, and that the Christians, however multiplied by zeal and power, did not exceed a fifth part of that great city. How different a proportion must we adopt when we compare the persecuted with the triumphant church, the West with the East, remote villages

[1] Lucian in Alexandro, c. 25. Christianity, however, must have been very unequally diffused over Pontus; since, in the middle of the third century, there were no more than seventeen believers in the extensive diocese of Neo-Cæsarea. See M. de Tillemont, Mémoires Ecclésiast. tom. iv. p. 675, from Basil and Gregory of Nyssa, who were themselves natives of Cappadocia.

[2] According to the ancients, Jesus Christ suffered under the consulship of the two Gemini, in the year 29 of our present era. Pliny was sent into Bithynia (according to Pagi) in the year 110.

[3] Plin. Epist. x. 97.

[4] Chrysostom. Opera, tom. vii. p. 658, 810 [edit. Savil. ii. 422, 529].

[5] John Malala, tom. ii. p. 144 [ed. Oxon.; p. 420, ed. Bonn]. He draws the same conclusion with regard to the populousness of Antioch.

with populous towns, and countries recently converted to the faith with the place where the believers first received the appellation of Christians! It must not, however, be dissembled that, in another passage, Chrysostom, to whom we are indebted for this useful information, computes the multitude of the faithful as even superior to that of the Jews and Pagans.[1] But the solution of this apparent difficulty is easy and obvious. The eloquent preacher draws a parallel between the civil and the ecclesiastical constitution of Antioch; between the list of Christians who had acquired heaven by baptism, and the list of citizens who had a right to share the public liberality. Slaves, strangers, and infants were comprised in the former; they were excluded from the latter.

The extensive commerce of Alexandria, and its proximity to Palestine, gave an easy entrance to the new religion. It was at first embraced by great numbers of the Therapeutæ, or Essenians, of the lake Mareotis, a Jewish sect which had abated much of its reverence for the Mosaic ceremonies. The austere life of the Essenians, their fasts and excommunications, the community of goods, the love of celibacy, their zeal for martyrdom, and the warmth though not the purity of their faith, already offered a very lively image of the primitive discipline.[2] It was in the school of Alexandria that the Christian theology appears to have assumed a regular and scientifical form; and when Hadrian visited Egypt, he found a church composed of Jews and of Greeks, sufficiently important to attract the notice of that inquisitive prince.[3] But the progress of Christianity was for a

[1] Chrysostom. tom. i. p. 592. I am indebted for these passages, though not for my inference, to the learned Dr. Lardner. Credibility of the Gospel History, vol. xii. p. 370.
[With regard to this, Milman says that the statements of Chrysostom with regard to the population of Antioch, whatever may be their accuracy, are perfectly consistent. In one passage he reckons the population at 200,000. In a second the Christians at 100,000. In a third he states that the Christians formed more than half the population. Gibbon has neglected to notice the first passage, and has drawn his estimate of the population of Antioch from other sources. The 3000 maintained by alms were widows and virgins alone.—O. S.]

[2] Basnage, Histoire des Juifs, l. ii. c. 20, 21, 22, 23, has examined with the most critical accuracy the curious treatise of Philo which describes the Therapeutæ. By proving that it was composed as early as the time of Augustus, Basnage has demonstrated, in spite of Eusebius (l. ii. c. 17), and a crowd of modern catholics, that the Therepeutæ were neither Christians nor monks. It still remains probable that they changed their name, preserved their manners, adopted some new articles of faith, and gradually became the fathers of the Egyptian Ascetics.

[3] See a letter of Hadrian in the Augustan History, p. 245. [Vopisc. Saturn. c. 1.]

long time confined within the limits of a single city, which was
itself a foreign colony, and till the close of the second century
the predecessors of Demetrius were the only prelates of the
Egyptian church.   Three bishops were consecrated by the hands
of Demetrius, and the number was increased to twenty by his
successor Heraclas.[1] The body of the natives, a people distinguished by a sullen inflexibility of temper,[2] entertained the new
doctrine with coldness and reluctance; and even in the time of
Origen it was rare to meet with an Egyptian who had surmounted
his early prejudices in favour of the sacred animals of his country.[3]
As soon, indeed, as Christianity ascended the throne, the zeal
of those barbarians obeyed the prevailing impulsion; the cities
of Egypt were filled with bishops, and the deserts of Thebais
swarmed with hermits.

A perpetual stream of strangers and provincials flowed into
the capacious bosom of Rome.   Whatever was strange or odious,
whoever was guilty or suspected, might hope, in the obscurity
of that immense capital, to elude the vigilance of the law.   In
such a various conflux of nations, every teacher, either of truth
or of falsehood, every founder, whether of a virtuous or a criminal
association, might easily multiply his disciples or accomplices.
The Christians of Rome, at the time of the accidental persecution
of Nero, are represented by Tacitus as already amounting to a
very great multitude,[4] and the language of that great historian
is almost similar to the style employed by Livy, when he relates
the introduction and the suppression of the rites of Bacchus.
After the Bacchanals had awakened the severity of the senate,
it was likewise apprehended that a very great multitude, as it
were *another people*, had been initiated into those abhorred
mysteries.   A more careful inquiry soon demonstrated that the
offenders did not exceed seven thousand; a number indeed
sufficiently alarming when considered as the object of public
justice.[5]   It is with the same candid allowance that we should
interpret the vague expressions of Tacitus, and in a former
instance of Pliny, when they exaggerate the crowds of deluded

---

[1] For the succession of Alexandrian bishops, consult Renaudot's History,
p. 24, etc. This curious fact is preserved by the patriarch Eutychius
(Annal. tom. i. p. 332, Vers. Pocock), and its internal evidence would alone
be a sufficient answer to all the objections which Bishop Pearson has urged
in the Vindiciæ Ignatianæ.

[2] Ammian. Marcellin. xxii. 16.

[3] Origen contra Celsum, l. i. p. 40 [c. 52, tom. i. p. 368, ed. Bened.]

[4] Ingens multitudo is the expression of Tacitus, xv. 44.

[5] T. Liv. xxxix. 13, 15, 16, 17.   Nothing could exceed the horror and
consternation of the senate on the discovery of the Bacchanalians, whose
depravity is described, and perhaps exaggerated, by Livy.

fanatics who had forsaken the established worship of the gods. The church of Rome was undoubtedly the first and most populous of the empire; and we are possessed of an authentic record which attests the state of religion in that city about the middle of the third century, and after a peace of thirty-eight years. The clergy, at that time, consisted of a bishop, forty-six presbyters, seven deacons, as many sub-deacons, forty-two acolythes, and fifty readers, exorcists, and porters. The number of widows, of the infirm, and of the poor, who were maintained by the oblations of the faithful, amounted to fifteen hundred.[1] From reason, as well as from the analogy of Antioch, we may venture to estimate the Christians of Rome at about fifty thousand. The populousness of that great capital cannot perhaps be exactly ascertained; but the most modest calculation will not surely reduce it lower than a million of inhabitants, of whom the Christians might constitute at the most a twentieth part.[2]

The western provincials appeared to have derived the knowledge of Christianity from the same source which had diffused among them the language, the sentiments, and the manners of Rome. In this more important circumstance, Africa, as well as Gaul, was gradually fashioned to the imitation of the capital. Yet notwithstanding the many favourable occasions which might invite the Roman missionaries to visit their Latin provinces, it was late before they passed either the sea or the Alps;[3] nor can we discover in those great countries any assured traces either of faith or of persecution that ascend higher than the reign of the Antonines.[4] The slow progress of the Gospel in the cold climate of Gaul was extremely different from the eagerness with which it seems to have been received on the burning sands of Africa. The African Christians soon formed one of the principal members

[1] Eusebius, l. vi. c. 43. The Latin translator (M. de Valois) has thought proper to reduce the number of presbyters to forty-four.

[2] This proportion of the presbyters and of the poor to the rest of the people was originally fixed by Burnet (Travels into Italy, p. 168), and is approved by Moyle (vol. ii. p. 151). They were both unacquainted with the passage of Chrysostom, which converts their conjecture almost into a fact.

[3] Serius trans Alpes, religione Dei susceptâ. Sulpicius Severus, l. ii. [p. 383, ed. Lugd. Bat. 1647]. With regard to Africa, see Tertullian ad Scapulam, c. 3. It is imagined that the Scyllitan martyrs were the first (Acta Sincera Ruinart. p. 34). One of the adversaries of Apuleius seems to have been a Christian. Apolog. p. 496, 497, edit. Delphin.

[4] Tum primum intra Gallias martyria visa. Sulp. Severus, l. ii. [l. c.] These were the celebrated martyrs of Lyons. See Eusebius, v. i. Tillemont, Mém. Ecclésiast. tom. ii. p. 316. According to the Donatists, whose assertion is confirmed by the tacit acknowledgment of Augustin, Africa was the last of the provinces which received the Gospel. Tillemont, Mém. Ecclésiast. tom. i. p. 754.

of the primitive church. The practice introduced into that province of appointing bishops to the most inconsiderable towns, and very frequently to the most obscure villages, contributed to multiply the splendour and importance of their religious societies, which during the course of the third century were animated by the zeal of Tertullian, directed by the abilities of Cyprian, and adorned by the eloquence of Lactantius. But if, on the contrary, we turn our eyes towards Gaul, we must content ourselves with discovering, in the time of Marcus Antoninus, the feeble and united congregations of Lyons and Vienne; and even as late as the reign of Decius we are assured that in a few cities only— Arles, Narbonne, Toulouse, Limoges, Clermont, Tours, and Paris—some scattered churches were supported by the devotion of a small number of Christians.[1] Silence is indeed very consistent with devotion; but as it is seldom compatible with zeal we may perceive and lament the languid state of Christianity in those provinces which had exchanged the Celtic for the Latin tongue, since they did not, during the three first centuries, give birth to a single ecclesiastical writer. From Gaul, which claimed a just pre-eminence of learning and authority over all the countries on this side of the Alps, the light of the Gospel was more faintly reflected on the remote provinces of Spain and Britain; and if we may credit the vehement assertions of Tertullian, they had already received the first rays of the faith when he addressed his Apology to the magistrates of the emperor Severus.[2] But the obscure and imperfect origin of the western churches of Europe has been so negligently recorded, that, if we would relate the time and manner of their foundation, we must supply the silence of antiquity by those legends which avarice or superstition long afterwards dictated to the monks in the lazy gloom of their convents.[3] Of these holy romances, that of the apostle St. James can alone, by its singular extravagance, deserve to be mentioned. From a peaceful fisherman of the lake of Gennesareth, he was transformed into a valorous knight,

---

[1] Raræ in aliquibus civitatibus ecclesiæ, paucorum Christianorum devotione, resurgerent. Acta Sincera, p. 130. Gregory of Tours, l. i. c. 28. Mosheim, p. 207, 449. There is some reason to believe that, in the beginning of the fourth century, the extensive dioceses of Liege, of Treves, and of Cologne, composed a single bishopric, which had been very recently founded. See Mémoires de Tillemont, tom. vi. part i. p. 43, 411.

[2] The date of Tertullian's Apology is fixed, in a dissertation of Mosheim, to the year 198. [Rather 199.—S.]

[3] In the fifteenth century there were few who had either inclination or courage to question whether Joseph of Arimathea founded the monastery of Glastonbury, and whether Dionysius the Areopagite preferred the residence of Paris to that of Athens.

who charged at the head of the Spanish chivalry in their battles against the Moors. The gravest historians have celebrated his exploits; the miraculous shrine of Compostella displayed his power; and the sword of a military order, assisted by the terrors of the Inquisition, was sufficient to remove every objection of profane criticism.[1]

The progress of Christianity was not confined to the Roman empire; and, according to the primitive fathers, who interpret facts by prophecy, the new religion, within a century after the death of its Divine Author, had already visited every part of the globe. " There exists not," says Justin Martyr, " a people, whether Greek or barbarian, or any other race of men, by whatsoever appellation or manners they may be distinguished, however ignorant of arts or agriculture, whether they dwell under tents, or wander about in covered waggons, among whom prayers are not offered up in the name of a crucified Jesus to the Father and Creator of all things." [2] But this splendid exaggeration, which even at present it would be extremely difficult to reconcile with the real state of mankind, can be considered only as the rash sally of a devout but careless writer, the measure of whose belief was regulated by that of his wishes. But neither the belief nor the wishes of the fathers can alter the truth of history. It will still remain an undoubted fact that the barbarians of Scythia and Germany, who afterwards subverted the Roman monarchy, were involved in the darkness of paganism; and that even the conversion of Iberia, of Armenia, or of Æthiopia, was not attempted with any degree of success till the sceptre was in the hands of an orthodox emperor.[3] Before that time the various accidents of war and commerce might indeed diffuse an imperfect knowledge of the Gospel among the tribes of Caledonia,[4] and among the borderers of the Rhine, the Danube,

[1] The stupendous metamorphosis was performed in the ninth century. See Mariana (Hist. Hispan. l. vii. c. 13, tom. i. p. 285, edit. Hag. Com. 1733), who, in every sense, imitates Livy; and the honest detection of the legend of St. James by Dr. Geddes, Miscellanies, vol. ii. p. 221.

[2] Justin Martyr, Dialog. cum Tryphon, p. 341 [c. 117, p. 211, ed. Bened.]. Irenæus adv. Hæres. l. i. c. 10. Tertullian adv. Jud. c. 7. See Mosheim, p. 203.

[3] See the fourth century of Mosheim's History of the Church. Many, though very confused circumstances, that relate to the conversion of Iberia and Armenia, may be found in Moses of Chorene, l. ii. c. 78-89.

[4] According to Tertullian, the Christian faith had penetrated into parts of Britain inaccessible to the Roman arms. About a century afterwards, Ossian, the son of Fingal, is *said* to have disputed, in his extreme old age, with one of the foreign missionaries, and the dispute is still extant in verse, and in the Erse language. See Mr. Macpherson's Dissertation on the Antiquity of Ossian's Poems, p. 10.

and the Euphrates.[1] Beyond the last-mentioned river, Edessa was distinguished by a firm and early adherence to the faith.[2] From Edessa the principles of Christianity were easily introduced into the Greek and Syrian cities which obeyed the successors of Artaxerxes; but they do not appear to have made any deep impression on the minds of the Persians, whose religious system, by the labours of a well-disciplined order of priests, had been constructed with much more art and solidity than the uncertain mythology of Greece and Rome.[3]

From this impartial though imperfect survey of the progress of Christianity, it may perhaps seem probable that the number of its proselytes has been excessively magnified by fear on the one side, and by devotion on the other. According to the irreproachable testimony of Origen,[4] the proportion of the faithful was very inconsiderable, when compared with the multitude of an unbelieving world; but, as we are left without any distinct information, it is impossible to determine, and it is difficult even to conjecture, the real numbers of the primitive Christians. The most favourable calculation, however, that can be deduced from the examples of Antioch and of Rome will not permit us to imagine that more than a twentieth part of the subjects of the empire had enlisted themselves under the banner of the Cross before the important conversion of Constantine. But their habits of faith, of zeal, and of union, seemed to multiply their numbers; and the same causes which contributed to their future increase served to render their actual strength more apparent and more formidable.

Such is the constitution of civil society, that, whilst a few persons are distinguished by riches, by honours, and by knowledge, the body of the people is condemned to obscurity, ignorance, and poverty. The Christian religion, which addressed itself to the whole human race, must consequently collect a far

---

[1] The Goths, who ravaged Asia in the reign of Gallineus, carried away great numbers of captives; some of whom were Christians, and became missionaries. See Tillemont, Mémoires Ecclésiast. tom. iv. p. 44.

[2] The legend of Abgarus, fabulous as it is, affords a decisive proof that many years before Eusebius wrote his history the greatest part of the inhabitants of Edessa had embraced Christianity. Their rivals, the citizens of Carrhæ, adhered, on the contrary, to the cause of Paganism, as late as the sixth century.

[3] According to Bardesanes (ap. Euseb. Præpar. Evangel.), there were some Christians in Persia before the end of the second century. In the time of Constantine (see his epistle to Sapor [Euseb.], Vit. l. iv. c. 13) they composed a flourishing church. Consult Beausobre, Hist. Critique du Manichéisme, tom. i. p. 180, and the Bibliotheca Orientalis of Assemani.

[4] Origen contra Celsum, l. viii. p. 424 [c. 69, tom. i. p. 794, ed. Bened.].

greater number of proselytes from the lower than from the superior ranks of life. This innocent and natural circumstance has been improved into a very odious imputation, which seems to be less strenuously denied by the apologists than it is urged by the adversaries of the faith; that the new sect of Christians was almost entirely composed of the dregs of the populace, of peasants and mechanics, of boys and women, of beggars and slaves, the last of whom might sometimes introduce the missionaries into the rich and noble families to which they belonged. These obscure teachers (such was the charge of malice and infidelity) are as mute in public as they are loquacious and dogmatical in private. Whilst they cautiously avoid the dangerous encounter of philosophers, they mingle with the rude and illiterate crowd, and insinuate themselves into those minds whom their age, their sex, or their education has the best disposed to receive the impression of superstitious terrors.[1]

This unfavourable picture, though not devoid of a faint resemblance, betrays, by its dark colouring and distorted features, the pencil of an enemy. As the humble faith of Christ diffused itself through the world, it was embraced by several persons who derived some consequence from the advantages of nature or fortune. Aristides, who presented an eloquent apology to the emperor Hadrian, was an Athenian philosopher.[2] Justin Martyr had sought divine knowledge in the schools of Zeno, of Aristotle, of Pythagoras, and of Plato, before he fortunately was accosted by the old man, or rather the angel, who turned his attention to the study of the Jewish prophets.[3] Clemens of Alexandria had acquired much various reading in the Greek, and Tertullian in the Latin, language. Julius Africanus and Origen possessed a very considerable share of the learning of their times; and although the style of Cyprian is very different from that of Lactantius, we might almost discover that both those writers had been public teachers of rhetoric. Even the study of philosophy was at length introduced among the Christians, but it was not always productive of the most salutary effects; knowledge was as often the parent of heresy as of devotion, and the description which was designed for the followers of Artemon

[1] Minucius Felix, p. 8 [ed. Lugd. B. 1652], with Wowerus's notes. Celsus ap. Origen, l. iii. p. 138, 142 [c. 49, tom. i. p. 479, ed. Bened.]. Julian ap. Cyril. l. vi. p. 206, edit. Spanheim.

[2] Euseb. Hist. Eccles. iv. 3. Hieronym. Epist. 83. [Ep. 70, tom. i. p. 424, ed. Vallars.]

[3] The story is prettily told in Justin's Dialogues. Tillemont (Mém. Ecclésiast. tom. ii. p. 384), who relates it after him, is sure that the old man was a disguised angel.

may, with equal propriety, be applied to the various sects that resisted the successors of the apostles. " They presume to alter the holy Scriptures, to abandon the ancient rule of faith, and to form their opinions according to the subtile precepts of logic. The science of the church is neglected for the study of geometry, and they lose sight of heaven while they are employed in measuring the earth. Euclid is perpetually in their hands. Aristotle and Theophrastus are the objects of their admiration; and they express an uncommon reverence for the works of Galen. Their errors are derived from the abuse of the arts and sciences of the infidels, and they corrupt the simplicity of the Gospel by the refinements of human reason." [1] Nor can it be affirmed with truth that the advantages of birth and fortune were always separated from the profession of Christianity. Several Roman citizens were brought before the tribunal of Pliny, and he soon discovered that a great number of persons of *every order* of men in Bithynia had deserted the religion of their ancestors.[2] His unsuspected testimony may, in this instance, obtain more credit than the bold challenge of Tertullian, when he addresses himself to the fears as well as to the humanity of the proconsul of Africa, by assuring him that if he persists in his cruel intentions he must decimate Carthage, and that he will find among the guilty many persons of his own rank, senators and matrons of noblest extraction, and the friends or relations of his most intimate friends.[3] It appears, however, that about forty years afterwards the emperor Valerian was persuaded of the truth of this assertion, since in one of his rescripts he evidently supposes that senators, Roman knights, and ladies of quality, were engaged in the Christian sect.[4] The church still continued to increase its outward splendour as it lost its internal purity; and, in the reign of Diocletian, the palace, the courts of justice, and even the army, concealed a multitude of Christians, who endeavoured to reconcile the interests of the present with those of a future life.

And yet these exceptions are either too few in number, or too

---

[1] Eusebius, v. 28. It may be hoped that none, except the heretics, gave occasion to the complaint of Celsus (ap. Origen, l. ii. p. 77 [c. 27, tom. i. p. 411, ed. Bened.]), that the Christians were perpetually correcting and altering their Gospels.

[2] Plin. Epist. x. 97. Fuerunt alii similis amentiæ, cives Romani. . . . Multi enim omnis ætatis, *omnis ordinis*, utriusque sexûs, et jam vocantur in periculum et vocabuntur.

[3] Tertullian ad Scapulam. Yet even his rhetoric rises no higher than to claim a tenth part of Carthage.

[4] Cyprian. Epist. 79 [80].

recent in time, entirely to remove the imputation of ignorance
and obscurity which has been so arrogantly cast on the first
proselytes of Christianity.[1] Instead of employing in our defence
the fictions of later ages, it will be more prudent to convert the
occasion of scandal into a subject of edification. Our serious
thoughts will suggest to us that the apostles themselves were
chosen by Providence among the fishermen of Galilee, and that,
the lower we depress the temporal condition of the first Christians, the more reason we shall find to admire their merit and
success. It is incumbent on us diligently to remember that the
kingdom of heaven was promised to the poor in spirit, and that
minds afflicted by calamity and the contempt of mankind cheerfully listen to the divine promise of future happiness; while, on
the contrary, the fortunate are satisfied with the possession of
this world; and the wise abuse in doubt and dispute their vain
superiority of reason and knowledge.

We stand in need of such reflections to comfort us for the loss
of some illustrious characters, which in our eyes might have
seemed the most worthy of the heavenly present. The names
of Seneca, of the elder and the younger Pliny, of Tacitus, of
Plutarch, of Galen, of the slave Epictetus, and of the emperor
Marcus Antoninus, adorn the age in which they flourished, and
exalt the dignity of human nature. They filled with glory their
respective stations, either in active or contemplative life; their
excellent understandings were improved by study; philosophy
had purified their minds from the prejudices of the popular superstition; and their days were spent in the pursuit of truth and the
practice of virtue. Yet all these sages (it is no less an object of
surprise than of concern) overlooked or rejected the perfection of
the Christian system. Their language or their silence equally
discover their contempt for the growing sect which in their time
had diffused itself over the Roman empire. Those among them
who condescend to mention the Christians consider them only as
obstinate and perverse enthusiasts, who exacted an implicit submission to their mysterious doctrines, without being able to

[1] [This enumeration ought to be increased by the names of several Pagans
converted at the dawn of Christianity, and whose conversion weakens the
reproach which Gibbon appears to support. Such are the Proconsul
Sergius Paulus, converted at Paphos (Acts xiii. 7-12); Dionysius, the
Areopagite converted with Damaris and others at Athens (Acts xvii. 34);
several persons at the court of Nero (Philip iv. 22); Erastus, received at
Corinth (Rom. xvi. 23) some Asiarchs (Acts xix. 31), and the philosophers,
Tatian, Athenagoras, Theophilus of Antioch, Hegesippus, Melito, Miltiades,
Pantænus, Ammonius, and others, all distinguished for their outstand-
ing genius and learning.—O. S.]

produce a single argument that could engage the attention of men of sense and learning.[1]

It is at least doubtful whether any of these philosophers perused the apologies which the primitive Christians repeatedly published in behalf of themselves and of their religion; but it is much to be lamented that such a cause was not defended by abler advocates. They expose with superfluous wit and eloquence the extravagance of Polytheism. They interest our compassion by displaying the innocence and sufferings of their injured brethren. But when they would demonstrate the divine origin of Christianity, they insist much more strongly on the predictions which announced, than on the miracles which accompanied, the appearance of the Messiah. Their favourite argument might serve to edify a Christian or to convert a Jew, since both the one and the other acknowledge the authority of those prophecies, and both are obliged, with devout reverence, to search for their sense and their accomplishment. But this mode of persuasion loses much of its weight and influence when it is addressed to those who neither understand nor respect the Mosaic dispensation and the prophetic style.[2] In the unskilful hands of Justin and of the succeeding apologists, the sublime meaning of the Hebrew oracles evaporates in distant types, affected conceits, and cold allegories; and even their authenticity was rendered suspicious to an unenlightened Gentile, by the mixture of pious forgeries which, under the names of Orpheus, Hermes, and the Sibyls,[3] were obtruded on him as of equal value with the genuine inspirations of Heaven. The adoption of fraud and sophistry in the defence of revelation too often reminds us of the

[1] Dr. Lardner, in his first and second volumes of Jewish and Christian testimonies, collects and illustrates those of Pliny the younger, of Tacitus, of Galen, of Marcus Antoninus, and perhaps of Epictetus (for it is doubtful whether that philosopher means to speak of the Christians). The new sect is totally unnoticed by Seneca, the elder Pliny, and Plutarch.

[2] If the famous prophecy of the Seventy Weeks had been alleged to a Roman philosopher, would he not have replied in the words of Cicero, " Quæ tandem ista auguratio est, annorum potius quam aut mensium aut dierum ? " De Divinatione, ii. 30. Observe with what irreverence Lucian (in Alexandro, c. 13), and his friend Celsus, ap. Origen (l. vii. [c. 14] p. 327), express themselves concerning the Hebrew prophets.

[3] The philosophers, who derided the more ancient predictions of the Sibyls, would easily have detected the Jewish and Christian forgeries, which have been so triumphantly quoted by the fathers, from Justin Martyr to Lactantius. When the Sibylline verses had performed their appointed task, they, like the system of the millennium, were quietly laid aside. The Christian Sibyl had unluckily fixed the ruin of Rome for the year 195, A. U. C. 948.

injudicious conduct of those poets who load their *invulnerable* heroes with a useless weight of cumbersome and brittle armour.

But how shall we excuse the supine inattention of the Pagan and philosophic world to those evidences which were presented by the hand of Omnipotence, not to their reason, but to their senses? During the age of Christ, of his apostles, and of their first disciples, the doctrine which they preached was confirmed by innumerable prodigies. The lame walked, the blind saw, the sick were healed, the dead were raised, dæmons were expelled, and the laws of Nature were frequently suspended for the benefit of the church. But the sages of Greece and Rome turned aside from the awful spectacle, and, pursuing the ordinary occupations of life and study, appeared unconscious of any alterations in the moral or physical government of the world. Under the reign of Tiberius, the whole earth,[1] or at least a celebrated province of the Roman empire,[2] was involved in a preternatural darkness of three hours. Even this miraculous event, which ought to have excited the wonder, the curiosity, and the devotion of mankind, passed without notice in an age of science and history.[3] It happened during the lifetime of Seneca and the elder Pliny, who must have experienced the immediate effects, or received the earliest intelligence, of the prodigy. Each of these philosophers, in a laborious work, has recorded all the great phenomena of Nature, earthquakes, meteors, comets, and eclipses, which his indefatigable curiosity could collect.[4] Both the one and the other have omitted to mention the greatest phenomenon to which the mortal eye has been witness since the creation of the globe. A distinct chapter of Pliny[5] is designed for eclipses of an extraordinary nature and unusual duration; but he contents himself with describing the singular defect of light which followed the murder of Cæsar, when, during the greatest part of a year, the orb of the sun appeared pale and

---

[1] The fathers, as they are drawn out in battle array by Dom Calmet (Dissertations sur la Bible, tom. iii. p. 295-308), seem to cover the whole earth with darkness, in which they are followed by most of the moderns.

[2] Origen ad Matth. c. 27, and a few modern critics, Beza, Le Clerc, Lardner, etc., are desirous of confining it to the land of Judea.

[3] The celebrated passage of Phlegon is now wisely abandoned. When Tertullian assures the Pagans that the mention of the prodigy is found in Arcanis (not Archivis) vestris (see his Apology, c. 21), he probably appeals to the Sibylline verses, which relate it exactly in the words of the Gospel

[4] Seneca Quæst. Natur. l. i. 15, vi. 1, vii. 17. Plin. Hist. Natur. l. ii.

[5] Plin. Hist. Natur. ii. 30.

without splendour. This season of obscurity, which cannot surely be compared with the preternatural darkness of the Passion, had been already celebrated by most of the poets [1] and historians of that memorable age.[2]

[1] Virgil. Georgic. i. 466. Tibullus, ii. 5, 75. Ovid. Metamorph. xv. 782. Lucan. Pharsal. i. 535. The last of these poets places this prodigy before the civil war.

[2] See a public epistle of M. Antony in Joseph. Antiquit. xiv. 12 [§ 3]. Plutarch in Cæsar. [c. 69] p. 471. Appian. Bell. Civil. l. iv. Dion Cassius, l xlv. [c. 17] p. 431. Julius Obsequens, c. 128. His little treatise is an abstract of Livy's prodigies.

EVERYMAN'S LIBRARY AND EVERYMAN PAPERBACKS: A Selection

indicates the volumes also in paperback: for their series numbers in Everyman Paperbacks add 1000 to the EML numbers given.

EUL stands for Everyman's University Library.

For copyright reasons some of the following titles are not available in the U.S.A.

BIOGRAPHY

ESSAYS AND CRITICISM

FICTION

HISTORY

LEGENDS AND SAGAS

POETRY AND DRAMA

RELIGION AND PHILOSOPHY

SCIENCES: POLITICAL AND GENERAL

TRAVEL AND TOPOGRAPHY